Offender Profiling

Second Edition

Robert D. Keppel

THOMSON
™

Australia · Canada · Mexico · Singapore · Spain · United Kingdom · United States

Offender Profiling
Robert D. Keppel

Executive Editors:
Michele Baird, Maureen Staudt &
Michael Stranz

Project Development Manager:
Linda de Stefano

Marketing Coordinators:
Lindsay Annett and Sara Mercurio

Production/Manufacturing Supervisor:
Donna M. Brown

Pre-Media Services Supervisor:
Dan Plofchan

Rights and Permissions Specialists:
Kalina Hintz

Cover Image
Getty Images*

The Adaptable Courseware Program
consists of products and additions to
existing Thomson products that are
produced from camera-ready copy.
Peer review, class testing, and
accuracy are primarily the responsibility
of the author(s).

Offender Profiling / Robert D. Keppel –
Second Edition
p. 280
ISBN-13: 978-0-0759-38875-8
ISBN-10: 0-0759-38875-X

International Divisions List

Asia (Including India):
Thomson Learning
(a division of Thomson Asia Pte Ltd)
5 Shenton Way #01-01
UIC Building
Singapore 068808
Tel: (65) 6410-1200
Fax: (65) 6410-1208

Australia/New Zealand:
Thomson Learning Australia
102 Dodds Street
Southbank, Victoria 3006
Australia

Latin America:
Thomson Learning
Seneca 53
Colonia Polano
11560 Mexico, D.F., Mexico
Tel (525) 281-2906
Fax (525) 281-2656

Canada:
Thomson Nelson
1120 Birchmount Road
Toronto, Ontario
Canada M1K 5G4
Tel (416) 752-9100
Fax (416) 752-8102

UK/Europe/Middle East/Africa:
Thomson Learning
High Holborn House
50-51 Bedford Row
London, WC1R 4LS
United Kingdom
Tel 44 (020) 7067-2500
Fax 44 (020) 7067-2600

Spain (Includes Portugal):
Thomson Paraninfo
Calle Magallanes 25
28015 Madrid
España
Tel 34 (0)91 446-3350
Fax 34 (0)91 445-6218

CONTENTS IN BRIEF

CONTENTS

LIST OF TABLES

INTRODUCTION

Offender Profiling is a collection of related readings in the field of crime assessment and profiling. It examines the process whereby experienced investigators, and others with direct knowledge of criminal activities, give advice to detectives about their cases under investigation. That advice includes information about the characteristics of the person who may have committed a crime (Criminal Personality Profile), specifics about linking cases through behavioral characteristics, determining the solvability factors for a particular investigation, and interview techniques for when the offender is questioned.

The term "Offender Profiling" was regularly used by members of the FBI's Behavioral Sciences Unit in the early 1980's to describe the process of drawing inferences about a suspect's characteristics from the details of his actions at scenes of murders and rapes. Notorious investigations that have used offender profiling include The Atlanta Child Murders, the USS Iowa Explosion, Green River Murders in Washington State, Nathaniel Code Murders in Louisiana, The Unabomber Cases, the Jon Benet Ramsey murder case in Boulder, Colorado, the Paul Keller Arson Series in Seattle, Washington, the DC Beltway Sniper Cases, and many others.

The public's familiarity with offender profiling is highlighted through the media's constant 24–7 coverage of high profile cases, making celebrities out of the criminal profilers they use as talking heads on television and radio. Also, the movie and television industry has glorified the profiling profession with such shows as Silence of the Lambs, Millennium, and Profiler. They may collectively try to personify the art and science of offender profiling, even though they do not truly represent typical profiles given in routine police investigations.

In spite of the media's often misrepresentation of offender profiling, many students have become infatuated with the process. Scholarship on offender profiling is at an elementary stage of development and, consequently, the literature is uneven in quality, scattered across a number of disciplines, and is somewhat disorganized. Research on the efficacy of profiling is virtually non-existent.

Offender Profiling synthesizes and organizes the best thinking on crime assessment and offender profiling, produced by a number of eminent scholars from a variety of disciplines, including psychology, psychiatry, criminology, geography, and criminal justice. The eight substantive sections cover a broad range of topics, including: 1) history origins of offender profiling, 2) methodologies of offender profiling (psychiatric, psychological, and criminal investigative), 3) behavioral characteristics of offenders, 4) crime assessment using method of operation and signature analysis, 5) profiling research, 6) statistical and geographical profiling and law enforcement data bases, 7) courtroom testimony and appellate court reviews and decisions, and 8) ethical considerations in profiling.

The book is designed for use in courses in criminology, criminal justice, psychology, and law, and other disciplines that address understanding violence, criminal typologies, offender profiling, and behavioral characteristics of criminals, as well as in criminal investigation training. *Offender Profiling* can be used as a primary or supplemental set of readings in a variety of classes on deviant behavior, crime, violence, homicide investigation, abnormal psychology, forensics that emphasize behavioral science, law enforcement, criminal justice, or homicide. Each of the readings included in Offender Profiling has undergone some minor editing, to make them more accessible to students, particularly those who may not be familiar with the substance of investigations and case law or the methodological and statistical procedures used in some research.

The editor brings together a unique combination of scholarship, teaching, and homicide investigation experience. Robert D. Keppel is an associate professor of criminal justice at Sam Houston State University where he teaches courses on Serial Murder, Criminal Investigation, Crime Scene Investigation, and Offender Profiling. He also is a visiting professor at Seattle University teaching Criminal Profiling, Forensic Science, Criminal Investigation, and Serial Murder. He retired as the Chief Criminal Investigator for the Washington State Attorney General's Office, with experience in over 2,000 homicide investigations over his career. He has a Ph.D. in Criminal Justice from the University of Washington, and has taught classes on homicide investigation and offender profiling at a number of colleges and universities, as well as in many training sessions for law enforcement personnel. He has collaborated with a number of eminent scholars on research, writing, and teaching about offender profiling.

HISTORICAL BACKGROUND AND OVERVIEW

In the past few years, offender profiling has grabbed the attention and imagination of the public and the media. Despite its roots in criminology and psychology, many in the field have remained skeptical of the usefulness, effectiveness, and legitimacy of offender profiling methods. In general, there is a lack of consensus on the accuracy, validity, and effectiveness of profiling practices and techniques. This lack of consensus and general confusion about offender profiling may be a direct outcome of the various definitions, terminology, approaches, and techniques.

Offender profiling has evolved over the past 100 years. The terminology, definitions, and approaches to profiling have also evolved. A look at the history and origin of offender profiling provides a basis for the questions, concerns, and research that develop out of profiling methods. *Section I: Historical Background and Overview* summarizes the historical developments in offender profiling, while describing the basic definitions, the terminology, divergent approaches, and issues and concerns in profiling.

Historical Origins of Offender Profiling (2005) examines the history and origin of offender profiling. It highlights examples of profiles of key cases from the 19th and 20th centuries, including profiles of Jack the Ripper, Peter Kurten, Adolph Hitler, the Mad Bomber, and the Boston Strangler. Authors Kristen Welch and Robert Keppel describe the contributions and the role of criminologists, psychologists, consulting detectives, medical examiners, forensic experts, and the FBI in the creation and evolution of modern profiling practices.

Correspondingly, Steven Egger presents a historical overview of criminal profiling and its implications from its use in World War II to its use in criminal investigations today in *Psychological Profiling: Past, Present, and Future*. He highlights Dr. James Brussels profiles of the Mad Bomber and the Boston Strangler. He discusses three critical dates in the development of psychological profiling, focusing on the contributions of the FBI and David Canter. Egger summarizes the criticisms and evaluations of psychological profiling. He concludes with a discussion on the future of criminal profiling.

Historical Origins of Offender Profiling

ROBERT KEPPEL AND KRISTEN WELCH

Introduction

The study of offender profiling compels us to understand it in spite of the filters provided by enormously popular television shows, such as *CSI, NYPD Blue, Millennium, Profiler, Law and Order, Missing without a Trace*, and *Cracker*. These shows have produced myths that are accepted not only as factually true, but have provided eager students with a skewed view of the realities of pursuing a profession in "profiling". When one looks back at the origin of profiling, the function of profiling has been around for over 100 years, but calling that function "criminal or psychological profiling" did not occur in the United States until the FBI's Behavioral Science Unit in the mid 1970's began training local law enforcement officers in the practical uses of criminal personality profiling.

Definition of Offender Profiling

There is a growing body of profiling literature on the various forms of profiling commonly used today, including investigative profiling, psychological profiling, psychiatric profiling, criminal profiling from crime scene analysis, and geographical profiling. As modern profiling techniques have evolved, so has the terminology. The practice used by law enforcement to identify suspects in unsolved crimes from crime scene characteristics has had several different names throughout history in addition to offender profiling:

- Applied Criminology
- Psychological Profiling
- Crime Scene Analysis
- Crime Assessment
- Crime Scene Assessment
- Criminal Profiling
- Criminal Personality Profiling

- Criminal Investigative Analysis
- Investigative Psychology
- Investigative Criminology

For the purposes of clarity, the term offender profiling and Howard Teton's (1995) definition of this technique provided in *The Encyclopedia of Police Science* and used by the FBI's Behavioral Science Unit, will be adopted in this article. Special Agent Teton, often depicted as the father of modern profiling techniques, describes offender profiling as "a method of identifying the perpetrator of a crime based on an analysis of the nature of the offense and the manner in which it was committed" (Teton, 1995, p.475). The underlying assumption of offender profiling is that the crime and the crime scene reflect the habits and personality of the offender. Correspondingly, in *The Police Dictionary and Encyclopedia,* author John J. Faye provides the following definition of profiling:

> **Psychological profile:** a description of the personality and characteristics of an individual based on an analysis of acts committed by the individual. The description may include age, race, sex, socioeconomic and marital status, educational level, arrest history, location of residence relative to the scene of the act, and certain personality traits. A profile is based on characteristic patterns of uniqueness that distinguish certain individuals from the general population. Regarding criminal acts, patterns are deduced from thoughtful analysis of wounds, weapon used, cause of death, position of the body. (1988: pp. 271–272)

Vernon Geberth (1981) defines a psychological profile as "an educated attempt to provide investigative agencies with specific information as to the type of individual who committed a certain crime" (p. 46). Similarly, Douglas, Ressler, Burgess, and Hartman (1986) describe the psychological profile as the identification of "the major personality and behavioral characteristics of an individual based upon an analysis of the crimes he or she has committed" (p. 405). The basic assumption of a psychological profile is that the crime scene reflects the personality and thoughts of the offender (Holmes & Holmes, 1998).

The origin of the term profiling in reference to investigative techniques is unclear. The actual practice of criminal profiling precedes the use of the term. The Oxford English Dictionary (OED) (2004) cites the earliest use of term profiling in an 1888 article in Scribners magazine by W.P.P. Longfellow entitled *One of the Secrets of Good Profiling,* in reference to the physical drawing of profiles. The OED also provides the following definition of the more modern technique of offender profiling:

> **Profiling** (*vbl. n*): orig. and chiefly *U.S.* **a.** The recording, itemization, or analysis of a person's known psychological, intellectual, and behavioral characteristics, esp. as documentation used (in schools, businesses, etc.) in the assessment of an individual's capabilities; (also) the compilation of databases which store such information and that can be used to identify any particular sub-group of people. (Oxford English Dictionary, 2004)

The word profile may be traced back even earlier to Blount's 1656 depiction of artistic representations in which places or objects are shown from a side view (Oxford English Dictionary, 2004). In all likelihood the use of the word profiling to apply to investigative techniques has grown out the use of profiles as character sketches of individuals' personalities and histories. The use of the word profiling to describe the current investigative technique may have evolved from the 1734 use of the word profile to illustrate the compilation of a biographical sketch or character study as exemplified by R. North in J. L. Clifford's 1969 *Biography as an Art*(Oxford English Dictionary, 2004). This is evidenced in the OED (2005) definition:

Profile: (n.)b. A biographical sketch or character study (common in journalistic use since 1920); a summary description or report.

Individuals have been compositing what became popularly known as "profiles" of historical figures, writers, and famous figures for at least 200 years (Oxford English Dictionary, 2005). The process of developing a report or a description of a person's characteristics based on crime scene characteristics would appear to be quite similar to the traditional definition of a profile as a biographical sketch of a person's characteristics, contributions, and life history. This is probably the strongest link to the modern use of the word profiling to identify the personality or psychological profile of individuals. Similarly, Special Agent Russell Vorpagel (1982), as a member of the FBI's Behavioral Sciences Unit, defined profiling as "a biographical sketch of behavioral patterns, trends, and tendencies" (p.156) of an offender in *Psychological Profiling and Crime Scene Behavioral Analysis: Painting Psychological Profiles: Charlatanism, Charisma, or a New Science?*

HISTORICAL BACKGROUND

The use of profiling as an investigative tool by detectives, investigative consultants, and the FBI has garnered a great deal of attention in recent years. Profiling has become the focus of more than speculation, prompting research and a body of literature, as well as the true crime shows, fictional narratives, and movies. Little attention, however, has centered on the origin of the investigative technique known as offender profiling with researchers typically only touching on the subject briefly in a paragraph or two at the beginning of their publications.

Much of the credit for the development and evolution of offender profiling as a legitimate law enforcement tool has been given to the FBI. However, many in the field cite earlier examples of profiling techniques, pointing to Dr. James Brussels 1956 profile of the Mad Bomber (Douglas, et al., 1986; Oremod, 1996) and Dr. Thomas Bond's 1888 profile of Jack the Ripper (Canter, 2004). In addition, many criminologists and criminal justice professionals acknowledge the work of early criminal anthropologists Jacob Fries, Cesare Lombroso, and Ernst Kretschmer as early contributors to profiling techniques (Douglas et al., 1986, Ressler et al., 1986). The following is a summary of the history of criminal profiling technique and chronicling early profiling efforts.

European Witch Hunts: The Witchcraze

While some modern profilers may trace the roots of profiling to early biological criminologists, even fewer researchers trace the origin of profiling to a much earlier date and vastly different aim. During the Spanish Inquisition and the years to follow, serious efforts were directed at identifying and eradicating witches. Most of Europe was faced with a witchcraze from 1450 to 1750 in which those individuals perceived to be witches were exterminated in huge numbers with estimates ranging from 200,000 to 9 million (Cyriax, 1993).

Endeavoring to control a quickly destabilizing society ridden by problems and uncertainties, the Church blamed witchcraft for the misfortunes that cursed the society. The witch hunt, which often relied on informants and accusations to identify those believed to practice witchcraft, also had a basic profile of a witch. The following is a typical profile, largely unwritten, of the characteristics used to identify witches in Europe from 1400's to 1700's:

1.1 PROFILE OF A WITCH

- Elderly female beyond child bearing range (later evolved to include younger women)
- Poor
- Lives on edge of town
- Displays knowledge of herbal medicines
- Mark of the Devil (insensitive spot)
- Steals men's potency, causing impotence in the surrounding areas
- Collects a great number of male members (penises) and keeps them in a birds nest or box. (Cyriax, 1993; Kramer & Sprenger, 1971)

The identification of witches was often conducted by professional "Witchpickers" who would torture their targets with long needles in the search of an insensitive "W spot" on their victim's bodies (Cyriax, 1993). One researcher credits the *Malleus Maleficarum* (The Witches Hammer), written circa 1487 as a manual for witch hunters, as an early tool for the profiling of witches due to its focus on the identification of witches. The Malleus Maleficarium (1971) is divided into three parts 1) discourse on the existences of witches and witchcraft, 2) types of witches and methods for identifying them, and 3) the examination and sentencing of witches. The second part of the text has been referred to as a "clinical diagnosis dedicated to uncovering and apprehending witches" (Zilboorg, 1935).

The *Malleus Maleficarium* (1971) is also responsible for reinforcing the belief that witches caused impotence and witch hunters need only look for communities in which men report impotence to locate witches. However, the identification of witches relied primarily on public outcry and accusation and the whims of the witchpickers, rather than the unwritten "profile" created from folklore and text such as the *Malleus Maleficarium* (Cyriax, 1993; Zilboorg, 1935). The first known written profile would come 300 years after the *Malleus Maleficarium* (1971) and was developed in the search for a serial killer, not for a witch.

Criminal Anthropology and Constitutional Theories

In *Psychological Services for Law Enforcement*, Theodore Blau (1994) reports examples of early profiling efforts similar to modern techniques in the beginning of the 19th century in the field of criminal anthropology. Similarly, former FBI Special Agent Howard Teton (1995), reports references in criminology literature to a "type of criminal psychology" as early as 1803 (p. 476). Several researchers have traced the origin of profiling to leading criminologists from the 19th and early 20th century (Blau, 1994; Brussel, 1968; Ressler & Shachtman, 1992; Teton, 1995). Criminal anthropology was a leading field in criminology in the United States from 1881 to 1911 (Henry & Einstadter, 1998), however criminal anthropology worldwide had an even earlier history. For example, Jacob Fries, who Howard Teton refers to as "the first student of criminology to relate the nature of crime to the personality of the individual", wrote a handbook on criminal anthropology in 1820 (Teton, 1995, p. 476).

Criminal anthropology is defined as "the scientific study of the relationship between human physical characteristics and criminality" (Schmalleger, 2004, p. 143). The basic premise of criminal anthropology is that the worst criminals are atavists, or genetic throwbacks from an earlier evolution, and are anatomically or physically different than other individuals (Henry & Einstadter, 1998; Lanier & Henry, 2004; Schmalleger, 2004). The leading criminologists in the field of criminal anthropology in the 19th and early 20th century argued that physical characteristics of offenders are linked to their criminal actions, that those who are criminal are genetic throwbacks in their physiology, thinking, and actions. In one of the first published works on criminal anthropology, *Anatomical Studies upon Brains of Criminals*, author Moriz Benedikt (1811) argued that the brains of criminals significantly deviated from the normal and that "man acts, thinks, feels, desires, and acts according to the anatomical construction and physiological development of his brain" (p. vii; Henry & Einstadter, 1998).

The idea that criminals were physically and mentally distinct from law abiding individuals (Dugdale, 1877; Hooten, 1939; Lombroso, 1876;Lombroso-Ferrero, 1911; Talbot, 1898) was expanded on to include the belief that different *types* of criminals, those who commit different categories of crimes, are also physically different from each other. This led to different profiles of criminals from the atavistic born criminal to the gentleman or normal criminal (Boeis, 1893; Henry & Einstadter, 1998; Lombroso-Ferrero, 1911; Parson, 1911) and included distinctions for murderers and thieves (Lombroso-Ferrero, 1911; Schmalleger, 2004). Cesare Lombroso and Ernst Kretschmer were two of the leaders in creating typologies and profiles of criminals that are most frequently credited for inspiring contemporary profiling of criminals (Blau, 1994; Brussel, 1968; Ressler & Shachtman, 1992; Teton, 1995).

CESARE LOMBROSO

Cesare Lombroso is best known as the founder of criminal anthropology for his study of the mind, body, and habits of the born criminal (Henry & Einstadter, 1998; Lanier & Henry, 2004; Schmalleger, 2004). Lombroso, an Italian physician, believed that criminals were throwbacks to a primitive era in human evolution and could be identified by atavistic characteristics. In furtherance of this belief, Lombroso created profiles of different types of criminals based on atavistic physical characteristics. For example, he differentiated between the physical and psychological characteristics of thieves, rapists, murderers, and the mentally ill including descriptions of their skin, jaws, teeth, ears, forehead, nose, tattoos and argot that he believed would be of use to identify or prosecute criminals and exonerate the innocent (Lombroso-Ferrero, 1911, 1972.)

In 1872, Lombroso developed a typology of criminals that included four classes: born criminals, criminals by passion, insane criminals, and occasional criminals, and identified 18 characteristics that indicated a born criminal (Lombroso-Ferrero, 1911, 1972; Lanier & Henry, 2004). Unlike modern profiles that focus on identifying a specific offender based on information gathered from the crime and crime scenes, Lombroso based his profiles on physical characteristics he believed were born in the criminal and pervaded a criminal type or class (Lombroso-Ferrero, 1911, 1972). As can be seen in the following profile of murderers, the significant difference between the profiles created by Lombroso and those created in the 20th century is that Lombroso aimed at identifying a class of criminals, rather than an individual offender.

LOMBROSO'S (1876) PROFILE OF MURDERERS

1. An aquiline beak of a nose

2. Fleshy swollen, and protruding lips

3. Small receding chin

4. Dark hair and bushy eyebrows that meet across the nose

5. Little or no beard

6. Displays an abundance of wrinkles, even in those younger than thirty

7. 4 to 5 times greater taste sensibility than the average person

8. A cynical attitude, completely lacking remorse

9. More likely to bear a tattoo

10. Attaches no importance to dress and are frequently dirty and shabby (Lombroso-Ferrero, 1972).

While he is well known for the *Criminal Man,* published in Italian in 1876 and later translated to English in 1911, his first work translated into English in 1895 focused on female criminals (Lombroso-Ferrero, 1972). In an era in which female offenders were largely overlooked, Lombroso dedicated an entire text to identifying characteristics of the female offender. Lombroso's *Female Offender* (1895), excerpted from the original Italian version *Criminal Woman, the Prostitute, and the Normal Woman* (1893), was the first and for years to come, the only text that discussed female criminality.

Lombroso contended that women were much less likely to be criminal, except for those that engaged in prostitution. He argued that the few born criminal females, however, were "more ferocious and terrible" than male offenders. He identified female offenders as those women totally lacking in feminine traits, contending that they typically displayed characteristics of voice, appearance, hair, and body closely resembling the opposite sex (Lombroso-Ferrero, 2004). Lombroso's ideas permeated criminological views on female criminality well into the 1970's.

Despite the obvious flaws and fallacies in Lombroso's theories and research, his work in criminal anthropology is a link in the history of offender profiling. In fact, some scholars and practitioners contend that early criminologists' attempts to develop criminal types and physical characteristics attributed to criminality are the precursors to modern profiling techniques. Some modern profilers have credited their work in the field to these criminologists (Brussel, 1968; Ressler & Shachtman, 1992; Teton, 1995).

ERNST KRETSCHMER

Robert Ressler points to the work of Ernst Kretschmer as an influence in the profiles he constructs (Ressler & Shachtman, 1992). Similarly, Dr. James Brussel (1968) credits Kretschmer for influencing the development of his profiles he constructed. Brussel incorporated physical characteristics into his profiles based on the idea that certain mental illnesses were associated with specific physical builds. This idea was directly descended from earlier criminologists, including Kretschmer.

Kretschmer was a proponent of constitutional theories which "explain criminality by reference to offenders' body types, genetics, or external observable physical characteristics" (Schmalleger, 2004). Kretschmer developed a typology of criminals and argued that a high correlation existed between body type, personality type, and criminality. As shown in the following example, Kretschmer's work is very similar to his predecessor, Cesare Lombroso.

Kretschmer's Somatotypology (1925)

Cycloid Personality	Schizoid Personality	Displastic Personality
heavyset, soft body type vacillate between normality and abnormality lack spontaneity & sophistication most likely to commit nonviolent property crimes	most likely have athletic, muscular bodies some can be thin and lean schizophrenic commit violent type of offenses	mixed group highly emotional often unable to control themselves mostly commit sexual offenses or crimes of passion

(Kretschmer, 1925; Schmalleger, 2004)

The research of criminologist Ernst Kretschmer played a role in the history profiling and influenced modern profilers, by its emphasis on the use of body types to identify offenders. In fact, Dr. James Brussel contends that he based his famous profile of the Mad Bomber in 1957 on Kretschmer's work (Brussel, 1968, p. 33). Based on crime scene details, Brussel believed that the Mad Bomber was suffering from paranoia. Kretschmer's study of ten thousand patients in mental hospitals indicated that 85% of patients suffering with paranoia had athletic body types, which lead Brussel to conclude that the Mad Bomber most likely had a symmetrical build (Brussel, 1968, pp. 32–33). While many believe the research of Lombroso and Kretschmer is dubious and unfounded at best, the underlying idea that characteristics of criminals can be classified to develop a list of traits that may lead to the identification of an offender has lead some experts to believe that Lombroso and Kretschmer contributed to what modern profiling is today.

Forensic Detectives, Medical Examiners, Coroners

The story of 19th century serial killer Jack the Ripper has inspired countless books and movies. It has grabbed the attention of investigators and the public for over 100 years, captivating the imagination and motivating a number of historical investigations into the unsolved murders. Today, the public is still enthralled with serial murders and this fascination has grown to include profiling techniques, as well as modern profilers (Keppel, Weis, Brown & Welch, 2005). Movies such as *Silence of the Lambs, Taking Lives, Murder by Numbers, Along Came A Spider, Kiss the Girls*, and *Bone Collector*, to name a few favorites, illustrate the fascination with investigations into serial murders utilizing offender profiling.

It is not surprising, therefore, to find that some of the earliest known written profiles were developed in the investigation of a serial killer. Unlike the heroes and heroines in modern movies however, the 19th century profilers didn't always get their man in the end. 19th century profilers typically relied more on crime scene details and information, whereas today's stars are portrayed with seemingly psychic powers that are almost infallible. In addition, the profilers of the 19th century were typically medical examiners and forensic detectives, whose profiles didn't wrap up the investigation neatly with a validation of their work in the apprehension of the suspect. The following sections illustrate the profiling efforts in the 19th century by medical examiners and forensic detectives.

1888: Dr. Thomas Bond's Profile of Jack the Ripper

With the release of Scotland Yard's home office files on the Jack the Ripper Murders in the late 1990's, came the earliest known profile of a killer. In November of 1888, Dr. Thomas Bond, a coroner for the Crown, submitted a letter to Scotland Yard following the murder of Mary Jane Kelly, pursuant to a request for his opinion considering the murders of several women in the Whitechapel area of London. Based on his observations of the Kelly murder scene and his subsequent autopsy of her, Dr. Bond provided characteristics about the killer, including the following profile of the murderer, commonly referred to as Jack the Ripper (Evans & Skinner, 2000; Sugden, 2002). In a letter to the Home Office dated 14 November 1888, Dr. Thomas Bond wrote:

1. All five murders were no doubt committed by the same hand. In the first four the throats appear to have been cut from left to right. In the last case owing to the extensive mutilation it is impossible to say in what direction the fatal cut was made, but arterial blood was found on the wall in splashes close to where the woman's head must have been lying.

2. All the circumstances surrounding the murders lead me to form the opinion that the women must have been lying down when murdered and in every case the throat was first cut.

3. In the four murders of which I have seen the notes only, I cannot form a very definite opinion as to the time that had elapsed between the murder and discovering the body, In one case, that of Berner's Street, the discovery appears to have been made immediately after the deed – In Buck's Row, Hanbury Street, and Mitre Square three or four hours only could have elapsed. [sic] In the Dorset street case the body was lying on the bed at the time of my visit, 2 o'clock, quite naked and mutilated as in the annexed report – Rigor mortis had set in, but increased during the progress of the examination. From this it is difficult to say with any degree of certainty the exact time that had elapsed since death as the period varies from 6 to 12 hours before rigidity sets in. The body was comparatively cold at 2 o'clock and the remains of a recently taken meal were found in the stomach and scattered about over the intestines. It is, therefore, pretty certain that the woman must have been dead about 12 hours and the partly digested food would indicate: that death took place about 3 or 4 hours after the food was taken, so one or two o'clock in the morning would be the probable time of the murder.

4. In all the cases there appears to be no evidence of struggling [sic] and the attacks were probably so sudden and made in such a position that the women could neither resist nor cry out. In the Dorset Street case the corner of the sheet to the right of the woman's head was much cut and saturated with blood, indicated that the fact may have been covered with the sheet at the time of the attack.

5. In the four first cases the murderer must have attacked from the right side of the victim. In the Dorsett Street case, he must have attacked from the front or from the left, as there would be no room for him between the wall and the part of the bed on which the woman was lying. Again, the blood had flowed down on the right side of the woman and spurted on the wall.

6. The murderer would not necessarily be splashed or deluged with blood, but his hands and arms must have been covered and parts of his clothing must certainly have been smeared with blood.

7. The mutilations in each case excepting the Berner's Street one were all of the same character and showed clearly that in all the murders, the object was mutilation.

8. In each case the mutilation was inflicted by a person who had no scientific nor anatomical knowledge. In my opinion he does not even possess the technical knowledge of a butcher or horse slaughterer or any person accustomed to cutting up dead animals.

9. The instrument must have been a strong knife at least six inches long, very sharp, pointed at the tip and about an inch in width. It may have been a clasp knife, a butcher's knife or a surgeon's knife. I think it was no doubt a straight knife.

10. The murderer must have been a man of physical strength and of great coolness and daring. There is no evidence that he had an accomplice. He must in my opinion be a man subject to periodical attacks of Homicidal and erotic mania. The character of the mutilations indicate that the man may be in a condition sexually, that may by called satyriasis. It is of course possible that the Homicidal impulse my have developed from a revengeful or brooding condition of the mind, or that Religious Mania may have been the original disease, but I do not think either hypothesis is likely. The murderer in external appearance is quite likely to be a quiet inoffensive looking man probably middle-aged and neatly and respectively dressed. I think he much be in the habit of wearing a cloak or overcoat or he could hardly have escaped notice in the streets if the blood on his hands or clothes were visible.

11. Assuming the murderer to be such a person as I have just described he would probably be solitary and eccentric in his habits, also he is most likely to be a man without regular occupation, but with some small income or pension. He is possibly living among respectable persons who have some knowledge of his character and habits and who may have grounds for suspicion that he is not quite right in his mind at times. Such persons would probably be unwilling to communicate suspicions to the Police for fear of trouble or notoriety, whereas if there were a prospect of reward it might overcome their scruples. (Evans & Skinner, 2001).

From this description of the perpetrator, the newspaper reporters drew erroneous conclusions and broadcast their own misinformed theory. Some of the conclusions and theories appear shocking and ludicrous today. The following comment was published in the Editorial column of the Manchester Evening News on Tuesday, 13 November 1888: "By the way, the theory is again revived that the perpetrator of the Whitechapel murders is probably a woman suffering from religious mania" (Evans & Skinner, 2001).

Dr. Bond's profile was very similar to the profiles of serial killers developed today. It was based on evidence and information from the crime scene and incorporating characteristics revealed by Dr. Bond's experience as an autopsy surgeon and his knowledge of violent crimes and crime scenes. This profile meets the earlier definition of profiling from the Oxford English Dictionary and the definition currently utilized by the FBI. It certainly meets Howard Teton's criteria of profiling as a "process of determining various aspects of a criminal's personality makeup from his or her choice of actions before, during, and after a criminal act" (1995, p. 475). While the accuracy of this profile of Jack the Ripper cannot be determined since the Whitechapel murders were never solved, it still earns Dr. Thomas Bond the title as the first profiler.

SIR ARTHUR CONAN DOYLE AND SHERLOCK HOLMES

Dr. Bond was not the only investigator to develop a profile of Jack the Ripper. While Sir Arthur Conan Doyle is probably best known as the author and creator of Sherlock Holmes, much less is known of Doyle's own forays into criminal investigations. As revealed by Peter Costello in *The Real*

World of Sherlock Holmes: The True Crimes Investigated by Arthur Conan Doyle (1991), Sir Arthur Conan Doyle was involved in the investigation of several violent crimes. Correspondingly, Harold Orel (1991) describes Doyle's life and involvement in a few key criminal cases, as well as his creation of fictional detective Sherlock Holmes.

Sir Arthur Conan Doyle was a medical man who trained under the tutelage of Dr. Joseph Bell at the University of Edinburgh. After years serving as a medical doctor, Sir Arthur Conan Doyle decided to try his hand at writing novels, including a fictional depiction of a consulting detective. While there has been some debate over Doyle's true inspiration for Sherlock Holmes in his detective novels, what is clear is his influence on modern criminal investigation (Teton, 1995; Douglas et al, 1986; Holmes & Holmes, 1996).

Edmund Locard, for example, recognized Doyle's influence and credits him as "the first to realize the importance of dust – I merely copied his method" (Teton, 1995, p. 476). In addition, modern profilers stress the importance of Doyle's fictional writings in originating psychological profiling (Teton, 1995) and illustrate the link between "fictional detective techniques and modern criminal profiling methods" (Douglas et al., 1986). The following is example of the fictional Sherlock Holmes powers of observation and an early attempt at profiling:

> Upon observing two men, "An old soldier, I perceive," said Sherlock. "And very recently discharged," said the older brother. "Served in India I see." "And a noncommissioned officer." "Royal Artillery, I fancy." "And a widower." The amazed Watson, thinking he was being had, asked them to explain. "Surely," said Sherlock, "it is not hard to see that a man with that bearing, expression of authority, and sun-baked skin is a soldier, is more than a private, and is not long from India." (Liebow, 1982, p. 133).

The resemblance between Doyle's fictional detective techniques and modern profiling may be a result of Doyle's own experiences. The strength of Sherlock Holmes was also strength of Sir Arthur Conan Doyle - attention to detail and power of observation (Costello, 1991; Hall, 1983; Holmes & Holmes, 1996; Liebow, 1982). Doyle was also a member of a small group called the Crimes Club, which discussed and investigated a number of cases. Members of the Crime Club showed an interest in the Jack the Ripper murders and arranged with the City of London Police Surgeon to visit the murder scenes (Costello, 1991, p. 61). Upon being asked his opinion of the murders, Doyle constructed a basic portrait of Jack the Ripper.

JACK THE RIPPER PROFILE

As revealed by Costello (1991) and Orel (1991), Doyle created a profile of Jack the Ripper that included the following points

- He has been in America.

- He is educated, not a toiler.

- He is accustomed to the use of a pen.

- Likely has a rough knowledge of surgery.

- Probably clothes himself as a woman to approach victims without arousing suspicion and to escape the crime without detection.

- There will be letters where he has written over his own name or documents that could be traced to him.

- Facsimiles of his handwriting from letters sent to the police should be published in the Newspapers so that someone may recognize the handwriting.

Doyle was known to have consulted with the police in over 28 cases (Costello, 1991). In one case, Doyle suspected that a husband was killing his wives in a case where both had met with accidents. He reportedly did not feel the facts fit the case and notified a friend at Scotland Yard. He was struck by the husband's disappearance and told his friend at Scotland Yard, "you might put more men on his track. If these deaths are not sheer coincidence, then this business isn't finished... You will have a creature to deal with who will be as rapacious a human as a pike that escapes being devoured by its parents-ruthless beyond all conjecture" (Costello, 1991, p. 141). While several authors contend that Sherlock Holmes was based on Sir Arthur Conan Doyle and his own detective experiences, still others point to Doyle's mentor Dr. Joseph Bell as a model for Sherlock Holmes.

Dr. Joseph Bell

Dr Joseph Bell was a surgeon, a medical examiner for the Crown, and instructor at Edinburgh in the 19th century (Liebow, 1982). While he taught his medical students many things, one of the lasting impressions was his emphasis on the powers of observation and attention to every detail. Students that worked with him in the infirmary report countless anecdotes of his almost psychic ability to read his patients, their present, their ailments, and their past. His powers did not include clairvoyance, but rather focused on the strengths of his observations and a never tiring focus on the patients (1982).

It was these strengths that would impress many of his students, including Arthur Conan Doyle (Orel, 1991). In a letter to Dr. Bell, Doyle credited Dr. Bell for inspiring the Sherlock Holmes persona. He writes the following in his 1982 letter to Dr. Bell:

> It is most certainly to you that I owe Sherlock Holmes and though in the stories I have the advantage of being able to place [the detective] in all sorts of dramatic positions, I do not think his analytical work is in the least exaggeration of some effects which I have seen you produce in the outpatient ward. (Hall, 1983, p. 78; Liebow, 1982, p. 172).

His profiling technique employed for the patients is well remembered and recorded by many of his students (Liebow, 1982; Hall, 1983). The technique he used was very similar to the analytical deductions more common in criminal investigations today. Dr. Bell used his observations of the patients he encountered along with his knowledge of the regions, dialect, argot, patterns of speech, tattoo's, and people's behaviors to make reasoned deductions and diagnosis similar to crime scene analysis. The following interaction between Dr. Bell and a civilian patient was recorded by Arthur Conan Doyle in his autobiographical *Memoirs* and reported by Liebow (1982), Hall (1983), and Orel (1991).

> "Well, my man, you've served in the army.'
> 'Aye, Sir.'
> 'Not long discharged?'
> 'No, Sir.'
> 'A Highland regiment?'
> 'Aye, Sir.'
> 'A noncommissioned officer.'
> 'Aye, Sir.'
> 'Stationed at Barbados.'

'Aye, Sir.'
'You see gentleman,' he would explain, the man was a respectful man, but did not remove his hat. They do not in the army, but he would have learned civilian ways had he been long discharged. He has an air of authority and he is obviously Scottish. As to Barbados, his complaint is of elephantitiasis, which is West Indian and not British.' To his audience of Watsons it all seemed very miraculous, until it was explained, and then it became simple enough. It is no wonder that after the study of such a character I used and amplified his methods when in later life I tried to build up a scientific detective who solved cases in his own merits. (Hall, 1983, p. 79; Liebow, 1982, pp. 132–133; Orel, 1991, pp. 5–6)

A similar example of Dr. Bell's method with his patients is provided by Trevor Hall (1983) in *Sherlock Holmes and His Creator* and in an article in *The Lancet* from August 1, 1956. Another former student of Dr. Bell, Emory Jones M.D. records the following incident in which Dr. Bell, as usual, made startling observations with no prior knowledge of the patient and without referring to intake papers:

"A woman with a small child was shown in. Joe Bell said good morning and she said good morning in reply.
'What sort of crossing di'ye have from Burntisland?'
'It was guid.'
'And had ye a guid walk up Inverleith Row?'
'Yes.'
'And what did you do with the other wain [child]?'
'I left him with my sister in Leith.'
'And would you still be working at the linoleum factory?'
'Yes, I am.'
'You see, gentleman, when she said good morning to me I noticed her Fife accent, and as you know, the nearest town in Fife is Burntisland. You notice the read clay on the edges of the soles of her shoes, and the only such clay within twenty miles of Edinburgh is in the Botanical Gardens. Inverleigh Row borders the garden and is her nearest way here from Leith. You observed that the coat she carried over her arm is too big for the child who is with her, and therefore she set out from home with two children. Finally, she has dermatitis on the fingers on her right hand which is peculiar to workers in the linoleum factory at Burntisland." (Hall, 1983, p. 81)

Dr. Bell's diagnosis and analysis was not limited to his patients at Longmore Hospital in Edinburgh. He also worked as a medical examiner and consultant to the Crown as a forensic expert (Liebow, 1982, p. 118). His obituaries, reports from students, several books, The Boston Medical and Surgical Journal, and newspaper reports account his work as a consulting medical detective and forensic expert for the Crown for over twenty years. In this capacity, he worked with Dr. Littlejohn, a prominent forensic expert, and consulted on several investigations. Little is known directly about his specific work in these investigations, as much was done confidentially. However, it has been recorded that he was instrumental in the murder trial of Dr. Eugene Chantrelle (Liebow, 1982, p. 119–122) and that after reviewing the case report he had given information and a suspect's name to Scotland Yard in the Jack the Ripper case the week before the murders ended (Liebow, 1982, pp. 167–169).

Consulting Detectives and Investigative Criminologists

Long before the 20th century FBI profilers and consulting detectives, investigators and criminologists of the 19th century were conducting very similar investigations emphasizing crime scene details and circumstances, and attempting to trace crime scene actions back to offender characteristics. In

19th century France, Francois Vidocq used investigative techniques and crime scene details to develop information about criminals. German Criminologist Hans Gross emphasized the importance of carefully studying criminal behavior and linking crime scene details to offender characteristics. Francois Vidocq and Hans Gross are the 19th century predecessors to modern profilers and contemporary profiling techniques.

FRANCOIS EUGENE VIDOCQ (1775–1857)

As a man with a criminal past of his own, Francois Vidocq understood the importance of getting into the criminal mind. He emphasized the importance of understanding the lifestyles, habitats, argot, and habits of various types of criminals. He influenced the way criminal investigations were conducted, by relying on sources of information, informants, undercover work, and crime analysis. Vidocq was originally known as an escape artist, who had no trouble escaping on numerous occasions, but later became a police spy. His criminal history was relatively minor and he had refused to participate in violent crimes brought him to the attention of the Criminal Division of the Paris Police.

Vidocq worked first as a secret informant and then as an undercover detective for the police. It was his idea to develop a unit of plainclothes detectives to infiltrate criminal groups, gather information on criminal activities, and investigate crimes (Edwards, 1977; Rich, 1935; Stead, 1953). He also stressed the importance of keeping files on known suspects and criminals. As illustrated by Samuel Edwards in the *Vidocq Dossier*. Vidocq urged for an undercover division of detectives:

> Ever since the middle ages members of the constabulary had worn identifying insignia that had over the centuries become full uniforms... How much better it would be, Vidoqc told his superiors if police officers assigned to criminal cases wore ordinary civilian attire. He envisaged the formation of a special bureau that would concentrate exclusively on the investigation and detection of crimes. Its memberships would be composed of men familiar with the methods and techniques of criminals, who would be aided in their work by files that identified every known robber, thief, forger, and confidence man. (1977, p. 37)

During his years with the French police, Vidocq spent countless hours developing informants for information on specific crimes, as well as insight into criminal thinking. He often used his own criminal background and knowledge to influence prisoners, gain information or confessions, create theories about the crime, and to develop strategies to apprehend offenders. While policing prior to Vidocq generally relied on eyewitness accounts and a good bit of luck, Vidocq developed new strategies for detecting and apprehending criminals. The French police wore distinct uniforms and relied on reactive policing, but Vidocq dispensed of the uniform and spent countless hours in criminal hangouts as part of his normal routine. He often worked in disguise, fooling even those who knew him, and developed several undercover personas (Edwards, 1977; Rich, 1935; Stead, 1953).

In 1811, Vidocq spearheaded the Surete Nationale and Police Judiciare of Paris. He had risen in the French police ranks to become the Chief of the Surete. Not surprisingly, he often recruited others with criminal pasts and sharp intelligence and cunning to work as undercover detectives. He is probably more famous, however, for the number of cases he solved and his almost supernatural power in detecting suspects in an investigation. These powers were far from supernatural, but relied on early profiling techniques and what has become the basis of criminal investigation today.

For example, Vidocq's most well known case involved a robbery of a butcher in 1821. Based on crime scene information and the victim's detailed account, Vidocq was able to identify and apprehend the robbers. The victim described the attack and how one robber fell to his knees during the scuffle. Vidocq deduced that the crime had been committed by a man named Raoul who was a smuggler with a bad reputation who ran a dram shop. What followed surprised everyone involved in the case, except Vidocq.

> At once he put Raoul's place under surveillance by Surete's agents and gave the men instructions to look out for a man that limped... Among the familiars of the dramshop, the agents reported was a man who walked with difficulty- as Chevalier Dupin observed Vidocq was a good guesser - and wore the kind of clothes the butcher had described. The agents shadowed him to his room... (Stead, 1953, p. 91)

After the surveillance, Vidocq went to take a look at the suspect. He recognized the limping suspect as Court, a man he'd arrested several times before for armed robbery. He was able to get an arrest warrant for both Raoul and Court, who later confessed to the robbery and attack on the butcher as well as a murder and other crimes (Stead 1953, pp. 91–94). Knowing there was a third accomplice to the confessed murder, Vidocq also developed an interview strategy that convinced the suspects to implicate their accomplice (Stead, 1953, pp. 94–95). This was not the only case where his knowledge of the criminals and criminal activities paid off. The following excerpt by Edwards (1977) is a typical example of Vidocq's knowledge of the criminals in France in which he details the habits and superstitions of criminals:

> The Surete and the uniformed police had less to do on Fridays than on any other day of the week, Vidocq said, because no criminal ever initiated a major enterprise on Fridays. If the first person passed on the street when a criminal went off to do a job was a priest, the project was postponed for at least twenty-four hours. This rule was observed by Protestants, Jews, and atheists, as well as Catholics. If the first person passed at the beginning of a work day was a nun, the job had to be put off for a week ... If he saw and retrieved a piece of iron, his enterprise would not fail. When a murder was planned, the killer had to sleep the previous night with some woman other than his wife or regular mistress, but he could go to bed only with his accustomed mate the night before perpetrating a major robbery ... A swindler drank no wine for three hours before fleecing a victim, and a wise burglar always drank a glass of caraway-flavored water before going to work (Edwards, 1977, pp. 93–94).

Vidocq stressed that observation was the first rule of criminal investigation. During a visit one morning with a known thieve named Hodot, Vidocq observed that the man's boots were extremely muddy and his clothes were wet. Since it had rained earlier in the day, Vidocq returned to the Criminal Division to determine if any burglaries had occurred. Upon learning of a burglary, he went out to the residence and found soft boot prints in the mud that appeared similar to Hodot's. He retrieved the boots from Hodot's apartment and matched the boots to the prints in the mud (Edward, 1977, pp. 40–41; Stead, 1953, pp. 42–47).

Following his years of service and his revolution of policing and criminal investigations, Vidocq opened his own offices as a private detective. He became known as one of the first consulting detectives. Significantly, Vidocq became a legend in the underworld of crime as someone with "mythical like powers" to develop leads and unearth the individual(s) behind any crime. What really lay beneath his omnipotence was his vast knowledge base of criminal behavior, logical reasoning, undercover work, and surveillance of suspects. The following is an example of just such a case:

> In the morning M. Prunaud hurried to my office and he had not finished telling me about his mishap, before I had named the authors of the robbery. "It can only have been committed," I said, "by Berthe, Mongodart, and their confederates." I at once put my agents on their heels and

> I ordered them to make sure whether they were spending money. A few hours afterward they announced to me that the two individuals on whom my suspicions rested had been met in a resort, in company of Toulouse and Reverand … they were newly dressed … their pockets were well filled for they had been seen with some girls. I knew their fence. I asked that a search be made of his domicile and the merchandise was discovered (Rich, 1935, p. 405)

One of the strongest points Vidocq made during his career was the importance of observation and gaining as much information as possible about various criminals and criminal types. In his memoirs, Vidocq explained, "from my duties I was interested in knowing as much as possible all of the professional thieves, both men and women" (Rich, 1935, p. 405) and when called to consult he reportedly could name the culprits before the victim could even finish their stories based on crime scene details. He would follow and watch the suspect to gain evidence, often ordering his detectives in a case involving theft to look for signs that the suspect had improved their financial situation, asserting the importance of locating incriminating evidence upon the individual (Edwards, 1977; Rich, 1935, pp. 404–406; Stead, 1953, pp. 89–95).

Vidocq wrote several books on criminals and criminal investigations in his years following the Surete. The ideas contained in his Memoirs would help revolutionize policing and Vidocq is credited for inspiring the New York detective bureau in 1854, Britain's Bow Street Runners, and even Scotland Yard(Edwards, 1977, pp. 170–171; Rich, 1935; Stead, 1953). Vidocq was not alone in his views of criminal investigation. His views are mirrored in the writings of Hans Gross, who shared many of Vidocq's perceptions about developing information on criminals, their activities and habits, as well as their method of operating. Like Francois Vidocq, Hans Gross stressed the importance of knowing everything about the criminal element and how they operated, using crime scene details to develop a rudimentary profile of the possible offender.

HANS GROSS

Born over a 150 years ago in Graz, Austria, Hans Gross has been described as "the father of criminal research" (Adam, 1934; Gross, 1911), and as a founding father of modern criminal profiling for his emphasis on the careful and thorough study of criminal behavior, criminal psychology, and crime scene characteristics (Gross, 1911; Gross, 1934). Gross received a degree in law, served as "untersuchungsrichter" or examining magistrate, and taught as a professor of criminal law at the University of Czernowitz and the German University at Prague. While a Professor of Criminology at the University of Prague, Gross wrote *Criminal Psychology* (1911) for judges, practitioners, and students, and one of the first textbooks on criminal investigation the late 1800's.

Handbuch fur Untersuchungsrichter, als System der Kriminalistik (1893) was adapted in the English version *Criminal Investigation: A Practical Textbook for Magistrates, Police Officers, and Lawyers* in 1906 and translated into a total of eight languages by 1908 (Adam, 1934; Gross, 1911; Gross, 1934). The goal of the book was to advise investigating officers on "how crimes were to be handled, investigated, and accounted for, to explain the motives at work, and the objects to be obtained" (Adam, 1934, p. xv). Gross described the construction and use of weapons, how to sketch crime scenes, taking fingerprint and other impressions, searching for blood evidence, analyzing handwriting, and determining injuries and cause of death.

More importantly for the history of profiling, he instructed investigating officers and magistrates on the behaviors and practices of criminals and witnesses, including the profiling of thieves and pickpockets, murderers, arsonists, and individuals perpetrating frauds, based on knowledge of criminal behavior and evidence from the crime scenes (Adam, 1934). Similar to modern profilers, Gross emphasized the relationship between the actions and the characteristics of offenders. As revealed by Douglas, Ressler, Burgess, & Hartman (1986) the "basic premise of criminal profiling is that the way a person thinks directs the person's behavior" (p. 405). In *Criminal Psychology* (1934), Gross illustrated the importance of determining the offender's character, his wishes and beliefs. He contended:

> Is it not known that every deed is an outcome of the total character of the doer? Is it not considered that the deed and the character are correlative concepts, and that the character by means of which the deed is to be established cannot be inferred from the deed alone?... Each particular deed is thinkable only when a determinate character of the doer is brought in relation with it – a certain character predisposes to determinate deeds, another character makes them unthinkable and unrelatable with this or that person. (1934, pp.55–56)

In the case of a pickpocket or theft at a ball, rout, or gathering in a home, Gross advised detectives to search for an innocent looking woman because females were often used as an accomplice to hide stolen items (Adam, 1934). Or if a burglary took place and the watchdog was unaccounted for, Gross advised investigators "to take stock of wandering people who are in the possession of a bitch and have been seen in the vicinity of the place of the crime" (Adam, 1934, p. 455), arguing that vagabonds and wandering tribes kept female dogs to lure away watchdogs. He also advised investigators to check suspects' clothes for the odor of a female dog in heat, contending that the criminal may rub the dog's sexual organs against their clothes to detract the watchdog from barking (Adam, 1934).

There are several examples in *Criminal Investigation*(1934) of early profiling techniques in the use of crime scene characteristics to determine the characteristics of the offender. For example, Gross instructed and advised officers to play close attention to details of the crime scene in a break in or theft, because the scene of the offense will provide insight into the criminal and his character. He stated the following about the importance of the scene and modus operandi:

> ... for in nearly every case, the thief has left the most important trace of his passage, namely, the manner in which he committed the theft. Every thief has a characteristic style or modus operandi which he rarely departs from; and which he is incapable of completely getting rid of; at times this distinctive feature that even the novice can spot it without difficulty, but ... Only a practiced, intelligent, and fervent observer is capable of distinguishing those traits, often delicate but identical, which characterize the theft, and drawing important conclusions from them (Adam, 1934, p. 472).

In addition, Gross directed officers to note the method and location of entry into the house, means of exit(s), equipment used, precautions taken inside the house to avoid detection or capture, evidence and methods of securing secondary pathways into or out of the house, physical evidence, how the thief carries out his work (with conscientious attention or laziness), and the process of going through items, as indicators of the offender's age, sex, experience, and ethnicity (Adam, 1934, pp. 448–509). For example, Gross (1934), stated that "one important characteristic of a thief and a method of distinguishing whether he be a novice or old offender, is the manner in which he covers his retreat" (p. 483). He emphasized those specific characteristics (point of entry, previous knowledge of the house, type of house chosen, specific room chosen, locking doors, and wedges/implements used to brace doors as precaution, and obstacles for intruders) that point to thief of gypsy origin (Adam, 1934, pp. 483–489). Gross also argued that officers should pay close attention to footprints:

> Next we obtain any other information such as footprints can furnish us: from which direction the thieves come, where have they got in, at what place have they got out, and –where have they posted their sentinels? If this work is carried out with care a mass of important points, with a little luck, may be at once established: such as sex, age, and even their origin-for the class of the shoe permits us to draw conclusions as to whether a person hails from town or country (Adam, 1934, p. 477).

Certain methods, Gross contended, will point to a certain type of offender and the professional habits of the criminal should be determined from the crime scene. In the following analogy, Gross described the process of determining the expertise and possible trade of the offender, based on his observations of workman in his house:

> Note the differences between the various methods, according to the trade to which he belongs. The locksmith will attack the lock itself, the joiner the wood of which the almirah or table is constructed; the locksmith will open the lock with a master key or if that does not do it, he will smash it; the joiner will try to raise the top of the table or lid of the cash box without touching the lock, or perhaps he will turn his attention to the joinings of the planks, or try to pull out the nails which hold the hinges to the doors; in short each workman works in his own way and when a workman of one class has done a job, the specialist can immediately say what that class is (Adam, 1934, p. 481).

Hans Gross contribution to criminal investigation, criminology, and criminal psychology did not end with his textbooks. He served as the editor of the *Archiv fur Kriminalanthropologie and Kriminalistic* and established the Museum of Criminology at the University of Graz. One of the first forensic journals, *Kriminologie,* was introduced by Gross, who also published several articles in *Anthropologie and Kriminologie* (Gross, 1911). His emphasis on investigating officers paying close attention to the crime scene, calling in specialists when necessary, establishing modus operandi characteristics, linking cases based on crime scene behaviors of criminals, and using crime scene characteristics to learn about the offender can be seen in contemporary profiling techniques and crime scene analysis.

PETER KURTEN: THE DÜSSELDORF VAMPIRE

In 1930 efforts were made to profile the Düsseldorf Vampire in Germany before Peter Kurten was apprehended. Kurten had been killing since his childhood, in the 1890's, but it was in Düsseldorf that he earned his greatest notoriety as a multiple rapist, vampire, killer, and arsonist. His trial in 1931 created an international sensation (Jenkins, 1994). 48 year old Kurten was charged with nine murders, seven assaults, and implicated in over 60 additional crimes. He was revealed as a sadist who killed, slashed, tortured, and even cannibalized countless young victims.

Kurten would frequently change his MO utilizing various approaches, weapons, and both indoor and outdoor crime scenes. He chose male and female, adult and child victims. One similarity was Kurten's desire for blood. His known crime scenes were soaked in blood and he was known to have asked the court assigned psychologist if he'd have time to feel the blood pumping from his body when he was decapitated.

Like many serial killers profiled today, Kurten had a long criminal history that included arson, burglary, and sexual assault. As in many modern serial cases, the police failed to initially recognize that the crimes were linked to the same killer, ruling many of the early disappearances as runaways, and deaths as accidents. Once it became obvious that a murderer was preying on the citizens of Düsseldorf, several conjectures about the killer flew through the countryside.

Beliefs about the Vampire of Düsseldorf varied widely in the community and in the police. While one detective profiled the killer as a single, male that was an obviously deranged madman in both appearance and demeanor, others discounted this view and supported the belief that no single killer could be responsible for all the crimes and that a "club of sadists" were carrying out the gruesome attacks (Nash, 1990). It was also believed that the killer was a frequent customer of the beer halls in Düsseldorf (Nash, 1990). As revealed in *The Sadist*, Dr. Karl Berg (1932) developed a profile of Peter Kurten following his arrest detailing Kurten's fascination with blood, torture, sex, and death. While the early profiles constructed of Kurten were largely inaccurate and proved useless, the attempts to profile Kurten by members of the police during Kurten's crimes and the psychological profile of Kurten created by Dr. Berg still qualify as offender profiling.

ADOLPH HITLER

In 1943, the CIA and the Office of Strategic Services hired Dr. Walter Langer, to produce a psychological profile of Adolph Hitler in the hopes it might predict his future decisions and actions and aid in his eventual interrogation. Dr. Langer based his profile of Hitler on research and interviews with those personally acquainted with Hitler. This resulted in a personality profile that focused on his parents influence, his libido, and his perceptions of himself (Holmes & Holmes, 1998; Langer, 1972).

Langer described Hitler as an egomaniac, with many of the characteristics of a schizophrenic, who saw himself as a savior with divine protection. Most interestingly, Langer predicted that Hitler would go to extreme lengths to avoid capture. He asserted that Hitler's mental condition would deteriorate and he would commit suicide if defeat was eminent, which proved an accurate prediction (Holmes & Holmes, 1998; Langer, 1972).

Langer's profile of Hitler provided to the Office of Strategic Services looked at information provided by informants, friends, associates, and Hitler himself and was based on Hitler's family background, Hitler's writings, and private and public statements made by Hitler The profile addressed how Hitler perceived himself, how the German people viewed him, and how he is known to his associates. The following is a part of the psychological profile of Adolph Hitler compiled by Dr. Langer in 1943.

PSYCHOLOGICAL PROFILE OF ADOLPH HITLER

- Believes in his own omnipotence and greatness - the greatest warlord, the greatest architect, the greatest authority of any leader over the German people, and he believes his destiny is to become immortal.

- Believes he is on a mission and had been sent to Germany by Providence.

- Sees himself as the messiah sent to lead Germany to glory, compares himself to Christ, and has a Messiah complex that leads him to believe he has extra-natural powers.

- Extremely secretive, even with close associates, distrusts men and women.

- Product of a domineering and abusive father and a libidinal attachment to an affectionate and loving mother (Oedipus Complex).

- Regards women as seducers, disloyal, and responsible for man's downfall

- He is a hysteric bordering on schizophrenia, he's not a paranoiac or insane, but is neurotic and depressed.

- He has dual and opposite personalities, a "Dr. Jekyl and Mr. Hyde" personality structure.

- He is not happy, but is harassed by doubts, misgivings, uncertainties, condemnations, loneliness, and guilt.

- Gratifies himself vicariously through fantasies and cannot repress unsocial impulses.

- Subject to procrastination.

- Fears being poisoned, assassinated, losing his health, gaining weight, treason, premature death, and fears his mission will fail.

- Probably impotent, possibly repressed homosexual feelings, he is an extreme masochist who derives pleasure from having a woman urinate and defecate on his face, he often plays the passive role, identifying more with his mother, and feels compelled to degrade himself.

- He fears and admires neither Stalin nor Churchill, but secretly admires Roosevelt.

- He is trying to solve personal conflicts and rectify injustices of his childhood.

- Connection between his sexual perversion and self loathing and anti-Semitism as he view the Jewish people as symbols of sex, disease, and his own perversion and identification with feminism.

- Creates his own strong, masculine image to compensate for insecurities, inferiorities, and guilt.

- Will fly into a rage if he feels his super-male personality and image challenged.

- Fears domination by others and cannot expose himself to defeat, he will refuse to accept or adjust to defeat. (Langer, 1943; Langer, 1972)

PROFILE OF HITLER AND HIS POSSIBLE FUTURE ACTIONS

- He is unlikely to seek refuge in a neutral country.

- If convinced he cannot win, he will lead his troops into battle and expose himself as a fearless and fanatical leader.

- Assassination will only make his myth and legend stronger and turn him into a martyr.

- He is borderline schizophrenic and may go insane when faced with defeat.

- Hitler will become more and more neurotic and his mental state will deteriorate as Germany suffers successive defeats.

- The most plausible outcome is that Hitler will commit suicide, not a simple suicide, but a dramatic and effective death scene. (Langer, 1943; Langer, 1972)

Modern Profiling

While Langer's 1943 profile of Adolph Hitler may be arguably the first known written psychological profile of a world leader, it was not the last. Psychological profiles of various world leaders, terrorists, and cult leaders have been constructed since WWII. For example, more recent psychological profiles have been constructed of Iraqi leader Sadaam Hussein (Post, 1991) and cult leader David Koresh (Wrightsman & Fulero, 2005). More commonly, however, psychological profiles have been used in the investigation of criminals.

Most of the profiles created in the 20th century have centered on strategies for locating, apprehending, and interviewing violent offenders including arsonists, kidnappers, hostage takers, sexual offenders, and serial murderers. The next section includes two such offender profiles, both incredibly accurate and both created by one of the most famous profilers of the 20th century, Dr. James Brussel. The concluding section covers the development of the psychological profiling program of the Federal Bureau of Investigation.

1950's: Dr. James Brussel and the Mad Bomber

Dr James Brussel, a New York psychiatrist and assistant commissioner of the New York State Department of Mental Hygiene worked with the New York police to develop a profile of the Mad Bomber. It is often reported that Dr. Brussel informed police to "look for a heavy man. Middle-aged. Foreign born. Roman Catholic. Single. Lives with a brother or sister. When you find him, chances are he will be wearing a double breasted suit, buttoned" (Douglas, 1995; Egger, 1999; Gerberth, 1996; Petherick, 2004). The most commonly reported profile constructed by Dr. Brussel contained the following characteristics:

- Male

- Harbors a grudge against Con Edison and believes himself to be permanently injured by the company

- Has been seriously ill with TB, chronic heart disease, or cancer.

- Was paranoid and delusional

- Middle-aged, probably around 50 years old

- He was neat, meticulous, and skilled at his work.

- Overly sensitive to criticism.

- Foreign born.

- High school education, but not college

- Of Slavic descent, probably Roman Catholic

- Lived in Connecticut

- Suffered from an Oedipal Complex, was likely unmarried and lived with a single female relative or relatives- not his mother. (Cyriax, 1993; Holmes & Holmes, 1996; Petherick, 2004)

In *Casebook of a Crime Psychiatrist*, Dr. Brussel (1968) explained the basic premise of his profiling technique stating "by studying a man's deeds, I have deduced what kind of man he might be" (p. 4). He described several of the cases he worked on, including the Mad Bomber case. He explained his role in the investigation, his profile of the Mad Bomber, and his deductions and reasoning in its construction. He included the following characteristics in his 1956 profile of the Mad Bomber:

BRUSSEL'S PROFILE OF THE MAD BOMBER

- Male
- Has knowledge of metalworking, pipefitting, and electricity,
- Suffered an injustice by Con Edison, which had rendered him chronically ill.
- Suffers from an insidious disorder, paranoia, and has a persistent and chronic disorder.
- Is pathologically self-centered
- Has no friends, male or female, is a loner
- Symmetric athletic body type, neither fat or skinny
- Is middle-aged (due to onset of illness and duration of bombings)
- Good education, likely high school education but not college
- Unmarried, possibly a virgin
- Distrusts and despises male authority, hates father
- Never progressed past the Oedipal stage of love for his mother due to her early death or separation from him
- Lives alone or with female mother-like relative
- Lives in Connecticut, is of Slavic descent, Roman Catholic and attends church
- Neat, tidy, and cleanshaven
- Quiet, polite, methodical, and prompt
- Has chronic illness, either heart disease, cancer, or tuberculosis, most probably heart disease
- Would be wearing a buttoned double-breasted suit when caught. (Brussel, 1968, pp. 30–46)

The only known written evidence of this profile, prior to the arrest of bomb suspect George Metesky, is a December 25, 1956 *New York Times* article by Philip J. Meagher, in which Dr. Brussel detailed the following profile of the Mad Bomber:

PROFILE OF THE MAD BOMBER REPORTED IN *NEW YORK TIMES* (1956)

- Single man
- Between 40–50 years old
- High school graduate

- Skilled mechanic who is neat with his tools

- An expert in civil or military ordinance

- An introvert who is unsocial but not anti-social

- Interested in women

- Cunning, moral, honest and religious

- Resentful of criticism of his work, but may conceal resentment, or he may flare up violently when criticized

- Contemptuous of others, he feels superior to critics

- Motive may be discharge or a reprimand, resentment keeps growing

- Present or former Consolidated Edison employee

- Progressive paranoia. (Meagher, 1956, p. 33).

There has been some controversy over the accuracy of this profile and it's consistency with George Metesky. However, the overwhelming majority of opinions (Brussel, 1968; Douglas et al., 1986; Egger, 1999; Newton, 2000; Petherick, 2004) report that Brussel's profile was astonishingly accurate, even down to the clothes worn at arrest. There have been inconsistencies in the reports over several details, including the double breasted suit worn at arrest and whether Metesky lived with his sisters.

Upon reviewing personnel files and letters sent to the police, handwriting and evidence revealed in the letters pointed to a former Con Edison employee, George Metesky; a man of Slavic descent with a grudge against the company (Brussel, 1968; Cyriax, 1993; Egger, 1999; Nash, 1990). Metesky was arrested at a Connecticut home, where he lived with two spinster sisters. He was wearing his pajamas when he was arrested, and not the popularly cited double breasted suit (Brussel, 1968).

Despite this slight deviation, the profile still proved accurate upon this point. When allowed by officers to dress before accompanying them to the station, Metesky donned a double breasted suit, neatly buttoned down the front, and a hat (Brussel, 1968:69). The officers reported that Metesky was polite, cleanshaven, and very neat. The profile was also accurate in that Metesky did have TB, was middle-aged (54 years old), unmarried, and Roman Catholic (Brussel, 1968, pp. 68–73; Cyriax, 1993).

George Metesky's mother had died during his youth, he was unemployed due to a chronic illness which he blamed on Con Ed., and he regularly attended church. In addition, George Metesky was found to be suffering from paranoia and was remanded to an asylum for insanity (Brussel, 1968, pp. 65–73). Metesky spent sixteen years in the state hospital before his release December 13, 1973 (Nash, 1990). Between 1957-1971, Dr. Brussel assisted the New York police and other law enforcement agencies on numerous occasions, including developing a profile for the Boston Strangler (Brussel, 1968).

1960's - THE BOSTON STRANGLER

Between June 1962 and January of 1964, 13 women were brutally raped and killed in Boston in what would become known as the Boston Strangler case (Brussel, 1968; Petherick, 2004). Women of various ages were attacked, strangled to death, and left in sexually degrading positions in their homes. Each of the crimes escalated in violence, degree of sexual offence, and varied in MO's. The escalating sexual violence and changes in MO's lead investigators to believe they were dealing with multiple offenders. In April of 1964, Dr. Brussel was asked to join a panel of professionals to solve the case of the Boston Strangler (Brussel, 1968). The panel came to the conclusion that the murders were committed by two separate offenders and developed the following profile of the Boston Strangler:

THE PANEL'S PROFILE OF THE BOSTON STRANGLER(S)

- 2 separate killers as indicated by changes in MO, both male

- 1 male strangles and kills only elderly females,

- 1 killer is homosexual and focuses on younger women

- both men are teachers

- the killers live alone

- they kill on scheduled holidays

- sexually inhibited

- products of traumatic childhoods with weak, distant fathers and cruel seductive mothers. (Brussel, 1968; Cyriax, 1993; Newton, 2000)

The panel's opinion and profile was disputed by Brussel, who believed the crimes were the work of a single offender and explained away the changes in MO. Brussel developed his own profile of the Boston Strangler that depicted a very different type of offender than the panel had described. He focused on the commonality within the crimes and explained that the changes in the MO and in the sexual assaults showed an escalating pattern as the offender matured and grew through the experience (Brussel, 1968). The following is the profile of the Boston Strangler constructed by Dr. Brussel in April of 1964:

DR. BRUSSEL'S PROFILE OF THE BOSTON STRANGLER

- One man whose MO has changed as he has matured and grown through the crimes.

- He transferred his schizophrenic feelings for mother to his younger victims.

- His approach of the victims in their apartment did not frighten them; he had possibly befriended his victims and was invited there or he knocked on the for offering a plausible story such as he was taking a poll or checking the plumbing.

- He attacks when the victim turns her back on him, because he views this as a symbol of rejection.

- He's a paranoid schizophrenic.

- Based on Kretschmer's studies and the strength exhibited by the strangling, he is well proportioned, muscular and powerful man.

- Late twenties or early thirties

- He'd be described as the average man and goes largely unnoticed, fading into the background.

- He is a cautious, neat, clean shaven, and tidy individual, he never leaves fingerprints or other clues, he has clean fingernails and dresses neatly.

- His hair is always combed and he tends it lovingly; girls would envy his hair.

- Obsessed with his relationship with the opposite sex, he wants women to be attracted to him rather than reject him.

- Italian or Spanish descent

- Average or better intelligence

- Unmarried and a loner

- The killer finished with Mary Sullivan & probably won't kill again. (Brussel, 1968)

In November 1964 Albert DeSalvo was arrested for a series of rapes known as the Green Man crimes. He had previously been arrested and convicted in connection to the Measuring Man crimes, which included various sexual offences (Brussel, 1968; Cyriax, 1993; Frank, 1966). Subsequent to his confession to the Boston Strangler murders to a psychiatrist at the psychiatric hospital in which he was institutionalized, police officials identified DeSalvo as the Boston Strangler and closed the file (Brussel, 1968; Cyriax, 1993; Frank, 1966; Summers, 2004). This decision was in part due to the confession and similarities between the crimes, but some argued that a key element was DeSalvo's striking resemblance to the profile developed by Brussel (Summers, 2004).

Although Albert DeSalvo was married, a family man who lived with his wife and children, he was also muscular, athletic, in his early thirties, Italian, and average looking (Brussel, 1968). Albert DeSalvo was very neat and clean, with scrubbed and clipped fingernails, and "meticulously combed and shaped" hair (Brussel, 1968, p. 161). He was heterosexual and boasted about his sexual powers (Brussel, 1968; Cyriax, 1993; Newton, 2000). In addition, as predicted by Dr. Brussel, the Boston Strangler killings seemingly stopped after Mary Sullivan's murder (Brussel, 1968; Cyriax, 1993; Summers, 2004).

Since DeSalvo was stabbed to death in his cell in 1973 and was never officially charged with the Boston Strangler murders, the accuracy of Brussel's profile was never confirmed (Cyriax, 1993; Frank, 1966). For years, the case stirred controversy and many argued that the Boston police closed the case of the Boston Strangler too soon (Sherman, 2003; Summers, 2004). Some credence was given to the claim that Albert DeSalvo was not the Boston Strangler when a 2001 DNA test revealed that semen evidence collected from the last known victim, Mary Sullivan, did not match Albert DeSalvo (Sherman, 2003). Questions about the accuracy of Brussel's profile and the true identity of the Boston Strangler still abound today (Sherman, 2003; Summers, 2004).

THE FBI: THE NATIONAL CENTER FOR THE ANALYSIS OF VIOLENT CRIME

In the United States, the act of profiling offenders evolved through the work of the FBI's profiling unit, once known as the Behavioral Science Unit (BSU). The BSU was formed in 1972 and led efforts to develop profiling as a law enforcement tool with the establishment of a psychological profiling program in 1978 (Egger, 1999; Wrightsman & Fulero, 2005). The BSU was eventually restructured under the National Center for the Analysis of Violent Crime (NCAVC) at the FBI Academy (Douglas et al., 1986). The FBI's BSU was the first of many profiling units in law enforcement agencies in the United States, generating innovative profiling techniques and the original research into profiling by interviewing 36 sexual homicide convicted offenders (Ressler et al., 1986).

Profiling research has explored the behavioral characteristics of several different types of offenders including serial murderers, rapists, hostage takers, terrorists, arsonists, bombers, voyeurs, cult leaders, exhibitionists, and pedophiles. It has largely focused on assault based crimes and homicides. Modern profiling has evolved out of the study of the bizarre behaviors and patterns of repeat offenders, such as serial murderers and serial rapists. The BSU accepted case files of unsolved crimes in an attempt to develop profiles of the personality and behavioral characteristics of unknown offenders so that police investigators could more easily understand the perpetrators they were seeking (Douglas et al., 1986). Attention was largely concentrated on serial murders due to the belief that cases with multiple crime scenes and more bizarre behavior would yield more information about the offender (Holmes & Holmes, 1996).

This understanding led members of the FBI's Behavioral Science Unit to study serial murderers in the hope that profiling techniques would help identify patterns within the crimes, link serial cases to one offender, and provide information that would assist in identifying the offender. In 1981, a study on the value of profiling was conducted by Howard Teton. His research assessed the results in 193 cases. Teton (1995) found that approximately 45% of the cases were solved, with investigators in 77% of the cases reporting that the profile significantly assisted in the investigations, and had actually led to the identification of the suspect in 17% of the cases (p. 476).

The FBI's Behavioral Science Unit's early experience with offender profiling was largely motivated by Howard Teton's work (Egger, 1999; Petherick, 2004). His initial approach to profiling was developed in 1970 during a lecture course entitled Applied Criminology. Teton had been working on the concept of profiling during the early 1960's, while working as a crime scene specialist for the San Leandro Police Department in California. His background included study at the School of Criminology at the University of California (Petherick, 2004; Wilson et al., 1997).

Spurred on by the work of Dr. James Brussel, a New York Psychiatrist, Howard Teton refined his profiling techniques in 1971. Special Agent Teton combined his own profiling approach centering on traditional crime scene investigation methods with Dr. Brussel's psychiatric approach. Teton's interest in Dr. Brussel's methodology had come from Dr. Brussel's role as a profiler in the New York Mad Bomber and Boston Strangler cases. Teton regards Dr. Brussel as the "first practitioner" of profiling in modern times and "a true pioneer of the field" (Teton, 1995, p. 476.)

Following a 1981 conference at Sam Houston State University, and spurred by the efforts of Pierce Brooks and Robert Keppel, the FBI established the Violent Crime Apprehension Program (VICAP). VICAP is a computerized database of characteristics of specific violent crimes that assists agencies in sharing information and linking cases (Howlett et al., 1986). Technological advances have led to the development of computerized programs, such as VICAP and the Homicide Investigation Tracking System (HITS), which assist in crime scene analysis and investigation (Keppel & Weis, 1993).

Technological advances have also influenced modern profiling through the creation of computerized programs that generate profiles of offenders based on crime scene information and known statistics. Many of the early profiling efforts in the FBI culminated in the development of a computer program called Profiler. Profiler analyzes known crime data and input on the specific crime(s), including crime scene details and victim information. Profiler output constitutes a basic profile of the offender and a reconstruction of the murder or violent crime. It has been reported that Profiler and the National Center for the Analysis of Violent Crime handles over 900 cases a year (Cyriax, 1993, p. 322).

CONCLUSION

Despite claims that offender profiling has a relatively short history, there is clear and convincing evidence of early attempts at profiling in the nineteenth century. While many credit the FBI with the concept of offender profiling, historical references to criminal profiling techniques can be traced back to early 20th century profiles of the Boston Strangler and the Mad Bomber by Dr. James Brussel, the personality profile of Adolph Hitler constructed by Dr. Walter Langer and the 1930 profile of the sadistic Vampire of Drusseldorf constructed by Dr. Karl Berg. A look at the 19th century also provided examples of offender profiling including the profiles of medical examiners Joseph Bell and Thomas Bond. The 19th century and the late 18th century also provided profiles based on the work of early investigators, consulting detectives, and practitioners such as Hans Gross, Francois Vidocq, and Sir Arthur Conan Doyle.

Profiling has its early roots in criminology, including the work of criminal anthropologists Lombroso, and Kretschmer. Early criminologists posited the ideal that criminal psychology could be identified by physical characteristics and early practitioners made the connection between crime scenes and the offenders' personality and psychological makeup. Throughout the history of profiling, criminologists, psychiatrists, detectives, investigative consultants, scholars, and researchers have contributed to today's profiling techniques. Although the exact origin of offender profiling cannot be easily pinpointed, it is clear that several individuals have played key roles in its evolution in the past century.

REFERENCES

Adam, J., & Adam, J.C. (1934). *Criminal investigation: A practical textbook for magistrates, police officers, and lawyers.* Adapted from Hans Gross's System der Kriminalistik. London: Sweet & Maxwell.

Ainsworth, P.B. (2001). *Offender profiling and crime analysis.* Portland, Oregon, Willan Publishing.

Benedikt, M. (1881). *Anatomical studies upon brains of criminals.* New York: William Wood & Company.

Blau, T.H. (1994). *Psychological services for law enforcement.* New York: John Wiley & Sons.

Boies, H.M. (1893). *Prisoners and paupers.* New York: Putnam.

Brussel, J.A. (1968). *Casebook of a crime psychiatrist.* New York: Bernard Geis Associates.

Canter, D. (2004) Offender profiling and investigative psychology. *Journal of Investigative Psychology and Offender Profiling, 1,* 1-15

Canter, D. (2003) *Mapping murder: The secrets of geographical profiling.* London: Virgin Books.

Costello, P. (1991). *The real world of Sherlock Holmes: The true crimes investigated by Arthur Conan Doyle.* New York: Carroll & Graf Publishers.

Cyriax, O. (1993). *Crime: An encyclopedia.* London: Andre Deutsch.

Douglas, J.E., Ressler, R.K., Burgess, A.W., & Hartman, C.R. (1986). Criminal profiling from crime scene analysis. *Behavioral Sciences and the Law, 4,* #4: 401-421.

Dugdale, R.L. (1877). *The Jukes: A study in crime, pauperism, disease, and heredity.* New York: Putnam & Sons.

Edwards, S. (1977). *The Vidocq dossier: The story of the world's first detective.* Boston, Massachusetts: Houghton Mifflin Company.

Egger, S.A. (1999). Psychological profiling: Past, present, and future. *Journal of Contemporary Criminal Justice, 15,* 242-261.

Evans, S.P., & Skinner, K. (2001). *The ultimate Jack the Ripper companion: An illustrated encyclopedia.* New York: Carroll & Graf Publishers.

Frank, G. (1966). *The Boston Strangler.* New York: The New American Library.

Fay, J.J. (1988). *The police dictionary and encyclopedia.* Springfield, Illinois: Charles C. Thomas Books.

Geberth, V.J. (1981). Psychological profiling. *Law and Order,* 46-49.

Geberth, V.J. (1996). *Practical homicide investigation.* Boca Raton, Florida: CRC Press.

Gross, H.G. (1934). *Criminal investigation: A practical textbook for magistrates, police officers, and lawyers.* Adapted by John Adam and J. Collyer Adam. London: Sweet & Maxwell.

Gross, H.G. (1911). *Criminal psychology.* Boston: Little, Brown, and Company.

Hall, T.H. (1983). *Sherlock Holmes and his creator.* New York: St. Martin's Press.

Henry, S., & Einstadter, W. (1998). *The criminological theory reader.* New York: New York University Press.

Holmes, R.M., & Holmes, S.T. (1996). *Profiling violent crimes: An investigative tool.* London: Sage Publications.

Hooten, E.A. (1939). *The American criminal: An anthropological study.* Cambridge, MA: Harvard University Press.

Howlett, J.B., Haufland, K.A., & Ressler, R.K. (1986). The violent criminal apprehension program – VICAP: A progress report. *FBI Law Enforcement Bulletin, 55*(12), 14-22.

Jackson, J.L. (1997). *Offender profiling: Theory, research, and practice.* New York: John Wiley & Sons.

Keppel, R.D., Weis, J.G., Brown, K.M., & Welch, K.L. (2005). The Jack the Ripper murders: A modus operandi and signature analysis of the 1888–1891 Whitechapel murders. *Journal of Investigative Psychology and Offender Profiling, 2,* 1-21.

Keppel, R.D., & Weis, J.G. (1993). *Improving the investigation of violent crime: The homicide investigation and tracking system.* National Institute of Justice: Research in Brief. U.S. Department of Justice.

Kramer, H., & Sprenger, J. (1971). *The malleus maleficarium.* New York: Dover Publishing.

Kretschmer, E. (1925). Physique and character. New York: Harcourt .

Langer, W.C. (1943). *A psychological analysis of Adolph Hitler: His life and legend.* Declassified Documents of the Office of Strategic Services. Accessed from the National Archives, Washington, D.C.

Langer, W.C. (1972). *The mind of Adolf Hitler.* New York: Basic Books.

Lanier, M.M., & Henry, S. (2004). *Essential criminology.* Boulder, Colorado: Westview Press.

Liebow, E. (1982). *Dr. Joe Bell: Model for Sherlock Holmes.* Ohio: Bowling Green University Popular Press.

Lombroso, C. (1911). *Crime: Its causes and remedies.* Boston: Little & Brown.

Lombroso, C., & Ferrero, G. (2004). *Criminal woman, the prostitute, and the normal woman.* London: Duke University Press.

Lombroso-Ferrero, G. (1972). *Criminal man: According to the classification of Cesare Lombroso.* Montclair, New Jersey: Patterson Smith Publishing.

Lombroso-Ferrero, G. (1911). *Criminal man.* Montclair, New Jersey: Patterson Smith Publishing.

Meagher, P. (1956, Dec. 25). 16 year search for madman. *New York Times, CVI,* #36: 1-31.

Nash, J.J. (1990). *Encyclopedia of world crime (Vol. III).* Wilmette, Illinois: Crimebooks Inc.

Newton, M. (2000). *The encyclopedia of serial killers.* New York: Checkmark Books.

Newton, M. (2003). *The FBI encyclopedia.* London: McFarland & Company, Inc. Publishers.

Orel, H. (1991). *Sir Arthur Conan Doyle: Interviews and recollections.* New York: St. Martin's Press.

Ormerod, D.C. (1996). The evidential implications of psychological profiling. *Criminal Law Review,* 863-877.

Parsons, P. (1909). *Responsibility for crime.* New York: Longmans, Green.

Petherick, W. (2004) Criminal profiling: How it got started and how it is used. Accessed online from Courttv at http://www.crimelibrary.com/criminal_mind/profiling/profiling2.

Pinizzotto, A.J. (1984). Forensic psychology: Criminal personality profiling. *Journal of Police Science and Administration, 12,* 32-40.

Post, J.M. (1991). Saddam Hussein of Iraq: A political psychological profile. *Political Psychology, 12,* 279-290.

Ressler, R.K., Burgess, A.W., Douglas, J.E., Hartman, C.R.,, & D'Agostino, R.B. (1986). Sexual killers and their victims: Identifying patterns through crime scene analysis. *Journal of Interpersonal Violence, 1,* 288-308.

Ressler, R.K., Burgess, A.W., Douglas, J.E., Hartman, C.R.,, & McCormack, A. (1986). Murderers who rape and mutilate. *Journal of Interpersonal Violence, 1,* 273-287.

Ressler, R.K., & Shachtman, T. (1992). *Whoever fights monsters.* New York: St. Martin's Press.

Rich, E.G. (1935). *Vidocq: The personal memoirs of the first great detective.* Cambridge, Massachusetts: Houghton Mifflin Company.

Schmalleger, F. (2004) *Criminology today, 3rd edition.* New Jersey: Prentice Hall.

Sherman, C. (2003). *A rose for Mary: The hunt for the real Boston Strangler.* Boston: Northeastern University press.

Stead, P.J. (1953). *Vidocq: A bibliography.* New York: Staples Press.

Sugden, P. (1995). *The complete history of Jack the Ripper.* London: Robinson.

Summers, C. (2004). The Boston Strangler. Accessed online from BBC news at http://www.bbc.co.uk/crime/caseclosed/strangler.shtml.

Talbot, E. (1898). *Degeneracy: Its causes, signs, and results.* New York: Walter Scott.

Tatar, M. (1995). *Lustmord.* New Jersey: Princeton University Press.

Teton, H. (1995). Offender profiling. In *The Encyclopedia of Police Science, 2nd edition* Ed. W.G. Bailey. New York: Garland Publishing.

Vorpagel, R.E. (1982). Painting psychological profiles: Charlatanism, charisma, or a new science? *The Police Chief,* 156-159.

Wilson, P.R., Lincoln, R., & Kocsis, R. (1997). *Validity, utility and ethics of criminal profiling for serial violent and sexual offenders.* Psychiatry, Psychology and the Law, 4, 1-12.

Wrightsman, L.S., & Fulero, S.M. (2005). *Forensic psychology.* Belmont, California: Thomson Wadsworth.

Zilboorg, G. (1935).*The medical man and the witch during the Renaissance.* New York: Cooper Square Publishers, Inc.

PSYCHOLOGICAL PROFILING

Past, Present, and Future

STEVEN A. EGGER

University of Houston-Clear Lake

The development of psychological profiling is examined from its use during World War II to its use today in criminal investigation. This historical analysis includes Dr. James Brussels's work on the Mad Bomber and the "Boston Strangler" cases and then highlights three important dates in the development of psychological profiling:1972, 1985, and 1994. This first date is when the Federal Bureau of Investigation began its pioneer development in psychological profiling. The second (1985) was psychologist Dr. David Canter's assistance to local police in England in the "Railway Rapist" case. And the third was the establishment of the first academic graduate degree program in investigative psychology by Dr. Canter at the University of Liverpool. Current profiling efforts include a discussion of the assumptions and goals of profiling and how the process of profiling is completed. Various critiques and evaluations of profiling are summarized. The future of profiling discusses issues of profiler licensing, standardizing the process, public versus private profilers, and profiling as an art or a science. New profiling techniques such as greater use of the computer in the profiling process and the decoding of narrative documents are included.

It is seldom that any man, unless he is very full-blooded, breaks out in this way through emotion, so I hazarded the opinion that the criminal was probably a robust and ruddy-faced man. Events proved that I had judged correctly.

—Sherlock Holmes, congratulating himself
on the accuracy of his psychological
profile in *A Study of Scarlet* by
Sir Arthur Conan Doyle (1887)

The terms *psychological profiling, offender profiling, criminal profiling* or *criminal personality profiling* have become almost household words when the public hears about serial killers or unsolved murders in the mass media or in works of fiction. Unfortunately, most of the public associates these terms with the blond psychic profiler seen on *The Profiler* on Saturday night television or the abilities of Frank Black seen on *Millennium* on Friday night television. Of course, there was Hannibal Lecter and Agent Starling working together on a profile of a serial killer in the film *The Silence of the Lambs*. All of these popular portrayals of profiling are inaccurate, and they are beginning to construct icons in our popular culture who promote the myth that profiling is a magical skill, frequently encompassing precognitive psychic ability. Fiction blurs with reality for the general public who expect profiling to be the answer to solving murders, rapes, and other violent crimes.

Geberth (1981) defines a psychological profile as "an educated attempt to provide investigative agencies with specific information as to the type of individual who committed a certain crime" (p. 46). Douglas, Ressler, Burgess and Hartman (1986) have defined profile analysis as the identification of the "major personality and behavioral characteristics of an individual based upon an analysis of the crimes he or she has committed" (p. 405). Copson (1995) argues that offender profiling should be defined as an approach to police investigations whereby an attempt is made to deduce a description of an unknown offender based on evaluating minute details of the crime scene, the victim, and other available evidence. Jackson and Bekerian (1997), in one of only two books dedicated to offender profiling, state that, "A profile is based on the premise that the proper identification of crime scene evidence can indicate the personality type of the individual(s) who committed the offense" (p. 3). They state that profilers [can] assist in investigations of violent sexual crime by addressing three questions:

1. What happened at the crime scene?

2. What type of person is most likely to have done this?

3. What are the most likely personality characteristics of such an individual? (p. 3)

Psychological profiling is an attempt to provide investigators with more information on the offender who is yet to be identified. Psychological profiling is currently also referred to as investigative profiling. The purpose of profiling is to develop a behavioral composite, combining sociological and psychological assessments of the offender. Profiling is generally based on the premise that an accurate analysis and interpretation of the crime scene and other locations related to the crime can indicate the type of person who committed the crime. Because certain personality types exhibit similar behavioral patterns (in other words, behavior that becomes routine), knowledge and an understanding of the patterns can lead investigators to potential suspects.

HISTORICAL DEVELOPMENT

To get a better understanding of the concept of profiling, its utility in a criminal investigation, as well as its future potential as an investigative tool, an understanding of the origins of psychological profiling is necessary. Profiling may have originated in fiction rather than fact; it may have begun in Edgar Allen Poe's creative mind as a tool for amateur detective C. August Dupin in his 1841 classic *The Murders of the Rue Morgue*. Profiling can also be seen in the fictional exploits of Sir Arthur Conan Doyle's Sherlock Holmes.

The first recorded use of a psychological profile occurred when Dr. W. C. Langer, a psychiatrist, was commissioned by the Office of Strategic Services to provide a profile of Adolph Hitler. Gathering all the information he could about Hitler, Langer offered a psychodynamic personality profile of the man, focusing on decisions that Hitler might make given certain scenarios. Langer's profile proved to be very accurate; it included Hitler's suicide when Berlin was taken by the Allies.

Following this use of profiling during World War II, profiling was next documented in 1957 when psychiatrist James Brussels was asked by the New York City Police Department to assist them in identifying the Mad Bomber, who was responsible for more than 30 bombings over a 15-year period. Brussels studied the crime scenes and analyzed the letters that the bomber had sent to the newspapers. Based upon this information, he told the police to "Look for a heavy man. Middle-aged. Foreign born. Roman Catholic. Single. Lives with a brother or a sister. When you find him, chances are he'll be wearing a double-breasted suit. Buttoned" (Douglas, 1995, p. 34). The police, matching this profile with a list of disgruntled current or former employees of the city's power company, identified and arrested the bomber. Prior to leaving his home for the police station, the bomber put on a double-breasted suit—buttoned. The only flaw in Brussels's profile was that the bomber lived not with a brother or a sister but with two maiden sisters.

Brussels explained his accuracy in this case by indicating that, normally, his function is to examine an individual and then try to make some reasonable predictions about how the person might act in a specific situation. In this case, Brussels stated he had reversed the process by trying to predict and describe an individual from the evidence of his actions. In 1964, Brussels used a similar technique in providing a profile of the Boston Strangler for the Boston Police Department. Albert DeSalvo, the man eventually identified as the strangler, fits Dr. Brussels's profile. Dr. Brussels's technique of interpreting the bizarre behavior of these killers and then translating this psychiatric knowledge into investigative realities had proven to be a very effective tactic in assisting law enforcement with these cases.

In 1976 and 1977, the Son of Sam terrorized New York city by shooting young couples as they sat parked in their cars at various locations throughout the city. In addition to the forensic experts who were asked to assist in providing a profile of this killer, Dr. Murray Miron of Syracuse University was asked to provide a psycholinguistic analysis of the notes sent by the Son of Sam to local newspapers. When David Berkowitz, the Son of Sam, was finally arrested, Miron's profile turned out to closely fit him (Geberth, 1996).

There have been three important dates in the development of profiling following the efforts of Dr. Brussel and a few other social scientists. The Federal Bureau of Investigation (FBI) became involved in psychological profiling in about 1972. Second, Dr. David Canter, a psychologist at Surrey University in England, was asked in 1985 to assist the Surrey Police, the London Metropolitan Police, and the Hertfordshire Police in the investigation of a series of 30 rapes and 2 murders. Third, Dr. Canter established the first academic graduate degree in investigative psychology at the University of Liverpool in 1994.

Howard Teten, an instructor at the FBI Academy, was teaching applied criminology when he began developing profiles for officers in his class who had unsolved cases in their jurisdictions. The bureau began to formally develop profiles shortly thereafter. Ressler, Burgess, & Douglas (1984) state that, "The FBI agents at the Behavioral Science Unit have been profiling murderers for approximately twelve years." However, it was not until 1978 that the FBI established a formal Psychological Profiling Program within its Behavioral Science Unit at the FBI Academy in Quantico, Virginia (Geberth, 1996). In 1982, the FBI Behavioral Science Unit received a grant from the National Institute of Justice, Department of Justice, to expand their profiling capabilities by building a file of taped interviews with convicted murderers (Porter, 1983, Ressler et al., 1984). As a result of this grant, the agents were able to interview 36 convicted sexual murderers representing solo, serial, and mass murderers. It should be noted here that a number of authors and researchers have characterized these 36 murderers as all being serial murderers, which was not the case.

In 1983, Sam Houston State University received a planning grant from the Office of Juvenile Justice and Delinquency Prevention and the National Institute of Justice, Department of Justice, for a National Missing/Abducted Children and Serial Murder Tracking and Prevention Program. Activities of this planning grant included task force and workshop activities to plan, develop, and implement a National Center for the Analysis of Violent Crime (Egger, 1998). A preliminary model of this center was to include training, research and development, criminal personality profiling, and the Violent Criminal Apprehension Program. Following three workshops conducted by the university, a specific plan was initiated within the Department of Justice to fund this national center at the FBI Academy in Quantico, Virginia within the Behavioral Science Unit. In 1984, the FBI received $3.3 million to support the organizational development of the center for 24 months. Under the agreed funding arrangement, the project stipulated, in part, to include for four major organizational components, research, training, investigative support (profiling), and information assistance (Office of Juvenile Justice and Delinquency Prevention [OJJDP] Interagency Agreement, December 19, 1983). In 1995, an additional unit, known as the Child Abduction and Serial Killer Unit (CASKU), was added to the center. The mission of CASKU is to assist law enforcement agencies in cases in which a child's safety is believed to be at risk. It is also responsible for responding to serial murder or mass murder cases when local police agencies request the center's assistance.

Following the FBI's pioneering efforts in the 1970s and 1980s, the agency has consistently maintained a very visible role through the mass media as criminal profilers who assist local police in catching serial killers. The agency's efforts continue to rely on its original 36 interviews referred to earlier, coupled with the experience of the FBI profilers. This research resulted in classification of offenders according to whether they are organized or disorganized. The organized offenders plan their crimes, display behavioral control at the scene of the crime, leave few or no clues, and select or target strangers. The disorganized offenders do not plan their crimes, and their crime scenes show evidence of haphazard behavior.

The second important development in the history of offender profiling occurred in the 1985 when David Canter, a psychologist at the University of Surrey in England, was approached by Detective Vince McFadden, head of the Surrey Police Criminal Investigation Division. McFadden requested Canter's assistance in a major inquiry of 2 murders and at least 30 rapes under investigation by the New Scotland Yard, the British Transport Police, and the Constabularies of Surrey and Hertfordshire. Canter agreed to help and was assigned a detective from the London Metropolitan Police and Surrey Constabulary to assist him. Canter developed a profile of the unidentified murderer-rapist who would be dubbed the Railway Rapist by the press. Canter's profile was remarkably accurate, and it proved very useful in the apprehension of the murderer-rapist John Duffy.

The development of the Railway Rapist profile was followed by 9 years of research, during which major theoretical concepts or theories were developed to bolster and strengthen the investigative psychological approach to offender profiling. In effect, during this time, Canter was developing empirical data from which to generalize. Canter's research focused on the search for feasible psychological principles that could be used to generate profiles to assist criminal investigations. This research was broken down into five basic aspects of the criminal transaction between offender and victim. These aspects are interpersonal coherence, significance of time and place, criminal characteristics, criminal behavior, and forensic awareness.

Interpersonal coherence addresses whether variations in criminal activity relate to variations in the ways that the offender deals with other people in noncriminal situations. Focusing on this aspect of the transaction highlights the selection of victims and the implied relationship of victim to offender. A coherence of behavior within a subgroup provides a series of assumptions for the investigator to test. The location and time of the criminal act may inform investigators about the way in which the offender conceptualizes temporal and spatial relationships. It may provide valuable information on the constraints of the offender's mobility. Addressing the characteristics of the criminal allows researchers to determine whether the nature of the crime and the way it is committed can lead to a classification of criminal characteristics. This may lead to common characteristics of a subgroup of offenders and provide some guidance for the direction of the investigation. The development of a person's criminal behavior may allow the police to backtrack the probable career of the unidentified offender and narrow the possibilities. Forensic awareness, a term coined by Rupert Heritage during his work with Canter, is displayed by the offender who attempts to mask or hide physical evidence of the crime from the police. It implies that the offender probably has had earlier contact with the police and has learned some of the techniques and procedures of criminalistics. This awareness should lead investigators to suspect that the offender has a criminal record.

Canter's research into the development of more accurate investigative profiles meant interpreting the "criminal's shadow" (see Canter, 1994). This shadow, or story of the criminal, which Canter refers to as the inner narrative, evolves from a series of cryptic signals given in the actions of the offender. These signals are as follows:

- The personal world that the offender inhabits

- The degree of care that the offender takes in avoiding capture

- The degree of experience that the offender shows in the crime

- The unusual aspects of the criminal act, which may reflect the type of person who may be recognized

- The habits of the offender, which may carry over into his daily life (adapted from Canter, as cited in Egger, 1998, p. 222)

During the period following the Duffy case, Dr. Canter tutored a small number of police officers who continued to refine and develop the application of Canter's theories and principles to serial crime in the United Kingdom. While at Surrey, Canter offered two conferences for police officers and academics from around the world to share their research on offender profiling. Shortly after the second conference, Canter and his colleagues moved to the University of Liverpool for the purposes of establishing graduate courses in investigative psychology. It was then, in 1994, that Canter and his faculty began offering master's and doctoral degrees in investigative psychology. The course very quickly became popular for police officers who wished to develop profiling skills, and whose agency was willing to send them and pay their tuition and salaries while they were in school. In addition, the more intelligent undergraduate students were screened for admission into the program due to the popularity of offender profiling and Dr. Canter's reputation in helping to solve the Duffy case.

Two other developments deserve mention in the history of offender profiling. The first development was the efforts of Dr. Milton Newton in the late 1980s, and the second was the research and dissertation of D. Kim Rossmo in 1995. In 1985, Dr. Milton Newton presented a preliminary analysis of his research entitled "Geoforensic Identification of Localized Serial Crime." In this research, Dr. Milton used geographic principles to determine the home or point of operation of a serial offender. This research was followed in 1987 by Newton's final and unpublished paper entitled "Geoforensic Analysis of Localized Serial Murder: The Hillside Stranglers Located" (Newton & Newton, 1987). In this work, Newton and his coauthor, E. Swoope, developed a method, through post hoc analysis, using a geographic procedure that includes locations of fatal encounters and body dumps; this method resulted in a near geographic hit on Angelo Buono's home, where many of the murder had actually taken place.

Newton's research, along with a military intelligence interrogation technique called *map tracking* and the criminal geography research of Brantigham and Brantigham (1978), became building blocks for the development of a supplemental tool to offender profiling; this is referred to as *geographic profiling*. Geographic profiling was invented by D. Kim Rossmo. *Crime geographic targeting analysis* (a more accurate label for this investigative tool) attempts to calculate the most likely residence of a serial criminal based on the geography of his or her crimes, including distance to crime research, demographical analysis, centrographic analysis, point pattern analysis, point spread analysis, crime site residual, spatial-temporal ordering, and directional analysis (Rossmo, 1995). This form of analysis requires a special software mapping program that can be run on a personal computer. At the very least, this profiling strategy can assist investigators in focusing their resources on specific geographic areas and narrow the alternative scenarios to explore.

CURRENT PROFILING EFFORTS

The process of profiling has been described in a number of ways. Holmes and Holmes (1998) define profiling by stating the assumptions and goals of profiling. They identify the four following assumptions made in the profiling process:

1. The crime scene reflects the personality of the offender. Thus, the assessment of the crime scene should aid police in determining the personality of the offender and narrowing the scope of the investigation.

2. The method of operation (MO) remains similar. The crime scene reflects a personality with pathology. To understand the crime, one needs to understand the criminal first. The MO—how the crime was committed—will certainly tell us facts about the offender and about the possibility of the crimes being related and committed by the same person.

3. The signature will remain the same. The signature is the unique manner in which the offender kills, the words that a rapist uses, how the crime scene is left, or some other indicator. (Regarding the second and third assumption, Holmes and Holmes differentiate the two by describing MO as a more general description of the crime, whereas the signature is the unique manner in which the offender commits his or her crime.)

4. The offender's personality will not change. Because most personality experts maintain that an individual's personality is set by the time he or she reaches teenage years, Holmes and Holmes argue that this is no different for the criminal offender.

In addition to assumptions made in the profiling process, Holmes and Holmes identify four goals of the profiling effort.

Narrow the scope of the investigation

Holmes and Holmes argue that even the most general of profiles can be of assistance to investigators, because if certain categories of suspects can be eliminated, such as women, males who are not White, or males who are divorced, the viable list of suspects will have been reduced by more than 50%. Another way of viewing this goal is to understand that the profiler is trying to give as specific a profile as possible in order for investigators to narrow their list of suspects to a manageable number of people.

Social and psychological assessments

A profile should contain basic information on social and psychological core variables of the offender's personality, including race, sex, social class, education, residence, marital status, type of vehicle, and other items included in the recommended interviewing strategy.

Psychological evaluation of belongings

When a suspect has been identified, the profiler should give the investigators information regarding what kind of physical or collateral evidence the offender may have in his or her possession. If certain evidence is found in the suspect's possession, the profiler should give recommendations for further investigative tactics.

Interviewing suggestions and strategies

The type of interview or interrogation given to a viable suspect is frequently a crucial decision made in the investigation of the case. Here, the profiler can suggest the body language to use or avoid, certain words to be used or avoided, and conditions that will draw the most information from the suspect. For instance, the author spent over 40 hours with serial killer Henry Lee Lucas, and prior to the first interview with Lucas, the author was warned not to use any form of profanity at all. Other interviewers of Lucas who did not heed this advice did not receive any assistance from Lucas (adapted from Holmes and Holmes, 1998, pp. 182–184).

McCann (1992) provides a briefer definition of profiling. "Criminal personality profiling is the process of analyzing various aspects of violent crime to derive a set of hypotheses about the characteristics of an unknown assailant. The ultimate goal of profiling is to assist in the successful apprehension and conviction of the perpetrator" (p. 475).

Wilson, Lincoln, and Kocsis (1997) delineate profiling into the three following types: diagnostic evaluations, crime scene analysis, and investigative psychology. Diagnostic evaluations are generally referred to today as criminal personality profiling and are done by psychiatrists or psychologists. These are professionals who have very little experience or knowledge of law enforcement or investigation. Their evaluations are generally based on their clinical practice, and drawn from their knowledge of personality theories and various psychological disorders as defined in the *Diagnostic Statistical Manual*. Profiles are constructed by diagnosing the probable psychopathology or personality type likely to have committed the crimes in question. The earliest recorded profiles of this type would include the Langer and Brussel profiles, as well as the profile of Jack the Ripper (Rumbelow, 1988). This approach, according to Wilson, Lincoln, and Kocsis, is individualist in nature and thus prevents adequate comparative assessment of validity and utility with the other types of profiling.

The second type of profiling, crime scene analysis, is a utilitarian approach developed by the FBI. It involves studying crime scenes and interviewing incarcerated offenders to develop typologies for certain offender categories. From recognizable patterns, baseline data of offender characteristics, and crime scene indicators, the FBI was able to create offender templates of disorganized asocial and organized nonsocial offenders. The disorganized type was frenzied and bizarre in the commission of crimes and possibly suffers from psychosis. The organized type tends to be methodical and cunning, with little regard for social welfare, and this type often displays self-centered attitudes or takes an immoral worldview. Recent research, such as Kocsis, Irwin, and Hayes (1997), found that these behavior syndromes might be better viewed on a continuum, with prototypes at either extreme.

This process of criminal personality profiling (or crime scene analysis) evolved into the following seven-step process:

1. Evaluation of the criminal act itself

2. Comprehensive evaluation of the specifics of the crime scene or scenes

3. Comprehensive evaluation of the victim or victims

4. Evaluation of preliminary police reports

5. Evaluation of the medical examiner's autopsy protocol

6. Development of a profile with critical offender characteristics

7. Investigative suggestions predicated on the construction of the profile (Douglas, 1997)

Most American writers and researchers are referring to the crime scene analysis model when they refer to offender profiling. Geberth (1996) identifies 22 possible factors from age to motive that can be determined from a criminal personality profile. Geberth also identifies the following six items necessary to creating a profile:

1. Crime scene photos

2. Information on the neighborhood or area

3. Medical examiner's report

4. Map of victim's travels prior to death

5. Complete investigative report

6. Background of the victim (adapted from Geberth, 1996, p. 720–721)

Wilson, Lincoln, and Kocsis (1997) cite three criticisms of crime scene analysis. First, the approach has no theoretical basis, and it simply reduces human behavior to a few observable parameters. Second, various descriptors used in the FBI's classification manual are not weighted and prioritized. Third, the information used in the development of this type of analysis is drawn exclusively from the United States, and it does not differentiate between urban and rural areas of the country. Notwithstanding these criticisms, the FBI model of profiling has been implemented, to one degree or another, by governmental entities in Canada, Australia, and the United Kingdom.

John Liebert, a Bellevue, Washington psychiatrist and a consultant to Seattle's Green River Task Force, is distrustful of psychological profiles put together by police agencies and the FBI. He states, "I think the state of the art [profiling] leaves a lot to be desired" (McCarthy, 1984, p. 1). Liebert urges police agencies involved in a serial murder investigation to utilize the services of a psychiatrist. He warns that "superficial behavioral scientific profiling that rigidly reduces serial murder to a few observable parameters can lead an investigation astray" (Lieber, 1985, p. 199).

Holmes and DeBurger (1988) warn against the trend of U.S. law enforcement agencies contacting federal agencies to assist them in profiles. They argue that because federal agencies have little experience in murder cases, it would be far better for local agencies to train their homicide investigators in the recognition of psychological motives and other characteristics of the unknown killer that can be inferred from the crime scene rather than using a specialist.

Levin and Fox (1985) characterize psychological profiles as vague and general, and thus useless in identifying the killer. They further argue that a profile should be used as a tool to focus on a range of suspects rather than point precisely to a particular suspect.

The FBI themselves urge caution in perceiving profiling as an automatic solution to a difficult case. Hazelwood, Ressler, Depue, & Douglas (1987) state that "Profiles have led directly to the solution of a case, but this is the exception rather than the rule, and to expect this will lead to failure in most cases. Rather, a profile will provide assistance to the investigator by focusing the investigation towards suspect possessing the characteristics described" (p. 147).

Notwithstanding the detractors and critics of offender profiling or crime scene analysis, most homicide investigators appear to be convinced of the potential value of the profile. Crime scene analysis has also received support from the psychiatric community. Dr. Park Dietz, a noted forensic psychiatrist and professor of law and behavioral science and psychiatry at the University of Virginia, argues that the FBI profiles have no peers. Dietz has stated, "I think I know as much about criminal behavior as any mental-health professional and I don't know as much as the bureau's profilers do" (Michaud, 1989, p. 42).

The third type of profiling, investigative psychology, does not use practical police experience or interview data with a range of offenders, but it uses techniques of social psychology, criminology, and forensic psychiatry. This profiling technique, developed by David Canter and Rupert Heritage at the University of Surrey, continually builds an empirical base from which to operate. This is different from the FBI's approach, which uses intuition and experience. In addition, investigative psychology relies more heavily upon victim information. Canter's research, the result of over 9 years of investigative profiling experience and data collecting, is based on two prominent concepts, the five-factor model and the circle theory, according to Wilson et al. (1997). The five-factor model reflects the five basic aspects of criminal transaction that were referred to earlier. These five aspects are interpersonal coherence, significance of time and place, criminal characteristics, criminal career, and forensic awareness. For example, offense variables from victim statements in sexual assault cases can be grouped around these five factors in a two-dimensional representation. It is from such a representation that predictions can be made about the offender. The circle theory, developed by Canter, allows for the prediction of an offender's residence, based on the spatial distribution of serial offenses. Two hypothetical models have been identified by Canter, the marauder model and the commuter model. Canter's study of 45 rapists revealed 39 who demonstrated the marauder model for an 87% accuracy rate. Some subsequent support for the marauder predictive model in rape cases was found in Australia, although it was found to be 16% less accurate (Kocsis & Irwin, 1997).

Overall, Wilson, Lincoln and Kocsis (1997) list three general conclusions to their critique and overview of criminal personality profiling. First, they state that profiling is reductive rather than productive. By this statement, they are referring to the fact that a profile can narrow the field of suspects, but it is not capable of specifically identifying one suspect. Second, they found that profiles could provide a wealth of data, but they may be incorrect in identifying key characteristics. In this case, they warn that this characteristic of profiling relies too heavily on data from convicted felons rather than those who are never caught.

Jackson and Bekerian (1997) view the current status of profiling as reflecting two methodological frameworks for analyzing behavior. One framework incorporates concepts and techniques of experimental psychology, such as hypothesis testing or statistical analysis of findings, and it is generally referred to as the scientific approach. Examples of this framework would include research on rape (Davies & Dale, 1995, 1996), evaluation of statistical modeling (Aitken, Connolly, Gammerman, Zhang, & Oldfield, 1995), prediction of offender profiles from victim and witness descriptions (Farrington & Lambert, as cited in Jackson & Bekerian, 1997), and discussion of life narratives (Canter, 1994). The second methodological framework relies on the concepts of clinical psychology and forensic psychiatry. In this framework, the profiler is making inferences about the unconscious psychological processes of the offender. Here, "Conclusions about the relationship of personality and behavior are drawn from multiple observations of single cases, rather than from population statistics that generalize across multiple cases" (Jackson & Bekerian, 1997). The primary example of this framework, aside from private psychological or psychiatric consultants, would be the FBI profiling approach described earlier.

The current ascendancy of profiling as a viable investigative tool is due, in large part, to exposure in the popular media and the over-sensationalism of its effectiveness rather than through positive empirical results (Davies, 1994; Wilson, Lincoln, & Kocsis, 1997). One of the first thing journalists ask about is whether a profile has been done. In many fictional mysteries, adventure-thrillers, or police procedurals, when a serial murder is suspected, the author had better have a profiler somewhere in the first 70 pages of the novel (Egger, 1998). For instance, the myth and infallibility of the psychological profile has most certainly been promoted by adaptation of the book, *The Silence of the Lambs* (Harris, 1988), into a very successful film starring Anthony Hopkins and Jodie Foster. Journalists, whether they are employed by newspapers or by television stations, seem to be infatuated with the term *profile*. To them, this term belongs in any report of crime in which the criminal has yet to be arrested. A profile is a summary of the offender for the public. The basic problem with this simplistic approach by the mass media is that there are no simple answers and that even complicated answers frequently provide only half answers. Another way of putting it is, sexy sound-bites do not a profile make!

A number of critics of profiling have voiced their concern over the lack of an overall evaluation of offender profiling. However, these critics do not indicate what standards profiling is being measured against. If we are assessing the effectiveness of profiling as a tool of criminal investigation rather than as a solution to a specific crime, the finding are very positive (Jackson, Van Hoppen, & Hebrink, 1993; Pinizzotto, 1984). If, on the other hand, we are measuring the extent to which profiling solves crimes, we can only point to anecdotal evidence provided by law enforcement agencies. Pinizzotto's study of the FBI's profiling techniques found that in 192 requests for offender profiles, 46% were deemed to be of benefit in the investigation but only 17% were of assistance in the actual identification of the suspect. This study also revealed that 77% of the respondents claimed that the profiles did give a clearer focus for their investigation process, bolstering the argument that profiling should be considered a tool of the investigator rather than a crime-solving technique. Jackson's study in the Netherlands also found that profiles are of benefit to police investigators. Over 97% reported that the profiles provided by the police intelligence service were useful, although these profiles did not provide actual resolution of the crimes profiled. In a subsequent evaluation, Pinizzotto and Finkel (1990) compared profiles for homicide and sexual assault cases by professional profilers, detectives, psychologists, and university students. No significant differences were found for the homicide cases, but the profilers were superior to the other groups in developing an accurate profile in the sexual assault cases.

McCann (1992) argues that three factors interfere with any adequate empirical evaluation of the success or failure of profiling techniques. First, mental health professionals often scrutinize their efforts with careful empirical observations, whereas police professionals use deductive reasoning and street experience to guide their investigations. Second, mental health professionals try to hold themselves to carefully designed research, whereas the police require efficient and rapid results. Third, the crimes that profiling is ideally suited for involve bizarre and serial behavior that frequently spans a large geographic area. This type of crime results in the lack of data coordination, because the crimes are scattered over time and distance; inconsistent classification; small samples; and difficulties in managing large amounts of data generated for each case.

In discussing diagnostic evaluations, crime scene analysis, and investigative psychology (or the three different approaches to profiling, according to Wilson, Lincoln, & Kocsis, 1997), it would appear that profiling, due to its popularity, has some validity. This is evident from the fact that, in addition to the FBI, the Royal Canadian Mounted Police, the Association of Chief Police Officers in the United Kingdom, and the Australian Bureau of Criminal Intelligence have concluded that "profiling is useful for crimes where there is some evidence of psychopathology in the offenders, such as lust killing or those where extensive mutilation is present."

Others have been more specific as to when an offender profile is useful. Geberth (1996) observes that profiling is "productive in crimes in which an unknown subject has demonstrated some form of psychopathology in his crime, for example: sadistic torture in sexual assault, evisceration, postmortem slashing and cutting, motiveless fire-setting, lust and mutilation murders, ritualistic crimes, and rapes" (p. 711). Holmes and Holmes (1998) provide a somewhat different list of crimes suitable for profiling.

- Sadistic torture in sexual assaults
- Evisceration
- Postmortem slashing and cutting
- Motiveless fire setting
- Lust and mutilation murder
- Rape
- Arson
- Bank robbery
- Sadistic and ritualistic crime
- Pedophilia (pp. 181–182)

THE FUTURE OF PROFILING

It is not unreasonable to predict that profilers will be licensed in the not-too-distant future, say 15 to 20 years from now. This, of course, will have to be preceded by a standardization of the process. Although a standardized training curriculum may not be implemented, surely a combination of education, training, and experience will be required in order to be licensed as a profiler. A licensing program, accreditation process, or registration of experienced certified profilers may be entirely feasible. It should be noted that the Association of Chief Police Officers in the United Kingdom has, in a few cases, certified individual graduates of Canter's program in investigative psychology as profilers.

In order for there to be any substantial progress toward the licensing of profilers and the standardization of the process, it will be necessary for profiling to become much more of a science than an art. The truth of this becomes more apparent as profiling experts become more common at criminal and civil trials. Since Daubert v. Merrel Dow Pharmaceuticals in 1993, when the U.S. Supreme Court held that the Frye ruling of 1923 was no longer law in the area of expert evidence, some legal scholars have begun to question the scientific nature of profiling and the nature of its acceptance in a courtroom.

Falsifiability, known or potential error rate, and peer review appear to be three of the major points or tests of the Daubert decision (1993). Falsifiability refers to the question of hypothesis testing. In other words, testing a false hypothesis to determine whether statements of scientific explanation are capable of empirical testing. Error rates would refer to the percentage of error in the calculations or predictions of the science. Peer review is self-explanatory. The question is whether offender profiling stands up to any of the tests according to the Daubert decision. The issue appears to be further complicated in Daubert v. Merrel Dow Pharmaceuticals because it is the judge who must evaluate scientific evidence before it is presented to the jury. The Supreme Court provided the following guidance to trial judges: "Whether an expert is proposing to testify to scientific knowledge that will assist the trier of fact to understand or determine the fact at issue." At the very least, the Daubert decision will require a great deal of clarification, as expert profilers are being used more and more by the bar in criminal as well as civil litigation.

As with many processes, and as we move into the 21st century, the computer is playing a greater role. Attempts have been made to computerize the process of offender profiling in the last few years; however, few have been successful. It is not unreasonable to expect that these efforts will bear greater fruit in the near future. Possibly the program with the greatest success in computerizing the profiling process has been the Surrey Police Behavioral Science Section's development of the Behavioral Analysis Data Management Autoindexing Networking System (BADMAN). This systems application, although initially set up for sexual assaultive crimes, will deal with a full range of crimes when it becomes fully operational. BADMAN currently provides decision support in four application areas.

- The identification of possible suspects

- Case linking by behavior

- Preparation of similar fact evidence

- Criminal profiling

In addition to computerized profiling, social scientists are making progress with forensic analysis of written documents. Hodges, Callahan, and Groesbeck are developing and experimenting with a concept that they refer to as "profile decoding." Profile decoding is based on Dr. Robert Langs' theory of the unconscious mind and the encoding of hidden communication. "Since the unconscious mind is always communicating at the same time the conscious mind is, each sentence or story from a patient [suspect or unidentified author] has two messages—a conscious literal message and a deeper encoded unconscious message" (Hodges, Callahan, & Groesbeck, 1999a, p. 2). This work is currently being applied to the JonBenet Ramsey kidnapping note. With this written document, these researchers are attempting to seek the identity and the motive of the author of the note by decoding and clarifying the hidden communication of the narrative of the note. This new profiling technique has the potential to increase law enforcement's forensic capabilities in dealing with ransom notes and other criminal writing.

Another issue facing offender profiling in the future is the extent to which profilers come from the private sector or the public sector. Some would argue that this is not a valid issue of concern because competition should drive out less competent and unqualified profilers. Competition should win out in the long run and increase the quality of profiling; however, because profiling is a relatively new field, the extent to which quality will prevail is problematic. In the meantime, criminologists, psychologists, psychiatrists, criminal investigators, retired law enforcement officers, as well as psychics and charlatans will continue to call themselves profilers and offer their services to the law enforcement community. Caveat emptor!

Some observers of profiling in the United States may argue that the art or science of profiling by the FBI, although significant and important, has not progressed or moved forward since its development of the asocial disorganized and nonsocial organized types in the late 1970s. In order to address that issue, Cleary and Rettig (1994) have expanded this typology to four types: methodical extrovert, methodical introvert, chaotic extrovert, and chaotic introvert. These typologies are then presented in two-dimensional space on a profiling matrix. To better explain their typologies, Cleary and Rettig show how known serial killers, Ted Bundy, Jerry Brudos, Edmund Kemper, Jeffery

Dahmer, Henry Lee Lucas, and Albert DeSalvo fit within these matrix profiles. Although interesting, this expanded typology has not been applied in a real profiling situation to ascertain its utility.

In reviewing the expanding literature and research on offender profiling, it becomes readily apparent that policing is becoming a knowledge industry. In an age of information and services, in a postindustrial age, policing must gather all the information possible and shape it into knowledge in a timely and effective manner so that it may provide a high level of service to its constituents. The better the profile is, the better its forensic capability.

Jackson and Bekerian (1997) argue that for profiling to reach its potential, two things must happen. First, profilers must better understand the requirements and needs of police investigation, which means that the issues of validity and reliability will have to be addressed in both scientific and investigative methodologies. Second, investigators must better understand the nature and use of profiles, requiring the investigator to have some understanding of the theory and research behind offender profiling techniques (pp. 6–7). Although these two requirements are indeed necessary, we should never lose sight of the profile's utility to law enforcement. The behavioral sciences have indeed contributed greatly to offender profiling as a tool for law enforcement. Now that this tool is readily available or within easy reach of the police, it needs to be sharpened and honed through refinement of research techniques and the further development of theoretical constructs so that it can increase the effectiveness of criminal investigations.

Psychological profiling is a relatively new tool in a criminal investigator's arsenal. In some cases, this tool is poorly understood by criminal investigators. Although not all investigators need to be trained profilers, a better understanding of how profiling is accomplished and how it may aid an investigation is recommended. Criminal investigators need to understand that, in some cases, a profile may reduce the universe of suspects to a much more manageable number. Profiles do not have to solve crimes; however, if they are successful, they can make the investigator's job easier.

REFERENCES

Aitken, C., Connolly, T., Gammerman, A., Zhang, G., & Oldfield, D. (1995). *Predicting an offender's characteristics: An evaluation of statistical modeling* (paper 4). London: Police Research Group Special Interest Series, Home Office.

Ault, R. L., & Reese, J. T. (1980, June 28). A psychological assessment of crime profiling. *FBI Law Enforcement Bulletin*.

Brantingham, P.J., & Brantingham, P.L. (1978). A theoretical model of crime site selection. In M.Krohn and R.Akers (Eds.), *Theoretical Perspectives*. Thousand Oaks, CA: Sage.

Canter, D. (1994). *Criminal shadows: Inside the mind of a serial killer*. London: Harper Collins.

Cleary, S., & Rettig, R.P. (1994, November). *A profiling matrix for serial killers*. Paper presented at the 46th meeting of the American Society of Criminology, Chicago, Illinois.

Copson, G. (1995). *Coals to Newcastle? Part 1: A study of offender profiling*. (Paper 7). London: Police Research Group Special Interest Series, Home Office.

Daubert v. Merrell Dow Pharmaceuticals, 61 U.S.L.W. 4805 (1993).

Davies, A. (1994). Editorial: Offender profiling. *Medical Science and Law, 34*, 185-186.

Davies, A., & Dale, A. (1995). *Locating the stranger rapist*. (Paper 3). London: Police Research Group Special Interest Series, Home Office.

Davies, A., & Dale, A. (1996). Locating the rapist. *Medicine, Science and the Law, 18*, 163-178.

Douglas, J. (1995). *Mindhunter: Inside the FBI's elite serial crime unit*. New York: Scribner.

Douglas, J. (1997). *Journey into darkness*. New York: Scribner.

Douglas, J., Ressler, R.K., Burgess, A.W., & Hartman, C.R. (1986). Criminal profiling from crime scene analysis. *Behavioral Sciences and the Law*, 4, 401-421.

Egger, S. A. (1998). *The killers among us: An examination of serial murder and its investigation.* Englewood Cliffs, NJ: Prentice Hall.

Geberth, V.J. (1981). Psychological profiling. *Law and Order*, 46-52.

Geberth, V.J. (1996). *Practical homicide investigation* (3rd ed.). Boca Rotan, FL: CRC Press.

Harris, T. (1988). *Silence of the lambs*. New York: St. Martin's.

Hazelwood, R.R., Ressler, R.K., Depue, R.L., & Douglas, J.E. (1987). Criminal personality profiling: An overview. In R. R. Hazelwood and A. W. Burgess (Eds.). *Practical aspects of rape investigation: A multidisciplinary approach* (pp. 137-149). New York: Elsevier.

Hodges, A.G., Callahan, P., & Groesbeck, C.J. (1999a). *Profile decoding: A psycho-dynamic reconstruction of the unconscious content of the Ramsey ransom note*. Unpublished manuscript.

Hodges, A.G., Callahan, P., & Groesbeck, C.J. (1999b). *A theory of unconscious communication applied to forensic cases*. Unpublished manuscript.

Holmes, R., & DeBurger, J. (1988). *Serial murder*. Newbury Park, CA: Sage.

Holmes, R., & Holmes, S. (Eds.). (1998). *Contemporary perspectives on serial murder*. Thousand Oaks, CA: Sage.

Jackson, J.L., & Bekerian, D.A. (1997). *Offender profiling: Theory, research and practice*. Chicester, UK: John Wiley & Sons.

Jackson, J., Van Hoppen, P.J., & Hebrink, J. (1993). *Does the service meet the needs?* Amsterdam: Netherlands Institute for the Study of Criminality.

Kocsis, R.N., Irwin, H.J., & Hayes, A. F. (1988). *Psychiatry, Psychology and the Law*, 5(1), 117-131.

Kocsis, R., & Irwin, H. (1997). An analysis of spatial patterns in serial rape, arson, and burglary: The utility of the circle theory of environmental range for psychological profiling. *Psychiatry, Psychology and Law*, 4, 195-206.

Levin, J., & Fox, J.A. (1985). *Mass murder*. New York: Plenum.

Lieber, J.A. (1985). Contributions of psychiatric consultation in the investigation of serial murder. *International Journal of Offender Therapy and Comparative Criminology*, 29, 187-199.

McCann, J.T. (1992).Criminal personality profiling in the investigation of violent crime: Recent advances and future directions. *Behavioral Sciences and the Law*, 10, 475-481.

McCarthy, K. (1984, June 28). Serial killers: Their deadly bent may be set in cradle. *Los Angeles Times*, p. A1.

Michaud, S.C. (1986, Oct. 26). The FBI's new psyche squad. *New York Times Magazine* (pp. 40, 42, 50, 74, 76, 77.

Michaud, S.G., & Hazelwood R., (1998). *The evil that men do*. New York: St. Martin's Press.

Newton, M.B., & Newton, D.C. (1985, October 18). *Geoforensic identification of localized serial crime*. Paper presented at the Southwest Division, Association of American Geographers meeting, Denton, Texas.

Newton, M.B., & Swoope, E.A. (1987). *Geoforensic analysis of localized serial murder: The Hillside Stranglers located*. Unpublished manuscript.

Odgers, S.J., & Richardson, J.T. (1995). Keeping bad science out of the courtroom: Changes in American and Australian expert evidence law. *UNSW Law Journal, 18*.

Pinnizotto, A.J. (1984). Forensic psychology: Criminal personality profiling. *Journal of Police Science and Administration*, 12, 32-37.

Pinnizotto A.J., & Finkel, N.J. (1990). Criminal personality profiling. *Law and Human Behavior, 14*, 215-233.

Porter, B. (1983, April). Mind hunters. *Psychology Today*.

Ressler, R.K. (1994). *Justice is served*. New York: St. Martin's Press.

Ressler, R.K., Burgess, A.W., & Douglas, J.E. (1984). *Serial murder: A new phenomenon of homicide*. Paper presented at the annual meeting of the International Association of Forensic Sciences, Oxford, England.

Ressler, R.K., Burgess, A.W., Douglas, J.E., & Depue, R. L. (1985). Criminal profiling research on homicide. In A. W. Burgess (Eds.), *Rape and sexual assault: A research handbook* (pp. 343-349). New York: Garland.

Rossmo, D.K. (1995). *Geographical profiling: Target patterns of serial murderers*. Unpublished doctoral dissertation, Simon Frasier University, Vancouver, British Columbia, Canada.

Rumbelow, D. (1988). *The complete Jack the Ripper*. London: Penguin.

Skrapec, C. (1984, December). *Psychological profiling and serial murderers*. Paper presented at the Doctoral Seminar on Psychopathology, Crime and Social Deviance, City University of New York.

Wilson, P., Lincoln, R., and Kocsis, R. (1997). Validity, utility and ethics of profiling for serial violent and sexual predators. *Psychiatry, Psychology and Law, 4*, 1-11.

Wilson, P., & Soothill, K. (1996). Psychological profiling: Red, green or amber? *The Police Journal*, 12-20.

Steven A. Egger is a professor of criminal justice at the University of Houston-Clear Lake. Nationally recognized as an expert on serial murder, Dr. Egger received his Ph.D. from Sam Houston University. Since that time, he has held several academic appointments in institutions of higher education. He was the former dean at the University of Illinois at Springfield. Dr. Egger is the author of two books on serial murder and is interested in the field of psychological profiling, especially when it involves a suspected serial murder case.

SECTION II

METHODOLOGIES OF OFFENDER PROFILING

Section II of *Offender Profiling* focuses on the various methodologies of offender profiling. Researchers have studied various approaches to offender profiling, to determine the most effective methodologies. Attempts at offender profiling, or inferring offender characteristics from crime scene behaviors have developed in part from investigators experience and knowledge of criminal behavior. Some researchers argue that these attempts have had mixed results and argue for the scientific study of offender profiling and the development of testable methodologies to determine the accuracy of profiling efforts.

For example, in *Psychology of Offender Profiling*, author David Canter (1995) discusses IP or Investigative Psychology and argues for a scientific approach to offender profiling drawing on psychological theories of criminal behavior. Canter illustrates a methodology which focuses on the psychological issues involved in profiling and how it diverges from a common sense approach developed by individual investigators in the field. He describes the relationship between sexual actions in assaults and the offenders' criminal history, as well as, the relationship between rapists' behaviors and offender characteristics to explain the profiling methodology as a canonical correlation. Canter contends there are underlying trends and consistencies in criminals' actions and provides two hypotheses central to profiling: 1) the offender consistency hypothesis and 2) the offence specificity hypothesis.

In *Criminal Profiling from Crime Scene Analysis* authors Douglas, Ressler, Burgess, and Hartman (1986) demonstrate the FBI approach to criminal profiling which seeks to determine the behavioral patterns of a suspect through investigative concepts. They describe this methodology as a criminal profile generating process that has the apprehension of the offender as its ultimate goal. Each of the process's six stages is explained in generating a profile of a murder suspect. The authors illustrate that this process of criminal personality profiling is a useful tool fro law enforcement in the investigation of violent crimes.

Author John Libert (1985) describes yet another methodology in *Contributions of Psychiatric Consultation in the Investigation of Serial Murder*. He discusses offender profiling from the psychiatric discipline in an effort to improve communication between investigators and psychiatric consultants in serial murder cases. This article provides a background explanation of profiling from a psychiatric perspective, illustrating the psychological terminology and reasoning related to serial murder. Libert describes the psychological formulations of serial murder, describing the language and concepts used by psychiatrists to explain sex and aggression in crimes. He demonstrates how these concepts are integrated into the construction of a profile of the serial murderer.

In the 1999 article *Profiling Killers: A Revised Classification Model for Understanding Sexual Murder* authors Keppel and Richard Walter present a classification model for sexually oriented murderers. They describe the homicide dynamics, homicide patterns, and suspect profiles of four types of rape murderers. These typologies include the power assertive, power reassurance, anger retaliatory, and anger excitation rape murderers. This article focuses on a crime classification model that incorporates the behaviors, motivations, and experiential learning of the offender and addresses the crime scene and behavioral characteristics that can assist law enforcement in prioritizing suspect leads and apprehending killers. In addition, Keppel and Walter provide insightful examples of each of the types of rape murderers to assist investigators in processing crime scenes and inferring offender and behavioral characteristics from crime scene details.

PSYCHOLOGY OF OFFENDER PROFILING

DAVID CANTER

Investigative Psychology Research Group
Department of Psychology
University of Surrey

ORIGINS

The term "Offender Profiling" was first regularly used by members of the FBI's Behavioural Science Unit, to describe the process of drawing inferences about a suspect's characteristics from the details of his[1] actions in a crime. Concerned mainly with rape and homicide (Hazelwood and Burgess, 1987; Ressler, et al 1988), they demonstrated that it was possible to draw general conclusions about the lifestyle, criminal history and residential location of a person who had committed a number of crimes, from careful examination of where, when and how those crimes had been committed.

Although the inference processes on which the FBI agents drew were illuminated by interviews they themselves had conducted with a few dozen convicted offenders, and by their own experiences of investigating many crimes, their process of inference derivation were broadly *deductive*, in the meaning of being based upon common sense as might be the basis of Judicial decisions. In the tradition of the detective novel, and other less fictional accounts of the solving of crimes, the processes that the FBI agents used focused on the clues derived directly from the crime scene. They drew upon general principles, drawn from everyday experience, to deduce the implications that the internal logic of a crime might have. So, for example, a well organised and planned crime would be hypothesised to be perpetrated by an individual who typically was well organised and planned his life (Ressler, et al 1988).

Subsequently, a number of studies, the majority of which have been conducted by the Investigative Psychology Research Group, at the University of Surrey, have been able to demonstrate that the valuable insights of FBI agents can be developed by using the *inductive* processes of science. By considering empirical results from the study of the actions of a large number of criminals it has been possible to propose both theories and methodologies that elaborate the relationships between an offender's actions and his characteristics.

Two interrelated issues need to be distinguished here. One is the common procedure of inferring general characteristics about a person from particulars of his or her behaviour. The second issue has its roots more clearly in the traditions of scientific psychology. This is the possibility of building psychological theories that will show how and why variations in criminal behaviour occur.

---

[1] All the criminals referred to in this chapter are male

The first meaning for "Offender profiling" with its origins in everyday experience, described the process whereby experienced investigators, and other people with direct knowledge of criminal activities, could give advice to detectives. As such, this procedure has roots that can be traced at least to biblical times. It is, therefore, not surprising that from the earliest years of criminal investigations, there have been attempts to draw upon similar ideas in order to give assistance to the conduct of enquiries. The senior medical officer at the time of the Jack the Ripper enquiry in 1888, provided suggestions about the characteristics of the offender in an attempt to help the police locate the killer (Rumbelow, 1988). Earlier in the nineteenth century the novelist Edgar Allan Poe, had given guidance, with a similar lack of success, to police investigations in the United States. Much of what is called 'profiling' today still has its roots in this application of 'common sense'.

In what follows, I will focus on the second meaning that is developing for 'offender profiling', dealing with the psychological issues involved.

CONSTRAINTS

There are constraints on both the information available to the police during an investigation and also on the type of information on which they can act. The constraints on the information available about the crime relate to the fact that only an account of what has happened, who the victim is, where it took place and when, is available to investigators. There is hardly ever any direct observation by the investigator, or the possibility of direct contact with the offender during the commission of the crime. This is very different from most areas of psychology, where the person of focal interest is available for close, direct observation and detailed questioning. If there is a victim who survives a crime, then that victim may be able to give the details of what occurred. But even in this case, it is unlikely that the victim can give any reliable information about the internal, cognitive processes of the perpetrator during the criminal acts. So the predictor variables are limited to those that are external to the offender.

The criteria variables (i.e. important features of the offender) are also restricted, because the information on which the police can act is limited to what is available to them in the investigative process. Details of a person's criminal history, as well as descriptions of age and appearance, occupational characteristics and domestic circumstances are all potentially available to investigating officers for any particular suspect. However, personality characteristics, detailed measures of intelligence, attitudes and fantasies are all more difficult for investigating officers to uncover. Similarly, in relation to giving guidance as to where detectives should look to find possible suspects, information about residential location, or recreational activities, for example, are more likely to be of immediate value than the issues with which psychologists are more conventionally concerned, such as locus of control or sexual predilections.

THE CANONICAL EQUATIONS

The methodological difficulties and the need for theory in this area can be illustrated by consideration of the inferential problem at the heart of profiling as a Canonical Correlation (cf. Tabachnick and Fidell, 1983). Such a procedure has the objective of analysing "the relationships between two sets of variables" (p. 146). In other words, it is an attempt to derive multiple regression equations that have a number of criterion variables as well as a number of predictor variables.

On one side of this equation are variables derived from information about the offence which would be available to investigators. On the other side, there are the characteristics of the offender that are most useful in facilitating the police enquiry. So, if $A_{1...n}$ represents n actions of the offender (including, for example, time, place and victim selection) and $C_{1...m}$ represents m characteristics of the offender, then the empirical question is to establish the values of the weightings ($F_{1...n}$ and $K_{1...m}$) in an equation of the following form:

$$F_1A_1 + ... + F_nA_n = K_1C_1 + ... + K_mC_m$$

If such canonical equations could be established for any subset of crimes then they would provide a powerful basis for police investigations, as well as raising some fascinating psychological questions about criminal behaviour.

The first step in producing such equations is to demonstrate that there are reliable relationships between A(ction)s and C(haracteristic)s, even at the one to one level. Indeed, the whole possibility of an empirically based approach to offender profiling depends upon the presence of these relationships.

A Study of the Relationship of Sexual Actions in Assaults and Offenders' Offence History

A number of studies conducted at the University of Surrey do show that this *a priori* assumption can be supported fairly readily. For example in an unpublished study of 60 serial rapists that I carried out with Rupert Heritage, we classified the first offence of each offender in terms of the presence or absence of four sexual aspects of the assault that had a frequency that was neither very high, nor very low in the sample: i.e., (i) insistence by the offender that the victim masturbate him, (ii) oral ejaculation by the offender (iii) aggression by the offender during the sexual activity and (iv) aggression after it. These four A(ction) variables were each independently correlated with two variables created on the basis of whether or not the offender had a criminal record for firstly, indecent exposure and secondly indecent assault. A further two C(haracteristics) variables were created to indicate the frequency of indecency convictions, thirdly, as a juvenile and fourthly as an adult. Each of the four A variables was then correlated with each of the four C variables.

Using conventional indicators of statistical significance, fifteen out of the sixteen values would be considered significant, providing definite evidence that the occurrence of certain actions during a sexual assault are more likely to be made by a man with a criminal history for indecency than not. But such results also raise many questions. For example in this instance frequency of juvenile convictions for indecency has the highest correlation with the sexual actions, but without extensive examination of a variety of other possible C variables and the relationships they have to each other it is difficult to tell how reliable such a correlation is likely to be with other samples. This correlation may drop considerably if the sample had a lower age range, for it may just be an artefact of the age of the offenders.

An Example of the Relationships Between Rapists' Behaviour and Offender Characteristics

Carrying out a further study on the same sample of sixty rapes, a number of characteristics beyond the criminal history of the offenders were considered; these were correlated with a range of distinct offence behaviours, such as wearing gloves, binding the victim and so on. The association coefficients in this case were not as high as for the previous analysis but the majority would pass conventional criteria for statistical significance. However, the problem that these results illustrate is that there are no uniquely strong relationships between a given A variable and a given C variable.

This means that there will be a mixture of correlations within the A variables and within the C variables that will contaminate any initial attempts to establish specific relationships between these two groups of variables.

These results, thus lend some support to the possibility of establishing empirical links between the A and C variables of the canonical correlation, for one type of crime at least. Other unpublished studies have indicated similar possibilities for burglary (Barker 1989), workplace crime (Robertson, 1993) and child abuse (Kirby, 1993 and Corstorphine, 1993). But in no case are there simple relationships between one A variable and one C variable. The central problems of canonical equations thus emerge. A variety of combinations of A weightings can just as validly give rise to a variety of combinations of C weightings. There is not one, but many possible relationships within any data set linking the A's to the C's. In concrete terms this could mean for instance that one pattern of behaviour could indicate a young man with little criminal history or just as readily an older man with a lot of criminal experience.

A second problem was identified by Tabachnick and Fidell (1983). This is the sensitivity of the solution in the A set of variables to the inclusion of variables in the C set. Minor variations in the variance or the inclusion of particular variables in the A set may radically change the weightings in the C set. So, for example, leaving out of the calculations an action because a witness or victim was not sure about it, could produce different proposals about the offender than if that action were included.

THE OFFENDER CONSISTENCY HYPOTHESIS

One hypothesis central to profiling is that the way an offender carries out a crime on one occasion will have some characteristic similarities to the way he carries out crimes on other occasions. If the inherent variations between contexts, for any aspect of human behaviour, is greater than the variations between people then it is unlikely that clear differences between individuals will be found for those behaviours. This hypothesis is applicable to the situation in which a person has committed only one crime. Even in that case a 'profile' has to be based upon the assumption that the criminal is exhibiting characteristics that are typical of him, not of the situation in which the crime was committed.

An Examination of the Linking of Three Rapes to one Offender

This can be illustrated by an exploratory study of 17 serial rapists carried out by Hammond (1990). For each rapist three rapes were selected, representing attacks that occurred in the early, middle and late stages of their series. For each rape 16 actions were identified to cover the range of actions that occurred in the rapes. Treating the actions as all or nothing occurrences within the whole sample the probability profile for each rape was drawn up. This consisted of the expected frequency of each action for each profile of actions, derived from the frequency of each action and the frequency of each profile. Joint probability calculations were then performed for each of the 51 (3×17) offences by comparing their actual dichotomous profiles with the expected frequency profile. This gave an index, presented as a probability, of the specificity of the three offences for each of the 17 individuals.

The results demonstrated that in less than 15% of the cases the probability was so low as to indicate, wrongly, that the offence was not committed by the offender convicted of it. Eleven out of the seventeen rapists (65%) had all their offences correctly attributed to them, showing consistency across all three offences. It is also interesting to note that in this small, exploratory study the first and third offences seemed to be more accurately identified than the middle offence. Indeed none of the third offences were assigned a probability below 0.72.

A small study such as this, that inevitably assumes all the convictions were 'safe', cannot be taken as evidence for offender consistency, but it does serve to show that such consistency can be demonstrated by the application of conventional probability theory to a mathematical profile of criminal actions. Such procedures could be developed both as analytic tools to help establish the conditions under which consistency did occur and even have the potential for contributing directly to criminal investigations.

An Illustration of The Comparison of a Target Offence with the Action Profiles of Other Offenders

Offender consistency has two components; the degree of variation within one offender's actions and the range of variation across a number of offenders. Although these two questions are distinguished by apparently small changes in emphasis there are potentially large differences in their implications. The actions that may be characteristic of a person across a series of offences may be quite different from those actions that help to discriminate him from other possible offenders in a large pool.

This can be illustrated by a study examining the actions of one rapist in relation to 45 others. This man was known to have committed 73 offences of many kinds, but for the purposes of this illustration his first known rape was examined. For this comparison ten aspects of rape were identified (drawing on the model of Canter and Heritage, 1989). Each of the 45 known rapists was assigned a characteristic profile by determining their modal behaviour across all the rapes for which they were convicted. The first rape of the target offender was then correlated with all the modal profiles of the 45 rapists, using the ten actions as the basis for the correlation.

Only 14 offenders produced correlations greater than 0.00. Only one offender, the target himself, obtained a perfect correlation. In this example, furthermore, only two others came close in their similarity coefficients. These results certainly illustrate that target offences can be linked to the characteristics patterns of their perpetrators, but much larger samples would be necessary to demonstrate the generality of these findings.

The Home Range Hypothesis

One set of actions of particular significance to police investigations are those that relate to the distance that an offender travels from home in order to commit the crime. The offender consistency hypothesis would lead to the proposal that there will be some structure, (identifiable pattern) to the locations at which an offender chooses to commit crimes. A number of studies have given general support to this proposition (reviewed in Brantingham and Brantingham, 1981; Evans and Herbert, 1989).

Recent studies (Canter and Larkin, 1993) have developed this proposition to show that there are reasonably precise relationships between the distances that rapists travel between their crimes (an A variable) and the distance they are travelling from home (a C variable). Barker (1989) has also shown similar relationships for burglars. The distances that rapists travel also appears to relate to other aspects of their offence, such as whether it is committed indoors or outdoors. Therefore by combining the purely geographical information with other aspects of the offence it has been possible to produce a data base search procedure that could narrow the area of likely residence of a known offender, on average, to less than a 3 km radius (Canter and Gregory, 1994). Whatever the eventual practical benefits of these studies their theoretical import is further to support the general proposition that the way an offender commits crimes is characteristic of that individual and distinguishable from the offence 'style' of other offenders committing similar crimes.

The Offence Specificity Hypothesis

If there is the possibility that an offender will reveal some consistency in any particular crime there is the further question about how much of a criminal specialist he is. Much of the criminology literature suggests that especially younger offenders are quite eclectic in their forms of crime, to the extent that individuals who have committed one type of crime are likely to have committed crimes of other types. Thus even establishing distinct groups of offenders on the basis of their types of crime may prove problematic.

A Study of the Specialisms of Juvenile Delinquents

The whole enterprise of deriving characteristics of offenders that could be reliable enough to be of utility in police investigation would be under serious threat if, as some argue, offenders are typically versatile in the types of offence that they commit. If a) opportunity and particular circumstances are seen to determine the particular crime that is committed, and b) social processes and aspects of individual learning give rise to a preparedness on the part of anybody to carry out a criminal act, but c) which particular act is carried out is as much due to chance and circumstance as to the propensities of the criminal, then no criminal could be distinguished from another. Such a perspective would argue that really any criminal could commit one of a great variety of different types of offence and therefore, it would not be possible to infer anything about the person from his or her particular crime.

Another argument, that is probably more relevant in relation to violent and obviously emotional crime, is the one that assumes these crimes are committed in states of impulsive, unplanned action. For these crimes it is postulated that people react in such an unstructured way that no aspect of their characteristics is likely to be revealed, other than possibly their characteristic impulsivity. For instance the location chosen will be a haphazard one that bears no relationship to other aspects of the individual's life. Similarly, their victims may be regarded as of no particular significance. The contrasting argument may be thought of as the *modus operandi* argument. The view that a criminal's actions are unique to him and therefore patterns and trends that allow the groupings of individuals are very unlikely. Any theory that is a basis for offender profiling will need to fit somewhere between the idiosyncratic perspective that is typical of *modus operandi* arguments and the generalist perspective that might be drawn from some criminological theories.

Approaches to Theory

The challenge is to establish the themes that will help to identify and explain the links between crime based consistencies and characteristics of the offender.

Cause or Relationship

Conceptually there are number of different roles that a theory can play in helping to link the A and the C variables. One is to explain how it is that the C variables are the cause of the A variables. A different theoretical perspective would be to look for some common third set of intervening variables that was produced by the C variables to cause the A variables. Yet a third possibility is that some third set of variables was the cause of both the A and the C variables. A variety of theoretical perspectives that reveal greater or lesser clarity on possible relationships between A and C are available.

a. Psychodynamic Typologies

Psychodynamic theories see the differences not so much in the crimes as in the internal emotional dynamics of the criminal, as reflected, for example, in the often quoted, rape typology of Groth and Birnbaum (1979), with its distinctions between offenders who are acting out their anger and those who are acting out desires for power. By their very nature, these theories are specific to particular types of crime. These tend to be crimes of violence and especially sexual crimes. There appear to be no attempts to apply similar psychodynamic consideration to say, burglary or fraud.

What this approach usually gives rise to is the proposal of a few broad types. In effect, a small number of simple equations that link the A and C variables are proposed. Each of these equations is shaped by a trend common to the A and the C variables; the need for power, anger, control and so on. These trends may be explained in term of displacement of anger from other targets, or the feeling of lack of power and the consequent compensatory search to obtain it illegally. Stephenson (1992) has reviewed such displacement compensation theories as general explanations of criminal behaviour and found little evidence for them. Such theories are the basis of the FBI typologies of rape and murder.

b. Personality Differences

An approach that emerges more directly from experimental psychology is the proposal that the A and the C variables will share underlying personality characteristics. Research conducted to explore this thesis has tended to focus on simple A variables; the crime for which a person has been convicted. Such studies compare people who have committed different crimes so, for example, robbers are compared with rapists, or burglars with child abusers. The comparison process of such studies need not have this artificial, quasi-experimental design to it, but people who have this type of hypothesis do tend to think in terms of some particular cause that has led a person to become involved in burglary or buggery and, therefore, there is a tendency to set the studies up as if a comparison of some direct causal influence were being examined.

Perhaps the most direct illustration of such an exploration is the work of Eysenck (1977), who argued that there are personality differences between different types of criminal. By comparing groups of people convicted of one particular offence on personality measurements, conclusions are drawn about the personality differences between different offenders.

The evidence for the variety of crimes in which any given individual is involved, throws some very real doubt on the possibility of explaining or predicting criminal characteristics from the particular type of crime that he or she carried out. Furthermore, any examination of the legal definition of crimes will demonstrate that there is some arbitrariness in terms of what the actual actions are that characterise a particular crime.

Despite these difficulties, however, it does seem unlikely that a person's personality is not reflected in some way in how he or she commits crimes. A person's intelligence or extraversion would be expected to have some bearing on what and how a criminal offends. The problem is identifying those 'real world' A and C variables that do have direct links to personality characteristics.

c. Career Routes

A rather different approach to distinguishing between offenders can be drawn from general, criminology theory. Here the idea is that a person starts off in his or her life of crime, much as the junior office worker may start off in a large organisation. A variety of opportunities are presented and a variety of experiences are gained. Through this process, the individual learns that he or she is particularly successful or particularly attracted to certain types of activities and so a form of specialism evolves. In this framework, people become muggers, burglars or rapists as their criminal career unfolds.

There is certainly broad evidence in support of this career conceptualisation. The criminological literature shows that when aggregates of crimes are examined, serious violent crimes are typically committed by offenders who are older than those involved in minor theft. Cohort studies (notably Farrington, 1986) have also indicated the variations in crimes that cohorts are involved in at different ages. However, for such an approach to be of direct value to profiling a number of detailed studies of individuals would be necessary in order to establish just what number and variety of career routes could be found through the criminal jungle.

This perspective offers two possible forms of elaboration of the canonical correlation by adding a temporal dimension. The most complex temporal elaboration is to propose that a matrix of equations would be necessary, in essence one equation for each stage in the criminal career. This would be a daunting research task requiring considerable resources and large data sets. A simpler framework deals with the C variables as aspects of the stage a criminal is at, i.e. what other criminal experiences he is likely to have.

d. Socio-Economic Sub-Groups

A more strongly socially oriented theory of offender differences would draw attention to the sub-groups from which they are likely to come. A detailed proposal of how "social profiles" could be drawn up for sexual mass murderers was presented by Leyton in 1983. He argued that the general social characteristics of sexual mass murderers were known, citing matters such as family breakdown and socio-economic status. Here, then, the link between the A and the C variables is postulated because they are both hypothesised to be the reflections of the same social processes of anomie and social breakdown. This perspective has potential for development if the social characteristics of sub-groups of offenders could be established. The difficulty is likely to be that most criminals are drawn from similar socio-economic circumstances so that discriminating between them in terms of these characteristics could prove very challenging. However, current studies (e.g. Robertson 1993) do suggest that in certain types of crime, notably work place crime and fraud, there may be quite strong differences in the types and styles of crime in relation to social sub-groups.

e. Interpersonal narratives

A further theoretical perspective (Canter 1994) is emerging which attempts to build links between the strengths of all the approaches outlined above. This approach sees any crime as an interpersonal transaction that involves characteristic ways of dealing with other people. It leads to hypotheses both about the range of crimes in which an individual will be involved and his or her characteristic ways of committing those crimes. Furthermore, it leads to hypotheses about consistencies between forms of criminal activity and other aspects of a criminal's life.

In essence, it is argued that although there will be some generality of criminal activity, common across a range of offenders who have committed similar types of crime, there will nonetheless be a sub-set, or repertoire, of criminal activity that an individual will tend to operate within. This will be reflected both in the types of crime committed, as well as the repertoire of actions engaged in for any particular type of crime. The origin of these interpersonal themes is hypothesised to have routes in the learning of styles of interpersonal interaction. Drawing on general theories in social psychology, it can be proposed that styles of transactions will essentially be directed against other people as objects to be abused, or as vehicles that provide an opportunity for some type of interpersonal exploitation.

Two sets of hypotheses can be derived from this conceptualisation. One set of hypotheses relates to the existence of sub-sets of interrelated activities. These may be classes of crimes which offenders tend to commit, or classes of behaviour that tend to be committed within a crime. An important point here is that individuals are expected to have overlapping sets of repertoires that will have characteristic themes associated with them. It is not expected that every person will fit distinctly into one type of offender or another.

The second set of hypotheses relates to predictions about the correlations between the themes that an offender exhibits and other characteristics that he might have. At the most elementary level this is an hypothesis about the characteristic style of criminal transaction. So, for example, a person who goes to some trouble to control his victim during the committal of a sexual offence, binding and gagging her, for example, would be hypothesised to be someone who has thought through the exploitation of others in order to avoid capture while escaping with a criminal act. Such a person, therefore, would be hypothesised as having a range of criminal history, including the committing of offences that there not necessarily of a sexual nature.

The study by Canter and Heritage (1989) shows one approach that can help develop the narrative perspective into a set of more precise, testable hypotheses. By content analysing the actions that occurred in 63 rapes they were able to identify 57 distinct actions. A subsequent analysis of the co-occurrence of these actions demonstrated that whilst there were a number of actions that were common to the great majority of sexual assaults there were also interpretable trends that characterised sub-sets of the less frequent actions. These trends were interpreted in terms of the interpersonal focus of the assault: a) the victim as an object of no concern to the offender, b) the victim as a target to be aggressively controlled, c) the victim as a sexual object, d) the victim as a source for criminal activity, and e) the victim as a person with whom a pseudo-relationship is desired. Heritage (1992) has been able to indicate that there may be important differences between the characteristics of these sub-groups, especially in terms of their previous criminal history and relationships with women.

CONCLUSIONS

The general experience of providing 'profiles' of offenders for police investigations has been drawn upon to formulate reasonably precise research questions. It has been shown that even the elementary models that underlie these questions have an inherent complexity to them, readily encapsulated in canonical equations. The demands on theory which these complexities generate are further extended by an awareness of the practical constraints under which any theory must be applied.

It has been proposed that central to all theory building in this area is the need to demonstrate consistencies within the actions of offenders and identifiable differences between them. Examples have been presented from a range of exploratory studies to show that there are indeed likely to be differences between offenders that are based upon consistencies in the actions of individual criminals. However, it is unlikely that rigid typologies of offenders will be empirically supported, rather there will be thematic trends to their actions that will be characteristic of both their target offence and other aspects of their personal history and life style.

Two points that emerge repeatedly from a number of studies help to give more shape to these general findings. The first is that the consistencies in a criminal's action broadly relate to whether his crimes involve some form of psycho-social, interpersonal contact or whether they may be described as psychologically distant exploitations of other people. The second is that the best predictor of later crime behaviour is indeed earlier criminal activity.

Taken together these two points put into high relief the central problem of recidivism; that it is rooted in psychologically entrenched ways of dealing with others. But they also point out the importance of going beyond general explanation of why people continue to offend and the need to explain why they continue to offend in a particular way.

REFERENCES

Barker, M. (1989). Criminal Activity and Home Range: A study of the spatial offence patterns of burglars. University of Surrey, M.Sc. dissertation (unpublished)

Brantingham, P.J., & Brantingham, P.L. (eds.) (1981). *Environmental Criminology*. Beverley Hills: Sage

Canter, D. (ed) (1985) *Facet Theory: Approaches to Social Research*. New York: Springer-Verlag

Canter, D. (1994). *Criminal Shadows*. London: HarperCollins

Canter, D., & Gregory, A. (1994, in press). Identifying the Residential Location of Rapists. *Journal of the Forensic Science Society*,

Canter, D., & Heritage, R. (1989) A Multivariate Model of Sexual Offence Behaviour. *The Journal of Forensic Psychiatry 1*, pp. 185-212.

Canter, D., & Larkin, P. (1993). The Environmental Range of Serial Rapists. *Journal of Environmental Psychology, 13*, pp. 63-69.

Corstorphine, E. (1993). *A Comparison of Sexual and Physical Abusers of Children*. University of Surrey: M.Sc. dissertation (unpublished)

Evans, D.J., & Herbert, D.T. (1989). *The Geography of Crime*. London: Routledge.

Eysenck, H. (1977). *Crime and Personality*. London: Paladin

Farrington, D. (1986). Stepping Stones to Adult Criminal Careers, in D. Olweus, J. Block, and M. Radke-Yarrow (eds) *Development of Antisocial and Prosocial Behaviour*. London: Academic Press. pp 359-384.

Groth, N., & Birnbaum, H. (1979). *Men who Rape: The Psychology of the Offender*. New York: Plenum.

Heritage, R. (1992). *Facets of Sexual Assault: First steps in investigative classifications*. University of Surrey, M. Phil dissertation (unpublished).

Hammond, S. (1990). *Statistical Approaches to Crime Linking*. University of Surrey: Internal Report

Hazelwood, R.R., & Burgess A. (eds.) (1987). *Practical Aspects of Rape Investigation: A Multidisciplinary Approach*. Amsterdam: Elsevier.

Herbert D.T. (eds.) (1989). *The Geography of Crime*. London: Routledge.

Kirby, S. (1993). *The Child Molester: Separating Myth from Reality*. University of Surrey: Ph.D. dissertation (unpublished).

Leyton, E. (1983). A Social Profile of Sexual Mass Murderers, in T. Fleming and L.A. Visano (eds) *Deviant Designations*. London: Butterworths.

Ressler, R.K., Burgess, A.W., & Douglas, J.E. (1988) *Sexual Homicide: Patterns and Motives*. Lexington: Lexington.

Robertson, A.R.T. (1993). *A Psychological Perspective on Blue-Collar Workplace Crime* University of Surrey, M.Sc. dissertation (unpublished).

Rumbelow, D. (1988). *The Complete Jack the Ripper*. London: Penguin.

Stephenson, G.M. (1992). *The Psychology of Criminal Justice*. Oxford: Blackwell.

Tabachnick, B.G., & Fidell, L.S. (1983). *Using Multivariate Statistics*. London: Harper & Row.

CRIMINAL PROFILING FROM CRIME SCENE ANALYSIS

JOHN E. DOUGLAS, M.S.,

ROBERT K. RESSLER, M.S.,

ANN W. BURGESS, R.N., D.N.Sc. AND

CAROL R. HARTMAN, R.N., D.N.Sc.

Since the 1970s, investigative profilers at the FBI's Behavioral Science Unit (now part of the National Center for the Analysis of Violent Crime) have been assisting local, state, and federal agencies in narrowing investigations by providing criminal personality profiles. An attempt is now being made to describe this criminal-profile-generating process. A series of five overlapping stages lead to the sixth stage, or the goal of apprehension of the offender: (1) profiling inputs, (2) decision-process models, (3) crime assessment, (4) the criminal profile, (5) investigation, and (6) apprehension. Two key feedback filters in the process are: (a) achieving congruence with the evidence, with decision models, and with investigation recommendations, and (b) the addition of new evidence.

> "You wanted to mock yourself at me! ... You did not know your Hercule Poirot." He thrust out his chest and twirled his moustache.
>
> I looked at him and grinned ... "All right then," I said. "Give us the answer to the problems—if you know it."
>
> "But of course I know it."
>
> Hardcastle stared at him incredulously ... "Excuse me, Monsieur Poirot, you claim that you know who killed thred people. And why? ... All you mean is that you have a hunch."
>
> I will not quarrel with you over a wood ... Come now, Inspector. I know—really know ... I perceive you are still sceptic. But first let me say this: To be sure means that when the right solution is reached, everything falls into place. You perceive that in no other way could things have happened."
>
> (Christie, 1963, pp. 227–228)

The ability of Hercule Poirot to solve a crime by describing the perpetrator is a skill shared by the expert investigative profiler. Evidence speaks its own language of patterns and sequences that can reveal the offender's behavioral characteristics. Like Poirot, the profiler can say, "I know who he must be."

This article focuses on the developing technique of criminal profiling. Special Agents at the FBI Academy have demonstrated expertise in crime scene analysis of various violent crimes, particularly those involving sexual homicide. This article discusses the history of profiling and the criminal-profile-generating process and provides a case example to illustrate the technique.

Introduction: History of Criminal Profiling

Criminal profiling has been used successfully by law enforcement in several areas and is a valued means by which to narrow the field of investigation. Profiling does *not* provide the specific identity of the offender. Rather, it indicates the kind of person most likely to have committed a crime by focusing on certain behavioral and personality characteristics.

Profiling techniques have been used in various settings, such as hostage taking (Reiser, 1982). Law enforcement officers need to learn as much as possible about the hostage taker in order to protect the lives of the hostages. In such cases, police are aided by verbal contact (although often limited) with the offender, and possibly by access to his family and friends. They must be able to assess the subject in terms of what course of action he is likely to take and what his reactions to various stimuli might be.

Profiling has been used also in identifying anonymous letter writers (Casey-Owens 1984) and persons who make written or spoken threats of violence (Miron & Douglas 1979). In cases of the latter, psycholinguistic techniques have been used to compose a "threat dictionary," whereby every word in a message is assigned, by computer, to a specific category. Words as they are used in the threat message are then compared with those words as they are used in ordinary speech or writings. The vocabulary usage in the message may yield "signature" words unique to the offender. In this way, police may not only be able to determine that several letters were written by the same individual, but also to learn about the background and psychology of the offender.

Rapists and arsonists also lend themselves to profiling techniques. Through careful interview of the rape victim about the rapist's behavior, law enforcement personnel begin to build a profile of the offender (Hazelwood, 1983). The rationale behind this approach is that behavior reflects personality, and by examining behavior the investigator may be able to determine what type of person is responsible for the offense. For example, common characteristics of arsonists have been derived from an analysis of the data from the FBI's *Crime in the United States* (Rider, 1980). Knowledge of these characteristics can aid the investigator in identifying possible suspects and in developing techniques and strategies for interviewing them. However, studies in this area have focused on specific categories of offenders and are not yet generalizable to all offenders.

Criminal profiling has been found to be of particular usefulness in crimes such as serial sexual homicides. These crimes create a great deal of fear because of their apparently random and motive-less nature, and they are also given high publicity. Consequently, law enforcement personnel are under great public pressure to apprehend the perpetrator as quickly as possible. At the same time, these crimes may be the most difficult to solve, precisely because of their apparent randomness.

While it is not completely accurate to say that these crimes are motiveless, the motive may all too often be one understood only by the perpetrator. Lunde (1976) demonstrates this issue in terms of the victims chosen by a particular offender. As Lunde points out, although the serial murderer may not know his victims, their selection is not random. Rather, it is based on the murderer's perception of certain characteristics of his victims that are of symbolic significance to him. An analysis of the similarities and differences among victims of a particular serial murderer provides important information concerning the "motive" in an apparently motiveless crime. This, in turn, may yield information about the perpetrator himself. For example, the murder may be the result of a sadistic fantasy in the mind of the murderer and a particular victim may be targeted because of a symbolic aspect of the fantasy (Ressler et al., 1985).

In such cases, the investigating officer faces a completely different situation from the one in which a murder occurs as the result of jealousy or a family quarrel, or during the commission of another felony. In those cases, a readily identifiable motive may provide vital clues about the identity of the perpetrator. In the case of the apparently motiveless crime, law enforcement may need to look to other methods in addition to conventional investigative techniques, in its efforts to identify the perpetrator. In this context, criminal profiling has been productive, particularly in those crimes where the offender has demonstrated repeated patterns at the crime scene.

THE PROFILING OF MURDERERS

Traditionally, two very different disciplines have used the technique of profiling murderers: mental health clinicians who seek to explain the personality and actions of a criminal through psychiatric concepts, and law enforcement agents whose task is to determine the behavioral patterns of a suspect through investigative concepts.

Psychological Profiling

In 1957, the identification of George Metesky, the arsonist in New York City's Mad Bomber case (which spanned 16 years), was aided by psychiatrist-criminologist James A. Brussel's staccato-style profile:

> "Look for a heavy man. Middle-aged. Foreign born. Roman Catholic. Single. Lives with a brother or sister. When you find him, chances are he'll be wearing a double-breasted suit. Buttoned."

Indeed, the portrait was extraordinary in that the only variation was that Metesky lived with two single sisters. Brussel, in a discussion about the psychiatrist acting as Sherlock Holmes, explains that a psychiatrist usually studies a person and makes some reasonable predictions about how that person may react to a specific situation and about what he or she may do in the future. What is done in profiling, according to Brussel, is to reverse this process. Instead, by studying an individual's deeds one deduces what kind of a person the individual might be (Brussel, 1968).

The idea of constructing a verbal picture of a murderer using psychological terms is not new. In 1960, Palmer published results of a three-year study of 51 murderers who were serving sentences in New England. Palmer's "typical murderer" was 23 years old when he committed murder. Using a gun, this typical killer murdered a male stranger during an argument. He came from a low social class and achieved little in terms of education or occupation. He had a well-meaning but maladjusted mother, and he experienced physical abuse and psychological frustrations during his childhood.

Similarly, Rizzo (1982) studied 31 accused murderers during the course of routine referrals for psychiatric examination at a court clinic. His profile of the average murderer listed the offender as a 26-year-old male who most likely knew his victim, with monetary gain the most probable motivation for the crime.

Criminal Profiling

Through the techniques used today, law enforcement seeks to do more than describe the typical murderer, if in fact there ever was such a person. Investigative profilers analyze information gathered from the crime scene for what it may reveal about the type of person who committed the crime.

Law enforcement has had some outstanding investigators; however, their skills, knowledge, and thought processes have rarely been captured in the professional literature. These people were truly the experts of the law enforcement field, and their skills have been so admired that many fictional characters (Sergeant Cuff, Sherlock Holmes, Hercule Poirot, Mike Hammer, and Charlie Chan) have been modeled on them. Although Lunde (1976) has stated that the murders of fiction bear no resemblance to the murders of reality, a connection between fictional detective techniques and modern criminal profiling methods may indeed exist. For example, it is attention to detail that is the hallmark of famous fictional detectives; the smallest item at a crime scene does not escape their attention. As stated by Sergeant Cuff in Wilkie Collins' *The Moonstone*, widely acknowledged as the first full-length detective study:

> At one end of the inquiry there was a murder, and at the other end there was a spot of ink on a tablecloth that nobody could account for. In all my experience . . . I have never met with such a thing as a trifle yet.

However, unlike detective fiction, real cases are not solved by one tiny clue but the analysis of all clues and crime patterns.

Criminal profiling has been described as a collection of leads (Rossi, 1982), as an educated attempt to provide specific information about a certain type of suspect (Geberth, 1981), and as a biographical sketch of behavioral patterns, trends, and tendencies (Vorpagel, 1982). Geberth (1981) has also described the profiling process as particularly useful when the criminal has demonstrated some form of psychopathology. As used by the FBI profilers, the criminal-profile-generating process is defined as a technique for identifying the major personality and behavioral characteristics of an individual based upon an analysis of the crimes he or she has committed. The profiler's skill is in recognizing the crime scene dynamics that link various criminal personality types who commit similar crimes.

The process used by an investigative profiler in developing a criminal profile is quite similar to that used by clinicians to make a diagnosis and treatment plan: data are collected and assessed, the situation reconstructed, hypotheses formulated, a profile developed and tested, and the results reported back. Investigators traditionally have learned profiling through brainstorming, intuition, and educated guesswork. Their expertise is the result of years of accumulated wisdom, extensive experience in the field, and familiarity with a large number of cases.

A profiler brings to the investigation the ability to make hypothetical formulations based on his or her previous experience. A formulation is defined here as a concept that organizes, explains, or makes investigative sense out of information, and that influences the profile hypotheses. These formulations are based on clusters of information emerging from the crime scene data and from the investigator's experience in understanding criminal actions.

A basic premise of criminal profiling is that the way a person thinks (i.e., his or her patterns of thinking) directs the person's behavior. Thus, when the investigative profiler analyzes a crime scene and notes certain critical factors, he or she may be able to determine the motive and type of person who committed the crime.

THE CRIMINAL-PROFILE-GENERATING PROCESS

Investigative profilers at the FBI's Behavioral Science Unit (now part of the National Center for the Analysis of Violent Crime [NCA VC]) have been analyzing crime scenes and generating criminal profiles since the 1970s. Our description of the construction of profiles represents the off-site procedure as it is conducted at the NCA VC, as contrasted with an on-site procedure (Ressler et al., 1985). The criminal-profile-generating process is described as having five main stages, with a sixth stage or goal being the apprehension of a suspect (see Fig. 4.1).

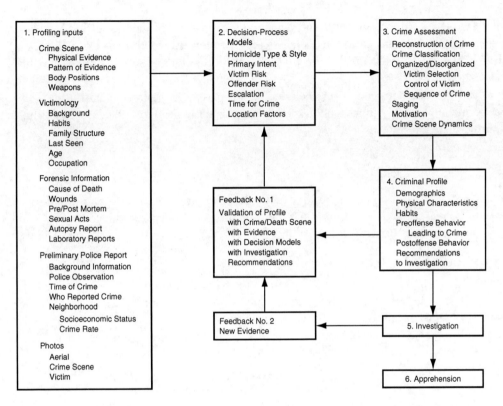

FIGURE 4.1

Criminal profile generating process.

Profiling Inputs Stage

The profiling inputs stage begins the criminal-profile-generating process. Comprehensive case materials are essential for accurate profiling. In homicide cases, the required information includes a complete synopsis of the crime and a description of the crime scene, encompassing factors indigenous to that area to the time of the incident such as weather conditions and the political and social environment.

Complete background information on the victim is also vital in homicide profiles. The data should cover domestic setting, employment, reputation, habits, fears, physical condition, personality, criminal history, family relationships, hobbies, and social conduct.

Forensic information pertaining to the crime is also critical to the profiling process, including an autopsy report with toxicology/serology results, autopsy photographs, and photographs of the cleansed wounds. The report should also contain the medical examiner's findings and impressions regarding estimated time and cause of death, type of weapon, and suspected sequence of delivery of wounds.

In addition to autopsy photographs, aerial photographs (if available and appropriate) and 8 × 10 color pictures of the crime scene are needed. Also useful are crime scene sketches showing distances, directions, and scale, as well as maps of the area (which may cross law enforcement jurisdiction boundaries).

The profiler studies all this background and evidence information, as well as all initial police reports. The data and photographs can reveal such significant elements as the level of risk of the victim, the degree of control exhibited by the offender, the offender's emotional state, and his criminal sophistication.

Information the profiler does *not* want included in the case materials is that dealing with possible suspects. Such information may subconsciously prejudice the profiler and cause him or her to prepare a profile matching the suspect.

Decision Process Models Stage

The decision process begins the organizing and arranging of the inputs into meaningful patterns. Seven key decision points, or models, differentiate and organize the information from Stage 1 and form an underlying decisional structure for profiling.

Homicide Type and Style

As noted in Table 4.1, homicides are classified by type and style. A single homicide is one victim, one homicidal event; double homicide is two victims, one event, and in one location; and a triple homicide has three victims in one location during one event. Anything beyond three victims is classified a mass murder; that is, four or more victims in one location, and within one event.

There are two types of mass murder: classic and family. A classic mass murder involves one person operating in one location at one period of time. That period of time could be minutes or hours and might even be days. The classic mass murderer is usually described as a mentally disordered individual whose problems have increased to the point that he acts against groups of people unrelated to these problems. He unleashes his hostility through shootings or stabbings. One classic mass murderer was Charles Whitman, the man who armed himself with boxes of ammunition, weapons, ropes, a radio, and food; barricaded himself on a tower in Austin, Texas; and opened fire for 90 minutes, killing 16 people and wounding over 30 others. He was stopped only when he was killed during an assault on the tower. James Huberty was another classic mass murderer. With a machine gun, he entered a fast food restaurant and killed and wounded many people. He also was killed at the site by responding police. More recently, Pennsylvania mass murderer Sylvia Seegrist (nicknamed Ms. Rambo for her military style clothing) was sentenced to life imprisonment for opening fire with a rifle at shoppers in a mall in October 1985, killing three and wounding seven.

The second type of mass murder is family member murder. If more than three family members are killed and the perpetrator takes his own life, it is classified as a mass murder/suicide. Without the suicide and with four or more victims, the murder is called a family killing. Examples include John List, an insurance salesman who killed his entire family on November 9, 1972, in Westfield, New Jersey. The bodies of List's wife and three children (ages 16, 15, and 13) were discovered in

TABLE 4.1 HOMICIDE CLASSIFICATION BY STYLE AND TYPE

Style	Single	Double	Triple	Mass	Spree	Serial
Number of Victims	1	2	3	4+	2+	3+
Number of Events	1	1	1	1	1	3+
Number of Locations	1	1	1	1	2+	3+
Cool-Off Period	N/A	N/A	N/A	N/A	No	Yes

their front room, lying side by side on top of sleeping bags as if in a mortuary. Their faces were covered and their arms were folded across their bodies. Each had been shot once behind the left ear, except one son who had been shot multiple times. A further search of the residence discovered the body of List's mother in a third floor closet. She had also been shot once behind the left ear. List disappeared after the crime and his car was found at an airport parking lot.

In another family killing case, William Bradford Bishop beat to death his wife, mother, and three children in the family's Bethesda, Maryland, residence in March 1976. He then transported them to North Carolina in the family station wagon where their bodies, along with the family dog's, were buried in a shallow grave. Bishop was under psychiatric care and had been prescribed antidepressant medication. No motive was determined. Bishop was a promising mid-level diplomat who had served in many overseas jobs and was scheduled for higher level office in the U.S. Department of State. Bishop, like List, is a Federal fugitive. There is strong indication both crimes were carefully planned and it is uncertain whether or not the men have committed suicide.

Two additional types of multiple murder are spree and serial. A spree murder involves killings at two or more locations with no emotional cooling-off time period between murders. The killings are all the result of a single event, which can be of short or long duration. On September 6, 1949, Camden, New Jersey, spree murderer Howard Unruh took a loaded German luger with extra ammunition and randomly fired the handgun while walking through his neighborhood, killing 13 people and wounding 3 in about 20 minutes. Even though Unruh's killings took such a short amount of time, they are not classified as a mass murder because he moved to different locations.

Serial murderers are involved in three or more separate events with an emotional cooling-off period between homicides. This type killer usually premediates his crimes, often fantasizing and planning the murder in every aspect with the possible exception of the specific victim. Then, when the time is right for him and he is cooled off from his last homicide, he selects his next victim and proceeds with his plan. The cool-off period can be days, weeks, or months, and is the main element that separates the serial killer from other multiple killers.

However, there are other differences between the murderers. The classic mass murderer and the spree murderer are not concerned with who their victims are; they will kill anyone who comes in contact with them. In contrast, a serial murderer usually selects a type of victim. He thinks he will never be caught, and sometimes he is right. A serial murderer controls the events, whereas a spree murderer, who oftentimes has been identified and is being closely pursued by law enforcement, may barely control what will happen next. The serial killer is planning, picking and choosing, and sometimes stopping the act of murder.

A serial murderer may commit a spree of murders. In 1984, Christopher Wilder, an Australian-born businessman and race car driver, traveled across the United States killing young women. He would target victims at shopping malls or would abduct them after meeting them through a beauty contest setting or dating service. While a fugitive as a serial murderer, Wilder was investigated, identified, and tracked by the FBI and almost every police department in the country. He then went on a long-term killing spree throughout the country and eventually was killed during a shoot-out with police.

Wilder's classification changed from serial to spree because of the multiple murders and the lack of a cooling-off period during his elongated murder event lasting nearly seven weeks. This transition has been noted in other serial/spree murder cases. The tension due to his fugitive status and the high visibility of his crimes gives the murderer a sense of desperation. His acts are now open and public and the increased pressure usually means no cooling-off period. He knows he will be caught, and the coming confrontation with police becomes an element in his crimes. He may place himself in a situation where he forces the police to kill him.

It is important to classify homicides correctly. For example, a single homicide is committed in a city; a week later a second single homicide is committed; and the third week, a third single homicide. Three seemingly unrelated homicides are reported, but by the time there is a fourth, there is a tie-in through forensic evidence and analyses of the crime scenes. These three single homicides now point to one serial offender. It is not mass murder because of the multiple locations and the cooling-off periods. The correct classification assists in profiling and directs the investigation as serial homicides. Similarly, profiling of a single murder may indicate the offender had killed before or would repeat the crime in the future.

Primary Intent of the Murderer

In some cases, murder may be an ancillary action and not itself the primary intent of the offender. The killer's primary intent could be: (1) criminal enterprise, (2) emotional, selfish, or cause-specific, or (3) sexual. The killer may be acting on his own or as part of a group.

When the primary intent is criminal enterprise, the killer may be involved in the business of crime as his livelihood. Sometimes murder becomes part of this business even though there is no personal malice toward the victim. The primary motive is money. In the 1950s, a young man placed a bomb in his mother's suitcase that was loaded aboard a commercial aircraft. The aircraft exploded, killing 44 people. The young man's motive had been to collect money from the travel insurance he had taken out on his mother prior to the flight. Criminal enterprise killings involving a group include contract murders, gang murders, competition murders, and political murders.

When the primary intent involves emotional, selfish, or cause-specific reasons, the murderer may kill in self-defense or compassion (mercy killings where life support systems are disconnected). Family disputes or violence may lie behind infanticide, matricide, patricide, and spouse and sibling killings. Paranoid reactions may also result in murder as in the previously described Whitman case. The mentally disordered murderer may commit a symbolic crime or have a psychotic outburst. Assassinations, such as those committed by Sirhan Sirhan and Mark Chapman, also fall into the emotional intent category. Murders in this category involving groups are committed for a variety of reasons: religious (Jim Jones and the Jonestown, Guyana, case), cult (Charles Manson), and fanatical organizations such as the Ku Klux Klan and the Black Panther Party of the 1970s.

Finally, the murderer may have sexual motives for killing. Individuals may kill as a result of or to engage in sexual activity, dismemberment, mutilation, evisceration, or other activities that have sexual meaning only for the offender. Occasionally, two or more murderers commit these homicides together as in the 1984–1985 case in Calaveras County, California, where Leonard Lake and Charles Ng are suspected of as many as 25 sex-torture slayings.

Victim Risk

The concept of the victim's risk is involved at several stages of the profiling process and provides information about the suspect in terms of how he or she operates. Risk is determined using such factors as age, occupation, lifestyle, physical stature, resistance ability, and location of the victim, and is classified as high, moderate, or low. Killers seek high-risk victims at locations where people may be vulnerable, such as bus depots or isolated areas. Low-risk types include those whose occupations and daily lifestyles do not lead them to being targeted as victims. The information on victim risk helps to generate an image of the type of perpetrator being sought.

Offender Risk

Data on victim risk integrates with information on offender risk, or the risk the offender was taking to commit the crime. For example, abducting a victim at noon from a busy street is high risk. Thus, a low-risk victim snatched under high-risk circumstances generates ideas about the offender, such as personal stresses he is operating under, his beliefs that he will not be apprehended, or the excitement he needs in the commission of the crime, or his emotional maturity.

Escalation

Information about escalation is derived from an analysis of facts and patterns from the prior decision process models. Investigative profilers are able to deduce the sequence of acts committed during the crime. From this deduction, they may be able to make determinations about the potential of the criminal not only to escalate his crimes (e.g., from peeping to fondling to assault to rape to murder), but to repeat his crimes in serial fashion. One case example is David Berkowitz, the Son of Sam killer, who started his criminal acts with the nonfatal stabbing of a teenage girl and who escalated to the subsequent .44-caliber killings.

Time Factors

There are several time factors that need to be considered in generating a criminal profile. These factors include the length of time required: (1) to kill the victim, (2) to commit additional acts with the body, and (3) to dispose of the body. The time of day or night that the crime was committed is also important, as it may provide information on the lifestyle and occupation of the suspect (and also relates to the offender risk factor). For example, the longer an offender stays with his victim, the more likely it is he will be apprehended at the crime scene. In the case of the New York murder of Kitty Genovese, the killer carried on his murderous assault to the point where many people heard or witnessed the crime, leading to his eventual prosecution. A killer who intends to spend time with his victim therefore must select a location to preclude observation, or one with which he is familiar.

Location Factors

Information about location—where the victim was first approached, where the crime occurred, and if the crime and death scenes differ—provide yet additional data about the offender. For example, such information provides details about whether the murderer used a vehicle to transport the victim from the death scene or if the victim died at her point of abduction.

Crime Assessment Stage

The Crime Assessment Stage in generating a criminal profile involves the reconstruction of the sequence of events and the behavior of both the offender and victim. Based on the various decisions of the previous stage, this reconstruction of how things happened, how people behaved, and how they planned and organized the encounter provides information about specific characteristics to be generated for the criminal profile. Assessments are made about the classification of the crime, its organized/disorganized aspects, the offender's selection of a victim, strategies used to control the victim, the sequence of crime, the staging (or not) of the crime, the offender's motivation for the crime, and crime scene dynamics.

The classification of the crime is determined through the decision process outlined in the first decision process model. The classification of a crime as organized or disorganized, first introduced as classification of Lust murder (Hazelwood & Douglas, 1980), but since broadly expanded, includes factors such as victim selection, strategies to control the victim, and sequence of the crime. An organized murderer is one who appears to plan his murders, target his victims, display control at the crime scene, and act out a violent fantasy against the victim (sex, dismemberment, torture). For example, Ted

Bundy's planning was noted through his successful abduction of young women from highly visible areas (e.g., beaches, campuses, a ski lodge). He selected victims who were young, attractive, and similar in appearance. His control of the victim was initially through clever manipulation and later physical force. These dynamics were important in the development of a desired fantasy victim.

In contrast, the disorganized murderer is less apt to plan his crime in detail, obtains victims by chance, and behaves haphazardly during the crime. For example, Herbert Mullin of Santa Cruz, California, who killed 14 people of varying types (e.g., an elderly man, a young girl, a priest) over a four-month period, did not display any specific planning or targeting of victims; rather, the victims were people who happened to cross his path, and their killings were based on psychotic impulses as well as on fantasy.

The determination of whether or not the crime was staged (i.e., if the subject was truly careless or disorganized, or if he made the crime appear that way to distract or mislead the police) helps direct the investigative profiler to the killer's motivation. In one case, a 16-year-old high school junior living in a small town failed to return home from school. Police, responding to the father's report of his missing daughter, began their investigation and located the victim's scattered clothing in a remote area outside the town. A crude map was also found at the scene which seemingly implied a premeditated plan of kidnaping. The police followed the map to a location which indicated a body may have been disposed of in a nearby river. Written and telephoned extortion demands were sent to the father, a bank executive, for the sum of $80,000, indicating that a kidnap was the basis of the abduction. The demands warned police in detail not to use electronic monitoring devices during their investigative efforts.

Was this crime staged? The question was answered in two ways. The details in one aspect of the crime (scattered clothing and tire tracks) indicated that subject was purposely staging a crime while the details in the other (extortion) led the profilers to speculate who the subject was; specifically that he had a law enforcement background and therefore had knowledge of police procedures concerning crimes of kidnaping, hiding the primary intent of sexual assault and possible murder. With this information, the investigative profilers recommended that communication continue between the suspect and the police, with the hypothesis that the behavior would escalate and the subject become bolder.

While further communications with the family were being monitored, profilers from the FBI's Behavioral Science Unit theorized that the subject of the case was a white male who was single, in his late 20's to early 30's, unemployed, and who had been employed as a law enforcement officer within the past year. He would be a macho outdoors type person who drove a late model, well maintained vehicle with a CB radio. The car would have the overall appearance of a police vehicle.

As the profile was developed, the FBI continued to monitor the extortion telephone calls made to the family by the subject. The investigation, based on the profile, narrowed to two local men, both of whom were former police officers. One suspect was eliminated, but the FBI became very interested in the other since he fit the general profile previously developed. This individual was placed under surveillance. He turned out to be a single, white male who was previously employed locally as a police officer. He was now unemployed and drove a car consistent with the FBI profile. He was observed making a call from a telephone booth, and after hanging up, he taped a note under the telephone. The call was traced to the residence of the victim's family. The caller had given instructions for the family to proceed to the phone booth the suspect had been observed in. "The instructions will be taped there," stated the caller.

The body of the victim was actually found a considerable distance from the "staged" crime scene, and the extortion calls were a diversion to intentionally lead the police investigation away from the sexually motivated crime of rape-murder. The subject never intended to collect the ransom money, but he felt that the diversion would throw the police off and take him from the focus of the rape-murder inquiry. The subject was subsequently arrested and convicted of this crime.

Motivation

Motivation is a difficult factor to judge because it requires dealing with the inner thoughts and behavior of the offender. Motivation is more easily determined in the organized offender who premeditates, plans, and has the ability to carry out a plan of action that is logical and complete. On the other hand, the disorganized offender carries out his crimes by motivations that frequently are derived from mental illnesses and accompanying distorted thinking (resulting from delusions and hallucinations). Drugs and alcohol, as well as panic and stress resulting from disruptions during the execution of the crime, are factors which must be considered in the overall assessment of the crime scene.

Crime Scene Dynamics

Crime scene dynamics are the numerous elements common to every crime scene which must be interpreted by investigating officers and are at times easily misunderstood. Examples include location of crime scene, cause of death, method of killing, positioning of body, excessive trauma, and location of wounds.

The investigative profiler reads the dynamics of a crime scene and interprets them based on his experience with similar cases where the outcome is known. Extensive research by the Behavioral Science Unit at the FBI Academy and in-depth interviews with incarcerated felons who have committed such crimes have provided a vast body of knowledge of common threads that link crime scene dynamics to specific criminal personality patterns. For example, a common error of some police investigators is to assess a particularly brutal lust-mutilation murder as the work of a sex fiend and to direct the investigation toward known sex offenders when such crimes are commonly perpetrated by youthful individuals with no criminal record.

Criminal Profile Stage

The fourth stage in generating a criminal profile deals with the type of person who committed the crime and that individual's behavioral organization with relation to the crime. Once this description is generated, the strategy of investigation can be formulated, as this strategy requires a basic understanding of how an individual will respond to a variety of investigative efforts.

Included in the criminal profile are background information (demographics), physical characteristics, habits, beliefs and values, pre-offense behavior leading to the crime, and post-offense behavior. It may also include investigative recommendations for interrogating or interviewing, identifying, and apprehending the offender.

This fourth stage has an important means of validating the criminal profile—Feedback No. 1. The profile must fit with the earlier reconstruction of the crime, with the evidence, and with the key decision process models. In addition, the investigative procedure developed from the recommendations must make sense in terms of the expected response patterns of the offender. If there is a lack of congruence, the investigative profilers review all available data. As Hercule Poirot observed, "To know is to have all of the evidence and facts fit into place."

Investigation Stage

Once the congruence of the criminal profile is determined, a written report is provided to the requesting agency and added to its ongoing investigative efforts. The investigative recommendations generated in Stage 4 are applied, and suspects matching the profile are evaluated. If identification, apprehension, and a confession result, the goal of the profile effort has been met. If new evidence is generated (e.g., by another murder) and/or there is no identification of a suspect, reevaluation occurs via Feedback No. 2. The information is reexamined and the profile revalidated.

Apprehension Stage

Once a suspect is apprehended, the agreement between the outcome and the various stages in the profile-generating-process are examined. When an apprehended suspect admits guilt, it is important to conduct a detailed interview to check the total profiling process for validity.

CASE EXAMPLE

A young woman's nude body was discovered at 3:00 p.m. on the roof landing of the apartment building where she lived. She had been badly beaten about the face and strangled with the strap of her purse. Her nipples had been cut off after death and placed on her chest. Scrawled in ink on the inside of her thigh was, "You can't stop me." The words "Fuck you" were scrawled on her abdomen. A pendant in the form of a Jewish sign (Chai), which she usually wore as a good luck piece around her neck, was missing and presumed taken by the murderer. Her underpants had been pulled over her face; her nylons were removed and very loosely tied around her wrists and ankles near a railing. The murderer had placed symmetrically on either side of the victim's head the pierced earrings she had been wearing. An umbrella and inkpen had been forced into the vagina and a hair comb was placed in her public hair. The woman's jaw and nose had been broken and her molars loosened. She suffered multiple face fractures caused by a blunt force. Cause of death was asphyxia by ligature (pocketbook strap) strangulation. There were postmortem bite marks on the victim's thighs, as well as contusions, hemorrhages, and lacerations to the body. The killer also defecated on the roof landing and covered it with the victim's clothing.

The following discussion of this case in the context of the six stages of the criminal-profile-generating process illustrates how this process works.

Profiling Inputs

In terms of *crime scene evidence*, everything the offender used at the crime scene belonged to the victim. Even the comb and the felt-tip pen used to write on her body came from her purse. The offender apparently did not plan this crime; he had no gun, ropes, or tape for the victim's mouth. He probably did not even plan to encounter her that morning at that location. The crime scene indicated a spontaneous event; in other words, the killer did not stalk or wait for the victim. The crime scene differs from the death scene. The initial abduction was on the stairwell; then the victim was taken to a more remote area.

Investigation of the *victim* revealed that the 26-year-old, 90-pound, 4′ 11″ white female awoke around 6:30 a.m. She dressed, had a breakfast of coffee and juice, and left her apartment for work at a nearby day care center, where she was employed as a group teacher for handicapped children. She resided with her mother and father. When she would leave for work in the morning, she would take the elevator or walk down the stairs, depending on her mood. The victim was a quiet young woman who had a slight curvature of the spine (kyhoscoliosis).

The *forensic information* in the medical examiner's report was important in determining the extent of the wounds, as well as how the victim was assaulted and whether evidence of sexual assault was present or absent. No semen was noted in the vagina, but semen was found on the body. It appeared that the murderer stood directly over the victim and masturbated. There were visible bite marks on the victim's thighs and knee area. He cut off her nipples with a knife after she was dead and wrote on the body. Cause of death was strangulation, first manual, then ligature, with the strap of her purse. The fact that the murderer used a weapon of opportunity indicates that he did not prepare to commit this crime. He probably used his fist to render her unconscious, which may be the reason no one heard any screams. There were no deep stab wounds and the knife used to multilate the victim's breast apparently was not big, probably a penknife that the offender normally carried. The killer used the victim's belts to tie her right arm and right leg, but he apparently untied them in order to position the body before he left.

The *preliminary police report* revealed that another resident of the apartment building, a white male, aged 15, discovered the victim's wallet in a stairwell between the third and fourth floors at approximately 8:20 a.m. He retained the wallet until he returned home from school for lunch that afternoon. At that time, he gave the wallet to his father, a white male, aged 40. The father went to the victim's apartment at 2:50 p.m. and gave the wallet to the victim's mother.

When the mother called the day care center to inform her daughter about the wallet, she learned that her daughter had not appeared for work that morning. The mother, the victim's sister, and a neighbor began a search of the building and discovered the body. The neighbor called the police. Police at the scene found no witnesses who saw the victim after she left her apartment that morning.

Decision Process

This crime's *style* is a single homicide with the murderer's primary intent making it a sexually motivated *type* of crime. There was a degree of *planning* indicated by the organization and sophistication of the crime scene. The idea of murder had probably occupied the killer for a long period of time. The sexual fantasies may have started through the use and collecting of sadistic pornography depicting torture and violent sexual acts.

Victim risk assessment revealed that the victim was known to be very self-conscious about her physical handicap and size and she was a plain-looking woman who did not date. She led a reclusive life and was not the type of victim that would or could fight an assailant or scream and yell. She would be easily dominated and controlled, particularly in view of her small stature.

Based upon the information on occupation and lifestyle, we have a low-risk victim living in an area that was at low risk for violent crimes. The apartment building was part of a 23-building public housing project in which the racial mixture of residents was 50% black, 40% white, and 10% Hispanic. It was located in the confines of a major police precinct. There had been no other similar crimes reported in the victim's or nearby complexes.

The crime was considered very *high risk* for the offender. He committed the crime in broad daylight, and there was a possibility that other people who were up early might see him. There was no set pattern of the victim taking the stairway or the elevator. It appeared that the victim happened to cross the path of the offender.

There was no *escalation* factor present in this crime scene. The *time* for the crime was considerable. The amount of time the murderer spent with his victim increased his risk of being apprehended. All his activities with the victim—removing her earrings, cutting off her nipples, masturbating over her—took a substantial amount of time.

The *location* of the crime suggested that the offender felt comfortable in the area. He had been here before, and he felt that no one would interrupt the murder.

Crime Assessment

The crime scene indicated the murder was one event, not one of a series of events. It also appeared to be a first-time killing, and the subject was not a typical organized offender. There were elements of both disorganization and organization; the offender might fall into a mixed category.

A reconstruction of the crime/death scene provides an overall picture of the crime. To begin with, the victim was not necessarily stalked but instead confronted. What was her reaction? Did she recognize her assailant, fight him off, or try to get away? The subject had to kill her to carry out his sexually violent fantasies. The murderer was on known territory and thus had a reason to be there at 6:30 in the morning: either he resided there or he was employed at this particular complex.

The killer's control of the victim was through the use of blunt force trauma, with the blow to her face the first indication of his intention. It is probable the victim was selected because she posed little or no threat to the offender. Because she didn't fight, run, or scream, it appears that she did not perceive her abductor as a threat. Either she knew him, had seen him before, or he looked nonthreatening (i.e., he was dressed as a janitor, a postman, or businessman) and therefore his presence in the apartment would not alarm his victim.

In the sequence of the crime, the killer first rendered the victim unconscious and possibly dead; he could easily pick her up because of her small size. He took her up to the roof landing and had time to manipulate her body while she was unconscious. He positioned the body, undressed her, acted out certain fantasies which led to masturbation. The killer took his time at the scene, and he probably knew that no one would come to the roof and disturb him in the early morning since he was familiar with the area and had been there many times in the past.

The crime scene was not staged. Sadistic ritualistic fantasy generated the sexual motivation for murder. The murderer displayed total domination of the victim. In addition, he placed the victim in a degrading posture, which reflected his lack of remorse about the killing.

The crime scene dynamics of the covering of the killer's feces and his positioning of the body are incongruent and need to be interpreted. First, as previously described, the crime was opportunistic. The crime scene portrayed the intricacies of a long-standing murderous fantasy. Once the killer had a victim, he had a set plan about killing and abusing the body. However, within the context of the crime, the profilers note a paradox: the covered feces. Defecation was not part of the ritual fantasy and thus it was covered. The presence of the feces also supports the length of time taken for the crime, the control the murderer had over the victim (her unconscious state), and the knowledge he would not be interrupted.

The positioning of the victim suggested the offender was acting out something he had seen before, perhaps in a fantasy or in a sado-masochistic pornographic magazine. Because the victim was unconscious, the killer did not need to tie her hands. Yet he continued to tie her neck and strangle her. He positioned her earrings in a ritualistic manner, and he wrote on her body. This reflects some sort of imagery that he probably had repeated over and over in his mind. He took her necklace as a souvenir; perhaps to carry around in his pocket. The investigative profilers noted that the body was positioned in the form of the woman's missing Jewish symbol.

Criminal Profile

Based on the information derived during the previous stages, a criminal profile of the murderer was generated. First, a physical description of the suspect stated that he would be a white male, between 25 and 35, or the same general age as the victim, and of average appearance. The murderer would not look out of context in the area. He would be of average intelligence and would be a high-school or college dropout. He would not have a military history and may be unemployed. His occupation would be blue-collar or skilled. Alcohol or drugs did not assume a major role, as the crime occurred in the early morning.

The suspect would have difficulty maintaining any kind of personal relationships with women. If he dated, he would date women younger than himself, as he would have to be able to dominate and control in the relationships.

He would be sexually inexperienced, sexually inadequate, and never married. He would have a pornography collection. The subject would have sadistic tendencies; the umbrella and the masturbation act are clearly acts of sexual substitution. The sexual acts showed controlled aggression, but rage or hatred of women was obviously present. The murderer was not reacting to rejection from women as much as to morbid curiosity.

In addressing the habits of the murderer, the profile revealed there would be a reason for the killer to be at the crime scene at 6:30 in the morning. He could be employed in the apartment complex, be in the complex on business, or reside in the complex.

Although the offender might have preferred his victim conscious, he had to render her unconscious because he did not want to get caught. He did not want the woman screaming for help.

The murderer's infliction of sexual, sadistic acts on an inanimate body suggests he was disorganized. He probably would be a very confused person, possibly with previous mental problems. If he had carried out such acts on a living victim, he would have a different type of personality. The fact that he inflicted acts on a dead or unconscious person indicated his inability to function with a live or conscious person.

The crime scene reflected that the killer felt justified in his actions and that he felt no remorse. He was not subtle. He left the victim in a provocative, humiliating position, exactly the way he wanted her to be found. He challenged the police in his message written on the victim; the messages also indicated the subject might well kill again.

Investigation

The crime received intense coverage by the local media because it was such an extraordinary homicide. The local police responded to a radio call of a homicide. They in turn notified the detective bureau, which notified the forensic crime scene unit, medical examiner's office, and the county district attorney's office. A task force was immediately assembled of approximately 26 detectives and supervisors.

An intensive investigation resulted, which included speaking to, and interviewing, over 2,000 people. Records checks of known sex offenders in the area proved fruitless. Hand writing samples were taken of possible suspects to compare with the writing on the body. Mental hospitals in the area were checked for people who might fit the profile of this type killer.

The FBI's Behavioral Science Unit was contacted to compile a profile. In the profile, the investigation recommendation included that the offender knew that the police sooner or later would contact him because he either worked or lived in the building. The killer would somehow inject himself into the investigation, and although he might appear cooperative to the extreme, he would really be seeking information. In addition, he might try to contact the victim's family.

Apprehension

The outcome of the investigation was apprehension of a suspect 13 months following the discovery of the victim's body. After receiving the criminal profile, police reviewed their files of 22 suspects they had interviewed. One man stood out. This suspect's father lived down the hall in the same apartment building as the victim. Police originally had interviewed his father, who told them his son was a patient at the local psychiatric hospital. Police learned later that the son had been absent without permission from the hospital the day and evening prior to the murder.

They also learned he was an unemployed actor who lived alone; his mother had died of a stroke when he was 19 years old (11 years previous). He had had academic problems of repeating a grade and dropped out of school. He was a white, 30-year-old, never-married male who was an only child. His father was a blue-collar worker who also was an ex-prize fighter. The suspect reportedly had his arm in a cast at the time of the crime. A search of his room revealed a pornography collection. He had never been in the military, had no girlfriends, and was described as being insecure with women. The man suffered from depression and was receiving psychiatric treatment and hospitalization. He had a history of repeated suicidal attempts (hanging/asphyxiation) both before and after the offense.

The suspect was tried, found guilty, and is serving a sentence from 25 years to life for this mutilation murder. He denies committing the murder and states he did not know the victim. Police proved that security was lax at the psychiatric hospital in which the suspect was confined and that he could literally come and go as he pleased. However, the most conclusive evidence against him at his trial were his teeth impressions. Three separate forensic dentists, prominent in their field, conducted independent tests and all agreed that the suspect's teeth impressions matched the bite marks found on the victim's body.

CONCLUSION

Criminal personality profiling has proven to be a useful tool to law enforcement in solving violent, apparently motiveless crimes. The process has aided significantly in the solution of many cases over the past decade. It is believed that through the research efforts of personnel in the FBI's National Center for the Analysis of Violent Crime and professionals in other field, the profiling process will continue to be refined and be a viable investigative aid to law enforcement.

REFERENCES

Brussel, J.S. (1968). *Casebook of a crime psychiatrist*. New York: Grove.

Casey-Owens, M. (1984). The anonymous letter-writer—a psychological profile? *Journal of Forensic Sciences, 29*, 816-819.

Christie, A. (1963). *The clocks*, pp. 227-228. New York: Pocket Books.

Geberth, V.J. (1981, September). Psychological profiling. *Law and Order*, pp. 46-49.

Hazelwood, R.R. (1983, September). The behavior-oriented interview of rape victims: The key to profiling. *FBI Law Enforcement Bulletin*, pp. 1-8.

Hazlewood, R.R., & Douglas, J.E. (1980, April). The lust murderer. *FBI Law Enforcement Bulletin*.

Lunde, D.T. (1976). *Murder and madness*. San Francisco, CA: San Francisco Book Co.

Miron, M.S., & Douglas, J.E. (1979, September). Threat analysis: The psycholinguistic approach. *FBI Law Enforcement Bulletin*, pp. 5-9.

Palmer, S. (1960). *A Study of murder*. New York: Thomas Crowell.

Reiser, M. (1982, March). Crime-specific psychological consultation. *The Police Chief*, pp. 53-56.

Ressler, R.K., Burgess, A.W., Douglas, J.E., & Depue, R.L. (1985). Criminal profiling research on homicide. In A.W. Burgess (Eds.), *Rape and sexual assault: A research handbook*, pp. 343-349. New York: Garland.

Rider, A.O. (1980, June). The firesetter: A psychological profile, part I. *FBI Law Enforcement Bulletin*, pp. 6-13.

Rizzo, N.D. (1982). Murder in Boston: Killers and their victims. *International Journal of Offender Therapy and Comparative Criminology*, 26(1), 36-42.

Rossi, D. (1982, January). Crime scene behavioral analysis: Another tool for the law enforcement investigator. Official proceedings of the 88th Annual IACP Conference. *The Police Chief*, pp. 152-155.

Vorpagel, R.E. (1982, January). *Painting psychological profiles: Charlatanism, charisma, or a new science? Official proceedings of the 88th Annual IACP Conference. The Police Chief*, pp. 156-159.

John E. Douglas, M.S., is Supervisory Special Agent, Federal Bureau of Investigation and Program Manager, Profiling and Consultation Program, National Center for the Analysis of Violent Crime, FBI Academy, Quantico, VA; Robert K. Ressler, M.S., is Supervisory Special Agent, Federal Bureau of Investigation and Program Manager, Violent Criminal Apprehension Program, National Center for the Analysis of Violent Crime, FBI Academy, Quantico, VA; Ann W. Burgess, R.N., D.N.Sc., is van Ameringen Professor of Psychiatric Mental Health Nursing, University of Pennsylvania School of Nursing, Philadelphia, PA; and Carol R. Hartman, R.N., D.N.Sc., is Associate Professor and Coordinator of the Graduate Program in Psychiatric Mental Health Nursing, Boston College School of Nursing, Chestnut Hill, MA. Preparation of this manuscript was supported by an Office of Juvenile Justice and Delinquency Prevention grant (84-JN-K010). The authors wish to acknowledge Allen G. Burgess, Cynthia J. Lent, and Marieanne L. Clark for contributions to this manuscript. Correspondence and reprint requests should be addressed to: John E. Douglas, FBI Academy, Quantico, VA 22135.

Contributions of Psychiatric Consultation in the Investigation of Serial Murder

JOHN A. LIEBERT

This article focusses on enhancing communication between investigative officers assigned to serial murder cases and their psychiatric consultants. In view of the interdisciplinary interest in this topic, it must be pointed out that my purpose in presenting this article is not for the validation of psychiatric diagnosis of psychodynamic formulations. For those who are primarily interested in the validity of psychiatric formulations as applied to violent crime and predictions of dangerousness, standard texts are recommended where metapsychological issues are thoroughly discussed, and the very important issues of the validity of psychiatry. The reader, if not already acquainted with the literature of "Anti-psychiatry", of Laing (1967), and the literature of Szasz (1961) can read these authors concerning the issues of validity in the field of psychiatric consultation to the criminal justice system. A well-known dilemma in clinical psychiatry is the retrograde reconstruction of clinical material, both fantasy and behavior, to presumed etiological antecedents. A definitive, unitary psychological model for serial murder does not exist today. Hence, this is an attempt to assist in communications between law enforcement personnel with the duty of investigating serial murder and their psychiatric consultants. The article is divided into three sections: 1) Overview, 2) Psychological Formulation of Serial Murder, 3) Profiling.

Overview

The problems of definition and identification in serial murder are issues best left to discussion by law enforcement and criminology experts. It is of note, however, that serial murders are identified at a point where a threshold of awareness is broken at the interface of the community and its police force. For example, a serial murder was identified retrospectively and prospectively when two separate reports of missing girls were entered with one police department, thereby initiating the "Ted Case" in Seattle. These two cases of missing persons were inactivated for lack of other suspects after Bundy's conviction for murder in Florida. It is typical in these cases for investigative doubt and confusion to persist for months concerning the actuality of a single murderer's responsibility for multiple victims over time and multiple police jurisdictions. The current Green River serial murder case in Washington State may span years and multiple states as did the "Ted" case which allegedly included Washington, Oregon, Wyoming, Colorado, Utah and

Florida. When an apprehension is made, unsolved murders going back decades may be brought to investigative light once the neighborhood of the suspect has been discovered.

The problem of definition in serial murder is subject to interpretation of the crime scene for theories regarding motivation for murder. The assumption formulated when conceptualizing apparently random events under the term *serial murder* is that one or more persons are murdering over a span of time and definable space and that there is a common denominator of motivation in the otherwise random appearing killings. The serial murder, therefore, must be conceptualized in terms of whether it appears to be motivated by lust (Bundy); terrorism (Atlanta); cultism (Zebra) or delutional thinking (Ecology, Santa Cruz). Psychiatric expertise may help in cases of terrorism, cults, and organized crime—such as child exploitation cases of lust murder where a pathological equivalent of coitus in the violent act of murder is compulsively repeated over time, appear especially appropriate for psychiatric consultation. For that reason, gangland slayings will not be discussed which may occur consecutively but have "rational" motivation.

Besides problems of definition and the identification of serial murder, the additional problem of excitement generated within a community upon identification far exceeds its morbidity and mortality risks. Excessive public excitement can create a self-feeding cycle between public sensibilities and newspaper coverage ultimately interfering with the process of investigation. Police administration must insulate the investigative staff from the demands for quick solutions and bizarre theories. Serial murders are notoriously difficult to investigate and require patient plodding work not popularized on television. Attention must be given to the possibility of a ritualized murder by a cult, terrorism, or the organized crime of "white slavery". The difficulty of defining a set of circumstances as serial murder, both spatially and temporally, indicates that organized murder of cultism or terrorism are apparently not operating. It is unlikely that bizarre symbolization of a ritualized cultist murder would go unnoticed long enough for an investigative staff to be in doubt as to whether a chain of serial murders exist. Likewise, a politically motivated group attempting to bring attention to itself or elicit change in the system via apparently random murders is extremely unlikely. *Serial murder is a product of extremely primitive emotions.* Investigators, however, must be alert for signs of symbolism at the crime scene which may link apparently random cases. The phases of the moon at which time the killings occur, for example, could have peculiar meaning to the killer without being a part of a cultist murder conspiracy. Without creating insensitivity to an apparent symbolic presentation at the crime scene, *murder theme* priorities must be set as early as possible. Evidence of symbolism within the spatial or temporal organization of the crime scene could provide clues regarding the identity of the killer. Excessive preoccupation with this can lead to wasteful distractions and disruptions in the investigation. Apparently motiveless serial killings of young males or females where intimate physical contact obviously preceded death, demands the investigation of Lust Murder. Retvitch (1965) explains in "Sex Murder and the Potential Sex Murderer",

> "Attacks and murders may be described by the police and courts as attempts at robbery and theft or assault and battery. The underlying sexual dynamics may be completely disregarded. In a case previously reported a man arrested for assault with intent to rob had attacked a woman with a black jack; he rationalized that he needed money and that a woman was the easier victim. Under intravenous sodium amytal, he revealed long-standing fantasies of tying female legs and that this was the purpose of the attack. A noose, a rifle and a book, *Psychopathia Sexualis*, found in his car were not considered clues. Only in isolated incidents were these cases examined as sex offenders."

To enhance the investigative focus on lust murder a psychiatrist or clinical psychologist may be consulted in order to make sense of an otherwise senseless killing spree.

Psychological Formulations of Serial Murder

If lust murder is the working hypothesis regarding apparently random violence, the clinician is expected to explain motivation and thereby help identify a suspect. Investigators need to be familiar with the language and concepts utilized by psychiatrists in their formulations of sex and aggression.

Rada (1978) in his publication, "Clinical Aspects of the Rapist" states,

> "Williams suggests that sexual crimes directed against females occur on a continuum from minor assaults at one end to lust murder at the other. The findings of other investigators, however, suggest that the rape-murderer and the lust murderer are quite different in terms of motives and personality dynamics. The rapist who murders rarely reports any sexual satisfaction from the murder and does not perform sexual acts on the dead victim. Rape murder occurs subsequent to sexual assault and does not appear to have sexual connotations itself. The lust murderer, on the other hand, frequently needs the murder to arouse his sexual interest and desires. Often he does not perform intercourse with the victim, dead or alive. He may, however, experience intense sexual pleasure and orgasm at the time of the murder—some compulsively dismember or disembowel the victim and masturbate to orgasm. J. Rhinehart points out that the potential sex killer may have committed previous offenses and may even have been caught, but his known criminal offenses usually do not arouse suspicion of a potential sex killer. The true sex killer is generally a very inept lover and can be a well-mannered, gentle, reserved, religious and timid man. Unlike the rapist, the great majority of lust murderers appear to be either overt or latent psychotics with poor control and explosive breaks with reality.
>
> I believe that the lust murderer and the rapist are basically different types of offenders and not simply a variance on a continuum. Rapists are capable of murder but usually for different reasons. In some rapists, however, there appears to be a progressive increase in aggresive fantasies toward women which over time may eventually lead to murder."

In a study of eight murders and thirty-four unprovoked assaults on women by males, Retvitch (1965) found introversive tendencies, feelings of isolation, detachment and lowering of reality boundaries to be among the most common findings in this series. Retvitch wrote:

> "In our material, 19 cases were considered schizoid or dynamically schizophrenic and nine cases overtly clinically schizophrenic. Five cases were diagnosed as mentally defective, and only ten cases could be classified in a category of personality pattern or personality trait disturbance. The psychiatric diagnoses are not precise, frequently overlap and should be viewed on a continuum rather than as a tightly fixed category.

Today, most likely many of these cases would be considered Borderline or Narcissistic Personality Disorders, or, the "Latent Pyschotics" of Rada's (1978) text.

Traditional resistance within the criminal justice system to the psychiatric concept of lust murder is evidenced in the discussion of diagnostic consideration. Retvitch (1965) has written:

> "In reviewing the literature one gains an impression that the great majority of recorded sadistic acts were perpetrated by either overt or latent psychotics with poor control or explosive breaks with reality, Vacher the Ripper was manifestly a case of paranoid schizophrenia with a history of hospitalization in an insane asylum for 'persecution mania'. Yet the experts of his time declared him 'sane' and a 'common criminal'. In the case of Verzeni, Krafft-Ebing quoted the experts as saying: 'There was nothing in his past that would indicate a mental disorder' but in describing his personality, the experts added: 'His character was peculiar; he was silent and inclined to be solitary'. In the case of John F. Roche, the newspapers reported the following 'Three psychiatrists found the 27-year plumber's helper sane and capable of standing trial'. Psychiatrists found Roche free of mental disorder and declared that in him the more primitive sadistic forces of murder, rape, etc. were mobilized into a habit pattern'. A week later one read: 'the sullen defendant told his lawyer that he would not cooperate with them, and throughout the day Roche

wrote and sat expressionless in his seat in front of two prison guards while prospective jurors were questioned, and shook his head negatively each time one of his attorneys tried to consult with him. Time after time he snarled answers to questions but most of the day he just sat grimly. 'Roche is not interested in a trial at all', said Mr. Murray. 'Talking to him is like sticking pins into an iceburg'. It is interesting that another expert diagnosed Roche as a case of schizophrenia which aroused the anger of the court."

In order to communicate with a psychiatric consultant about the latent psychotic individual, a familiarity with the concepts of Borderline and Narcissistic personality underpinnings and Clinical Disorders and their manifestations is necessary. Research on psychological separation and individuation is crucial for understanding how destructive aggression can be intertwined with bonding abnormalities between child and mother. Preoedipal aggression in psychiatric language distinguishes aggression unique to the parent/child relationship preceding the onset of identification and the triangular, competitive relationships between child and parents known as the oedipal period beginning at age three. Preoedipal developmental issues emphasize the diadic relationship between mother and child. It is this diadic development preceding the competitive, triangular strivings of the Oedipal Period that is of primary concern in the psychogenesis of Latent Psychotic Borderline or Narcissistic Personality Disorder. McDevitt (1983) described deviant sadomasochistic interactions between the male child and his mother during this preoedipal period including obviously painful pinching. Lansky (1983) further develops the relationship between impulsive behavior and attachment in his paper, "The Explanation of Impulsive Action". According to Lansky, impulsive behavior can be considered restorative, because the impulse can restore emotional equilibrium in adults suffering from disorders of attachment in the preoedipal first three years of life. He describes a profound sense of "absence" in adult attachment disorders followed by restoration of more normal feelings following impulsive behavior. Podolsky (1965) in "The Lust Murderer", has stated:

> "the typical lust murder characterized by 1) periodic outbursts due to recurring compulsions by paroxysmal sexual desires, 2) nearly always cutting or stabbing, particularly the breasts or genitals, frequently with sucking or licking of the wounds, biting of the skin and sometimes a desire to drink the blood and eat the flesh of the victim, 3) sometimes erection and ejaculation followed by violation of the victim—often there is no attempt at intercourse, 4) behavior usually returns to normal until the next outburst".

The columnist, Lerner (1957) wrote, "In many cases of sexual brutality and murder the sex act is never committed. Violence serves as a substitute for it".

Retvitch (1965) has elaborated on the restorative function of violent sexual impulses.

> "Either murder or assault on a female is an expression of a compulsive need and provides satisfaction with or without accompanying sexual manifestations such as erection and ejaculation. The assaults are usually repetitive and are frequently committed in a similar ritualistic manner . . . the accumulation of tensions released through the attack may be of long duration or it may be a displacement of suddenly induced, hostile emotions from mother or mother-surrogate to the victim. Krafft-Ebing in reporting the case of the 20-year-old-male who stabbed girls in the genitals stated, 'For a while he succeeded in mastering his morbid cravings, but this produced feelings of anxiety, and perspiration would break out on his entire body.' "

The restorative value of impulsive behavior for reintegration of personality may explain Podolsky's (1965) findings that "behavior usually returns to normal until the next outburst after the lust murder". The intertwining of sadomasochistic aggression and attachment anomalies evidenced in the early childhood observations of McDevitt (1983) may lead to a clearer psychodynamic formulation of sadomasochistic aggression in the Latent Psychotic or Borderline and Narcissistic

Personality Disorders. It is the aggressive and destructive elements of the early mother and child relationship that are "introjected", or, absorbed excessively into the personality structure of the Borderline or Narcissistic Personality Disordes and remain *unmetabolized* as dissociated elements, or elements that can be split off and "projected" outward on the external world. Hence the Narcissistic or Borderline Personality Disorder has incorporated too much of the bad from the maternal relationship and can split this "introjected" badness from his own personality and perceive it as originating from outside. In this psychodynamic formulation, the individual no longer possesses the "badness"—it is the other person, the female victim who "has it". He may either project his introjected, dissociated badness on to his victim and justify his own violence or displace his violence toward his bad mother on to the victim and destroy the mother's badness. The lack of sound personality boundaries in these individuals creates confusion regarding the location of the "badness" between people. In absorbing elements of the badness and aggression of mother and recycling of this badness through projection or displacement, female targets become psychotic disorganization with a lack of realistic perception and true identification of the potential victim. The latent psychotic in the process of lust murder is unlikely to have adequate personality integration and reality testing to know the nature of the victim as an actual human being or target of his own aggression. Kernberg (1982), discussing sexual aggression and introjection in his article, "An Ego Psychology and Object Relations approach to the Narcissistic Personality", has stated,

> "One prognostically crucial dimension along which one can explore narcissistic personality structures is the extent to which aggression has been integrated into the psychic apparatus. Aggression may be integrated into the pathological, grandiose self, or it may remain restricted to the underlying, dissociated, and/or repressed primitive object relations against which the pathological grandiose self represents the main defensive structure. One may, in fact, describe the developmental sequence of this integration of aggression into the psychic apparatus including, 1) primitive dissociation or splitting of aggressively invested object relations from libidinally invested object relations, 2) later condensation of such primitive aggressive object relations with sexual drive derivatives in the context of polymorphous, perverse sexual striving and 3) predominant channeling of aggression into a pathlogical, narcissistic character structure with direct investment of aggression by the pathologic grandiose self ... When primitive aggression is directly infiltrated in the pathological, grandiose self, a particularly ominous development occurs perhaps best described as characterological sadism. In this last group we find narcissistic patients whose grandiosity and pathological self idealization are reinforced by the sense of triumph over fear and pain achieved by inflicting fear and pain on others. We also find cases where self esteem is enhanced by the direct sadistic pleasure of aggression linked with sexual drive derivatives. Some of these narcissistic personalities may pursue joyful types of cruelty ... A final factor that has crucial prognostic significance is the extent to which the antisocial trends are built into the patient's narcissistic character pathology ...
>
> Antisocial tendencies go hand and hand with a lack of integration and normal superego functions, and also with a lack of development of a modulated capacity for depressive reaction. The quality of object relations is also an inverse relation to antisocial trends. Naturally when antisocial trends are present in the patients who also present a sadistic infiltration of the pathological grandiose self or direct expressions of severely sadistic sexual behavior, the prognosis is significantly worsened."

It seems likely that the contemporary concepts of Narcissistic or Borderline Personality Disorders with antisocial, sadistic impulse disorders are referred to in the literature as latent psychotics and lust murder. It is the clinical elucidation of rage, violence, aggression, and sadomasochistic sexual perversion, or polymorphous perverse sexuality, which Kernberg developed from his clinical research. Psychoanalysis cannot prove causative linkage between the clinical manifestations of sexual perversion, violence and sadomasochism presented by their adult patients and events from the mother-child diad of the first three years of life; yet well organized clinical case material can be dramatically convincing. It is this function, clinical effectiveness of psychoanalytic reconstruction from adult symptom to childhood event that is the traditional psychodynamic foundation for conceptualizing lust murder and latent psychosis.

It is the fusion of destructive impulses from disorganized sexual impulses evolving out of the preoedipal matrix of these individuals, together with the incapacity for empathic bonding typical of the sociopath, that provides a motivational model for comprehension of the serial lust murderer. With this model the investigative staff may be able to better comprehend the unobtrusive, superficially adjusted individual in society who appears to behave and relate normally but is incapable of true social integration, true intimacy or consistent psychological integration. It is this individual who may appear to be a "good family man" and a "good citizen" but one driven by a crescendoing evolution of antisocial, aggressive sexual impulsivity into a repetitious pattern of lust murder. It is this person who can be transiently psychotic and, via impulsive behavior such as murder and yet reintegrate to a superficial appearance of social and psychological adjustment. It is this individual who charges fragmentary sexual behavior, such as collecting female shoes, with destructive aggression.

Guttmacher's (1963) series of sexually aggressive offenders shows the relevance of polymorphous perverse sexual behavior, or the predilection of a substitute for intercourse, in the histories of these men, i.e., fetishism. Guttmacher (1963) has written:

> "Only one case had a previous conviction for exhibitionism. Of great importance for prediction of potential violence with sexual motivation seem to be the following combination of factors:
> 1) unprovoked assaults on women, particularly choking or stabbing, 2) offenses of breaking and entering committed solo and in bizarre circumstances, 3) fetishism of female underclothing ... confusion of sexual identity as elicited on projective tests.... and blurring of reality boundaries.

It is certainly not proven in the cases of lust murderers that history of polymorphous perverse or, synonymously, paraphilic behavior is a common antecedent to the murdering; however, lust murderers are frequently uncooperative in volunteering psychological information. The *Comprehensive Textbook of Psychiatry*, (1980), defines paraphilia as follows:

> "Paraphilias are characterized by specialized sexual fantasies, masturbatory practices, sexual props and requirements of the sexual partner. The special fantasy, with its unconscious and conscious components, is the pathognomonic element, arousal and orgasm being variously dependent upon the active elaboration of the illusion. The influence of the fantasy, of its elaborations on behavior, extend beyond the sexual sphere to pervade the person's life. Paraphilia, also referred to as perversion and sexual deviation, at one end of the spectrum shades into the psychosis and gender identity disorders ... Overall, paraphilia shares more common grounds with Borderline Personality Disorders ... in fetishism the sexual focus is on objects such as shoes, gloves, corsets or hose that are intimately associated with the human body and are relatively indestructible. The particular fetish is linked to somebody closely involved with the patient during his childhood and has some quality closely associated with that loved, needed and traumatizing person. It serves the magical, hence fetish, bridge to relatedness, as a binder against aggression and as a representation of the female phallus.

> Sexual activity may be directed toward the fetish itself, such as masturbation, with or into a shoe, or the fetish may be incorporated in sexual congress with, for example, the demand that high heel shoes be worn.

> Fetishization has been viewed as the central process in all sexual arousal, perverse and normal. Stoller, however, broadened fetishization to a more general process of dehumanization and believed that the fetish stands for the human, rather than solely for the missing maternal phallus. McDougal also suggested that fetishism is one concrete means of compensating for the gap in

reality sense left by the disavowed sexual reality, that is, disavowal of the anatomical distinction between the sexes."

The individual who is borderline in character structure—and so sociopathic and incapable of social bonding as to be capable of multiple murder—likely manifests fetishist behavior early in his criminal career. For that reason, Guttmacher's (1963) cases may have shown a high incidence of "fetishism of female underclothing, expressions of hatred, contempt and fear of women, primitive fantasy life, confusion of sexual identity and a high incidence of offenses of breaking and entering, committed solo and in bizarre circumstances". The multilated victim of lust murder can be conceptualized therefore as a failure of the fetish. For example, Podolsky (1965) says,

> "In a crime pronounced as sexual murder; the type of injuries is of considerable importance; the most frequent are multilation of the genital organs or the cutting out thereof; next comes disembowelment, the plunging of a stick or umbrella into the vagina or anus, the tearing out of the hair, the severing of the breast and throttling ...
>
> In genuine cases of sexual murder, the killing replaced the sexual act. There is, therefore, no sexual intercourse at all. Sexual pleasure is induced by cutting, stabbing and slashing the victim's body, ripping open her abdomen, plunging the hand into the intestines, cutting out and taking away her genitals, throttling her, sucking her blood. These horrors, which surpass in frightfulness everything that has been committed by human beings even under the effects of war psychosis, constitutes, so to speak, pathological equivalents of coitus."

Weinsel and Calef (1972) have formulated an hypothesis which further assists in bridging the phenomena of the paraphilias with lust murder,

> "Mention should also be made of the role of the necrophelia theme in that group of sexual perversions (paraphilias) which, loosely, are considered together under the label of 'bondage' fantasies and practices. Here too the helplessness of the sexual object is the crucial dynamic element: most frequently the object is tied-up or bound in some other fashion; but the numerous variations include the object's being a slave, being drugged or anaesthetized, asleep, hypnotized or paralysed. Sexual gratification for these individuals is often possible only when the object is in this helpless condition, for practical purposes—dead! We recognize that no one single determinant is responsible for such fantasies and behavior, and both the products or regression from an oedipal conflict and more primitive pregenital (preoedipal) fixations play some role in the formation of these tendencies. Further, it is our experience that at least in some of these cases the wish to re-enter and to explore the interior of the mother's body may be an important dynamic ingredient; and it is our further impression that the more immediate causal element is related to the traumatic impact of viewing the paternal phallus together with a defensive identification with it. It should be added that in all of these fantasies the mechanism of turning passive into active is a crucial factor."

Here we begin to see the bizarre destructive acts of the lust murderer as primitive aggression fused with the polymorphous, perverse sexuality described by Kernberg (1982) as well as the possible final outcome of crescendoing development of paraphilia to ultimate breakdown of the binding power of the fetish, hence personality disintegration and resultant psychosis. Therefore, masturbation into a shoe which has been burglarized from a woman's bedroom may be only a quantitative leap from disembowelment in terms of disavowal of sexual reality. The lust murderer who mutilates and disembowels his victim, in other words, is dehumanizing his victim, and denying the threat of sexual differences to a far greater extreme than the foot fetishist. Mutilation and disembowelment of the victim in lust murder and the foot fetish, however, share similar paraphilic roots in the service of the magical functions in the Borderline Personality Disorder, or latent psychotic, who is defending from psychological disintegration. Stoller (1980) in his discussion of Transsexualism describes brutally violent hypermasculinity in primitive tribal warriors whose attachment with their mothers was so powerful that denial of female identification, through hypermasculine aggression and dehumanization of the female, was necessary for defense against symbiotic anxiety, and, consequently, dissolution of psychological boundaries and ultimate psychosis.

Profiling

In order for a psychiatrist to be of assistance in the investigation of serial murder there must be a clear and frank discussion of the nature of the process being investigated. If investigative personnel believe that a serial murderer is basically a bad person who behaves offensively because he has chosen a particularly nefarious habit, the psychiatrist can be of little assistance. Psychiatrists are only of value in serial murder investigations if there is receptiveness within the investigative staff to a mutual learning process concerning lust murder. The repulsive nature of this crime, particularly if associated with necrophilia or mutilation, may result in resistances within the staff that can lead to wasteful diversions. Evidence can be missed or destroyed to avoid disgust or threatening emotional feelings. Acceptance that the Borderline or Narcissistic Personality Disorder with severe sociopathic and sadistic trends can commit murder as a substitute for normal erotic pleasure or even nonviolent perversion is the foundation for exploration of motivation in serial murders. With a mutually respectful desire to learn about the bizarre world of the lust murderer the investigator and psychiatric consultant can enhance their sense of "type" for a suspect. The investigator is less likely to make a mistake in judging the grandiosity of pathological narcissism and the manipulativeness of sociopathy with "normalcy". The lust murderer can present a facade of relationships and effective, perhaps, even superior performance. Not infrequently, he will be in the bright-superior intelligence range and, therefore, potentially a skilled imposter. Ted Bundy served as a government sexual-assault expert and a crisis clinic counselor. This does not mean that the lust murderer, despite his appearance of superior function and normal relationships, is otherwise a normal person who has consciously selected a criminal career in life. The lust murderer has primitive personality abnormalities making him incapable of normal intimacy. I know of no lust murderer who was in intensive psychotherapy and therefore provided evidence of his capacity to bond in a human relationship. Lust murderers may be able to maintain effective facades as imposters, immitating normal people, but they are not normal enough to tolerate the intensive bonding demands to meaningful psychotherapy. The not uncommon expectation that a serial murderer is the intimate acquaintance of practicing psychiatrists is, of course, totally contradictory to the psychodynamic formulation of lust murder. Lust murder represents the extreme sadomasochistic and sociopathic end of the Borderline-Narcissistic Personality Disorder spectrum—consequently the least treatable part of the spectrum. Their inability to attach, hence their intolerance of intimacy, may be manifested in their propensity to drive great distances frequently crossing state lines. The clinical manifestation of disturbed bonding in sociopathic personality disorders along with manifestations of confused and fragmented, or polymorphous perverse sexuality may be observed in the suspects' prior histories. Sensitivity to polymorphous perverse sexuality in these individuals, hence to fetishistic and paraphilic sexual behavior, will lead to concentration on these aspects of a suspect's biography. This perspective on lust murder is, of course, questionable practical value, because the vast majority of personality disorders who manifest sadomasochistic behavior and polymorphous perverse behavior are extremely unlikely to commit serial murder, but ruling them in or out while ignoring this dimension is reckless.

As previously mentioned, there may be resistance within the criminal justice system to uncovering sexual motivation for crime. To assume that previous convictions and F.B.I. rap sheets are in any way a comprehensive and valid representation of a person's predilections for violent offenses is inexcusable within this type of investigation. Any suspect with a history of burglary or assault must be thoroughly investigated for a history which has either been distorted by the court or inadequately investigated. These individuals have extremely damaged self images. Therefore, any manifestation of normalcy is in fact that of an imposter. They are devious in their apprehension of victims. It is not coincidental that Ted Bundy worked in a sexual assault program or Wayne Williams as a talent scout. Their heightened ability to be effective imposters and dedicate this skill to a successful predatory existence is an important factor of their narcissistic and sociopathic personality structure. Devices as disguises, impersonations, and other manipulations of the environment are not uncommon, in contrast to the authenticity of their own identity which they cannot experience. Sensitivity to the manifestations of sadomasochism and polymorphous perverse sexual behavior is likewise of importance to the coroner's office. To examine the victim of a serial murder case without looking carefully for evidence of symbolic mutilation, vampirism or oral aggression and cannibalism in the form of bite marks suggests a non-professional orientation. The bite marks in the Chi Omega case which resulted in the conviction of Ted Bundy, were nearly destroyed.

Summary and Suggestions:

Lust murder cases appear to be increasing. It is unrealistic to expect urban and suburban police departments to invest major resources of tracking these individuals with the hope of reducing the vulnerability to society. It is doubtful that a full-time metropolitan intelligence department can be dedicated to the tracking of serial murders. It is important that one investigator, within a region, be highly trained and educated regarding this type of crime. If a network of experience and information is available regionally and/or nationally, police departments can turn to these agencies for assistance in the event their communities are victimized by a serial lust murderer. The value of this type of accessibility depends on liason between specialized investigative resource for lust murder and the administrations of the various departments. All too often investigations are disrupted and confused by interdepartmental breakdowns in communication.

The value of specialized resources depends upon the soundness of information and assistance provided. Behavioral science profiling can be superficial, phenomenological and, perhaps, even worse, distracting. There is no evidence that we know enough about lust murderers to make very many phenomenological generalizations. True, some cross state lines, but Wayne Williams did not, even though he drove a great deal. Many lust murderers are extremely bright and extraordinarily clever; yet some are nearly retarded. Lust murders have been know to infiltrate the investigation. Their major interest revolves around their potential apprehension. Superficial behavioral scientific profiling that rigidly reduces serial murder to a few observable parameters can lead an investigation astray. It is better to search for what distinguishes any given serial murder in its uniqueness, then build a profile of a potential suspect against the psychopathology of the Narcissistic or Borderline Personality disorders particularly the severe forms. Their biographies will likely show overt but, perhaps, subtle antisocial, polymorphous perverse and sadistic trends not registered often on police records. The mutual study of suspects' biographies by investigators with a psychiatric consultant can reduce wasteful diversions and rigidity within the investigation.

REFERENCES

Comprehensive Textbook of Psychiatry. (1980). Baltimore., Md. Williams and Wilkins Co.

Guttmacher, M. (1963). Dangerous Offenders., *Crime and Delinquency, 9,* 381-390.

Kernberg, O. (1982). An Ego Psychology and Object Relations Approach to the Narcissistic Personality. In The American Psychiatric Association, *Psychiatry, 1982, Annual Review.* Washington, D.C.: American Psychiatric Association Press (510-523).

Laing, R. (1967). *The Politics of Experience.* London: Penguin.

Lansky, M. (1983). The Explanation of Impulse Action. Paper presented at the Seventh World Congress of Psychiatry, Vienna, Austria.

Lerner, M. (1957). New York Post, Apr. 22.

McDevitt, J. (1983). Emergence of Hostile Aggression and Its Modification during the Separation Individuation Process. Paper presented to the Seattle Psychoanalytic Society.

Podolsky, E. (1965). The Lust Murderer, *Medico-Legal Journal, 33,* 174-178.

Rada, R. (1978). *Clinical Aspects of the Rapist,* New York: Grune & Stratton.

Retvich, E. (1965). Sex Murder and the Potential Sex Murderer. *Diseases of the Nervous System, 26,* 640-648.

Stoller, R. (1980). Cross Cultural Observations about General Identity. Paper presented to the Seattle Psychoanalytic Society.

Szasz, T. (1961). *The Myth of Mental Illness.* New York: Harper & Row.

Weinshel, E., & Calet, V. (1972). On Certain Neurotic Equivalents of Necrophilia. *International Journal of Psycho-Analysis, 53,* 67-75.

PROFILING KILLERS: A REVISED CLASSIFICATION MODEL FOR UNDERSTANDING SEXUAL MURDER

ROBERT D. KEPPEL AND RICHARD WALTER

Generally, murder classifications have failed to be useful for investigators in identifying perpetrators of murders. Based on the experience of the authors, this article extends the definitions of four previously recognized rape-offender typologies (power-assertive, power-reassurance, anger-retaliatory, and anger-excitation) into classifications for sexually oriented killers. These types of murderers and their crime scenes are described through the dynamics of their behaviors, homicidal patterns, and suspect profiles. Each typology is followed by an actual case example that fits that particular type of killer. By identifying crime scene and behavioral factors of these killers, the homicide investigator will be more equipped to process murder scenes, prioritize leads, and apprehend killers. Unlike earlier efforts at crime scene classification, the present work addresses the behaviors, motivational continuum, and the effects of experiential learning by the perpetrators. The relative frequency of the four types within a population of murderers at the Michigan State Penitentiary is revealed.

W hen the motivation for a murder is unknown and the identity of the killer has not been established, it is hard to explain the critical questions of who, what, when, where, why, and how. Without such information, the public is left with the uneasy feeling that the police have not caught the killer and another murder is possibly forthcoming. This lack of knowledge has created a forensic investigative dilemma since the beginning of police inquiries.

Past efforts to address unsolved murders by developing theories of investigations have not been empirically studied (Keppel & Weis, 1994). Researchers and investigative practitioners have attempted to analyze murder and the people who commit it by constructing self-styled categories of killers that were hypothetical inferences developed from some individual case studies of convicted murderers and limited experience at investigating violent crimes. In their *Crime Classification Manual*, Douglas, Burgess, Burgess, and Ressler (1992) discussed a wide range of information focused on concept identification. The killers were categorized into groups in which one expected outcome became the single and significant identifier. For example, a lust killing is described as a sexually oriented killing. Similarly, a murder arising from a business dispute was called a power or greed killing.

Unfortunately, although their typologies of murderers have descriptive value, they have failed to provide investigators with the elements necessary for crime scene assessment. For example, greed may have been the original motivation for killing an elderly woman and classified as such.

This type of characteristic does not explain the motivation if the woman was also severely beaten, stabbed, and placed into a sexually degrading and posed position. Although general indicators may apply to a myriad of circumstances, the static descriptors of these types of classification systems only address the obvious. They do not address the hidden and inferred behavior of the killer.

In addition, other authorities, such as Holmes and Holmes (1996), cited typologies of serial murderers that were labeled *visionary, mission, hedonistic*, and *power/control*. These categories have a wide range of function, are of limited service to investigative work, and are unsupported by empirical study.

Very few police investigators use the typologies in the *Crime Classification Manual* (Douglas et al., 1992) or those developed by Holmes and Holmes (1996) to generalize about a population of murderers. In fact, the major homicide tracking systems such as the Federal Bureau of Investigation's (FBI) Violent Criminal Apprehension Program (VICAP); the Homicide Investigation Tracking System (HITS) in Washington, Oregon, and Idaho; and the Royal Canadian Mounted Police's (RCMP) Violent Crime Linkage Analysis System (VICLAS), which are centralized data bases for homicide information, do not use either typology to classify murderers (*HITS Murder Form*, 1995; Johnson, 1994; *VICAP Form*, 1991). The reason is that because the *Classification Manual*'s and Holmes and Holmes's characteristics of killers and crime scenes are not rich in detail, their utility in aiding investigators to apprehend killers is limited.

Homicide investigators have noted generally that crime classification systems have provided little assistance in solving a particular murder (Copson, 1995; Copson, Badcock, Boon, & Britton, 1997; Geberth & Turco, 1997; Keppel, 1995; Keppel & Birnes, 1995; Morneau & Rockwell, 1980). This is the problem! That is, despite a general description of incidents of murder, the information from homicide classification systems currently mentioned in the literature does not address the key issues relating to the offender's identity. Also, this information does not affect his apprehension. Accordingly, when the logical flow is broken or incomplete between theories and reality, the direction and function of the classification concepts become defused, limited, and sometimes meaningless. Therefore, despite best intentions, the end result may be that the homicide investigator is left with some abstract notions, a dead body, and an unknown offender.

Given the dynamic and synergetic components of two or more murders committed over time by the same person, a systematic look at a viable murder continuum offers the opportunity to explore elements left at the crime scene by the killer. Here, the investigator can assign meaning to (a) the presence or absence of evidence, (b) methods of operation, (c) signature, (d) the comfort zone of the killer (the place the killer feels at ease), and (e) an inferred motive for the murder. In addition, there may be indicators for emotional intensity, rationale for the murder, and a constellation of additional factors associated with the known and specific type of killer responsible for a certain murder. If used properly, a dynamic classification system can be applied to the murder. The system can then provide information that could be further analyzed to determine methods of approach in the investigative process of the murder. It also may provide reasons for inaccuracies, additional crime scene analysis, and behavioral indicators of the killer.

The intent of criminal profiling, crime scene assessment, or psychological profiling, as it is sometimes called, is to identify the key crime scene and behavioral factors related to the killer, thereby enabling the homicide investigator to more effectively analyze murder scenes, interview killers, prioritize leads, and apprehend killers (Warren, Hazelwood, & Dietz, 1996). It is the focus of this article to (a) identify and define certain typologies within a rape-murder classification, (b) explain the homicidal pattern of the killer within that typology, (c) offer profile characteristics of the killer within each typology, and (d) give a specific example of a murder case scenario that typifies the killer within each typology. Therefore, the investigator will be informed of specific crime scene indicators that describe clearly each of the categories or typologies of killers. In turn, those very indicators will help homicide detectives perform their own crime scene assessment without the long wait sometimes associated with obtaining a profile from an outside expert.

In 1977, Groth, Burgess, and Holmstrom developed a classification system for rapists based on empirical research, and Hazelwood and Burgess (1987) refined and used those same categories for analyzing rape cases 10 years later. Although only addressing issues within a classification of rapists, not rape-murderers, their dynamic model focused on the purpose and style of attack and the conceptual and emotional factors of the behaviors of rapists.

Hazelwood and Burgess (1987) originally described four categories of rapists with their classification: (a) power-assertive (PA), (b) power-reassurance (PR), (c) anger-retaliatory (AR), and (d) anger-excitation (AE). Although these categories at the time related only to rapists and their behavior, the authors expanded those same categories to the crime of rape-murder.

Background

Based on their experience in analyzing and investigating many murder and rape-murder cases and interviewing numerous rape-murderers, the authors undertook a project to add to Hazelwood and Burgess's (1987) preexisting rapist categories that would, in turn, enable homicide detectives to use the descriptions of the homicidal pattern and profile for each type of killer in their murder cases. This was accomplished by taking known examples of murder cases that fell within each category and describing their crime scenes in detail.

The major problem in the project was to develop meaningful characteristics in each category that dealt with the deceased victim. When Hazelwood and Burgess (1987) created their categories, they based them largely on what the offender said or did not say to the living victim/witness. In the case of murder, very few, if any, words exchanged between the offender and the victim are known to investigators. Therefore, the crime scene detail, which reflects the behavior of the offender, is vital to each of the new rape-murder categories.

What follows is detailed information about each category. The categories are divided into three different sections: dynamics, homicidal pattern, and suspect profile. Then, each category will be accompanied by an example of a known rape-murder case for that specific category. See Table 6.1 for a comparison of the dynamic characteristics of the four categories.

TABLE 6.1   COMPARISON OF THE DYNAMIC CHARACTERISTICS OF THE FOUR CLASSIFICATIONS

Power-Assertive	Power-Reassurance	Anger-Retaliatory	Anger-Excitation
Rape is planned; murder is not planned	Rape is planned; murder is not planned	Rape and murder are planned	Rape and murder are planned
Power interest	Power interest	Anger driven	Anger driven
Increasing aggression with the victim ensures control power	Acts out fantasy and seeks reassurance from the victim	Seeks revenge for his anger toward another person by attacking a symbolic victim	Engages in pro-longed torture, exploitation, and/or mutilation; this energizes the killer's fantasy life

POWER-ASSERTIVE RAPE-MURDER

Dynamics

The power-assertive rape-murder is a series of acts in which the rape is planned, whereas the murder is an unplanned response of increasing aggression to ensure control of the victim. The acts within the rape-assault are characterized by forceful aggression and intimidation. Specific to the expression of virility, mastery, and dominance, a direct and overpowering assault is necessary and often results in multiple antemortem rapes of the victim.

For the homicide itself, the central issue becomes one of maintaining control over a vulnerable victim by an exaggerated machismo overreaction. To quickly overcome a victim's resistance, the killer may say, "You don't want to get hurt. Just give up." Characteristically, the killer demonstrates mastery by taking charge or command by the use of an assertive image and dominating violence. For the individual killer or his followers, the finality of the killing ensures the success of the killer's power and control through the elimination of the threat posed by the victim and the secrecy of the performed acts. Because of the satisfaction that the rape-murder gives the killer, he analyzes, plans, and seeks methods to improve his aggressive and masculine image in his everyday life and in times of murder.

Homicidal Pattern

The homicidal pattern in the power-assertive murder is characterized by the sating of power needs through sexual assault and murder. Once the perpetrator has decided to commit either the initial or a repeat rape-murder, the methods for victim selection and acting out will be determined by previous experience, the stress of internal pressures, and opportunity. Accordingly, in selecting the victim, the perpetrator may choose one by opportunity and surprise. Often, the victim is a stranger who is available by surprise on the street or through a breaking and entering into a home. If the rape-assault occurs in a home and the husband is present, he may be required to watch the assault or participate.

When the victim has been assaulted on his/her own territory, the body is left undisturbed. Alternately, when the victim has been abducted from an outside location, the killing and disposal sites vary. That is, when the killing was perpetrated elsewhere, the body was generally dumped.

If the perpetrator has coconspirators, there is often evidence of multiple sexual assaults. That evidence in or around the victim's body can be found in the recovery of ejaculate that is later analyzed and determined to come from several persons.

Consistent with his need to overpower and portray an image of the military warrior, detectives will find that clothing is torn off the victim. In addition, the killer will brandish weapons of symbolic importance to him. Generally, his preferred weapon is part of his normal image. The weapon may be a knife or rope or something else and is easily concealed. He views weapons as an extension of his own power and therefore will bring them to the crime scene and take them with him after the murder.

The victim, male or female, may show evidence of bruises from beating and pummeling at the death scene. When the perpetrator senses a challenge to his control and masculine image—or a revelation of his internal weaknesses—he may become even more violent. Here, extreme forms of violence will occur short of what he, in his own mind, considers to be deviant, perverse, and atypical of his self-image. Although violence inflicted on the victim may have been severe, there is generally no mutilation of the body; that would be perverse in his mind. With this in mind, investigators must be cautious when interviewing the power-assertive killer. If the perpetrator senses that he may be seen as a pervert, he may instantly turn off during the interview process and refuse any further contact with authorities.

After the killing has occurred, the perpetrator does not maintain contact with the victim. On departing from the crime scene, he often will leave an organized crime scene—as defined by the FBI behavioral scientists and Geberth (1996)—in an effort to cover up and protect his identity. Because the crime scene reflects his image of being in the clear from suspicion, he can emotionally exculpate himself from any responsibility for the murder and repeat it within a short time span. Although he remains intellectually precocious and alert, his desire for power will demand credit for the killing. That is, the murder does not count unless someone knows or suspects him of the killing. Therefore, due to his need for glory and recognition, he may betray his secret to a bar patron, fellow worker, admirer, cell-mate, and sometimes the police.

Suspect Profile

In the power-assertive type of killer, the offender is usually in his early 20s and somewhat emotionally primitive. He is primarily preoccupied with projecting a macho image and orients his life accordingly. Despite a wide range of physical characteristics and types, the power-assertive offender is sensitive to his characteristics of masculinity. Therefore, he often is a body builder and portrays a muscular image and/or displays tattoos for a show of machismo and power. In addition to displaying a confident body posture, the offender cruises in his well-attended car, carries weapons, and shows an arrogant and condescending attitude to others. Although a heavy use of alcohol and drugs may be used to bolster the offender's courage and power, he does not abuse these substances to the point of blacking out.

Although the offender may associate with people, he is not seen as a team player. Socially, he may not be a hermit but at times because of his level of frustration with social contacts, he lives on the edge of being a loner. Although he may have an active interest in sports, they are generally limited to individual contact events such as wrestling, judo, and karate. For the most part, he seeks to gain power and displays a winner-take-all attitude. Although he may have a history of multiple marriages and relationships, he does not view them as successful.

In demonstrating his potential for power, he has a history of perpetrating crimes such as burglary, theft, and robbery. Unless the criminal history has resulted in a mental health referral, he may have had no contact with mental health workers.

Educationally, he is typically a school dropout. Based on the limits of the masculine image, his sexual preferences will not accommodate the variety of materials contained in hard-core pornographic literature. He is especially conflicted over unconventional sexual interest and may display a strong antihomosexual attitude. For the most part, if he reads magazines, they will likely be *Playboy* and *Penthouse* types of literature.

Although he may have served in the Marines or the Navy, his service record is generally poor, and he may have terminated his service prematurely. He is generally viewed as antisocial.

Case Example

In 1986, a 40-year-old woman began walking down a Sydney, Australia, street in the early evening. Suddenly, she was grabbed by an unknown male who pulled her head back by the hair and said to an unseen accomplice, "What about this one?" In response, the coconspirator said, "No, she's too old." The aggressor then retorted, "You said long black hair." Again, the unseen voice said, "She's too old." At this point, the woman was set free. She reported this incident to the police.

Later that night, an Australian beauty queen with long black hair was scheduled to return by train from a visit with her sister. She failed to return. The next day, she was discovered in a fenced field on the outskirts of Sydney. Her body was found about 150 yards from a gravel road. The body was face down with its arms crisscrossing the head as though carried and dropped into that position. Her legs were spread open. The body was nude and no clothing was found in the surrounding area. There were three major cuts on the ventral side of the neck. The head was nearly severed from the body. The ventral side of the hands showed severe defense wounds from a knife. The forensic examination of the body revealed anal, oral, and vaginal sexual assaults. There was no evidence of any postmortem mutilation.

In this case, there is evidence of a planned assault on a preselected type of victim. Although long black hair appeared to be a criteria for selection, the age of the victim may have also been an influence. Although the first woman was rejected, the criminals continued to search for a woman who would meet their criteria.

In part, the follow-up investigation may have targeted a specific individual. But because of the evidence of multiple rape assaults, all of which were antemortem, investigators must also consider that the victim was abducted and sexually assaulted by multiple offenders.

Although the victim suffered severe defense wounds, there were no significant signs of beating or pummeling of the body. Based on the report of the first victim, multiple sexual assaults, and pattern style, the investigation indicated that probably three to five persons committed the murder. Although each member of the group has the obligation to surmount the victim in sexual assault, it is likely that the leader of the group would save the ultimate act of cutting the victim's throat for himself. Here, he rises above equals. Of note, he did not remove the head . . . that would have been perverse.

Based on this information regarding the power-assertive type, the New South Wales Police were advised that the leader and his associates would likely brag about the killings at the local bar. Again, a suspect profile was given to the investigators. After 11 days of investigation, a total of five suspects confessed to the killing. The leader of the group had a criminal history of exploitative crimes, confident body posture, use of alcohol, and ill-fated relationships. In addition, he was an educational dropout and needed to be validated by followers. Finally, because his followers also needed to validate their victory, they revealed their crime through bar talk, thus tipping the police onto them.

POWER-REASSURANCE RAPE-MURDERER

Dynamics

In the power-reassurance rape-homicide, a planned, single rape attack is followed by an unplanned overkill of the victim. Motivated by an idealized seduction and conquest fantasy, the killer focuses on acting out a fantasy and seeks verbal reassurance of his sexual adequacy. When the victim does not yield to the killer's planned seduction scenario, a sense of failure and panic thrust him into a murder/assault. In the murder/assault, he gains control and lessens the threat over the situation in which the victim was not compliant. After killing his unrequited lover, the murderer may act out his sexual fantasies through exploratory postmortem mutilation.

The power-reassurance type tries to express his sexual competence through seduction. When that fails, the subsequent killing permits him to reintroduce the fantasy system for further sexual exploration that he was not allowed to do prior to the killing. The quest for sexual competency and personal adequacy dominates any fantasy drawings he may do.

Homicidal Pattern

In planning the rape, the power-reassurance type selects and watches a female victim. He may choose a casual acquaintance, neighbor, or stranger. No matter which type of victim, he applies his fantasies to that victim. In the power-reassurance rape-homicide, the murder occurs after the attempted rape has failed and the perpetrator feels a need for emotional catharsis and victim control. Although the offender has no intent to harm or degrade the victim, the failure of the rape-assault and the rejection from the victim panics him into a homicide overkill. Believing that he can act out sexual fantasy and reality, he prepares a scenario of misbeliefs designed to seduce the victim into validating his sexual competence. When the victim does not follow his plan, he feels threatened and attacks the victim.

Often, the selected victim is 10 or 15 years older or younger than the perpetrator. If the victim is the same age as the killer or outside his preferred age range, she may be considered damaged goods.

The power-reassurance type uses threats and intimidation to gain initial control and sometimes enters the crime scene with a weapon. But, usually the first time he attacks, a weapon is not preselected and brought to the scene. The second time, he may bring a gun and display it but will not fire it due to the noise. The third time, the weapon may be a knife.

After the initial attack on the victim, the offender tries to act out the preprogrammed fantasy. In this respect, he has been called the *polite and gentleman rapist* due to the verbal dialogue that he tries to carry on with the victim. During the assault, he may ask the victim to remove her clothing and be quite polite with other such requests. While assuring her that he is not going to hurt her, he seeks reassurances of his sexual competency from her. Typically, he may ask, "Is this nice; do you like this; is this pleasing to you; am I better than …?"

When the killer finds his sexual competence threatened through ridicule, challenge, and counterattack, he loses control of the situation and kills the victim through pummeling and manual strangulation. Because he fears the revelation of his failure at sex, he initiates the homicidal attack to control the victim and protect his self-image.

Because the incomplete sexual assault does not validate his sexual competency, he will often explore the mysteries and curiosities of sex on the postmortem body. Consequently, there is sometimes mutilation of the body coupled with evidence of ritualism. Because his fantasies have been shunted by the unsuccessful rape, there often is not any evidence of sperm at the murder crime scene. Nevertheless, the postmortem activities and ritualisms can satisfy and reinforce him. From his point of view, the killing was a success. Therefore, when the need arises, it can be acted out repeatedly until his needs are satisfied.

As a result, the behavior of the power-reassurance murderer may be episodic in nature with one or more killings within a cluster of similar offenses. Notably, when the offender views the murder as successful, he may attempt to extend the relationship with that victim by collecting small souvenirs and newspaper clippings to enhance his imagined relationship. Finally, the reader should be aware that nighttime is the friend of fantasy development. Therefore, the offender acts out in the nighttime hours because that's when he feels most comfortable.

Suspect Profile

In considering the age of the power-reassurance murderer, the general acting out age is in the mid-20s range. Of course, the age can be variable and conditional on circumstances such as the incarceration of the offender for other crimes during his mid-20s. Although intellectually equal to other types of offenders, the murderer relies excessively on fantasies that allow opposing ideas to come in close proximity. This often makes the offender appear dull and somewhat emotionally scattered. He prefers to satisfy his needs through certain fantasies rather than risk rejection. As a consequence, he is often plagued by an inadequate sex life and uses sexual fantasies and relationships to overcome the dysfunction and pain of reality.

In developing his extensive repertoire of rape fantasies, he borrows notions from erotic pornography and a long history of substitutions for sexual activity such as window peeping, fondling of clothing, and obsessive daydreaming. Developmentally, the onset of absorbing fantasies may have started in the early juvenile years. Because his fantasies have taken him into a private world, he is generally viewed as socially isolated with no male or female friends. He is viewed as a loner and a weirdo. Generally, he is an unmarried person without a history of normal sexual activities.

Educationally, he may be identified as an underachiever who suffers from a learning disability but who still squeaks through the system. His military service will not be marked with unusual problems. He will simply be viewed as a nona-chieving passive soldier who takes orders.

Because he does not have any interest in athletic activities, he will often compensate for his lack of machismo through compulsive behaviors. Mentally, he may have had a professional referral because he does not live up to what he is capable of achieving.

Due to the dominating influences of fantasy activities, his life tends to leave him an immature person who views life as a spectator not a participant. In other words, he lacks the confidence to participate. He feels inferior and cannot tolerate criticism of team members. Again, because his activities are dominated by compressed and edited illusions, he often bypasses the social inter-mediate steps in developing normal social-sexual interactions.

Given the excessive energies directed toward his own self-stimulation, the offender may live at home and try to subsist on little income. If income is not available, he may perform menial labor to support basic needs. Accordingly, he often lives, works, and plays in a neighborhood familiar to him. A common form of transport would be walking. However, if the subject does have a car, it would likely be an older model in need of repair and care.

The subject's criminal record may reflect his interest in fetish activities, unlawful entry, and larcenies. Basically, the killer is fantasy driven and once the satisfaction is over, he leaves the disorganized crime scene (Geberth, 1996) laden with very valuable evidence.

Case Example

A 24-year-old subject had a 10-year history of alcoholism and unemployment. During a summer evening, the subject was drinking in a local park and chanced upon a 14-year-old female. After a brief encounter, he wrestled her to the ground and sexually assaulted her. Later, when the victim reported the incident to police, she denied that he sexually penetrated her. When the subject was interviewed by the police, he insisted that penetration had taken place.

Subsequently, the subject was convicted of criminal charges and given a brief prison sentence. Prior to parole, the subject was interviewed about the offense. Amongst many issues discussed, he reported his sexual interest in women who were in their 50s, 60s, or 70s. Against advice, the subject was paroled.

Approximately 1 month after parole, he was jailed for drunk and disorderly. Following his release from jail, he resumed a lifestyle pattern of drinking, minimal employment, and socially floating in a fantasy world.

At age 26, the subject found himself in a bar admiring a 65-year-old woman. During the course of the evening, he watched her and made several unsuccessful attempts to make conversation with her. After the bar closed, the woman said goodbye to her friends and started to walk the eight blocks to her home. En route, the subject approached the victim and expressed interest in having sex with her. In response, she refused his offer by chiding and laughing at him. He persisted and followed her to her home. Once there, he again reiterated his dream of having sexual relations with her. According to the subject, she reportedly stated, "Fuck off! Go home and grow a penis, little boy!" At that time, he forced his way into the house and beat the victim into unconsciousness. He then searched the premises and found a shovel with which to chop her body. After inflicting wounds to her body and head with the shovel, he put her in the closet and left the scene.

Following the discovery of the body, the police investigation led to the subject. After explaining to the detectives that he only intended to "love her," he confessed and explained the murder. On returning to prison with a life sentence for murder, the subject stated, "It's your fault! You knew my fantasy for older women and should not have released me!" Soon after his return to prison, the subject began experimenting with asphyxial autoeroticism and bloodletting. These behaviors were basically his efforts at self-mutilation.

In this example, the subject sat in the bar and activated an overidealized seduction and conquest of a 65-year-old female. Although he planned a sexual rendezvous that would reassure his sexual competence against a history of inadequacy, the implementation of the plan met with unaccounted-for resistance. Faced with failure and the fractured fantasy scenario, he exploded into a rage. He pummeled the victim with his fist into death or a near-death state. Following the combative stage of the killing, he then mutilated the body with a shovel. He then left the crime scene. As in his first offense, although semen was not at the crime scene, the subject reported feeling sexually sated and satisfied. That is, from his point of view, the killing was an unfortunate necessity on the way to fantasy satisfaction.

ANGER-RETALIATORY RAPE-MURDERER

Dynamics

In the anger-retaliatory rape-murder, the rape is planned and the initial murder involves overkill. It is an anger-venting act that expresses symbolic revenge on a female victim. Nettled by poor relationships with women, the aggressor distills his anguish and contempt into an explosive revenge on the victim. Although the assault is not predicated on a fantasy system, it is often precipitated by a criticism or scolding from a woman with power over him. In the attempt to express revenge and retaliation for being disciplined, the aggressive killer will either direct his anger at that woman or redirect his anger to a substitute woman. Because the latter type of scapegoating retaliation does not eliminate the direct source of hate, it is likely that it will be episodically repeated to relieve internal stresses. Dynamically, the rape-homicide is committed in a stylized violent burst of attack for the purposes of retaliation, getting even, and revenge on women (Keppel, 1997).

Homicidal Pattern

The homicidal pattern is characterized by a violent sexual assault and overkill of a victim. Inasmuch as the actual source of the killer's anger is a woman who belittles, humiliates, and rejects the subject, the fatal hostility may not be directed at a mother, wife, or female supervisor but at an unsuspecting substitute victim whom the killer has sought out. In these instances, it is likely that the victim would come from his own age group or older. Often, the substitute victim comes from areas in which the aggressor may live or work. That is, while conducting routine, everyday living, the aggressor may find a potential victim who reminds him of his mother or girlfriend. A chance meeting could occur at a grocery store or through general cruising of a neighborhood. When a potential victim is selected, he will keep in mind the location and living circumstances of the victim.

Alternatively, the aggressor tends to act out against the actual victim directly rather than through a substitute when that actual (targeted) victim is a younger person. The selection of this type of victim may be a dismissive female clerk who says "no" and/or a child who threatens to expose inappropriate sexual behaviors. Again, the perpetrator tends to choose victims from familiar areas. Once angered by the intended target, the perpetrator may choose a preselected substitute victim as a symbolic vehicle for resolving his internal stresses.

In approaching the crime scene, the killer usually walks. However, if necessary, he may drive to the crime scene area and approach the last 200 feet on foot. The anger-retaliatory killer may have some type of ruse to get inside the victim's door, but once the victim is isolated, he confronts her.

Armed with a barrage of accusations, he responds to the victim's denial of him by hitting her in the mouth and about the face. As the assault becomes more combative, the aggressor may use weapons of opportunity (knives, statuary, etc.) to brutalize the victim.

Depending on the aggressor's age, experience, and internal stresses, the rape-assault may be incomplete because of an inability to get an erection. Therefore, semen may not be found at the crime scene. In either case, the subject is intent on sating his anger through percussive acts of assault with fists, blunt objects, or a knife.

Regardless of whether the victim is alive or dead, the assault continues until the subject is emotionally satisfied. As his anger begins to cool, he places the body into a submissive position by placing it on its side away from the door, face down, putting an artifact or cloth across the eyes, or placement in a closet with the door closed. Generally, following the intense expression of anger, the subject tends to leave a disorganized crime scene, and the improvised murder weapon may be found within 15 feet of the body. Just prior to leaving the crime scene, the perpetrator often takes a small trinket or souvenir.

When the subject views the sexual assault and murder as a success, he often leaves the crime scene with a feeling of having been cleansed and renewed. Because the subject has transferred the blame of the murder onto the victim, he does not experience any sense of guilt. Accordingly, he does not own any feelings of wrongdoing. In fact, quite the contrary is true. That is, he can develop a sense of sentimentality over the victim and help search for the victim with tears in his eyes.

Suspect Profile

In the anger-retaliatory type, the offender is usually in the mid-to-late-20s and somewhat younger than his victims. He is seen as an explosive personality who is impulsive, quick-tempered, and self-centered. In dealing with people, he is not reclusive but a loner in the midst of a crowd. Generally, his social relations are superficial and limited to many drinking buddies. Socially, he is a person whom no one really knows. Although a sportsman, he prefers playing team contact sports.

Conflicted over his relationship with women, he may often feel dependent and aggressively resistant to them. When challenged by women, he may use various forms of aggression to get even and degrade them. If he has been married, his marital relationship may have been ill-fated or may be in some phase of estrangement. In the marriage, there has generally been a history of spousal abuse. Rather than dealing with the problems in the marriage, he will often avoid them by seeking extramarital liaisons. For the most part, these relationships are unsatisfactory.

Sexually, he is frustrated and may be impotent. Often, he links eroticized anger with sexual competence. Although he may use *Playboy* and similar types of magazines for curiosity, he does not use pornographic materials for stimulation.

When his aggressive feelings toward women are linked with impulsive behavior, he may develop a history of committing crimes such as assault and battery, wife beating, felonious assault, and reckless driving. Humiliated by disciplinary violations, he is usually a school dropout who has not lived up to his potential. If he has joined the military services, his unsettled behavior often results in a discharge from service. Consistent with these behaviors, his free-floating anger is the cause of many difficulties with authority. Mentally, his unpredictable behavior may have resulted in his being referred to a mental health worker.

Case Example

In 1990, a 28-year-old female victim and her three children had lived for 2 years with the 28-year-old male subject. The victim was aware that the subject had a history of felonious assault and several domestic violence charges made by girlfriends that were later dismissed. As for her own relationship, she reported to friends that the subject was becoming more violent and would choke her. For her own protection, she advised her three children that if need be, they should call 911.

On one day, the victim allowed her three children to visit at a friend's home. Later that evening, the victim and subject visited at the home of the victim's husband and girlfriend. While there, they ran out of liquor and the men offered to go to the store. While away, the victim expressed concerns about her boyfriend to her husband's girlfriend.

When the men returned, the subject suggested that they sneak around and see what the women were talking about. When the victim discovered the men were eavesdropping, she was not amused and began to insult the men. Reportedly, she insinuated that the men had had sex with one another while they were out getting the alcohol. They were not amused. Nevertheless, the evening continued until approximately 2 in the morning, at which time the victim and subject returned to their residence. Later, according to the subject, he and the victim got into bed and began the usual foreplay of ripping off each other's underwear. He claimed that she continued to hit and scratch him. Noting that he only had one arm because of a failed suicide attempt, he claimed that to protect himself, he placed both of her arms on her stomach and laid on top of her. After several minutes, she said, "I'm sorry." Accepting that as an invitation to sexual behavior, he claimed that he entered the vagina for a period of time. This was followed by anal intercourse and a return to the vagina. Following the completion of the sexual act, he claimed that the victim did not appear to be breathing. He then dragged her into the bathtub and splashed water to revive her. She did not revive. He then called an alternative girl-friend and indicated that he may have hurt the victim quite badly. He then asked the alternative girlfriend if he could come over and visit her. She said no. He then expressed a feeling of depression and decided to commit suicide by drowning. He claimed that he drove to a lake 1 1/2 hours away from home and walked into the water up to his neck. He then had second thoughts and thought the victim might still be alive. Therefore, he returned but found her dead. He then called 911 and reported the circumstances to the police.

When police arrived, they asked him what happened. He responded, "I guess I just fucked her to death." When police examined the scene, they found the victim's nude body on its side facing the inner wall. The body had bruise marks, a large vaginal tear, and tunneled rectum. There was dried blood between the body and the drain of the bathtub. Inasmuch as the forensic evidence challenged the subject's description, the police made a search of the scene for a weapon of opportunity. Following much discussion, a baseball bat was ruled out. Ultimately, it was determined that the subject had placed his fist inside her and caused an internal rupture. Eventually, at trial, he admitted anger at the victim and sexually assaulting her. However, the defense counsel insisted that it was an accident due to the size of his phallus rather than a fist. The subject was convicted. He later appealed and received a reduced sentence.

In this case, the victim and subject were the same age. The subject had a record of assaults against women. The instant offense appears to have been sparked by the victim's challenge of his masculinity with her husband. When given the ability to link anger and sexuality, the subject burst into a violent attack and overkill of the victim. Although it is unknown whether he actually got an erection, it is known that he used a weapon of opportunity: his only fist and arm. The placement of the body was consistent with an absolute demand for submission. The subject left a disorganized crime scene. Following the assault and killing, the subject called a girlfriend for help rather than the police. During the police investigation, the subject expressed sentimental concern for the victim.

ANGER-EXCITATION RAPE-MURDER

Dynamics

The planned sexual assault and homicide are designed to inflict pain and terror on the victim for gratification by the perpetrator. The prolonged torture of the victim energizes the killer's fantasies and temporarily satisfies a lust for domination and control. Precipitated by highly specialized fantasies, the perpetrator selects the victim, male or female, and escalates violence through various acquired and learned incremental levels of ritualistic carnage. Dynamically, the approach of the victim, exploitation of naivete, torture, and mutilation all serve to appease the perpetrator's insatiable appetite for the process of killing.

For unlike other murderers, the luxury of sadism is found in the art and process of killing, not the death. In some instances, the actual death may be anticlimactic. However, in the execution of crimes, the excitement is heightened by the realization of a rehearsed scenario of eroticized anger and power that has been building in his fantasy life until he steps across the line into the reality of murder. Again, sadistic murder is comprised of a series of recognizable deviancies that coalesced into a ritualistic satisfaction. Inasmuch as the development of the process requires an investment of acquired skills, energy, and time, the intent becomes one of indulgent luxury rather than the end goal of a dead body.

Homicidal Pattern

In the anger-excitation rape-homicide, the homicidal pattern is characterized by a prolonged, bizarre, ritualistic assault on the victim. Sponsored by a plan of action, the fantasy of the assault is put into action with an equipped murder kit. Often, the victim may be a stranger who fits his needs for a symbol, such as a nurse, a prostitute, a child, a student, or a matriarch. Also, he may be attracted to victims who meet certain criteria such as long blond hair, specialized shoes, or a tramp image. When preparing to encounter the victim, the organized offender can invoke a disarmingly charming manner and dispel most immediate fears from the victim.

To activate the assault process, the subject will use a con or ruse to dupe the victim from the time of contact until the victim is isolated. At that time, he will begin to display vacillating mood shifts that confuse the victim. He then will drop the mask. He may tell her in a very matter-of-fact, monotone voice "I'm going to kill you" just to watch the look of terror on the victim's face. When he sees the victim becoming terrorized, he goes into a fantasy, and a methodical love for torture is demonstrated through acts of sexual ritual and experimentation. Here, while showing variant forms of dependency, dread, and degradation, the offender is only limited by imagination. Most commonly, bondage and domination play a significant role in the killing process.

In addition, there may be evidence of antemortem cuttings, bruises, and various forms of incomplete strangulation, body washing, shaving, and burns. Although some offenders may attempt perimortem sex, the evidence of ejaculate in the body is not likely at this stage. After the victim has been bludgeoned and strangled, the likelihood for postmortem experimental sexuality increases. Here, it is most likely that one will find evidence of secondary sexual mechanisms. The evidence of sexual exploration is revealed by localized brutalization, skin tears, and inserted objects into the body. In addition, he may leave the body in a bizarre state of undress after possibly cutting the clothing off. In some cases, the clothing could be fetish items that he would take as souvenirs. In some cases, the perpetrators will leave clothing neatly folded alongside the body. In others, they may harvest the body of parts. These parts and souvenirs taken from the crime scene may provide materials for later extravaganzas of masturbation. (Generally, this type of perpetrator divides the murder into phases in which the first part documents the art of killing and the second phase is a later reverie of masturbation with souvenirs.)

Eventually, when the crime has been completed and the perpetrator has been satisfied, he will carefully repack his ropes, knives, and specialized tools of torture into his murder kit for safekeeping. Alert to not leaving any signs at the crime scene, he may move the body to a second location to conceal it. Again, to distance himself from detection, he may bury the body in a shallow grave or dump it in a location familiar to him where he is comfortable. Again, to avoid detection, the organized offender tends to commit offenses distant from his usual activities. Accordingly, when he needs added stimulation, he may attempt to interject himself into the criminal investigation.

Suspect Profile

In the anger-excitation type, the age range of the perpetrator is considered somewhat variable. Although most perpetrators commit their first homicide by the age of 35, it is possible that a late bloomer or an undetected perpetrator could do so earlier. Characteristically, the organized offender is often a well-appearing person who is bright and socially facile with others. Based on the ability to appear conventional and law abiding, he can cunningly deceive others. Because he has the ability to separate a general lifestyle from his criminal interest, he may enjoy a good marriage. In the marriage, he may perform as a dutiful and conventional husband. Financially, he is identified as an adequate provider. His work history may be tumultuous until he finds a position with minimum supervision. Sometimes, he may show a penchant for mechanical interest and working with his hands. If so, he may seek employment in the semiskilled trades such as auto mechanics, carpentry, or a specialty factory position. In his daily habits, he is often compulsive and structurally organized. Educationally, he may have 2 years of college and/or graduated. On serving in the military services, he will be identified as doing well. Often, his military success may have resulted in his being identified as "good officer material."

Based on his exceptional ability to organize, he can successfully segment his criminal interest into a private world of protected ritualisms. Often, his ritual for paraphernalia and souvenirs are contained in a private chamber of horrors. This specialty place may be a dark closet, room, basement, or hole in the ground. Also, he may use an abandoned barn, cabin, or garage. Inside the specialty area, he will keep the victim's souvenirs, murder kit, and favored pornographic materials. Characteristically, the pornographic materials will depict a look of terror and scantily dressed victims. Most often, the literature shows bondage and sadism. Because the specialty area is designed to help the perpetrator manufacture and refine fantasies, it may contain a wide range of masochistic and sadistic clues. Although alcohol is not indicated, it is possible that the perpetrator will use chemical drugs to fuel his fantasies.

Case Example

While hiking along a ridge of low mountains above a large city, a surprised witness looked down a cliff and saw a nude body trussed in ropes. When police arrived, they found a 21-year-old female nursing assistant tied in a crouched position. When they turned the body over, they saw a nylon cord tied to the right wrist and both ankles. The head had been cut off cleanly at the base of the neck. The fingers had been cut off both hands in the area of the knuckles. A bone-colored Playtex bra and similarly colored blouse was wound around both arms. A crime scene search of the immediate area could not locate the head or missing fingers. Several months later, they were found approximately 6 miles away. The body parts and jewelry were comingled into several plastic bags.

Meanwhile, after some difficulty in identifying the body, the police traced the victim's known whereabouts. Based on accounts from friends and witnesses, police learned that the victim and a female friend had gone to a bar for an evening's entertainment. While there, a friend noticed a man looking in their direction. Eventually, that man was identified. The subject was a handsome 22-year-old male scheduled to be married in 1 week to a chaste bride-to-be. As he became a focus of police attention, the subject became nervous and withdrew $2,000 from a joint account held with his girlfriend. He also borrowed her car and disappeared for several months. Later, her car was found parked in front of a police station. Eventually, after consulting a lawyer and his family, he appeared at the police station.

Meanwhile, the car revealed a number of forensic specimens linking him to the murder. In addition, police went to his home and found that it had been thoroughly cleaned. Nevertheless, they were able to locate the victim's blood in the bathtub and other samples of her blood throughout the apartment. When confronted with a number of forensic specimens linking him to the murder, he told police that the victim voluntarily went with him to his home from the bar. While there, drug dealers arrived and killed the victim. He was then forced by drug dealers to behead the victim and dispose of her body. Consequently, after the beheading and draining of the victim's blood down the bathtub drain, he tied her and tossed her over the cliff. He then disposed of her head and fingers away in another location. He reported that this was necessary because the drug dealers had threatened to kill him if he did not cooperate. Needless to say, his story could not be corroborated. Instead, the crushed skull, scratches from a knife in the bathtub, blood stains, pliers, hacksaw tool marks, evidence of a massive cleanup effort, and the attempt to hide other evidence convinced police and the jury that he acted alone in committing the diabolical murder. While in prison, he repeated his prepared story, and a number of people supported him. Consequently, despite many objections, he was recently paroled. (Prior to the instant offense, there is circumstantial evidence that he may be linked to two nurses who have gone missing and have never been discovered.)

In this example, there is evidence of targeting a nurse, use of a con or ruse, and the isolation of the victim before acting out the crime. While in the comforts of his own home and available tools, he acted out a planned attack of terror and pain on the victim. There was also evidence of bondage, domination, submission, and *pic-querism*. Picquerism is a secondary sexual mechanism in which satisfaction is gained by penetrating the body through cutting, slicing, and tearing of the body parts. In the postmortem activities, there was evidence of trussing up the body, disposal in a neutral location, and the separation of the head with fingers and jewelry in a separate location. Evident from the description, the satisfaction did not end with the death but extended into postmortem activities and beyond. Certainly the subject derived a great deal of satisfaction at avoiding police, leaving the suspect vehicle with evidence in front of the police station, and the effort at surmounting them by creating a phantom scenario. Finally, this killing not only satisfied internal needs but it also helped protect him from a pending marriage and the expectation to perform conventional sexual practices. For him, sadistic sexual fantasies were an art form and a lifestyle.

SUMMARY AND DISCUSSION

For many years, the authors have performed crime scene assessments for homicide investigators based on the rape-murderer classifications mentioned earlier. Another important question about the four categories is: How widespread is each of the four categories among a population of murderers? To answer this question, the authors examined the frequency of the four categories within the population of murderers incarcerated in the Michigan state prison system. Having that information would assist law enforcement officers in knowing how common each type of rape-murderer is.

For a point of reference, in October 1995, the Michigan Department of Corrections reported a prison population of 41,584 prisoners. At that time, the number of prisoners serving sentences for homicide was 5,928 (14%). This figure represented only those prisoners serving homicide sentences at that particular time and did not account for the total number who have served throughout history. Of the total number of homicide offenders in prison, 2,476 or 42% had committed sexually related murders.

Within that aggregate number of homicides, a survey was conducted to determine the frequency for each category among convicted murderers. This was accomplished by assessing each inmate on entry or reviewing the intake files of previously committed inmates to determine their most appropriate rape-murderer category. The findings of the research revealed the following results: power-assertive = 38% (n = 904), anger-retaliatory = 34% (n = 807), power-reassurance = 21% (n = 599), and anger-excitation = 7% (n = 166).

Based on the assumption that most murderers have the capacity for rational thought in a variety of emotional responses, there exists choice, determination, and a foundation for behavior patterns. Given their ability to learn, interpret, and modify behaviors, their characteristics and details of their crimes are formed into specific patterns. When individual idiosyncrasies and levels of social maturity are factored into their violent behavior, the result may be a complex mixture of knowledge, intentions, and behavioral outcomes. Therefore, when an investigator examines a crime scene, the presence or absence of evidence may reveal recognizable patterns that are indicative to that specific offender.

The rape-murder classification system described here was built on an interactive and dynamic template of conceptual and emotional constructs. Infused with the learning from factually based cases and perpetrator interviews, there existed a wide range of information related to precrime, crime, and postcrime behaviors. These behaviors were recognized within the continuums of the four typologies: power-assertive, power-reassurance, anger-retaliatory, and anger-excitation. Within each one of these rape-murderer types, a number of recognizable factors became evident and interrelated to cause and effect.

In addition, depending on their motivation and internal inhibitions, the perpetrators in each typology may and do regulate the rate of murder. In some instances, the perpetrator may simply kill one person. However, when fueled by power and anger, the use of murder can become a preferred mode of problem resolution for the perpetrator.

In the case of the repeat offender, each typology has a pattern of reoccurrence consistent with its killer's individual fantasies. For instance, the repeat power-assertive may show an increase in violence and/or systematic decrease in time between offenses. As for the power-reassurance, the schedule depends on fantasy preparation time, satisfaction, and feeding off the memory. If any one of these factors has changed, it is likely that the perpetrator will commit repeat offenses to gain satisfaction. Under these conditions, one may find a cluster of activity followed by a long absence before the murders are repeated. Alternately, the anger-retaliatory is emotionally driven and conditioned to the expression of anger. When a particular victim and/or set of circumstances does not fill the need, the perpetrator may commit cluster killings until his needs are fulfilled. Generally, the timing between clusters lessens with experience. In reference to anger-excitation, the repeat offender is the most fickle and sanguine in killing. It can be said that as a lengthy predatory jackal who refines skills of hunting to eat better, so it is for the anger-excitation rape-murderer. Accordingly, when the satisfaction from the killings become brief and situational, the killing rate increases.

Finally, the earlier described murder classification system offers the investigator an ability for understanding the behavioral parameters of the perpetrator of an unsolved rape-murder. That is, given a set of circumstances, analysis of facts, inferences, and patterns, the details of the classification system can give the detective an informed direction for further investigation. The common rape-murderer is characteristically a repeat offender and this behavior is consistent with his rapist equivalent in sexual assault cases. Both have patterns that can be recognized within the rape continuum. Here, the crime scene itself becomes the initiation point for pattern recognition, evidence collection, decision making for follow-up, and strategy planning for interviews with suspects. If the category for a particular rape-murderer is identified correctly, the perpetrator can be his own accuser.

REFERENCES

Copson, G. (1995). *Coals to Newcastle? Part 1: A study of offender profiling* (Police Research Group Special Interest Series, Paper 7). London: Home Office Police Department.

Copson, G., Badcock, R., Boon, J., & Britton, P. (1997). Articulating a systematic approach to clinical crime profiling. *Criminal Behaviour and Mental Health, 7,* 13-17.

Douglas, J.E., Burgess, A.W., Burgess, A.C., & Ressler, R.K. (1992). *Crime classification manual.* Lexington, MA: Lexington Books.

Geberth, V.J. (1996). *Practical homicide investigation: Tactics, procedures, and forensic techniques* (3rd ed.). Boca Raton, FL: CRC Publishing.

Geberth, V.J., & Turco, R.N. (1997). Antisocial personality disorder, sexual sadism, malignant narcissism, and serial murder. *Journal of Forensic Sciences, 42*(1), 49-60.

Groth, A.N., Burgess, A.W., & Holmstrom, L.L. (1977). Rape: Power, anger, and sexuality. *American Journal of Psychiatry, 134,* 1239-1243.

Hazelwood, R.R., & Burgess, A.N. (1987). *Practical aspects of rape investigation: A multidisciplinary approach.* New York: Elsevier North-Holland.

HITS murder form. (1995). Seattle, WA: Washington State Attorney General's Office.

Holmes, R.M., & Holmes, S.T. (1996). *Profiling violent crimes: An investigative tool.* Thousand Oaks, CA: Sage.

Johnson, G. (1994). VICLAS: Violent crime linkage analysis system. *RCMP Gazette, 56*(10), 5-22.

Keppel, R.D. (1995). Signature murders: A report of several related cases. *Journal of Forensic Sciences, 40,* 658-662.

Keppel, R.D. (1997). *Signature killers.* New York: Pocket Books.

Keppel, R.D., & Birnes, W.J. (1995). *The riverman: Ted Bundy and I hunt the Green River killer.* New York: Pocket Books.

Keppel, R.D., & Weis, J.P. (1994). Time and distance as solvability factors in murder cases. *Journal of Forensic Sciences, 39,* 386-401.

Morneau, R., & Rockwell, R. (1980). *Sex, motivation, and the criminal offender*. Springfield, IL: Charles C Thomas.

VICAP form. (1991). Washington, DC: Federal Bureau of Investigation.

Warren, J.I., Hazelwood, R.R., & Dietz, P.E. (1996). The sexually sadistic killer. *Journal of Forensic Sciences, 41*, 970-974.

Robert D. Keppel, Ph.D.
Visiting Associate Professor
Seattle University
Criminal Justice Program
P.O. Box 222000
Seattle, WA 98122
USA

Richard Walter, M.A.
Psychologist, Michigan State Prison
710 South Dexter Drive
Lansing, MI 48910
USA

R.D. Keppel and R.A. Walter, *International Journal of Offender Therapy and Comparative Criminology*, Vol. 43, No. 4, 1999. Copyright © 1999 by Sage Publications, Inc. Reprinted by Permission of Sage Publications, Inc.

BEHAVIORAL CHARACTERISTICS OF OFFENDERS

Section III addresses the behavioral characteristics of offenders in an attempt to help investigators understand the underlying trends and patterns of certain types of offenders that may be revealed at a crime scene. Researchers have shown that offender profiling can be useful in investigating violent crimes. The articles in Section III attempt to present a psychological profile of certain types of offenders by exemplifying the behavioral characteristics of offenders of several violent crimes, including the sexual homicide of elderly females, sexually sadistic homicides, non-serial sexual murders, targeted violence, juvenile kidnappings, child pornography, child sexual abuse, and sexual offenses committed by juveniles.

The articles in this section provide aggregate characteristics of offenders of various crimes to assist law enforcement in creating a profile of the offender based on the type of crime committed. Statistical information is provided based on known offender characteristics to show the most likely type of offender to commit a certain type of crime. While this is can be a valuable tool to assist law enforcement in the investigation of violent crimes, linking a specific offender to a profile based on aggregate characteristics of known offenders of these crimes has not been as accepted by the courts. As seen in *Section V*, profiling efforts based on aggregate characteristics of offenders based on the type of crime have not been successfully introduced at trial.

In the first article, authors Safarik, Jarvis, and Nussbaum (2002) reveal the offender and victim characteristics in the sexual homicide of elderly females. Since the sexual homicide of elderly females is a relatively rare phenomenon, there hasn't been much research addressing this issue. This has been of little assistance to the law enforcement investigators that are faced with these types of rare violent crimes. In *Sexual Homicide of Elderly Females: Linking Offender Characteristics to Victim and Crime Scene Attributes*, the authors try to rectify this problem through empirical analysis of 128 sexual homicide cases. Safarik, Jarvis, and Nussbaum examine the characteristics of elderly women who were murdered based on characteristics of 110 offenders and crime scene details. The authors conduct an in-depth analysis of crime scene attributes to highlight victim and offender information and reveal a picture of the victim and offender demographics in the sexual homicides of elderly females. These efforts are aimed at assisting investigators in developing predictive information about the offender in furtherance of the investigation of these cases.

In the second article, Warren, Hazelwood, and Dietz (1996) study the sexually sadistic serial murders. They describe the characteristics and crime scene behaviors of twenty sexually sadistic serial murderers believed responsible for 149 murders in the United States and Canada. This study examines the relationship between the character pathology and arousal of offenders with the control and degradation of others. The article also reveals commonalities and patterns within sadistic murders. The authors provide offender demographics and crime scene behaviors of sexually sadistic killers, including the level of planning, location information, captivity, paraphilia, sexual bondage, sexual acts, torture, and method of death most likely in these cases.

In the third article, *Profiles in the Offending Process of Non-serial Sexual Homicides*, authors Beauregard and Proulx (2002) move the focus away from serial sexual killers. The aim of the study was to create a typology of nonserial sexual homicides based on offense, offender, and victim characteristics. They reveal the offender characteristics most prevalent in nonserial sexual homicides by studying and empirically analyzing the crimes of 36 murderers of females 14 years or older. The authors utilized cluster analysis to examine the offending process. They identify two pathways into the offending process of nonserial sexual murders: 1) the sadistic pathway; and 2) the anger pathway; as well as the attendant behavioral characteristics of these two types of offenders. Beauregard and Proulx compare and contrast their results with the FBI typology of murderers; Warren, Hazelwood, and Dietz's (1996) study of sexually sadistic killers; and Gratzer and Bradford's (1995) study of sadistic and non-sadistic sexual killers.

The fourth article in Section III is a 1995 National Institute of Justice: Research in Action brief entitled *Threat Assessment: An Approach to Prevent Targeted Violence*. Authors Fein, Vossekuil, and Holden identify characteristics of offenders involved in stalking cases, workplace violence, and attacks of threats of attacks on public figures and officials. The aim of the article is to assist law enforcement in the identification and offenders of targeted violence and the prevention of these types of crimes. The authors emphasize the history and observable behavioral characteristics of those most likely to commit targeted violence, in addition to the triggering events precipitating acts of violence. Focusing on proactive policing, the authors discuss investigative tools and approaches that can be used to recognize, evaluate, and manage the risks of targeted violence before crimes occur.

The final article in Section III spotlights the characteristics of offenders in the kidnapping, of children. In the June 2000 Office of Juvenile Justice and Delinquency Prevention Report (OJJDP) *Kidnapping of Juveniles: Patterns from NIBRS*, authors David Finkelhor and Richard Ormrod describe the types of kidnappings reported to NIBRS by law enforcement in 1997. They identify and describe three types of offenders and corresponding offender, offense, and victim characteristics in the abduction of juveniles based on statistical analysis of reported crimes.

The reader should note that knowledge of the profiles and information in this section is a useful tool for understanding offenders, prioritizing leads, and investigating crimes, but a profile generated of a specific offender based on this aggregate information will generally not be accepted at trial. While statistical information on known characteristics may help officers understand the most likely behavioral characteristics of the offender group, it does not rule out or point out characteristics of a specific offender and is therefore, not a conclusive link. As revealed in *Sections IV* and *Section V*, individual-specific profiles containing characteristics of the offender based on crime scene information and details have had more success at the trial and appellate level.

SEXUAL HOMICIDE OF ELDERLY FEMALES

Linking Offender Characteristics to Victim and Crime Scene Attributes

MARK E. SAFARIK AND JOHN P. JARVIS
Federal Bureau of Investigation

KATHLEEN E. NUSSBAUM
University of Liverpool

The FBI consults regularly on the investigation of extraordinarily violent and unusual homicide cases. Although overall awareness of elderly victimization throughout the United States has greatly increased over the past decade, little attention has been focused on elderly female victims of sexual homicides and the offenders who commit these crimes. Law enforcement agencies are often faced with rarely seen and excessively violent crime scenes as they attempt to solve these homicides. This in-depth study examines the characteristics of 128 elderly women who were murdered by 110 offenders as well as the characteristics of the attendant crime scenes. An empirical analysis of crime scene attributes, victim characteristics (including severity of victim injuries), and offender demographics produces significant predictive information about offender characteristics that may assist law enforcement investigations of such cases.

Case 1

A 77-year-old widow was sexually assaulted and murdered in her bedroom. The medical examiner identified three separate causes of death. The offender strangled the victim into unconsciousness, severely fractured her skull using a nearby clock he removed from the bedroom dresser, and then repeatedly stabbed her in the face, chest, and vagina with a butcher knife he obtained from the kitchen. A 20-year-old male living two blocks away was arrested.

Case 2

A 19-year-old offender, while walking by the apartment of a 76-year-old woman at 2 a.m., noticed a light on and began peeping through the windows. He saw her sitting alone watching television. He smashed out the front door window, reached in, and unlocked the door. He blitz attacked the victim,

Authors' Note: The viewpoints expressed herein are solely those of the authors and do not reflect the official position of the Department of Justice, the Federal Bureau of Investigation, or the University of Liverpool. The authors are particularly grateful to Alan Jacobson who offered editorial guidance on this manuscript. We also wish to thank both colleagues and anonymous reviewers for their detailed, constructive comments offered on earlier drafts. Finally, an earlier version of this work was presented at the American Society of Criminology Meetings held in San Francisco, California, November 14th through 19th, 2000.

shattering her jaw as he knocked her unconscious to the floor. He ripped off her clothing, raped her vaginally, then anally, and finally assaulted her vaginally with an umbrella lying nearby. He used a piece of glass from the broken window to cut her throat. He returned to a friend's house covered in blood and told him he had just killed an "old lady." He was convicted and sentenced to life in prison.

Case 3

A 70-year-old woman was found dead, lying on her bed in a blood-spattered bedroom of a rural farm house. She suffered 28 stab wounds to the face, neck, and chest. The offender had pushed her night clothes above her breasts and spread her legs. She was nude except for the night shirt. After killing her, he placed a pillow over her face. No semen was located at the scene. Ten years later, investigators still pursue leads in this woman's death, and her daughters are haunted on a daily basis because the offender remains unidentified.

INTRODUCTION

Most law enforcement agencies in the United States seldom face the unenviable task of investigating the brutal sexual assault-homicide of an elderly female member of their community. However, this crime does occur, and its prevalence may increase as the nation's population ages. Although law enforcement agencies respond to violent criminal behavior on a daily basis, even the most experienced homicide investigator is rarely prepared for the extreme brutality and sexual degradation that is sometimes unleashed on one of the most vulnerable and fragile community citizens: the elderly female.

That an elderly woman has been viciously sexually assaulted appears, on its surface, to be incongruous with what the public at large and even most law enforcement officers associate with a sexual assault offense. Sexual assault, in the minds of many lay and professional people, is believed to be motivated by sexual arousal and desire on the part of the offender (Groth & Birnbaum, 1979). Rape and sexual assault are in fact distortions of human sexuality (Groth, 1978). When the victim is an elderly female, these distortions cause us to question the more traditional avenues of investigating these types of homicides. This perception can pose serious difficulties as law enforcement attempts to establish initial investigative directions for solving these cases.

Because of the relative infrequency of these cases and the lack of research in this area, investigators often encounter difficulties when trying to investigate a sexual homicide involving an elderly female victim.[1] Complicating this is a lack of knowledge with respect to offenders who perpetrate these heinous crimes. Empirical research, perhaps leading to investigative decision support systems, is needed to assist law enforcement in rapidly identifying and apprehending these offenders. Specifically, analysis and study of readily obtainable crime scene, victim, and demographic variables may be useful in supporting such goals. The research offered here examines cases of elderly female sexual homicide to identify patterns in the behavioral aspects of the victims, offenders, their interactions within the context of the crime and to link offender characteristics to

---

[1] *Sexual homicide* is defined as

the killing of a person in the context of power, sexuality, and brutality with evidence or observations that include a sexual nature. These include: victim attire or lack of attire; exposure of the sexual parts of the victim's body; sexual positioning of the victim's body; insertion of foreign objects into the victim's body cavities; evidence of sexual intercourse (oral, vaginal, or anal); and evidence of substitute sexual activity, interest, or sadistic fantasy. (Ressler, Burgess, & Douglas, 1988, p. 1) victim and crime scene attributes. Thus, the goal is to distinguish factors that are specific to these cases and then to examine their usefulness in guiding the investigative efforts to identify these offenders. Before examining the elderly sexual homicide data, a review of the research surrounding the scope and nature of crimes against the elderly, with special attention to sexual assault and homicide, is necessary to insure a fuller understanding of these difficult cases.

CRIMES AGAINST THE ELDERLY

Both Bureau of Justice Statistic studies and the National Crime Survey reflect that crimes against the elderly tend to be more serious in nature than those against younger persons (Bureau of Justice Statistics, 1994). Older victims of violent crimes are more likely to be attacked by total strangers (Kennedy & Silverman, 1990; Muram, Miller, & Cutler, 1992) and are most likely to be victimized in their own homes. They are less likely to try to protect themselves during a crime and are more likely to sustain injuries. These findings are confirmed by numerous studies that discuss the general problem of victimization of the elderly and by specific research addressing violent offenses (Antunes, Cook, Cook, & Skogan, 1977; Faggiani & Owens, 1999; Fox & Levin, 1991; Lent & Harpold, 1988; Nelson & Huff-Corzine, 1998).

These studies also demonstrate that in particular ways elderly women are inherently more vulnerable to crime than younger women. First, they are more likely to live alone. Nearly 80% of elderly persons who live alone are female due in large part to an increased risk of widowhood and longer life expectancy (Taeuber & Allen, 1990). Second, "Vulnerability is related to physical size and strength; elderly females are less capable of fleeing or resisting a physical attack than a younger person" (Nelson & Huff-Corzine, 1998, p. 135). As women age, they experience skeletal, neuro-muscular, and other systemic changes (Davis & Brody, 1979). These age-related changes restrict mobility and reduce women's abilities to escape or defend themselves against an assailant. As Moen (1996) noted, this may be particularly true of the older members of the aged population (75 years and older) who are dis-proportionately female and living alone.

This notion of vulnerable victims is also characteristic of the routine-activities perspective offered in criminology (Cohen & Felson, 1979). That is, considering the interaction of available victims, motivated offenders, and the lack of guardianship may offer an understanding of how these incidents occur. Elderly women, perhaps as a consequence of widowhood, are more likely than younger females to lack the guardianship common to children and younger women with parents, boyfriends, and husbands and thus are more likely to be perceived by motivated offenders as suitable targets.

This vulnerability conception is further supported by the work of Longo and Gochenour (1981), which indicates that some rapists select elderly victims because of their vulnerability (see also Davis & Brody, 1979). Furthermore, the idea that predators often choose prey for particular reasons based on some set of criteria is not unique to criminal behavior. In nature, predators continually assess a victim's vulnerability (chance of successful capture and killing) and accessibility (likelihood of detection and deterrence) in the course of their daily activities (Boudreaux, Lord, & Jarvis, 2001). Our contending theory in these cases of sexual homicide is that offenders are no different and engage in similar decision-making assessments.

However, an abundance of definitive literature is lacking, perhaps largely due to an emphasis on broad categories of both violent and property offenses and an inability to adequately distinguish between crimes against males and females. A thorough search of the literature found that any extensive focus on violence against elderly women was limited. However, some discussion of the few studies that were found is merited.

Sexual Assault of the Elderly Female

The sparse research literature relative to sexual assault of the elderly female reveals that these victims are much more likely to be injured or killed compared to other victims of similar crimes (Davis & Brody, 1979; Gerry, 1983; Kerschner, 1976; Pollock, 1988). Some studies examine rapists (Hazelwood & Burgess, 1995; Warren et al., 1998), but few focus specifically on those who rape the elderly (Fletcher, 1977; Groth, 1978; Muram et al., 1992; Pollock, 1988). Pollock (1988) conducted the only study to date that was found to contrast those who commit sexual offenses against older women with those who victimize younger women. His findings clearly identify predatory rapists who purposefully select older women. According to this study, when a rapist attacks an older woman, the rape or sexual assault is likely to be "a particularly brutal act largely motivated by rage or sadistic intent" (p. 530). He also suggested that apparently motiveless violent attacks on elderly women may be cases of sexual assault.

Many elderly women are unaware of their vulnerability to sexual assault and perceive sexual assault as a sexually motivated crime, directed primarily at young and promiscuous women who somehow contribute to being selected as victims through their actions and behaviors (Groth, 1978; Hazelwood, 1987). More recent research suggests that sexual assault is motivated by the need to express power or anger or a combination of both (Groth, Burgess, & Holmstrom, 1977; Hazelwood & Warren, 1990, 2000; Pollock, 1988). This power or anger may be expressed as a need to punish, dominate, and control the victim. The offender is rarely seen as seeking sexual gratification from his assaults. Consistent with this notion, Groth's (1978) examination of case files of sexual assaults of older victims found that offenders use physical force, including beating, stabbing, and killing their victims, in 60% of the cases. Groth suggested that the elderly female represents an authority figure or is the actual woman over whom the assailant wants power. Sexuality is the method used to effect revenge or express his hostility and anger. Groth, like Pollock (1988), noted that the sexual assault of older victims is often an exceptionally violent crime that is "more an issue of hostility than sexual desire" (Groth, 1978, p. 213). For the moment, however, consider the information noted above relative to sexual assaults and the following research findings relative to homicides involving elderly female victims.

Elderly Female Homicide

Homicide of elderly females is generally a rare phenomenon. According to the FBI (2000), 15,553 homicides in the United States were reported to the police in 1999. Of these homicide victims, 812 were determined to be elderly (60 years of age or older), and more than half of this total (499) were identified as females. Elderly female homicides that became known to the police constituted just more than 3% of all homicides in the United States in 1999 (FBI, 2000). According to the annual publication, FBI Uniform Crime Reports (UCR), this percentage has been fairly stable over the past decade. Although homicide may result from a confrontation between an offender and a victim in the course of another crime, most homicide studies do not focus exclusively on the elderly. Many of the studies cited in this research are largely limited to aggregate analyses regarding both male and female victims with little attention to the importance of both qualitative and quantitative analyses. Conversely, the studies that have examined homicide of the elderly concentrate on the types of homicide, which, in most cases, do not exhibit an identifiable sexual component.

ELDERLY FEMALE SEXUAL HOMICIDE

There are many difficulties in obtaining reliable statistics relative to the number of elderly sexual homicides. One of the most problematic of these involves the identification of the offense as a homicide without note of the subordinate offense of rape or sexual assault (Brownmiller, 1975).[2] Other difficulties include the lack of necessary investigation to identify the sexual behavior, poor communication between investigators and other personnel relative to understanding the sexual nature of the offense, and classification errors in official data entries (see Burgess, Hartman, Ressler, Douglas, & McCormack, 1986). Although official statistics are elusive, one demographic fact is inescapable: Census data show that an increasing proportion of the baby boom generation will be aging into the elderly population in the coming years (U.S. Bureau of the Census, 1999). Coupled with people living longer, this suggests that the incidence of violent victimization of elderly females may also increase. This is further evidenced by nearly 75% of people older than the age of 65 being women (U.S. Bureau of the Census, 1999).

As with all criminal behavior, examination of any factors that may assist law enforcement in rapidly identifying and apprehending responsible offenders and protecting potential victims has merit. In addition, because cases of the type described here are generally uncommon, when such cases occur, law enforcement must be cognizant of and use the most effective investigative tactics and strategies available.

From a practitioner's perspective, the current body of knowledge regarding elderly female sexual homicide is derived principally from experiential patterns observed by homicide investigators. Their experience and collective training have helped them form a consensus regarding these kinds of cases. In particular, it is believed that the age of the victim and offender appear to be quite disparate. That is, elderly victims are most often killed by younger offenders. The typical intraracial nature of violent crime seems to be conditional in these cases; that is, the race of the offender seems to be dependent on specific case factors rather than on the general expectation that an offender is the same race as the victim. The excessive violence exhibited in a number of these cases, the excessive injury that results from this violence, and a perceived ambiguity between burglary or robbery and sexual homicide as motivations are attributes that may be distinct from other violent crimes. To further investigate these contentions, as well as for the reasons stated earlier, cases of elderly female sexual homicide are examined.

DATA AND METHOD

Data were collected from two sources. First, we examined the data available from the Supplementary Homicide Reports (SHR) as collected by the FBI UCR from 1976 to 1999. These data served to provide a brief statistical description of the 604 cases that were identified during that period. However, many details of the crime scene, the nature and extent of victim injuries, and similar case attributes were not available from the SHR. Therefore, we turned to the ongoing data collection efforts of the National Center for the Analysis of Violent Crime (NCAVC) to acquire data on incident, victim, and offender details in cases of this nature that are not available in the SHR. This

---

[2] This hierarchy rule of official reporting may be more common in historical Uniform Crime Report data than will be so in the future. The redesigned uniform crime-reporting program known as the National Incident-Based Reporting System suspends such rules and allows for full reporting of collateral offenses (see Chilton & Jarvis, 1999a, 1999b).

NCAVC data, therefore, serve as the principal data source for the research conducted here. The NCAVC case data reflecting the types of cases examined here were identified through various sources. Cases were identified through the FBI's Violent Criminal Apprehension Program, brought forward by law enforcement through their participation in the FBI's National Academy Training Program, and through the operational activities of the FBI's NCAVC. The cases represent submissions from 30 states, with California, Georgia, Washington, Florida, New York, New Jersey, and Texas providing a large number. These sources identified 128 solved cases involving a female 60 years of age or older who was determined to be a victim of a sexual homicide.[3] The 110 offenders in these cases have been convicted and are responsible for at least one sexual homicide of an elderly female.[4]

Following Burgess et al. (1986), this study involved a comprehensive review of the behavioral and psychological details of the 128 sexual homicides through analysis of the offenders' physical, sexual, and, when known, verbal behavior with the victim (see also O'Toole, 1999). This also includes a complete study of the victim, a thorough evaluation of the crime scene, and an in-depth investigation of the nature and scope of the interactions between the victim and the offender.

These records were very comprehensive and usually contained investigative, autopsy, and forensic and evidence analysis reports; crime scene and autopsy photographs, diagrams, sketches, and maps; victimology information; offender background; and any confessions or admissions by the offender. Psychological evaluations of the offender were provided in a number of the cases. In addition, investigators who worked on these cases were contacted to clarify or provide supplemental information not identified in the police reports.

Clearly, for both statistical and methodological reasons, it would be impossible to fully examine every aspect of these incidents with the relatively small number of cases available. Nonetheless, examination of the data was conducted in two stages. First, the descriptive information available from these incidents was examined in an effort to fully depict the relative frequencies of specific victim, offender, and offense attributes that comprise the behavior evident in these cases. Typical variables examined included, but were not limited to, demographics, injury, weapon use, and so forth. Through this analysis, links between the attributes are suggested.

Second, for the purposes of this research, we narrowed our focus to four dependent variables: race of offender, age of offender, relationship of victim to offender, and distance of offender's residence (in blocks) from that of the victim. These dependent variables were selected for analysis because these attributes are most likely to assist law enforcement investigators confronted with solving such cases (Safarik, Jarvis, & Nussbaum, 2000). Each dependent variable was then examined separately using logistic regression models. Particular attention was given to the degree of probability to which each independent variable could contribute to the explanation of variance in the dependent variable. The set of independent variables represents crime scene and victim characteristics and specific offender behavioral attributes.

---

[3] One 55-year-old victim was included because she was found to be the victim of an offender who specifically targeted elderly females for sexual homicide. Despite this victim's age, she had the physical appearance of a significantly older woman.

[4] One offender was positively identified through DNA analysis but field to Mexico to avoid apprehension.

RESULTS

Initial analyses of the SHR data revealed 604 cases reported to law enforcement over the 24-year period.[5] The data associated with these SHR cases showed 81% of the victims to be White; offender race, when known, to be approximately 45% White and 55% non-White; a predominate use of personal weapons (hands, fists, and feet) rather than firearms (2.8%); and when it could be established, a stranger was most often, 54% of the time, found to have been the assailant. Further analysis of the circumstances of these incidents reported in the SHR showed that 92% of the cases involved a rape of the victim, with just 8% involving some other sexual offense. Finally, the age of the offender was found, on average, to be 27 years of age. Although these demographic results are useful for describing the overall nature of these cases, virtually no further detailed investigative information about these cases is available to explore potential relationships between crime scene, victim, and offender attributes. Therefore, analyses of the NCAVC data were undertaken to extend the demographic results available from the SHR.

Analyses of NCAVC case data examined the descriptive statistical properties of all candidate variables to be included in the analysis. These results, as shown in Table 7.1, are largely consistent with findings from the SHR and suggest that the average offender was more likely non-White, age 25 or older, living within six blocks of the victim, and not known to the victim. These demographics depict an average offender in these data; however, it is important to note that variation in these attributes was also evident as shown by the standard deviations in Table 7.1.

The Offenders

The offender population includes 48 White (44%), 46 Black (42%), 14 Hispanic (13%), and 1% others.[6] Of note is the absence of Asian offenders. The offenders range in age from 15 to 58. Blacks offend interracially 77% of the time, Hispanics 80%, and Whites only 4%. Of the offenders, 56% live within six blocks of the victim, with nearly 30% living on the same block. Of Hispanic offenders, 85% live within six blocks of the victim. Overall, 81% of the offenders travel to the scene on foot. And 93% of Blacks and 85% of Hispanics were on foot.

The offenders in many respects are found to be quite similar. For instance, 90% have criminal records, with burglary (59%) making up the highest proportion. However, property and violent offenses are found to be approximately equally represented among those with criminal histories. It should be noted that just 21% are found to have sex offenses in their criminal histories, a key point for law enforcement when considering the background of potential suspects. In terms of their employment skill levels, 93% are unskilled, with nearly 70% unemployed. Of the offenders, 93%

---

[5] The Supplementary Homicide Reports data, although limited in investigative case details, do provide an opportunity to examine trends. Examination of the reported cases since 1976 suggests a marked decline in the number of elderly female sexual homicides that came to the attention of law enforcement by the late 1990s. However, as we have noted, these statistical data must be viewed with caution as it is not uncommon for sexual behavior in homicide cases to sometimes remain unidentified or undetected until much further investigation.

[6] Although comparable national estimates for offenders are not collected, arrest information by race is available through the FBI Uniform Crime Reports. Examination of these data shows more involvement of Whites (53%) among all arrestees for murder/ nonnegligent man-slaughter. Similar involvement of other races (47%) was found. Caution should be taken relative to these Uniform Crime Reports data, however, because this information reflects all homicide arrests rather than just those committed against the elderly. Contrasts are further clouded by the inability of these data to show which of these cases may have involved a sexual component to the crime. The Supplementary Homicide Reports analysis, however, was consistent with the demographic composition reported here.

TABLE
7.1   DESCRIPTIVE STATISTICS FOR DEPENDENT AND INDEPENDENT VARIABLES

Variable	% of Cases	M	SD
Offender race		0.41	0.49
Non-White	59		
White	41		
Took items		0.72	0.45
Took items	69		
No items taken	26		
Neighborhood composition		0.58	0.50
Primarily White	57		
Less than 80% White	42		
Offender age		1.60	0.50
Between 15 and 24 years old	43		
25 or older	57		
Victim's state of dress		3.09	7.91
Fully dressed	5		
Partially nude	77		
Nude	16		
Injury Severity Score[a]		47.40	16.93
Offender distance		0.42	0.50
Within 6 blocks	54		
More than 6 blocks	39		
Homicide Injury Scale[b]		4.58	7.87
Neighborhood composition		0.58	0.50
Primarily White	57		
Less than 80% White	42		
Offender knew victim		0.55	0.50
Knew victim	52		
Did not know victim	42		
Victim's body left		1.02	5.78
Uncovered	57		
Covered	33		
Altered	9		
Method of entry		0.40	0.49
No force used	56		
Force used	37		
Time of day		0.20	0.13
Between 8 P.M. and 8 A.M.	66		
Between 8 A.M. and 8 P.M.	22		

NOTE: Offender race, 0 = non-White, 1 = White; took items (from crime scene), 0 = none taken, 1 = items taken; neighborhood composition, 0 = 79% or less White, 1 = 80% or more White; offender age, 1 = between 15 and 24 years old, 2 = older than 25; victim's state of dress (when found at crime scene), 1 = fully dressed, 2 = partially dressed, 3 = nude; offender distance (from victim's residence), 0 = 6 blocks or less, 1 = more than 6 blocks; offender knew victim, 0 = victim unknown to offender, 1 = victim known to offender; victim's body left (at crime scene), 0 = uncovered, 1 = covered, 2 = altered; method of entry, 0 = no force, 1 = forcible entry; time of day, 0 = 8 P.M. to 8 A.M., 1 = 8 A.M. to 8 P.M.

have 12 years or fewer of formal education, and 19% of that group have 8 years or fewer. Of those who attended high school, the majority had spotty attendance records and poor academic performance. Many simply dropped out after a couple of years. Also, 93% had a history of substance abuse, with no race or age trends noted. The drug abused most often was alcohol (85%), followed by marijuana (54%) and cocaine (44%).

Finally, 45% of the offenders confessed to the crime subsequent to their arrest, and 19% made some kind of an admission relative to the crime yet continued to deny responsibility for the homicide. In terms of racial differences, Whites were observed to have confessed nearly twice as often as Blacks, and Blacks made some sort of admission more than twice as often as Whites.

The Victims

Analysis of the victims revealed several important observations. The mean age was 77. Although the victim population was disproportionately White (86%), both Blacks (9%) and Hispanics (4%) were also victimized. Similar to the offender data, Asian victims were rare: Only a single Asian victim was identified. Of the victims, 94% were killed in their own residences. Although 14% of the victims had lived in their neighborhoods from 4 to 9 years, 73% had lived there at least 10 years, and many had lived there substantially longer. Contributing to their vulnerability, 81% of the victims had no additional home security beyond locks normally found on doors and windows.

Qualitative analyses of these cases suggests the possibility that variation in the degree of injury suffered may be a useful measure to analyze offender behavior. In an effort to identify a way these cases could be compared using the severity of the victim's injuries, a scale was created to quantify the severity of injuries directly related to the cause(s) of death. This scale, called the Homicide Injury Scale, draws on available medical examiner data and ranks injury severity from internal injuries only (1) to multiple excessive external injuries with multiple causes of death (6). Not relying solely on this convention, a second measure, the Injury Severity Score, is also used by adapting an injury scale developed by Baker, O'Neill, Haddon, and Long (1974). The Injury Severity Score is currently used by the Centers for Disease Control.[7] Both of these derived measures, the Homicide Injury Scale and the Injury Severity Score, are then applied to the victim data. It should be noted that the correlation between these measures was determined to be .77. Mean injury levels were 4.6 and 47.4, respectively, and reflect more rather than less severe injury. These measures are then used in subsequent analyses in an effort to further the examination of offender characteristics.

Turning to cause of death (COD) determinations, strangulation (63%) was found to be the most frequent, followed by blunt force trauma (38%). Death by a firearm (1%) was the least frequent. Variations in this pattern by race were also examined, but no significant differences were found.

The Incidents

Some of the limited findings relative to violent victimization of the elderly were also found in the data. In particular, there are some consistencies in the dynamics of the victimization. Of the offenders, 40% gained entrance through unlocked doors or windows, and 20% were freely admitted

---

[7] Original scoring is based on location and severity of the injury on the body, with scores ranging from 1 (*minor*) to 6 (*unsurvivable*). Modifications to this scoring scheme were required when coding cause of death injuries in homicides with a resulting minimum value of 25 (a single body region sustaining a critical/fatal injury) and a maximum of 75 (at least three body regions receiving critical/fatal injuries). A full discussion of the original scoring scheme can be found by referencing Baker, O'Neill, Haddon, and Long (1974), Baker and O'Neill (1976), and Yates (1990). The authors are continuing work examining the merit of scoring injuries in homicides, and further details on the scoring scheme adopted here are available on request.

to the residence. Close to 40% used force on a door or window to gain entry. Of White offenders, 38% entered through unlocked windows or doors, and 36% gained entry through admittance by the victim or by the use of a ruse or con scheme. Of Black offenders, 48% used force, and only 10% were admitted by the victim through use of a ruse or con. White offenders were either admitted by the victim or used a ruse/con almost four times as often as Black offenders. In contrast, Black offenders were nearly twice as likely as White offenders to use force to gain access to their victims.

Analysis of offender behavior at the crime scene indicates that 77% of the offenders brought nothing with them to the scene. When they did bring something, the items consisted mostly of weapons (10%) or tools (8%). In contrast, they removed property 72% of the time, mostly small easily accessible items such as cash and jewelry. Offenders left the body of the victim uncovered 57% of the time. White and Hispanic offenders were most likely to leave the victim uncovered (64%), in essence, discarding her body where they last interacted with her. Black offenders were more likely to cover the body (43%), and White offenders were least likely (21%). The approach used by 82% of the offenders was found to be a blitz attack (the immediate and overwhelming use of injurious force to physically incapacitate the victim). Nearly 70% killed their victims between 8 p.m. and 4 a.m., with the greatest percentage (39%) occuring after midnight.

Offenders were found to have sexually assaulted their victims vaginally (65%) and anally (24%). Black offenders sexually assaulted both vaginally (71%) and anally (29%) more often than White offenders, who assaulted at 58% and 16%, respectively. Hispanic offenders ($n = 14$) assaulted anally 36% of the time, more often than either Blacks or Whites, but the significance of this finding is hampered by consideration of the small sample ($n = 5$). Overall, these offenders inserted foreign objects into the victim's body 22% of the time, with White offenders responsible for just more than half of those cases. Of note, more than half of all foreign object insertions were perpetrated by offenders younger than 24 years of age.[8] Finally, semen was identified in only 48% of the cases, with no differences noted for race or age. Sexual activity, without the presence of semen, was noted in the remaining 52% of cases. This sexual activity in addition to vaginal, anal, and oral assault included fondling the sexual areas of the body, foreign object insertion, and posing the victim to expose sexual areas, among others.

Linking Offender Characteristics

These results provide a baseline for judging the degree to which various independent variables may increase the likelihood of accurately assessing offender characteristics. In more complex analyses, following Warren et al. (1999), logistic regression models are employed to examine the performance of various independent variables in predicting four offender characteristics as shown in Table 7.2 (offender race, offender age, distance from offender's residence to victim's residence, and victim-offender relationship). The percentage correctly classified in these models represents the degree of accuracy that was obtained using the indicated independent variables. Our results are encouraging, with each model resulting in about 60% to 70% classification accuracy. Particular attention should be given to the improvement of prediction accuracy that results from inclusion of crime scene or victim attributes as explanatory variables. Using this approach, the model classification accuracy and performance of various independent variables for the demographic attributes in question are shown in Table 7.2.

---

[8] This corresponds with the analysis of Ressler et al. (1988), which suggested that sexual homicide offenders that engage in foreign object insertion do so as a form of sexual substitution or sexual exploration, which may correspond with a sexually inadequate or immature offender. Such a description would suggest a younger offender as found here.

TABLE 7.2

LOGISTICAL REGRESSION RESULTS FOR DEPENDENT VARIABLES OF INTEREST

Variable	B	Odds Ratio	χ^2	% Corrected Classified	Adjusted R^2
Offender race			21.630**	69.4	.219
Took items**	−0.97	0.38			
Neighborhood composition**	1.70	5.51			
Constant	−0.78	—			
Offender age			20.180**	65.6	.196
Victim's state of dress**	−1.90	0.15			
Injury Severity Score*	−0.02	0.98			
Constant	0.53	—			
Offender distance			13.251**	72.3	.141
Homicide Injury Scale**	−0.30	0.74			
Neighborhood composition**	1.23	3.40			
Constant	0.09	—			
Offender knew victim			5.063**	61.0	.054
Victim's body left*	−0.51	0.60			
Constant	0.51	—			

NOTE: For variable definitions, SEE TABLE 1. In all analyses reported here, the predictors were entered as single blocks. Stepwise procedures yielded slightly different parameter estimates, but the overall fit of the models did not vary significantly.

*$p < .10$. **$p < .05$.

Our results demonstrate that by considering the independent variables shown in Table 7.1, items taken from the crime scene and neighborhood composition, the ability to predict offender race increases. Prediction likelihood of an offender's race increases from 0.60 (not reported in the table) to 0.69. Thus, determining the racial homogeneity of the neighborhood where the crime took place increases the odds by 5.5 of correctly predicting offender race. Although other candidate variables and diagnostics (including auto-correlation, specification errors, multicollinearity, etc., as in all analyses in Table 7.2) were examined, this model was found to be adequate for predicting offender race. A similar analysis of offender age improved classification accuracy from 0.57 to 0.66. The independent variables of the victim's state of dress (clothed, unclothed, etc.) and the Injury Severity Score were found to have significant influence on predicting the offender's age category.

Analysis of the distance between the offender's residence and the victim's was also conducted, with the independent variables of neighborhood composition and the Homicide Injury Scale improving classification accuracy from 0.57 to 0.72, or approximately 25%. This suggests that the proximity of the offender's residence to the crime scene is significantly influenced by the racial homogeneity of the neighborhood. Interracial offending of Blacks against Whites (77%) occurs more in heterogeneous communities. White against Black offending was found to be virtually nonexistent in heterogeneous communities. Recognizing the intraracial nature of these crimes only appears to be applicable if the victim is Black. If the victim is White, the intraracial aspect of violent offending does not appear to be as germane.

Finally, an analysis of the relationship between the offender and the victim revealed an increase in classification accuracy from 0.55 to 0.61. The variable of how the victim's body was left at the crime scene (uncovered, covered, or altered) had statistical significance in the prediction of victim-offender relationship. Stronger findings in this particular analysis may have been found if not for a lingering difficulty defining relationships between offenders and their victims as will be discussed later.

DISCUSSION AND CONCLUSION

Pollock (1988), among others, noted that there have been few studies that systematically examine those who commit sexual offenses against older women. This study responds to this scarcity of knowledge by examining sexual homicides of elderly women.

To understand the importance of these results, it is also necessary to look beyond the statistically significant findings and correlations and look at the other substantive findings that may be important for understanding these cases. Through an exhaustive and detailed examination of each crime scene, an attempt was made to relate the criminal behavior exhibited in these scenes with the known characteristics and behavioral patterns of the offenders. Many of the descriptive findings here are also consistent with other studies that have explored violent victimization of the elderly (Faggiani & Owens, 1999; Fox & Levin, 1991; Kennedy & Silverman, 1990; Nelson & Huff-Corzine, 1998). Although some of the observations of the data cannot be applied to all cases (for primarily methodological reasons), there are others that may support law enforcement efforts to gain investigative direction.

This analysis reveals several points that merit further elaboration. The most important of these being the comparison of the results to law enforcement's anecdotal beliefs, victim location and routine activities theory, defining stranger versus acquaintance, community composition and inter-racial offending, levels of homicidal injury, classifying sexual homicide offenders, and financial gain versus sexual/homicide motives.

First, despite that the offenders in these cases are diverse in age and split relatively evenly between Black and White offenders (with a less significant contribution by Hispanic offenders), many aggregate demographic characteristics are found to be strikingly similar. These observations are consistent with the experience of investigators who have anecdotally described violent offenders of the elderly as younger offenders, assaulting the victims at or close to the victims' residences, living within close proximity to the crime scene, and generally unknown to the victim.

Second, elderly violent crime victims sustain their injuries at their residences anywhere from 82% (Hochstedler, 1981) to 100% (Pollock, 1988) of the time for sexual assault and 52% for violent crimes overall (Antunes et al., 1977) and 34% for robbery of females (Faggiani & Owens, 1999). A similar result is identified here with 94% of these women killed at home. Although only 56% of offenders lived within six blocks, fully 81% (higher for Blacks and Hispanics) initiated the assault by walking to the scene. This implies that a majority of the offenders had some pretense to be in the vicinity of the victim prior to the crime thus providing them an opportunity to initiate the assault on foot. Although 14% of the victims had lived in their neighborhoods 4 to 9 years, 73% had lived there at least 10 years and many substantially longer. This suggests that in conjunction with longevity in their neighborhoods, these victims were well-known to many residents in the area as well as individuals who routinely engaged in the activities of daily life there. Unfortunately, this longevity may have produced unrecognized risk to the victim. Rossmo (1999) suggested that motivated offenders may sometimes create "mental maps" of neighborhoods when they identify potentially suitable victims. *Mental mapping* is the process by which an offender catalogs victim information in a mental "card file" to facilitate a return to that victim in the future (p. 89).

Third, relationship classifications of stranger and acquaintance are particularly problematic (Riedel & Rinehart, 1996). Stranger classifications are prevalent in widely used national data sets such as the UCR and the National Crime Victimization Survey, but a gray area may exist between stranger and acquaintance classifications. Stronger findings in this particular analysis may have been found if not for a lingering difficulty defining relationships between offenders and their victims. Many offenders labeled as strangers may in fact be marginally acquainted with their victims. This acquaintance may have arisen out of a former service performed by the offender (gardening, lawn care, odd jobs, etc.), from common routine activities engaged in by the victim and offender (e.g., common bus stops, shopping areas, commuting patterns of the victim and offender), or other commonalties that brought them into visual contact, making them acquaintances by sight but more accurately classified as "apparent" strangers. Therefore, although stranger classifications were common in the data and are commonly found in many data sets relative to crimes of violence, it is theorized that this frequency may be overstated (see Safarik et al., 2000). Within this study, few crimes occurred between absolute strangers. This does not imply that a prior relationship existed between the offender and victim but rather that the offender was aware of where the victim lived (prior to the crime) and perceived her to be alone and vulnerable.

Fourth, the paradigm of intraracial offending in violent crimes as identified in UCR data (FBI, 2000) has been observed for many years. However, intraracial offending patterns by these offenders appear to be dependent on specific conditional case factors. The most notable of these seems to be the homogeneity of the neighborhood. This result is not surprising because the racial composition of communities tends to be reflected in residential patterns. Offending patterns appear to be no different. This study reiterates the intraracial nature of offending in homogenous communities shown in existing experiential data (Safarik et al., 2000). In contrast, White victims of Black and Hispanic offenders lived in neighborhoods characterized by investigators as transitional. These transitional neighborhoods were thought to have undergone a socioeconomic change from middle to lower class. Often accompanying such a change are other demographic transformations that result in social disorganization and increased criminal activity. The elderly may also experience emotional or economic issues that detract from their willingness to move to a different location. However, because these victims may be cognizant of changes in their neighborhoods and sense more potential dangers as a result, they may also be aware of their vulnerability and more likely to take proactive steps to secure their residences. The intraracial offending pattern among White offenders and the observation that Whites are nearly four times as likely as Blacks to be admitted by the victim may suggest that because the offenders were the same race, these victims were more easily lulled into a false sense of security and hence dropped their guard. No Hispanic offender either used a ruse or was admitted by the victim.

Fifth, most studies of homicide examine weapon use, or more broadly the COD, as a characteristic of homicidal behavior. UCR data consistently reveal that firearms are the leading cause of homicidal death in all age categories except children ages 1 to 4. Elderly victimization research confirms that firearms are the leading COD among the elderly. Death by strangulation is rarely seen, comprising only 4% of elderly homicide victims (Fox & Levin, 1991). This is in marked contrast to the findings from this study. Firearms (1%) are virtually never seen, but strangulation accounted for 63% of these victims' deaths. Despite the extensive examination of weapon use and COD, little if any homicide research has examined the degree of injury. Most studies assume either no variation in injury because every victim suffered a lethal injury, or they consider only the COD. The level of injury exhibited in a number of the cases in this study was found to be excessive and is an attribute believed to be distinct from other violent crimes. As noted earlier, both Groth (1978) and Pollock (1988) found similar results in earlier studies. Although the Homicide Injury Scale and the Injury Severity Score metrics are somewhat different, both of these measures provide quantitative evidence supporting the differentiation of levels of homicidal injury as an attribute of these cases. The data examined here also reveal that many of these victims suffered multiple, severe, and excessive injuries. Many died from brutal and horrific injuries in excess of what would be necessary to cause death. This excessive violence is commonly referred to as *overkill* (Douglas, Burgess, Burgess, & Ressler, 1992, p. 254). As noted earlier, the mean for both injury metrics approximated the range of the scale synonymous with overkill.

Sixth, Hazelwood and Dougla's (1980) work, which offers a categorization of sexual murderers on a continuum from organized to disorganized, may have relevance here. Applying this typology, these offenders are found to be overwhelmingly consistent with the disorganized typology. In addition, more recent work by Hazelwood and Warren (2000) extends earlier work and establishes a new typology of impulsive and ritualistic offenders. The descriptive assessment of the impulsive offender is remarkably consistent with the majority of the offenders in this study. Salfati (2000) and Salfati and Canter (1999) offered a model of homicide behavior that appears to provide empirical support for categorizing patterns or themes of behavior at the crime scene into either an expressive or instrumental style or a combination of the two. These offenders and their crime scene behavior suggest consistency with the instrumental classification. The collective attributes of these offenders and their crime scenes, as found in Table 7.3, manifest the characteristics associated with the disorganized, impulsive, and instrumental offender typologies. Such classifications may provide investigative direction to law enforcement.

Seventh, the literature on violent crime suggests that elderly women are simply the unfortunate victims of nonviolent offenders, primarily motivated by financial gain, who have randomly targeted their residences for the commission of either a property crime (e.g., burglary) or a robbery (Faggiani & Owens, 1999; Falzon & Davis, 1998; Fox & Levin, 1991; Hochstedler, 1981; Nelson & Huff-Corzine, 1998; Lent & Harpold, 1988). In the process of committing this purported financial crime, the offender inadvertently discovers an elderly female. He then changes his primary motive resulting in him not only sexually assaulting her but murdering her as well. The observation that 72% of the offenders in this study removed something from the crime scene may appear on the surface to support earlier research. However, from both a behavioral and experiential perspective, such a scenario stands in stark contrast to what has been observed in detailed reviews of these cases. The suggestion of a financially motivated crime gone awry is contradicted by the observation that the preponderance of the behavior was directed at the victim in furtherance of not only the sexual assault but the effort required to kill her. Not only was the majority of the interaction occurring with the victim, but chronologically, it was occurring first. The removal of property occurred subsequent to the homicide. In addition, there was a lack of balance between the effort expended to sexually assault and murder the victim and the subsequent search for and theft of property. The items taken were generally located after a cursory search in the immediate vicinity of the victim and consisted mostly of cash and jewelry. The theft of property was, in most cases, an afterthought. This was supported by forensic examination of the crime scenes, admissions to uninvolved third parties, and admissions or confessions to police.

Clearly, offenders can have more than one motive when they engage in a specific criminal activity. They can also change the motive or add other criminal objectives that they had not thought of previously. Although this appears to be the case with some of these offenders, this study provides support contrary to the literature and suggests that the selection of these women was premeditated. The majority of the offenders fully intended to sexually assault and murder these women prior to the initiation of the crime, and this intent superseded their intent to steal. Supporting this interpretation, Groth's (1978) earlier work relating to elderly rape victims revealed that one third of the offenders who sexually assaulted elderly women reported their intention was to physically injure the victim.

TABLE
7.3

TABLE 7.3 CONTRASTS OF INCIDENT CHARACTERISTICS WITH DESCRIPTIVE TYPOLOGIES

Attribute	Disorganized[a]	Impulsive	Instrumental	Elderly Sexual Homicide Offender
Crime scene attributes				
Body disposition	Left at death scene Not transported Left in view Partially undressed or naked		Left at death scene Not transported Left in view Partially undressed or naked	Left at death scene Not transported Left in view Partially undressed or naked
Criminal sophistication	Criminally unsophisticated	Criminally unsophisticated		Criminally unsophisticated
Planning	Little or no planning, spontaneous offense	Little or no planning, spontaneous offense		Little or no planning, spontaneous offense
Evidence consciousness	Leaves evidence at scene	Leaves evidence at scene		Leaves evidence at scene
Organization	Scene appears random and sloppy with no set plan for deterring detection	Scene appears random and sloppy with no set plan for deterring detection		Scene appears random and sloppy with no set plan for deterring detection
Protects identity	No measures taken to protect identity	No measures taken to protect identity		No measures taken to protect identity
Approach	Sudden violence to victim (blitz attack) to gain control	Sudden violence to victim (blitz attack) to gain control		Sudden violence to victim (blitz attack) to gain control
Sexual activity	Sexual activity at scene, usually postmortem		Sexual activity at scene	Sexual activity at scene, usually postmortem
Weapon	Weapon used from scene and often left		Weapon used from scene	Weapon used from scene and often left
Forensic Evidence	Leaves forensic evidence	Leaves forensic evidence	Leaves forensic evidence	Leaves forensic evidence
Cause of death	Most often death results from strangulation and blunt force trauma		Most often death results from strangulation and blunt force trauma	Most often death results from strangulation and blunt force trauma
Use of restraints	Minimal	Minimal		Minimal
Other activity			Property taken, financial gain	Property taken, financial gain
Level of force	Often excessive or brutal	Often excessive or brutal		Often excessive or brutal
Paraphilic behavior	Absence of paraphilic behavior (e.g., bondage or sadism)	Absence of paraphilic behavior (e.g., bondage or sadism)		Absence of paraphilic behavior (e.g., bondage or sadism)

(continued)

TABLE 7.3 CONTINUED

Attribute	Disorganized[a]	Impulsive	Instrumental	Elderly Sexual Homicide Offender
Motivation		Underlying theme of anger		Underlying theme of anger
Offender attributes				
Work history	Poor work history			Poor work history
Skill level	Unskilled work			Unskilled work
Employment			Unemployed	Unemployed
Criminal history		Arrest history diverse and generally antisocial Depending on age, history will reflect a multiplicity of crimes with no specific theme	Criminal histories with both property and violent offenses Burglary or theft convictions	Arrest history diverse and generally antisocial Depending on age, history will reflect a multiplicity of crimes with no specific theme Criminal histories with both property and violent offenses Burglary or theft convictions
Intelligence	Lower intelligence			Lower intelligence Most have only some high school
Travel and search patterns	Lives or works near death scene	Travels shorter distance to offend Offends over smaller area		Lives or works near death scene Association with area Travels shorter distance to offend, half live within 6 blocks
Social skills	Socially incompetent			Socially incompetent
Substance abuse		Abuse of alcohol		Abuse of drugs and/or alcohol

NOTE: Although certain attributes under the three headings are shown by an empty cell, this does not mean that the attribute is not applicable to that categorization. The attributes listed were only those identified in the literature.

[a] "This disorganization may be the result of youthfulness of the offender, lack of criminal sophistication, use of drugs and alcohol" (Douglas, Burgess, Burgess, & Ressler, 1992, p. 128). The offenders in this study are usually characterized by at least one of these attributes.

Source: Hazelwood and Warren (2000) and Salfati (2000).

We have shown that empirical support for linking offender characteristics with victim and crime scene attributes has merit. The application to the sexual homicide of elderly females was evident in this data set. Although this study was limited to some of the basic elements of behavioral assessments of these types of criminals, other data collection efforts and analyses may yield different results (Muller, 2000; Salfati, 2000; West, 2000). Nonetheless, this effort shows specific support for the potential to identify offender characteristics from incident, victim, and crime scene variables.

The failure to carefully review and analyze all the behavioral interactions of elderly female homicides may contribute to at least some cases being improperly classified as nonsexual homicides without note of the subordinate offense of sexual assault. Consideration of the totality of the offense behavior, including the sexual components, rather than simply noting whether the victim was raped or semen was forensically identified, will likely result in more accurate classification of these cases as sexual homicides. The homogeneity of many of the crime scene attributes and the consistency with characteristics of the disorganized, impulsive, and instrumental offender should provide law enforcement with a well-informed position from which to start their investigation. In addition, analysis of readily available victim and crime scene attributes can provide statistically significant contributions for discerning important offender characteristics.

REFERENCES

Antunes, G.E., Cook, F.L., Cook, T.D., & Skogan, W.G. (1977). Patterns of personal crime against the elderly: Findings From a national survey. *The Gerontologist, 17*, 321-327.

Baker, S.P., & O'Neill, B. (1976). The Injury Severity Score: An update. *Journal of Trauma, 16*, 882-885.

Baker, S.P., O'Neill, B., Haddon, W., & Long, W.B. (1974). The Injury Severity Score: A method for describing patients with multiple injuries and evaluating emergency care. *Journal of Trauma, 14*(3), 187-196

Boudreaux, M.C., Lord, W.D., & Jarvis, J.P. (2001). Behavioral perspectives on child homicide: The role of access, vulnerability, and routine activities theory. *Trauma, Violence and Abuse, 2*(1), 56-76.

Brownmiller, S. (1975). *Against our will: Men, women and rape.* New York: Simon & Schuster.

Bureau of Justice Statistics. (1994). *Elderly crime victims: National Crime Victimization Survey.* Washington, DC: U.S. Department of Justice, Office of Justice Programs.

Burgess, A.W., Hartman, C.R., Ressler, R.K., Douglas, J.E., & McCormack, A. (1986). Sexual homicide: A motivational model. *Journal of Interpersonal Violence, 1*(3), 251-272.

Chilton, R., & Jarvis, J. (1999a). Using the National Incident-Based Reporting System (NIBRS) to test estimates of arrestee and offender characteristics. *Journal of Quantitative Criminology, 15*(2), 207-224.

Chilton, R., & Jarvis, J. (1999b). Victims and offenders in two crime statistics programs: A comparison of the National Incident-Based Reporting System (NIBRS) and the National Crime Victimization Survey (NCVS). *Journal of Quantitative Criminology, 15*(2), 193-205.

Cohen, L.E., & Felson, M. (1979). Social change and crime rate trends: A routine activity approach. *American Sociological Review, 44*, 588-608.

Davis, L.J., & Brody, E.M. (1979). Rape and older women—A guide to prevention and protection (DHEW Publication No. ADM 82-11-1195). Washington, DC: U.S. Government Printing Office.

Douglas, J.E., Burgess, A.W., Burgess, A.G., & Ressler, R.K. (1992). *Crime classification manual: A standard system for investigating and classifying violent crimes*. New York: Lexington Books.

Faggiani, D., & Owens, M.G. (1999). Robbery of older adults: A descriptive analysis using the National Incident-Based Reporting System. *Journal of the Justice Research and Statistics Association, 1*(1), 97-117.

Falzon, A.L., & Davis, G.G. (1998). A 15 year retrospective review of homicide in the elderly. *Journal of Forenisc Sciences, 43*(2), 371-374.

Federal Bureau of Investigation. (2000). *Crime in the United States*. Washington, DC: U.S. Government Printing Office.

Fletcher, P. (1977). Criminal victimization of elderly women—A look at sexual assault. Syracuse, NY: Rape Crisis Center of Syracuse.

Fox, J., & Levin, J. (1991). Homicide against the elderly: A research note. *Criminology, 29*, 317-327.

Gerry, D.P. (1983, April). *The effects of rape on three age groups of women: A comparison study*. Paper presented at the Southern Gerontological Association Meeting, Atlanta, Georgia.

Groth, A.N. (1978). The odler rape victim and her assailant. *Journal of Geriatric Psychiatry, 2*, 203-215.

Groth, A.N., & Birnbaum, H.J. (1979). *Men who rape*. New York: Plenum.

Groth, A.N., Burgess, A.W., & Holmstrom, L.L. (1977). Rape: Power, anger, and sexuality. *American Journal of Psychiatry, 134*, 1239-1243.

Hazelwood, R.R. (1987). Analyzing the rape and profiling the offender. In R.R. Hazelwood & A.W.Burgess (eds.), *Practical aspects of rape investigation* (pp. 169-199). New York: Elsevier North-Holland.

Hazelwood, R.R., & Burgess, A.W. (eds.). (1995). *Practical aspects of rape investigation; A multidisciplinary approach* (2nd ed.). Boca Raton, FL: CRC.

Hazelwood, R.R., & Douglas, J.E. (1980). The lust murderer. *FBI Law Enforcement Bulletin, 49*(4), 18-22.

Hazelwood, R.R., & Warren, J. (1990). The criminal behavior of the serial rapist. *FBI Law Enforcement Bulletin, 59*(2), 1-17.

Hazelwood, R.R., & Warren, J. (2000). The sexually violent offender: Impulsive or ritualistic? *Aggression and Violent Behavior, 5*(3), 267-279.

Hoclistedler, E. (1981). *Crime against the elderly in 26 cities*. Washington, DC: U.S. Department of Justice, Bureau of Justice Statistics.

Kennedy, L.W., & Silverman, R.A. (1990). The elderly victim of homicide: An application of routine activity theory. *Sociological Quarterly, 31*, 305-317.

Kerschner, P.A. (1976, October). *Rape and the elderly; An initial analysis*. Paper presented at the Annual Meeting of the Gerontological Society, New York.

Lent, C.J., & Harpold, J. (1988). Violent crime against the aging. *FBI Law Enforcement Bulletin, 57*(7), 11-19.

Longo, R.E., & Gochenour, C. (1981). Sexual assault of handicapped individuals. *Journal of Rehabilitation, 47*(3), 24-27.

Moen, P. (1996). Gender, age, and the life course. In R. Binstock & L. George (eds.), *Handbook of aging and the social sciences* (pp. 171-187). San Diego: Academic Press.

Muller, D. (2000). Criminal profiling: Real science or just wishful thinking. *Homicide Studies, 4*(3), 234-264.

Muram, D., Miller, K., & Cutler, A. (1992). Sexual assault of the elderly victim. *Journal of Interpersonal Violence, 7*(1), 70-76.

Nelson, C., & Huff-Corzine, L. (1998). Strangers in the night: An application of the lifestyle-routine activities approach to elderly homicide victimization. *Homicide Studies, 2*(2), 130-159.

O'Toole, M.E. (1999). Criminal profiling: The FBI uses criminal investigative analysis to solve crimes. *Corrections Magazine, 61*(1), 44-46.

Pollock, N.L. (1988). Sexual assault of older women. *Annals of Sex Research, 1,* 523-532.

Ressler, R.K., Burgess, A.W., & Douglas, J.E. (1988). *Sexual homicide: Patterns and motives.* Lexington, MA: Lexington Books.

Riedel, M., & Rinehart, T.A. (1996). Murder clearances and missing data. *Journal of Crime and Justice, 19,* 83-102.

Rossmo, K.D. (1999). *Geographic profiling.* New York: CRC.

Safarik, M.E., Jarvis, J.P., & Nussbaum, K.E. (2000). Elderly female serial sexual homicide: A limited empirical test of criminal investigative analysis. *Homicide Studies, 4*(3), 294-307.

Salfati, G.C. (2000). The nature of expressiveness and instrumentality in homicide: Implications for offender profiling. *Homicide Studies, 4*(3), 265-293.

Salfati, G.C., & Canter, D.V. (1999). Differentiating stranger murders: Profiling offender characteristics from behavioral styles. *Behavioral Sciences and the Law, 17,* 391-406.

Taeuber, C.M., & Allen, J. (1990). Women in our aging society: The demographic outlook. In J. Allen & A.J. Pifer (eds.), *Women on the front lines: Meeting the challenge of an aging America* (pp. 11-46). Washington DC: Urban Institute.

U.S. Bureau of the Census. (1999). *1999 Census of Population: Characteristics of the population.* Washington, DC: Government Printing Office.

Warren, J., Reboussin, R., Hazelwood, R.R., Cummings, A., Gibbs, N.A., & Trumbetta, S.L. (1998). Crime scene and distance correlates of serial rape. *Journal of Quantitative Criminology, 14,* 35-59.

Warren, J., Reboussin, R., Hazelwood, R.R., Gibbs, N.A., Trumbetta, S.L., & Cummings, A. (1999). Crime scene analysis and the escalation of violence in serial rape. *Forensic Science International, 100,* 37-56.

West, A. (2000). Clinical assessment of homicide offenders: The significance of crime scene in offense and offender analysis. *Homicide Studies, 4*(3), 219-233.

Yates, D.W. (1990). Scoring systems for trauma. *British Medical Journal, 301,* 1090-4

Mark E. Safarik is a supervisory special agent and serves in the Federal Bureau of Investigation's National Center for the Analysis of Violent Crime's behavioral analysis unit. He specializes in the behavioral analysis of violent crime with an emphasis on homicide and has conducted extensive research on the sexual homicide of elderly women. He works closely with law enforcement agencies throughout the United States as well as internationally. He has been an FBI agent for 18 years. Prior to becoming an FBI special agent, he was a detective with the Davis, California, Police Department. His law enforcement career spans 25 years.

John P. Jarvis is assigned to the behavioral science unit of the Federal Bureau of Investigation where his principal responsibilities include training, research, and consultation in crime analysis and the behavioral sciences. He holds a Ph.D. in sociology from the University of Virginia, and his primary research interests include trend analysis, measurement of crime, and issues related to deviance and social control.

Kathleen E. Nussbaum is a graduate student in investigative psychology at the University of Liverpool. She holds an undergraduate degree from New York University and has served as a research intern with the Federal Bureau of Investigation's National Center for the Analysis of Violent Crime. The work for this article began during her internship and has continued with general issues of violence and profiling of elderly violent crimes.

Mark E. Safarik, John P. Jarvis and Kathleen E. Nussbaum, *Journal of Interpersonal Violence,* Vol. 17, No. 5, 2002, pp. 500-525. Copyright © 2002 by Sage Publications, Inc. Reprinted by Permission of Sage Publications, Inc.

THE SEXUALLY SADISTIC SERIAL KILLER

JANET I. WARREN,[1] D.S.W., ROBERT R. HAZELWOOD,[2] M.S. AND PARK E. DIETZ,[3] M.D., M.P.H., AND PH.D.

This article explores characteristics and crime scene behavior of 20 sexually sadistic serial murderers. The pairing of character pathology with paraphilic arousal to the control and degradation of others is examined as it manifests itself in their murders. Commonalities across murders and across murderers are highlighted, i.e., the execution of well-planned murders, the use of preselected locations, captivity, a variety of painful sexual acts, sexual bondage, intentional torture, and death by means of strangulation and stabbing.

> "I did and perpetrated them [the murders] following [the dictates] of my imagination and my thought, without the advice of anyone, and according to my own judgment and entirely for my own pleasure and physical delight, and for no other intention or end."
>
> —Baron Gilles de Rais (1400's) (1)

Throughout history, there have been isolated, but highly publicized cases of serial murder. Jack the Ripper, a source of on-going inquiry and speculation, became famous following a series of prostitute murders in London, England, in 1888. In the 1950s, Ed Gein provided the prototype for the movie, *Silence of the Lambs*, by using the skin of his murder victims to fashion face masks and articles of clothing. Most recently, Jeffrey Dahmer shocked America when the body parts of multiple male victims were found in his apartment in Milwaukee, and he confessed not only to having sex with the corpses but eating muscle tissue of his victims.

In 1970, Brittain attempted to offer a "clinical description of the sadistic murderer," a significant number of who had murdered multiple times (2). Drawing from case studies, he suggested that the sadistic murderer was an introspective, solitary, and prudish person who rarely showed any signs of overt violence. His developmental history was characterized by an ambivalent relationship to his mother, a punitive relationship with his father, and general difficulty in relating socially to others. Brittain suggested that, sexually, this type of offender experienced a rich fantasy life and

---

[1] Janet I. Warren, Associate professor of Clinical Psychiatric Medicine, Institute of Law, Psychiatry and Public Policy, University of Virginia, Charlottesville, Virginia.
[2] Robert R. Hazelwood, FBI (Retired), Vice-president, The Academy Group, Manassas, Virginia.
[3] Park E. Dietz, Clinical professor of Psychiatry and Biobehavioral Sciences, U.C.L.A. School of Medicine, President, Threat Assessment Group, Inc., and President, Park Dietz & Associates, Newport Beach, California.
Received for publication 29 Jan. 1996; revised manuscript received 26 March 1996; accepted for publication 28 March 1996.

reported a history of cross-dressing, fetishism, and homosexual activity but was "often impotent" in his heterosexual relationships. He was described as being cruel to animals; interested in black magic, Nazism, and weapons; and "excited by cruelty in books and films." Brittain contended that the sadistic murderer was likely to offend following a loss of self-esteem, experienced relief in response to his murder, and behaved "normally" after it. He killed by asphyxia or multiple stabbings. Prognostically, Brittain observed that this type of murderer was often a model prisoner or patient but "given the opportunity he is likely to murder again and he knows it."

MacCullough, Snowden, Wood, and Mills discussed the interrelationship between sadistic fantasy, sadistic behavior, and criminal offending (3). They argue that the wish to control lies at the heart of sadism and define sexual sadism as "the repeated practice of behavior and fantasy which is characterized by a wish to control another person by domination, denigration or inflicting pain for the purpose of producing mental pleasure and sexual arousal (whether or not accompanied by orgasm) in the sadist."

Drawing from patients at Park Lane Hospital in Liverpool, England, MacCullough et al. identified 16 individuals who had been diagnosed as psychopathic and who had been convicted of a sexually motivated crime. Eighty-one percent of the offenders had been masturbating to fantasies of rape, buggery, kidnap, bondage, flagellation, torture, and killing for extended periods of time before their offenses. The majority of the offenders reported nonaggressive sexual fantasies following puberty, but one to seven years after the onset of puberty, sadistic content began to appear, accompanied by a "substantial" increase in masturbatory activity. A significant number of the offenders described their sadistic fantasies as being progressive in nature with the fantasies continually being changed to maintain their efficacy as a source of arousal and pleasure. The authors comment: "this increase in the power of fantasies was accomplished by increasing the sadistic context and also by including fantasy based on previous behavioral 'try-outs' of the main fantasy sequence." The offenders reported acting out discrete components of the sexually sadistic fantasy over extended periods of time before their patterns of violent offending coalesced. Offenses that did not appear overtly sadistic were considered covertly sadistic "because they are part of an escalating sequence of sadistic behavior, which, if unchecked, can ultimately lead to loss of life." These offenders were all characterized from an early age by difficulties in social relatedness that developed after puberty into a problem of relating erotically. In describing this formative process, these authors comment: "fantasy of successful control and dominance of the world can be conceptualized as an operant which increases the probability of its own recurrence by the relief which it gives from a pervasive sense of failure." In assessing this pairing of fantasy with progressive behavioral enactment, MacCullough et al. caution that "if a man presents with sadistic sexual fantasies, admits to previous tryouts (which may have resulted in recordable offenses), and demonstrates a pattern of progression of offending and fantasy, then progression to killing would appear to be a strong possibility."

In 1985, Levin and Fox undertook to study mass murder, a phenomenon they defined as involving either a simultaneous mass slaying or a series of killing with at least four victims (4). Drawing from a sample of 42 offenders, they concluded that the mass murderer is typically a white male in his late twenties or early thirties; in cases of serial murder, he kills by beating or strangulation. According to Levin and Fox, the sexually motivated offender is "more evil than crazy"; he is described as traveling from state to state, "searching for victims whom he can rape and sodomize, torture and dismember, stab and strangle." Emphasizing that this particular type of offender is seldom driven by hallucinations or delusions, Levin and Fox assert that he is most often a sociopathic personality devoid of guilt or conscience and intent upon controlling and dominating others.

In 1986, Dietz drew from case examples and research in progress to develop a typology of serial, mass, and sensational homicides (5). The term "serial murder" was used to refer to cases in which a single perpetrator killed others in five or more separate incidents. According to Dietz, the serial killer is often a psychopathic sexual sadist who kills strangers by means of strangulation, stabbing, or beating, because these means of death allow greater intimacy than projectile weapons. Dietz argued against the diagnostic labeling of these men as borderline personality disorders, emphasizing that "these men enjoy killing people." Dietz recognized additional categories of serial killers: crime spree killers; functionaries of organized crime; custodial poisoners and asphyxiators; and the "supposed psychotics."

Leyton wrote that the serial killer uses murder to provide both "revenge and a life-long celebrity career" in a social context that highlights worldly ambition, success and failure, and "manly avenging violence" (6). Drawing from detailed narratives of Kemper, Bundy, de Salvo, and Berkowitz, he argued against "clumsy" psychiatric attempts to find these men insane, asserting that their motivations "transcend mere catharsis and temporary gratification: their aim (being . . .) a more ambitious one, a kind of sustained subpolitical campaign directed towards 'the time-lessness of oppression and the order of power'."

In 1988, Ressler, Burgess, and Douglas published the results of interviews with 36 sexual murderers, most of whom murdered multiple times (7). The authors examined the developmental history, motivational dynamics, and crime scene behavior that characterized certain notorious killers and determined that the men in their sample were not only aware of their long-standing preoccupation with murder, but also "devoted to violent, sexualized thoughts and fantasies." Examining the progressive development of these fantasies from childhood through adolescence into adulthood, the authors conclude that these men murdered "because of the way they think," and that the motivation for sexual murder lay in their internally driven and pervasively active fantasy life. The authors suggested that childhood sexual trauma may be a predisposing factor to murder and that deviant fantasies precede the sexually violent crimes of these men.

Holmes and DeBurger, using the FBI's classification scheme, asserted that the serial murderer was the most heinous and perplexing of violent offenders (8). Highlighting four classificatory themes (the background of the offender, his victims, the methods used, and the location of the victims), they suggest four subcategories of serial murder: the visionary type; the mission-oriented type; the hedonistic type; and the power-control-oriented type. They apparently attempt to differentiate the psychotic serial killer from the sexually motivated, characterologically-disturbed serial killer, but the basis on which they attribute particular motives to certain well-known offenders is unclear.

In 1989, Prentky, Burgess, Rokous, and Austin attempted to explore further the role of fantasy in serial sexual murder. Using part of the sample interviewed by Ressler et al., as well as cases from the Treatment Center for Sexually Dangerous Persons in Massachusetts, they compared 25 sexual murderers who had killed at least three times with 17 sexual murderers who had killed only once (9). They found that the serial sexual murderers reported more compulsive masturbation, indecent exposure, and voyeuristic activity and had a significantly higher incidence of fetishism and cross-dressing. The serial killers were also characterized by more consuming violent fantasies and a consistently better planned and more organized crime scene. Highlighting the importance of internal drives to an understanding of repetitive sexual murder, Prentky et al. emphasized the need to understand further why "some individuals move from fantasy to behavior and others do not . . .".

Langevin, most recently, has sought to describe the behavior of "sex killers" (10). Observing that they are, in many respects, demographically similar to killers in general, he notes that they are characterized by two unique aspects of their modus operandi; i.e., they more often choose strangers as victims and tend to use strangulation as their preferred method of murder. Drawing on an earlier study of 13 sex killers, he observed that 31% appeared to be driven by pure sexual release, whereas an additional 69% fused a sexual motive with anger. Diagnostically, most of the murderers were suffering from some type of character disorder, and 75% met diagnostic criteria for sexual sadism. Although both sex killers and a group of sexual aggressors tended to suffer from multiple paraphilias (including voyeurism, exhibitionism, and frottage), sex killers were engaged in transvestism more often than nonsex killers and nonhomicidal sexual aggressors. Eighty percent of the sex killers reported running away from home as children, 83% had temper tantrums, and 60% had alcoholic fathers. Langevin reported no difference in intelligence between the three groups, but indicated that 40% of the sex killers showed some abnormality in the right temporal horn area of the brain and a trend toward an elevated level of testosterone.

Interspersed throughout these various attempts to understand serial murder, is an implicit or explicit recognition of the sexual component of some types of repetitious homicide. Although the terms vary depending on the author's discipline, descriptors such as "sexual homicide," "sadism," and "paraphilic murder" repeatedly occur in accounts of many of the most virulent serial murderers. Dietz has been perhaps the most definitive in asserting that the blending of sexual sadism with psychopathic character pathology results in the phenomenon of men who "enjoy killing."

To explore one subgroup of serial killers more fully, we compiled data on 20 sexually sadistic serial murderers. Some of these data (16 subjects) were compiled as part of the Dietz, Hazelwood, and Warren study of sexually sadistic criminals (11). The 20 men selected for the present study were responsible for 149 murders throughout the United States and Canada.

METHOD

The data were compiled from case files obtained by the FBI's National Center for the Analysis of Violent Crime through their case consultations or research efforts. Cases were included in the sample if: a. the perpetrator demonstrated an enduring pattern of sexual arousal to images of suffering or humiliation and b. the offender killed at least three victims in at least three incidents separated by time, place, or both. For each case, information was available from a variety of sources, including police investigation reports, crime scene photographs, victim statements, reports of interviews with families, confessions, psychiatric reports, trial transcripts, presentencing reports, descriptions generated by the offenders (i.e., manuscripts, diaries, sketches, audiotapes, and videotapes), interviews with the offender, and/or published book-length biographies of the offender. All data reported represent minimum estimates of the actual frequency of the variables studied; the data were collected from sources of information not designed specifically for research.

RESULTS AND DISCUSSION

Nineteen of the 20 offenders were white males (see Table 8.1). This over-representation of Caucasians in sexually motivated serial crimes is a pattern observed in other research (Warren J, Reboussin R, Hazelwood R, Gibbs N, Trumbetta S, Escalation in violence in serial rape, unpublished). Although blacks are known to commit serial rape and murder in an instrumental fashion, for example, in the context of burglaries or robberies, the fantasy-driven crimes of the sexual sadist do not appear to be represented proportionally in this population. This pattern may reflect a different process of development of sexual identity among the two groups, a different potential for developing paraphilic preferences, or both.

TABLE 8.1	CHARACTERISTICS OF 20 SEXUALLY SADISTIC SERIAL MURDERERS		
		n	%
Male		20	100
White		19	95
Middle class background		13	65
Parental infidelity and/or divorce		10	50
Stable employment		15	75
Homosexual experience in adulthood		11	55
Paraphilic interest in peeping, obscene phone calls, or indecent exposure		9	45
Paraphilic interest in fetishism, bondage, or transvestism		5	25
Evidence of violent fantasies		16	80
Shared sexual partners		7	35
Indoctrination of compliant victims		7	35
Married at time of offense		10	50
Posthigh school education		6	30
Drug/alcohol abuse		8	40
Violent theme collections		15	75
Interest in security/law enforcement		7	35
Psychotic symptoms		1	5
Arrest history		7	35

Anthropological studies of serial murder highlight the lower class origins and the oppressive inequality of the early life of this particular group of offenders. This study found that 65% of the sample came from middle- or upper-middle class families. The available information indicates, however, that at least 50% also came from families characterized by infidelity and divorce. These findings suggest that sexually sadistic serial murder is not related to lower class origins, but may be associated with a chaotic or unstable early life experience.

Interestingly, 65% of the sample had no arrest record before being arrested for murder. This pattern is unlike other types of aggressive sex offenders whose criminal histories are often characterized by a lengthy constellation of property and personal crimes. This pattern supports either the specificity of these offenders' criminal intent or their skill at avoiding detection, and highlights the difficulty of law enforcement in identifying them early in their criminal careers.

Still, not all of the crimes of sexual sadists are designed to fulfill their sexual desires. For example, some of the subjects in this study had engaged in armed robbery, illegal arms deals, drug trafficking, counterfeiting, and other crimes for profit. One of the subjects committed three known murders, none of which can be proven to have been committed in the course of sexually sadistic acts. One victim was a wife whom he had tortured sexually for years, but asphyxiated merely because he got tired of her and wanted a new wife. A second victim was an adolescent female whose body was skeletonized; he remained silent about stabbing her. A third victim was the female relative of a woman he intended to kill.

Abel, Becker, Cunningham-Rathner, Mittelman, and Rouleau's study of paraphilic behavior has indicated that individuals plagued by one paraphilia generally suffer either simultaneously or sequentially from three or four additional paraphilias over the course of their lives (12). Not unexpectedly, in this sample, a significant proportion of the men demonstrated an interest in paraphilic activities in addition to those reflecting sexual sadism. These included voyeurism, obscene phone calls, exhibitionism, fetishism, and/or cross-dressing. Over half of the men also reported homosexual experiences as adults. The multifaceted nature of the sample's sexual behavior is consistent with the clinical hypothesis that perversions may be polymorphous and reflective of some underlying disorganization or lack of unification in the development of the sexual libido. Recent research, by Hucker, Langevin, Dickey, Handy, Chambers, and Wright, associates sexual aggression and sexual sadism with neurological abnormalities in the right temporal horn of the brain (13). Prentky and Burgess discuss the role of the limbic system, serotonin, and sex hormones in the manifestation of sexually aggressive behavior (14). These preliminary findings or propositions invite further inquiry as to whether the well-documented clustering of paraphilic behaviors might emanate from subtle yet significant neurological or biochemical dysfunctions.

Many writers have emphasized the role that violent fantasies play in the occurrence of sexually sadistic behavior. Drawing from the sketches, videos, and pornography that were accumulated by these men, at least 85% of the sample had violent fantasies that seemed to remain consistent over significant periods of time. These fantasies contain a ritualized, repetitious core that is highly arousing to the sexual sadist. The assimilation of this core fantasy into ritualized, repetitious behavior across successive murders suggests that this internal representation is the script followed by the offender during his crimes. Evidence of such scripted behaviors can be instrumental in linking offenses perpetrated by the same offender.

A previous study by Hazelwood, Warren, and Dietz suggests that sexual sadists are particularly apt at seducing women into becoming compliant accessories to their violent fantasies or criminal acts (15). Within the current sample, 35% of the men enacted their core fantasies with women with whom they were having ongoing relationships; two of the 20 men eventually introduced their spouses into their murders. As discussed by Wilson and Seaman, Charlene Williams, a competent boutique owner became an accessory to murder for her husband, Gerald Gallego (16). Hazelwood, Warren, and Dietz described the process by which such indoctrination occurs and suggested that the sexually sadistic offender often manifests an unusual degree of insight into ways by which others can be influenced and controlled. The psychopathic underpinning of such exploitive behavior is highlighted.

The current study found that 75% of the sexually sadistic serial murderers kept collections of a violent theme of one type or another. These included audiotapes, videotapes, pictures or sketches of the individual's sadistic acts, or crimes with others, bondage material that was used in the various killings, sexually sadistic pornography, detective magazines, and various types of weapons. The nature of these collections and the sexual interests of these murderers cannot help but bring to mind Freud's assertions regarding the dynamic association between anal eroticism, sadistic behavior, and obsessive patterns of behavior. On a more practical level, the importance of these materials in the investigation and eventual prosecution of these offenders cannot be overemphasized. Hazelwood and Warren recommend that these collections be sought when applying for search warrants and conducting investigations, as their discovery can constitute irrefutable proof of the perpetrator's guilt (17).

As indicated in Table 8.1, only one serial murderer exhibited any type of psychotic behavior (i.e., hallucinations, delusions, or thought disorder). This clearly contradicts some of the earlier writing which associated these bizarre types of murder with insanity (18). As discussed in the earlier study of sexually sadistic criminals, the majority of these men engaged in extensive patterns of antisocial behavior in adult life, suggesting that their willingness to commit crimes for sexual gratification stems from character pathology rather than psychosis.

Perhaps, the most unsettling aspect of the murders committed by these men is the meticulous and precise nature of their execution. As indicated in Table 8.2, the majority of the murders were carefully planned (95%) and involved a preselected location (80%), the use of a torture kit (70%), prolonged captivity of at least some victims (65%), and recording of the offense by various means (45%). These activities clearly reflect a preferred mode of murder for these offenders that has been carefully thought out and choreographed over time. The obsessional and highly ritualized nature of these offenses seems to require the establishment of a preselected location and prolonged interaction with the victim.

As summarized in Table 8.2, the sexual acts that accompany the murders include a multiplicity of assaultive activities including rape, fellatio, sodomy, and foreign object penetration. Certain of the sexual acts apparently derive from a desire to humiliate and cause pain to the victim (65% perform anal intercourse, 65% insert foreign objects into the victim anally or vaginally). Sexual bondage also occurs in the murders of 95% of the offenders. This interest in sexual bondage is of

TABLE 8.2 CHARACTERISTICS OF THE OFFENSES OF 20 SEXUALLY SADISTIC SERIAL MURDERS.

	n	%
Careful planning of offenses	19	95
Impersonation of a police officer in the commission of the offense	3	15
Use of a con or ruse in approaching victim	16	80
Victim taken to preselected location	16	80
Victims kept in captivity for 24 h or more	13	65
Victim bound, blindfolded, or gagged	20	100
Use of a torture kit	14	70
Sexual bondage of victim	19	95
Anal intercourse with victim	13	65
Foreign object penetration	13	65
Variety of sexual acts (i.e., vaginal intercourse, fellatio, anal intercourse, foreign object penetration)	18	90
Penile penetration	19	95
Postmortem sexual assault	0	0
Verbal/behavioral scripting during offense	14	70
Sexual ritual	19	95
Intended torture	20	100
Asphyxiation as primary means of killing	12	60
Stabbing as primary means of killing	6	30
Gunshot as primary means of killing	1	5
Postmortem mutilation	1	5
Trophies (belonging to victim)	13	65
Partner assisted in crime	4	20
Concealed victim's corpse	13	65
Recorded the offenses	9	45
Single state or province murders	15	75
Multiple state or province murders	5	25

paraphilic significance to these men and, by their account, represents the subjugation and control of the victim that is central to their sexual arousal. There was only one instance of postmortem mutilation and no instances of necrophilic sexual activity, distinguishing these offenders from necrophilic serial killers such as Ted Bundy, Arthur Shawcross, or Joel Rifkin.

The means of death used by these murderers are personal and intimate. Sixty percent of the sample used strangulation or other types of asphyxiation as their primary means of killing, while 30% stabbed their victims to death. Only one individual in the sample used projectile weapons in murdering his boy victims. In 100% of the cases, intentional torture was inflicted on the victim before death. The types of torture, as noted in the earlier study by Dietz, Hazelwood, and Warren, included beating, biting, whipping, the insertion of foreign objects, painful bondage, electrical shock, asphyxiation, and burning (11). The process of seeing the victim suffer, of having the experience of pain, terror, and humiliation reflected back to the sadist, is central to the intent and arousal of this particular type of murderer.

Levin and Fox asserted that certain types of serial murderers move from state to state trying to find victims to rape, sodomize, and torture (4). In the current sample, only 25% murdered in more than one state or province; 75% contained their offenses to a single city, state, or province. This finding contradicts the vagabond image of the serial murderer and suggests that the majority of men are able to murder repeatedly in a relatively restricted area, and through the well-planned nature of these murders, avoid detection for long periods of time.

The victims of these murders seem to fall into consistent categories (see Table 8.3). Seventy percent of the men killed only female victims; 15% killed only male victims. A minority killed both male and female victims and/or adult and child victims. In 80% of the cases, the abduction of victims involved fairly complex scenarios to gain access to the victim. These cons or tricks involved such ploys as impersonating a police officer, enticing children into playful activities, and arranging for models through photographic studies. As in other studies of serial offenders, the majority of these sexually sadistic murderers killed only strangers (19). This element of their modus operandi is of great importance in their continued success at avoiding apprehension. The fact that four of the offenders also murdered individuals known to them, however, also suggests, as does their involvement with "compliant victims," that they are not always careful to avoid detection.

TABLE 8.3 CHARACTERISTICS OF THE VICTIMS OF 20 SEXUALLY SADISTIC SERIAL MURDERERS.

	n	%
Female victims only	14	70
Male victims only	3	15
Female and male victims	3	15
Any child victims (15 years and under)	10	50
Stranger victims only	16	80
Similarities among victims (age, appearance, intelligence, or circumstances)	10	50

The nature of the data did not allow for an examination of the first murder committed by each man, which would seem to be a pivotal point. The research of MacCullough et al. suggests that the sadistic fantasy has been in existence for years and that the first murder represents the culmination of many prior imaginary reenactments (3). One of the murderers in the current sample, however, described experiencing death in a nonsexual context for the first time. He wrote:

> "I stood there looking at him on the ground and I was suddenly feelings of power. I realized I held this man's life in my hands ... I thought I'm like God ... I too have the power to give life or take it away' ... I got down on my knees and took the rock and hit him again as hard as I could. I watched his forehead cave in from the force of the blow and the blood and brains splattered over the road ... I never thought it would be so easy to kill a person, or that I would enjoy it. But it was easy and I was enjoying the feeling of supremacy. A supremacy like I had never known before."

Clearly, this man did not experience the visceral abhorrence that would accompany such an experience for many; rather, he stumbled upon an exhilaration that made him feel "like God." Over time, he sought his exhilaration in sexual homicides of three women. Further study of "first murders" might shed light upon the rewards that cause some killers to seek the experience repetitively.

CONCLUSIONS

These data on 20 sexually sadistic serial murderers suggest that they represent a group of serial murderers whose demographics, offense behavior, and victim acquisition techniques are surprisingly consistent. Ninety-five percent were white males and 65% from middle class origins. They repeatedly executed murders that reflect careful planning, the use of prese-lected locations, captivity, a variety of painful sexual acts, sexual bondage, intentional torture, and death primarily by means of strangulation or stabbing. Their murders were consistent over time and reflect sexual arousal to the pain, fear, and panic of their victims. They choreographed assaults that allowed them to intrude upon and control their victim's deaths. One of the men, who murdered victims by manual strangulation, told of breathing air into his dying victim so that he could watch more closely her dawning realization that he was, in fact, going to kill her. This sense of being Godlike and in control of the life and death of another human being is reported by some of the men as one of the most exhilarating aspects of their sexual experiences and of their crimes. There was little postmortem mutilation and no necrophilic sexual activity.

The careful planning and execution of the murder occurs both in voluntary imaginings (fantasy) and in practical preparations for each crime. Whether masturbating to the fantasy or committing the crime, they hope for and sometimes achieve climax at the time of the victim's death. This type of reinforcement is obviously powerful, and no doubt, contributes to the offender's interest in reoffending. These men report that the actual murders become the fantasy material for subsequent masturbation, which reinforces the sadistic arousal pattern and the desire to murder and causes them to remain at risk for future violence.

This research suggests that the sexually sadistic killer represents one distinctive type of serial murderer whose expertise and thoroughness makes him a particularly dangerous threat to society.

REFERENCES

Wolf, L. The life and crimes of gilles de Rais, 1400. New York: Potter.

Brittian, R. The sadistic murderer. Med Sci Law 1970;*10*:198-207.

MacCulloch, M.J, Snowden, P.R, Wood P.J.W, Mills H.E. Sadistic fantasy, sadistic behaviour and offending. Br J Psychiatry 1983;*143*:20-9.

Levin J, Fox J. Mass murder: America's growing menace. New York: Plenum, 1985;*229*.

Dietz PE. Mass, serial, and sensational homicides. Bull NY Acad Med 1986;*62*:477-91.

Leyton E. Hunting humans: The rise of the modern multiple murderer. New York: Penguin, 1986;*331*.

Ressler R, Burgess A, Douglas J. Sexual homicide: Patterns and motives. Lexington: Health, 1988;*33*.

Holmes R, Deburger J. Serial murder. Newbury Park: Sage, 1988.

Prentky R, Burgess AW, Rokous F, Lee A. The presumptive role of fantasy in serial sexual homicide. Am J Psychiatry1989;*146*(7):887-91.

Langevin R. The sex killer. In: Burgess A, editor. Rape and sexual assault volume *III*. New York: Garland, 1991.

Dietz PE, Hazelwood RR, Warren J. The sexually sadistic criminal and his offenses. Bull Am Acad Psychiatry Law 1990;*18*:163-78.

Abel GG, Becker JU, Cunningham-Rather J, Mittellman M, Rouleau JL. Multiple paraphilic diagnoses among sex offenders. Bull Am Acad Psychiatry Law 1988;*16*(2):153-68.

Hucker SJ, Langevin R, Dickey R, Handy L, Chambers J, Wright S. Cerebral damage and dysfunction in sexually aggressive men. Ann Sex Res 1986;*1*:33-7.

Prentky RA, Burgess AW. Hypothetical biological substrates of a fantasy-based drive mechanism for repetitive sexual aggression. In Burgess A, editor. Rape and sexual assault volume *III*. New York: Garland, 1991.

Hazelwood RR, Warren J, Dietz PE. Compliant victims of the sexual sadist. Aust Fam Physician 1993;*22*(4):474-79.

Wilson C, Seaman D. The serial killers: A study in the psychology of violence. London: Carol, 1990.

Hazelwood RR, Warren J. The relevance of fantasy in sexual crimes investigation. In: Hazelwood RR, Burgess A, editors. Practical aspects of rape investigation: A multidisciplinary approach, revised ed. New York: Elsevier, 1995. In press.

Revitch E. Sex, murder and the potential sex murderer. Diseases of the nervous system 1985;*26*:640-8.

Warren J, Hazelwood RR, Reboussin R. Serial rape: The offender and his rape career. In Burgess A, editor. Rape and sexual assault volume *III*. New York: Garland, 1991.

Address requests for reprints or additional information to
Janet Warren, D.S.W.
Institute of Law
Psychiatry and Public Policy
Box 100, Blue Ridge Hospital
Charlottesville, VA 22908

PROFILES IN THE OFFENDING PROCESS OF NONSERIAL SEXUAL MURDERERS

ERIC BEAUREGARD AND JEAN PROULX

The aim of this study was to investigate specific pathways in the offending processes of nonserial sexual murderers and to examine possible relationships with different precrime, peri-crime, and postcrime factors. Included in this study were 36 offenders who have committed at least one sexual murder against a female victim and they were classified using cluster analysis. Participants using the sadistic pathway planned their offenses and used physical restraints during the offenses. Furthermore, they mutilated and humiliated their victims. Finally, they hid the bodies of the victims. Participants using the anger pathway had not premeditated the homicide. Mutilation, humiliation, and physical restraints were less predominant with these participants than with those using the sadistic pathway. Moreover, these offenders were more likely to leave the bodies at the crime scenes after the killings occurred. These two profiles are compared with empirical studies addressing sexual homicide.

The first scientific study of sexual homicide was *Psychopathia Sexualis*, published in 1886/ 1998 by Richard von Krafft-Ebing. From Gilles de Rays to Jack the Ripper, Krafft-Ebing presented a comprehensive collection of case studies to gain insight into the phenomenon of lust murder. Unfortunately, he did not present any explanation for such crimes.

Brittain (1970), as a psychiatrist, based his study of the sadistic sexual murderer on his clinical experience. The aim of his study was not to theorize on sadism but to offer a description of the psychosocial profile of this particular type of murderer. According to Brittain, the sexual murderer presents a narcissistic and egocentric personality with some obsessive traits, which often will be reflected on the crime scene. This individual feels he is different from others and will have a tendency to remain alone. This type of murderer habitually presents more than one paraphilia, such as cross-dressing, fetishism, and masochism. Behaviors of cruelty against animals are also observed. Finally, the killing happens habitually after a threat to self-esteem. The crime is planned, and the victim is chosen randomly or for reasons unknown to others.

Other researches have followed, offering new clinical typologies of the sexual murderer (Bénézech, 1997; Geberth, 1996; Holmes & De Burger, 1988; Money, 1990; Revitch & Schlesinger, 1989). Although very interesting, these typologies did not include behaviors and attitudes that were

NOTE: Correspondence should be addressed to Eric Beauregard, School of Criminology, University of Montreal, C.P. 6128, Succursale Centre-Ville, Montreal, Quebec, Canada, H3C 3J7; phone: 450-478-5977; e-mail: eric.beauregard@sympatico.ca.

only known to the offenders. Also, in most of these studies, the size of the sample was unknown and the number of variables included was limited. Finally, these studies are not based on an empirical classification method.

The FBI Typology

One particular study tried to overcome these limitations. This typology was developed at the FBI Behavioral Science Unit, in large part through the work of Ressler and his colleagues (Burgess, Hartman, Ressler, Douglas, & McCormack, 1986; Ressler, Burgess, & Douglas, 1988; Ressler, Burgess, Douglas, Hartman, & D'Agostino, 1986; Ressler, Burgess, Hartman, Douglas, & McCormack, 1986). These researchers interviewed convicted murderers to learn about modus operandi, crime scene characteristics, methods employed to escape detection, and criminal profiles. The typology they proposed (see Table 9.1) contains two principal types of murder: organized (or nonsocial) and disorganized (or asocial). This classification grew out of a study of 36 sexual murderers who collectively were responsible for 118 victims.

Although the FBI typology is, in our opinion, one of the most complete and detailed classifications of sexual homicide available today, it is not without certain faults. Above all, their study focused on the crime phase and the crime scene but neglected the precrime phase.

TABLE 9.1 CRIME SCENE AND PROFILE CHARACTERISTICS OF ORGANIZED AND DISORGANIZED MURDERERS

Organized	Disorganized
Crime scene variables	
Offense planned	Spontaneous offense
Victim a target stranger	Victim or location known
Personalized victim	Depersonalized victim
Controlled conversation	Minimal conversation
Crime scene reflected overall control	Crime scene random and sloppy
Restraints used	Minimal use of restraints
Aggressive acts prior to death	Sexual acts after death
Body hidden	Body left in view
Weapon or evidence absent	Evidence or weapon often present
Transports victim or body	Body left at death scene
Profile characteristics variables	
Good intelligence	Average intelligence
Socially competent	Socially immature
Skilled work preferred	Poor work history
Sexually competent	Sexually incompetent
Inconsistent childhood discipline	Harsh discipline in childhood
Controlled mood during crime	Anxious mood during crime
Use of alcohol with crime	Minimal use of alcohol
Living with partner	Living alone
Mobility with car in good condition	Living or works near crime scene
Followed crime in news media	Minimal interest in news media
May change jobs or leave town	Minimal change in lifestyle

Source: Ressler, Burgess, and Douglas (1988).

As further criticism, Godwin (1998) noted that rather than explaining the differences between organized and disorganized murderers, this typology describes different levels of aggression in sexual homicide. Furthermore, the mixed sexual homicide was added to the typology as a residual category for homicides that did not fit into the other two. Finally, the authors of the FBI typology neglected to provide any explanation regarding the methodology and the clinical and/or statistical analyses used to identify their two principal types of sexual murderers.

The Sadistic Murderer

Recent studies have emphasized a particular type of sexual homicide: the sexually sadistic murderer. Warren, Hazelwood, and Dietz (1996), for instance, examined a sample of 20 sexually sadistic serial murderers drawn from the records of the National Center for the Analysis of Violent Crime (NCAVC). The authors described the principal characteristics of the murderers, their crimes, and their victims. Their results showed that all (100%) of the murderers were men, 95% were White, 75% held a steady job, 70% presented with paraphilias, and 75% collected violent material.

Regarding the crimes themselves, results indicated that 95% of the offenses were highly planned and that 80% involved the use of a con or manipulative strategy to come in contact with victims. Moreover, in 80% of the cases, victims were taken to preselected locations; in 100%, victims were bound, blindfolded, or gagged; in 90%, there was sexual intercourse; in 95%, a sexual ritual occurred; and finally, in 100%, traces of torture were found on the bodies of the victims. As to the victims, 70% were women, 80% were complete strangers to the offenders, and 50% presented certain similarities between them.

In another study on the subject, Gratzer and Bradford (1995) compared 30 sexually sadistic murderers from the NCAVC in the United States with 29 sexually sadistic murderers and 28 nonsadistic sexual offenders from the Royal Ottawa Hospital (ROH) in Canada. Results indicated that a significantly greater proportion of murderers from the NCAVC had bound, blindfolded, or gagged their victims; raped them anally; and forced them to perform fellatio. Furthermore, murderers from the NCAVC were more likely than those from the ROH to commit serial homicides, impersonate police officers, be assisted by a partner, keep victims in captivity for 24 hours or more, and tell victims what to say during the offense. They were also more likely to perform a variety of sexual acts on victims, record the offenses, keep personal items belonging to victims, and conceal victims' corpses.

Finally, Gratzer and Bradford (1995) also investigated differences between the two groups of sadistic murderers with respect to torture. They reported that proportionally more sexually sadistic murderers from the NCAVC penetrated their victims with foreign objects, rendered their victims unconscious through asphyxiation, and beat them.

AIM OF STUDY

Research on sexual homicide conducted to date reveals certain limitations. First, none of the studies of sexual homicide explored in detail the three dimensions of the crime, namely, the offender, the offending process, and the victim. Also, the vast majority of these studies were carried out with participants who had killed more than two victims. This suggests that the primary concern of the research was serial murderers rather than sexual homicide in general. Last, studies of sexual homicide and the typologies derived from them are lacking in empiricism. Most of the researchers who have developed a typology of sexual homicide based their classification on clinical or intuitive judgment, thereby making it almost impossible to verify the validity of their clustering procedures.

The aim of this study was to create a typology of nonserial sexual homicides based on characteristics regarding offense, offender, and victim and using a quantitative methodology, cluster analysis, and a large number of variables relative to the offending process. Furthermore, we verified the precrime and postcrime factors associated with each type of sexual murder.

METHOD

To qualify for this study, participants had to meet at least one criterion of the definition of sexual homicide used by Ressler and colleagues (1986, 1988). In short, evidence or observations had to indicate that the murder was of a sexual nature. This included the following: (a) victim's attire or lack of attire, (b) exposure of the sexual parts of the victim's body, (c) sexual positioning of the victim's body, (d) insertion of foreign objects into the victim's body cavities, (e) evidence of sexual intercourse (oral, anal, vaginal), and (f) evidence of substitute sexual activity, interest, or sadistic fantasy.

We solicited all sexual murderers incarcerated in the province of Quebec in 1998. Of these, 51 consented in writing to participate in the research project; 32 refused. For the purposes of this study, we retained only participants who had killed women 14 years or older. We did not consider murderers who had killed children (13 years or younger) or male adults. This left us with 36 sexual murderers of women 14 years or older.

Each of the 36 participants was interviewed by two male criminologists on the following topics: crime-phase variables (e.g., crime scene variables, acts committed while committing the crime), emotions (e.g., affects before, during, and after the crime), attitudes toward their crimes (e.g., admit all acts committed, negative consequences for victim, responsibility), disinhibitors (e.g., deviant sexual fantasies, alcohol, drugs, pornography), occupational problems (e.g., compulsive work, loss of job), and relationship problems (e.g., loneliness, separation, familial difficulties). Before the interview, we reviewed all the information contained in participants' institutional records. This allowed us to corroborate the information that participants provided during the semistructured interview. In the event of a discrepancy, precedence was always given to official data. We also reviewed police reports of the sexual murders. We went to different police agencies to gather as much information as possible to reconstruct the offenses. We also consulted the autopsy reports and, on occasion, the crime scene photographs.

RESULTS

To determine the best variables to use in developing a typology, we ran chi-square tests on all combinations of the 24 variables of the modus operandi included in our questionnaire. Of the variables, nine were significantly related to other variables. We then entered these nine variables in a K-mean cluster analysis and obtained two profiles of offending processes that discriminate between the two groups. We chose the terms *sadistic* and *anger* as labels for the profiles based on the salient characteristics of the modus operandi for the participants in the two groups. To arrive at a better understanding of these two profiles, we analyzed the relationships between these profiles and all the other variables investigated during the interview, namely, precrime, crime, and postcrime variables.

TABLE 9.2	DISTRIBUTION OF PARTICIPANTS IN TWO PROFILES OF THE OFFENDING PROCESS BY CRIME-PHASE VARIABLES		
		Anger (%) (n = 20)	Sadistic (%) (n = 16)
Premeditated offense**		5	81
Victim unknown to offender (ns)		70	94
Victim selected**		0	79
Victim humiliated**		11	82
Victim mutilated*		10	44
Use of physical restraints during offense*		5	38
Duration of offense more than 30 minutes*		53	87
Victim's body left on crime scene*		84	44
High risk of being apprehended**		35	80

**$p < .01$.
*$p < .05$.
ns = not significant.

As one can see in Table 9.2, 44.4% of our sample (16 participants) fell under the sadistic profile. For these participants, the homicides were premeditated and the victims, often strangers, were selected and humiliated. Physical restraints were used to control victims, and victims' bodies were mutilated. These homicides lasted more than 30 minutes, which increased offenders' risk of being apprehended by the police. After victims died, these offenders often moved the corpses.

Murderers in the anger profile made up 55.6% of our sample (20 participants). These homicides were unplanned, and victims were not preselected. These offenders did not humiliate, use physical restraints against, or mutilate their victims. These homicides lasted less than 30 minutes for almost half of the participants, thereby decreasing the risk of being apprehended. Finally, the bodies of the victims were often left at the crime scenes.

Table 9.3 gives percentages for the crime-phase variables not included in the cluster analysis. Results showed that offenders in the sadistic profile sometimes dismembered the bodies of their victims, which was never the case in the anger profile. Furthermore, victims in anger sexual homicides were more often left on their backs. In sadistic sexual homicides, on the other hand, victims' bodies were sometimes concealed.

Table 9.4 gives the distribution of participants in the two profiles according to emotions felt before, during, and after the crimes. For offenders in the anger profile, anger was predominant before the crime, compared with 33.3% of those in the sadistic profile. A significantly higher proportion of offenders in the sadistic profile, however, reported positive affect before their crimes. Positive affects included joy, sexual arousal, calm, and well-being.

Table 9.5 presents the percentage of participants in the two profiles of the offending process according to variables regarding attitudes of the murderers toward their offenses. Offenders in the anger profile more often gave themselves up to the police than did those in the sadistic profile. Also, under police interrogation, offenders in the anger profile more often admitted all the acts committed against their victims. Finally, all the murderers in the anger profile admitted responsibility for their crimes, compared with 73.3% of those in the sadistic profile.

TABLE 9.3 DISTRIBUTION OF PARTICIPANTS IN TWO PROFILES OF THE OFFENDING PROCESS BY OTHER CRIME-PHASE VARIABLES

	Anger (%) (n = 20)	Sadistic (%) (n = 16)	Total (%) (n = 36)	Phi
Search for distinctive characteristics in victim	25.0	41.7	31.3	0.174
Evidence of premortem torture	10.5	33.3	20.6	0.280
Evidence of postmortem torture	15.8	33.3	23.5	0.205
Use of weapon during offense	80.0	68.8	47.1	0.112
Sexual intercourse during offense	80.0	76.9	78.6	−0.037
Resistance from victim	80.0	92.3	84.8	0.168
Offense committed in evening	70.0	56.3	63.9	−0.142
Corpse of victim dismembered	0.0	18.8	8.8	0.334*
Victim's body left on her back	76.9	33.3	63.2	−0.420
Corpse of victim concealed	0.0	18.8	8.8	0.330

*p < .05.

TABLE 9.4 DISTRIBUTION OF PARTICIPANTS IN TWO PROFILES OF THE OFFENDING PROCESS ACCORDING TO AFFECT BEFORE, DURING, AND AFTER CRIME

	Anger (%) (n = 20)	Sadistic (%) (n = 16)	Total (%) (n = 36)	Phi
Anger before crime	83.3	33.3	63.3	−0.508*
Anger during crime	55.6	53.8	54.8	−0.017
Anger after crime	6.3	0	3.7	−0.163
Calm before crime	5.6	16.7	10.0	0.181
Calm during crime	0	7.7	3.2	0.215
Calm after crime	18.8	36.4	25.9	0.197
Positive affect before crime	11.1	41.7	23.3	0.354**

*p < .05.
**p < .01.

TABLE 9.5 DISTRIBUTION OF PARTICIPANTS IN TWO PROFILES OF THE OFFENDING PROCESS ACCORDING TO VARIABLES REGARDING ATTITUDES TOWARD THEIR CRIMES

	Anger (%) (n = 20)	Sadistic (%) (n = 16)	Total (%) (n = 36)	Phi
Give himself up after committing crime	85.7	25	53.3	−0.607*
Admit crime when arrested	61.1	33.3	48.5	−0.277
Admit all acts committed during offense	100	81.3	91.7	−0.337*
Admit negative consequences for victim	95	75	86.1	−0.287
Admit responsibility	100	73.3	88.6	−0.415*
Admit having a sexual problem	27.8	50	38.2	0.228

*p < .05.

Table 9.6 shows the percentage of participants in the two profiles according to disinhibitor variables. As we can see, there were no significant differences between the two profiles. However, we observed that 50% of offenders in the sadistic profile admitted having sexual fantasies 48 hours before the crime compared with 21.1% of those in the anger profile. Moreover, we noted that almost all the sexual murderers in our sample admitted using alcohol prior to their crimes and that about half of the participants admitted using drugs hours before committing the homicides.

Table 9.7 gives the percentage of participants in the two profiles according to occupational problems 48 hours and 1 year prior to their crimes. Murderers in the anger profile reported significantly more problems of idleness 48 hours before their crimes compared with those in the sadistic profile. Regarding the other variables, there were no significant relationships.

Table 9.8 gives the percentage of participants in the two profiles with respect to variables concerning relationship problems. Offenders in the anger profile experienced significantly more loneliness problems 48 hours before their crimes compared with those in the sadistic profile. Murderers in the sadistic profile, on the other hand, experienced significantly more separation problems 48 hours before the homicides.

TABLE 9.6 **DISTRIBUTION OF PARTICIPANTS IN TWO PROFILES OF THE OFFENDING PROCESS ACCORDING TO DISINHIBITOR VARIABLES**

	Anger (%) ($n = 20$)	Sadistic (%) ($n = 16$)	Total (%) ($n = 36$)	Phi
Use of alcohol hours before crime	85.0	78.6	82.4	−0.083
Use of drugs hours before crime	52.6	50.0	51.5	−0.026
Use of prescription drugs hours before crime	15.0	0	9.1	−0.255
Use of pornography hours before crime	0	0	0	
In a strip club hours before crime	5.3	14.3	7.7	0.150
Deviant sexual fantasies involving victim (48 hours)	5.0	20.0	11.4	0.233
Deviant sexual fantasies involving victim (1 year)	0	0	0	
Deviant sexual fantasies involving person other than victim (48 hours)	21.1	50.0	33.3	0.303
Deviant sexual fantasies involving person other than victim (1 year)	33.3	33.3	33.3	0.000

TABLE 9.7 **DISTRIBUTION OF PARTICIPANTS IN TWO PROFILES OF THE OFFENDING PROCESS ACCORDING TO VARIABLES REGARDING OCCUPATIONAL PROBLEMS**

	Anger (%) ($n = 20$)	Sadistic (%) ($n = 16$)	Total (%) ($n = 36$)	Phi
48 hours before crime				
Compulsive work	5.6	6.7	6.1	0.023
Loss of job	0	13.3	6.1	0.278
Occupational problem of idleness	38.9	0	21.2	−0.474**
1 year before crime				
Compulsive work	11.1	6.7	9.1	−0.077
Loss of job	16.7	20.0	18.2	0.043

**p < .01.

TABLE 9.8 DISTRIBUTION OF PARTICIPANTS IN TWO PROFILES OF THE OFFENDING PROCESS ACCORDING TO VARIABLES REGARDING RELATIONSHIP PROBLEMS

	Anger (%) (n = 20)	Sadistic (%) (n = 16)	Total (%) (n = 36)	Phi
48 hours before crime				
Loneliness problems	22.2	0	12.1	−0.339*
Separation problems	0	26.7	12.1	0.407*
Conjugal difficulties	16.7	0	9.1	−0.289
Familial difficulties	5.6	0	3.0	−0.161
Perceived rejection	52.9	50.0	52.0	−0.027
Other relational problems	5.6	6.7	6.1	0.023
1 year before crime				
Loneliness problems	27.8	0	15.2	−0.386*
Separation problems	22.2	26.7	24.2	0.052
Conjugal difficulties	27.8	13.3	21.2	−0.176
Familial difficulties	27.8	6.7	18.2	−0.273
Perceived rejection	58.8	37.5	52.0	−0.199
Other relational problems	5.6	6.7	6.1	0.023

*$p < .05$.

In the year preceding their murders, offenders in the anger profile experienced significantly more loneliness problems than did those in the sadistic profile. Finally, we observed that about half of our sample of sexual murderers felt rejection 48 hours and 1 year before committing the crimes.

DISCUSSION

The study conducted by the FBI identified two types of serial sexual murderers based on crime-phase and crime-scene characteristics. Despite the difference in the number of victims between the studies, it is interesting to compare our two profiles with their two murderer types. The organized sexual murder shares certain similarities with the sadistic profile. In both cases, the homicide is highly planned, physical restraints are used, and the victim is unknown to the offender. Moreover, the offense is committed in a controlled manner, the offender demands the victim's submission, and there is evidence of physical aggression before the death of the victim. Afterward, the victim's body is moved and concealed in a different location from the crime scene. The anger profile and the disorganized sexual murder share the following characteristics: absence of planning, absence of physical restraints, and absence of moving the victim's body.

There are, however, three significant differences between the pathways and their corresponding FBI types. First, in our study, mutilation was characteristic of the sadistic pathway. In the FBI study, on the other hand, this was more frequently associated with the disorganized murderer. We might venture that this difference is due to the organized murderer's need to control. In this way, acts of mutilation do not reflect one person's control over a crime scene. For the organized murderer, this could be a way to escape a hazardous crime scene and thus prevent evidence of fingerprints left on the victim's body.

The second feature separating the two studies is directly related to the first one. Our results suggest that the sadistic murderer runs a higher risk of being caught by the police after the offense. Results from the FBI study, on the other hand, indicated that the disorganized murderer is more likely to be caught after the crime, essentially because of all the evidence left at the crime scene. We believe, however, that this difference is due to the fact that this variable does not measure the same thing in the two studies. As mentioned earlier, the FBI study used the presence of evidence or of the weapon at the crime scene to estimate risk of apprehension. In our study, however, we estimated that risk of apprehension would be greater if the crime phase lasted longer and if the victim's body was moved to another location after the murder.

Finally, the third aspect that distinguished our two profiles from the two FBI profiles concerns the positioning of the victim's body after the homicide. The disorganized offender is known to position the victim's body in a sexually explicit manner to shock and offend the people who discover the corpse. This practice is not consistent with the behavior of the anger murderer, who instead leaves the deceased victim on her back at the crime scene. It may be that this particular behavior of the disorganized murderer is due to his mental state at the time of the homicide. According to Ressler et al. (1988), the disorganized murderer presents certain similarities with the psychotic offender, including loss of contact with reality. Offenders in the anger profile, on the other hand, present some characteristics of the borderline personality disorder (e.g., emotional instability, impulsiveness), which may explain why they commit their crimes impulsively and run away from the crime scene once the victim is dead.

We also compared our results with those obtained by Warren et al. (1996), who described the characteristics of 20 sexual sadists. Their findings showed that sadistic murderers carefully planned their offenses (95%), used physical restraints (100%), had sexual intercourse with the victims (90%), and mutilated the bodies in 100% of the cases. They also reported that the offenders' victims were women in 70% of the cases and strangers in 80%. By comparison, our study revealed that 81% of the sadistic murderers planned their offenses, 38% used physical restraints to control victims during the offenses, and 77% had sexual intercourse with the victims. We also observed that 44% mutilated the victims, who in 94% of the cases were strangers.

We believe the discrepant figures between the two studies can in large part be attributed to the fact that Warren et al. (1996) focused specifically on serial sexual sadists. It is well recognized that the offending processes of serial sexual murderers are highly planned and repetitive and aim to fulfill their sexual fantasies. Moreover, we know that their offending processes become more sophisticated and more violent with each subsequent homicide (Gratzer & Bradford, 1995).

This difference between serial sexual sadistic murderers and nonserial sexual sadists was well illustrated in the study by Gratzer and Bradford (1995). These authors suggested three hypotheses. The first is that the sexual sadists from the NCAVC were higher functioning than were those from the ROH, as evidenced by the fact that a greater proportion of the former were married, had more than a high school education, and had established a reputation as a solid citizen. The second hypothesis is that the higher functioning sadists from the NCAVC were able to avoid detection for a greater length of time. This allowed an escalation in sadistic behavior, with each new offense fueling increasingly deviant and elaborate sadistic fantasies. Finally, these differences may be related to characterological differences. In this regard, the authors noted that the serial sadists from the NCAVC presented with more features of a narcissistic personality, including grandiosity, lack of empathy, and demand for admiration from victims. By contrast, the sadists from the ROH presented with more features of an antisocial personality disorder. These characterological differences reflect the different crime characteristics of the two groups: Sadists from the NCAVC committed more elaborate crimes, and those from the ROH committed more impulsive crimes (Gratzer & Bradford, 1995).

The only study of sexual homicide aside from ours to have investigated the affective state of murderers was the one conducted by the FBI, and even then, only affect before the crime was explored. The results of this study indicated that organized murderers felt more angry and depressed and less afraid and confused than did disorganized murderers. Although we looked at affect before, during, and after the crime, only the precrime results yielded significant differences. These differences suggest that anger murderers feel anger before the crimes, whereas sadistic murderers have a positive affect. Offenders in the anger profile tend to commit their crimes in reaction to something that upsets them; they commit their crimes in a burst of rage. Offenders in the sadistic profile, on the other hand, commit crimes that arouse them or that they enjoy doing.

Two hypotheses may help explain the differences in the affect results between these two studies. First, the FBI researchers may not have been investigating the affect variables in the same manner that we did; indeed, they may not have covered positive affects. Second, it is also possible that the pathological character and motivations of serial sexual murderers are different from sexual murderers who killed only one victim.

Our study also examined attitudes of murderers after their crimes. We observed that offenders in the anger profile give themselves up to the police after committing the crimes, collaborate during the investigations, admit all the acts committed during the offenses, and also admit their responsibility for the homicides more often than do offenders in the sadistic profile. We ventured that this was related primarily to differences in personality between the two types of murderer. We also hypothesized that murderers in the anger profile were marked by a borderline personality. This type of personality is characterized by impulsive acts and inappropriate and intense anger. Beck and Freeman (1990) mentioned that when murderers with this type of personality become conscious of the irrationality of their acts, they feel guilt and remorse. We believe that personality type might explain why anger murderers act this way after their crimes.

Last, our results showed murderers in the anger profile to be vulnerable to guilt. Furthermore, the fact that they did not bother to remove evidence suggests impulsivity on their part. Thus, an investigator who must question this type of murderer could take advantage of these two weaknesses and increase the chances of obtaining a confession from the murderer.

CONCLUSION

Our study enabled us to identify two profiles in the offending process in a sample of 36 sexual murderers of women 14 years or older. However, this research contains certain limitations. The most important, in our opinion, is the small number of participants that took part in the study. Even if the other studies conducted so far did not involve a larger number of participants, we know that we must be careful in interpreting and generalizing these results. A cross-validation study with another sample is certainly an interesting option. Unfortunately, other databases on sexual murderers mainly include serial sexual murderers, whereas our sample included primarily nonserial sexual murderers (34 out of 36). In addition, due to our sampling procedure, our sample of sexual murderers is close to a population of sexual murderers of women incarcerated in the province of Quebec in 1998. In fact, we assessed 36 of these 46 sexual murderers. Consequently, our sample is quite representative of the sexual murderer population in Quebec. As to the other studies of sexual murderers (e.g., NCAVC database), sampling procedure did not permit us to conclude that their samples are representative of the population of sexual murderers in the place and at the time where data had been gathered. Finally, because data collection in other studies was based on interview protocols different from our protocol, variables are probably not defined in the exact same way as in our study. Thus, a cross-validation study is not actually possible.

The typology of sexual homicides that we proposed, however, is based on a quantitative method and on a wide variety of variables concerning offense, offender, and victim. Consequently, we believe that it can be useful to criminologists, psychologists, and all other clinicians whose work places them in contact with this clientele. We also believe that this classification could serve the purposes of police investigation. It could be used in criminal investigative analysis (profiling) to help investigators classify the characteristics of the crime, victim, and offender to identify potential suspects (Homant & Kennedy, 1998; Knight, Warren, Reboussin, & Soley, 1998). It could then help investigators in the interrogation of these suspects.

ACKNOWLEDGEMENTS

The views expressed are those of the authors and are not necessarily those of the Correctional Service of Canada. We wish to thank Jean-Pierre Guay, Marc Ouimet, and Maurice Cusson for their comments on this study. We also wish to thank Paul DiBiase for his substantive and stylistic editing.

REFERENCES

Beck, A.T., & Freeman, A. (1990). *Cognitive therapy of personality disorders*. New York: Guilford.

Bénézech, M. (1997). L'homicide sexuel: Diagnostic et classement criminologique [Sexual homicide: Diagnostic and criminological classification]. *Journal de Médecine Légale Droit Médical, 40*(4), 289-294.

Brittain, R. (1970). The sadistic murderer. *Medicine, Science and the Law, 10*, 198-207.

Burgess, A.W., Hartman, C.R., Ressler, R.K., Douglas, J.E., & McCormack, A. (1986). Sexual homicide: A motivational model. *Journal of Interpersonal Violence, 1*, 251-272.

Geberth, V.J. (1996). *Practical homicide investigation: Tactics, procedures, and forensic techniques* (3rd ed.). Boca Raton, FL: CRC Press.

Godwin, M. (1998). Reliability, validity and utility of extant serial murderer classifications. *The Criminologist, 22*, 194-210.

Gratzer, T., & Bradford, J.M. (1995). Offender and offense characteristics of sexual sadists: A comparative study. *Journal of Forensic Sciences, 40*, 450-455.

Holmes, R.M., & De Burger, J. (1988). *Serial murder*. Newbury Park, CA: Sage.

Homant, R.J., & Kennedy, D.B. (1998). Psychological aspects of crime scene profiling: Validity research. *Criminal Justice and Behavior, 25*, 306-319.

Knight, R.A., Warren, J.I., Reboussin, R., & Soley, B.J. (1998). Predicting rapist type from crime scene variables. *Criminal Justice and Behavior, 25*, 30-46.

Krafft-Ebing, R.V. (1998). *Psychopathia sexualis. The complete English-language translation*. New York: Arcade. (Original work published 1886)

Money, J. (1990). Forensic sexology: Paraphilic serial rape (biastophilia) and lust murder (erotophonophilia). *American Journal of Psychotherapy, 44*, 26-37.

Ressler, R.K., Burgess, A.W., & Douglas, J.E. (1988). *Sexual homicide: patterns and motives*. New York: Free Press.

Ressler, R.K., Burgess, A.W., Douglas, J.E., Hartman, C.R., & D'Agostino, R.B. (1986). Sexual killers and their victims: Identifying patterns through crime scene analysis. *Journal of Interpersonal Violence, 1,* 288-308.

Ressler, R.K., Burgess, A.W., Hartman, C.R., Douglas, J.E., & McCormack, A. (1986). Murderers who rape and mutilate. *Journal of Interpersonal Violence, 1,* 273-287.

Revitch, E., & Schlesinger, L.B. (1989). *Sex murder and sex aggression; Phenomenology, psychopathology, psychodynamics and prognosis.* Springfield, IL: Charles C Thomas.

Warren, J.I., Hazelwood, R.R., & Dietz, P.E. (1996). The sexually sadistic serial killer. *Journal of Forensic Sciences, 41,* 970-974.

Eric Beauregard, M.Sc.
Ph.D. Candidate
School of Criminology
University of Montreal
Montreal, Canada

Jean Proulx, Ph.D.
School of Criminology
University of Montreal
Montreal, Canada

E. Beauregard and J. Proulx, *Journal of offender therapy and comparative criminology*, August, vol. 46, no. 4, 2002, pp. 386-99.

THREAT ASSESSMENT: AN APPROACH TO PREVENT TARGETED VIOLENCE

ROBERT A. FEIN, PH.D.,

BRYAN VOSSEKUIL, AND GWEN A. HOLDEN

On April 25, 1993, 25 abortion protesters gathered at the Brookline home of a doctor who performed abortions at the Preterm Health Services clinic on nearby Beacon Street.

It was a Sunday afternoon, just a few weeks after antiabortion activist Michael Griffin had gunned down Dr. David Gunn at a Pensacola, Florida abortion clinic. The protesters sensed that Gunn's murder, the first in the abortion war, had somehow changed the movement—a clear escalation of the violence.

As Mary Schumacher, then the executive director of Operation Rescue in Massachusetts, led the group in prayer, she described how Griffin could not be "prolife" if he killed someone. She called Gunn's death a "tragedy" and asked the protesters to pray for him.

Just then one of the protesters—a young man with a face twisted in anger—interrupted the prayer. "You need a talking to," he said to Schumacher.

After the prayer, the man confronted Schumacher and spoke about the failure of the Catholic Church to fight hard enough against abortion. "How can you say that Gunn's death was a tragedy? He was killing the innocent. Griffin was a hero as far as I'm concerned," Schumacher remembers the man saying, his voice filled with rage.

"I remember it well, especially the part when he said Griffin was a hero," said Schumacher, referring to her 1993 encounter..."It was not the kind of conversation you forget. I even alerted a police officer that day about it. You could tell the guy was not stable."

Boston Globe, 1/8/95 (emphasis added)

The man described in the *Boston Globe* article who was reported to the police that day in 1993 was John C. Salvi III. Less than a year later, on December 30, 1994, Salvi allegedly opened fire on the Preterm and Planned Parenthood clinics in Brookline, Massachusetts, killing two and wounding five persons. Salvi has been charged with committing an act of "targeted violence," a term that refers to situations in which an identifiable (or potentially identifiable) perpetrator poses (or may pose) a threat of violence to a particular individual or group.

Increasingly, Americans have been confronted with such incidents of targeted violence, both actual or threatened. Behaviors characterized as "stalking," workplace violence, and attacks on public figures and officials are frequently reported in the media. Recently, those reports have concerned

10.1 *Highlights*

In the past 5 years, violent crimes involving stalking, workplace violence, and attacks or threatened attacks on public figures and officials have been prominent in the news. Law enforcement and security professionals are turning to prevention as an important component of control strategy. This Research in Action discusses operational and investigative tools and approaches that can be effectively used to recognize, evaluate, and manage the risks oftarget–ed violence before crimes occur.

OF SPECIAL INTEREST:

- Threats of violence arise from feelings or ideas that range from the mean-spirited to the messianic. Sometimes a threat is backed by the will and capacity to do harm; at other times, a voiced threat may amount to nothing but emotional "venting." However, violent acts can be committed when no prior threat has been uttered. For law enforcement and security officers, recognizing the difference between "making" and "posing" a threat is crucially important.

- Perpetrators of violence often have a traceable history of problems, conflicts, disputes, and failures. Violent behavior may be triggered by these individuals' perception that it provides a means to rectify or avenge an injustice or wrongdoing. Targeted violence can be premeditated or opportunistic when a situation arises that facilitates or permits the violence or does not prevent it from occurring.

- The first component of threat assessment case management involves developing a plan that moves the subject away from regarding violence as a viable option.

- Information about a subject's coping ability during periods of great stress, including any contemplated or attempted violence against others or self, is of special interest in a threat assessment investigation. Other behavioral data—such as obsessive or undue interest in a potential target, or efforts made to secure or practice with weapons—also is helpful.

- Interviews of subjects should be considered as part of the investigation's overall strategy. However, sometimes an interview may stimulate the interest, and may even increase the desperation or anxiety level, of a subject and thus could precipitate violence when it may not have occurred otherwise.

- The target in a threat assessment case needs to be evaluated in terms of vulnerability to attack, job and personal lifestyle, fear of the subject, and degree of sophistication with regard to the need for caution.

- Documentation of data and consultation with experts are key aspects in implementing a case management strategy.

- A case can be considered for closing when the subject is deemed to no longer be a threat. Questions should be asked regarding what changed circumstances could trigger the subject to move toward violent behavior.

---

violent attacks occurring in settings (such as health clinics, schools, the workplace, or a Long Island commuter train) where unsuspecting victims believed themselves to be safe. Often the perpetrators of these attacks are subsequently found to have given advance notice of their violent inclinations.

INVESTIGATIVE AND OPERATIONAL TECHNIQUES

Traditional law enforcement activities aim at apprehending and prosecuting perpetrators of violence *after* the commission of their crimes. In most circumstances, the primary responsibility of law enforcement professionals is to determine whether a crime has been committed, conduct an investigation to identify and apprehend the perpetrator, and gather evidence to assist prosecutors in a criminal trial. However, when police officers are presented with information and concern about a *possible future* violent crime, their responsibilities, authority, and investigative tools and approaches are less clear. "Threat assessment" is the term used to describe the set of investigative and operational techniques that can be used by law enforcement professionals to identify, assess, and manage the risks of targeted violence and its potential perpetrators.

"Making" versus "posing" a threat

Individuals utter threats for many reasons, only some of which involve intention or capacity to commit a violent act. However, a person can present a grave threat without articulating it. The distinction between *making* and *posing* a threat is important:

- Some persons who make threats ultimately pose threats.

- Many persons who make threats do not pose threats.

- Some persons who pose threats never make threats.

Targeting the victim

Postponing action until a threat has been made can detract attention from investigation of factors more relevant to the risk of violence, e.g, a potential perpetrator's selection of possible targets. Data from two recent studies suggest that at least some approachers—and attackers—of public officials/figures show an interest in more than one target.[1] U.S. Secret Service experience indicates that a number of would-be Presidential assassins, such as Arthur Bremer and John Hinckley, considered several targets, and changed targets, before finally making an attack. Data on relationship stalking murders and work-place violence murders point to suicide, as well as homicide, as a possible outcome.[2] These examples suggest that, in some cases, the perpetrator may ultimately become his or her own final target.

---

[1] Dietz, P.E. and D.A. Martell, "Mentally Disordered Offenders in Pursuit of Celebrities and Politicians," National Institute of Justice, Washington, D.C., 1989, 83–NI–AX–0005; Dietz, P.E., D.B. Matthews, D.A. Martell, T.M. Stewart, D.R. Hrouda and J. Warren, "Threatening and Otherwise Inappropriate Letters to Members of the United States Congress," *Journal of Forensic Sciences*, 36 (September 5, 1991):1445-1468; Dietz, P.E., D.B. Matthews, C. Van Duyne, D.A. Martell, C.D.H. Parry, T.M. Stewart, J. Warren and J.D. Crowder, "Threatening and Otherwise Inappropriate Letters to Hollywood Celebrities," *Journal of Forensic Sciences*, 36 (January 1, 1991):185-209; and Fein, R.A. and B. Vossekuil, "The Secret Service Exceptional Case Study Project: An Examination of Violence Against Public Officials and Public Figures," National Institute of Justice, study in progress, 92–CX–0013.

[2] For example, both Thomas McIlvane, in the Royal Oak, Michigan post office attack, and Alan Winterbourne, in the Oxnard, California unemployment office attack, killed themselves.

LEGAL SANCTIONS

The threat of sanctions, such as a long prison sentence, may not deter a person who desperately desires revenge or is prepared to die to achieve his objective. Passage of enforceable laws that define and prohibit behaviors that could presage violent attacks is one important step in preventing such attacks. Forty-nine States have passed antistalking laws in the past 4 years, and the National Institute of Justice, together with the National Criminal Justice Association, published a model antistalking law.[3] Additionally, authorities in some jurisdictions are reviewing various threat and harassment laws to determine whether they might apply to threat-of-violence situations. However, laws by themselves are unlikely to prevent stalking, workplace, or public figure–centered violence, unless law enforcement and security professionals know how to identify, evaluate, and manage persons at risk of committing these violent acts.

FUNDAMENTAL PRINCIPLES OF THREAT ASSESSMENT

Notwithstanding the growing importance of threat assessment for law enforcement and security professionals, systematic thinking and guidance in this area have been lacking. The law enforcement and security communities currently do not have clearly articulated processes or procedures to steer their actions when they are made aware of threat-of-violence subjects and situations. Without guidelines for making threat assessments, otherwise competent law enforcement professionals may be less thoughtful and thorough than they might be in handling such incidents. To fill the void, this report presents four fundamental principles that underlie threat assessment investigation and management. They are followed by a model and process for conducting comprehensive threat assessment investigations.

- Violence is a process, as well as an act. Violent behavior does not occur in a vacuum. Careful analysis of violent incidents shows that violent acts often are the culmination of long-developing, identifiable trails of problems, conflicts, disputes, and failures.

- Violence is the product of an interaction among three factors:

  a. The *individual* who takes violent action.

  b. *Stimulus or triggering conditions* that lead the subject to see violence as an option, "way out," or solution to problems or life situation.

  c. *A setting that facilitates or permits the violence*, or at least does not stop it from occurring.

- A key to investigation and resolution of threat assessment cases is identification of the subject's "attack-related" behaviors. Perpetrators of targeted acts of violence engage in discrete behaviors that precede and are linked to their attacks; they consider, plan, and prepare before engaging in violent actions.

- Threatening situations are more likely to be successfully investigated and managed if other agencies and systems—both within and outside law enforcement or security organizations—are recognized and used to help solve problems presented by a given case. Examples of such

---

[3] National Criminal Justice Association, *Project to Develop a Model Anti-Stalking Code for States*, National Institute of Justice, Washington, D.C., 1993.

systems are those employed by prosecutors; courts; probation, corrections, social service, and mental health agencies; employee assistance programs; victim's assistance programs; and community groups.

FUNCTIONS OF A THREAT ASSESSMENT PROGRAM

The three major functions of a threat assessment program are: identification of a potential perpetrator, assessment of the risks of violence posed by a given perpetrator at a given time, and management of both the subject and the risks that he or she presents to a given target.

IDENTIFYING THE PERPETRATOR

The process of identifying a potential perpetrator involves: (1) defining criteria that could lead to a person becoming a subject of a threat assessment investigation; (2) determining the areas within the law enforcement or security organization that will be responsible for receiving information about possible subjects and conducting threat assessment investigations; (3) notifying those individuals and organizations that might come in contact with—or know of—potential subjects about the existence of a threat assessment program; and (4) educating notified individuals and organizations about the criteria for bringing a concern about potential violence to the attention of investigators.

ASSESSING THE RISKS

The second goal of a threat assessment program is to evaluate the risks persons under suspicion may pose to particular targets. Risk assessment involves two primary functions: investigation and evaluation.

Investigation

The primary objective of a risk assessment investigation is to gather information on a subject and on potential targets. Multiple sources of information should be consulted to learn about a subject's behavior, interests, and state of mind at various points in time:

- Personal interviews with the subject.

- Material created or possessed by the subject, including journals and letters, and materials collected by the subject, such as books and magazines, that may relate to the investigation.

- Persons who know or have known the subject, including family members, friends, coworkers, supervisors, neighbors, landlords, law enforcement officers, social service or mental health staff, and previous victims of unacceptable behavior (including violence) committed by the subject.

- Record or archival information, including police, court, probation, and correctional records; mental health and social service records; and notes made by those aware of the subject's interest in a particular target, such as security personnel, managers, victims, or colleagues.

Information about the subject

At the beginning of a threat assessment investigation, it is important to secure detailed descriptions of the subject's behaviors and actions that prompted other persons to notice the subject. The kinds of information useful for threat assessment include data about overwhelmingly or unbearably stressful experiences and the subject's ability to cope at such times. Behavioral data about the subject's motives, intentions, and capacities is critical; of particular importance is information about attack-related behaviors:

- The subject has expressed interest in possible targets, including particular, identifiable targets.

- The subject has communicated with or about potential targets.

- The subject has considered and/or attempted to harm self or others.

- The subject has secured or practiced with weapons.

- The subject has followed or approached potential targets, either with or without weapons, at events or occasions.

Interviewing the subject

Whether to interview the subject of a threat assessment investigation can be a key question; the decision depends on several factors:

- The investigator's need for information.

- The facts leading to initiation of investigation.

- The investigator's legal standing in relation to the subject.

- The resources available to the investigator.

- The investigator's training and experience in interviewing.

- The stage of the investigation.

- The investigator's strategy for resolving the case.

A decision to interview a subject should be made on the basis of case facts. Generally, when there has been face-to-face contact between subject and target or the subject has communicated a threat to the target, an interview is a good idea. An interview under such circumstances may have several goals. It may signal that the subject's behavior has been noticed, permit the subject's story to be related to a third party, gather information that is the basis for corroboration, and provide an opportunity for communicating that the subject's behavior is unwelcome, unacceptable, and must cease.

Any interview is a vehicle for gathering information about the subject that can be used to assess the threat that a subject poses and to manage that threat. Therefore, threat assessment interviews are most productive if they are conducted respectfully and professionally. The task of the investigator is twofold: to gather information about the subject's thinking, behavior patterns, and activities regarding the target(s) and to encourage change in the subject's behavior. By showing an interest in the subject's life that is neither unduly friendly nor harsh, an investigator can increase the likelihood of the interview's success.

10.2   *Possible Indicators of Potential Trouble*

- "My former spouse keeps calling me, cursing, and hanging up."

- "Coworkers report that Jones seems obsessed with getting even with Rogers."

- "Smith is talking about blowing away the Governor. I think he has a gun. He was just turned down on the appeal of his case for worker's compensation."

- "The Judge got her fifth letter this year from Harris telling her that he loves her passionately."

- "The CEO's office just got a call from Doe saying that the Chairman's life is in danger."

- "I know I only met him once, but I know that he loves me; once his wife is out of the way, we can be together always."

In some cases, however, an interview may intensify the subject's interest in the target or increase the risk of lethal behavior. For example, a subject who has written a letter to a celebrity professing undying love and formally proposing marriage, *but who has engaged in no other known behavior in relation to the celebrity*, may have his or her interest stimulated by an interview. Without an interview, the subject's interest may dissipate. Similarly, a desperate and suicidal subject, self-perceived as having been abandoned, who has been stalking a former partner, may sense that time is running out and be prompted by an interview to engage in more extreme behavior before "they put me away. In such a circumstance, the investigator may need to expend additional resources, perhaps increasing security for the target, arranging hospitalization or arrest of the subject, or monitoring or surveilling the subject. Subject interviews, therefore, should be considered and conducted within the context of overall investigative strategy.

Information about the target

A man who, over days and weeks, has been following a secretary whom he met once, but with whom he has no relationship, appears to have picked out a potential target. An employee, fired by a manager whom he blames for discriminating against him and causing the breakup of his family, has told former coworkers that he will "get even"; once again, a potential target appears to have been selected. To prevent violence, the threat assessment investigator requires information on the targeted individual. Relevant questions about the target might include:

- Are potential targets identifiable, or does it appear that the subject, if considering violence, has not yet selected targets for possible attack?

- Is the potential target well known to the subject? Is the subject acquainted with a targeted individual's work and personal lifestyle, patterns of living, daily comings and goings?

- Is the potential target vulnerable to an attack? Does the targeted individual have the resources to arrange for physical security? What might change in the target's lifestyle or living arrangements that could make attack by the subject more difficult or less likely, e.g., is the targeted individual planning to move, spend more time at home, or take a new job?

- Is the target afraid of the subject? Is the targeted individual's degree of fear shared by family, friends, and/or colleagues?

- How sophisticated or naive is the targeted individual about the need for caution? How able is the individual to communicate a clear and consistent "I want no contact with you" message to the subject?

EVALUATION

A 2-stage process is suggested to evaluate information gathered about the subject and the potential target(s). In the first stage, information is evaluated for evidence of conditions and behaviors that would be consistent with an attack. The second stage of evaluation seeks to determine whether the subject appears to be moving *toward* or *away* from an attack. After analyzing the available data, the threat assessor is left with these questions:

- Does it appear more or less likely that violent action will be directed by the subject against the target(s)? What specific information and reasoning lead to this conclusion?

- How close is the subject to attempting an attack? What thresholds, if any, have been crossed (e.g., has the subject violated court orders, made a will, given away personal items, expressed willingness to die or to be incarcerated)?

- What might change in the *subject's* life to increase or decrease the risk of violence? What might change in the target's situation to increase or decrease the risk of violence?

CASE MANAGEMENT

The first component of threat assessment case management involves developing a plan that moves the subject away from regarding violence against the target as a viable option. Such a plan is likely to draw on resources from systems within the threat assessment unit's parent organization, as well as those outside it. The second component is plan implementation. The best developed and supported case management plan will be of little use in preventing violence if the plan is not implemented and monitored. The plan must remain flexible to accommodate changes in the subject's life and circumstances. The final management component is formal closing of the case.

Case plan development

Once an evaluator determines that a given subject presents a risk of violence to a targeted individual, the next task is to develop a plan to manage the subject and the risk. The evaluator then proceeds to identify those internal and external systems that may be helpful in managing the problems presented by the subject. In certain situations, such as those in which the subject has been stalking an identifiable target in a jurisdiction that has an enforceable and effective anti-stalking law, the best way to prevent violence and minimize harm to the targeted individual may be to prosecute the case vigorously. A good relationship between threat assessment investigators and prosecutors can influence the priority assigned to the case and the extent to which prosecutorial and judicial processes facilitate its resolution. Such relationships also may affect the court's disposition of the case, including sentencing of a convicted offender.

Even conviction and imprisonment, however, do not guarantee that the target will be safe from the subject. If the subject has been unable or unwilling to let go of the idea of a relationship with the target, or if the subject attributes the pains and misfortunes of his or her life to the targeted individual, it may make sense to consider strategies by which the subject is encouraged to change the direction, or intensity, of his interest. A subject engaged in activities that bring success and satisfaction is less likely to remain preoccupied with a failed relationship. Family, friends, neighbors, or associates may play a role in suggesting and supporting changes in the subject's thinking and behavior. In addition, mental health and social service staff may be of great assistance in aiding the subject to formulate more appropriate goals and develop skills and strengths that are likely to result in life successes.

At least one aspect of a case management plan concerns the target. If the subject is to be prohibited from contact with the target, the target needs to understand what to do (i.e., whom to call and how to contact the official handling the case) if the subject initiates direct or indirect contact.

Case management implementation

The most carefully crafted plan will have little effect if it remains in the investigator's files and is not translated into action.

Although no procedures or techniques can guarantee that a subject of comprehensive threat assessment will not attempt violent action toward a target, two activities are known to help reduce the risk of violence, and, in the instance of a bad outcome, assist the threat assessment team in any post-incident review.

First, documentation of data and reasoning at every stage of a threat assessment investigation is essential. Undocumented or poorly documented information-gathering and analysis are suspect in and of themselves, and they provide little foundation for review or for efforts to learn from—and improve on—experience. Without clear documentation, investigators are left with only their recollections, which can be both partial and faulty and are subject to criticism as retrospective reconstruction. A carefully and comprehensively documented record may be criticized for imperfect data-gathering or flawed analysis, but such a record also demonstrates both thoughtfulness and good faith—critical questions in any postincident review.

Second, consultation at every major stage of the threat assessment process can be a significant case management tool. Consultants may be members of the threat assessment unit or external experts. To be effective, a consultant should be knowledgeable in areas relevant to the case and be known and trusted by the investigators. For example, in a case where a subject has a history of diagnosed mental disorders and the primary investigator is unfamiliar with mental health language and concepts used in the records, an expert in psychology or psychiatry can provide invaluable insight and advice.

In addition to providing special expertise, consultants may notice and ask about questions in a case that remain to be explored or answered. Even proficient investigators are occasionally vulnerable to "missing the forest for the trees." A consultant, such as a fellow threat assessment specialist who has not been involved with the case, may offer a comment that can redirect or sharpen an ongoing investigation. In the event of a bad outcome, use and documentation of consultant expertise may demonstrate that the threat assessment team sought additional perspectives and ideas and did not get stuck with "tunnel vision."

Closing the case

The final task of threat assessment case management is closing the case. When a threat assessor determines that the subject has moved far enough away from possible violent action toward the target to no longer cause appreciable concern, the case can be considered for closing. At this time, it may be important to ask:

- What has changed in the subject's life that appears to lessen the likelihood that the subject is interested in or will attempt violent action toward the target?

- Which components of the case management plan seemed to affect the subject's thinking or capacity to initiate violent action, and to what extent?

- What life circumstances might occur that would again put the subject at increased risk of contemplating, planning, or attempting violent action toward the original target or other potential targets?

- Are there supports in place (or that can be developed) that will be known and available to the subject at a future time when the subject is again at risk of moving toward violent behavior?

While social commentators and analysts may debate the myriad reasons that lead to growing national concern about targeted violence, law enforcement and security organizations are increasingly being called on to examine individual situations and make judgments and determinations about the risks of violence that one person might present to an identifiable target. In cases related to stalking behaviors, workplace violence, attacks on public officials and figures, and other situations where targeted violence is a possibility, comprehensive and carefully conducted threat assessment investigations can safeguard potential targets, deter potential attackers, and serve the public.

Points of view in this document are those of the authors and do not necessarily reflect the official position of the U.S. Department of Justice.

Robert A. Fein, Ph.D., a Visiting Fellow at the National Institute of Justice, is a Consultant Psychologist for the U.S. Secret Service; Bryan Vossekuil is Assistant Special Agent in Charge, Intelligence Division, U.S. Secret Service; and Gwen A. Holden serves as Executive Vice President of the National Criminal Justice Association.

"Threat Assessment: An Approach to Prevent Targeted Violence" by Robert A. Fein, Ph.D., Bryan Vossekuil, and Gwen, National Institute of Justice Research in Action, 1995.

KIDNAPING OF JUVENILES: PATTERNS FROM NIBRS

DAVID FINKELHOR AND RICHARD ORMROD

The Office of Juvenile Justice and Delinquency Prevention (OJJDP) is committed to improving the justice system's response to crimes against children. OJJDP recognizes that children are at increased risk for crime victimization. Not only are children the victims of many of the same crimes that victimize adults, they are subject to other crimes, like child abuse and neglect, that are specific to childhood. The impact of these crimes on young victims can be devastating, and the violent or sexual victimization of children can often lead to an intergenerational cycle of violence and abuse. The purpose of OJJDP's Crimes Against Children Series is to improve and expand the Nation's efforts to better serve child victims by presenting the latest information about child victimization, including analyses of crime victimization statistics, studies of child victims and their special needs, and descriptions of programs and approaches that address these needs.

The kidnaping of children has generated a great deal of public concern, not to mention confusion and controversy. These crimes, from the kidnaping of the Lindbergh baby to the abduction and murder of Adam Walsh, have been some of the most notorious and highly publicized news stories of recent history, occupying a central place in the fears and anxieties of parents. Yet, an ongoing debate has raged over how frequently such crimes occur, which children are most at risk, and who the primary offenders are.

Part of the problem has been confusion about the definition of kidnaping. While lengthy ransom abductions and the tragic recovery of bodies have molded the public's perception of the crime, in a strict legal sense, kidnaping also involves both short-term and short-distance displacements, acts common to many sexual assaults and robberies. Kidnaping occurs whenever a person is taken or detained against his or her will and includes hostage situations, whether or not the victim is moved. Moreover, kidnaping is not limited to the acts of strangers but can be committed by acquaintances, by romantic partners, and, as has been increasingly true in recent years, by parents who are involved in acrimonious custody disputes.

Confusion about kidnaping has been exacerbated by the absence of reliable statistics about the crime. Kidnaping is not one of the crimes included in the Federal Bureau of Investigation's (FBI's) national Uniform Crime Reporting (UCR) system, and individual States or other jurisdictions have rarely made any independent tally of kidnaping statistics. As a result, a national picture of, or even a large data set about, this crime from the law enforcement perspective has been unavailable. In the past, several attempts were made to collect abduction data, but they were limited in scope or time. For example, OJJDP's 1988 National Incidence Studies of Missing, Abducted, Runaway, and

11.1   *A Message From OJJDP*

The kidnaping of a child is a crime that tears at the fabric of society. Until recently, the nature and scope of the problem have been unclear because existing crime data collection systems—such as the FBI's Uniform Crime Reporting (UCR) system and OJJDP's National Incidence Studies of Missing, Abducted, Runaway, and Thrown-away Children—do not collect law enforcement data on kidnaping.

Fortunately, that is about to change. In partnership with the Bureau of Justice Statistics, the FBI is supplanting the UCR with the National Incident-Based Reporting System (NIBRS). This will enhance

our understanding of youth abduction and create a comprehensive picture of kidnaping offenses.

This Bulletin describes the offense of kidnaping of juveniles, using 1997 NIBRS data. Among other significant findings, the analysis reveals that such abductions are relatively uncommon, that there are three distinct kinds of perpetrators, and that the rate of juvenile kidnaping peaks in the afternoon.

The better we understand this serious crime, the more effective our efforts will be to prevent and respond to it. NIBRS promises to be an important tool in that process.

Thrownaway Children (NISMART) estimated the number of family and nonfamily abductions for a single year but contained no police data on family abductions (Finkelhor, Hotaling, and Sedlak, 1990, 1991). The Washington State Attorney General's Office has compiled data on abduction homicides known to police, and the FBI has a database on the very serious kidnaping cases that have been reported to it (Hanfland, Keppel, and Weis, 1997; Boudreaux, Lord, and Dutra, 1999).[1] However, despite these various data sources, a broad picture covering the full spectrum of kidnaping offenses that are reported to and investigated by law enforcement has not been available.

THE NATIONAL INCIDENT-BASED REPORTING SYSTEM

Fortunately, a comprehensive national database on kidnaping and other crimes is beginning to emerge. The FBI, in partnership with the Bureau of Justice Statistics, is supplanting the UCR with the more comprehensive National Incident-Based Reporting System (NIBRS), which collects detailed information on crimes known to the police. One of the improvements introduced by NIBRS is the inclusion of specific data on kidnaping. NIBRS offers an outstanding opportunity to learn more about the nature and extent of this crime, about which so few data have been available in the past.

This Bulletin describes the crime of kidnaping of juveniles (youth ages 17 and younger) as it appears in statistics reported by law enforcement agencies using NIBRS for 1997, the most recent reporting year for which NIBRS data are currently available. An analysis of data on 1,214 juvenile kidnapings from the jurisdictions in 12 States that participated in NIBRS in 1997 reveals the following:

---

[1] Several small-scale studies have also analyzed a series of infant abductions and child molestation abductions (Burgess and Lanning, 1995; Lanning and Burgess, 1995; Prentky et al., 1991).

- Kidnaping makes up less than 2 percent of all violent crimes against juveniles reported to police.

- Based on the identity of the perpetrator, there are three distinct types of kidnaping: kidnaping by a relative of the victim or "family kidnaping" (49 percent), kidnaping by an acquaintance of the victim or "acquaintance kidnaping" (27 percent), and kidnaping by a stranger to the victim or "stranger kidnaping" (24 percent) (figure 11.1).

- Family kidnaping is committed primarily by parents, involves a larger percentage of female perpetrators (43 percent) than other types of kidnaping offenses, occurs more frequently to children under 6, equally victimizes juveniles of both sexes, and most often originates in the home.

- Acquaintance kidnaping has features that suggest it should not be lumped with stranger kidnaping into the single category of nonfamily kidnaping, as has been done in the past.

- Acquaintance kidnaping involves a comparatively high percentage of juvenile perpetrators, has the largest percentage of female and teenage victims, is more often associated with other crimes (especially sexual and physical assault), occurs at homes and residences, and has the highest percentage of injured victims.

- Stranger kidnaping victimizes more females than males, occurs primarily at outdoor locations, victimizes both teenagers and school-age children, is associated with sexual assaults in the case of girl victims and robberies in the case of boy victims (although not exclusively so), and is the type of kidnaping most likely to involve the use of a firearm.

- Relatively little kidnaping involves weapons.

- Only one death and a few major injuries were associated with juvenile kidnaping reported to NIBRS.

NIBRS data on kidnaping have some important limitations. Conclusions drawn from these data must be used with caution. Although the patterns and associations discovered are real, they apply only to the jurisdictions reporting and are not necessarily representative of national patterns and dynamics of crime. Also, NIBRS relies on local law enforcement agencies to collect data, and it is

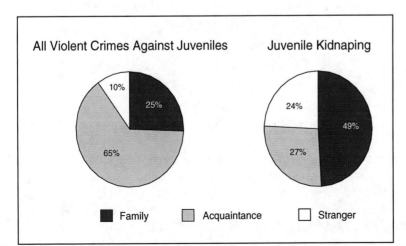

FIGURE 11.1

All Violent Crimes Against Juveniles and Juvenile Kidnaping, by Offender's Relationship to the Victim

Source: Federal Bureau of Investigation, 1997.

The National Incident-Based Reporting System

The U.S. Department of Justice is supplanting its Uniform Crime Report (UCR) system with a more comprehensive National Incident-Based Reporting System (NIBRS). Although NIBRS holds great promise, it is still far from a national system. Its implementation by the FBI began in 1988, and participation by States and local agencies is voluntary and incremental. By 1995, jurisdictions in 9 States had agencies contributing data; by 1997, the number was 12; and by the end of 1999, jurisdictions in 17 States submitted reports, providing coverage for 11 percent of the Nation's population and 9 percent of its crime. Only 3 States (Idaho, Iowa, South Carolina) have participation from all local jurisdictions, and only 1 city with a population currently greater than 500,000 (Austin, TX) is reporting, leaving the crime experiences of large urban areas particularly underrepresented.

Nevertheless, the system is assembling large amounts of crime information and providing a richness of detail about juvenile victimizations that was previously unavailable. The patterns and associations these data reveal are real and represent the experiences of a large number of youth. The 1997 NIBRS data file contains information on 364,830 violent crimes against individuals, with 79,028 of these against juveniles.

A more detailed discussion of the NIBRS data can be found in the authors' recently published OJJDP Bulletin, Characteristics of Crimes Against Juveniles (NCJ 179034).

not clear how systematic agencies are in their recording of kidnaping. Because kidnaping is not included in UCR data, agencies may not yet code for kidnaping as thoroughly as they might for other crimes. Moreover, jurisdictions may vary in how regularly they charge offenders with the crime of kidnaping. The elements of kidnaping exist in a wide range of criminal incidents—sexual assaults, robberies, and physical assaults—yet some jurisdictions, for a variety of possible reasons such as training, tradition, or local statutes, may charge or record the crime of kidnaping more or less frequently than other crimes.

Nonetheless, current NIBRS data provide a picture of the types of incidents law enforcement agencies in participating jurisdictions across the country are recording for statistical purposes as the crime of kidnaping. This perspective of current law enforcement practices is important in and of itself because, unlike public perceptions and prevailing stereotypes, it represents the actual juvenile kidnaping that police in these jurisdictions deal with on a day-to-day basis.

JUVENILE KIDNAPING—A RARE OCCURRENCE

Data indicate that kidnaping of juveniles is a relatively rare crime in NIBRS jurisdictions. It constitutes only one-tenth of 1 percent of all the crimes against individuals, 1 percent of all crimes against juveniles, and 1.5 percent of all violent crimes against juveniles recorded in the database. Kidnaping is dwarfed by the much more common crimes of simple and aggravated assault, larceny, and sex offenses, which make up most of the crimes against juveniles (Finkelhor and Ormrod, 2000). Both the limited coverage of NIBRS and the fact that kidnapings represent a very small percentage of all crimes make it impossible to project a reliable national estimate of kidnaping incidents. Nonetheless, the 1,214 juvenile kidnaping cases in the 1997 NIBRS data provide a larger database than has been previously available for examining the characteristics of this crime.

Kidnaping is widely recognized to involve very different dynamics and motives depending on the identity of the perpetrators and age of the victim (Boudreaux, Lord, and Dutra, 1999; Finkelhor, Hotaling, and Sedlack, 1990; Forst and Blomquist, 1991). Previous research and current public policy divide kidnaping into two categories: family abductions and nonfamily abductions. Family abductions are usually committed by parents who, in the course of custodial disputes, take or keep children in violation of custody orders (Plass, 1998). Nonfamily abductions are generally thought to involve efforts, primarily by strangers, to isolate children in order to commit another crime, such as sexual assault or robbery.

Three Types of Perpetrators

In contrast, the criminal kidnaping of juveniles, as recorded by police in the NIBRS jurisdictions, is divided into three relatively large categories: family kidnaping (49 percent), acquaintance kidnaping (27 percent), and stranger kidnaping (24 percent) (figure 11.1). Compared with all violent crimes against juveniles, kidnaping has substantially higher percentages of both family and stranger perpetrators, but the high percentage of acquaintance kidnapings is striking given previous characterizations of this crime that have emphasized only the family and stranger elements.

In the NIBRS jurisdictions, family kidnaping perpetrators are usually parents (80 percent), almost always adults (98 percent), and often female (43 percent) (figures 11.2 and 11.3). Although not a majority of family kidnaping perpetrators, females commit a substantially larger portion of the family abductions than they do of acquaintance abductions (16 percent), stranger abductions (5 percent), or violent crimes in general (24 percent).

Stranger perpetrators are predominately males (95 percent) and predominately adults (90 percent) (figures 11.2 and 11.3). Acquaintance kidnaping has the largest proportion of juvenile offenders (30 percent) and a somewhat higher percentage of female offenders than stranger kidnaping (16 percent and 5 percent, respectively). Data from the NIBRS jurisdictions provide limited information about the characteristics of some offenders in the acquaintance category. Eighteen percent are categorized as boyfriend, which suggests a quite distinct dynamic, whereas two other subdivisions—friend (7 percent) and acquaintance (73 percent)—although more ambiguous, suggest different degrees of intimacy or familiarity.

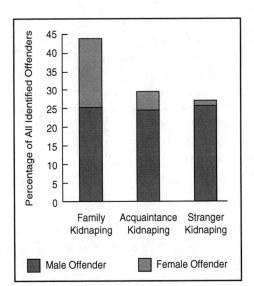

FIGURE 11.2

Juvenile Kidnaping, by Offender's Relationship to the Victim and Offender's Gender

Note: What may appear to be inconsistencies in the proportions of the three types of juvenile kidnaping presented in figures 11.1 and 11.2 are the result of the different methods of analyzing NIBRS data used in each figure. Figure 11.1 analyzes incidents of juvenile kidnaping. Figure 11.2 analyzes juvenile kidnaping offenders. Thus, for example, in part because one kidnaping incident may involve more than one offender, figure 11.1 shows that 49 percent of all juvenile kidnapings are committed by family members, while figure 11.2 shows that 44 percent of all kidnaping offenders are family members.

Source: Federal Bureau of Investigation, 1997.

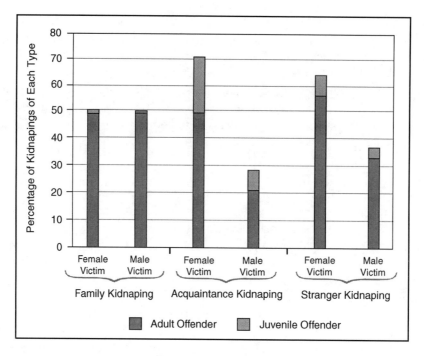

FIGURE 11.3

Juvenile Kidnaping, by Offender's Relationship to the Victim, Victim's Gender, and Offender's Age Group
Source: Federal Bureau of Investigation, 1997.

Family perpetrators kidnap males and females in approximately equal proportions (figure 11.3). Acquaintance perpetrators kidnap substantially more females than males (72 percent and 28 percent, respectively). Stranger perpetrators also kidnap more females than males but not quite so disproportionately as acquaintances (64 percent and 36 percent, respectively).

Victim Age Patterns

The three categories of kidnaping also have distinct patterns with respect to the age of victims. In the NIBRS incident reports, family kidnaping has its peak occurrence for children under age 6 (43 percent), while a large majority of acquaintance kidnaping victimizes teenagers (youth ages 12 to 17) (71 percent). Stranger kidnaping is more equally split between teenage and elementary school-age victims (57 percent and 32 percent, respectively). However, the risks for children of different ages appear to have a complex interplay (figure 11.4). Children under the age of 6 are primarily targets of family kidnaping, which peaks at about age 2 and declines thereafter. The risk of kidnaping by a stranger is comparatively low for pre-schoolers but rises throughout the elementary school years and reaches its peak around age 15. Acquaintance kidnaping is the predominant problem for teenagers, displacing stranger kidnaping as their biggest threat.

Location

NIBRS provides only crude data about the location of crimes, particularly a crime like kidnaping that may have an originating, intermediate, and destination locale (for example, a child taken from a street, driven in a car, brought into a residence, and then raped). NIBRS allows multiple-location

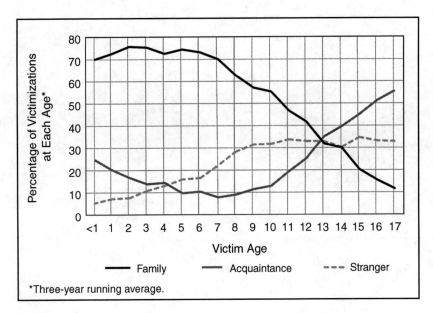

FIGURE 11.4

Juvenile Kidnaping, by Victim's Age and Offender's Relationship to the Victim

Source: Federal Bureau of Investigation, 1997.

coding for multiple-offense crimes, but only 1 percent of incidents involving kidnaping have multiple locations recorded in NIBRS data. The information on location does, however, show clear-cut associations between the offender's relationship to the victim and the location of the kidnaping.

In the NIBRS jurisdictions, family kidnaping, consistent with the stereotype, is associated primarily with homes and residences (84 percent) (figure 11.5). Stranger kidnaping, by contrast, is associated primarily with outdoor locations (58 percent)—streets, highways, parks, waterways, and other public areas. Like family kidnaping, most acquaintance kidnaping takes place at homes and residences (63 percent), but unlike family kidnaping, a substantial percentage of acquaintance kidnaping also occurs in outside locations (22 percent). It is important to note that schools are an unusual site for abduction, even family abduction (only 5 percent of family, 4 percent of acquaintance, and 3 percent of stranger kidnaping occur at school).

Additional Offenses

In other studies, nonfamily kidnaping is generally associated with other offenses, such as robbery or sexual assault, and is in fact a means of facilitating those offenses. One advantage of NIBRS over UCR is its ability to code multiple crimes associated with a single incident. Overall, 19 percent of the juvenile kidnaping reported in NIBRS jurisdictions is associated with another violent crime. This makes it the most common crime to be paired with an additional offense. These additional offenses provide some perspective on the motives of kidnaping offenders.

Most additional offenses associated with kidnaping occur in conjunction with acquaintance and stranger kidnaping, but the types of offenses vary somewhat according to the gender of the victim (figure 11.6). For female victims, sex crimes were the predominant adjunct to kidnaping, occurring

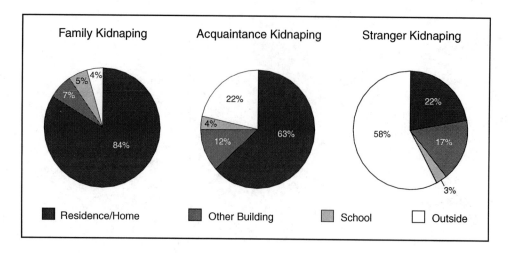

FIGURE 11.5

Juvenile Kidnaping, by Offender's Relationship to the Victim and Type of Location

Note: Percentages may not total 100 percent because of rounding.
Source: Federal Bureau of Investigation, 1997.

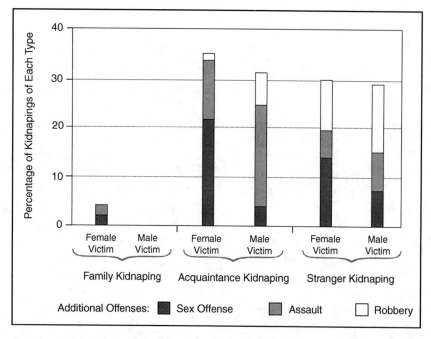

FIGURE 11.6

Juvenile Kidnaping With Additional Offenses, by Victim's Gender, Offender's Relationship to the Victim, and Type of Additional Offense

Source: Federal Bureau of Investigation, 1997.

in 23 percent of the kidnapings by acquaintances and 14 percent of the kidnapings by strangers reported to NIBRS in 1997. For male victims, robbery and assault were the additional offenses most likely to accompany kidnaping, although some sex offenses also occurred.

Family kidnaping tends not to be associated with any other crime. In this type of kidnaping, none of the offenses against boys and only 5 percent of the offenses against girls were linked to an additional violent crime.

Weapon Usage

For the most part in NIBRS jurisdictions, kidnaping is a weaponless crime (figure 11.7). Approximately 14 percent of acquaintance kidnapings and about 23 percent of stranger abductions involved weapons, mostly guns. The use of weapons in family abductions was quite rare (less than 2 percent).

Injuries and Deaths

Injuries occurred in only 12 percent of all kidnapings recorded by police in participating jurisdictions. They were most frequent in acquaintance abductions (24 percent) and least frequent in family abductions (4 percent) (figure 11.8). Major injuries (for example, severe lacerations, broken bones, unconsciousness) were extremely rare, occurring in only 2 percent of all kidnapings. Only one fatal outcome to a kidnaping was recorded in the 1997 NIBRS data. When interpreting figure 11.8, however, it must be kept in mind that these abductions were not necessarily crime episodes of long duration or ones in which a child was officially declared missing. They could have involved episodes during which a child was transported a short distance or into a building or car in order to accomplish a sexual assault or robbery. NIBRS has no usable information about whether the child victim was at any time in the episode reported missing or about the distance or duration of the kidnaping.

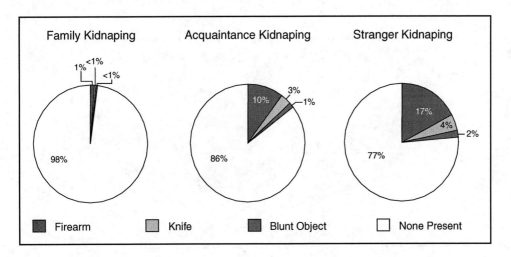

FIGURE 11.7

Juvenile Kidnaping, by Offender's Relationship to the Victim and Presence of Firearm, Knife, or Blunt Object

Note: Percentages may not total 100 percent because of rounding.
Source: Federal Bureau of Investigation, 1997.

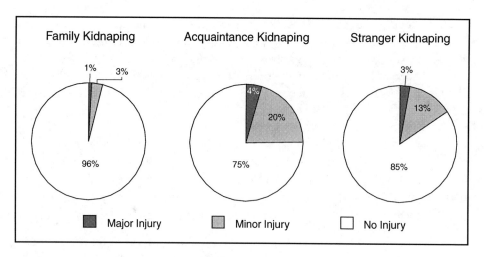

FIGURE 11.8

Juvenile Kidnaping, by Offender's Relationship to the Victim and Victim's Injury

Note: Percentages may not total 100 percent because of rounding.
Source: Federal Bureau of Investigation, 1997.

Time of Day

Rates for all crimes against children peak in the afternoon (Snyder and Sickmund, 1999), and kidnaping is no exception: 41 percent of all juvenile kidnapings in NIBRS jurisdictions occur during afternoon hours (noon to 6 p.m.). The main difference among the three types of kidnaping is that acquaintance and stranger kidnaping are somewhat more likely than family kidnaping to occur in the evening (6 p.m. to midnight) or nighttime (midnight to 6 a.m.) hours (46 percent, 41 percent, and 30 percent, respectively) (figure 11.9).

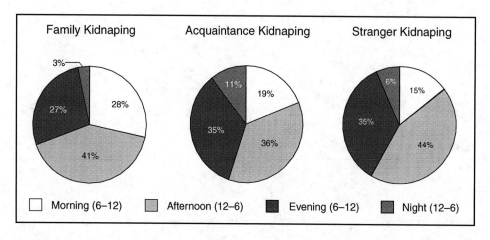

FIGURE 11.9

Juvenile Kidnaping, by Offender's Relationship to the Victim and Time of Day

Note: Percentages may not total 100 percent because of rounding.
Source: Federal Bureau of Investigation, 1997.

IMPLICATIONS

NIBRS data from the jurisdictions reporting in 1997 suggest that the current practice of differentiating the crime of kidnaping into only two categories (family and non-family) needs to be changed. The two components of the conventional nonfamily category—acquaintance kidnaping and stranger kidnaping—seem to be different types of offenses, at least as they appear in law enforcement data. The specific characteristics of acquaintance kidnaping, which has not yet been separately profiled, need to be better delineated and understood.

Acquaintance kidnaping in data from NIBRS jurisdictions distinguishes itself from stranger kidnaping in a variety of important ways (table 11.1). First, it involves more juvenile offenders and somewhat more female offenders. Second, it occurs more often with teenage victims, while more stranger kidnaping victimizes school-age children (the complement of "teenage victim"). Third, acquaintance kidnaping is much more likely to occur at a home or residence, while stranger kidnaping most often occurs in outdoor locales. Finally, acquaintance kidnaping victims suffer a higher rate of injury. These substantial differences highlight that acquaintance kidnaping is both a separate and serious form of kidnaping.

Unfortunately, because of the limited categories of information available in NIBRS, it is impossible to draw confident conclusions about the dynamics and motives that might specially characterize acquaintance kidnaping. Nevertheless, NIBRS data are consistent with case material suggesting that certain specific types of crimes are encompassed within the acquaintance kidnaping category. For example, one specific type of acquaintance kidnaping is the situation where boyfriends or former boyfriends kidnap girlfriends (32 percent of the acquaintance kidnaping of teenage female victims) to seek revenge for being spurned, force a reconciliation, commit a sexual assault, or perhaps evade parents who want to break up the relationship. Another type of acquaintance kidnaping is related to gang activity: for example, the situation where teenagers abduct other teenagers in order to intimidate, recruit, or retaliate against them. A third type of acquaintance kidnaping involves family friends or employees (for example, babysitters) who remove children from their home for the purpose of sexual assault or perhaps retaliation against the family. Such variety of offenders and motives may make acquaintance kidnaping more difficult to typify than family or stranger kidnaping, but it is nevertheless instructive in that it highlights the importance of obtaining data on a larger number of cases for the purposes of profiling.

TABLE 11.1   KEY DIFFERENCES BETWEEN ACQUAINTANCE AND STRANGER ABDUCTIONS

	Percentage of Victimizations With Characteristic	
Characteristic	Acquaintance (*n* = 244)	Stranger (*n* = 221)
Any juvenile offender	27	8
Any female offender	17	5
Teenage victim	71	57
Home or residence location	63	22
Outside location	22	58
Injury to victim	25	15

Source: Federal Bureau of Investigation, 1997.

There is no easy explanation for why acquaintance kidnaping involves more injury than stranger kidnaping. It may be the combination of more teenage victims who would be inclined to resist and the fact that intimidation is a more common motive for these crimes, which results in the use of more force and thus more injury. It may also be that police are less likely to think of kidnaping as an element in an acquaintance crime (and thus less likely to record kidnaping as an additional offense in the NIBRS database) unless the victim is injured.

It is also instructive to examine the discrepancies between the pictures of nonfamily kidnaping presented in NIBRS data and those found in the data collected by the earlier NISMART, which conducted an independent review of police files (abduction, missing persons, homicide, and sexual assault files) in 1988 (Finkelhor, Hotaling, and Sedlak, 1990). NISMART data record fewer acquaintance and juvenile perpetrators but substantially more weapon usage. Another significant discrepancy is in the percentage of kidnaping incidents associated explicitly with sexual assault. In NISMART, sexual assault appeared to be a motive in two-thirds of the nonfamily abductions known to police (Asdigian, Finkelhor, and Hotaling, 1995), whereas in NIBRS, only 15 percent of nonfamily kidnaping (of both male and female victims) was coded with the additional crime of sexual assault.

There are several possible explanations for these differences. The methodology used in NISMART to look for abductions was to directly sample police departments' sexual assault files but not their general assault or robbery files, which may have exaggerated the portion of kidnaping that was associated with sexual assault. At the same time, NISMART's direct access to police files may have revealed sexual assault motives or intentions that are not captured when officers apply NIBRS codes. It is certainly surprising that so much of the stranger and acquaintance kidnaping recorded in NIBRS has no other crime associated with it, because these types of kidnaping are generally considered as primarily a method to facilitate other offenses. One problem might be that law enforcement officials, continuing the UCR tradition with its single-code limit, do not take advantage of the multiple crime codes allowed under NIBRS and fail to record adjunct or secondary offenses. For whatever reason, NIBRS may underrep-resent the motive of sexual assault and the presence of other crimes in acquaintance and stranger kidnaping.

Another conspicuous discrepancy between NIBRS and NISMART data concerns the relative occurrence of family and nonfamily abduction. The NISMART data suggest that the overwhelming majority of abductions were committed by family members (Finkelhor et al., 1990), whereas family abductions actually constitute only a slight minority of all kidnapings recorded in NIBRS. However, the NISMART family abduction estimates come from a national household survey, not police records, and, although 44 percent of the families surveyed indicated they had contacted police, relatively little is known about how such reports are recorded or tabulated in crime statistics. The discrepancy between the NISMART and NIBRS data suggests that many, if not most, calls to police about family abductions are not recorded as crimes.

Findings on kidnaping from the NIBRS jurisdictions also are inconsistent with other kidnaping studies—for example, those based on FBI data or national inquiries of police investigators (Boudreaux, Lord, and Dutra, 1999; Hanfland, Keppel, and Weis, 1997)—concerning characteristics such as the identity of perpetrators or the incidence of serious injury and death. These differences can almost all be traced to the different samples selected in different studies—for example, samples of kidnaping homicides. What is really highlighted by all of these comparisons is the absence of a consensus about how segments of the population of kidnaped children should be aggregated or subdivided for most useful policy analysis. NIBRS data provide yet another, but by no means a complete or conclusive, perspective on the problem.

The inconclusiveness of findings about kidnaping point to the main policy needs in this area. First, substantially more research about this crime—which has attracted a large amount of public attention but rather little scientific study or profiling—is needed. Second, research about the problem would benefit if those studying and collecting data about it would adopt a common set of definitions and categories within which to subdivide and analyze it. This uniformity has been achieved in regard to other crimes (e.g., sexual assault) in recent years as a result of national data systems like the UCR, but kidnaping was outside the purview of this system. The inclusion of kidnaping in NIBRS offers the opportunity to achieve that uniformity now. Third, in the light of this and in order to increase the usefulness of NIBRS for the study of kidnaping, NIBRS may need to make a special effort to help local agencies report kidnaping in uniform and consistent ways, since it is a crime that may be handled in disparate fashions from jurisdiction to jurisdiction.

CONCLUSION

NIBRS, as it grows, will increasingly facilitate new insights into the dynamics of crime. This may be nowhere more apparent than in dealing with the crime of kidnaping, for which there have been few data sources. Although the quality of NIBRS data on kidnaping is unclear, this new national database will allow a more systematic analysis of kidnaping across jurisdictions and over time. The availability of such data may even prompt efforts to better define and categorize the crime of kidnaping and to improve the reliability of its coding. These are small but crucial steps on the path to improving law enforcement's understanding of and response to this crime.

REFERENCES

Asdigian, N.L., Finkelhor, D., & Hotaling, G.T. (1995). Varieties of non-family abduction of children and adolescents. *Criminal Justice and Behavior*, 22(3), 215-232.

Boudreaux, M.C., Lord, W.D., & Dutra, R.L. (1999). Child abductions: Age-based analyses of offender, victim, and offense characteristics in 550 cases of alleged child disappearance. *Journal of Forensic Sciences* 44(3):531-545.

Burgess, A.W., & Lanning, K.V. (1995). *An Analysis of Infant Abductions*. Alexandria, VA: National Center for Missing and Exploited Children.

Federal Bureau of Investigation. (1997). *National Incident-Based Reporting System (NIBRS)*. (12 States only). Computer file. Tabulations undertaken by Crimes Against Children Research Center.Washington, DC: U.S. Department of Justice, Federal Bureau of Investigation.

Finkelhor, D., Hotaling, G.T., & Sedlak, A. (1990). *Missing, Abducted, Runaway, and Thrownaway Children in America: First Report*. Washington, DC: U.S. Department of Justice, Office of Justice Programs, Office of Juvenile Justice and Delinquency Prevention.

Finkelhor, D., Hotaling, G.T., & Sedlak, A. (1991). Children abducted by family members: A national household survey of incidence and episode characteristics. *Journal of Marriage and the Family*, 53(2), 805-817.

Finkelhor, D., & Ormrod, R. (2000). *The Characteristics of Crimes Against Juveniles*. Bulletin. Washington, DC: U.S. Department of Justice, Office of Justice Programs, Office of Juvenile Justice and Delinquency Prevention.

Forst, M.L., & Blomquist, M. (1991). *Missing Children: Rhetoric and Reality*. New York, NY: Lexington Books.

Hanfland, K.A., Keppel, R.D., & Weis, J.G. (1997). *Case Management for Missing Children Homicide Investigation.* Washington State: Attorney General of Washington.

Lanning, K.V., & Burgess, A.W. (1995). *Child Molesters Who Abduct: Summary of the Case in Point Series.* Alexandria, VA: National Center for Missing and Exploited Children.

Plass, P.S. (1998). A typology of family abduction events. *Child Maltreatment, 3*(3), 244-250.

Prentky, R.A., Knight, R.A., Burgess, A.W., Ressler, R., Campbell, J., & Lanning, K.U. (1991). Child molesters who abduct. *Violence and Victims, 6*(3), 213-224.

Snyder, H.N. & Sickmund, M. (1999). *Juvenile Offenders and Victims: 1999 National Report.*

David Finkelhor and Richard Ormrod. "Kidnapping of Juveniles: Patterns from NIBRS" in *Juvenile Justice Bulletin,* June 2000), pp. 1-8. Office of Juvenile Justice and Delinquency Prevention, U.S. Department of Justice.

CRIME ASSESSMENT USING METHOD OF OPERATION AND SIGNATURE ANALYSIS

Section IV: Crime Assessment Using Method of Operation and Signature Analysis is a collection of three articles focused on the identifying offender characteristics and linking cases through crime scene analysis. This section focuses on enhancing understanding of the basic terminology and the use of crime scene analysis. Several case examples are provided to demonstrate the process and effectiveness of crime scene analysis in the investigation of violent crimes such as serial and sexual murders. Crime scene analysis based on modus operandi (MO) and signature characteristics can assist in the investigation of violent serial crimes by identifying offender characteristics, linking cases, prioritizing leads and suspects, and developing apprehension and interview strategies. Unlike most profiling efforts of law enforcement, crime scene analysis has been introduced as evidence at trial in several criminal cases in the United States.

In *Violent Crime Scene Analysis: Modus Operandi, Signature, and Staging*, authors John Douglas and Corrine Munn (1992) discuss the language of crime scene analysis, providing definitions and examples of modus operandi, signature aspects, and staging. They emphasize the importance of MO and signature aspects in linking cases and illustrate the use of crime scene details and behavioral clues that suggest staging. Several cases linked by offender signature analysis are described, including those of serial offenders Ronnie Shelton, Nathaniel Code, and David Vasquez. Additionally, Douglas and Munn detail the reasons for staging and various signs of staging investigators may encounter at crime scenes.

Robert D. Keppel further illustrates the successful use of crime scene analysis in the 1995 article *Signature Murders: A Report of the 1984 Cranbrook, British Colombia Cases*. Keppel highlights the differences between Modus Operandi and signature by providing definitions and examples of each. MO refers to those actions of the offender which are necessary to commit the crime, while actions beyond those necessary to commit the crime reflect the offender's signature. Keppel describes how crime scene analysis was used to link the two crime scenes of a killer to each other and to one offender, detailing aspects of MO and signature revealed in the two murders. Signature analysis of the crime scenes revealed the distinctive calling card of Terrence Wayne Burlingham. In addition, Keppel used the Homicide Investigation and Tracking System (HITS) to link the two crime scenes by statistically estimating the rarity of crime scene and signature characteristics prominent in the two crimes.

VIOLENT CRIME SCENE ANALYSIS: MODUS OPERANDI, SIGNATURE, AND STAGING

JOHN E. DOUGLAS, Ed.D.
Special Agent, Chief of the Investigative Support Unit, FBI Academy

CORINNE MUNN
Served as Honors Intern, FBI Academy

Most crime scenes tell a story. And like most stories, crime scenes have characters, a plot, a beginning, a middle, and hopefully, a conclusion. However, in contrast to authors who lead their readers to a predetermined ending, the final disposition of a crime scene depends on the investigators assigned to the case. The investigators' abilities to analyze the crime scene and to determine the who, what, how, and why govern how the crime scene story unfolds.

To ensure a satisfactory ending, that is, the apprehension and prosecution of the violent crime offender, investigators must realize that the outcome depends on their insight into the dynamics of human behavior. Speech patterns, writing styles, verbal and nonverbal gestures, and other traits and patterns give shape to human behavior. These individual characteristics work in concert to cause each person to act, react, function, or perform in a unique and specific way. This individualistic behavior usually remains consistent, regardless of the activity being performed.

Since the commission of a violent crime involves all the dynamics of "normal" human behavior, learning to recognize crime scene manifestations of behavioral patterns enables investigators to discover much about the offender. It also provides a means by which investigators can distinguish between different offenders committing the same types of offense.

There are three possible manifestations of offender behavior at a crime scene–modus operandi, personation or signature, and staging. This article addresses each of these manifestations in order to demonstrate the importance of analyzing a crime scene in terms of human behavior.

MODUS OPERANDI

In 1989, Nathaniel Code, Jr., a Shreveport, Louisiana, man, was convicted of murder. The jury determined that on three separate occasions between 1984 and 1987, Code murdered a total of eight people. The jury returned a guilty verdict, even though several disparities existed among the three crime scenes.

For example, the offender gagged the first victim with a piece of material obtained at the crime scene, but brought duct tape to use on the seven victims in the other two incidents. Also, the killer stabbed and slashed the first victim, whereas the victims of the other two crimes were also shot and showed signs of ligature strangulation. The victims ranged in age from 8 years to 74 years and included both sexes; however, all were black. And, the offender took money from one crime scene, but not the other two.

Considering the evidence found at the three crime scenes, could one man be linked to all of the murders? Wouldn't such differences in modus operandi (M.O.), which is the offender's actions while committing the crime, and victimology (characteristics of the victims) eliminate the connection to one offender?

When attempting to link cases, the M.O. has great significance. A critical step in crime scene analysis is the resulting correlation that connects cases due to similarities in M.O. But, what causes an offender to use a certain M.O.? What circumstances shape the M.O.? Is the M.O. static or dynamic?

Unfortunately, investigators make a serious error by placing too much significance on the M.O. when linking crimes. For example, a novice burglar shatters a locked basement window to gain access to a house. Fearing that the sound of a window breaking will attract attention, he rushes in his search for valuables. Later, during subsequent crimes, he brings tools to force open locks, which will minimize the noise. This allows him more time to commit the crimes and to obtain a more profitable haul.

As shown, the burglar refined his breaking-and-entering techniques to lower the risk of apprehension and to increase profits. This demonstrates that the M.O. is a learned behavior that is dynamic and malleable. Developed over time, the M.O. continuously evolves as offenders gain experience and confidence.

Incarceration usually impacts on the future M.O.s of offenders, especially career criminals. Offenders refine their M.O.s as they learn from the mistakes that lead to their arrests.

The victim's response also significantly influences the evolution of the M.O. If a rapist has problems controlling a victim, he will modify the M.O. to accommodate resistance. He may use duct tape, other ligatures, or a weapon on the victim. Or, he may blitz the victim and immediately incapacitate her. If such measures are ineffective, he may resort to greater violence or he may kill the victim. Thus, offenders continually reshape their M.O. to meet the demands of the crime.

In the case of Nathanial Code, M.O. and victimology alone would have failed to link him to each of the eight murders. But Code left more than gags, duct tape, and bodies with gunshot wounds and slashed throats at the crime scenes; he left his "calling card." Investigators found this "calling card" or signature aspect at every crime scene, and thus, were able to link Code to the offenses.

THE SIGNATURE ASPECT

The violent, repetitive offender often exhibits another element of criminal behavior during the crime–the signature aspect or "calling card." This criminal conduct is a unique and integral part of the offender's behavior and goes beyond the actions needed to commit the crime.

Fantasies of offenders often give birth to violent crime. As offenders brood and daydream, they develop a need to express these violent fantasies. When they are finally acted out, some aspect of each crime demonstrates a unique, personal expression or ritual based on these fantasies. However, committing the crime does not satisfy the needs of offenders, and this insufficiency compels them to go beyond the scope of the offense and perform a ritual. When offenders display rituals at the crime scene, they have left their individualized "calling card."

How do crime scenes manifest this "calling card" or signature aspect? Basically, crime scenes reveal peculiar characteristics or unusual offender input that occur while the crime is being committed.

For example, a rapist demonstrates his signature by engaging in acts of domination, manipulation, or control during the verbal, physical, or sexual phase of the assault. The use of exceptionally vulgar or abusive language, or preparing a script for the victim to repeat, represents a verbal signature. When the rapist prepares a script for a victim, he dictates a particular verbal response from her, such as "Tell me how much you enjoy sex with me," or "Tell me how good I am."

The use of excessive physical force shows another aspect of a subject's signature. One example of signature sexual behavior involves the offender who repeatedly engages in a specific order of sexual activity with different victims.

The signature aspect remains a constant and enduring part of each offender. And, unlike the M.O., it never changes. However, signature aspects may evolve, such as in the case of a lust murderer who performs greater postmortem mutilation as he progresses from crime to crime. Elements of the original ritual become more fully developed. In addition, the signature does not always show up at every crime scene because of unexpected contingencies, such as interruptions or an unexpected victim response.

The investigator may not always be able to identify signature aspects. Violent offenses often involve high-risk victims or decomposition of the body, which complicates recognizing the signature aspects of an offender.

MODUS OPERANDI OR SIGNATURE ASPECT?

The following scenarios are fictitious accounts. They are used to show the difference between a M.O. and a signature aspect.

A rapist enters a residence and takes a woman and her husband captive. The offender orders the husband to lie face down on the floor and then places a cup and saucer on his back. He tells the husband, "If I hear the cup move or hit the floor, your wife dies." The offender then takes the wife into the next room and rapes her.

In another situation, a rapist enters the house, orders the woman to phone her husband, and tells her to use some ploy to get him to come home. Once the husband arrives, the rapist ties him to a chair and forces him to watch the assault on his wife.

The rapist who used the cup and saucer developed an effective modus operandi to control the husband. However, the other rapist went beyond just committing the rape. He satisfied his fantasies fully by not only raping the wife but also by humiliating and dominating the husband. His personal needs compelled him to perform this signature aspect of the crime.

In Michigan, a bank robber makes the bank tellers undress during the robbery. In Texas, another bank robber also forces the tellers to undress, but he also makes them pose in sexually provocative positions as he takes photographs. Do both of these crimes demonstrate a signature aspect?

The Michigan robber used a very effective means to increase his escape time, i.e., causing the tellers to dress before they called the police. When interviewed, they offered vague, meager descriptions because their embarrassment prevented them from having eye contact with the robber. This offender developed a very clever M.O.

However, the Texas robber went beyond the required action to commit his crime successfully. He felt compelled to enact the ritual of requiring the tellers to pose so that he could snap photographs. He left his signature on the crime. The act of robbing the bank itself did not gratify his psychosexual needs.

LINKING CASES

When attempting to link cases, the M.O. plays an important role. However, as stated previously, the M.O. should not be the only criteria used to connect crimes, especially with repeat offenders who alter their M.O. through experience and learning. Usually, first offenses differ considerably from subsequent offenses. However, the signature aspect stays the same, whether it is the first offense or one committed 10 years later. The ritual may evolve, but the theme remains constant.

The signature aspect should receive greater consideration than victim similarities, although these should never be discounted when attempting to link cases to a serial offender. Physical similarities of victims are often not important, especially when linking crimes motivated by anger. The offender expresses anger through rituals, not by attacking a victim who possesses a particular characteristic or trait.

CASES LINKED BY OFFENDER SIGNATURE

Ronnie Shelton: Serial Rapist

Ronnie Shelton committed as many as 50 rapes. When convicted of 28 of them, he received a prison sentence in excess of 1,000 years.[1] Both his verbal communication and sexual assaults manifested his signature.

Verbally, Shelton was exceptionally degrading and exceptionally vulgar. In addition, he would make such comments as "I have seen you with your boyfriend," "I've seen you around," or "You know who I am." Thoughts of Shelton lurking around their neighborhoods terrorized the victims.

However, it was the sexual assault itself that occupied the central position in Shelton's ritual. He would rape his victims vaginally, then withdraw and ejaculate on their stomachs or breasts. Shelton would also frequently masturbate over the victims or between their breasts or force them to masturbate him manually. Then, he would use their clothing to wipe off the ejaculation. He also forced many of his victims to have oral sex with him and then insisted that they swallow the ejaculation. The combination of these acts displayed Shelton's signature.

Shelton's M.O. consisted of entering the victim's dwelling through a window or patio entrance that faced a wooded area or bushes offering concealment. He wore a ski mask, stocking, or scarf. He convinced the victims that he was not there to rape but to rob them. However, when he had the victim under control, he would return to the rape mode. The victim would comply because she had seen his propensity for violence by his earlier actions, such as throwing her on the floor or holding a knife to her throat. In addition, Shelton would say to the victims, "Keep your eyes down," "Cover your eyes," or "Don't look at me and I won't kill you (hurt your kids)." Before he left, he would verbally intimidate them with such warnings as "Don't call the police or I'll come back and kill you." These characteristics served as Shelton's M.O., whereas his former actions were his signature that linked him to 28 sexual assaults.

---

[1] SA Douglas has qualified as an expert in criminal investigative analysis and has provided testimony in the area of signature crime analysis during the following court proceedings: State of Ohio v. Ronnie Shelton, State of Louisiana v. Nathaniel Code, and State of Delaware v. Steven B. Pennell.

Nathaniel Code: Serial Killer

Nathaniel Code, Jr., killed eight times on three separate occasions. The first homicide, a 25-year-old black female, occurred on August 8, 1984. Code stabbed her nine times in the chest and slashed her throat.

Approximately a year later, on July 19, 1985, Code killed four people–a 15-year-old girl, her mother, and two of their male friends. Code nearly severed the girl's head from her body. He asphyxiated the mother and draped her body over the side of the bath tub. Code then shot one of the males in the head, leaving him in a middle bedroom; the other male, who was found in the front bedroom, was shot twice and had his throat slit.

The last killing took place on August 5, 1987. The victims were Code's grandfather and his 8-year-old and 12-year-old nephews. The boys died of ligature strangulation. Code stabbed his grandfather five times in the chest and seven times in the back.

The changes in Code's M.O., exhibited from case to case, show how the M.O. is refined. For example, in the first murder, Code gagged the victim with material found at the scene; the next time, he brought duct tape.

Code also kept his victims under surveillance to obtain information on them, especially with the second killings. In that case, he brought a gun to the scene to dispose of the males, who posed the greatest threat to him. Since the last victims, an elderly man and two children, posed little threat to him, Code did not use a gun on them.

All eight killings occurred in single family dwellings. In each dwelling, the air conditioners and/or televisions were on, which drowned out the noise as he entered through a door or window. Code quickly gained and maintained control of the victims by separating them in different rooms.

Nathaniel Code had a very distinctive "calling card," one aspect of which were the injuries inflicted on the victims. Code employed a very bloody method of attack and overkill. He could have simply murdered each victim with a single gunshot wound–a clean kill involving very little "mess." Instead, Code slaughtered his victims by slashing their throats with a sawing motion that resulted in deep wounds. Although brutal, the attack didn't satisfy his ritual; all victims sustained additional injuries, with the exception of the 15-year-old girl. One male victim suffered gunshot wounds to the chest, while another received multiple stab wounds to the chest. Code wounded nearly all the victims far beyond what was necessary to cause death (overkill).

The physical violence and bloody overkill satisfied Code's need for domination, control, and manipulation. He positioned each victim face down, which supports this theory. Code even forced the mother to witness her daughter's death as part of this ritual of control, which was formed from his rage. In fact, forensic tests found the daughter's blood on the mother's dress. If the victim's response threatened his sense of domination, Code reacted with anger and the excessive violence that led to overkill.

The last signature aspect of Code's crimes probably best illustrates his unique "calling card"– the ligatures. Code used both an unusual configuration and material. In all three cases, he bound the victims with electrical appliance or telephone cords acquired at the scene. Code could have brought rope or used his duct tape, but the use of these cords satisfied some personal need. Using a handcuff-style configuration, he looped the cord around each wrist and then the ankles, connecting them to the wrists by a lead going through the legs.

The dissimilarities of these cases involves the M.O., not the signature aspect. The use of a gun with threatening males present reveals an adaptive offender. At the time of the grandfather's homicide, additional financial stressors affected Code, evidenced by the theft of money from his grandfather's residence. These financial stressors influenced Code's M.O., not his "calling card."

Physical characteristics, age, and even sex do not enhance or diminish the ritual driven by rage. Code's ritual of anger required control and domination of his victims, so victimology was not as important. Code, like Ronnie Shelton, the serial rapist, selected victims he could control, manipulate, and on whom he could project his anger.

Importance of Offender Signature

Understanding and recognizing the signature aspects is vital in the apprehension and prosecution of an offender, especially a serial offender. No one appreciates the importance of recognizing an offender's "calling card" more than David Vasquez.

In 1984, Vasquez pled guilty to the murder of a 34-year-old Arlington, Virginia, woman. The woman had been sexually assaulted and died of ligature strangulation. The killer left her lying face down with her hands tied behind her back. He used unique knots and excessive binding with the ligatures, and a lead came from the wrists to the neck over the left shoulder. The body was openly displayed so that discovery offered significant shock value.

The offender spent considerable time at the crime scene. He made extensive preparations to bind the victim, allowing him to control her easily. His needs dictated that he move her around the house, exerting total domination over her. It appeared that he even took her into the bathroom and made her brush her teeth. None of this behavior was necessary to perpetrate the crime; the offender felt compelled to act out this ritual.

Vasquez had a borderline I.Q. Believing this would make it difficult to prove his innocence, his lawyers convinced him that he would probably receive the death sentence if the case went to trial. Instead, Vasquez opted for life imprisonment by pleading guilty.

Three years later, in 1987, police discovered a 44-year-old woman lying nude and face down on her bed. A rope bound her wrists behind her back, and a ligature strand tightly encircled her neck with a slip knot at the back. It continued over her left shoulder, down her back, and then was wrapped three times around each wrist. Forensics revealed that she died of ligature strangulation, and that she had been sexually assaulted. The offender left the body exposed and openly displayed. He appeared to have spent a considerable amount of time at the crime scene. This homicide occurred 4 blocks from the 1984 murder.

David Vasquez had been imprisoned 3 years when the 1987 murder occurred. At the request of the Arlington, Virginia, Police Department, the National Center for the Analysis of Violent Crime (NCAVC) conducted an extensive analysis of these two murders, a series of sexual assaults, and several other killings that occurred between 1984 and 1987. Eventually, the NCAVC linked these offenses through analogous signature aspects of another local suspect. Physical evidence later corroborated this connection and determined that the "calling card" left at the 1984 homicide did not belong to David Vasquez. As a result of this finding, the Commonwealth of Virginia released Vasquez from prison and exonerated him of the crime.

Staging

When investigators approach a crime scene, they should look for behavioral "clues" left by the offender. This is when investigators attempt to find answers to several critical questions. How did the encounter between the offender and victim occur? Did the offender blitz (ambush) the victim, or did he use verbal means (the con) to capture her? Did the offender use ligatures to control the victim? What was the sequence of events? Was the victim sexually assaulted before or after death? When did the mutilation take place–before or after death? Did the offender place any item at the crime scene or remove something from the crime scene?

As investigators analyze crime scenes, facts may arise that baffle them. These details may contain peculiarities that serve no apparent purpose in the perpetration[2] of the crime and obscure the underlying motive of the crime. This confusion may be the result of a crime scene behavior called staging. Staging occurs when someone purposely alters the crime scene prior to the arrival of the police.

Reasons for Staging

Principally, staging takes place for two reasons–to direct the investigation away from the most logical suspect or to protect the victim or victim's family. It is the offender who attempts to redirect the investigation. This offender does not just happen to come upon a victim, but is someone who almost always has some kind of association or relationship with the victim. This person, when in contact with law enforcement, will attempt to steer the investigation away from himself, usually by being overly cooperative or extremely distraught. Therefore, investigators should never eliminate a suspect who displays such distinctive behavior.

The second reason for staging, to protect the victim or the victim's family, occurs for the most part in rape-murder crimes or autoerotic fatalities. This type of staging is performed by the family member or person who finds the body. Since perpetrators of such crimes leave their victims in degrading positions, those who find the bodies attempt to restore some dignity to the victim. For example, a husband may redress or cover his wife's body, or in the case of an autoerotic fatality,[3] a wife may cut the noose or the device suspending the body of her husband.

Basically, these people are trying to prevent future shock that may be brought about by the position, dress, or condition of the victim. In addition, they will often stage an autoerotic fatality to look like a suicide, perhaps even writing a suicide note. They may even go so far as to the make it appear to be a homicide.

For both types of crime scene investigations, rape-murders and autoerotic fatalities, investigators need to obtain an accurate description of the body's condition when found and to determine exactly what the person who found the body did to alter the crime scene. Scrutiny of forensic findings, crime scene dynamics, and victimology will probably reveal the true circumstances surrounding the deaths.

Finally, at some crime scenes, investigators must discern if the scene is truly disorganized or if the offender staged it to appear careless and haphazard. This determination not only helps to direct the analysis to the underlying motive but also helps to shape the offender profile. However, recognition of staging, especially with a shrewd offender, can be difficult. Investigators must examine all factors of the crime if they suspect it has been staged. This is when forensics, victimology, and minute crime scene details become critical to determine if staging occurred.

"Red Flags"

Offenders who stage crime scenes usually make mistakes because they arrange the scene to resemble what they believe it should look like. In so doing, offenders experience a great deal of stress and do not have the time to fit all the pieces together logically. As a result, inconsistencies in

---

[2] P.E. Dietz, M.D. and R.R. Hazelwood,"Atypical Autoerotic Fatalities," Medicine and Law, *1*, 1982, 301-319.

[3] ibid

forensic findings and in the overall "big picture" of the crime scene will begin to appear. These inconsistencies can serve as the "red flags" of staging, which serve to prevent investigations from becoming misguided.

To ensure this doesn't happen, investigators should scrutinize all crime scene indicators individually, then view them in context with the total picture. Crime scene indicators include all evidence of offender activity, e.g., method of entry, offender-victim interaction, and body disposition.

When exploring these issues, investigators should consider several factors. For example, if burglary appears to be the motive, did the offender take inappropriate items from the crime scene? In one case submitted to the National Center for the Analysis of Violent Crime (NCAVC), a man returning home from work interrupted a burglary in progress. The startled burglars killed him as he attempted to flee. But, an inventory of the crime scene determined that the offenders did not steal anything, although it did appear that they started to disassemble a large stereo and TV unit.

Further examination of the crime scene revealed that they left smaller, and easily transported, items of far greater value (jewelry, coin collection, etc.). The police subsequently determined that the victim's wife paid the burglars to stage the crime and kill her husband. She, in fact, was having an affair with one of the suspects.

Another factor to consider is the point of entry. Did the point of entry make sense? For example, did the offender enter the house through a second-story window, even though there was an easier, less conspicuous entrance that could have been used? Why did the offender increase his chance of being seen by potential witnesses who might alert authorities?

Investigators should also consider whether the offender put himself at high risk by committing the crime during the daylight hours, in a populated area. If the crime scene is a place of residence, they should also evaluate any obvious signs of occupancy, such as lights on in the house, vehicles in the driveway, etc.

Case Scenario

The following case scenario brings to light some "red flags" that investigators should look for at a crime scene.

One Saturday morning, in a small Northeastern city, an unknown intruder attacked a man and his wife. By placing a ladder against the house, the suspect made it appear that he had climbed to a second-story window, removed the screen, and entered the residence. All this occurred in a residential area during a time when neighbors were doing their weekend chores and errands.

The husband claimed that he heard a noise downstairs, so he went with a gun to investigate. A struggle with the intruder ensued, during which the husband was left unconscious by a blow to the head.

Presumably, the intruder then went upstairs and killed the wife by manual strangulation. He left the body with a nightgown pulled up around the victim's waist, implying that he sexually assaulted her. The couple's 5-year-old daughter remained unharmed, asleep in the next room.

While processing the crime scene, detectives noted that the ladder made no impression in the moist soil near the house, although it did when they tried to climb the ladder. Also, the intruder positioned the ladder with the rungs facing away from the house, and many of the rungs on the wooden ladder had rotted, making it impossible for it to support anyone weighing over 50 pounds.

In addition, the crime scene raised questions that could not be answered logically. Why didn't the offender choose to enter the residence through a first-story window to decrease the possibility of detection by both the occupants and neighbors? Why did the offender want to burglarize the residence on a Saturday morning when there was a good chance that he would be seen by neighbors? Why did the intruder choose a residence that was obviously occupied (several vehicles were in the driveway)?

Inside the residence, other inconsistencies became apparent. For example, if the intent was murder, the intruder did not seek his victim(s) immediately, but went downstairs first. He also did not come equipped to kill because, according to the one witness, the husband, he never displayed a weapon. Also, the person posing the most threat, the husband, received only minor injuries.

By analyzing the crime scene, which revealed excessive offender activity, it became apparent that there was no clear motive for the crime. Therefore, based on the numerous inconsistencies found at the crime scene, NCAVC criminal investigative analysts conclud-ed that the husband staged the homicide to make it appear to be the work of an intruder. He was eventually convicted of his wife's murder.

Forensic "Red Flags"

Forensic results that don't fit the crime should also cause investigators to consider staging. Personal assaults should raise suspicion, especially if material gain appears to be the initial motive. These assaults could include the use of a weapon of opportunity, manual or ligature strangulation, facial beating (depersonalization), and excessive trauma beyond that necessary to cause death (overkill). In other words, do the injuries fit the crime?

Sexual and domestic homicides usually demonstrate forensic findings of a close-range, personal assault. The victim, not money or property, is the primary focus of the offender. However, this type of offender will often attempt to stage a sexual or domestic homicide that appears to be motivated by personal gain. This does not imply that personal assaults never happen while a property crime is being committed, but usually these offenders prefer quick, clean kills that reduce the time spent at the scene.

Forensic red flags are also raised when there are discrepancies between witness/survivor accounts and forensics results. For example, in one case, an estranged wife found her husband in the tub with the water running. Initially, it appeared as if he slipped and struck his head on a bathroom fixture, which resulted in his death by drowning. However, toxicological reports from the autopsy showed a high level of valium in the victim's blood. Also, the autopsy revealed several concentrated areas of injury or impact points on the head, as if the victim struck his head more than once.

Subsequently, investigators learned that the wife had been with the victim on the evening of his death. She later confessed that she laced his dinner salad with valium, and when he passed out, she let three men into the house. These men had been hired by the wife to kill the victim and to make it look like an accident.

Often, investigators will find forensic discrepancies when an offender stages a rape-murder, that is, positioning the body to infer sexual assault. And if the offender has a close relationship with the victim, he will only partially remove the victim's clothing, never leaving her completely nude. However, despite the position of the body and the removal of some of the victim's clothes, an autopsy can confirm or deny whether any form of sexual assault took place, thereby determining if the crime scene was staged.

If investigators suspect a crime has been staged, they should look for signs of association between the offender and the victim. Or, as is frequently the case with domestic violence, the involvement of a third party, who is usually the one who discovers the victim. For example, in the case involving the husband who staged his wife's murder to make it look like the crime was committed by an intruder, the husband did not immediately check on his wife and daughter once he regained consciousness. Instead, he remained downstairs and called his brother, who went upstairs and discovered the victim. Offenders will often manipulate the discovery of victims by a neighbor or family member, or conveniently be elsewhere when the victim is discovered.

CONCLUSION

Violent crime scenes require investigators to be "diagnosticians." They must be able to analyze crime scenes for the messages they emit and understand the dynamics of human behavior displayed at crime scenes. Investigators must also be able to recognize the different manifestations of behavior, so they can ask the right questions to get valid answers.

By approaching each crime scene with an awareness of these factors, investigators can steadily improve their ability to read the true story of each violent crime scene. By doing so, they will be more knowledgeable and better equipped to apprehend the violent crime offender.

John E. Douglas and Corinne Munn, "Violent Crime Scene Analysis: Modus Operandi, Signature, and Staging' in FBI Law Enforcement Bulletin, February 1992.

CASE REPORT SIGNATURE MURDERS: A REPORT OF THE 1984 CRANBROOK, BRITISH COLUMBIA CASES

CHAPTER

13

ROBERT D. KEPPEL,[1] PH.D.

Two females, Denean Worms and Brenda Hughes, were murdered in separate events in Cranbrook, British Columbia in 1984 within three months of each other. Terrence Wayne Burlingham was found guilty of both murders and appealed. The Supreme Court of Canada granted Burlingham a new trial in the Worms case, but forbid the use of Burlingham's confession and introduction of the murder weapon into evidence. The Crown counsel requested an evaluation of the two murders to determine if they were committed by the same person. The analyses of those murders revealed that they were linked by a personal "signature" of the killer. The murder cases reported here demonstrate a control-oriented signature. The killer used a .410 shotgun as his method of control and death, engaged in overkill of each victim by shooting them twice in the head, and left the victims in sexually degrading positions. Another signature feature was the absence of typical wounds to the victims which would be expected from a serial sex offender. All of these characteristics, in combination, accounted for this killer's personal expression.

Background

Terrence Wayne Burlingham appealed his conviction for the first-degree murder of Denean Worms, age 20, committed in October, 1984 at Cranbook, British Columbia. Burlingham had been convicted earlier of the first-degree murder of Brenda Hughes, age 16, committed in December 1984, also at Cranbrook. This appeal concerned only the trial and conviction for the murder of Denean Worms. At the time of the Worms appeal, Burlingham was serving his sentences of life imprisonment without eligibility for parole for 25 years on both convictions (1).

The Supreme Court of Canada provided the following case information. In both murders, committed only a few months apart, each victim was a young woman who had been violated sexually. Each was found naked, and was shot twice in the head at contact range with a .410 shotgun. Ms. Worms was killed by No. 5 pellets; Ms. Hughes, by No. 6 pellets (1).

Burlingham was arrested almost immediately after Ms. Hughes was found dead. In the course of his interrogation, he confessed to the killing of Ms. Hughes and took police authorities to his parents' home, where a sawed-off .410 shotgun and some No. 6 pellet shells were found. As the officers believed that Burlingham was also responsible for the death of Ms. Worms, they continued

[1]Chief criminal investigator, Washington State Office of the Attorney General, 900-4th Avenue, Suite 2000, Seattle, WA 98164. Received 23 April 1999; and in revised form 1 June 1999; accepted June 1 1999.

185

their interrogation. By this time, however, he had consulted a lawyer (who was not counsel at trial or his counsel on appeal), who advised him to say nothing to the police (1).

As recorded through testimony, it was reported that the investigating officers made many disparaging remarks to Burlingham about his counsel during their interrogation. Among other things, they questioned his loyalty, commented adversely upon his proposed legal fees, and criticized or ridiculed his absence on a weekend. The officers suggested to Burlingham they were more trust-worthy than a lawyer (1).

When the officers found they were not making any headway with this approach to Burlingham's interrogation, they consulted with Crown counsel of British Columbia, but not counsel for Burlingham, and then they offered Burlingham a deal. If Burlingham would cooperate by admitting to the Hughes murder, or by supplying physical evidence for this crime, they would reduce the charge for the death of Ms. Worms, but not for that of Ms. Hughes to second-degree murder. The accused then made some incriminating admissions in the Hughes murder and took the police to where a second .410 shotgun, the murder weapon, was found under the ice in the Kootenay River (1).

Notwithstanding this "deal," Burlingham was charged with the first-degree murder of Ms. Worms. It appears that Crown counsel only authorized the officers to say that a plea of guilty to second-degree murder would be accepted, not that the accused would be charged with second-degree murder (1).

The outcome of his appeal was that Burlingham was awarded a new trial on the Worms case in 1995. Significantly, the Supreme Court of Canada's rulings prevented the Crown Counsel from using Burlingham's confession to police and evidence (the .410 shotgun) derived from that confession at the new trial (1). Because the police mislead Burlingham, the only evidence that can be used is evidence from the crime scene and any new evidence and testimony. Therefore, prior to the retrial of Burlingham on one count of first-degree murder in the Worms homicide, Crown Counsel from British Columbia contacted this author and requested a signature analyses of the two murders to determine if they were committed by the same person. The Crown's theory was that evidence of the killer's signature in the two murders would be considered new evidence. The analysis could not include any information about Mr. Burlingham or evidence about why he was connected to either case because a credible signature analysis cannot consider that evidence.

For purposes of linking murder cases, regardless of whom criminal justice authorities have field charges against, experts have been called upon to testify about certain crime scene characteristics that have proved to be significant in various crimes. Experts have noted changes and similarities in a killer's method of operation or *modus operandi* (MO) (2–6). In particular, the way a murder is committed, for the most part, is influenced to some extent by the victim's response to the killer's actions. The MO of a killer includes only those actions necessary to perpetrate the murder. Many serial murderers are not satisfied with just committing the murder but feel compelled to go further. Actions beyond those necessary to commit the killing demonstrate behavior unique to that particular killer. The killer's personal expression is called his signature. Unlike MO, the signature remains constant (2–4, 7–10).

Signature murder testimony has been admitted at trial and upheld under appellate scrutiny in the United States several times. Those adjudicated cases are *State of Louisiana v. Nathaniel Code* (8,11), *State of Delaware v. Steven Pennell* (8,12), *State of California v. Cleophus Prince* (8,13), and *State of Washington v. George Russell* (8,9,14). Also, in *State of Washington v. Robert Parker* in 1998, the court refused to permit a required separation of charges in a pre-trial hearing. This decision was based in part on signature murder testimony. The Burlingham case was to be the first occasion when signature testimony would be used to link one murder to another in a Canadian court.

The materials used for the Worms and Hughes murders analyses were police reports from the initial investigation of the crime scenes and victims' backgrounds, crime scene diagrams, evidence reports, crime laboratory examination reports, autopsy reports, and photographs. The following facts were examined in the analyses from the Worms and Hughes murder cases.

Introduction to the Details of the Murders

The Cranbrook, British Columbia vicinity averaged less than one murder per year for the ten-year period preceding 1984. In that year, however, the locale experienced two separate atypical murders within ten kilometers of each other during a three-month period. Brenda Hughes lived twelve blocks south and five blocks west from the location where Denean Worms was last seen alive, a disco in Cranbrook.

Details of the Denean Worms Murder Case

The body of a 20-year-old white female was found October 16, 1984 at 1800 hours by target shooters at a gravel pit/shooting area outside Cranbrook. Police investigators discovered that she was nude except for white gym socks on her feet. The body was covered with a tree stump and several boards.

The victim was identified as Denean Worms. She was 5´3˝ tall, and weighted 140 lbs. She had dark brown curly hair, cut short, and brown eyes. She was last seen on Wednesday, Oct. 10, 1984 at 0150 hours, leaving a disco, in Cranbrook, BC. She was reported to be last seen wearing blue jeans, a white shirt and/or red vest, and running shoes. She worked at the disco as part-time cleaning staff and shared a nearby apartment with a male roommate.

Investigators located three blood-stained areas on the grounds near her body. Blood stain pattern #1 was 7.4 m away, blood stain pattern #2 was 4.5 m away, and blood stain pattern #3 was 2.7 m away. At pattern #1, 23 shotgun pellets, six metal pieces, and five pieces of teeth were recovered. This evidence revealed to investigators that the victim was initially shot at the location of pattern #1, then drug to the location where her body was found. Several kilometers away, back toward town, the victim's purse and shoes were found.

Autopsy results indicated that Worms was shot twice. Gunshot wound #1 through the left hand, exited the planar surface, and re-entered the left side of her face. It was determined that Gunshot #1 was the first shot fired. Gunshot wound #2 was an entry wound to the right side of the victim's head near her ear. It was *coup de grace* style. Both shots were fired from a .410 shotgun. There were no shotgun casings found at the scene. Multiple lineal abrasions were present over her back. They were consistent with being found on a person who had been dragged over a rough irregular surface. Semen was discovered in the vaginal area.

Details of the Brenda Hughes Murder Case

Brenda Hughes was a 16-year-old white female who lived with her family in Cranbrook, B.C. She was described as being 5´7˝ tall and weighing 120 lbs. She had brown hair and hazel-colored eyes. On Dec. 30, 1984, the victim's father, mother, and brother, left their home at about 1045 hours. She remained behind because she wanted to take a shower. The front door of the residence was left locked, but the carport entrance to the basement was left unlocked. The victim was last seen wearing pink night clothes.

At approximately 1230 hours, the family returned home from church. They entered the residence through the carport entrance, which was still unlocked. They immediately noticed blood on the head of the family's dog. The mother found the victim on the couch in the downstairs family room. The pink night clothes, which the victim was last seen wearing, were found in her brother's bedroom floor. Three dollars had been taken from his wallet, which was left on the dresser in his upstairs bedroom. The mother's purse was found on top of a toilet. It had been opened and appeared to have been gone through by someone. A gray-metal locking box was missing from the floor of the master bedroom closet. The father found that the victim's hair was wet, thus confirming that she had taken a shower. He noted that the volume to the stereo had been turned down, which was not normal for his daughter. He also noted that one load of wash had been done and removed from the washing machine, while another load had been washed and left in the machine.

Blood found on the stairway walls was determined to be the victim's blood deposited by the dog's fur. There was no splatter that came directly from the victim. A dented wallboard on the stairway wall was not there prior to the murder. There was no other evidence of a struggle. A pillow that had served as a buffer between the victim's head and gun barrel was also found.

The victim was found nude on the family room couch. She was face-down with her left side visible. Her head was resting against the armrest-pillow on the couch. Her left arm was bent with her hand near her shoulder. Her right hand was resting on top of her buttocks. She had sustained two gunshot wounds to the left side of her head. Gunshot wound #1 was an entrance wound to the left ear area. Plastic wrapping, cloth wadding, and lead pellets of the shotgun shell from a .410 shotgun were found inside her head. Gunshot wound #2 was located about 2 cm above gunshot wound #1. It is near contact in type. Lead pellets, plastic wrapping, and cloth wadding from a .410 shotgun were found inside victim's head. There were no exit wounds. As in the first case, no shotgun casings were found at the scene. A small fresh bruise was found in the posterior left mid-calf area. Semen was found in the vaginal area.

Signature Analyses

The following discussion summarizes the author's report to the Crown counsel in *R. v Terrance Wayne Burlingham*. The main question was: What features distinguished the killer's *modus operandi* and signature?

The distinction between a killer's MO and signature is important, particularly in these cases where the MO varies substantially between the first murder and the second murder. For example, in the Worms case, the killer picked up the victim on her way home from the bar. She was taken from public view so the killer could privately attack. But, in the Hughes case, the victim was raped and murdered in her own home. Thus the killer changed his MO from the first case to the second.

Whether the killer operated outdoors versus indoors was an additional characteristic of his MO. In Worms' case, the killer left her outdoors in an area from which he could escape without being detected. In the Hughes case, the killer appeared to feel very comfortable with a victim indoors. With that change in approach, the killer altered his MO.

Another MO factor was the killer's decision regarding transporting his victim from one location to another. Whereas he chose to transport Worms from one site to another, the killer chose not to do so with the second victim. By attacking Hughes and leaving her in her own home, the killer avoided the uncomfortable and risky situation of transporting Hughes' body from her home to another location.

Rape-murderers are driven by their anger and power. They need to express their emotions through control over their victims. After studying the case files of thousands of killers and interviewing many violent offenders, such as the one in these cases, the author concluded that most signature killers know they are committing a crime, but that knowledge is secondary in importance to the sexual excitement of terrorizing victims. The key to the signature in these cases was the manner in which the offender accomplished immediate and sustained domination and terror to the victims. The distinguishing signature of the killer in these cases is as follows.

First, in both cases, the offender demonstrated pre-planning and vast experience by his actions. Carrying any version of a sawed-off .410 shotgun is highly intimidating and terror producing. It wasn't necessary for him to carry such a power-oriented weapon when other weapons could have been used. The offender in these cases needed the terror that such a weapon produces with its size and ferocity, resulting in dominance over any victim. The .410 shotgun is not the weapon of choice by most killers, and certainly not the weapon of choice by most sexually-oriented murderers (15). This weapon was pre-selected and brought to the scene of each murder. The use of a .410 shotgun to intimidate his victims was one element of this killer's signature.

Second, it was necessary for the killer to leave both victims nude in sexually degrading positions. The intent of the killer was to present these victims as disposable, serving no value, and tools of ridicule. Therefore, the victims were not allowed any sense of decency by the killer. In Worms case, she was left nude, thrown away like a piece of trash, covered by a stump and boards in a reasonably remote area. But she was not left as though the killer didn't ever want her found. If the killer didn't want Worm's body found, he would have used more thorough and more elaborate concealment. In Hughes' case, the killer left her nude and prone on a sofa in her own home for relatives to discover. Leaving both bodies in positions that the finder would believe was sexually degrading and, also, demonstrating to the finder that the victims were extremely vulnerable, was a signature of this killer.

Third, the absence of damage to each victim's body is vital evidence of this killer's signature. In each case, there was no evidence of a struggle, binding, strangulation, physical torture, or post-mortem mutilation. The overpowering presence of the .410 shotgun rendered both victims helpless and, therefore, demonstrated this killer's need for complete compliance without the use of other implements or assaults. Many rape-murderers do not refrain from other types of violence. The failure of Worms' killer to use such violence, as evidence by the lack of pre-fatal and postmortem wounds is unusual. Physical assault and mayhem are common in rape-murder crimes. The unique absence of damage reflecting a struggle or torture is a signature for this type of offender. When one considers rape-murderers in general, to find no additional marks other than the death producing injuries is exceptionally rare.

Finally, the placement and number of gunshots to each victim's head is a signature element of this killer. The killer chose (felt he had) to fire a second shot, even though the first shot proved fatal in both cases. Additionally, the near-contact and *coup de grace* type wounds to the left side of each victim's head indicate this killer's need to assure himself that the victims were indeed dead. The additional shot reflects force beyond what was necessary to commit the murder.

In these two control-type rape-murders, the killer acted in a way that established his highly personalized signature. The author's conclusion was that both victims were killed by the same killer.

HITS DATA SEARCH

Independent from the above analyses, a computer search was performed to determine how frequently the main characteristics of these two murders have been seen in other murders. The search was conducted in the Homicide Investigation Tracking System's (HITS) data base. HITS is a central repository of homicide cases for the states of Washington and Oregon. It also contains additional murder cases from other states, British Columbia, and other provinces. This information is gathered from law enforcement officers and their reports (4,16). The search was conducted on March 17, 1998. At that time, there were 5960 murder records in the HITS data base. The following results of those searches were:

Total murder records	5960
Female victims	2295
Victims left nude	284
Major trauma to the head	56
Weapon was a shotgun	0

The most extraordinary finding for murders in which women were found nude, raped, and shot in the head was that, as of March 1998, no murder victims, shot with a shotgun had appeared in the entire HITS data base. The search findings clearly support the initial analyses that murderers who rape and murder female victims, leave them nude, and shoot them in the head with a shotgun are truly rare.

DISCUSSION

The single most important issue for the signature killer is control. Signature killers use a specific series of actions to assume and exert control. Some take pleasure in luring the unsuspecting victim through deception to a safe place where they can establish control. Other killers need immediate confirmation that control has been established and use overpowering implements and actions to achieve it (2,3,8). In the Worms and Hughes cases, the killer used a sawed-off .410 shotgun to gain control.

The central thread of Burlingham's signature was the imposing, and therefore controlling, nature of the .410 shotgun. Burlingham and a friend stole two guns two days before Denean Worms was murdered. One of these guns was the .410 shotgun used on Worms. Burlingham showed the shotgun to his friend a few days later, by which time the barrel had been substantially sawed off. Eventually, Burlingham hid the shotgun in the Kootenay River. His need for that type of weapon did not diminish. In fact, it was a requirement for his next homicide. Therefore, he used another .410 shotgun at the Hughes murder scene. That particular shotgun he had stolen from another burglary of a home while the people were asleep.

An interesting feature at both murder scenes was that no expended shell casings were found. Burlingham was careful at the Worms scene to retrieve the expended shotgun shell ejected from the first shotgun blast. This demonstrated an effort to not leave evidence. The second shotgun was double-barreled so the gun did not eject the expended rounds.

Investigative follow-up work and crime laboratory analyses further corroborated the opinion that the same person committed both murders. As mentioned earlier, given the Canadian Court's ruling, if evidence was to be introduced, it would have to be new testimony unrelated to Burlingham's confession or to evidence derived from that confession. While my analysis was being performed, Crown counsel and investigators realized that DNA testing had not been completed in 1984. So the semen samples found in both victims were tested and compared to Burlingham's DNA. Burlingham's blood sample positively linked him to the semen found inside the vaginas of both victims.

Finally, facing insurmountable new evidence against him, Terrence Burlingham pled guilty to the murder of Denean Worms.

Signature murder testimony is yet to be offered in the Canadian judicial system.

Acknowledgments

This analysis was possible thanks to the outstanding cooperation of Dennis Parsons of the Royal Canadian Mounted Police and the prosecutorial work of Dana Urban of the British Columbia Crown Counsel's Office. Also, Dr. W. R. Currie is recognized for his thorough postmortem exminations. The author acknowledges Richard Walter, Michigan State Prison Psychologist, former FBI agents John Douglas, Gregory Cooper, and Roy Hazelwood, FBI agent Larry Ankrom of the National Center for the Analysis of Violent Crime, and Vernon Geberth retired Captain with the New York City Police Department for their work in the area of signature crimes.

REFERENCES

Regina v. Terrence Wayne Burlingham, B.C.J. No. 1986, Vancouver Registry: CA006715, 1993.

Douglas, J.E., Burgess, A.W., Burgess, A.G., & Ressler, R.K. Crime classification manual, New York: Lexington Books, 1992.

Douglas, J.E., & Munn, C. Violent crime scene analysis. Homicide Investigators Journal, Spring 1992:63–9.

Geberth, V.J. Practical homicide investigation: tactics, procedures, and forensic techniques. Boca Raton: CRC Publishing, 1996.

Hanfland, K.J., Keppel, R.D., & Weis, JP. Case management for missing children homicides, Seattle: Washington State Attorney General's Office, May 1997.

Keppel, R.D., & Weis, J.P. Murder: A multidisciplinary anthology of readings. Orlando: Harcourt Brace Custom Publishing, 1999.

Keppel, R.D., & Birnes, W.J. The Riverman: Ted Bundy and I hunt the Green River Killer. New York: Pocket Books, 1995.

Keppel, R.D., & Birnes, W.J. Signature killers. New York: Pocket Books, 1997.

Keppel, R.D. Signature murders: A report of several related cases. Forensic Sci 1995:40(4);658-62.

Hazelwood, R., & Michaud, S.G. The evil that men do. New York: St. Martins Press, 1999.

State of Louisiana v. Nathaniel Code, 627 So.2d 1373, (1994).

State of Delaware v. Steven B. Pennell, Del.Super., 584 A.2d 513, (1989).

State of California v. Cleophus Prince, 9 CAL.APP.4th 1176, 10 CAL.RPTR.2D 855, (1992).

State of Washington v. George W. Russell, 125 Wash.2d 24, 882 P.2D 747 (1994)

Keppel, R.D., & Walter, R.A. Profiling killers: A revised classification model for understanding sexual murder. J Offender Therapy and Comparative Criminology 1999;43(4):417-37.

Keppel, R.D., & Weis, J.P. Time and distance as solvability factors in murder cases. J Forensic Sci 1994;39(2):386-401.

Additional information and reprint requests:
Robert D. Keppel, Ph.D.
President
Institute for Forensics
800-Fifth Avenue, Suite 4100
Seattle, WA 98104

COURTROOM TESTIMONY AND APPELLATE COURT REVIEW

Section V: Courtroom Testimony and Appellate Court Review addresses several of the legal issues concerning the use of profiling and crime scene analysis evidence in criminal trials. Much of the focus in today's courts centers around the admissibility of profiling evidence and expert witness testimony in linking serial cases to one another and to the same offender. Typically, expert witness testimony and evidence based on profiling practices have not been allowed in criminal cases in the United States and in England. English courts in particular, have adopted strict interpretations on the admissibility of evidence in criminal cases.

In the United States, however, there has been limited success in introducing expert witness evidence based on modern profiling practices or crime scene analysis. This section focuses on the reasoning behind the court's standards for the introduction of expert witness testimony, the reasoning behind judicial decisions in appellate court reviews, and the implications for the court decisions on the introduction of expert witness testimony pertaining to crime scene analysis. In addition, the George Russell criminal case and appeal is provided as an example of recent court holdings on the admissibility of evidence.

Authors Alison, Bennel, Mokros, and Ormerod (2002) argue for the use of extreme caution in using profiling evidence in criminal investigations and argue strongly against the admissibility of all expert witness testimony based on profiling evidence. *The Personality Paradox, in Offender Profiling: A Theoretical Review of the Processes Involved in Deriving Background Characteristics from Crime Scene Actions* addresses the validity and reliability of profiling evidence used in criminal investigations and its subsequent inadmissibility in criminal cases. The authors argue that the majority of modern profiling procedures rely on outdated beliefs about personality and broad personality types are probably useless in predicting criminal behavior.

Allison et al. contend that efforts to determine offender characteristics such as socio-demographic information based on appraisals of personality types in conjunction with crime scene information are unreliable and of little use to investigators. In addition, an argument is made for using more scientific methods to derive offender information from crime scene evidence. The authors emphasize the inclusion of situational factors and victim role information, such as the significance of Person x Situation interactions in generating offender behavior. They conclude that modern profiling techniques should incorporate contemporary trait approaches and that profiling evidence should not be admitted in criminal trials until research shows that profiling has predictive validity.

A transcript of the pretrial testimony of consulting detective and expert witness Robert Keppel in the George Russell criminal case is provided in *Testimony of Robert Keppel in State of Washington v. George Russell* (1991). Included is the prosecutions direct examination of the witness: Keppel's qualifications as a consultant, definitions of key terms (serial murder, modus operandi, signature, posing, and staging); findings in the Pohlreich, Beethe, and Levine homicides; HITS of the homicides; and the MO and signature in the Russell case. The defense cross examination is also provided, including questions concerning the use of crime scene analysis, profiling, and crime solvability.

Cross examination questions focused on distinguishing between the use of profiling and crime scene analysis in the investigation of the homicides. Critical in this case is establishing a factual base of the facts and issues in question to support the admissibility of the testimony. This is an excellent example of how testimony based on crime scene analysis has been admitted in criminal cases in the United States.

Finally, in *State v. Russell* (1994), 125 Wash. 2d 24, the reader has the opportunity of reviewing the appeal of criminal case in which the admissibility of expert testimony based on evidence from crime scene analysis is one of the base for appeal. George Russell appealed his homicide conviction to the Supreme Court of Washington on the basis of several points, arguing that the trial court had erred in admitting expert witness evidence at trial and excluding evidence of other suspects and crimes. The facts of the criminal case, including information pertaining to each homicide is provided, as well as findings of the trial court's decisions to admit expert witness testimony of crime scene analysis.

Upon review of the lower courts decisions and reasoning, the appeals court found that the lower court had not erred in admitting expert witness testimony of HITS analysis and the rarity of posing, and that the Frye standard did not apply to the type of information given in this case. The court found that the lower court had followed the standard for admissibility of evidence by establishing that 1) the witness was an expert, and 2) the evidence provided was beneficial to the jury. The Supreme Court of Washington, upon reviewing each point and issue of the appeal, affirmed the trial courts decision and upheld George Russell's conviction.

THE PERSONALITY PARADOX IN OFFENDER PROFILING: A THEORETICAL REVIEW OF THE PROCESSES INVOLVED IN DERIVING BACKGROUND CHARACTERISTICS FROM CRIME SCENE ACTIONS

LAURENCE ALISON,

CRAIG BENNEL,

ANDREAS MOKROS AND

DAVID ORMEROD

Most approaches to offender profiling depend on a naive trait perspective, in which the task of predicting personality characteristics from crime scene actions relies on a model that is nomothetic, deterministic, and nonsituationist. These approaches rest on two basic premises: behavioral consistency across offenses and stable relationships between configurations of offense behaviors and background characteristics. Research supports the former premise but not the latter. Contemporary trait psychology reveals that this is probably due to the fact that Person x Situation interactions have an effect on offense behavior. When profiling reports rely on a naive trait approach, such reports should be used with caution in criminal investigations and not at all as evidence in court until research demonstrates its predictive validity.

Many of the individuals who have been involved directly in providing offender profiles for investigations highlight the notion that profiling involves the derivation of personality characteristics from crime scene actions. They claim that the aim of offender profiling is to derive an offender's likely characteristics from the way in which he or she committed a particular crime, thus helping the police to identify the perpetrator (Blau, 1994). For example, Douglas, Ressler, Burgess, and Hartman (1986) described this as "a technique for identifying the major personality and behavioral characteristics of an individual based upon an analysis of the crimes he or she has committed"

(p. 405). According to Pinizzotto and Finkel (1990), an offender profile "focuses attention on individuals with personality traits that parallel traits of others who have committed similar offences" (p. 216). Turvey (1999) referred to offender profiling as the "process of inferring distinctive personality characteristics of individuals responsible for committing criminal acts" (p. 1). Finally, Rossmo (2000) claimed that the profiling process is based on the premise that the "interpretation of crime scene evidence can indicate the personality type of the individual(s) who committed the offence" (p. 68).

Previous evaluations of offender profiling have focused on post hoc assessments of accuracy based on the degree to which police officers claimed they were [*116] satisfied with the advice that they received. For example, a number of reviews of profiling have been carried out primarily on the basis of opinions of detectives about its utility (Britton, 1992; Copson, 1995; Douglas, 1981; Goldblatt, 1992; Jackson, Van Koppen, & Herbrink, 1993). Broadly speaking, all of these reviews concluded that investigators approved of the advice given and found it useful in various ways. However, none of these reviews are definitive and all were somewhat limited in the extent to which they were able to obtain a representative sample of profiles. They were also limited by the fact that they relied almost entirely on the subjective opinions of the investigators subsequent to the conclusion of the case.

In contrast to these evaluations of offender profiling that have focused primarily on product-related issues, few studies or theoretical reviews have considered the profiling process itself or the premises on which profiling methods are founded. Therefore, the goal in this article is to review the validity of the assumptions integral to the process of profiling. In particular, we demonstrate that much of what is considered standard practice in offender profiling falls short of current understanding in psychology about various psychological processes and principles, and therefore profiling practices do not meet basic expert witness standards under Federal Rule of Evidence 702, as recently interpreted.

The following points highlight the general argument advanced in this article as to why the derivation of background characteristics from crime scene actions is unlikely to be a valid and reliable process: (a) Most current profiling methods rely on a naive and outdated understanding of personality and the trait approach; (b) global traits, or broad personality types, are unlikely to be useful in predicting criminal behavior; (c) it is unlikely that the classification of offenders into broad personality types would enable the profiler to relate clusters of socio-demographic characteristics to different types; (d) a theoretical framework that emphasizes the importance of Person x Situation interactions in generating behavior may lead to a more productive research endeavor; and (e) profiling should be used with extreme caution in criminal investigations, and not at all as evidence in court, until research demonstrates its predictive validity.

Points (a) through (c) demonstrate how common profiling standards and practices would preclude such material being used in court in cases in which the profile is adduced to infer that, because the defendant is a particular type of individual, it is more probable that this defendant committed the crime. Points (a) through (c) reflect the contemporary personality theorist's perspective that such inferences are not possible. Moreover, other reliability factors, some of which correspond to criteria set out in *Daubert v. Merrell Dow Pharmaceuticals, Inc.* (1993), all militate against profiling advice being used in court. These factors include the extent to which the principle has been tested, the extent to which (a) the principle has been published and subjected to peer review and (b) the witness's specialized field of knowledge has gained acceptance with the general scientific, technical, or specialized community. It is appropriate for psychologists trained in areas such as personality psychology and social psychology to form part of a relevant scientific community to evaluate such reports because many statements in offender profiles purportedly rely on various psychological principles and processes.

THE PROFILING PROCESS RELIES ON A NAIVE TRAIT APPROACH

Many statements contained within offender profiles tend to attribute behaviors to underlying, relatively context-free dispositional constructs within the offender. This practice bears a strong resemblance to traditional trait theories of personality that were common in psychology before the 1970s (Mischel, 1968). As is the case with traditional trait theories, the theory underpinning most forms of offender profiling is nomothetic in its attempt to make general predictions about offenders. It is also deterministic in its assumption that all offenders' behaviors are affected in predictable ways. Finally, it is largely nonsituationist in its belief that behavior is thought to remain stable in the face of different environmental influences.

The Profiling Process Explained

The assumption regarding primary traits is that they are stable and general in that they determine a person's inclination to act consistently in a particular way (stable) across a variety of situations (general). As the notion of behavioral dispositions implies, traits are not directly observable. Rather, they are inferred from behavior (Mischel, 1999). In the case of profiling, these latent phenomena are inferred from crime scene actions. An example illustrates how tautological this argument can be. If a crime is particularly violent, this leads to the conclusion that the offender is particularly aggressive. Similarly, aggressive offenders commit any given crime in a particularly violent way. Thus, traits are both inferred from and explained by behavior.

A more sophisticated but similar example comes from the work that Turvey (1999) referred to in his discussion of motivational typologies, in which he outlined a variety of rape types (power reassurance, power assertive, anger retaliatory, anger excitation, and profit) on the basis of previous research by Groth (1979) and Burgess and Hazelwood (1995). He stated, for example, that "power assertive" offender actions "suggest an underlying lack of confidence and a sense of personal inadequacy, that are expressed through control, mastery and humiliation of the victim, while demonstrating the offender's sense of authority" (Turvey, 1999, p. 173). These offenders, according to Turvey, "may begin to do things that might lead to their identification" (p. 174). Although Turvey added the appropriate caveat that, "all too often, investigators and criminal profilers use … offender classifications to label a rapist's behavior with a single investigative 'diagnosis' " (p. 181), such classification systems have been used and remain in use for that very purpose.

For example, in a report prepared in the case of the Scarborough rapist (Paul Bernardo), a Federal Bureau of Investigation (FBI) profiler claimed that in observing the first eight offenses of the unknown offender, the offender could be classified as a "sexual sadist" (*http://www.corpus-delicti.com/court_bernardo_warrant.html*). This led the profiler to conclude that the following characteristics (and many others) could be predicted on the basis of such a classification system: male, White, parental infidelity or divorce, married at the time of the offense, known for cross-dressing, military experience, and a fascination with police work. Similar examples are abundant in some of the advice given to police forces in the United Kingdom, although the most significant case in the last [*118] decade was the advice provided by a psychologist in the Rachel Nickell murder enquiry.

In the Rachel Nickell enquiry, a clinical psychologist provided the police with an offender profile claiming that he was able to deduce from the crime scene both the murderer's sexual fantasies and a range of background characteristics. Examples of statements from the profile include the notion that the offender would be a lonely individual who was socially and sexually inept, would live nearby and probably alone, and that the offender would be interested in unusual and isolated hobbies (Britton, 1997). When the police eventually focused on a suspect whom they believed fit the profile, a man who had also been identified by a number of witnesses as being near the scene of the crime at the time of the murder, a covert operation known as Operation Edzell was set up.

This operation involved a female undercover officer befriending the suspect through a lonely hearts club the suspect was known to have joined prior to the murder. The operation was purportedly designed to establish whether the suspect would divulge sexual fantasies to his newly found partner that corresponded with those predicted in the psychologist's profile of the murderer. After an exchange of numerous letters between the undercover officer and the suspect, which slowly became more sexually explicit on both parts, the enquiry team were convinced that the sexual fantasies expressed in the suspect's letters fit the profile allegedly constructed at the beginning of the enquiry (the profiler in this case wrote his original profile on a white board, the details of which were erased, and therefore it is impossible to ascertain whether the original profile matched the profile that was subsequently written down). When the suspect was prosecuted for the murder, however, the judge ruled the evidence of the undercover operation inadmissible. Subsequent to this decision, no further evidence was offered against the suspect. Although there was no attempt to use the profile as the basis for evidence, it is difficult to ignore the possibility that it may have shaped the sequence of events in the enquiry and the way in which the undercover operation was conducted. (See Ormerod, 1996a, 1996b, for further details of this case.)

The methods and propositions described in these last two examples, that clusters of specific characteristics about the offender can be derived from examining crime scene actions, are not unique. Indeed, many of the most widely recognized and often-used experts in the United States, United Kingdom, and several other European countries have made similar claims (Asgard, 1998; Boon, 1997; Douglas, Burgess, Burgess, & Ressler, 1992; Douglas et al., 1986). They reflect the belief that the same behavioral dispositions that determine the style of crime scene behavior are reflected in more general, non-offense patterns in the individual's life. In fact, some profiling advice claims that these dispositions are linked directly with certain demographic features. Figure 1 exemplifies the supposed relationship between offense behavior, latent traits, and demographic features.

The most frequently cited theory of offense behavior in terms of this simple model is exemplified in the FBI's proposition of differences between "organized" and "disorganized" offenders (Douglas et al., 1986). The implication for adherence to such a simple model is that, for example, offenders will vary according to the degree of "organizational control" over a victim, and this will also reflect a stable trait emergent in other features of the offender's life. Therefore, factors [*119] such as social maturity, intelligence, and previous convictions can all be "profiled" on the basis of the level of organization observed at the crime scene.

This process is illustrated in a quotation from Douglas et al. (1992) in which they stated that "the crime scene is presumed to reflect the murderer's behavior and personality in much the same way as furnishings reveal the homeowner's character" (p. 21). However, for the over 200 classification categories of murder, rape, and arson that they presented in their *Crime Classification Manual*, it was also conceded by the authors that "at present, there have been no systematic efforts to validate these profile derived classifications" (Douglas et al., 1992, p. 22). Despite their acknowledgment, this theory and its derivations enjoy a consistent presence in the literature on serial killing and sexual assault (e.g., Badcock, 1997; Britton, 1997; Hickey, 1997; Holmes & DeBurger, 1988). Furthermore, they have been referred to in the advice given by profilers in police investigations (Alison, Smith, & Eastman, 2001) and, although fairly consistently rejected on appeal in the United States (Ormerod, 1996a), attempts have been made to use the process in criminal proceedings.

Research on the Profiling Process

In a comparative study of profilers, groups of homicide detectives, psychologists, and students, Pinizzotto and Finkel (1990) described the steps that lead to profiling inferences. They stated that professional profilers: (a) assess the type of criminal act with reference to individuals who have committed similar acts previously, (b) thoroughly analyze the crime scene, (c) scrutinize the background [*120] of the victim as well as any possible suspects, and (d) establish the likely motivations of all parties involved. Finally, a description of the perpetrator is generated, as the fifth step, from the characteristics supposedly connected with such an individual's "psychological make-up" (p. 216).

It is argued that the inferential process accomplished in the five steps described above can be represented in the question series, "What?" to "Why?" to "Who?" (Pinizzotto & Finkel, 1990). On the basis of crime scene material (What), a particular motivation for the offense behavior is attributed to the perpetrator (Why). This, in turn, leads to the description of the perpetrator's likely characteristics (Who). This simple "What" to "Why" to "Who" inference assumes that the supposed specific motivations that drive the initiation of the offense are consistently associated with specific types of background characteristics of the offender (e.g., "If Motivation X, then Characteristics A, B, C, and D"). This practice is problematic because it is not clear how a profiler moves from one point to the next (i.e., what rules of thumb connect each inferential leap; Pinizzotto & Finkel, 1990). Moreover, profilers commonly do not specify which (if any) behavioral, correlational, or psychological principles they rely on. Therefore, labels such as "organized" and "disorganized" (Ressler, Burgess, Douglas, Hartman, & D'Agostino, 1986) may simply be the result of a readiness to attribute a latent trait to a set of crime scene behaviors despite the lack of clear evidence for the existence of such factors.

Furthermore, Prentky and Burgess (2000) criticized the practice of developing offender profiles by identifying two potential problems: (a) the difficulty involved in the correct classification of the offender based on extremely limited material and (b) the inability to draw reliable conclusions based on "nothing more than what one knows about a particular subtype" (p. 194). As yet, there have been very few attempts to evaluate the evidence for the feasibility of such inferences in relation to offender profiling. One recent study that has attempted to do this demonstrated that there was no evidence to support the hypothesis that subsets or clusters of behaviors were associated with subsets or clusters of offender background characteristics (Mokros & Alison, in press).

THE PERSONALITY PARADOX

The readiness to invoke dispositions rather than explain behavior in terms of situational influences has been described by some as a disparity between intuition and empiricism (i.e., an intuitive belief within most people that behavior is cross-situationally consistent vs. much empirical evidence that suggests it is not; Bem & Allen, 1974). Bem and Allen (1974) have called this disparity "the personality paradox" and, according to their observations, individuals are prone to infer stable dispositions from behavior even though evidence has consistently demonstrated that global trait constructs fail to accurately predict behavior over time and across specific situations. It is possible, therefore, that this inappropriate heuristic has perpetuated the use of such inappropriate methods in offender profiling because many of the individuals who currently provide profiling advice have little academic understanding of personality and of the difficulties associated with inferring behavior from global traits. In some cases, profilers openly admit [*121] that opinions about offenders are based on intuition and experience rather than scientific evidence.

This personality paradox is exemplified in the definitions of profiling outlined at the outset of this article and in statements such as the following:

> Profiling rests on the assumption that at least certain offenders have consistent behavioral traits. This consistency is thought to persist from crime to crime and also to affect various non-criminal aspects of their personality and lifestyle, thus making them, to some extent, identifiable. (Homant & Kennedy, 1998, p. 328)

Similarly, the traditional view of personality dispositions leads to the assumption that "individuals are characterized by stable and broadly generalized dispositions that endure over long periods of time and that generate consistencies in their social behavior across a wide range of situations" (Mischel, 1990, p. 112).

Empirical tests, however, generally yield little supportive evidence for this traditional trait view (Mischel, 1968). In a number of classic studies carried out in the 1920s and 1930s (Dudycha, 1936; Hartshorne & May, 1928; Newcomb, 1929), behavioral consistency was tested by observing people's social behavior as it occurred across a variety of natural settings. The intercorrelations among behaviors composing a particular trait concept rarely exceeded .30, leading many theorists to question not only popular trait theories (e.g., Mischel, 1968; Peterson, 1968; Vernon, 1964) but also the very concept of personality (Epstein, 1979). More recent studies, such as the often-cited Carleton College study, also support these earlier findings insofar as the two global trait concepts of friendliness and conscientiousness mostly failed to allow predictions of behavior across specific situations (Mischel & Peake, 1982). As in the earlier studies, the mean intercorrelations of items were positive but very low (.13 and .08, respectively).

Beyond the lack of empirical support for high levels of behavioral consistency, the traditional trait perspective has been criticized on other grounds. Briefly, these include the following: (a) analysis of variance studies (summarized in Bowers, 1973) demonstrating that much of the variation in behavior across situations can be attributed to situational influences or Person x Situation interactions (however, see Golding, 1975, and Clweus, 1977, for criticisms of these studies); (b) the circularity in reasoning that emerges when one tries to explain behavior from a traditional trait perspective (Bandura, 1969; Cervone & Shoda, 1999a, 1999b); and finally, (c) recent findings suggesting that there exist important forms of personality coherence that traditional trait models fail to capture, in particular, forms of personality coherence that are manifest at the individual (idiographic) level but not at a general (nomothetic) level (Cervone & Shoda, 1999a, 1999b; Zelli & Dodge, 1999).

On the basis of evidence concerning the traditional trait approach, one would not expect a task such as offender profiling, in which global traits are derived from specific actions (or vice versa) to be possible. Moreover, the profilers' task is even more ambitious than this: Many profilers make inferences about characteristics that are not appropriate for a psychological definition of traits. Rather, profilers include features such as the offender's age, gender, ethnicity, marital status, degree of sexual maturity, and likely reaction to police questioning (Annon, 1995; Ault & Reese, 1980; Grubin, 1995; Homant & Kennedy, 1998).

ASSUMPTIONS UNDERLYING OFFENDER PROFILING

Two basic assumptions underpin the profiling methods discussed so far. First, the actions of any given offender are consistent across offenses, or, in statistical terms, intraindividual behavioral variation across offenses is smaller than inter-individual behavioral variation (the consistency assumption). Clearly, if the behavior of the same offender varied more than between offenders, it would not be logical to look for a common denominator that summarized the behavioral tendencies of one offender. The second assumption is that similar offense styles have to be associated with similar background characteristics. For example, aggressive individuals are aggressive both in their offense behavior and in the way they act in other (non-offese) situations (the homology assumption). These two assumptions relate to the necessary (consistency) and sufficient (homology) conditions for offender profiling to be valid and useful.

The Consistency of Offense Behavior

Offenders' behavioral consistency has been examined in a variety of ways. Traditionally, criminological research has adopted a molar approach, defining behavioral consistency as the probability that an individual will repeatedly commit similar types of offenses (Farrington, 1997). Being less occupied with legal nomenclature, psychological research, in contrast, has emphasized a molecular analysis of criminal behavior. In this context, behavioral consistency has been defined as the repetition of particular aspects of behavior if the same offender engages in the same type of offense again (Canter, 1995).

Numerous studies have provided some support for the notion of offender consistency. For example, one study examined the consistency of behaviors displayed by different burglars of residential properties (Green, Booth, & Biderman, 1976). On the basis of 14 aspects of the crimes, such as "location of entry," "method of entry," and "value of property taken," Green and his colleagues were able to use cluster analysis to accurately assign 14 out of 15 cases of burglary to the three actual perpetrators. Similarly, studies have suggested that behavioral consistency exists in the crime scene behaviors of serial rapists, though only to a limited degree (Canter, 1995; Craik & Patrick, 1994; Grubin, Kelly, & Brunsdon, 2001; Wilson, Jack, & Butterworth, 1996). Thus, there does appear to be some, albeit limited, evidence supporting the consistency assumption in offender behavior.

The Homology of Offense Behavior and Offender Characteristics

The second premise is that the manner in which an offense is committed corresponds with a particular configuration of background characteristics. This differs from the more humble findings that relate to bivariate measures of association, examples of which include Davies, Wittebrood, and

Jackson's (1998) and House's (1997) observations on the relationship between previous convictions and certain crime scene actions of rapists. Davies et al. used odds ratios and base rates (i.e., probabilities derived from percentages), and House reported percentages, to describe the relationship between pairs of crime scene actions and previous convictions. For example, Davies et al. noted that offenders who display [*123] awareness of forensic procedures by destroying or removing semen have a likelihood of a previous conviction for a sexual offense that is almost four times higher (exact odds ratio = 3.96) than those offenders who do not take such precautions.

However, these simple relationships between a given action and a given characteristic are very different from the far more ambitious accounts that are often referred to by practitioners and researchers in the profiling field (e.g., see Blau, 1994; Douglas et al., 1986; Pinizzotto & Finkel, 1990). In these cases, attempts were made to profile clusters of background features from crime scene actions to develop a psychological portrait of the offender. They were concerned with multivariate forms of prediction in which particular configurations or sets of actions were linked to particular sets of characteristics. When tested, however, the results were not very promising.

In the study by Davies et al. (1998), the integration of a range of crime scene actions as predictors within logistic regression models failed to show a substantial improvement over the information obtained through simple base rates in the majority of instances. Similarly, in the study by House (1997), the 50 rapists in his sample appeared relatively homogeneous with respect to their criminal histories, regardless of whether they acted in a primarily aggressive, pseudo-intimate, instrumental/criminal, or sadistic manner during the sexual assault. More recent studies have also failed to discover any relationships between specific behavioral themes of rape behavior and subsets of offender background characteristics (Mokros & Alison, in press).

TOWARD A CONTEMPORARY MODEL OF OFFENDER PROFILING

Most varieties of offense behavior for which profiling may be of relevance involve intense, relatively short-lived, and potentially traumatic interactions that are generally characterized by the diametrically opposed interests of the offender and victim. Therefore, the influence of situational factors and the role of the victim should not be neglected. A theoretical framework that emphasizes the importance of Person x Situation interactions in generating behavior may provide a more productive model for offender profiling.

Unlike traditional trait approaches that conceptualize traits as stable attributes within each person that determine how we behave, contemporary trait approaches view traits as probable "if ..., then ..." relations between clusters of behaviors and clusters of situations (Mischel, 1990; Wright & Mischel, 1987a). The contemporary view on traits, therefore, is not a challenge "to the *existence* of dispositions, but to the assumptions about their nature" (Mischel, 1990, p. 131). The central problem with traditional trait approaches, as perceived by contemporary trait psychologists, is the "limited utility of inferring broad, context-free dispositions from behavioral signs as *the* basis for trying to explain the phenomenon of personality, and for predicting an individual's specific behavior in specific situations" (Mischel, 1990, p. 131).

Thus, the analysis of behavior from a contemporary trait perspective extends beyond the idea of drawing on underlying context-free dispositional constructs in an attempt to explain and predict behavior. Instead, the approach takes account of contextual details. The primary unit of observation is "not the unconditional [*124] probability of trait-relevant behavior, p(B), ... rather, it is the conditional probability of a certain behavior or category of behaviors given a certain condition or set of conditions has occurred, p(B C)" (Wright & Mischel, 1987a, p. 1161).

Conditional trait theorists also recognize that behavior categories and situation categories will often vary in the degree to which they are "well defined or fuzzy" (Wright & Mischel, 1987a, p. 1161). In the criminal domain, for example, behavior categories (e.g., hostility) will often consist of a range of specific offense behaviors, with some being highly typical of the category (e.g., the use of physical violence) and some being more peripheral (e.g., the use of verbal violence; Bennell, Alison, Stein, Alison, & Canter, 2001). Likewise, situation categories (e.g., a high-risk event) in the criminal domain will consist of various contexts that are highly typical (e.g., a victim screaming for help when the attack is taking place in public) as well as contexts that are more peripheral (e.g., a victim screaming for help when the attack is taking place indoors). Even the links between behavior categories and situation categories will vary "in the degree to which they are necessary and sufficient [e.g., if encountered by serious resistance, physical violence *will* result] versus probabilistic [e.g., if encountered by serious resistance, physical violence *might* result, with probability *p*]"; Wright & Mischel, 1987a, p. 1161). The probabilistic nature of these links will, in part, determine what affects the behavioral consistency of offenders across their crime series and how consistent offenders are between their criminal and noncriminal life.

Challenges for a Contemporary Model of Offender Profiling

One of the primary challenges for contemporary trait psychologists is to understand very clearly the relationship between people's behavior, on the one hand, and the situations they typically encounter, on the other. In the words of Wright and Mischel (1987a), contemporary trait psychologists must "identify the categories of conditions in which predictable behaviors relevant to some dispositional domain are most likely to be observed" (p. 1162). This has proven to be an extremely difficult task in the noncriminal domain, but it would be even more difficult to accomplish in the investigative domain. In the investigative domain, very little is ever known about the context within which any given crime takes place beyond the time of occurrence, the location where the offense was committed, and some information about the victim—contextual features that profilers are often encouraged to examine (Douglas et al., 1992).

However, possible ways of accomplishing this task in the noncriminal domain are slowly beginning to emerge and may prove useful in the profiling context. For example, it is possible to conduct interviews with people to determine directly from them the situational features they consider relevant to particular behaviors they exhibit. In one study, adults and children were asked to generate "if ..., then ..." contingencies to describe why they think people behave the way they do (e.g., "If Sally is teased, then she becomes withdrawn"; Wright & Mischel, 1987b). Cluster analyzing these "if ..., then ..." contingencies proved to be a useful way of identifying important situational features and relevant situation-behavior links in a noncriminal context (Wright & Mischel, 1987b). This approach has the potential to reduce the number of "if ..., then ..." statements needed to predict behavior by showing how it is possible to generalize from one [°125] "if ..., then ..." contingency to another one located within the same taxonomic group. This is extremely important, considering the potentially large number of "if's" that would be needed to represent every situation an individual may encounter (Shoda, 1999).

A similar approach could also be applied in the profiling context by interviewing offenders about the circumstances they consider relevant to behaviors they exhibit (e.g., "If I encounter a victim who physically resists me, then I become very hostile," or "If I find myself in a situation where there is a high risk of getting caught, then I become very controlling"). The problem is that previous research in the noncriminal domain suggests that these classification systems may not account for every individual, nor may they be "sensitive enough to the important nuances of each situation that may critically affect their psychological meaning" (Shoda, 1999, p. 162). The same sorts of problems would be likely to arise in the profiling context as well.

In addition to identifying relevant "if's" and "then's," recent studies have begun to indicate that the nature of the "if's" in these situation-behavior contingencies is extremely important to consider. For example, studies that have examined how surface level categorizations of situations affect behavior have yielded poor results (Lord, 1982; Shoda, Mischel, & Wright, 1994). Situational similarity, defined purely by the physical features of situations (e.g., during dinner, in the office, at the park, etc.), does not appear to influence noncriminal behavioral consistency (Shoda, 1999). Instead, the psychological meaning of specific situations to particular individuals must be established to generate any valid inferences (Shoda, 1999). In one study, focusing on the types of interpersonal interactions taking place across situations has proved productive (Shoda et al., 1994), whereas, in another, focusing on the competency demands characteristic of particular situations proved a valid and useful way of defining situations (Wright & Mischel, 1987a). Thus, an important development would be to assess the psychological relevance of situational properties that might emerge in criminal activity. When doing this, it might not be sufficient to simply know that a crime was committed against a young woman, outdoors, during the night. Instead, the psychologically active ingredients (Shoda et al., 1994) making up these criminal situations may need to be identified and taken into account.

Some Cautionary Notes

Although contemporary trait approaches may be more suitable for making inferences about personality features on the basis of crime scene actions, we should add some cautionary notes about the extent to which this approach may or may not be useful in the course of a criminal investigation or in court.

One would have to consider what is commonly termed the *bandwidth-fidelity* or *abstraction* issue (Hampson, 1995). This originated with Cronbach and Gleser's (1957) discussion of the bandwidth-fidelity trade-off, which refers to "the differences in precision of [personality] measurement at different levels of abstraction" (Hampson, 1995, p. 95). As Hampson (1995) stated:

> Where an abstract personality trait is involved [e.g., conscientiousness], then measurement will be imprecise in the sense that the prediction of specific behaviors [e.g., punctuality] will be relatively poor. Nevertheless, predictions can be [°126] made for a wide range of behavior. ... In contrast, where a less abstract trait is involved, such as punctuality, then prediction of specific punctual behaviors will be good. However, this fidelity is gained at the expense of bandwidth: knowing a person's punctuality is only predictive of a small range of behaviors. (p. 95)

The bandwidth-fidelity trade-off connects directly with current concerns regarding levels of differentiation in offending behavior (Canter, 2000). Examining offense behaviors at a very general level (e.g., in terms of broad psychological themes underlying offender-victim interactions) may be productive in the sense that one might be able to predict very general information about an offender's background. For example, there has been some success in demonstrating how, in cases of arson, particular configurations of actions (or behavioral themes) are associated with different underlying themes within an offender's background (e.g., whether the arsonist has a general history of psychiatric problems, or whether the offender has a long history of previous offenses; Canter & Fritzon, 1998). However, evaluating offense behavior at this aggregate level probably means that profilers will not be able to predict very specific background characteristics. For example, Douglas et al.'s (1992) accounts of the offender having an "uncharacteristically detailed, precise, airtight alibi" (p. 25) or that the offender will be "considered odd by those who know him" (p. 130) are probably a little ambitious. Thus bandwidth is gained at the expense of fidelity.

There are many studies of sexual offenders that support the aggregate level of research. For example, it has been demonstrated in one study that rapists display significantly diverse facets of personality disorder depending on their level of physical violence as demonstrated in their crime scene behavior (Proulx, Aubut, Perron, & McKibben, 1994). Among the findings reported in this study was the observation that more violent offenders score significantly higher on the histrionic, narcissistic, antisocial, and paranoid subscales than do the less violent offenders. Similar results have been reported for another sample of rapists (Langevin, Paitich, & Russon, 1985). In addition, when Knight, Warren, Reboussin, and Soley (1998) derived a set of crime-scene behavior variables from a sample of rapists and then applied these items to predict motivational characteristics for a second sample of rapists, they were somewhat successful in predicting the individuals who could be classified as *expressive, aggressive, antisocial*, and *sadistic* types (Knight & Prentky, 1990).

In a more recent study, rapists were assigned to one of three groups (*sadistic, opportunistic*, and *anger* rapists) according to their respective modus operandi (Proulx, St.-Yves, Guay, & Ouimet, 1999). In this study, they found that substantial differences existed between the sadistic and the opportunistic types with respect to personality disorders. The sadistic offenders were more likely to have avoidant, schizoid, and dependent tendencies, whereas the opportunistic offenders were characterized as narcissistic, paranoid, and antisocial. This study indicates that it may be possible to discriminate between rapists on the basis of their crime scene actions and that such differentiation may be reflected in personality. Such a procedure could properly be referred to as a psychological profile because it refers exclusively to particular psychological constructs. In contrast, the current use of the term **psychological profiling** to refer to demographic characteristics is [* 127] a misnomer. Whether the former types of profiling could prove valuable to law enforcement agencies remains to be seen.

Therefore, three main objectives for future research emerge. The first objective is to explore the relationship between personality, as defined through dispositional concepts, and crime scene actions. These dispositional concepts need to take the form of measurable psychological constructs, such as aggressiveness or hostility, rather than demographic features. Only then is the second step possible: assessing whether these dispositions function as moderators of offender background characteristics. Finally, an alternative theoretical framework for exploring the relationship between crime scene actions and characteristics of offenders can be explored that avoids the previous major flaws of the traditional, global trait perspective, such as its neglect of situational influences. In this regard, contemporary trait approaches may provide a more useful model for offender profiling.

INVESTIGATIVE AND LEGAL IMPLICATIONS

In this article, we illustrate why the evidence for relying on a nomothetic, deterministic, and nonsituationist model of offender profiling is not compelling. Thus, any claim involving the derivation of specific clusters of characteristics of the offender on the basis of an evaluation of the crime scene must be treated with a degree of skepticism. Despite this, and despite the admission by many profilers that their work is little more than educated guesswork, the utility of profiling seems to be generally accepted as valid. Relatively recent reports suggest that the FBI currently has 12 full-time profilers who collectively are involved in about 1,000 cases per year (Witkin, 1996). Few studies have considered whether such profiling advice may actually be an impediment to an enquiry, and there are some commentaries on *Regina v. Stagg* (1994) as to how that may have been the case (Alison & Canter, 1999; Ormerod, 1996a). In contrast, most of the evaluation studies have suggested that police officers were relatively happy with the advice received and found it useful despite the fact that it very rarely led to the identification of the offender (Copson, 1995).

The arguments that investigators commonly present for the utility of profiling include statements such as, "It helps narrow the suspect search," "It gives another point of view," and "It helps us understand the offender" (Alison et al., 2001). These comments highlight the possibility that profiling can be of some help and, clearly, with the attendant caveats about profiling standards and appropriate knowledge of how to use such advice, investigations may well benefit from external input of this sort. However, investigators should be wary of (a) reports that rely on broad generalizations about behavior, (b) very specific statements about the likely characteristics of the offender, and (c) claims about the motivations behind the offense. This may lead to an inappropriate focus on a subpopulation of possible suspects, the mismanagement of resources, and a delay in the successful resolution of the case. The argument is not that all profiling advice is poor but, rather, that many of the most influential claims about offenders in the last few decades have been based on intuition, outdated and ill-informed concepts about personality, or on very small-scale studies that are methodologically controversial. Thus, commonly used terms such as *organized/disorganized* (Ressler et al., 1986), *visionary type murderers* (Holmes & DeBurger, 1988), and *power [° 128] reassurance rapists* (Burgess & Hazelwood, 1995) should be treated with extreme caution, particularly in cases in which the profiler claims that these typologies are associated with specific sets of background characteristics.

In terms of using offender profiles in court, there are more persuasive reasons to exclude testimony that relies on such simple classification systems. Although there have been no cases to date in the United Kingdom that have incorporated such advice, there have been several attempts to do so in the United States (Ormerod, 1996a, 1999). The majority of these attempts have involved expert witnesses providing evidence in relation to the consistency assumption discussed earlier rather than the homology assumption, which is also integral to the process of profiling. Recent examples include a number of cases in which attempts were made by former FBI agents to link offenses to a particular offender on the basis of so-called signature aspects of offense behavior (Douglas & Munn, 1992).

One such case involved 2 counts of murder in which substantial physical and circumstantial evidence was available that linked the defendant to two of the murders. In addition to this evidence, the trial court accepted testimony provided by an FBI agent that each of the 3 murders in question had characteristic behavioral similarities that suggested they were the work of the same offender (*Delaware v. Pennell*, 1991). On appeal before the Delaware Supreme Court, the defendant's counsel argued that the testimony provided by the FBI agent did not meet the standards of the test then imposed as a standard for all scientific evidence to be adduced before the court–the *Frye* test–and therefore it should not be admissible in court. The court affirmed the original ruling, however, stating that the *Frye* test did not apply in this case because the FBI agent's linkage analysis was based solely on his own knowledge and experience and not on scientific tests for which the *Frye* test would typically be applied.

In a similar case involving 4 counts of murder, evidence provided by an FBI agent was admitted at the pretrial hearing to support the State's position that another set of crimes (consisting of 4 additional murders that the defendant was also charged with) were, in fact, connected to the crimes the defendant was being tried for. The FBI agent testified that, based on various ritual aspects of the murders that were (in the agent's opinion) particularly rare, the 8 murders were the work of one person. The agent did not testify before the jury, but his testimony was accepted by the trial judge as evidence on the issue of suspect identity. On appeal before the Louisiana Supreme Court, the court found no error in the trial court's ruling to accept the FBI agent's linkage analysis (*Louisiana v. Code*, 1993).

Unlike these two previous cases, in a more recent case (*New Jersey v. Fortin*, 2000), the Superior Court of New Jersey reversed an earlier ruling that permitted a former FBI agent's linkage analysis to be used as evidence. The case involved 1 murder and 1 attempted murder; the FBI agent provided testimony that due to distinct similarities across the crimes in question, the two crimes were the work of the same offender. Despite the fact that such evidence had been used in the previously cited cases, the court was not persuaded that these techniques were sufficiently reliable for use in this particular case because of the many differences that existed between the crimes in question.

Finally, in a case that involved evidence being admitted that was related more directly to the homology assumption, a former FBI agent provided testimony as [*129] to the classification of offenses according to the organized/disorganized dichotomy. The former agent contended that the 9 crimes for which the defendant was being charged fit a mixed category, displaying elements of both themes. The defendant's counsel highlighted the disorganized characteristics in an effort to prove the defendant's diminished responsibility. However, in cross-examination, the State elicited testimony from the expert that some of the crimes displayed signs of organization, thereby indicating a lack of mental illness. Under appeal to the Supreme Court of North Carolina, the defendant's counsel contended that the cross-examination was improper as it was prejudicial and had no probative value (*North Carolina v. Wallace*, 2000). However, the court concluded that the cross-examination was permissible, as the jury had been given proper instructions to limit their consideration of the expert's testimony.

Thus, in some cases, advice regarding the consistency of offense behavior has been considered sufficiently reliable and relevant to be helpful to the jury, and in others it has been rejected. However, as far as we are aware, in no case has profiling evidence been successfully used to provide evidence probative of guilt or innocence. Ormerod (1996a, 1999) has comprehensively outlined the number of hurdles that the expert testimony would have to overcome to be able to introduce such evidence, at least in U.K. courts. Much of Ormerod's discussion is in relation to *Regina v. Stagg* (1994), but the points made are applicable to any case in which attempts are made to introduce profiling evidence in court. There are questions over relevance, whether the advice is expert evidence, whether it can be used as similar fact evidence, and whether its potential for prejudicial influence outweighs its probative value.

Ormerod (1999) noted that for a profile about the guilt of a specific defendant to be legally relevant, it must render the facts at issue (the commission of the crime by *this* defendant) more probable. Thus, in Ormerod's view, it is not sufficient to state that the defendant possesses the qualities of the *type* of individual who could have committed the offense because the jury must evaluate whether the defendant matching the description is *the* offender. Even if the profiling advice were based on very specific details, such as those in the Paul Bernardo case outlined earlier, using these details to prove the guilt or innocence of the offender would not be possible because there is no reliable evidence to suggest that such forms of profiling are possible. Indeed, the arguments against the homology assumption suggest that it is very *unlikely* that such details could be inferred from crime scene characteristics.

With hard scientific or technical evidence, one must consider the reliability of the evidence. A ballistics expert is allowed to testify about the likelihood of the match between the offense bullet and the defendant's gun only because he or she can demonstrate by reliable means that the tests are accurate. This is quite different from the evidence of a fortune-teller, for example. If the police sought to rely on the fortune-teller's evidence to demonstrate that it was more probable that the defendant committed the crime, the court would reject the evidence as irrelevant. There is no reliability in the evidence, therefore, it has no foundation on which to make its claim. Where does that leave a profiler who relies not on the hard science of ballistics but on spurious and outdated psychological principles? Given the arguments outlined in this article regarding the inappropriateness of the homology assumption, it is improbable that a profiler would be able to demonstrate [°130] with sufficient strength any claim that he or she can reliably and consistently identify character traits from crime scenes. The evidence would lack a reliable foundation.

In *Regina v. Stagg* (1994), the judge also questioned whether profile evidence was sufficiently well accepted as a scientific method according to strict definitions in Daubert v. Merrell Dow *Pharmaceuticals, Inc.* (1993). Although the English courts have not been overly concerned with this issue, the concern has been more prevalent in U.S. courts, particularly in light of recent developments. In broad terms, federal standards on the admissibility of expert testimony require that to be considered expert evidence, the proffered witness (a) must qualify as an expert by knowledge, skill, experience, or training; (b) must testify to scientific, technical, or other specialized knowledge; and (c) his or her testimony must assist the trier of fact. In cases following the *Daubert* criteria for admitting scientific evidence, the following facts must be considered: whether the method consists of a testable hypothesis, whether the method has been subject to peer review, the known potential rate of error, the existence and maintenance of standards controlling the technique's operation, whether the method is generally accepted, the relationship of the technique to methods that have been established to be reliable, the qualifications of the expert witness testifying on the basis of the methodology, and the nonjudicial uses of the method.

If the foregoing criteria were applied to the many opinions about likely offender characteristics on the basis of types of classification systems endemic in some profiling methods, the "reliability" of profile evidence would be extremely controversial. As outlined earlier, the few studies that have assessed success rates have been limited and have relied heavily on subjective opinions of the investigating officers. Moreover, rates of "success" are difficult to evaluate because it is extremely difficult to assess the extent to which the profile aided in the identification of the offender. Where efforts have been made to extract such information, results are not encouraging. For example, in Copson's (1995) study, profiles assisted in less than 25% of cases in solving the case, and in only 5 cases out of 184 (2.7%) did the profile lead to the identification of the offender. Studies have also indicated that profilers do not process crime scene information differently from any other group (e.g., students, police officers) in which they are untrained in profiling methods (Pinizzotto & Finkel, 1990).

Courts in the United Kingdom, at least, are aware of the potential prejudicial value of statements that appear to come from authoritative sources but are not necessarily any more helpful than jurors' own opinions (Ormerod, 1999). A particular danger may lie in Bem and Allen's (1974) demonstration that individuals readily attribute behavior to global traits and that much profiling advice appears to reinforce this inappropriate heuristic. Therefore, a profiler proffering advice on types of offenders, and how these classifications relate directly to sets of characteristics, may be particularly prone to prejudicial thinking because it exploits inaccurate laypersons' perspectives of behavior.

However, is it possible that arguments could be made to admit expert testimony on offender profiling on the basis of a more flexible application of standards, as outlined in *Kumho Tire Co. v. Carmichael* (1999)? The plaintiffs in this case argued that the court's application of the *Daubert* criteria was too inflexible, resulting in the exclusion of testimony regarding visual observations [°131] made by an expert with extensive experience in tire failure analysis. On the basis of patterns of wear and tear on tires, the plaintiffs sought to use the expert to support the view that the tire that blew out on a minivan driven by Carmichael, thereby leading to a fatal accident, was defective. The issue regarding the admission of the expert testimony centered on whether observations based on extensive visual and tactile practical experience represent a standard of knowledge sufficient to comprise technical or other specialized knowledge beyond the knowledge of the jurors.

Profilers with extensive practical case experience may argue that this standard of knowledge applies to them and thus affords them the privileged position of commenting on offenses that the layperson would have little or no opportunity to experience. This tacit knowledge may indeed lead to a greater appreciation of the multivariate factors that underpin various forms of offending behavior. However, if an offender profiler were to present profiling evidence in court, it would be essential for them to make clear that their testimony was based on personal opinion and experience rather than scientific evidence. As O'Connor and Krauss (2001) made clear, the burden would be on profilers to know what their limits are and to effectively articulate these limits to the court.

It seems improbable that any individual would have experienced a sufficient number of cases to enable him or her to offer the level of detailed advice that exists in many profiling reports. Many profilers comment on crimes that are exceptionally rare, such as sexual homicide. Therefore, by definition, they would not have had the opportunity to work on hundreds of such cases. Moreover, for reliable conclusions, each case used to proffer an opinion would have to be similar in nature to the profiled case. Due to the behavioral complexity involved in such cases, it is unlikely that any individual expert would have encountered enough cases that are sufficiently similar to be considered "extensive practical experience." There is a qualitative and quantitative lack of experience in the field. Given the research reviewed in this article, one could reasonably argue that these limits are so overwhelming as to make any evidence based on offender profiles inappropriate for use in court, under federal approach to expert evidence, even with the flexibility of the approach outlined in *Kumho Tire Co. v. Carmichael* (1999).

CONCLUSION

In terms of its evidential value, profiling cannot circumvent the problems of legal relevance if it is adduced to seek to show that, on the basis of a profile constructed from the crime scene, it is more probable that a particular defendant committed the crime. Few profilers would or could claim, on the basis of experience (or, indeed, any method), that they could single out the actual perpetrator. As Ormerod (1996b) stated, "This above all other hurdles appears to be the one almost guaranteed to trip up the psychological profile" (p. 350). Ormerod (1996b) concluded with a quote from Smith (1993), which warned that psychological profiling "does not of course provide the identity of the offender, but it can indicate the *type* of person being sought, i.e., the type most likely to have committed a crime possessing certain unique characteristics" (p. 245). However, the arguments outlined in this article assert that, because many contemporary profiling methods rely on a naive trait approach, even Smith's more humble claim [*132] is overly optimistic. The notion that particular configurations of demographic features can be predicted from an assessment of particular configurations of specific behaviors occurring in short-term, highly traumatic situations seems an overly ambitious and unlikely possibility. Thus, until such inferential processes can be reliably verified, such claims should be treated with great caution in investigations and should be entirely excluded from consideration in court.

REFERENCES

Alison, L.J., & Canter, D.V. (1999). Professional, legal and ethical issues in offender profiling. In D.V. Canter & L.J. Alison (Eds.), *Profiling in policy and practice* (pp. 21-54). Aldershot, England: Ashgate.

Alison, L.J., Smith, M., & Eastman, O. (2001, January). *Toulmin's philosophy of argument and its relevance to offender profiling.* Paper presented at the 6th International Investigative Psychology Conference, University of Liverpool, Liverpool, England.

Annon, J.S. (1995). Investigative profiling: A behavioral analysis of the crime scene. *American Journal of Forensic Psychology, 13,* 67-75.

Asgard, U. (1998). Swedish experiences in offender profiling and evaluation of some aspects of a case of murder and abduction in Germany. In Case Analysis Unit (BKA) (Eds.), *Method of case analysis: An international symposium* (pp. 125-130). Weisbaden, Germany: Bundeskriminalamt Kriminalistisches Institut.

Ault, R.L., & Reese, J.T. (1980). A psychological assessment of crime profiling. *FBI Law Enforcement Bulletin, 49,* 22-25.

Badcock, R. (1997). Developmental and clinical issues in relation to offending in the individual. In J.L. Jackson & D.A. Bekarian (Eds.), *Offender profiling: Theory, research and practice* (pp. 9-41). Chichester, England: Wiley.

Bandura, A. (1969). *Principles of behavior modification.* New York: Holt, Rinehart & Winston.

Bem, D.J., & Allen, A. (1974). On predicting some of the people some of the time: The search for cross-situational consistencies in behavior. *Psychological Review, 81,* 506-520.

Bennell, C., Alison, L.J., Stein, K.L., Alison, E.K., & Canter, D.V. (2001). Sexual offences against children as the abusive exploitation of conventional adult-child relationships. *Journal of Social and Personal Relationships, 18,* 149-165.

Blau, T.H. (1994). Psychological profiling. In T.H. Blau (Ed.), *Psychological services for law enforcement* (pp. 261-274). New York: Wiley.

Boon, J. (1997). Contribution of personality theories to psychological profiling. In J.L. Jackson & D.A. Bekarian (Eds.), *Offender profiling: Theory, research and practice* (pp. 43-59). Chichester, England: Wiley.

Bowers, K. (1973). Situationism in psychology: An analysis and a critique. *Psychological Review, 80,* 307-336.

Britton, P. (1992). *Review of offender profiling.* London: Home Office.

Britton, P. (1997). *The jigsaw man.* London: Bantam Press.

Burgess, A., & Hazelwood, R. (Eds.). (1995). *Practical aspects of rape investigation: A multidisciplinary approach* (2nd ed.). New York: CRC Press.

Canter, D.V. (1995). Psychology of offender profiling. In R. Bull & D. Carson (Eds.), *Handbook of psychology in legal contexts* (pp. 343-355). Chichester, England: Wiley.

Canter, D.V. (2000). Offender profiling and criminal differentiation. *Legal and Criminological Psychology, 5,* 23-46.

Canter, D.V., & Fritzon, K. (1998). Differentiating arsonists: A model of firesetting actions and characteristics. *Legal and Criminological Psychology, 3,* 73-96.

[*133] Cervone, D., & Shoda, Y. (1999a). Beyond traits in the study of personality coherence. *Current Directions in Psychological Science, 8,* 27-32.

Cervone, D., & Shoda, Y. (1999b). *The coherence of personality: Social-cognitive bases of consistency, variability and organization.* New York: Guilford Press.

Copson, G. (1995). *Coals to Newcastle: Part 1. A study of offender profiling.* London: Home Office, Police Research Group.

Craik, M., & Patrick, A. (1994). Linking serial offences. *Policing, 10,* 181-187.

Cronbach, L.J., & Gleser, G.C. (1957). *Psychological tests and personnel decisions.* Urbana: University of Illinois.

Daubert v. Merrell Dow Pharmaceuticals, Inc., 509 U.S. 579, 113 S. Ct. 2786 (1993).

Davies, A., Wittebrood, K., & Jackson, J.L. (1998). *Predicting the criminal record of a stranger rapist.* London: Home Office, Policing and Reducing Crime Unit.

Delaware v. Pennell, 584 A. 2d 513 (Del. Super. Ct. 1989).

Douglas, J.E. (1981). *Evaluation of the (FBI) psychological profiling program.* Quantico, VA: FBI Academy, Institutional Research and Development Unit.

Douglas, J.E., Burgess, A.W., Burgess, A.G., & Ressler, R.K. (1992). *Crime classification manual: A standard system for investigating and classifying violent crime.* New York: Simon & Schuster.

Douglas, J.E., & Munn, C. (1992). Violent crime scene analysis: Modus operandi, signature, and staging. *FBI Law Enforcement Bulletin, 62,* 1-20.

Douglas, J.E., Ressler, R.K., Burgess, A.W., & Hartman, C.R. (1986). Criminal profiling from crime scene analysis. *Behavioral Sciences and the Law, 4,* 401-421.

Dudycha, G.J. (1936). An objective study of punctuality in relation to personality and achievement. *Archives of Psychology, 204,* 1-319.

Epstein, S. (1979). The stability of behavior: I. On predicting most of the people most of the time. *Journal of Personality and Social Psychology, 37,* 1097-1126.

Farrington, D.P. (1997). Human development and criminal careers. In M. Maguire, R. Morgan, & R. Reiner (Eds.), *The Oxford handbook of criminology* (2nd ed., pp. 361-408). Oxford: Oxford University Press.

Golding, S. (1975). Flies in the ointment: Methodological problems in the analysis of the percentage variance due to persons and situations. *Psychological Bulletin, 82,* 278-288.

Goldblatt, P. (1992). *Psychological offender profiles: How psychologists can help the police with their enquiries.* Surrey, England: University of Surrey.

Green, E.J., Booth, C.E., & Biderman, M.D. (1976). Cluster analysis of burglary M/Os. *Journal of Police Science and Administration, 4,* 382-388.

Groth, A.N. (1979). *Men who rape: The psychology of the offender.* New York: Plenum.

Grubin, D. (1995). Offender profiling. *Journal of Forensic Psychiatry, 6,* 259-263.

Grubin, D., Kelly, P., & Brunsdon, C. (2001). *Linking serious sexual assaults through behavior.* London: Home Office, Research, Development and Statistics Directorate.

Hampson, S.E. (1995). *The construction of personality: An introduction* (2nd ed.). London: Routledge.

Hartshorne, H., & May, M.A. (1928). *Studies in the nature of character: Vol. 1: Studies in deceit.* New York: Macmillan.

Hickey, E.W. (1997). *Serial murderers and their victims* (2nd ed.). New York: Wadsworth.

Holmes, R.M., & DeBurger, J. (1988). *Serial murder.* Newbury Park, CA: Sage.

Homant, R.J., & Kennedy, D.B. (1998). Psychological aspects of crime scene profiling: Validity research. *Criminal Justice and Behavior, 25,* 319-343.

House, J.C. (1997). Towards a practical application of offender profiling: The RNC's criminal suspect prioritization system. In J.L. Jackson & D.A. Bekerian (Eds.), [*134] *Offender profiling: Theory, research and practice* (pp. 177-190). Chichester, England: Wiley.

Jackson, J.L., Van Koppen, P.J., & Herbrink, J.C.M. (1993). *Does the service meet the needs? An evaluation of consumer satisfaction with specific profile analysis and investigative advice as offered by the Scientific Research Advisory Unit of the National Criminal Intelligence Division (CRI), The Netherlands*. Leiden: NSCR.

Knight, R.A., & Prentky, R.A. (1990). Classifying sexual offenders: The development and corroboration of taxonomic models. In W.L. Marshall, D.R. Laws, & H.E. Barbaree (Eds.), *The handbook of sexual assault: Issues, theories, and treatment of the offender* (pp. 27-52). New York: Plenum.

Knight, R.A., Warren, J.I., Reboussin, R., & Soley, B.J. (1998). Predicting rapist type from crimescene variables. *Criminal Justice and Behavior, 25*, 46-80.

Kumho Tire Co. v. Carmichael, 119 S. Ct. 1167 (1999).

Langevin, R., Paitich, D., & Russon, A.E. (1985). Are rapists sexually anomalous, aggressive, or both? In R. Langevin (Eds.), *Erotic preference, gender identity, and aggression in men: New research studies* (pp. 17-38). Hillsdale, NJ: Erlbaum.

Lord, C.G. (1982). Predicting behavioral consistency from an individual's perception of situational similarities. *Journal of Personality and Social Psychology, 42*, 1076-1088.

Louisiana v. Code, 627 So. 2d 1373 (La. 1993).

Magnusson, D., & Endler, N.S. (1977). Interactional psychology: Present status and future prospects. In D. Magnusson & N.S. Endler (Eds.), *Personality at the crossroads: Current issues in interactional psychology* (pp. 3-35). Hillsdale, NJ: Erlbaum.

Mischel, W. (1968). *Personality and assessment*. New York: Wiley.

Mischel, W. (1990). Personality dispositions revisited and revised: A view after three decades. In L. Pervin (Eds.), *Handbook of personality: Theory and research* (2nd ed.; pp. 111-134). New York: Guilford Press.

Mischel, W. (1999). *Introduction to personality* (6th ed.). Fort Worth, TX: Harcourt Brace.

Mischel, W., & Peake, P.K. (1982). Beyond deja vu in the search for cross-situational consistency. *Psychological Review, 89*, 730-755.

Mokros, A., & Alison, L.J. (in press). Is profiling possible? *Legal and Criminological Psychology*.

Newcomb, T.M. (1929). *Consistency of certain extrovert-introvert behavior patterns in 51 problem boys*. New York: Columbia University, Teachers College, Bureau of Publications.

New Jersey v. Fortin, 162 N.J. 517 (2000).

North Carolina v. Wallace, 351 N.C. 481 (2000).

O'Connor, M., & Krauss, D. (2001). Legal update: New developments in Rule 702. *American Psychology-Law Society News, 21*, 1-18.

Olweus, D. (1977). A critical analysis of the modern interactionist position. In D. Magnusson & N.S. Endler (Eds.), *Personality at the crossroads: Current issues in interactional psychology* (pp. 221-233). Hillsadale, NJ: Erlbaum.

Ormerod, D. (1996a). The evidential implications of psychological profiling. *Criminal Law Review, 92*, 863-877.

Ormerod, D. (1996b). Psychological profiling. *Journal of Forensic Psychiatry, 7*, 341-352.

Ormerod, D. (1999). Criminal profiling: Trial by judge and jury, not criminal psychologist. In D.V. Canter & L.J. Alison (Eds.), *Profiling in policy and practice* (pp. 207-261). Aldershot, England: Ashgate.

Peterson, D.R. (1968). *The clinical study of social behavior*. New York: Appleton-Century-Crofts.

[*135] Pinizzotto, A.J., & Finkel, N.J. (1990). Criminal personality profiling: An outcome and process study. *Law and Human Behavior, 14*, 215-233.

Prentky, R.A., & Burgess, A.W. (2000). *Forensic management of sexual offenders*. New York: Kluwer Academic/Plenum.

Proulx, J., Aubut, J., Perron, L., & McKibben, A. (1994). Troubles de la personnalite et viol: Implications theoriques et cliniques [Personality disorders and violence: Theoretical and clinical implications]. *Criminologie, 27,* 33-53.

Proulx, J., St-Yves, M., Guay, J.P., & Ouimet, M. (1999). Les aggresseurs sexuels de femmes: Scenarios delictuels et troubles de la personnalite [Sexual aggressors of women: Offence scenarios and personality disorders]. In J. Proulx, M. Cusson, & M. Ouimet, *Les violences criminelles* (pp. 157-185). Sainte-Foy, Quebec, Canada: Les Presses de l'Universite Laval.

Regina v. Stagg. (1994). CCC 14th September.

Ressler, R.K., Burgess, A.W., Douglas, J.E., Hartman, C.R., & D'Agostino, R.B. (1986). Sexual killers and their victims: Identifying patterns through crime scene analysis. *Journal of Interpersonal Violence, 1,* 288-308.

Rossmo, D.K. (2000). *Geographic profiling.* Boca Raton, FL: CRC Press.

Shoda, Y. (1999). Behavioral expressions of a personality system: Generation and perception of behavioral signatures. In D. Cervone & Y. Shoda (Eds.), *The coherence of personality: Social-cognitive bases of consistency, variability, and organization* (pp. 155-181). New York: Guilford Press.

Shoda, Y., Mischel, W., & Wright, J.C. (1994). Intraindividual stability in the organization and patterning of behavior: Incorporating psychological situations into the idiographic analysis of personality. *Journal of Personality and Social Psychology, 67,* 674-687.

Smith, C. (1993). Psychological offender profiling. *The Criminologist, 244,* 224-250.

Turvey, B. (Ed.). (1999). *Criminal profiling: An introduction to behavioral evidence analysis.* New York: Academic Press.

Vernon, P.E. (1964). *Personality assessment: A critical survey.* New York: Wiley.

Wilson, M., Jack, K., & Butterworth, D. (1996). *The psychology of rape investigations: A study in police decision making.* Liverpool, United Kingdom: University of Liverpool, Department of Psychology.

Witkin, G. (1996). How the FBI paints portraits of the nation's most wanted. *U. S. News & World Report, 32.*

Wright, J., & Mischel, W. (1987a). A conditional analysis of dispositional constructs: The local predictability of social behavior. *Journal of Personality and Social Psychology, 53,* 1159-1171.

Wright, J., & Mischel, W. (1987b). Conditional hedges and the intuitive psychology of traits. *Journal of Personality and Social Psychology, 55,* 454-469.

Zelli, A., & Dodge, K.A. (1999). Personality development from the bottom up. In D. Cervone & Y. Shoda (Eds.), *The coherence of personality: Social-cognitive bases of consistency, variability, and organization* (pp. 94-126). New York: Guilford Press.

Testimony of Robert Keppel in State of Washington v. George W. Russell (1991)

Pretrial Testimony

Before The Honorable Patricia Aitken, Judge of the Superior Court for King Country, Department Number 30.

Appearances of Counsel

For the State: Rebecca Roe and Jeffrey Baird, Deputy Prosecuting Attorneys

For the Defense: M. Schwartz and B. Hampton, Attorneys at Law

Seattle, Washington, August 14, 1991

(Partial Transcript.)

MS. ROE: State calls Detective Keppel.

Robert D. Keppel, called as a witness by and on behalf of the state, having been first duly sworn, was examine and testified as follows:

DIRECT EXAMINATION

By Ms. Roe:
Could you please state your name and spell your last name for the record.

A. Robert D. Keppel, K E P P E L.
Q. What's your occupation?
A. I'm the chief criminal investigator for the office of the attorney general.
Q. That is for the State of Washington?
A. Yes.
Q. Mr. Keppel, could you please give us a brief educational background.
A. I have a Bachelor's Degree in police science from Washington State University. I received that in 1966. I have a Master of Arts in police science and administration from Washington

State in 1967. I have a master of education in adult education from Seattle University in 1979. I'm currently a Ph.D. candidate at the University of Washington in their individual Ph.D. program.

Q. Could you tell us a little bit about the program you are in now.

A. The program requires that you be in a graduate school for at least thirty hours at the University of Washington. I was in the higher education graduate school of study. Then you can apply for a specialized individual Ph.D. based upon your own personal interests. My interests were in the area of murder investigation, so it required me to be in more than one school of the university. I had to make application for that.

Q. Which schools at the university is your Ph.D. program a part of?

A. It is a part of sociology, which focuses on murder. It is a part of psychology, psychiatry, dentistry, pathology, anthropology and law.

Q. Ultimately what will your Ph.D. be in, should you be successful in this pursuit?

A. It will say "Criminal Justice," but the focus is on investigation of murder.

Q. Are you at this time working on a dissertation towards the end of receiving your Ph.D.?

A. Yes.

Q. What is that on?

A. It has to do with the effects of time and distance factors on the major components found within a murder incident, on solvability.

Q. Could you give us an idea, after you graduated from school, of your work background?

A. I started with the King Country sheriff's department at the time, in 1967, in July, as a police officer. Then I was there six months. I got drafted in the army. I was in the army for three years, in the military police. Subsequently I came back to the King County sheriff's office. I was there until March of 1952. Then I left in March of 1982 and I've been with the attorney general's office since.

Q. When you were at the King County Police, did some portion of your career there involve being a homicide detective?

A. Yes, eight years' worth.

Q. Since you have gone to the state attorney general's office what has been your area of focus?

A. Murder investigation and governmental corruption.

Q. Interesting combination. Since you've been at the attorney general's office have you been involved in establishing what is called the H.I.T.S. program?

A. Yes, I have.

Q. Could you describe, first of all, what does that stand for and what it is?

A. H.I.T.S. stands for Homicide Information and Tracking System. Basically it is a system designed to help local law enforcement coordinate information about murder cases, whether it be linking a potential case up with another case, or whether individual facts about an offender, or a description that has to do with linking that particular fact up to a murder investigation. We have since been expanded also to include sexual assault cases.

Q. What kind of information does that require? What are you regularly obtaining from law enforcement agencies in the H.I.T.S. program?

A. We have a form that we use to collect the information from. Each law enforcement agency that has a murder investigation in the state, after they've investigated the case for a period of time, would fill out this form and submit it to us. The form has 255 fields of information on it that relate to the characteristic of murder.

Q. Do you go through those? Do you actually look at those as they're submitted?

A. I used to be the one to do that. Instead of one, we have eleven people. There are several people that do that within our unit.

Q. Are you the supervisor of that unit?

A. Yes.

Q. How does the H.I.T.S. program fit in with the VICAP program?

A. VICAP started essentially before H.I.T.S. I was on the national planning committee for the VICAP program. The VICAP program deals strictly with tracking serial murder cases only from one jurisdiction to another. The entire hundred eighty-nine fields of the VICAP form are found somewhere within the context of our H.I.T.S. form. So, we cooperate on a daily basis with VICAP by submitting to them the fields that they think are necessary to track serial cases.

Q. You do that based on the information that is submitted to you on the H.I.T.S. form?

A. Yes.

Q. Can you indicate how you got involved in the idea of tracking?

A. It started back in 1974 when the Ted Bundy murder cases began in the Seattle area, the ones that we knew began in the Seattle area. We were in a position of not knowing who the offender was, having very little physical evidence that would lead directly to an offender, in our possession. Yet, we had two separate body-find locations, multiple bodies found at each of those locations. There was indications from the approaches of various victims that had seen a similar suspect. That was the major connection between these two locations, which totaled three bodies at the Issaquah site and four bodies at the Taylor Mountain site. We never did identify, until Ted Bundy's final confessions, one of the bodies at the Issaquah site. We were interested in the fact that things seemed to have stopped in the Seattle area and wanted to expand out into other jurisdictions, mainly in our own state and throughout the Pacific Northwest, and anywhere else to try and find cases that were similar to what we had experienced here. In that process, it was rather manual and slow, and rather laborious, in that you actually had to call people on the phone, send letters out of inquiry, finding people that weren't there in the office that day, so we had to call back. It took us nearly a little over two years to accumulate 90 cases that were close in MO characteristic to what we had. Those 90 cases, we're finding to this day, we didn't find them all either. Even in our own state we keep coming up with evidence of more cases, back in Ted Bundy's era, that we missed back there in that communication. A lot of problems with interdepartmental communications, cooperation back then, seem to be that murder investigation facts were the privy of one jurisdiction, and they're very parochial in their attitude, which laid up a lot of barriers to finding all the possible cases. There was a good chance that in those cases, because of the information they gathered in their investigations outside of Seattle, that there may appear certain suspect information that we would relate back to our cases. For instance, if we would find a case in Utah that Theodore Bundy was a suspect in, and we were to check back in our own suspect files and were to find a Theodore Bundy, maybe that isn't the reason we haven't made the connection to Theodore Bundy who is a suspect. There may be a partial description given in the other cases. Maybe the last time a person is seen they get into a tan Volkswagen bug. That's all the information that is present. We go through our data, look for a tan Volkswagen bug, who is it registered to, what do we have, and we might be able to come up with a name. We didn't have the specific information to deal with 3500 suspects in basically eight cases to be able to identify those features that would come out.

Q. How long has H.I.T.S. been in existence?

A. It began in its infancy, probably when VICAP began, in June of 1985. We used their forms and didn't have any additional fields than what they collected. Subsequent to that date, they changed their form, reduced it. I saw a need over and beyond what VICAP collected. And the reasons that they collect their information is to be able to give detectives answers on individual questions, individual cases, not necessarily just serial in nature or multiple in nature, or whatever you want to call it. So we created a proposal to get a federal grant to initiate the H.I.T.S. System in September of 1987. We were successful in obtaining that grant, which also includes a major project on solvability, because you just can't get a grant from the National Institute of Justice without having a research component with it. We are currently in the process of doing that research project.

Q. Are you aware whether or not you get a reasonably complete number of forms related to the homicides that occur in this state?

A. I think, of the agencies that have homicides, we probably get a hundred percent cooperation from them, especially back in history. We have a process of identifying what the cases are and where they are. But, frankly, in our major research period, which was from '81 until the end of 1986, there were 1309 murder cases that were discovered in the state of Washington for that period of time. We were only able to code or fill out forms on 1295 of 'em. So we were unable to locate the case files for the remainder. More recently, after the research period, because we had our own people going out and filling out forms, helping people fill out forms, more recently we have hired five investigators and a supervisor to assist with that process. Now we don't require that the minute a murder goes down they fill out the form. We want them to investigate the case for a period of time so they will have something to put on the form, have results that we can use in our analysis through the H.I.T.S. system. There are certain cases that we don't have, that date back to probably 1989, 1990, but they're very few. Probably the ones that are closed and people have not seen the need, they're not unsolved, so they don't come to us with the case reports.

Q. Have you had opportunities during the course of your experience to give training to various groups on the subject of crime scene investigation, serial homicide, et cetera?

A. Yes.

The Clerk: State's Exhibit 76 is marked for identification.

By Ms. Roe:

Handing you State's Exhibit Number 76 marked for identification, is that your curriculum vitae?

A. Yes, it is.

Q. Is that reasonably current as to the kinds of training and presentations you have given in the area of crime scene analysis?

A. Yes.

Ms. Roe: State offers Exhibit 76.

By Ms. Roe:

Do you know how recently this was prepared?

A. That was done probably about four weeks ago.

Q. It is current as of four weeks ago?

A. Yes.

Q. Including the most recent entry being a June 28th, 1991, faculty instructor on homicide investigation training for the Washington Defender Association?

A. Yes.

Ms. SCHWARTZ: No objection.

Ms. ROE: State offers Exhibit 76.

THE COURT: Exhibit 76 will be admitted.

We'll be in recess for 15 minutes. (Recess taken.)

By Ms. Roe:

Mr. Keppel, could you indicate as either an investigating detective or part of the H.I.T.S. program, or as a consultant to other jurisdictions, whether you have had a significant amount of experience with serial murder investigations?

A. What I would call significant, yes.

Q. In numbers?

A. Yes.

Q. Any idea of numbers?

A. Investigations? Probably over fifty.

Q. And other incidents of being asked to consult on cases?

A. Yes.

Q. Are some of those consultations that you were involved in listed in the CV?

A. Just a few of the more famous ones.

Q. Like Wayne Williams?

Q. Yes. Could you define for us your operating definition of "serial murder"?

A. Well, mine doesn't differ too much from that presented in the FBI's literature. I would just like to state it is only a guideline.

It is basically three or more victims, which include usually one offender and three separate events, three separate locations, with elements of premeditation, planning, some elements of fantacies. But I don't believe that that definition is all inclusive. There is certainly—You could have two murders and still be classified, in my mind, as a serial case. You could have one murder and, like, a first degree assault, first degree rape, attempt kidnapping, that goes along with one murder. It is a series of events, so the framework is there for a serial case.

Q. Have you had experience, either as an investigating detective or as a consultant, with an aspect of serial crimes known as signature crimes?

A. Yes.

Q. How would you define that?

A. Well, a signature is an action or sometimes called, among some of the law enforcement officers, as a modus operandi. But I define it more strictly to those events that only the offender can replicate and no one else can. It is impossible for anyone else to do anything exactly the way the offender left his signature, or calling card, whatever you want to call it.

Q. Can it be words, conduct, or both?

A. Yes, it can be.

Q. Is it fair to say that a signature is unique to that particular person?

A. Absolutely to the offender.

Q. Have there been kinds of cases that you investigated or consulted on that involved people who had a certain aspect of the commission of their crimes that involved a signature?

A. Yes.

Q. How would you—How do you distinguish, if you do, the idea of signature from modus operandi that term?

A. Modus operandi has evolved from the early days. Probably signature was included in that. We have seen the need today to be able to separate the two, because in the early days people relied on exact MO to relate one case to another. For instance, if you had a burglary case where the guy was using a pipe wrench on the front door, regardless of any other characteristic that went along with that burglary, if it happened in a geographical location, a proximity that was near this other one, you would think the same offender did it because of that MO; however, in murder the MO characteristics have been known to change over time, changed out of necessity. So when you compare one case to another, you may not be particularly focusing on exact MO, as much as you would be focusing on changes. Some things that would be, for instance, in the method of death, the offender may use a gun one time, find out it makes too much noise, decides he wants to use something more quiet, so he progresses to a quite implement. The characterization of modus operandi is experienced over time by the offender and can change, and it is very dynamic.

Q. Were you asked to consult on this particular series of homicides, Pohlreich, Beethe and Levine?

A. Yes.

Q. Did you have the H.I.T.S. forms regarding these three crimes?

A. Yes, I did.

Q. In addition to the H.I.T.S. forms and other information that you may have learned in either formal or informal conversations with detectives, what other information were you provided on which you rely?

A. Crime scene photographs, all of the case materials, follow-up reports by detectives, statement forms, evidence forms, some diagrams, lab request forms, lab result forms.

Q. At least at the point in time when you were examining this material, a complete set of discovery at that time?

A. Yes, all three cases.

The Clerk: State's Exhibits 77, 78 and 79 are marked for identification.

Ms. Roe: I would ask you to identify State's Exhibit 77, 78, and 79, if you can.

The Witness: These are the actual printouts of the H.I.T.S. forms on Pohlreich, Beethe and Levine.

Ms. Roe: State offers Exhibits 77, 78 and 79.

Ms. Schwartz: No objection.

The Court: Exhibits 77, 78 and 79 will be admitted.

By Ms. Roe:

Mr. Keppel, have you formed an opinion whether or not the same person was responsible for all three of these crimes?

A. Yes, I have.

Q. What is that opinion?

A. My opinion is that all three murders were committed by the same person.

Q. To what degree of certainty do you have that opinion?

A. As high as possible.

Q. Could you indicate first, in general, what the various bases of that opinion are, then we'll go through those individually.

A. Basically, there are three dominant areas and some sub areas that you have to pay attention to. The first area is the open display of the victim's body.

The second area would be how the body is placed in an unusual position, either staged or posed;.
The third dominant area is the fact of sexual insertion of a foreign object. The sub areas of importance are geography, timing and the incidents of murder like that throughout Washington state.

Ms. Roe:

I will start with the aspect of these crimes of posing and ask you to take a look at these photos from the various cases.

Q. First of all, in the Pohlreich case, with reference to State's Exhibits 26, 27 and 28, could you indicate what aspects of posing you find in those photos.

Ms. Schwartz: Perhaps, Your Honor, I could approach the bench and see those?

The Court: Certainly, yes.

The Witness: First of all, I think I need to make a distinction between staging and posing, what that is. Our question on our form that deals with that is something that says "unusual position of the body." That usually refers to the fact that if you were to commit a murder and you were to shoot somebody and they would naturally fall in that position and you would leave them there and escape, whatever position that body is left in is immediately what happened after the manner of death is executed. There are certain things that happen after the death, in order to pose or stage a body. Posing refers directly to the body itself. Like you would pose for a picture with certain things on or off, implements in your hand. Staging refers more to the crime scene itself. For instance, I could, if I was a murderer, go out and stage a crime scene of a murder that looks like an accident or a suicide. So you would stage the whole scene in that manner. You would use the surroundings of the room, car, grounds, or whatever. The posing refers directly to the body itself. I won't deal with the open display right now, because we're just talking about posing. Posing, to we, would be something that is an unnatural position that the body is left in. It is my experience that when a person carries a body to a position and the body, in my opinion, has not been murdered right there in the final location where the body has been found, she's been murdered in another place, the offender has situated—

Mr. Baird: Excuse me, I'm sorry. This is not by way of objection. We don't know what object is referred to here.

Ms. Roe: Sorry, State's Exhibit 28.

The Witness: State's Exhibit 28.

Someone other than the victim has placed her hands in a particular position, placed her legs in a particular position, namely crossing them, and placed an object over the face, which appears to be a lid to a soft drink. Inside the hand is a pine cone.

The Court: Exhibit?

The Witness: That's Exhibit 27.

Ms. Roe: I will ask you to take a look at State's Exhibits 29, 30 and 31, which relate to the Carole Beethe homicide, and ask you what aspects of posing you see in those photos.

The Witness: State's Exhibit 29, the pillow over the top of the head, the legs exentuated in a spread eagle position, almost exentuated spread eagle position. And, of course, a long rifle or firearm placed in the sexual area. Also on her feet are a pair of red high heel shoes. That also would indicate a posing of the victim.

Ms. Roe:

For the record both victims you described are nude?

A. Yes.

Q. Other than the high heel shoes?

A. Yes.

Q. Could you indicate in State's Exhibits 32, 33 and 34, which are photographs of Andrea Levine, what aspects of posing of the body you have observed in those photos?

A. State's Exhibit 34 shows her, again, spread eagle on the bed. The sex manual underneath her left arm and the vibrator, I guess you call those things, in her mouth orifice.

Q. Detective Kepple, in your experience can you indicate how common or uncommon this kind of posing is? I'm including in that specifically distinguishing staging, how common or uncommon is posing of bodies in this manner?

A. It's very rare.

Q. How many cases have you been involved in, would you say, that involved posing, during the 20 years you've been involved as a detective?

A. I have seen numerous examples at seminars that I have gone to throughout the United States. My particular involvement, where I have seen somebody posed, is limited to probably less than ten.

Q. That's out of what kind of numbers of cases?

A. Actually, where I've been called in as a consultant or personally investigated, probably well over a thousand.

Q. You referred in your initial discussion—I'm sorry, before I leave that area, I would like to ask you whether the fact that each of the three bodies is posed somewhat differently, affects your opinion that the same person is responsible for posing them all?

A. No, it doesn't.

Q. Why not?

A. Mainly because, you see, in conjunction with the other components also, a change over time in the types of posing. What is most recognizable about these three is that all the implements used in the actual posing were items that were generic to the surroundings where the death took place, right at that scene. They were not brought to the scene by the offender, in the traditional sense of him calculating ahead of time exactly what he needed for that purpose. In each of these areas all of the aspects of posing and the equipment and the sexual insertion are all things that are right there at that scene.

Q. You referred initially to the aspect of the bodies being openly displayed; can you indicate what you mean by that?

A. Yes. When a murder investigation is submitted it comes in basically with three separate alternatives to be checked in the disposition of the body.

One is that the body was concealed, that the offender took painstaking efforts to hide the body from its discovery. That could be in a house where he used a closet, attic, subflooring, basement, as in the John Daisey cases. There is an effort to conceal the victim. It could be out in the woods, it could be covered with leaves, could be buried, but there is an effort at concealment.

The next area is that the offender was unconcerned as to whether or not the body was found. In those types of cases we see the more traditional type murders of the husband murdering the wife, where they don't have much choice because there are witnesses around. In all of those cases the unconcern has to do with the fact that there are witnesses there, so why worry about it?

Then you have the last aspect, which is open display. That means that the offender took some effort to assure that even within the residence, or outside someplace, that because of the position the body is in, the location it would be found, and found in the position that he left it in.

So, each of these three cases, to me, display or exhibit the open display attitude. The outside area in the Pohlreich case where she is near a Dumpster in the parking lot, in the back, would indicate that the offender had a period of time where he spent arranging the body in the position it was in so somebody would discover it there. If he did not want that body found, he would have hid the body, probably thrown it in the dumpster or taken it out in the woods and dumped it, or some other place. But there was an intentional aspect here that needs to be brought out.

In the two cases inside the houses, the offender took no steps to remove the victims from the bed. The bed is a common place where people are found. If you are going to look for somebody you will knock on the door and go in and see if she is there. You know they will be there. If the offender wanted to do something in those houses, he may have wanted to remove the victims from the position they were in and hide them in an attic, in some other location in the basement, outside, underneath wood, buried out back, but you see none of that in these cases.

Q. You've also referred to the third basis being the sexual insertion; can you define that and distinguish that, if you would, from rape, what we typically think of as rape?

A. Sexual insertion of a foreign object is something other than normal intercourse. The offender uses some implement other than his normal apparatus to rape the victim with, basically enter the victim in orifices that are commonly construed as sexual orifices, like the mouth, the vaginal area and the anal area. To some extent, in some outrageous cases, they cut open portions of the body and insert things.

Q. In the Pohlreich case what evidence did you see that there had been that kind of penetration?

A. The autopsy report indicated that there was—Well, Exhibit 27, on the back, is the anal cavity. It is quite a violent wound in that particular area, which indicated something other than normal intercourse took place, a foreign object insertion was there at some time.

Q. You've also indicated that to a somewhat lesser degree that geography and time fit into your opinion. Could you explain how the fact that these occurred where they did—By the way, are you familiar with this area of King County?

A. Yes.

Q. The area that is involved in these cases?

A. Yes, I am.

Q. How does the time and geography fit into your analysis here?

A. Well, whenever we look at murder cases that could be related we look, naturally, at the location where the victim was found, the location where the victim was last seen. If we get fortunate maybe somebody saw the point of contact between the offender and the victim. Those areas in this case are very, very close in proximity in the Bellevue area. As you go back in history and examine cases around the Bellevue area, Bellevue is not known to be the murder capital of the world. There are very few murder cases. When you consider the parameters around Bellevue, I'm talking about unincorporated King County, areas that have Bellevue addresses, Redmond addresses, Kirkland addresses, throughout history all of these areas have been rather low on the murder rate scale in comparison to the City of Seattle. So, when you look at geography, you look at that particular area, and the area has had absolutely no murders like this in its history.

In addition to that, the other cases that may have occurred in time and frequency throughout the history of our state, if you were to take the year 1990 and look at cases that are openly displayed, look at cases where there is sexual insertion of a foreign object, look at cases where posing is involved, there are no cases in 1990 in the whole state, except those three.

Now, if you further that parameter out into the whole state, back in history, and the familiarity I have with all the data throughout our state indicates that the act of posing is rate in the context of all the cases we have. The act of sexual insertion is rare. And the act of open display is a little bit more prominent than either sexual insertion or posing.

When you take in combination all three of those aspects and you look at the history of our state back to 1981, which is where most of our data is, there are no cases which have all of those three elements present other than these three.

Q. You are familiar with the fact that in the Pohlreich case the indications are that the last point of contact, if you will, was in a bar as opposed to the Beethe and Levine cases where it appears the victims were attacked in a burglary-type thing in their home. Does the fact of that difference, in point of contact, does that have an impact on your opinion that the same person is responsible for these?

A. No.

Q. Why not?

A. Mainly because an offender is thinking about his choices. The choices he's comfortable with are the areas that he has most frequent contact with. So, the relationships, no matter if they are close, casual or first time in a bar situation, are something that maybe a person is comfortable with.

The fact that Pohlreich was once at Papagayo's and never seen again until her body was found is important to the aspect that each of these three victims were known throughout their history to have been in each of these locations. They had previous contacts with Cucina, Factoria, The Pub, the Black Angus. They all seemed to intermingle. These places are not far apart in proximity. They are what I would classify as hangouts to meet people. So, a person who is going to approach somebody in a bar in that circumstance is comfortable with that. What that person may not be comfortable with his where the actual location of the murder took place. For instance, in the Pohlreich case the distance from Papagayo's to the Black Angus is further than one would naturally want to walk, so a vehicle could be involved. When you add that aspect to the case and you have a place or another location where the murder occurred, that significance of that crime scene for wanting to do it again reduces because maybe the actions inside the car weren't appropriate. Maybe something happened that the person needed to change. So, you get a change in the actual MO from outdoors to indoors because the offender feels more comfortable burglarizing a house. More than likely, I would expect this offender has a history of that type of activity and feels comfortable with it. I would expect that the aspect of the outdoors versus the indoors doesn't affect my opinion at all.

Q. Does the fact that there appears to be progression in the level of violence, in the level of gratuitous harm to the victims, that that increases, so therefore it is different from one to another, does that affect your opinion that the same person is responsible for all three?

A. No, it doesn't.

Q. Why not?

A. When you take a look at the types of violence inflicted you see a progression. Actually, it is a decreasing progression, when you think of the role of the victim. You have a little bit of resistance and some questioning on the part of the offender, as far as the value of the method of death is concerned, because you have a strangulation and you have a beating. In my experience people aren't—unless you are prepared for strangulation, you have a fight on your hands unless you have a person bound, so things go awry. Naturally you see a participation there, where the victim is in a struggle and something is happening. In the Beethe case you also see some, albeit small, evidence of some defense wounds.

In the third case you see less of a role on the part of the victim, because there are absolutely no defense wounds. She was virtually murdered in her sleep without knowing what happened. You see a decreasing amount of role of the victim. On the other hand you see an increasing amount of the violence on the part of the offender. That goes in basically two ways, the initial way to get the person dead in the beginning, to the post-offense behavior where you would expect the victim is dead and now more things happen.

As you look at Pohlreich, with strangulation and some beating, then you progress to Beethe where there is quite a bit of beating, then you progress to Levine where there is even more beating, yet more stabbing, and some other things done. You see a natural progression forward. In the MO you would expect that to happen as the offender becomes more in tune with what he wants to do at those scenes and what satisfies his needs the most.

Ms. Roe: Thank you, no further questions at this time.

CROSS-EXAMINATION

By Ms. Schwartz:

Mr. Keppel, let me ask you this: Did you become involved in crime scene analysis—is that what you term this methodology, by which you try to determine whether a series of crimes are caused by the same person, is that crime scene analysis?

A. That's term I've heard. When I first started it was called something different, it was called applied criminology. It was taught at the FBI Academy. I attended a two-week presentation there by the staff of the Behavioral Sciences Unit. At that time the whole concept was in its infancy.

Q. When was that?

A. In 1975. Since that time their theories and their methods of doing things have been published, presented at seminars where I've been in attendance. So, I gained the knowledge they have about the methods and tactics they use in, I think what they call now, crime scene assessment.

Q. It is still the Behaviorial Sciences Unit?

A. Yes.

Q. That's still Mr. Douglas' unit?

A. It wasn't Mr. Douglas' unit when I first became involved.

Q. They also do profiling-type work?

A. Yes, they do.

Q. What is profiling?

A. Well, I understand they have a particular technique they use to take a case, not necessarily a series case, and look at the crime scene, look at the victim's background, look at the evidence and the evidence results, and be able to give some sort of, what I call a Kentucky windage estimate, of what the offender is really like and what you would expect to find once you arrest him.

Q. That's based on an analysis of what they find at the scene; clues?

A. Right.

Q. Try to come up with kind of a personality profile?

A. Right.

Q. Do they also use that, as far as you know from lectures and material you've read, do they use that in the factoring in whether several crimes are committed by the same person?

A. They use some of the same data. But certainly the focus is not, when you look at whether or not two crimes are necessarily related, it is a lot different than if you only have one there.

Q. When you look at a scene, like you did in these cases, would it be correct you are trying to work backwards and figure out from the scene what was being done by the offender, what was going on with the offender when he did what he did; is that fair to say?

A. You look at what the offender did and what the victim was doing at the time. The relationship of the geography. All of the basic possibilities of the components of murder. I usually view murder as an incident, and that incident contains certain components, of which there are basically five. You have the elements around where the victim was last scene, time, location, witnesses, things like that. You have the point of contact between the offender and the victim. You have what I would call an initial assault, where there may be a very harmonius relationship at the time of contact but there comes a time when the victim becomes aware things aren't going her way. The initial assault takes place, it could be a kidnapping, slapping around, whatever, then there comes the death inflicting injuries. Then there is the body recovery site itself. As an investigator, you would seek the elements of each of those five components, trying to find out as much information as you could about all those components.

Q. All of that contributes to your opinion as to whether certain crimes were or were not related, is that right?

A. Yes.

Q. Was this approach to crimes developed by the Behaviorial Sciences Unit, at the same time by yourself, as a crime solving methodology or crime solving approach?

A. Well, they have—their major approach is crime solvability, and mine.

Q. That's your goal?

A. Yes, because it also is an understanding of what happened at the crime scene, who the potential offender is. It may give you direction for investigation.

Q. Meaning how to develop a suspect, would that be correct?

A. Right.

Q. Profiling really is an attempt to develop a suspect, isn't it?

A. It is an attempt to develop what the suspect might be like. I don't think they can put a name with anybody.

Q. A personality type that is a likely suspect; would that be fair to say?

A. I usually don't like the word "personality."

Q. A background, a general profile of a likely candidate for a suspect?

A. Characteristics of a person.

Ms. Schwartz: Okay.

Q. That's looking at the same factors that you look at when you look at the question of whether certain crimes are related, is it not?

A. Yes, it is.

Q. One of things you look at is interaction with the body after the death; is that fair to say?

A. Yes.

Q. You defined the term "modus operandi," and you described what a signature is. Is there a term called "ritual" that is one of the terms used in connection with this kind of work?

A. Well, ritual to me—

Q. Is that a term that is used?

A. I've heard it used, yes.

Q. What is that?

A. It applies to a ceremonial type of event where things are more obvious, beliefs in Satan, beliefs in a certain sect, things like that come out. The normal ritual—We all have rituals that we go by. If somebody disturbs mine in the morning, I'm liable to have a bad day.

Q. Is the term "ritual" used in connection with interaction with the body, for example?

A. It can be, yes.

Q. Has it been?

A. I think it has been.

Q. Are you familiar with Mr. Douglas' use of that term in some of the writings he has done?

A. Yes. In fact, he described this very event as ritual.

Q. This particular crime?

A. Yes.

Q. Any particular one of these or all of them?

A. Well, things like this. I don't know exactly what he said about this, but I've seen in his writings before where somebody who staged a body in this position and also spends a considerable amount of time doing it. There is a certain amount of ritualism to that event that the person has to do. Just like I have to brush my teeth everyday, this person has to do some sort of sexual insertion.

Q. The sexual insertion can be a ritual?

A. It can be, according to Douglas, yes.

Q. The reason behind the ritual is some kind of need that the offender has?

A. Absolutely.

Q. He's gratifying that need by performing this ritual with the body?

A. Yes.

Q. Do you know if any profiling was done in this case, or these cases I should say?

A. I don't know.

Q. You didn't do any, I take it?

A. No.

Q. When did you first come in contact with these three homicides, or were there different dates for the different homicides?

A. I personally had no role in either receiving the H.I.T.S. forms or entering them, or looking at them, or anything, until I was approached by the prosecutor to examine the cases for this proceeding. That was in, I think, the end of January of '91. I had the materials for about— until we met on February 7th. I gave my opinion to them at that time.

Q. For approximately two weeks you had a great deal of material concerning all three cases; is that fair to say?

A. Yes.

Q. At the time, when you received the material on these cases from the prosecutor, was it your understanding that they already had a suspect? In fact, they already charged a suspect?

A. There was a charge, yes. But the fact that that suspect was charged had no bearing on my analysis to see if all three cases were committed by the same person or not.

Q. That's the same person that is charged now, is that right?

A. Yes.

Q. Looking at the Beethe case, do you see elements of a ritual type behavior there with the body?

A. Yes.

Q. Would that be the shotgun inserted into the vaginal orifice?

A. Yes.

Q. The spreading of the legs; is that part of the ritual?

A. Yes.

Q. Possibly the positioning of the arms?

A. The positioning could make a difference, yes.

Q. What other kinds of ritual behavior do you see there?

A. Attempts at covering up the face.

Q. The wrapping around the face?

A. Uh-huh.

Q. How about the red shoes; does that play a role in this?

A. I would say most definitely.

Q. What is the significance of the shoes—Let me ask you first: Did you believe those shoes were placed on the body after the person was dead?

A. Yes.

Q. Go ahead and explain.

A. It is my experience that a lot of serial killers have what is called a shoe fetish. Either presence or absence of shoes means something. They may not mean anything to the investigators right away, but to the offender it means a lot. I have seen offenders who have oodles of shoes at their house. I have seen those that have underwear at their house. It is part of their ritual, to be able to observe or see and have this as part of their own sexual fantacies of seeing females nude with shoes on.

Q. Would the fact they are red high heel shoes be particularly significant?

A. Not necessarily.

Q. In the Levine case, the dildo would be part of a ritual?

A. I think the sexual insertion in an orifice is part of that post-death behavior that you are talking about. The implement that is used makes no difference. It's the concept behind the implement that makes all the difference.

Q. The interaction with the body with the implement, putting something in the body, is that what it is?

A. Absolutely.

Q. Did you see evidence in the Beethe and Levine cases that a considerable amount of time had been spent with the body after the death?

A. Yes.

Q. In Levine that is reflected by the many wounds, knife-type wounds?

A. Right.

Q. Is it your understanding those were inflicted after the death?

A. Yes.

Q. All of them?

A. I think so.

Q. Can you say about how long the killer would have spent with the body after the death, with Levine?

A. My estimate is probably well over a couple of hours.

Q. Plus maybe; is that fair to say?

A. Yes.

Q. Is there an element of fantacy that you see in both Levine and Beethe?

A. Yes.

Q. Can you say what you see there that shows elements of fantacy?

A. I think that is in combination with what you see, what you consider the signature on these cases, is the fact that the offender has a particular need. The need is expressed only in terms of what their thinking is. In this case, the fantacies, whether it is contrived, whether it is thought about, whether it is conscious or unconscious, it is thought about doing this to victims.

Q. It is thought about beforehand?

A. Oh, yes.

Q. It is planned out beforehand, is that right?

A. My guess is that it has been. But in this case he's sophisticated enough to use the implements that are already at that particular scene rather than going to the extent of actually taking something with him there to do it with.

Q. Would it be fair to say the second crimes are sexually oriented crimes?

A. So is the first one.

Q. You think all three are?

A. Yes.

Q. How important is the modus operandi in trying to decide if crimes are related, generally speaking, if you can answer that?

A. I think it becomes very important to the aspect of not all the time is a signature recognizable in some cases. Without the signature, you are falling back on what MO characteristics are present. The MO characteristics are governed by time, decomposition. Things that might be available at one time period wouldn't be available in the next. We get a lot of cases that the MO characteristics are few and far between, skeleton found in the woods is a lot different than a fresh body found in a house. It may have a lot more data. What is important about MO, when looking from one case to another, regardless of the fact that the signature could be there or not, is that you are looking for changes. You are looking for are the changes logical? Do they make sense from one case to the next? Certainly an increasing amount of violence from one case to the next is what you would look for. You could look for methods of approach to the victim that may be more convenient. Those changes over time, with whatever becomes more apropos to the offender's desires. For instance, meeting somebody in a bar then finally attacking somebody in their house in the middle of the night in their bed is quite a convenient change for the offender. You would look for those changes in MO, then the general characteristics of MO, too. You would look at those probably not quite as strong, but strong, like the sex of the victim, the height, the weight, and all this kind of stuff.

Q. If all of these crimes, the three of them, had involved nighttime burglaries with the victim in her bed, would you still say they appeared to be related?

A. If all of them—

Q. If Pohlreich had been murdered like Beethe and Levine in her bed at night, would that cause you to change your opinion?

A. Probably not. But I don't know that the—What I see here is the fact that you have an escalation and a changing MO. You might want to look around for another case, if Pohlreich was in bed.

Q. Say there was a number four victim found in her bed, in the same general area, and the body appeared to be positioned; would you think to look to see if that crime could also be related?

A. I would look to see if it is related, yes.

Q. You would look for the kinds of characteristics that you already described here?

A. Yes.

Q. You are not saying that because Pohlreich is not in bed and because that crime has a slightly different MO, that that causes you to think more that that is related than if it were the same MO? Either way you would think they were related, is that right?

A. I feel that because of the escalation of the events, that Pohlreich is very much related.

Q. Are you aware of two other assault cases where—that occurred in early September where young women were attacked in their apartments, or entering their apartments, in the same general area, also white females, and in those cases where the injuries were by some object, a rock, or some heavy hard object, blows to the head; are you aware of such cases?

A. Other than the one you described to me?

Q. Meaning when we talked to you in your office?

A. Yes.

Q. Have the prosecutors or police made you aware of those two other incidents?

A. The fact they exist, yes. I've never looked at the case materials in any of those.

Q. Let's assume a hypothetical, that there is an apartment complex within a mile of the Beethe residence. There are a lot of apartments in the complex, ground floor apartments, not particularly secure. That on two occasions, within two weeks of the Levine murder, white females are attacked in the manner I described by a black person, a person described to be a black person, with a description that does not rule out the suspect in this case, approach-ing from behind and striking the victim in the head from the back with some object causing head injuries. One being inside the apartment, the other being the woman attempting to enter the apartment. Both victims are white females. Would you look to investigate to see if those matters could be related?

A. Yes, I would look to investigate those matters.

Q. How knowledgeable are you of assault-burglary type crimes in Bellevue within the last year?

A. Not very.

Q. You are not familiar with the statistics there?

A. No.

Q. Would it be fair to say the various area around Bellevue is not an area known for a high instance of violent crime?

A. In comparison to my knowledge of other areas, no it is not.

Q. You mentioned you had never seen or heard of a case in the state of Washington that involved all three of the characteristics of foreign insertion, posing of the body and open display; are you familiar with the Charles Campbell case?

A. Yes.

Q. Didn't that case involve all three of those?

A. When you talked to me we discussed two of those characteristics, we talked about posing and sexual insertion. We did not speak about display.

Q. You testified those three were not observed in other cases?

A. The detectives who filled out that form in Charles Campbell did not feel that the offender openly displayed those victims.

Q. You are speaking of detectives filling out a form, that's the H.I.T.S. form?

A. Right.

Q. Would it be fair to say there is a certain degree of subjectivity in the filling out of the forms?

A. Yes.

Q. By the detectives?

A. Yes.

Q. So it is whether they perceive posing or open display that is what goes into your data base, is that correct?

A. That's correct.

Q. Are you aware now, or do you have an opinion now, as to whether there was an open display in Campbell?

A. I have not studied that case to know that that might be—That might be a possibility, but I have not looked at it.

Q. A lot of the cases you have looked at, I'm referring now specifically to the Green River killer investigation that you were involved with, involved the finding of bodies or parts of a body that were fairly well decomposed; is that fair to say?

A. Yes.

Q. You were involved in the Green River killer investigation?

A. Yes.

Q. In fact, you were very much involved in that?

A. I still am the consultant.

Q. On the task force?

A. Yes.

Q. You were on the task force at the time?

A. I began on the task force in January of '84. The murders actually started in' 82.

Q. You were on the task force for how long?

A. Two years.

Q. Are you familiar with the posed body that was found as one of the Green River victims, I believe it was by the name of Carol Kristinson?

A. I would say yes, very familiar.

Q. Is there a reservation?

A. Whether or not she's a Green River victim? I think so.

Q. Is that a reservation that you have or is that shared by other members of the task force?

A. It is shared by a lot of members of the police department. The lists you refer to that have victims on them are mainly political in nature, so the actual beliefs of detectives is we're going to investigate all these cases and hopefully find one offender and see if this offender that maybe killed Kristinson may be involved in the others. You can't eliminate the facts of the Kristinson case from your fact pattern, because of where she is from, her life style. If you were to find an offender in that case, you would want to see if that offender was eligible for any of the Green River victims.

Q. Are you saying that there has been some debate among the task force members and yourself, at least as to some of the Green River victims, whether in fact they were in fact all Green River victims?

A. Well, if you—Excuse me, yes, there is.

Q. What did you start to say?

A. Well, I wouldn't call it debate, I would call it constructive criticism of what we're doing. If we are going to look at the whereabouts of offenders and look at specific dates and times where we know people probably disappeared and were killed on the date that they disappeared, in those cases we would probably want to keep Kristinson in that list because she's fresh, and we got a pretty good time and date that she was last seen. Of the forty-nine victims on that list there is probably only twenty two or twenty three that have good time and dates that we could verify as to their disappearance and possibly their death.

Q. In those cases—

The Court: Let me ask a question, would it be better to go over to tomorrow morning with this witness, Ms. Schwartz?

Ms. Schwartz: I can't answer if it would be better. I don't have a whole lot longer to go on this witness, maybe 15 minutes.

Ms. Roe: I would rather finish today. I have another officer who is very brief, and the defense has indicated they may stipulate to his testimony, the officer who gave the defendant his rights in May of 1990. There is a problem with coming back.

The Court: Do you have a problem coming back to court tomorrow?

The Witness: Yes.

The Court: We'll take a few minutes to see if there is a stipulation. Perhaps we can give the court reporter a rest, then go ahead. Perhaps we can take a brief recess. Keep in mind our court reporter has been taking very difficult testimony all day. We'll be in very brief recess.
(Recess taken.)

Ms. Roe: We very reached a stipulation that we can take care of in the morning, if that's okay?

The Court: Certainly.
If you would resume the stand, please.
By Ms. Schwartz:

I'll open up another line of inquiry. Mr. Keppel, you mentioned that Pohlreich was killed elsewhere from where she was found; is that your opinion?

A. Yes. Elsewhere could be another location at the parking lot, undiscovered in a car nearby, or wherever, but where she was found right there, I don't believe she was killed.

Q. Can you tell us why you believe that?

A. Well, for one thing there is very little disturbance, other than what the offender would do to lay the victim down, to position the body in the way it is in, and to find a little lid to put on the face. I would expect that probably, with the amount of struggle going on there, that there would have been some evidence of involuntary excretion, things that come out when people die, and stuff like that, someplace, and it is not there.

Q. Given the manner of death, that is likely to have occurred wherever she was killed, is that fair?

A. Yes.

Q. Urine, defecation?

A. It could be. But what I'm talking about is the resistance of asphyxiation causes things to come out, so it should be found someplace.

Q. Are you aware of the—You have the autopsy report on Pohlreich?

A. Yes.

Q. Do you have that with you?

A. No.

Q. Do you recall from the autopsy report that there were abrasions to the front of the body?

A. Not specifically, no.

Q. Showing you State's Exhibits Number 27 and 28, do you see in these pictures, either one of them, evidence of abrasions on the front of the body?

A. Yes.

Q. Can you describe where those abrasions are located on the body?

A. On the knees area.

Q. I'll show you—That was on State's Exhibit 28?

A. Yes.

Q. Handing you State's Exhibit 27, do you see evidence of abrasions in State's 27?

A. Yes, I do.

Q. Where do you see that in twenty seven?

A. On the back of the hands.

Q. Are those abrasions? Are you familiar with what happens when there are abrasions post-mortem, as opposed to before death, as far as the evidence of the abrasion itself, how it looks?

A. Not specifically.

The Clerk: Defendant's Exhibit 80 is marked for identification.

Ms. Schwartz:

Handing you what's been marked for identification as Defendant's Exhibit Number 80, is this the King County medical examiner's autopsy report on Ms. Pohlreich?

A. Yes, it is.

Q. Did you look at the autopsy report in your examination of this case in arriving at your conclusion?

A. Yes.

Q. Would it help you to refresh your recollection, as to the abrasions on the body, to take a look at the report?

A. It might, yes.

Q. Do you want to look through it? I believe there are highlights on there that were probably not on the one you looked at. If you would look at the first page. Do you note the evidence of abrasions in addition to the ones you described?

A. Yes, there is evidence of abrasion over the right breast.

Q. Anything else?

A. The feet are soiled by dirt.

Q. The top of the foot?

A. Scattered abrasions are noted over the surface, which take on a yellowish-brown postmortem type appearance.

Q. Does that sound right to you, yellowish-brown would be postmortem abrasions?

A. I would have to accept the autopsy report on its face value. Postmortem abrasion in this case would indicate to me that something is happening after she's dead.

Q. You did accept the autopsy report at face value in analyzing these cases, is that right?

A. Yes.

Q. What is it that the abrasions after death tell you, the abrasions on the front of the body after death?

A. Well, in that particular place, that she was someplace else, she had to be dragged on her knees, could be on the parking lot when she is taken out of the car. Could be, if she was killed someplace else in the parking lot at that location.

Q. Are the abrasions on the front of the body, the breasts, the knees, consistent with the body being dragged along the ground on its face, face down?

A. Could be, yes.

Q. Is that a reasonable explanation for those abrasions?

A. Yes.

Q. Of course, the body was not found face down, so it would have to have been turned over and placed where it was, is that correct?

A. Yes.

Q. Did you at one time have the opinion that the Pohlreich case was possibly a sexual encounter gone bad?

A. I don't think there is any evidence about the existence of that in the beginning. It looks to me like there is a problem with the offender learning how to manipulate death and execute death, and that there is sexual assault involved. If we knew more about the preparation there, that conclusion might be a little more clear.

Q. Was there evidence in that case of interaction with the body after death, after the body was dead?

A. Yes.

Q. That would be the position; is that what you're saying?

A. Placing of the arms and the objects, yes.

Q. The object being the pine cone?

A. Yes.

Q. There was no other object, is that right?

A. The one across the face.

Q. Have you ever seen a pine cone before used as an object, placed in connection with a body in some kind of signature?

A. Pine cone?

Q. Fir cone; whatever it was?

A. No.

Q. Does that have any known symbolic or ritualistic value as far as murder is concerned?

A. No.

Q. You mentioned that there is a postmortem insertion in Pohlreich also?

A. There was at one time a foreign object insertion, yes.

Q. That's with the body, that's another interaction with the body after death?

A. Yes.

Q. Do you have any idea what that object was?

A. No, I don't.

Q. You mentioned that the offender in these cases found all these objects, or whatever he used, he found them at the scene; do you know that to be a fact in Pohlreich?

A. Naturally there is a possibility, since the object is not there, that it is something from another area. That's a possibility. There is a possibility that it was at that area and it wasn't there at the time the police found the scene. Maybe it was there and they didn't collect it because they didn't recognize it for what it should be.

Q. There was no evidence in Pohlreich, was there, that there was an object at the scene that was inserted postmortem, is that correct?

A. No.

Q. There was certainly evidence of that fact, in both the Beethe and Levine cases, is that right?

A. Right.

Q. You described a signature, and as I understand it, it is pretty much like we think of a signature something that only the person can do, maybe somebody else could try to copy, but only the person whose signature it is can actually do it, is that right?

A. That's a fairly good analogy, yes.

Q. Is that why the term "signature" was coined to describe what happens in these cases?

A. I would imagine.

Q. I think you said only the offender can replicate it, is that right?

A. Yes.

Q. Going to the Mary Pohlreich case; do you feel there is an intentional degrading of the body in that case?

A. An intentional degrading? Absolutely.

Q. What do you see about that case that tells you that it is an intentional degrading?

A. For one thing, she's left openly displayed in a nude manner, not on her back, or with— excuse me, on her back, she's not placed in just a dump fashion. If you were an offender and you are going to murder somebody and leave them someplace, and you just want to dump the body and get out, you are leaving the area right away. However, in this case you see elements of degrading this female, defilement, almost coyly crossing the legs and leaving them out in the open like this. Crossing the hands over and covering up the face, almost like he didn't want them to see again.

Q. Have you ever testified before on this subject in court, as to your belief or opinion that certain murders were in fact committed by the same individual?

A. No.

Q. Have you ever been asked to testify before on that subject?

A. Yes.

Q. You mentioned you had in your possession a lot of material from the prosecutor's office, among that material was there something called victimology or victim profiles?

A. It seems to me there was some summary of a victim included with that.

Q. Would they be attached to the H.I.T.S. form?

A. No.

Q. That would have been provided by the detectives separately?

A. Right.

Q. Did you rely on the victim profiles in arriving at the conclusion that these matters were related?

A. No.

Ms. Schwartz: That's all I have, Your Honor.

Ms. Roe: Couple questions, Your Honor.

REDIRECT EXAMINATION

By Ms. Roe:

Mr. Keppel, you were asked to describe the elements of Beethe and Levine, that, using counsel's word, is evidenced by a ritual; what evidence did you see of that in the Pohlreich case?

A. Well, you still see the amount of postmortem activity that was accomplished, and the need on the part of the offender to put this person in a particular position. The ritual of placing them and actually the need to have to do that is what that person has to do. So, crossing the legs, crossing the arms, putting the pine cone there, placing the thing over the face, is something that is consistent throughout. Although there is less time around each of those victims, as you proceed from Pohlreich up to Levine, where the offender has spent a lot more time with the victim.

Q. It progresses?

A. It progresses, right.

Q. Can you think of one good reason why he would not have taken the amount of time with Ms. Pohlreich's body that he would have with Beethe and Levine?

A. A very good reason is that that place is a public place. He has to act fairly fast. There is traffic. It is a parking lot area. There are apartment houses behind where she's found. There is not only vehicle traffic but foot traffic.

Ms. Roe: Thank you, no further questions.

RECROSS EXAMINATION

By Ms. Schwartz:

Given that you testified that this victim is left in a public place, do you see the same evidence of planning or fantacy behavior in the Pohlreich case that you see in the Beethe or Levine cases?

A. I see slightly less because of the importance of the progression of planning. As you go up with the characteristics that are there, that I testified about, there is more death-inflicting injuries. There is more time with each of these victims.

Q. Wouldn't it be correct that your hypothesis, is that what it is is a hypothesis of progression with these victims, could be true only if you assume that the same person committed the crimes?

A. No.

Q. Different people could commit crimes in progression?

A. I guess I don't understand your question.

Q. There is only a progression if it is the same person doing the crimes, isn't that right?

A. Right. I see what you mean.

Ms. Schwartz: That's all.

Ms. Roe: Nothing further.

The Court: You may be excused.

Court will be in recess.

(Court recessed for the evening.)

Testimony of Robert Keppel in State of Washington v. George W. Russell (1991).

STATE V. RUSSELL

125 Wash.2d 24, 882 P.2d 747 (WASH 1994)
The STATE of Washington, Respondent, v. George W. RUSSELL, Appellant.
No. 60673–1.
Supreme Court of Washington,
En Banc.
Oct. 13, 1994.

D efendant was convicted on three counts of first-degree murder, in the Superior Court, King County, Patricia Aitkin, J. Defendant appealed. The Supreme Court, Madsen, J., held that: (1) trial court did not err by ordering that there be joinder of three counts, each involving separate murder; (2) trial court did not err in admitting expert testimony; (3) trial court did not err in admitting evidence of other assaults; and (4) deputy prosecutor's reference to "cat killing," allegedly conducted by defendant's witness, and to defendant's future dangerousness, while improper, did not require new trial.

Affirmed.

Andersen, C.J., dissented and filed opinion in which Johnson and Smith, JJ., concurred.

Utter, J.,, concurred in dissent and filed opinion.

26. Criminal Law 369.15, 673(5)

In determining admissibility of other crimes to prove identity, trial court must determine that evidence is relevant to identity and that any prejudice is outweighed by probative value, and must then properly limit purpose for which jury may consider evidence. ER 404(b).

27. Criminal Law 369.15

Evidence of other crimes is relevant on issue of identity only if method employed in commission of both crimes is "so unique" that proof that an accused committed one of the crimes creates high probability that he also committed other crimes with which he was charged, or in other words device used must be so unusual and distinctive as to be like a signature. ER 404(b).

28. Criminal Law 369.15

Evidence in each of three counts of murder, involving separate witnesses, would have been admissible as other crimes evidence to show identity had counts been severed and tried separately, as required before counts could be joined; in each case there was a victim killed by violent means who was then sexually assaulted and posed, naked, with aid of props and murders occurred within few weeks of one another in small geographic area. CrR 4.3(a); ER 404(b).

29. Criminal Law 620(6)

Prejudice to defendant resulting from joinder of three counts of murder, each involving separate victim, was outweighed by need for judicial economy; trial court found that great deal of evidence, particularly from those witnesses acquainted with defendant during period of time in which crimes were committed, would be repeated in each trial if motion to sever had been granted. CrR 4.3(a).

30. Criminal Law 620(6)

Trial court did not err by declining murder defendant's motion to sever one of three counts, each involving separate victim; strength of case sought to be severed was approximately same as that of other counts, defendant failed to show that joinder affected his decision whether to testify, evidence of each count would have been admissible had separate trials been held, and judicial economy favored joinder. CrR 4.3(a).

31. Criminal Law 469.1, 4.77.1

Expert testimony which does not involve new methods of proof or new scientific principle's from which conclusions are drawn, and is thus not subject to *Frye* test under which acceptance of method in scientific community must be established, can be admitted if witness qualifies as expert and if expert testimony would be helpful to trier of fact. ER 702.

32. Criminal Law 474.5

Acknowledged experts in scene of crime evidence could offer testimony as to frequency of instances in which perpetrator of murder arranged corpses into a "pose," for purposes of establishing that same individual had killed three posed victims, even though it was claimed that witnesses relied upon computer programs listing various characteristics of homicides and that acceptability of programs in scientific community should have been established, as required under *Frye* test; computer programs did not involve new method of proof or scientific principles, but were simply sophisticated record-keeping systems. ER 702.

33. Criminal Law 488

Expert witnesses testifying as to rarity of instances in which perpetrator will position corpse into a "pose" did not impermissibly produce numerical evidence tending to show that it was defendant who had posed corpses of three murder victims, even though witnesses had cited data from computer studies as to number of times that perpetrators had posed corpses; experts had relied on computer databases as support for conclusions that posing was rare, and not for establishing statistical probability of defendant's guilt, and experts had relied more on case materials and personal experience than database. ER 702.

34. Criminal Law 449.1, 465

In order for lay witnesses to give opinion testimony, witness must have personal knowledge of matter forming basis of opinion, testimony must be based rationally upon option of witness, and opinion must be helpful to jury. ER 602, 701.

35. Criminal Law 455

Detectives who had observed bodies left in degrading positions after death could give lay opinion testimony that bodies seemed posed and one detective could state that only once in his career had he ever seen another murder scene involving posing; detectives had testified regarding their personal knowledge of crime scenes and their perception of three murders at issue. ER 602, 701.

36. Criminal Law 470(2)

Expert witnesses could give their opinion that three murders involving "posing" of corpses in degrading situations were committed by same perpetrator, even though murder defendant claimed that it constituted opinion on ultimate facts of case; evidence was admissible under rule allowing identity evidence, and permissible inferences from evidence could not be excluded, and in any event defendant had opened door to line of inquiry by attempting to emphasize differences between the three killings involved.

37. Criminal Law 662.4

Trial court did not violate confrontation rights of murder defendant by allowing expert witness to testify as to rarity of cases in which corpses were "posed" after death, by reference to computerized survey results, without providing defendant with access to police reports from which computer database was compiled; original defense request for access to computer system had specifically disavowed request for police reports, defense expert had reviewed data with prosecution's expert, and prosecution witness himself did not have access to police reports and was basing his conclusion on data interpreted by another person. U.S.C.A Const. Amend. 6; West's RCWA Const. Art. 1, § 22 as amended by Amend. 10.

38. Criminal Law 359

Before evidence tending to show that another party may have committed a crime may be admitted there must, be such proof of connection or circumstances as tends clearly to point out someone besides one charged as guilty party.

FACTS

Count 1—Mary Ann Pohlreich

On Friday, June 22, 1990, Mary Ann Pohlreich went to Papagayo's, a Bellevue night club, with two friends. The three drove in Pohlreich's car. Her two friends left Pohlreich at Papagayo's at approximately 9:30 p.m.

Early the next morning, Pohlreich's body was found. partially inside the dumpster coral area in the parking lot behind the Black Angus restaurant, about a mile from Papagayo's. Pohlreich's body was unclothed, but she was wearing two pieces of jewelry. There was a Frito Lay dip container lid over her right eye and forehead, her arms were folded over her stomach, her legs were extended and crossed at the ankles, and she had a pine cone in one of her hands.

Though there were a number of significant injuries, the King Country medical examiner determined that the most likely cause of death was manual strangulation. Pohlreich's skull fracture and numerous facial injuries appeared to have been inflicted by a fist. Pohlreich's liver had two widely separated lacerations, and she had a distinct anal tear that the medical examiner opined was caused by a solid, nonhuman object. Pohlreich had a blood alcohol level of.14 percent at the time of her death.

Pohlreich's purse, sweater, and car were found at Papagayo's. The police discovered that on the evening of Pohlreich's death George Russell went to Papagayo's with his friend Smith McLain to have dinner. Once there, Russell and another friend talked to Pohlreich. After dinner, Russell borrowed the keys to McLain's truck, explaining that he had to change into a shirt with a collar as required on Papagayo's dance floor. Russell had a duffle bag in the truck.

A Bellevue police officer was working off duty that night as a doorman at Papagayo's. He often spoke with Russell, a frequent patron of the nightclub. That night he saw Russell twice: once shortly after he began his shift at 10:30 p.m. and again approximately an hour later. On the second occasion, Russell told the officer that he was going to take "this girl" over to her place to get something. Verbatim Report on Appeal, at 4042, 4052. The officer did not see the woman well enough to identify her; however, he described her size as being similar to Pohlreich's, and he noticed that the woman seemed very intoxicated.

Russell did not return to Papagayo's that evening with the truck. McLain was upset and spent the rest of the evening waiting for him at the Overlake Denny's where it was customary for Papagayo's patrons to go after closing. At around 5:30 a.m., McLain found a ride home.

On the morning that Pohlreich's body was discovered, Russell telephoned the McLain residence. Russell said that he had been out looking for McLain all night. At approximately 6 a.m., McClain's sister, Shawn Calvo, saw Russell return in her brother's truck. Russell told her that he had borrowed the truck to drive a friend home and then could not find McLain. During this conversation Calvo noticed a reddish-orange stain on the passenger seat of the truck. Russell explained that his friend had vomited clam chowder in the truck. Russell declined Calvo's offer of a ride home and walked away with his duffle bag.

McLain woke up after Russell had left and went out to inspect his truck. He smelled a strong offensive odor that reminded him of vomit or the smell of a deer gutted after a hunting kill. Russell called McLain that morning and told him that he had thrown up in the truck after drinking too much. Russell informed McLain that he had driven a woman home in the truck because he did not want to be seen in the woman's Porsche.

Russell had spoken previously about the woman with the Porsche. That woman was Tamara Francis. Francis testified that she knew Russell but had never left Papagayo's with him.

The police also discovered that Russell had been a regular customer at the Black Angus, where Pohlreich's body was discovered, from 1989 until March 1990; when he was banned from the restaurant. Russell was very angry about that decision.

On October 11, 1990, almost 31/5 months after Pohlreich's murder, the police removed the interior of Smith McLain's truck. While the interior had been cleaned and detailed during the summer, the floormats had not. McLain had removed the floormats, which were made from house carpet remnants, from his truck and had put them in the garage because they smelled so bad.

The upholstery in McLain's truck reacted positively for blood and HO and A antigens which matched the HO and A antigens in the vaginal swab taken at the Pohlreich autopsy. Both antigens could have been contributed by Pohlreich herself who was a type A secretor. Russell was type O; although he could have been the source of the HO antigens, he could not have contributed the A antigens.

The State also sent the vaginal swab and upholstery samples for DNA testing. Because of the poor quality of the samples, the laboratory conducted a polymerase chain reaction (PCR) test. The PCR test results indicated that neither Russell nor McLain could have been the source of the blood in McLain's truck, but that Pohlreich could have been. The testing also revealed that only Russell, of all the comparison samples, could have been the donor of the sperm.

In addition to the sperm and blood samples, one negroid hair, consistent with Russell's, was found in the debris on the sheet in which Pohlreich's body was wrapped. Five fibers found in the pubic combings were consistent with the truck carpet as was one fiber from the sheet debris. Another fiber in the sheet debris was consistent with the truck's upholstery.

Count 2—Carol Beethe

Carol Beethe was employed as a bartender at Cucina Cucina, a restaurant in Bellevue. She lived in a condominium with her two children. Beethe's ex-husband, Paul, lived nearby. On August 8, 1990, Beethe spoke with Paul at around 9:30 p.m. At 10:30 p.m. she spoke with her boyfriend, Mike Suell, with whom she was planning to go on a vacation. At midnight she met another friend at the restaurant where he was the bartender. Beethe left at approximately 2:15 a.m.

At 4:30 a.m. Beethe's daughter Kelly heard someone in the hall of the family's condominium, and then saw the person shine a flashlight in the bathroom, her sister's bedroom, and her own bedroom. Kelly assumed that the person was Mike Suell.

When Kelly awoke at 8:30 a.m., her mother was not up as she usually was, her bedroom door was locked, and Kelly could not wake her. When Kelly went outside to open the sliding glass door to her mother's room, she saw her mother and became scared. She called her father who came over and entered the room through a sliding glass door.

Beethe was on her back on the bed. The bedspread was pulled down to the foot of the bed. Her body was unclothed except for a pair of red high-heeled shoes. Her feet were together with legs spread and knees bent. Blood had been smeared on her legs in a manner that resembled "finger painting." Verbatim Report on appeal, at 3290. A rifle had been placed resting symmetrically between Beethe's legs, resting on her shoes. The firearm penetrated approximately five or six inches into her vagina. Her left arm was bent upward at the elbow, while her right arm was bent down at the elbow, nearly touching her hip. Beethe's head was wrapped in a plastic bag and covered with a large pillow.

The medical examiner ascertained that Beethe's death had been caused by head injuries. The head injuries were inflicted by an instrument swung with considerable force in rapid succession. The blows left distinct "Y" shaped marks and crushed the entire left side of Beethe's skull. Beethe had also been struck many times with a knee or fist in the torso. Her ribs were broken and her liver was lacerated.

Testimony suggested that Beethe and Russell were acquaintances. One witness testified that both Russell and Beethe frequented the Overlake Denny's. A waitress at the Black Angus testified that on two occasions she was talking to Beethe about a "situation.between George [Russell] and I" and saw Russell glaring at them. Verbatim Report on Appeal, at 4893–99. (This occurred before

Russell was banned from the Black Angus). After the murders, Russell told friends that he knew the victim of the second murder and that she was a bartender at the Cucina Cucina restaurant in Bellevue.

When Beethe's body was found, she had rings on her right hand but not on her left hand. At the time of her death, Beethe owned two wedding ring sets, one from her mother and one from her previous marriage. The rings were kept in a jewelry box in Beethe's bedroom, but they were never located after her death. During their investigation, the police published photographs of the rings in a Bellevue newspaper. At trial, one of the State's witnesses testified that Russell had tried to sell him rings that resembled the missing set.

Beethe's family also informed the police that she had a half dozen small Crown Royal bags in the top drawer of her dresser containing silver dollars and other change from tips. When police allowed Paul to reenter his ex-wife's house he noticed the Crown Royal bags were missing.

About three weeks after Beethe's murder, Russell and a friend drove to a wooded area on Mercer Island. Russell informed his fiend that he had to pick up some money owned him. Russell stepped out of the car and returned with a paper bag full of silver dollars and change.

Forensic evidence did not reveal any of Russell's fingerprints in Beethe's residence. A fabric glove impression left on the sheet of her bed suggested that the murderer wore gloves. Negroid hairs were discovered on Beethe's sheet, pillow and underwear, but the fragments were not suitable for comparison.

Count 3—Andrea Levine

Andrea Levine rented a basement apartment in the home of Robert Hays and his wife. On Thursday, August 30, 1990, Hays saw Levine after she returned from work. Later that evening, Levine met her boyfriend at a Kirkland restaurant, where the two discussed plans to go to the San Juan Islands. Levine declined a ride and drove herself home to pack at about 1:30 a.m.

Hays and his wife awoke on Friday morning at about 5 am. Hays opened the back door to let their dog out. The dog began barking wildly. Hays stepped out to investigate and saw a dark figure about 25 to 30 feet away. It was dark and Hays could see only an adult with a white form, approximately two-thirds of the width of the person, on or in front of the individual's abdomen. Hays called out and the person fled. Hays chased the person a short distance but stopped because he was unarmed. He called the police who examined the yard but did not check Levine's apartment.

The following Monday, Hays' wife entered Levine's apartment because one of Levine's cats appeared hungry. As she walked down the hallway, she smelled something like old blood coming from the bedroom. She opened the door and discovered Levine's body. Levine was on her back, on the bed. Her face was turned toward her left shoulder. Her legs were spread with knees straight. Her right arm extended above her shoulder while her left arm rested by her side. Under Levine's left forearm was the book *More Joy of Sex*. A plastic dildo was partially inserted into Levine's mouth.

The medical examiner determined that Levine had died from severe multiple head wounds inflicted with an object such as an iron bar. Levine's body was covered with postmortem stab wounds. Forensic evidence revealed the presence of a single negroid public hair at the crime scene. This hair could not be matched to any samples taken from Russell, although Russell could not be excluded, either. No fingerprints could be found, suggesting to the police that someone had "wiped the scene down." Verbatim Report on Appeal, at 5286, 5304–05.

At trial the State presented evidence showing that Russell knew Levine. On one occasion, Levine's boyfriend drove her home in her truck and Russell followed in the boyfriend's car. A few weeks later, Russell and some friends drove out to Renton to help Levine put a new battery in her truck. Russell rode back to Kirkland with Levine. On a third occasion, Levine was at a bar and Russell came over to talk. After Levine's murder Russell made disparaging remarks about her, stating that she "slept around," that she "used men," and that she was a "whore." Verbatim Report on Appeal, at 5464.

On the Labor Day weekend after Levine was killed, Russell and some friends went to Canada. On August 30, the night before they left, the group stayed at a motel. Russell left during the night dressed in dark pants, white tennis shoes, a dark blue sweatshirt, and a dark cap. He said something about going to work. He returned at about 6 a.m. wearing the same clothing. Russell did not have a car. Levine lived about a mile from the motel by car, but the walling distance was shorter.

A friend of Russell's testified that she received a ring from Russell several days after Labor Day. She wore the ring several times and then gave it to a friend who pawned it. The police later retrieved the ring from the Pawn shop. Levine's sister-in-law identified the ring as one that she had given to Levine.

Police brought the ring to a jewelry store where an employee identified it as one he had worked on for Levine in February 1990. The owner of the jewelry store also testified that Levine had brought the ring in to be worked on.

Russell was arrested eight days after Levine's murder based on some outstanding misdemeanor warrants. After interviewing Russell, the police charged him with the murders of Mary Ann Pohlreich, Carol Beethe, and Andrea Levine. Russell raises several issues in this appeal. Other facts will be discussed where relevant to the issue presented....

[26] The final factor is whether evidence of each count would be cross admissible under ER 404(b) if severance were granted. ER 404(b) permits evidence of other crimes to show identity; motive, intent, preparation, plan, knowledge, absence of mistake or accident, opportunity, or an alternative means by which a crime could have been committed. *State v. Lord* 117 Wash.2d 829, 872 n. 11, 822 P.2d 177 (1991), *cert. denied*—U.S.—, 113 S.Ct. 164, 121 L.Ed.2d 112 (1992). Such evidence is not admissible "to prove the char.ater of a person in order to show action in conformity therewith". ER 404(b); *State v. Smith*, 106 Wash.2d 772, 775, 725 P.2d 951 (1986). Of relevance here is identity. In determining the admissibility of other crimes to prove identity, a trial court must determine that the evidence is relevant to identity and that any prejudicial effect is out-weighted by the probative value. It must then properly limit the purpose for which the jury may consider the evidence. *Smith*, 106 Wash.2d at 772, 725 P.2d 951; *Watkins*, 53 Wash.App. at 270, 766 P.2d 484.

[27] Evidence of other crimes is relevant on the issue of identity only if the method employed in the commission of both crimes is "so unique" that proof that an accused committed one of the crimes creates a high probability that he also committed the other crimes with which he is charged. *Hernandez*, 58 Wash.App. at 799, 794 P.2d 1327 (citing *Smith*, 106 Wash.2d at 777, 725 P.2d 951). In other words, the device used must be so unusual and distinctive as to be like a signature. *State v. Coe*, 101 Wash.2d 772, 777, 684 P.2d 668 (1984) (citing *McCormick's Evidence* § 190, at 449 (Edward W. Cleary gen. ed., 2d ed. 1972)); *see also State v. Lynch*, 58 Wash.App. 83, 88, 792 P.2d 167, *review denied*, 115 Wash.2d 1020, 802 P.2d 126 (1990).

[28] The trial court found cross admissibility on the basis of signature and entered the following written findings:

1. Each crime bears the perpetrator's unique signature, comprised of the manner in which these women were killed, the elaborate manner in which they were posed after their deaths, and the proximity in time and place of the three murders.

2. Evidence of each crime is highly probative of the identity of the murderer in each of the other crimes; the probative value of this evidence greatly outweighs its prejudice to the defendant.

Clerk's Papers, at 407. The trial court also cited the opinions of two criminal investigators who testified during the severance hearing that the three homicides bore the same signature and were committed by the same person.

Russell now contends that the factors identified in finding of fact 6 do not meet the test for signature crimes, and that no unique signature was identified by the trial court. The State counters by citing other "signature" cases in which the criminal methods were less distinctive than those employed here. See *State v. Laureano*, 101 Wash2d 745, 682 P.2d 889 (1984) (evidence of prior robbery admissible under ER 404(b) where crimes committed 3 weeks apart where both involved forcible entry into family residences by three persons dressed in army fatigues (though not the same three) and where both involved firearms and similar use of a shotgun); *see also Lynch* (two prior robberies admissible where all crimes involved wearing a brown wig, similar time of day, a red 10-speed bicycle, display of a gun tucked in a waistband, and theft of car keys from victims); *but see Hernandez*, 58 Wash.App. at 799, 794 P.2d 1327 (no showing of unusual or unique manner sufficient to show identity where robber entered the store, pulled a knife, asked for money and fled upon receiving it).

We find that the factors cited by the trial court support the finding that certain evidence in this case was quite unique. Each count involved a victim killed by violent means who was then sexually assaulted and posed, naked, with the aid of props. The murders occurred within a few weeks of one another in a small geographic area. We agree with the trial court and with the expert witnesses that these similarities were not due simply to coincidence. Accordingly, we do not regard the trial court's conclusion as to cross admissibility as an abuse of discretion.

[29] Finally, the court must weigh any prejudice to the defendant resulting from joinder against the need for judicial economy. The trial court found that apart from the evidence of signature, "a great deal of evidence, particularly from those witnesses who were acquainted with the defendant during the period of time in which these crimes were committed, would be repeated in each trial if the defendant's motion to sever Count I from the others is granted." Clerk's Papers, at 407–08. The court thus concluded that judicial economy was served by a single trial on all counts.

[30] Excluding pretrial motions, this case took 33 days to try. Considering our evaluation of the other severance factors we cannot find that the prejudice resulting from joinder in this case outweighed considerations of judicial economy. Accordingly, we conclude that the trial court did not abuse its discretion in denying Russell's motion for severance.

IV

The fourth issue the Defendant raises is whether the trial court erred in admitting expert and lay testimony regarding the rarity of posed murder victims. Russell here raises several arguments regarding this testimony. We will first address Russell's contention that the expert testimony was inadmissible because the State's experts improperly relied on unproven scientific methodologies in determining that the same person committed all three murders.

At issue here are references made by John Douglas and Robert Keppel to the HITS and VICAP computer programs during their testimony regarding the rarity of posing. These programs use forms, filled out by local law enforcement officers, listing the various characteristics of homicides in Washington and the nation respectively. The trial court found that the expert testimony referring to

HITS and VICAP did not involve novel scientific evidence and was, therefore, subject only to the requirements of ER 702:

[31] As stated earlier, expert testimony is admissible under ER 702 if the witness qualifies as an expert and if the expert testimony would be helpful to the trier of fact. *Kalakosky*, 121 Wash.2d at 541, 852 P.2d 1064; *State v. Cauthron*, 120 Wash.2d 879, 890, 846 P2d 502 (1993). Testimony which does not involve new methods of proof or new scientific principles from which conclusions are drawn need not be subjected to the *Frye* test. *State v. Ortiz*, 119 Wash.2d 294, 311, 831 P2d 1060 (1992); *State v. Young*, 62 Wash.App. 895, 906, 802 P2d 829, 817 P2d 412 (1991). Decisions based on ER 702 are reviewed under the abuse of discretion standard. *Kalakosky*, 121 Wash2d at.541, 852 P2d 1064.

[32] In the case at bar, the trial court ruled that both Keppel and Douglas were widely recognized as authorities in crime scene analysis. Both men have extensive experience in serial crime analysis and investigation. The court then found that their testimony would not involve the application of a new scientific technique and that a *Frye* hearing was unnecessary. Finally, the court ruled that the testimony concerning the rarity of posing would be helpful to the jury under ER 702:

> The jury does not have the specialized knowledge of how common the problem is or how often there is sexual penetration, open display of bodies, or the posing of the body after death. So I think it is within the scope of an opinion of somebody's experience to indicate whether these are common or not common or unique. I would find that the relevance of the testimony, as it goes to the identity of the perpetrator, and the inference to be drawn, is that the same person committed all three homicides.
>
> Verbatim Report on Appeal, at 2331.

We agree with the trial court that the *Frye* test clearly was inapplicable to the expert testimony regarding the HITS and VICAP programs. These programs are nothing more than sophisticated record-keeping systems. The court correctly analyzed the admissibility of this testimony under ER 702 and we find no abuse of discretion in the admission of the experts' testimony.

[33] Russell also objects to this testimony on the ground that it was statistical. Neither expert expressed his opinion about the rarity of posing in precisely quantified terms, though Douglas testified as to the number of cases on VICAP and Keppel testified as to the number of cases on HITS. Russell maintains, however, that by specifying the extent of these databases, Keppel and Douglas implicitly testified that Russell was guilty as a matter of mathematical probability.

We first note that there is no prohibition against using well-founded statistics to establish some fact that will be useful to the trier of fact. *State v. Briggs*, 55 Wash.App. 44, 62–63, 776 P2d 1347 (1989) (citing *People v. Collins*, 68 CaL2d 319, 332, 66 Cal.Rptr. 497, 438 P2d 33 (1968)). Second, both experts relied on the databases primarily as support for the conclusion that posting is a rare occurence and not for the conclusion that there was a statistical probability that Russell committed the murders. Finally, both experts relied more on case materials and personal expertise than on the databases in forming their opinions and both expressed their opinions in non-quantifiable terms.

Russell next contends that the trial court erred in allowing three laywitnesses to testify about the rarity of posing and thus to reinforce the expert testimony. In addition to Keppel and Douglas, three detectives testified that each of the bodies seemed posed and only one said he had ever seen another murder scene involving posing.

[34] This court recently explained the appropriate conditions for admissibility of lay testimony as follows:

> Under Rule 701 and Rule 602, the witness must have personal knowledge of matter that forms the basis of testimony of opinion; the testimony must be based rationally upon the perception of the witness; and of course, the opinion must be helpful to the jury (the principal test).

Ortiz, 119 Wash.2d at 308–09, 831 P2d 1060 (citing *McCormick's Evidence* 29 (Edward W. Cleary gen. ed., 3d ed. 1984)).

[35] We have already concluded that the court did not abuse its discretion in finding testimony regarding the rarity of posing helpful to the trier of fact. The detectives testified regarding their personal knowledge of crime scenes, and their perceptions of the three murders at issue. While the testimony may have been cumulative, we do not see that its admission rises to the level of an abuse of discretion.

[36] The defense argues further that the State's expert testimony amounted to expert opinion on the ultimate question of guilt. The State points out, however, that if the testimony was improper, the defense opened the issue when it presented testimony that the murders were not related.

These arguments bring us once again to Russell's challenge that this expert testimony was improperly admitted under ER 404(b) to show identity and thus to prove that the same person committed all three murders. In her pretrial ruling the judge limited the experts by allowing them to testify only that the criminal methods employed in each case were unique and rose to the level of signature evidence. The experts were precluded from testifying that they thought that the same person committed all three crimes.

During the course of trial, the court modified this ruling when defense counsel, during cross examination of State's expert Keppel, asked whether he knew of any other cases related to these three murders. The State objected because the line of questioning went beyond the scope permitted by the court. The court told the defense:

> You may do that. Then they have the right to come back on redirect and ask if these three cases are related, which they have not done. They have not gone into the relationship among the three cases. If you want to relate. . .the Pohlreich case to other cases, then I think in all fairness they can come back and relate the three cases to each other.

Verbatim Report on Appeal, at 5770. When the defense pursued the issue of the similarities and differences among these three murders and others, the court allowed Keppel to testify on redirect that in his opinion all of the murders were committed by the same person. Keppel based his opinion on the posing and on the facts. that all the victims were nude, all were female, and all were killed within a short period of time of their contact with the offender. He also observed that each crime involved the sexual insertion of a foreign object and that the offender needed to display these victims and ensure their discovery. Russell did not raise an ER 404(b) objection to this line of testimony.

Later, the State's other expert, John Douglas, also testified that all of the victims were posed and that all of the murder scenes exhibited the same signature. Douglas based his opinion regarding signature on the facts that all of the victims had been posed in degrading and humiliating positions and on the fact that the murders occurred within a 67-day period within a small geographical area. Again, Russell raised no ER 404(b) objection but instead, in cross examination, sought to emphasize the differences between Pohlreich's murder and the other two murders. Douglas agreed that there were differences among the crimes, but explained on redirect that the differences were insignificant compared to the similarities. "The significant part is the posing of the victims, the posing in this degrading type of position, that is critical." Verbatim Report on Appeal, at 6042.

The defense then called Robert Gebo as an expert witness who testified that, at one point, he had believed that the Pohlreich and Beethe murders were not connected. On cross examination, the prosecution elicited Gebo's current opinion that all of the murders were committed by the same person. The court overruled defense counsel's objection and motion to strike, and again ruled that Gebo's testimony on direct brought the issue of whether the homicides were related onto the field of play.

In considering Russell's contention that these experts improperly gave opinions on the ultimate question of guilt, we observe that the purpose of showing identity under ER 404(b) is to demonstrate the probability that the same person committed the crime. *Coe*, 101 Wash2d at 777–78, 684 P2d 668; *Smith*, 106 Wash.2d at 778, 725 P.2d 951. Having found the expert testimony admissible to show identity, we will not rule inadmissible the inference to be drawn from such evidence. Moreover, the express assertions that the same person committed the three murders were invited by defense counsel. Once the defense brought up the issue of whether these crimes were related to other crimes, the court properly ruled that the State could, in turn, ask the experts whether the crimes were related to one another and had been committed by one person. *See State v. Gefeller*, 76, Wash.2d 449, 455, 458 P2d 17 (1969); *State v. Crenshaw*, 27 Wash. App. 326, 333, 617 P2d 1041 (1980), *aff'd* 98 Wash2d 789, 659 P2d 488 (1983). We find no error in the court's ruling.

In a related argument, the defense complains that Gebo improperly based his change of opinion on the totality of the evidence against Russell, and that his testimony thus doubly invaded the province of the jury. The trial court cured any error in this regard by allowing the State to call Gebo as a rebuttal witness so that he could explain that his change of opinion was based not on information relating to Russell but on the views of his colleagues, Robert Keppel and John Douglas. The defense now claims that Gebo was lying. We have no way to assess this claim and will not consider it further.

[37] Russell next contends that the trial court's denial of discovery of police reports from which the HITS data is drawn violated his Sixth Amendment right of confrontation. The Sixth Amendment and Const. art. 1, § 22 (amend. 10) grant criminal defendants the right to confront and cross-examine adverse witnesses. *State v. Hudlow* 99 Wash.2d 1, 15, 659 P2d 514 (1983); *State v. Boast* 87 Wash2d 447, 453, 553 P.2d 1322 (1976).

ER 703 governs the bases of opinion testimony given by experts:

> The facts or data in the particular case upon which an expert bases an opinion or inference may be those perceived by or made known to the expert at or before the hearing. If of a type reasonably relied upon by experts in the particular field in forming opinions or inferences upon the subject, the facts or data need not be admissible in evidence.

ER 705, in turn, governs the disclosure of the facts underlying an expert's opinion and provides as follows:

> The expert may testify in terms of opinion or inference and give reasons therefor without prior disclosure of the underlying facts or data, unless the judge requires otherwise. The expert may in any event be required to disclose the underlying facts or data on cross examination.

ER 703 thus permits expert opinion testimony based on hearsay data that would be otherwise inadmissible in evidence, while ER 705, which is identical to Federal Rule of Evidence 705, authorizes the admission of expert opinion testimony without the prior disclosure of the facts or data which underlie the opinion. *See* 11 James W. Moore & Helen I. Bendix, *Federal Practice* § 705.10, at VII-70 (2d ed. 1976); *see also* Robert H. Aronson, *Evidence in Washington.* 705–3 (2d ed. 1993) (under ER 705, trial court has discretion to require an expert to disclose the basis for opinion).

Initially, the defense requested access to the HITS system and specifically disavowed any request for police reports of cases included in that system. The State offered to allow a reputable defense expert review the data with Keppel, and Keppel reviewed the database with defense counsel for several hours. The trial court granted the defense's discovery request for forms in the relevant categories, *e.g.*, posing/unusual position, sexual insertion, ritual. After access to the HITS system was provided, the defense requested a variety of police reports referenced in HITS. The defense argues that the trial court's denial violated the confrontation clause.

Keppel himself did not have access to the actual police reports in the HITS system. The trial court reasoned that meaningful cross examination was possible without access to the police reports by pointing out that Keppel was basing his conclusions on data interpreted by another person.

Other Washington cases have allowed the admission of expert opinion based on data interpreted by another. See *State v. Ecklund* 30 Wash.App. 313, 318, 633 p.2d 933 (1981); *Tennant v. Roys*, 44 Wash.App. 305, 311, 722 p.2d 848 (1986). We see no abuse of discretion or violation of the confrontation clause resulting from a similar admission here. The State allowed the defense to review the same data on which Keppel relied. Keppel himself did not have access to the actual police reports that make up the databases; moreover, he did not base his opinions exclusively on the databases. We hold that Russell was not denied due process and find no abuse of discretion in the trial court's denial of discovery of the police reports underlying the HITS system.

V

[38]Russell next argues that the trial court erred in excluding evidence of other suspects and other crimes which he contends would connect another person with the three murders at issue.

Washington law on this point is clear:

> While evidence tending to show that another party may have committed the crime may be admissible, before such testimony can be received there must be such proof of connection . . . 1or circumstances as tend clearly to point out someone besides the one charged as the guilty party.

State v. Kwan, 174 Wash. 528, 532–33, 25 P.2d 104 (1933) (citing *State v. Downs*, 168 Wash. 664, 667, 13 p.2d 1 (1932)); *see also State v. Mak*, 105 Wash.2d 692, 716, 718 P.2d 407, *cent, denied* 479 U.S. 995, 107 S.Ct. 599, 93 L.Ed.2d 599 (1986). The trial court's decision on admissibility of this type of evidence is reviewed for abuse of discretion.Mak, at 717, 718 P.2d 407.

Accordingly, we affirm the judgment of the trial court and uphold the defendant's convictions in this case.

BRACHTENBACH, DOLLIVER, DURHAM and GUY, JJ., concur.

PROFILING RESEARCH

While offender profiling has garnered a lot of attention, both as a viable investigative technique for law enforcement and an entertainment tool for television, movies, and media, little empirical research has focused on profiling. *Section VI: Profiling Research* illustrates the various types of studies examining offender profiling. These studies seek to strengthen crime scene analysis and offender profiling procedures, and examine the validity of these techniques. The following are examples of current research in the field, the efforts of inquisitive scholars from the fields of criminology, psychology, criminal justice, and law, and the types of questions they attempt to answer

In *Investigative Case Management for Missing Children Homicides*, Hanfland, Keppel, and Weis describe crime characteristics and solvability factors in 600 missing children homicides. The primary goal of the study was to better assist investigators in making decisions and developing strategies that lead to the timely capture of killers of abducted children. They identify the frequencies of when the child is reported missing, when the abducted child is killed, victim characteristics, victim-offender relationships, offender characteristics, the Modus Operandi motivations, cause of death, investigative characteristics, murder incident sites, and series characteristics. Their results and identification of several solvability factors have serious implications for the process of investigating child abductions and missing children homicides.

In *The Nature of Expressiveness and Instrumentality in Homicide: Implications for Offender Profiling* (2000), Gabrielle Salfati examines the classification of crime scene behaviors and offender characteristics homicide cases to strengthen the scientific study of offender profiling. Her study investigated the possibility of developing a model of homicide behavior to use as the basis of establishing the validity of offender profiling. The study analyzed 247 single offender/single victim homicides using Small Space Analysis Statistics. Since a number of homicide cases revealed common behaviors, these behaviors were not used to discriminate between cases. Salfati differentiates between expressive actions and instrumental actions at the crime scene, classifying crime scene characteristics and offender characteristics for comparison. She concludes by discussing the implications the results have for offender profiling.

In *Psychological Aspects of Crime Scene Profiling: Validity Research* (1998), authors Homant and Kennedy describe crime scene profiling and question the validity of profiles. The authors provide a review of the literature on offender types and the ability to generalize behavioral characteristics at a crime scene to offender characteristics. They distinguish between the process of crime scene profiling and four other types more commonly referred to: 1) psychological profiling, 2) offender profiling, 3) equivocal death analysis, and 4) geographic profiling. They describe the goals of profiling procedures, review the theoretical basis of profiling, and examine various studies of profiling. Then, Homant and Kennedy address the validity and reliability of crime scene profiling by reviewing recent studies.

In the 1995 article *Coals to Newcastle: Police Use of Offender Profiling*, author Gary Copson discusses his research on law enforcement perceptions of the usefulness of offender profiling. This article developed out of Copson's awareness that little empirical research had been conducted on the usefulness of inferring offender characteristics from offense characteristics. Copson (1995) provides a review of the previous studies focusing on an assessment of the usefulness and accuracy of offender profiles. Based on a review of the research, he concluded that past studies relied mostly on the opinions of the detectives who have used profiling advice and revealed a measure of approval for the potential of offender profiling, but none of the cases should be regarded as definitive.

Deciding that accuracy, or the predictive value, of a profile is not the sole source of usefulness to investigators; Copson focused his study on determining the relative usefulness of a profile on the basis of the users' judgment of the profiling advice. His study assessed professional judgments of the profiling service rendered in 184 criminal cases in Great Britain. He found that the majority of detectives (83%) found the profiling advice they received operationally beneficial, although only half (53%) found that it contributed anything of value to the information supplied to the profiler and only a few (14%) stated that it assisted in solving the case. He concludes his findings with several recommendations for police officers considering commissioning profiling advice.

INVESTIGATIVE CASE MANAGEMENT FOR MISSING CHILDREN HOMICIDES: REPORT II

KATHERINE M. BROWN,[1] ROBERT D. KEPPEL,[2]
JOSEPH G. WEIS,[3] AND MARVIN SKEEN[4]

INTRODUCTION

Child abduction murder is every parent's worst nightmare. To compound the problem, child abduction murders are incredibly difficult to solve and deeply impact law enforcement officials involved in the investigation. According to the National Center for Missing and Exploited Children (NCMEC), abductions resulting in a child's death present many investigative and emotional obstacles for law enforcement officers (National Center for Missing & Exploited Children, 2000). Hanfland, Keppel and Weis (1997) state that the rarity of child abduction murders, even among criminal homicides, and their complex, emotion-laden, high profiles, makes them extremely difficult to investigate.

The 1979 abduction of seven-year-old Etan Patz, and the 1981 abduction and murder of six-year-old Adam Walsh, terrified parents throughout the nation. Unfortunately, as a result of those events, inflated and unsubstantiated numbers of missing children were widely reported to be over 2 million per year. The numbers of children who were abducted and then murdered were erroneously reported to be as high as 5,000 per year.

The public outcry over concern for the safety of America's children contributed to the establishment of the National Center for Missing and Exploited Children (NCMEC) by the United States Congress. To the contrary, careful research has shown that between 40 and 150 incidents of child abduction murder occur each year, which is less than one half of one percent of the murders committed nationally. On average, there is one child abduction murder for every 10,000 reports of a missing child (Finklehor, Hotaling & Sedlak, 1992).

Missing and Abducted Children Statistics

Missing children cases are typically placed into five categories: family abduction, nonfamily abduction, runaways, throwaway or abandoned children, and children who become lost or injured (Baker, Burgess, Rabun, & Nahirny, 2002). In 1988, an estimated 354,100 family abductions occurred.

[1]Sam Houston State University, Huntsville, Texas, USA
[2]Seattle University, Seattle, Washington, USA
[3]University Of Washington, Seattle, Washington, USA
[4]Washington State Attorney General's Office, Seattle, Washington, USA

Forty-six percent of those abductions involved concealment of a child, out of state transportation, or the intent to keep the child indefinitely or to permanently alter custody. During this period, an estimated 3,200 to 4,600 nonfamily abductions were known to police (Finklehor et al., 1992). Unfortunately, less than 5.0% of those types of cases are reported to police (Hanfland, et al., 1997), and they are more likely to result in harm or death. Approximately 200 to 300 of them were stereotypical kidnappings in which the child was transported a distance of more than 50 feet or kept over night. An estimated 446,700 children ran away during this period and approximately 127,100 children were told to leave their home or were abandoned (Finklehor et al., 1992).

Unfortunately, it is extremely difficult to gather accurate information on child abduction for a variety of reasons. Existing studies on child abduction are limited in scope, and there are discrepancies in the statistical information produced. Boudreaux, Lord and Etter (2000) propose an explanation for the deficiencies in data on child abduction:

> First, a number of highly publicized stranger abduction cases in the early 1980s resulted in a social climate of heightened concern and emotion regarding the safety of children. This yielded overestimated initial incidence rates of child abduction (Best & Thibodeau, 1997; Finklehor et al., 1990). Second, early statistics combined many different types of child abduction (e.g., family and nonfamily abductions) and age groups of children (e.g., preteen and teenaged children), impeding researchers' abilities to identify specific critical issues and draw clear conclusions regarding the dynamics of child abduction. Third, many child abductions are not reported to law enforcement agencies such as the Federal Bureau of Investigation (FBI) or child assistance agencies such as the National Center for Missing & Exploited Children (NCMEC). Finally, data collection has been hindered by variations in state laws (e.g., definitions) and the use of different data collection methods. Locating child abduction case files within law enforcement agencies can be particularly cumbersome because abductions may be filed under other crime categories (e.g., homicide and sexual assault). (p. 64)

Definitions

There is no consistent, standard social scientific definition of child abduction. According to Fass (1999, p. 9), "our definition of the crime (even, indeed, the courts' definition) has been historically derived." According to Boudreaux et al. (2000), the definition is problematic for two reasons:

> (a) there is no single accepted definition of child abduction (i.e., the legal definitions of the terms child and abduction can vary from jurisdiction to jurisdiction), and (b) there are different forms of child abduction, each with inconsistent terms, which if not specifically defined, can cause confusion (e.g., parental abduction, family abduction, stereotypical abduction, missing children, and kidnapped children). (p. 64)

In addition, legal definitions of child abduction vary widely across jurisdictions.

Finklehor et al. (1992) propose that the definition of child abduction should be "the coerced unauthorized movement of a child, the detention of a child, or the luring of a child for the purposes of committing another crime" (p. 228). The National Incidence Studies of Missing, Abducted, Runaway, and Thrownaway Children (NISMART) (2002) defines stereotypical kidnapping as: "A nonfamily abduction perpetrated by a slight acquaintance or stranger in which a child is detained overnight, transported at least 50 miles, held for ransom or abducted with intent to keep the child permanently, or killed" (p. 2) and nonfamily abduction as:

> (1) An episode in which a nonfamily perpetrator takes a child by the use of physical force or threat of bodily harm or detains the child for a substantial period of time (at least 1 hour) in an isolated place by the use of physical force or threat of bodily harm without lawful authority or parental permission, or (2) an episode in which a child younger than 15 or mentally incompetent,

and without lawful authority or parental permission, is taken, detained or voluntarily
accompanies a nonfamily perpetrator who conceals the child's whereabouts, demands ransom, or
expresses the intention to keep the child permanently. (p. 2)

There has been disagreement over the amount of distance required to transport a child in order to establish an abduction (Finklehor et al., 1992). According to Forst and Blomquist (1991), some jurisdictions follow the "any movement" rule, while some jurisdictions abide by the "incidental rule" in which movement in the context of another crime is incidental. To add to the confusion, some definitions depend on the motivation of the offender, and there is even disagreement about the definition of child (Lanning, 1995). The confusion and ambiguity regarding definitions contribute significantly to difficulties in collecting rigorous data on child abduction murder. However, those obstacles are not insurmountable

SUMMARY

This report discusses the findings from a research project which examined the investigations of more than 800 child abduction murders. The report is particularly salient to homicide detectives who are confronted with an unsolved murder case involving child abduction. Results from this study will help police investigators identify strategies and implement tactics to focus investigations that will improve their ability to solve child abduction murder cases.

METHODOLOGY

Introduction

The data used in this study were collected through a cooperative agreement between the Washington State Attorney General's Office and the Office of Juvenile Justice and Delinquency Prevention, United States Department of Justice. The objective of the collaborative research project was to examine murders of abducted children. The data set will be referred to as the Child Abduction Murder (CAM) dataset. This report, the second of two, updates the data and findings of a prior three year research project that examined the investigations of murders of more than 600 abducted children. The findings of the previous study are referred to in this study as the Hanfland et al., 1997 report. The original study, as well as the follow-up data collection and analyses, were conducted by criminal justice professionals with extensive murder investigation and research backgrounds.

Child Abduction Murder Data

The CAM data were collected from 227 municipal police department and county sheriff's offices in the United States with a service population of 100,000 or more, or that had fifteen or more murders reported to the Federal Bureau of Investigation's (FBI) Uniform Crime Report (UCR) in 1987 (Hanfland et al., 1997). The department head, detective division commander, or a detective of each of the agencies meeting the above criteria was contacted by telephone and asked to participate in the data collection project. To follow-up, an introductory letter and a formal request for case information was mailed to identified agencies, with a resulting initial response rate of 75% (Hanfland et al, 1997).

An additional teletype was sent to each police agency in the United States at three different time intervals on different days of the week, with a request to contact the coordinator of the project. Basic screening information was then recorded about the cases. Additional methods were employed to identify relevant cases for the study. Appropriate state and federal agencies were contacted and asked for case information. Homicide detectives across the country were also contacted for additional information (Hanfland et al., 1997).

Initially, data were collected by interviews with the detectives and the review of investigative case files from 1,025 cases. Responses were received from both large and small agencies and departments. The agencies were representative of all regions of the country, covering 44 states. Of the original 1,025 cases, 621 cases were found to meet the criteria established for inclusion in the original data collection collaboration (Hanfland et al., 1997). A second stage of the research, described in this report, was designed to expand the original CAM data set. Over a number of months, more than 200 additional cases have been collected, resulting in 833 child abduction murder cases from 1968 to 2002. The additional cases came from police departments and county sheriff's offices of all sizes.

Case Criteria

The cases of murder in the original CAM data set were chosen for inclusion based on the following criteria:

1. The victim was *younger than* 18-years-old (except as described in #3 below), whose body had been recovered, or if the body had not been recovered, the killer was identified, tried, and convicted; and

2. The police agency receiving the initial contact about the case, whether as a missing, abducted, runaway, or dead body case, acted on the premise that abduction was a possibility;

3. The case was part of a series in which at least one victim in the series met the above stated criteria (Hanfland et al., 1997, p. 14).

Additionally, cases were included that were not considered "closed" in the traditional sense. If the reporting agency believed that abduction was a possibility, and began investigating the case as a child abduction, it was included in the data set. The murders of abducted children to be examined in this report were selected from the CAM dataset based on the following criteria: the victim was 17-years-old or *younger*, whose body had been recovered, or if the body had not been recovered, the killer was identified, tried, and convicted. A total of 735 cases met all of the criteria and were the focus of analyses.

Data Collection Instrument

The CAM data collection instrument was designed by homicide investigators, Dr. Robert D. Keppel, Kenneth Hanfland, and Dr. Joseph G. Weis, a criminologist. It was used to collect information on 412 items representing the essential characteristics of the murder of an abducted child and of its investigation (See Hanfland et al., 1997). The instrument was designed to evaluate the criminal investigation process, including the initial response of the police agency, basic investigation, extended investigation, physical evidence, geographical considerations, and victim and offender information. It was field tested on ten cases of child abduction resulting in murder, after which a few problems were identified and corrected.

Data Integrity

After the data collection instrument was received from participating agencies, it was reviewed for validity and internal consistency. The data were then entered into a database designed specifically for the project. To ensure data integrity, a printout was generated from each new computer record, and was visually compared with the original data collection instrument. Any necessary corrections were made by the data entry clerk, and the resulting printout and the original data collection instruments were given to the project coordinator for an additional review for errors. Any additional errors were corrected, and the form was placed in a file (Hanfland et al., 1997, p. 17).

Resulting Data

The data set used for this research was collected with the purpose of determining proper and effective avenues of investigation in missing and abducted children cases. In order to determine which factors were effective investigation tools, information on solved cases was collected. Information on unsolved cases was also collected to examine the differences in solved and unsolved cases. Thirty-five percent of the cases of child murder from the original CAM data set were unsolved at the time the data were collected. The original CAM dataset contained 577 case investigations with a total of 621 victims (some cases had multiple victims) and 419 killers. Of the 735 cases analyzed for this report, 27.4% were unsolved at the time of data collection.

Definitions

Defining the terms used in this research project was critical. In order to select appropriate variables for analysis in our study, certain terminology was defined: abduction, components of the murder incident, time and distance intervals, and solved cases. Once the terminology was defined and the proper parameters set, appropriate variables were selected for statistical analysis.

Abduction

For purposes of this research, abduction was defined as:

1. The victim was kidnapped.

2. The victim was detained and his/her freedom of movement was restricted.

3. victim of domestic violence was reported by the family (or someone else) as a missing child.

4. The police were initially of the opinion that the victim was taken or held against his or her will, whether or not that turned out to be the case in the end (Hanfland et al., 1997, p. 14).

Components of the Murder Incident

1. The Victim Last Seen Site (VLS) was defined as the location where and time when the victim was last seen. The VLS was determined from eyewitness information and records indicating when and where the victim was last seen alive.

2. The Initial Contact Site (IC) was defined as the place where and time when the killer initially contacted the victim. The IC was established from evidence indicating that the killer first met the victim at a certain time and at a specific location during the course of the murder incident.

3. The Murder Site (MS) was defined as the place where and time when the victim sustained the death-producing injuries.

4. The Body Recovery Site (BR) was defined as the location where and time when police, medics, or witnesses found the victim, dead or alive, prior to transportation to a medical facility or morgue (Keppel, 1992; Keppel & Weis, 1993a).

Solvability

In the CAM data set, solvability was defined and measured two ways: "Has the offender been arrested, or does probable cause exist for an arrest?" and "Has the investigation resulted in a conviction?" For the analyses here, solvability was based on investigations resulting in an arrest. Cases with a "Yes" to the question "Has the offender been arrested, or does probable cause exist for an arrest?" at the time of coding were considered "solved," cases with a "No" to that question were considered "unsolved." Cases with "Unknown" as the answer to the question were considered to have missing data and were not included in the analysis.

Purpose of the Study

According to Hanfland et al. (1997), the rarity of these types of cases has allowed a body of "commonly held beliefs" to develop that has little-to-no basis in fact. Hence, detectives, case managers, police executives, and the media sometimes operate from a position of false assumptions and misperceptions. Homicide investigators, through no fault of their own, sometimes fail to realize that the investigations of the murders of abducted children are very different from the other murders they usually investigate. Consequently, they sometimes make decisions about the direction of the investigation that are not "high percentage" choices. For example, some detectives believe that in any murder of a child the logical suspect is a parent and, therefore, they devote a considerable amount of resources to proving that the killer was the father. But this research shows that the parents are the least likely suspects in an abduction murder of a child. This kind of false assumption is made, in part, from lack of experience with these types of cases and because there is very little empirical research on these types of child murders and their investigations from which detectives can draw guidance. This research will help investigators make those decisions, identify the strategies, and implement the tactics that will lead to the more certain and timely capture of the killers of abducted children.

Data Analysis

Throughout the report data are presented as simple percentages. Often comparisons are made with "all murder cases" and, at times, with "all child murders," which include domestic child abuse murders, mutual combat murders, and others that do not involve abduction. Percentages are used to provide a sense of how often or how rarely a characteristic or circumstance can be expected in these types of cases. The logic is that knowing the "spread" will help the detective make better decisions and prioritize courses of action. In most cases, simple descriptive frequencies were run on appropriate variables. Where the impact of a variable on solvability was examined, a cross-tabulation was performed to test statistical significance.

The CAM dataset utilized for the second stage research consists of 833 child abduction murders. Of those cases, 735 victims are 17-years-old or younger with 516 of those victims being single-victim murder cases rather than part of a series. Of the 735 cases analyzed, 27.4% remained unsolved at the time of data collection. Table 17.1 summarizes the characteristics of the CAM data set that was used as the basis for the data analyses discussed in this report.

TABLE 17.1 CAM DATA SET

	All Cases in CAM Dataset		Victims ≤ 17-Years-Old	
	N	%	N	%
Solved	589	74.1	527	72.6
Unsolved	206	25.9	199	27.4
Disposition Unknown	38	4.6	9	1.2
Total N	833		735	

VICTIMS

Introduction

The existing research on the rarity of child abduction murders, particularly those committed by non-family killers, shows clearly that most law enforcement jurisdictions in the United States will not be called on to investigate a child abduction murder. In fact, most homicide investigators will never investigate a child abduction murder over their entire career. However, it is prudent for investigators to be prepared. These investigations can put enormous strain on even the best prepared detectives, investigations, and jurisdictions. Their typically emotion-laden, volatile, high profile characteristics present unique challenges to law enforcement.

Initial Police Involvement

Police involvement in the child abduction murder investigations in this study began with the report and identification of the victim as a "missing child" in 60.2% of the cases. The case investigation was initiated by the recovery of a dead body in 20.3% of the cases. Only 8.5% of the investigations began as reports of a runaway child, and 9.7% as abduction investigations.

As illustrated in Table 17.2, most reports to the police of a missing, runaway, or abducted child were made relatively soon after the child was missed. Of the children reported missing, 19.6% of the

TABLE 17.2 PERCENT OF MISSING CHILDREN REPORTS WITHIN TIME PERIODS

Case Reported to Police	%
Immediately	19.6
Within 1 Hour	27.5
Within 2 Hours	42.9
Within 4.5 Hours	68.4
Within 24 Hours	86.6
>24 Hours	99.0

victims were reported missing "immediately," 42.9% within two hours, and 86.6% within 24 hours of being missed. Two hours lapsed before reports were made in 56.2% of the cases, and at least a whole day passed in 12.5% of the cases. Unfortunately, 1.0% of cases never have a missing person report filed.

These reporting delays are important to the course of the investigation. The data show that delays are much more critical in child abduction murders than in other types of investigations, because missing children who *are* murdered are killed quickly after their abduction.

When an Abducted Child is Killed

Missing children were killed within a very short period of time after their abduction. Table 17.3 illustrates that 46.8% of the victims, incredibly, were dead within one hour after the abduction, 76.2% within three hours, and 88.5 % within 24 hours after being abducted.

TABLE

17.3   **WHEN AN ABDUCTED CHILD IS KILLED**

Time Period	%
<1 Hour	46.8
Within 3 Hours	76.2
Within 24 Hours	88.5
Within 7 Days	97.9
Within 30 Days	100.0

There is a misconception that killers keep children alive for long periods of time after an abduction. Clearly, this misconception is not supported by the data. Hours and even minutes are critical in an abducted child investigation. While the murder of an abducted child is rare, immediate reporting of the abduction and swift investigative measures may ensure that the child is recovered alive.

The dictum that the first 24 to 48 hours of an investigation are the most critical must be modified in child abduction cases. An absent child should be reported to authorities immediately. Police should concentrate their investigative resources as quickly as possible once a child is reported missing. Swift action by law enforcement may increase the odds that a child is found alive, and if the child is murdered, will improve the probability that the killer is caught.

In addition to information about the time lapse between when a child is missing and when the absence is reported to police, this research has identified unique characteristics of child abduction murder victims. This information will assist investigators in identifying and differentiating potential murder victims from the vast majority of missing children who eventually turn up alive and well. This information will help investigators prioritize investigative resources.

VICTIMS OVERVIEW

The typical child abduction murder victim was a white (74.5%) female (74.0%), approximately 11 years old (M=11.52). They were predominantly from a middle class (35.2%) or "blue collar" (35.8%) family, living in an urban (29.3%) or suburban (35.2%) neighborhood, in a single-family residence

(71.1%). The victim's relationship with family was good (49.8%), and the family situation was not considered high risk (83.5%). In summary, the typical child abduction murder victim was an 11 year-old, white, female from a middle class or "blue collar" family with good family relationships.

Victim's Race and Gender

As found in the previous first stage analysis, the race of child abduction murder victims is not significantly different from all murders victims — both are predominantly White. Table 17.4 illustrates this similarity.

TABLE 17.4 VICTIM RACE

	Child Abduction	All Murders
White	74.5%	66.0%
Black	14.3%	17.0%
All Other	11.2%	17.0%

The gender of child abduction murder victims differs significantly from the gender of victims in all child murders and murders in general. The first stage findings indicated that child murder victims were more likely to be female (55.0%), while only 38.0% of murder victims in general were female. But the second stage analysis indicated that child abduction murder victims were predominantly female (74.0%), reversing the typical relationship between the gender of victim and murder. Table 17.5 shows the differences in gender by type of murder.

TABLE 17.5 VICTIM GENDER

	Child Abduction Murders	All Child Murders	All Murders
Female	74.0%	55.0%	38.0%
Male	26.0%	45.0%	62.0%

Victim's Age

According to Hanfland et al. (1997), approximately one-half of all children who are murdered are between the ages of 15 and 17-years-old. Among child abduction murder victims, only 22.2% of victims are older teenagers between the ages of 16 and 17-years old. Table 17.6 illustrates the age distribution of child abduction murder victims. The mean age of victims is 11.52. About 10% of the victims are children five-years-old and younger, a group smaller than one might expect, based on

TABLE 17.6	DISTRIBUTION OF VICTIMS BY AGE GROUPS	
Victim Age Group	**%**
1 to 5-years-old	10.1
6 to 9-years-old	21.5
10 to 12-years-old	20.7
13 to 15-years-old	25.5
16 to 17-years-old	22.2

the common perception that it is "little kids" or "young children" who are most vulnerable and selected most often as victims. Older children (6–9), preteens (10–12), young teens (13–15), and older teens (16–17), each constitute about 20% of the victims of child abduction murders. Only a slight majority of the victims in this sample (52.3%) were not yet teenagers at the time of their death.

Lifestyle of Victims

There is also a public misconception that children who are killed during an abduction are particularly vulnerable or high risk victims, but most of the victims (67.5%) are described by those who know them as "normal kids." On the other hand, approximately one-third (32.5%) of the victims are not considered average kids. Only 16.9% of the victims are described as street kids and 13% as runaways. As one might expect, those types of victims are typically teenagers rather than younger children. Community resources focused on run-away children and at-risk children who are prone to live on the street would be prudent preventive measures.

SUMMARY

It is vitally important to identify which children are most at risk for child abduction murder. It is also imperative that the offender is examined and, hopefully, better understood. The next chapter discusses the characteristics of the typical child abduction murderer.

KILLERS

Introduction

Just as child abduction murder victims are unique; their killers are unique among murderers. Those who kill abducted children share many characteristics with other types of murderers, but they differ in important ways that suggest a different etiology to their predatory behavior. Their unique characteristics call for different investigative strategies. This chapter will focus on the personal and social attributes and behavior of child abduction killers.

Killer Attributes

In addition to their unique choice of victim—the substantial overselection of female victims — child abduction killers are unique among murderers in general. Hanfland et al. (1997) have characterized child abduction murderers as "social marginals." Child abduction killers are not:

> active, successful participants in mainstream, conventional social life, but, rather, they occupy a position in society that is, indeed, on the "edge, brink, border, precipice, or margin." They are not integrated, personally or socially, into the kinds of relationships or activities that produce and sustain effective self or social controls. Their personal and social attributes establish and define their social marginality. (Hanfland et al., 1997, p. 32)

Killer's Age

The mean age of child abduction murderers is 27.8 years old. Table 17.7 shows the distribution of child abduction offenders by age group. Only 12.2% of the offenders were juveniles (under 18), and only 10.1% over 40 years old. The great majority of offenders (65.8%) were young adult men between 18 and 30 years old. The oldest offender in this sample was 61-years-old with the youngest offender being 9-years-old. Contrary to the belief that these killers are "dirty old men," the evidence shows that they are more similar in age to killers in general — young adults.

TABLE 17.7   DISTRIBUTION OF KILLERS BY AGE GROUPS

Killer Age Group	%
< 18-years-old	12.2
18 to 20-years-old	21.2
21 to 25-years-old	22.3
26 to 30-years-old	22.3
31 to 40-years-old	23.4
> 40-years-old	10.1

Killer's Race

The race of the killers in this sample was predominantly white (69.8%). Only 19.1% are black and the remaining 11.0% are other racial/ethnic groups, when adjusted for the missing race identification of 158 killers. The results on the race of killers support the earlier first stage findings, that there were no important differences in race between child abduction killers and other killers. Table 17.8 shows the racial breakdown of child abduction murder killers compared to murderers in general.

TABLE 17.8	KILLER RACE	
	Child Abduction	**All Murders**
White	69.8%	75.0%
Black	19.1%	20.0%
All Other	11.0%	5.0%

Killer's Gender

Murders are a predominantly male phenomenon, with the great majority of victims and killers being male. The first stage research observed that child abduction murderers are even more likely to be male — 98.5% of child abduction murder killers are males, compared to 87% of murderers in general. By including the additional cases collected in stage two of the study, 96.1% of the killers are male, still a substantial overrepresentation of male killers. These murders are carried out, almost exclusively, by males, and perpetrated typically against young females. There are also a number of indicators of *social marginality* among these killers, including marital status, residential status, employment and occupation, lifestyle, problem behavior, and criminal behavior.

Killer's Marital Status

Only 16.9% of the killers were married at the time they committed the murder. Another 13.2% were divorced, meaning that 83.0% of the killers formed no intimate attachments or bonds with another person at the time of the abduction and subsequent murder. The marital status of the killers is illustrated in Table 17.9.

TABLE 17.9	MARITAL STATUS OF KILLER
Marital Status	**%**
Single	69.8
Married	16.9
Divorced	13.2

Killer's Residential Status

Contrary to perceptions that killers who kill children are "loners," only 17.1% of the killers lived alone, while 74.8% lived with someone. It is perhaps a little unusual that 33.2% of them lived with their parents. Table 17.10 describes the killers' living arrangements.

The killers in this sample also changed their residence frequently. The majority of them moved at least once within the five years preceding the murder (79.7%). Of this group, 44.5% of killers changed residences three or more times, and 19.7% moved five or more times.

TABLE 17.10 LIVING ARRANGEMENTS OF KILLER	
Living Arrangement	**%**
Living with Parents	33.2
Living Alone	17.1
Living with Spouse and/or Children	17.1
Living with Girlfriend/Boyfriend	14.2
Living with Other Roommates	10.3
Other	8.2

Killer's Employment and Occupation Status

This transient nature may be related to their uneven employment history. Approximately half (48.3%) of child abduction murderers were unemployed at the time of the murder, and if they were employed, they worked in unskilled or semi-skilled labor occupations. Table 17.11 describes the most common occupations of killers at the time they committed the murder.

TABLE 17.11 KILLER OCCUPATIONS	
Occupation	**%**
Construction Worker	26.4
Food Industry Worker	7.5
Service Industry	6.9
Student	6.6
Truck Driver	6.6
Auto Maintenance	3.7

Killer's Lifestyles

Only 10.1% of the killers were described as "model" citizens and a mere 3.9% were active in church or civic groups. In fact, 20.1% of the killers were on probation or parole for another offense at the time they committed the child abduction murder. Many of them (30.2%) were described as "strange" by others who knew them, 14.7% were described as "friendly to children," and 16.0% were considered reclusive. Table 17.12 reveals other behaviors of the killers that are considered outside the norm by our society. A number of them abused alcohol (24.6%), used and abused drugs (22.1%) or were sexually promiscuous (15.5%), according to others who knew them and, before they were identified as a child abduction killer, characterized their behaviors and identity.

Killer's Past Behavior

Child abduction murderers experience more serious personal behavioral problems than the typical killer. Over three-fourths of them (78.5%) had a recognized and identified history of at least one serious behavioral problem. The child abduction murderers in this study differed significantly from

TABLE 17.12 PERCEIVED LIFESTYLE OF KILLERS

Perceived Lifestyle	%
Described as "Strange"	30.2
Alcohol Abuser	24.6
Drug User/Abuser	22.1
Reclusive	16.0
Sexually Promiscuous	15.5
Friendly To Children	14.7
Transient/Semi-transient	11.9

TABLE 17.13 PERSONAL PROBLEMS OF THE KILLERS

	Child Abduction	All Murders
Sexual Problems	30.4%	3.0%
Alcohol Problems	23.8%	27.0%
Drug Problems	22.3%	14.0%
Mental Problems	18.4%	13.0%

general murder killers in the extent of their problems (Table 17.13). Almost one-third (30.4%) of the killers of abducted children suffered from "sexual problems," in contrast to an extremely low rate among general murder killers (3.0%). The former are ten times more likely than the latter to have a history of identified sexual problems.

Killer's Prior Crimes

In addition to victim and killer demographic and behavioral characteristics, information was collected regarding the killer's criminal background and motivation to commit murder. A large percent of the murderers had a substantial history of prior crimes against children (46.0%). Table 17.14 shows the types of crimes committed against children by these killers.

These killers clearly demonstrated violent predispositions toward children prior to the child abduction murder. Sexual assaults (21.0%) and rapes (13.3%) were the crimes most frequently committed before against children. Incredibly, the murder of another child was committed

TABLE 17.14 PRIOR CRIMES AGAINST CHILDREN BY KILLERS

Prior Crimes	%
Sexual Assault (Non-Rape)	21.0
Rape (or attempt)	13.3
Murder (or attempt)	10.7
Kidnap	6.5
Assault	6.1

previously by 10.7% of the killers in this study. An additional 6.5% had also previously kidnapped children. Sexual assault of the victim occurred in 62.8% of these child abduction murder cases — those easily characterized as acts of violent, sexual predation on children.

Custody Status

In spite of the substantial evidence of prior crimes of violence against children, approximately half (50.8%) of child abduction killers, like murderers in general (66.0%), are *not* in any "official custody status" at the time of the extant murder. A slightly higher percent of child abduction killers (20.1%) are either on parole or probation when they kill as compared to 17.0% of all murderers. While most child abduction killers may not be immediately accessible in the custodial system, they are slightly more likely than other murderers to be found in the active files of the correctional or judicial systems.

SUMMARY

Child abduction killers can be characterized as social marginals who have a propensity to commit crimes of violence against children. Most of them exhibit weak social bonds to conventional contexts, relationships, and activities, strong predictors of involvement in crime. Individuals with weak social controls are more likely to commit child abduction murders given the appropriate motivation and opportunity. The victim-killer relationship discussed in the next chapter illustrates opportunities available to the killer in greater detail.

VICTIM-KILLER RELATIONSHIP

Introduction

It is vitally important to understand the demographics of both the victim and killer in the study of the murder of abducted children. However, it may be more important to understand the victim-killer relationship in order to protect our children. The following chapter will present an overview of the relationship between the child abduction murder victims and their killers.

Victim-Killer Relationship

Of the cases in which the victim-offender relationship was known ($n = 585$), child abduction murderers were strangers to the victim in 44.4% of the cases, and were family friends or acquaintances in 41.9% of the cases. The killer was an intimate or family member of the victim in 13.7% of the cases (Table 17.15). As with adults, children are at a higher risk from those that they know (55.6%) than from strangers (44.4%).

TABLE 17.15 VICTIM-KILLER RELATIONSHIP

Relationship	Child Abduction Murders	All Child Murders	All Murders
Stranger	44.4%	5.0%	20.0%
Friend/Acquaintance	41.9%	28.0%	42.0%
Family/Intimate	13.7%	67.0%	38.0%

The killers were strangers to the victim in 44.4% of the cases, in contrast to 5.0% of all child murders and 20.0% of murders in general. Victims are much more likely to be killed by family members in child murders (67.0%) than in child abduction murders (13.7%).

Victim-Killer Relationship by Age and Gender

The victim-killer relationship was also examined by age and gender. The victim-killer relationship varies by the age and gender of the victim. Table 17.16 shows the victim-killer relationship for females by age group. The youngest females (1 to 5 years-old) were most likely killed by a friend or an acquaintance (49.0%). In contrast, older female victims (10 to 17-years-old) were more likely to be killed by strangers.

TABLE 17.16 FEMALE VICTIM-KILLER RELATIONSHIP BY AGE GROUP

| Relationship | Victim Age Group | | | | |
	1–5	6–9	10–12	13–15	16–17
Stranger	15.7%	33.0%	41.6%	37.2%	40.2%
Friend/Acquaintance	49.0%	39.4%	32.7%	28.4%	22.7%
Family/Intimate	17.6%	8.3%	11.9%	7.4%	14.4%
Unknown	17.6%	19.3%	13.9%	27.0%	22.7%

Table 17.17 shows the differences in the victim killer relationships for males. The youngest victims (1 to 5 years-old) were almost as likely to be killed by family members (34.8%) as they were by strangers (30.4%). The youngest victims were least likely to be killed by friends or acquaintances. The older male victims (16 to 17-years-old) were almost as likely to be killed by strangers (41.9%) as friends or acquaintances (48.4%). In this sample, family or intimates did not kill male teenagers, but only younger boys.

TABLE 17.17 MALE VICTIM-KILLER RELATIONSHIP BY AGE GROUP

| Relationship | Victim Age Group | | | | |
	1–5	6–9	10–12	13–15	16–17
Stranger	30.4%	36.7%	35.3%	28.6%	41.9%
Friend/Acquaintance	26.1%	34.7%	39.2%	40.0%	48.4%
Family/Intimate	34.8%	14.3%	7.8%	0%	0%
Unknown	8.7%	14.3%	17.6%	31.4%	9.7%

The overall victim-killer relationship by gender is shown in Table 17.18. Females were most often killed by strangers (35.9%), while males were most likely killed by friends or acquaintances (37.9%). Both genders were least likely to be killed by a family member or intimate.

TABLE 17.18	VICTIM-KILLER RELATIONSHIP BY VICTIM GENDER	

	Victim Gender	
Relationship	Female	Male
Stranger	35.9%	34.7%
Friend/Acquaintance	32.0%	37.9%
Family/Intimate	11.1%	10.5%
Unknown	21.1%	16.8%

SUMMARY

The differences in the victim-killer relationship by age and gender of the victims can be more clearly seen when the different types of murders and modus operandi are examined in light of the research findings in the following chapter. The next chapter will detail the killer's motivation for abducting the child. In addition, how the killer selected the victim will be examined.

KILLER MOTIVATION AND VICTIM SELECTION

Introduction

Surprisingly, over half (58.4%) of the prior crimes committed by an killer against children had a *modus operandi* (MO) that was similar to the extant murder. For example, a child abduction killer who lures the child away by asking for help locating a lost pet is very likely to lure away the next victim in a similar way. The similarities in MOs produced other surprises: They were most alike, by a large margin, in the "commission of the offense," or the way the crimes were committed (Table 17.19). In the cases that had similar MOs, the priors were committed in similar ways — for example, the choice of weapon was the same across different crimes committed by a killer.

There is a misconception that child abduction killers are looking for a child with a certain appearance. Contrary to murder in general, child abduction killers were much less likely to select certain types of victims based on personal characteristics. A mere 7.2% of prior crimes were committed against similar victims. The killers were even less likely (5.2%) to approach their victim

TABLE 17.19	MODUS OPERANDI (MO) SIMILARITIES BETWEEN OTHER CRIMES AND EXTANT MURDER

MO	%
Commission of the Crime	16.5
Victim Characteristics	7.2
Specific Acts Committed	5.7
Approach to Victim	5.2

in similar ways. Finally, 16.5% of the prior crimes against children were similar to the extant murder in the kinds of specific acts that were performed during the commission of the crimes. For example, the killer used rope to bind and control a kidnap victim, as well as the subsequent murder victim.

These findings regarding the similarity of MOs across the majority of crimes committed by child abduction killers show that there is more consistency in the MOs of child abduction killers than expected, especially compared to other types of murderers. The data also suggest that there may be a greater predisposition to serial offending among child abduction killers.

Sexual Motivation

Child abduction murderers share a characteristic with classic serial killers — both show a sexual component to their motivation to kill. More than two-thirds (69.2%) of child abduction murders involve a sexual motive, compared to only 5% of all murders and 14% of child murders. Almost one-half (46.3%) of the child abduction murders are classified as rapes and 21.9% as other sexual assaults. As one would expect in these types of murders, a large group (27.8%) are kidnappings, which is approximately 15 times greater than in all child murders and 30 times greater than in murders in general.

Some of the kidnappings also include a secondary sexual component, because there is physical evidence that almost two-thirds (62.8%) of the child abduction murder victims had been sexually assaulted, compared to only 7.0% percent of all murder victims and 15.0% of all child murder victims. The dramatic differences in the role of sexual motivation and conduct across the different types of murder clearly demonstrate the unique role that sex plays in child abduction murders. The great majority of these killers would qualify as sexual predators in most states.

Pornography

There is a common belief in our society that pornography plays an important role in the process of motivating sex killers and lust killers. Interestingly, approximately one-quarter of the killers in this study used pornography (24.8%), and pornography was a "trigger" for the murder in 20.7% of the cases. This is an increase in the use of pornography as a trigger over the 4% reported for the first stage data (Hanfland et al., 1997). It may be that the role of pornography in the sexual motivation of these murders is more prevalent, but is still not common. It could also reflect differences in the selection of the first and second stage cases. One explanation for the low reliance on pornography could be that child abduction killers have a predisposition to engage in these types of violent and sexual acts with children as a deep-seated element of their flawed characters, making the exposure to pornographic materials unnecessary in the process of "getting motivated" to commit the murder.

Crises and Stressors

Some observers of murder have proposed that certain kinds of personal problems — usually revolving around employment or marriage — may serve as "precipitating crises" that contribute to the motivation of the killer. In the case of child abduction murders, there is evidence of at least one precipitating crisis (or stressor) in the life of the killer in 25.4% of the cases. What is striking is that of those cases, the usual crises or stressors emphasized in the literature do not seem to be as important as others that seem to resonate with the character of the killers and with their choice of predominantly female victims. For example, only 4.9% involved marital problems, 3.8% involved employment problems, and 6.0% involved financial problems.

This research shows that 11.3% of the child abduction murderers had a "conflict with a female," and 8.4% with "criminal/legal problems." The majority of these killers have extensive criminal histories, so it is not surprising that their related criminal/legal problems might be implicated somehow in the motivation to commit murder. We also know that there is a dramatic, disproportionate preponderance (74.0%) of young, vulnerable female victims.

Choosing and Controlling the Victim

Table 17.20 indicates that the child abduction murderers overwhelmingly chose their victims because the opportunity presented itself (40.3%). Killers rarely chose their victims for their physical characteristics (9.7%) or because of a prior relationship with the victim (14.4%). Killers had a specific motivation to murder a particular victim in only 12.7% of the cases.

TABLE 17.20   How Killer Chose Victim

Choice	%
Victim of Opportunity	40.3
Prior Relationship with Victim	14.4
Specific Motivation	12.7
Physical Characteristics	9.7

Table 17.21 indicates that some killers initiated contact with their victims through deception (27.3%) and others through normal activities (22.9%). Only 12.9% of the killers contacted their victims through other illegal or criminal activity. In 34.2% of the cases the manner of initial contact is unknown. The initial victim-offender contact most often took place in a suburban (32.9%) area, and least often in a rural area (16.7%) see Table 17.22. Table 17.23 illustrates the differences in area of initial contact by type of murder.

TABLE 17.21   How Killer Initiated Contact with Victim

Method	%
Through Deception	27.3
Through Normal Activity	22.9
Through Illegal/Criminal Contact	12.9
Other	2.7
Unknown	34.2

Typically, killers came into contact with the victim because the offender lived in close proximity to the victim (26.3%). An additional 16.4% came into contact with their victim because of other criminal activity. Table 17.24 shows the reasons the killer was at the victim contact site.

TABLE
17.22 AREA OF INITIAL VICTIM-KILLER CONTACT

Area	%
Suburban	32.9
Urban	50.5
Rural	16.7

TABLE
17.23 AREA OF INITIAL VICTIM-KILLER CONTACT BY TYPE OF MURDER

Area	Child Abduction Murders	All Child Murders	All Murders
Urban	50.5%	17.0%	31.0%
Suburban	32.9%	74.0%	58.0%
Rural	16.7%	9.0%	11.0%

TABLE
17.24 WHY KILLER WAS AT THE VICTIM CONTACT SITE

Reason	%*
Lived in Area	26.3
Criminal Activity	16.4
Normal Social Activity	13.9
Normal Non-social Activity	10.2
Meeting Victim Intentionally	4.7
Other	2.2
Unknown	27.9

*Percentages will not equal 100%. More than one reason may indicate why the killer was at the victim contact site.

The majority of killers gained control over the victim by using direct physical assault (47.2%). An additional 2.1% used verbal threats, with deception (11.6%) and victim incapacity (11.1%) used equally as often to gain control of their victims. Table 17.25 illustrates the methods of control used by these child abduction murderers.

Binding of Victim

There is evidence that child abduction killers are 6 to 12 times more likely than other murderers to "bind" their victims. Child abduction killers bound their victims in one-fourth (24.0%) of the cases,

TABLE 17.25 **HOW KILLER GAINED CONTROL OF VICTIM**	
Method	**%**
Direct Physical Assault	47.2
Deception	11.6
Victim Incapacity	11.1
Verbal Assault	2.1
Unknown	30.6

compared to only 2.0% in child murders and 4.0% in all murders. The much more frequent binding of child abduction murder victims reflects both control and sexual elements. Binding a victim makes control easier, and for uncooperative, strong victims it may be absolutely necessary. For child victims, this control function of binding is less critical. But in these types of murders, with their strong sexual component, the binding (or "bondage") is more likely to serve more primary and secondary sexual functions. These victims are being bound less to physically control them than to fulfill the sexual fantasies and needs of the killers.

The source of the binding material is known in 96.8% of the cases involving binding. In those known cases, 16.2% of the killers brought the binding material with them to the crime scene. This has evidentiary implications for matching binding material found in the possession of the killer after he is identified.

Cause of Death

Death by strangulation was the leading cause of death of victims (33.2%), followed by blunt force trauma (23.9%), and stabbing/cutting (23.3%). Firearms, a frequent cause of death in general murders, only accounted for 11.8% of child abduction murder victim deaths. Table 17.26 lists common causes of death for victims, and Table 17.27 compares the common causes of death in general murders and child murders, according to Hanfland et al., (1997), to the causes of death in this analysis.

TABLE 17.26 **CAUSE OF DEATH**	
Cause	**%***
Strangulation – Ligature and Manual	33.2
Blunt Force Trauma	23.9
Stabbing/Cutting	23.3
Asphyxia – Unknown Means	12.2
Firearm	11.8
Drowning	3.7

*Percentages will not equal 100%. More than one cause of death may have been indicated. Only the most common causes of death were reported above.

TABLE 17.27   CAUSE OF DEATH BY TYPE OF MURDER

Cause of Death	Child Abduction Murders	All Child Murders	All Murders
Strangulation	33.2%	13.0%	9.0%
Blunt Force Trauma	23.3%	37.0%	18.0%
Stabbing/Cutting	23.9%	9.0%	23.0%
Firearms	11.8%	16.0%	43.0%

Unusual Acts

There is a common belief that killers who commit murders that are out of the ordinary are involved in a variety of unusual acts during the murder incident, ranging from cult rituals to "posing" victims to grotesque mutilation. In general, the data suggest that child abduction murders are not characterized by unusual, bizarre, or weird acts and rituals. There is almost no evidence that unusual ceremonies or acts had been performed at the crime scene (e.g., evidence of ritual (1.1%), masochistic acts (1.1%), burnt candles, dead animals, satanic symbols). The extreme rarity of these kinds of acts in child abduction murders is consistent with what is found for all murder cases.

Body Disposal/Recovery

The geographic location of the body disposal site chosen by killers is shown in Table 17.28. These child abduction killers chose rural areas for the body disposal location in 52.6% of the cases.

TABLE 17.28   AREA OF BODY RECOVERY

Area	%
Rural	52.6
Suburban	20.5
Urban	14.8
Inner City	12.2

The choice of a rural location for body disposal contrasts with findings by Hanfland et al. (1997) for all murder cases (Table 17.29). Killers in general murders chose suburban body disposal locations in about half of all cases (54.0%), but rural locations in only in 22% of the murders.

Child abduction killers deliberately chose the body disposal location in 48.0% of cases. It was a random selection in 32.6% of cases. As shown in Table 17.30, killers were forced by circumstances to choose the body disposal location in only 10.4% of the murders. Killers concealed the victim's body in 55.4% of cases, and unconcerned with the location of the body in 36.4% of cases. As illustrated in Table 17.31, the victim's body was simply left in the open in only 8.1% of cases, and in an unusual position even less often (3.2%).

TABLE 17.29 AREA OF BODY RECOVERY SITE BY TYPE OF MURDER

Area	Child Abduction Murders	All Child Murders	All Murders
Urban	27.0%	14.0%	25.0%
Suburban	20.5%	61.0%	54.0%
Rural	52.6%	26.0%	22.0%

TABLE 17.30 HOW KILLER SELECTED BODY DISPOSAL SITE

Selection	%
Deliberately Selected	48.0
Random/Arbitrary Choice	32.6
Forced by Circumstances	10.4

TABLE 17.31 HOW KILLER DISPOSED OF BODY

Selection	%
Concealed	55.4
Unconcerned	36.4
Open	8.1

Post Offense Behavior

After the murder is committed and the body disposed of, the killer apparently engages in a variety of behaviors that are related to the murder, which for many of them constitute a prelude to apprehension and arrest. The killers do a number of things after the murder (See Table 17.32). A surprising 23.7% of child abduction killers return to the body disposal site. Some killers leave

TABLE 17.32 POST OFFENSE BEHAVIOR OF KILLERS

Behavior	%
Returned to Body Disposal Site	23.7
Left Town	16.1
Confided in Someone	16.1
Followed Case in Media	14.3
Interjected Self Into Investigation	10.0
Contacted Victim's Family	9.7
Contacted Police or Media	9.7
Changed Residence	8.3

town right after the murder (16.1%) or confide in someone about their involvement in the murder (16.1%). Some follow the case in the media (14.3%). Ten percent actually interjected themselves into the murder investigation in some way. Each of the behaviors may provide valuable leads for investigators to pursue.

In 15% of the cases, the killer kept the body longer than necessary to dispose of it, and kept it in convenient and accessible places where it could be concealed, moved quickly, and/or "played" with. The killer kept the body in his residence (53.0%), in his car (21.0%), or in a variety of other places within easy reach. However, contrary to beliefs about murderers, especially serial killers who prolong their relationship with the victim, these child abduction killers only held onto the bodies for very short periods of time. Of the bodies that were kept by the killer, 32.1% were in his possession for three hours or less, and 56.6% for 24 hours or less. So, it is likely that most of the bodies were being kept only until they could be disposed of safely. Only 15.1% of the bodies that were kept by the killer were in his possession for more than a week. It is likely that in these cases there was a reason other than delayed disposal — for example, to play out sexual fantasies with the corpse or to treat it like a trophy — for keeping the body. And this is a very small number of cases.

More striking is the number of child abduction killers who returned to the body disposal site. Almost one-fourth (23.7%) of the killers return to the body disposal site after a significant period of time. Of those killers who do return, an incredible 83.3% do so prior to the discovery of the body, and 33.1% do so within three days after the murder. Clearly, a significant proportion of child abduction killers return to the body disposal site, particularly soon after the murder has occurred. As one would expect, very few return after the body has been discovered and reported in the media. But an opportunity exists — albeit for a short period of time — for investigators to observe potential suspects between the time the body is reported to the police and, then, made public by the media.

INVESTIGATION

Introduction

The previous chapters detailed valuable information about the victims, killers, their relationship, the killer's motivation and how the killer chose their victim. In addition to this information, variables relating to the actual investigation process may prove valuable to detectives. A descriptive analysis of the variables affecting abducted child murder investigations will be explored in the following sections.

Police Refusal to Accept a Missing or Runaway Child Report

The data for this study showed that a law enforcement agency refused to accept an initial report for a missing or runaway child in less than two percent (1.8%) of child abduction murder cases. Because this number was sufficiently small, it can not be determined whether the refusal to accept the initial missing or runaway child report had any effect on the investigations. Fortunately, the refusal to accept an initial report about a missing or runaway child was rare.

Multiple Police Agencies

Some murder victims were reported to be missing from within one law enforcement agency's jurisdictional boundary and the body was subsequently discovered within another jurisdiction. While this is not unusual, what has not been well understood is to what extent that actually happens. Of the murders studied in this project, 64.0% of the victim bodies were discovered within the jurisdictional boundaries of the law enforcement agency that received the initial missing/ abduction report. In short, almost two-thirds of the victims apparently did not cross law enforcement jurisdictional boundaries in the course of events that led to the discovery of the body. On the other hand, 36.0% of the killers transported victims and dumped their bodies in jurisdictions different from where they were first contacted, assaulted, or killed. It is a common belief that such crossing of jurisdictional lines would have a negative impact on the outcome of the investigation. What was found was that, while the investigation was at times made more complicated for the detectives, there is no statistical difference in the clearance rates between those cases that crossed jurisdictional lines and those that did not.

Unknowing Witnesses

Unknowing witnesses are witnesses that saw some aspect of the crime, but at the time did *not* realize that they were witnessing part of a crime or potential abduction. It was discovered that this is quite common — there were unknowing witnesses in 32.9% of the cases. This would indicate that a neighborhood or area canvass would be of great importance in generating investigative leads.

Neighborhood Canvass

"Neighborhood canvass" means the checking, by police, around the area of the victim's last known location and/or the location the victim was known to be going, or around any site determined to be important to the investigation, in an effort to locate witnesses or to obtain facts about the circumstances. This typically involves going door-to-door, person-to-person. An area search differs from a neighborhood canvass in that the latter typically involves going from door to door to contact potential witnesses, while the former is more likely part of the actual search for the victim and/or physical evidence. These two activities may occur simultaneously or separately, depending on circumstances. They are separated here for greater specificity.

A neighborhood canvass was conducted within less than 2.5 hours of a report of an abducted or a missing child in 62.1% of the cases. A canvass was conducted in less than 12 hours in 70.4% of the cases. But in over 21.0% percent of reported abducted or missing children investigations, no neighborhood canvass was conducted.

What was not collected in this research was information on who actually conducted the neighborhood canvass. However, it is a common practice in law enforcement to have uniformed patrol officers conduct the initial neighborhood canvass. Whether or not this is done is usually a simple issue of manpower availability. Unfortunately, most police agencies do not have Standard Operating Procedures for these types of cases, and patrol officers frequently are not given specific guidance as to what to ask the people they interview. It is also unfortunate that in many cases there is no follow-up canvass by detectives.

On the surface, the lack of a neighborhood canvass may not appear to be a critical factor in these types of investigations. However, it may be one of the most critical factors uncovered in this research project, especially when combined with what we know from the data concerning murder incident sites. We know that the victim's last known location is usually very close to the site of the initial contact between the killer and the victim. When the police did not know the initial contact site, the solvability rate dropped to 23.9%. When the initial contact site was known, the solvability rate increased to 79.7%.

The initial contact site is the location at which there is potentially the greatest chance for a witness to observe the killer and the victim together. This site is where the killer may be most likely to expose himself to observation by others. There are quite often witnesses, some unknowing, to the initial contact, as evidenced by the fact that agencies that conducted thorough neighborhood canvasses discovered those witnesses and obtained their statements.

The initial neighborhood canvass is also an opportunity for law enforcement officials to put everyone contacted "on-the-record." A useful technique in conducting a neighborhood canvass is to provide patrol officers and detectives printed questionnaires that include specific questions, including the identification of everyone who lives in each residence. The completion of these questionnaires facilitates easy reporting of the results of the interviews of each house/business, and the content of subsequent interviews can be compared with the initial statements. Such comparisons can identify inconsistent statements and persons who have left the area since the initial canvass. It is worth pointing out that in 33.5% of the cases examined in this research, a physical description of the killer was obtained *before* he was identified. In those cases the clearance rate increased by 15.0%.

Area Search

The area most commonly searched (98.0% of the cases) was the area in which the victim was last seen. It was searched within five hours in 72.9 percent of the cases. Searching resulted in finding evidence or leads in 45.5% percent of the murders. Of course, when evidence or leads were found by searching, cases had a higher solution rate than those in which no evidence or leads were found.

Like the neighborhood canvass, the initial area search is frequently conducted by uniformed patrol officers. Later searches are often conducted with volunteers, such as Explorer Scouts or Search and Rescue teams. However, experience has found that explicit instructions on what the searchers are looking for are missing from these searches.

For every child abduction murder a police agency handles, there could be hundreds to thousands of reports of a missing child. This issue is important because it is easy for officers responding to a missing child call to think in terms of a lost child, and not the possibility of an abduction murder. A lost child is usually thought to be alive, not dead. With a lost child mindset, one could overlook the body of a murdered child that has been concealed, or inadvertently destroy evidence when murder is not considered as a possibility.

There are examples of cases in which officers made contact with the killer at his residence and, unknown to the officers, the body of the victim was on the premises at that moment. While there is no way to know that while talking with a *potential witness* at his front door, at least one of the cases included a search of the killer's residence in which the body was in a box and missed by investigators. The chances of such things happening are slight, but officers should always remain mindful of the possibility.

The research confirms that the body of the victim is the single most important source of physical evidence that can be connected to the killer. It also tells us that 55.4% of the victims' bodies are concealed when they are disposed of by the killer. These two facts make a thorough area search very important in the investigation. (See the section on the Body Recovery Site for further discussion of investigative implications related to the area search.)

Who Discovered the Body of the Victim?

It is important to examine who finds the body of a child abduction murder victim. Table 17.33 shows that in the majority of cases the victim's body was found by an innocent passerby or by the police. The killer claimed to have "discovered" the body in about three percent (2.8%) of the cases.

TABLE
17.33 **WHO DISCOVERED VICTIM'S BODY**

Body Discovery	%
Passerby	55.3
Police	25.4
Search Party	5.9
Relative/Acquaintance of Victim	4.4
Killer	2.8
Fire Department/Aid Crew	2.2
Witness to Death	1.7

Investigative Steps in the First 48 Hours

The investigative activities of the critical first 24 to 48 hours of the murder investigations were classified into seven general categories, as listed in Table 17.34. Collecting information is by far the most common investigative activity (87.2%). Circumstances in the early stages of an abducted child murder case can vary from simply accepting a missing child report and conducting no immediate investigation, to immediately dispatching officers to the area and conducting a neighborhood canvass and an area search, to a full-scale crime scene investigation and arrest of the killer.

TABLE
17.34 **MAJOR INVESTIGATIVE STEPS IN THE FIRST 48 HOURS**

Investigative Step	%
Collected Information	87.2
Searched	51.4
Collected Evidence	40.3
Disseminated Information	24.8
Direct Contact With Killer	14.1
Organizational Changes	3.9
Other	3.8

Police Contact with Killer

Law enforcement contact with or knowledge of anyone who may physically be around some aspect of the murder, crime scene, or body disposal site is critical to investigations. Alarmingly, the evidence shows that the police had contact with the killer about some aspect of the murder — *before* he became the prime suspect — in *half* of the cases. The police often do not realize or know that they have come that close to the killer — probably early in the investigation when many names are being recorded, interviews are being done, canvassing is taking place, records are being searched, tips are being received, and so on. Police need to know this when conducting the investigation of a child abduction murder — the killer's name may be in their possession in a substantial proportion of cases, and probably early in the investigation.

Equally surprising, the data show that the killer's *name* became known, not necessarily as the suspect, very early in the course of most investigations of child abduction murder. In 21.9% of the cases, the killer's name came up immediately, in 39.8% within 24 hours, and in 57.0% within a week. This might be cause for alarm, but there is other evidence that the police are on the trail of the killer relatively early in the investigation as well.

Police focused on the killer as a suspect or person of interest almost immediately at the beginning of the investigation in 17.7% of the cases, and within one and one-half days in an additional 39.9%.But, unfortunately, there is a dramatic drop-off — after a month from the beginning of the murder investigation, there is still no primary suspect in more than 34.7% of the murders. Fortunately, it also means that by a month's end, investigators have focused on the killer in a large majority of cases.

Physical Evidence

Physical evidence linked to the killer was collected in 67.2% of the cases. While there is a correlation between the gathering of physical evidence and solvability, physical evidence by itself does not ensure solution. The most common evidence collected that is related to the killer is hair (Table 17.35). Strands of the killer's hair were collected in 26.1% of the cases of child abduction murder. When we look at hair evidence in all murder cases, it is present in only 18.0% of the cases, and that includes killer, victim, animal and "unknown" hair evidence.

The most common evidence collected in all murder investigations is a weapon (39.0%). In child abduction murders, weapons are collected in only 20.0% of the cases. This is consistent with cause of death data that show children are killed less often with a weapon and more often by human physical agency.

TABLE 17.35   PHYSICAL EVIDENCE RELATED TO KILLER

Evidence	%
Hair	26.1
Weapons	20.0
Prints (Finger and Shoe)	18.0
Semen	17.2
Fibers	15.9
Blood	14.3

Discarded Evidence

In addition to evidence that was residual, or that was inadvertently left behind by the killer, the killer often (24.2%) deliberately discards physical evidence after the murder that is found by the police. Of that discarded evidence, 36.0% of it was found along the roads on which the killer traveled in the course of the murder, body disposal, or escape. It is important to note that 56.5% of the evidence found along a road was within one mile of the body recovery site. Increased clearance rates are observed when discarded evidence was found by the police in general murders. This has important investigative implications for child abduction murder investigations.

In a child abduction murder, there is a good chance that there is discarded physical evidence along the road within one mile of the body disposal site, and that improves the odds of case solution. Is it worth the effort to do that kind of search? That depends on the circumstances surrounding the case. The detectives at the scene have to make that decision. But, now there is strong evidence that it might pay off in catching the killer to have a set of objective criteria to apply during consideration of investigative options.

Polygraph

The use of the polygraph in investigations of murder of abducted or missing children is fairly common (47.1%). While it is a common practice, its utility is in question. As shown in Table 17.36, the polygraph was used to test acquaintances (26.3%) and family members (22.7%) of the victim. However, in 33.8% of the cases in which the polygraph was used, a person *other than* the accused showed "deception" on the test. Interestingly, of those persons who showed deception, 13.3% were family or friends of the victim, the two groups most often polygraphed.

TABLE 17.36   RELATIONSHIP OF PERSONS POLYGRAPHED TO VICTIM

Relationship	%*
Acquaintances	26.3
Family Members	22.7
Strangers	19.2
Neighbors	7.2

*Percentages will not equal 100%. The relationship of other persons polygraphed to the victim was either unknown or unrecorded in some cases.

When two additional facts are considered, the use of the polygraph becomes more clouded: 1) The younger the victim, the less likely police believe the polygraph helps the investigation; but 2) The younger the victim, the more likely the family/friends of the victim will be polygraphed. So it seems that those who are more likely to be polygraphed are more apt to show a "false deception." And, the less likely the polygraph may help the case, the more likely it is to be used.

Overall, the use of the polygraph was perceived by detectives to have helped the investigation in 62.1% of the cases, while in 9.0% of the cases detectives believed that it was inconclusive or led the investigation in a false direction. This discussion is not intended to be a condemnation of the use of the polygraph. It is intended to provide facts on which to base future decisions regarding whether or not the polygraph is appropriate in a specific abducted child murder investigation.

News Media

Anyone familiar with criminal investigations understands that media involvement sometimes disrupts orderly investigation. At times there tends to be a distrust of the news media by law enforcement officers. There are many concerns about the media; for example, fear of inappropriate information being released, telling the suspect what the police know or do not know, or that media representatives will interfere with the progress of the investigation. Of the detectives interviewed, 46.8% believed that the media coverage of the investigation was "excessive."

Those concerns have led many police agencies to establish a Media Relations Officer, either as a full time position or as a position appointed on a case-by-case basis for potentially high visibility investigations. We know from experience that a designated media relations officer generally makes for a smoother working relationship with the news media. However, there is absolutely no correlation between whether a law enforcement agency has a media relations officer and the clearance rates of the murders of abducted children.

In spite of the law enforcement concerns, and in spite of the high profile nature of these types of murder, the police used the news media in one way or another in 74.9% of these abducted child murder cases. The most common use of the media was in an attempt to locate witnesses. Even while using and cooperating with the news media, there is a fear in law enforcement that news media involvement may hinder the investigation in one way or another. To justify their suspicions, homicide detectives point to examples of media interference hurting an investigation. In actuality, in child abduction murder investigations, the media effect on the criminal investigation is more positive than negative. As shown in Table 17.37, in 58.6% of these cases, the media involvement had no effect at all.

TABLE 17.37 EFFECT OF MEDIA COVERAGE ON THE INVESTIGATION	
Effect	**%**
No Effect	56.8
Helped	32.9
Hindered	6.2
Effect Unknown	4.1

However, in 32.9% of the cases, the investigating detective believed that the use of the media helped the investigation, usually by bringing a witness forward. The detective felt that the media hindered or hurt the investigation in only 6.2% of the cases. An argument can be made that any hindrance is too often, but we will learn shortly that there are other institutions that have a more negative impact on the investigations.

Outside Forces That Created Problems for the Investigation

As demonstrated in Table 17.38, the three most frequently identified outside forces that created any kind of problem during investigations were another outside law enforcement agency, news media, and the family of the victim.

TABLE 17.38 PROBLEMS CAUSED BY OUTSIDE FORCES	
Outside Forces	**%**
Police Agencies	9.9
News Media	9.1
Family of Victim	5.0
Community/Political Pressure	2.8
Lawyers	1.3

Red Herrings

A "red herring" is something that diverts attention from the matter at hand. An example of a red herring in a murder investigation might be a vehicle that detectives believe to be the killer's vehicle, and a major commitment of manpower has been devoted to finding it, at the expense of other avenues of inquiry, only to learn later that the car was not involved.

Red herrings were reported in 38.0% of the investigations. They ranged from "good" suspects, to physical evidence, to erroneous polygraph results. While troublesome and time consuming for the investigation, the presence of a red herring had no statistical effect on the clearance rate of the cases.

MURDER INCIDENT SITES

Introduction

Keppel and Weis (1993) conceptualize the crime of murder as an incident. Each murder incident includes multiple sites or locations of contact between the offender and the victim, as well as potential witnesses. The investigation of a murder should emphasize the search for information about the major sites of a murder incident. The presence of information that establishes the existence of each site, coupled with when and where each site is located within the incident, and the manner in which their relationships affect each other, greatly influences the solution of murder investigations.

According to Keppel and Weis (1993), the follow-up investigation of a murder involves the gathering of information about the various components that are locations of victim-killer contact. The types of information crucial to the investigation, in order of their usual occurrence within the murder incident are:

1. where and when the victim was last seen,

2. where and when the offender initially contacted the victim,

3. where and when the murder took place, and

4. where and when the body was recovered.

Components of the Murder Incident

Each of these components occurs in a murder and, therefore, each is important to a murder investigation. The components are defined as:

1. The Victim Last Seen Site (VLS): the location where and time when the victim was last seen. The VLS was determined from eyewitness information and records indicating when and where the victim was last seen alive.

2. The Initial Contact Site (IC): the place where and time when the killer initially contacted the victim. The IC was established from evidence indicating that the killer first met the victim at a certain time and at a specific location during the course of the murder incident.

3. The Murder Site (MS): the place where and time when the victim sustained the death-producing injuries.

4. The Body Recovery Site (BR): the location where and time when police, medics, or witnesses found the victim, dead or alive, prior to transportation to a medical facility or morgue (Keppel, 1992; Keppel & Weis, 1993).

Information about the location and the time of each site within the sequence of the murder incident has an impact on case solvability. In most murder cases, the events occur simultaneously, and the research suggests that all events are located in the same place and not separated by distance or spans of time (Hanfland et al., 1997; Keppel & Weis, 1993).

Separation of Components by Time and Distance

The sites within incidents of murder may become separated in time and distance in two ways. First, the offender may attempt to consciously separate time and distance. The killer may believe that the separation of murder components will delay the discovery of various sites, perhaps for a long time, contributing to the destruction of evidence. The separation may also inhibit the investigation by creating communication and cooperation problems among police agencies, because the locations are not within the authority of one jurisdiction. Second, the offender may simply unintentionally separate the location of components over time and distance.

Investigative Implications

The information which identifies the location and time of each site is vitally important to investigations. The confirmation through evidence of the date, time, and location of a site prior to the identification of a possible suspect enables the investigator to more accurately check thewhereabouts and verify alibis of a suspect against the time and location of that site (Hanfland, et al., 1997).

Keppel and Weis (1993) found that when any information on the dates and locations of the four murder incident sites was known, the probability of case solution increased. The study also showed a strong positive correlation between knowing the dates of occurrences for the murder incident locations and the ability to identify a perpetrator. Another important finding was that case solvability increases as the time separating pairs of murder incident sites decreases. The study supported their hypothesis that the more investigators know about the distances between the pairs of the murder incident sites, the more likely a case will be solved. The research also showed that when the distance between the locations was less than 200 feet, the solvability increased substantially. Finally, the research showed that when the times and distances decrease among pairs of murder incident sites, the solvability increases (Keppel, 1992).

The conclusions regarding time and distance in the Keppel and Weis (1993) research supported what experienced murder investigators have learned through their observations of murder cases. The more information detectives have about a case, especially about the murder incident sites, the more likely it will be solved. Their study showed that it was not "just any information" that will enhance solvability — some information is more valuable and useful than other information in murder investigations.

SEPARATION OF COMPONENTS IN CHILD ABDUCTION MURDERS

When Time is Known

Because information known about each site is critical to the basic model for child abduction murder investigations, the murder incident components were examined by time and distance separation. The murder incident component about which "time" is most often known was the Victim Last Seen Site (98.9%), followed by the Body Recovery Site (98.6%), Initial Contact site (87.5%), and the Murder Site (84.5%). This knowledge is detailed in Table 17.39.

TABLE 17.39 MURDER INCIDENT COMPONENT TIME KNOWN

Murder Incident Component	%
Victim Last Seen	98.9
Initial Contact	87.5
Murder	84.5
Body Recovery	98.6

When Place is Known

The murder incident component about which "location" is most often known was the Body Recovery Site (98.4%), followed in order by the Initial Contact Site (78.2%), Victim Last Seen site (78.1%), and the Murder Site (69.4%). Table 17.40 illustrates these findings.

TABLE 17.40 MURDER INCIDENT COMPONENT PLACE KNOWN

Murder Incident Component	%
Victim Last Seen	78.1
Initial Contact	78.2
Murder	69.4
Body Recovery	98.4

When Time or Place is Known

The murder incident component about which "time *or* location" is most often known was the Victim Last Seen Site (99.3%), followed by the Body Recovery Site (99.0%), Initial Contact Site (93.5%), and the Murder Site (91.3%). Table 17.41 indicates the results of this analysis.

This order is unique to child abduction murder investigations. In general murder, Keppel (1992) found that the location of the Body Recovery Site was the location most often known

TABLE 17.41	MURDER INCIDENT COMPONENT TIME OR PLACE KNOWN

Murder Incident Component	%
Victim Last Seen	99.3
Initial Contact	93.5
Murder	91.3
Body Recovery	99.0

followed by the Murder Site, Victim Last Seen Site and the Initial Contact Site. The data indicates that in child abduction murder investigations the order switches to the Victim Last Seen Site as the location about which information is most likely known. This is due to the nature of the victim. Children are missed more quickly than adult victims in some cases, especially small children who are usually in the presence of a caregiver. It is also not surprising that in these types of investigations that the percentage of knowledge about murder incident locations is higher than in general murders because of the high-profile nature of child abduction murder investigations.

When Both Time and Place are Known

An examination of the murder incident components about which both time and place were known produced a decrease in the known percentages. The murder site about which both time and location is most often "known" was the Murder Site (98.0%), followed by the Victim Last Seen Site (77.7%), Body Recovery Site (77.2%), and the Initial Contact Site (62.6%) as indicated in Table 17.42. The Initial Contact Site is the murder incident component least identified by time and place in child abduction murders. This is not surprising given that much of this information is gathered from witness statements or statements by the killer.

TABLE 17.42	MURDER INCIDENT COMPONENT TIME AND PLACE KNOWN

Murder Incident Component	%
Victim Last Seen	77.7
Initial Contact	62.6
Murder	98.0
Body Recovery	72.2

Time Interval Between Incidents

In addition to "knowing" about the time and place of the murder incident components, the actual time span between murder incident components was examined. The time spans between the Victim Last Seen Site to Initial Contact Site, Victim Last Seen Site to Murder Site, and Initial Contact Site to Murder Site, were then coded into one of the following time interval categories:

1. 0 to 29:59 minutes

2. 30 to 59:59 minutes

3. 1 to 4:59:59 hours

4. 5 to 24 hours

5. > 24 hours

The Victim Last Seen Site to Body Recovery Site, Initial Contact Site to Body Recovery Site, and Murder Site to Body Recovery Site were coded into one of the following categories:

1. 0 to 7:59 hours

2. 8 to 15:59 hours

3. 16 to 23:59 hours

4. 24 to 47:59 hours

5. 48 to 71:59 hours

6. 72 to 167 hours

7. 7 to 14 days

8. 15 to 30 days

9. > 30 days

The categories are based on the natural breaks in the frequency distribution of the CAM data.

It is interesting to note that the time span between when a victim was last seen and the initial contact with the killer is less than 30 minutes in over three-fourths of the child abduction murder investigations. The time span is illustrated in Table 17.43.

The data also indicate a very short time frame between when the initial contact between the victim and the killer occurred and when the victim is murdered. The abducted child is murdered in under 5 hours in 85.1% of cases as illustrated in Table 17.44. The victim is murdered in less than 30 minutes after he or she was last seen in 30.8% of cases.

The bodies of abducted children are recovered within 24 hours of when the victim was last seen in 37.6% of cases, within 48 hours in 49.4% of cases and within a week in 68.5% of cases (See Table 17.45). And, as Table 17.46 indicates, 38.1% of abducted children are murdered within the first half following

TABLE 17.43 TIME SPAN BETWEEN VICTIM LAST SEEN AND INITIAL CONTACT

Time span Interval	%
0 to 29:59 minutes	76.3
30 to 59:59 minutes	7.9
1 to 4:59:59 hours	10.8
5 to 24 hours	4.1
> 24 hours	.9

TABLE

17.44 TIME SPAN BETWEEN VICTIM LAST SEEN AND MURDER

Time span Interval	%
0 to 29:59 minutes	30.8
30 to 59:59 minutes	16.5
1 to 4:59:59 hours	35.6
5 to 24 hours	13.5
> 24 hours	3.6

TABLE

17.45 TIME SPAN BETWEEN VICTIM LAST SEEN AND BODY RECOVERY

Time Span	%
0 to 7:59 hours	17.9
8 to 15:59 hours	11.0
16 to 23:59 hours	8.7
24 to 47:59 hours	11.8
48 to 71:59 hours	6.4
72 to 167 hours	12.7
7 to 14 days	8.7
15 to 30 days	6.1
> 30 days	16.7

TABLE

17.46 TIME SPAN BETWEEN INITIAL CONTACT AND MURDER

Time span Interval	%
0 to 29:59 minutes	38.1
30 to 59:59 minutes	15.2
1 to 4:59:59 hours	31.8
5 to 24 hours	11.5
> 24 hours	3.4

their abduction. The bodies of abducted children are recovered within 24 hours of when the killer and victim had their initial contact in 39.0% of cases, within 48 hours in 52.6% of cases and within a week in 73.0% of cases. The time frame between when the initial contact and when the victim's body is recovered is illustrated in Table 17.47.

The bodies of abducted children are recovered within 24 hours of when the murder occurred in 46.4% of cases, within 48 hours in 57.6% of cases and within a week in 76.3% of cases. The time frame between when the murder and when the victim's body is recovered is illustrated in Table 17.48.

TABLE
17.47 TIME SPAN BETWEEN INITIAL CONTACT AND BODY RECOVERY

Time Span	%
0 to 7:59 hours	20.1
8 to 15:59 hours	10.0
16 to 23:59 hours	8.9
24 to 47:59 hours	13.6
48 to 71:59 hours	6.1
72 to 167 hours	14.3
7 to 14 days	7.2
15 to 30 days	5.4
> 30 days	14.5

TABLE
17.48 TIME SPAN BETWEEN MURDER AND BODY RECOVERY

Time span Interval	%
0 to 7:59 hours	26.1
8 to 15:59 hours	11.4
16 to 23:59 hours	8.9
24 to 47:59 hours	11.2
48 to 71:59 hours	5.8
72 to 167 hours	12.9
7 to 14 days	6.1
15 to 30 days	4.3
> 30 days	13.2

Distance Between Sites

The distance between murder incident components was also examined. In the first stage analysis, the distance between each pair of murder components was measured in feet or miles for each pair of components. Then the actual distance was placed into one of the following categories before inclusion in the CAM dataset:

1. 0 feet to 199 feet,

2. 200 feet to < ¼ mile,

3. ¼ mile to < 1½ mile,

4. 1½ mile to < 12 miles,

5. > 12 miles.

Table 17.49 indicates the distance between the Initial Contact Site and the Victim Last Seen Site.

TABLE 17.49 DISTANCE BETWEEN VICTIM LAST SEEN SITE AND INITIAL CONTACT SITE

Distance	%
0 feet to 199 feet	64.2
200 feet to 1/4 mile	15.9
> ¼ mile to 1 1/2 miles	8.3
> 1½ miles to 12 miles	7.2
> 12 miles	4.4

This distance is 199 feet or less in 64.2% of murders. The distance between the Victim Last Seen Site and the Murder Site is 199 feet or less in 26.6% of child abduction murder cases (See Table 17.50).

TABLE 17.50 DISTANCE BETWEEN VICTIM LAST SEEN SITE AND MURDER SITE

Distance	%
0 feet to 199 feet	26.6
200 feet to 1/4 mile	19.2
> ¼ mile to 1 1/2 miles	13.7
> 1½ miles to 12 miles	24.5
> 12 miles	16.0

The killer transports the victim more than one-fourth mile from where the victim is last seen in 54.2% of cases. The victim is transported under one-fourth mile in 45.8% of murders. Table 17.51 indicates the distance between where the victim is last seen and where their body is recovered. The victim's body is recovered at a distance of over one-fourth mile in 67.3% of the murders. The victim's body is recovered within 199 feet in only 15.8% of cases.

TABLE 17.51 DISTANCE BETWEEN VICTIM LAST SEEN SITE AND BODY RECOVERY SITE

Distance	%
0 feet to 199 feet	15.8
200 feet to ¼ mile	16.8
> ¼ mile to 1½ miles	13.4
> 1½ miles to 12 miles	30.5
> 12 miles	23.4

The distance between where the victim and the killer had their first contact and where the victim is murdered is less than 199 feet in 34.0% of murders. The distance between the Initial Contact Site and the Murder Site is illustrated in Table 17.52. The distance between the Initial Contact Site and the Murder Site is greater than one-fourth mile in 51.8% of murders. The victim's

TABLE 17.52 DISTANCE BETWEEN INITIAL CONTACT SITE AND MURDER SITE

Distance	%
0 feet to 199 feet	34.0
200 feet to ¼ mile	14.3
> ¼ mile to 1½ miles	11.5
> 1½ miles to 12 miles	24.4
> 12 miles	15.9

body is recovered over one and one-half miles away from where the initial contact with the killer occurred in 53.5% of the murders. The distance between the Initial Contact and the Body Recovery Site is indicated in Table 17.53. The distance between the Murder Site and the Body Recovery Site is less than 199 feet in 69.1% of the murders as shown in Table 17.54. (The killers inform police where the Murder Site was or confirm its location in their statement to police in 55.9% of cases).

TABLE 17.53 DISTANCE BETWEEN INITIAL CONTACT SITE AND BODY RECOVERY SITE

Distance	%
0 feet to 199 feet	19.7
200 feet to ¼ mile	15.2
> ¼ mile to 1½ miles	11.6
> 1½ miles to 12 miles	28.7
> 12 miles	24.8

TABLE 17.54 DISTANCE BETWEEN MURDER SITE AND BODY RECOVERY SITE

Distance	%
0 feet to 199 feet	69.1
200 feet to ¼ mile	6.1
> ¼ mile to 1½ miles	4.5
> 1½ miles to 12 miles	10.8
> 12 miles	9.6

Finally, the distance between each of the murder incident component sites was examined in relation to the other murder incident component sites. Table 17.55 illustrates this comparison. The distance between the Initial Contact Site and the Victim Last Seen Site is less than 199 feet in 64.2% of the murders. The distance between the Murder Site and the Body Recovery Site is less than 199 feet in 69.1% of the murders.

TABLE 17.55 DISTANCE BETWEEN MURDER INCIDENT SITES			
	Initial Contact	**Murder**	**Body Recovery**
Victim Last Seen	< 199 feet (64.2%)	> ¼ mile (54.2%)	> ¼ mile (67.3%)
Initial Contact		> ¼ mile (51.8%)	> ¼ mile (65.1%)
Murder			< 199 feet (69.1%)

The distance is greater than one-fourth mile between the Victim Last Seen Site and Murder Site (54.2%) and the Initial Contact Site and the Murder Site (51.8%) in just over one-half of the murders. A majority of the cases show a distance of greater than one-fourth mile between the Victim Last Seen Site and the Body Recovery Site (67.3%) and between the Initial Contact Site and Body Recovery Site (65.1%).

ANALYSIS OF DISTANCE BY MURDER INCIDENT COMPONENT

Distance clearly has an impact in murder investigations of abducted children. In order to more fully understand the investigative implications how distance between murder incident component locations, the murder incident components will be examined individually. A detailed analysis follows.

Victim Last Seen Site

The victim's last known location is within one-fourth mile of the Initial Contact Site in 79.4% of the child abduction cases. Also, in 40.3% of the murders, the Victim Last Seen Site is less than 200 feet from the *victim's* home. In 36.1%, the Victim Last Seen Site is within one-fourth mile of the *offender's* home. The data show that the typical victim is near his or her home when last seen prior to the abduction, and that often; the killer is not far away.

Initial Contact Site

Even though these types of murders most often involve stranger relationships, in 57.2% of the cases, the victim lived less than ¼ of a mile from the Initial Contact Site and 200 feet from the Initial Contact Site in 35.0% of them. In 36.5% of the murders, the killer lived within one-fourth mile of the Initial Contact Site. The initial contact between the killer and the victim is also typically very close to the victim's last known location. In fact, it is located within less than 200 feet in 63.8% of cases. After the initial contact is made, the victim is taken or transported some distance away and killed. The victim's body is then disposed of very near the Murder Site.

The Initial Contact Site, and knowledge about its location and time of occurrence, is the single most important site in terms of its effect on the outcome of the investigation. If the Initial Contact Site is not discovered by police, the clearance rate drops to 23.9%. If the Initial Contact Site is discovered by police, the clearance rate is 79.7%.

We visited this issue briefly when the importance of the neighborhood canvass was discussed. At that time we learned that the initial contact site is where there is probably the greatest chance for a witness to observe the killer and the victim together. This is where the killer is most likely to expose and connect himself to the victim, to be observed by a witness.

In 79.4% of the murders, the Initial Contact Site is within one-fourth mile of the victim's last known location. If the Initial Contact Site is not found, the witnesses who might put the killer with the victim are not identified. This information is so important that it is recommended that the neighborhood canvass be comprehensive and thorough and followed up with a repeat canvass.

Why was the killer at the Initial Contact Site? The killer was in the area because he lived in the area (26.3%), was involved in normal social activity (13.9%), or was there for some other purposeful activity like working (10.2%). The child abduction may make more sense in light of this information because the research shows that 40.3% of the victims were "victims of opportunity." The fact that the killer belongs in the area of the Initial Contact Site in almost half of the cases suggests that officers conducting the neighborhood canvass should not only ask the question, "What did you see that was unusual?" but should also ask, "What did you see that was usual?" Or, simply, "What and who did you see?"

Murder Site

Unfortunately, the site of the actual murder is known less frequently than any other site. For investigative effectiveness, without the Murder Site, the police have less evidence to tie to any particular offender. This study has shown that the Murder Site is the richest site in terms of physical evidence collection. It is second in importance only to the actual body of the victim for evidence that is connected to the killer.

If the Murder Site is so important, why do we find it in only 69.4 percent of the murders of abducted children? The data do not provide a specific answer to that question. It is likely that in some of the cases, the searchers didn't know where to look. We now know that for over two-thirds (68.9%) of the murders, the distance between the Murder Site and the Body Recovery Site is less than 200 feet (one-half of an average city block) (Table 17.51).

It was stated above that the Murder Site is the most important site in terms of physical evidence associated with the killer. We know that it is quite often within 200 feet of the body recovery site. Armed with this information, it is recommended that investigators do a fine-focus search over the 200 feet in every direction from the Body Recovery Site. While the distance between the Murder Site and the Body Recovery Site is very short in the majority of the cases, the distance between the Murder Site and the Initial Contact Site is more variable. However, in 52.0% of the cases the distance is greater than one-fourth mile, and in 40.7% it is greater than one and one-half miles.

Body Recovery Site

The terms "Body Recovery Site" and "Body Disposal Site" will be used interchangeably in this report, depending on the context and whether it is from the point of view of the police or the killer. For the location of the Body Recovery Site, the general geographical areas were shown previously in Table 17.28. Of particular note, it was discovered for abducted children murders that even though the body recovery sites were found in all of the geographical locations, they were more often found in rural areas. This contrasts with all murder cases, in which rural body disposal is much less frequent. (See Table 17.29.)

The killers deliberately chose the Body Disposal Site for their own reasons (48.0%). In 32.6% of the cases, the choice of the Body Disposal Site was purely random, while in 10.4%, the killer was forced by outside circumstances to use a certain site. In general murder cases, the killer is typically

(69%) unconcerned whether or not the body is found. However, murders of missing or abducted children are quite different.

The most telling information about the location of the child's body is that the killers dispose of them mostly by concealment (55.4%), while concealment of the body is present in only 14.0% of all murder cases (Hanfland et al., 1997). The implication for investigation is that when the police are searching for the body of a murdered abducted child, they should pay close attention to ground that has been disturbed for burial purposes, and should move material available to conceal victims, such as broken tree branches or large portions of discarded rugs.

In 62.7% of the cases, the Body Recovery Site is further than one and one-half miles from the victim's home. Interestingly, the younger the victim, the closer the body is found to the victim's home. The body was found at the victim's residence in only 2.9% of cases, and 5.4% at the killer's residence.

SERIES CASES

Introduction

There were 116 series cases examined in this study. The data were analyzed in two ways. The first involved comparisons *between* the series and non-series cases. For example, is the ratio of male to female victims the same? The second analysis entailed an examination of the individual cases *within* a series. This approach was an effort to identify "flags" that would aid in the linking of cases. Basically, it was an attempt to find a "common thread" within a series.

Comparisons of Series and Non-Series Cases

There are several MO and investigative issues that are similar between series and non-series murders of abducted children. Following are some of those *similarities*:

1. Concealment of victims' bodies when disposed of;

2. Consistent rate of body parts being removed;

3. Average distance from the initial contact site to the body recovery site;

4. Average distance from the victims' last known location to the body site;

5. The rate of sexual assault; and

6. The rate at which "red herrings" show up in the investigation

There are also *dissimilarities* between series and non-series cases:

Victims' Gender

When the victims' gender is examined, the data show that there is a difference in victim selection. Males are over-selected in the series cases. In non-series cases, males represent almost one-fourth of the victims, while in series cases they represent almost one-third of the victims. Table 17.56 shows that 31.9% of the series victims are males, compared to 24.8% male victims in non-series cases, a difference of 7.1%.

TABLE
17.56 **VICTIM GENDER BY SERIES AND NON-SERIES CASES**

	Series	Non-Series	Total
Female	68.1%	75.2%	70.0%
Male	31.9%	24.8%	30.0%

Victim-killer Relationship

The series killer is more likely to be a stranger to the victim and less likely to be an acquaintance than in non-series cases. Table 17.57 shows that the stranger relationship jumps from 28.3% in non-series cases to 71.3% in series cases. The important investigative implication is in prioritizing leads. If it is reasonably suspected that the case at hand is in a series, strangers (71.3% of series killers) should become the major focus as suspects. On the other hand, if it is suspected that it is a non-series case, strangers (28.3% of non-series killers) and acquaintances (36.2% of non-series killers) should be given equal consideration as suspects.

TABLE
17.57 **VICTIM-KILLER RELATIONSHIP BY SERIES AND NON-SERIES CASES**

Relationship	Series	Non-Series	Total
Stranger	71.3%	28.3%	66.7%
Friend/Acquaintance	20.0%	36.2%	22.2%
Family/Intimate	6.1%	11.9%	11.1%

Killers' Personal Problems

Table 17.58 shows that of those series killers with a history of personal problems, 58.0% of them had a history of sexual problems, more than twice the rate for non-series killers (25.3%). Here, too, there are investigative implications that go to the issue of evaluating potential suspects. If the child abduction murder is known to be part of a series; the presence of a history of sexual problems in the background of a suspect should statistically make him a better suspect than one without such a background.

TABLE
17.58 **PERSONAL PROBLEMS OF KILLERS BY SERIES AND NON-SERIES CASES**

	Series	Non-Series
Sexual Problems	58.0%	25.3%
Drug Problems	33.9%	20.1%
Alcohol Problems	30.4%	22.6%
Mental Problems	25.9%	17.1%

Prior Crimes Against Children

Dramatically, 76.9% of the series killers had committed prior crimes against children, while one-half that many (38.9%) of the non-series killers had victimized children before. And as discussed earlier, a substantial portion of those priors were violent crimes against children. Again, there are investigative implications that impact the evaluation of potential suspects. Prior arrest records and police contact records should be considered carefully when evaluating and prioritizing suspects, particularly evidence of prior crimes against children.

Linking Cases

Being able to determine whether two or more murders (or other types of offenses) were committed by the same killer is often helpful in an investigation. Linking cases can be an objective, scientific process when it is done by matching physical evidence, such as latent prints, DNA, or spent bullets. Unfortunately, all cases do not have physical evidence for scientific comparison, and we then enter the realm of subjectivity and uncertainty.

One of the aims of this research project was to identify elements in child abduction murders that would, absent physical evidence, make the linking process more objective. To some extent that aim has been fulfilled by the information that has been discovered about series killers. This information will allow us to make better judgments about whether an arrested killer might be a series killer. Knowing the facts of the case for which he was arrested may help find other cases for which he is responsible. However, the more difficult task of linking unsolved cases continues to be more subjective.

After hundreds of factors were reviewed and thousands of calculations were made, only a couple of factors emerged that may lend some objectivity to the task of linking unsolved cases: binding of the victim and gender of the victim. It was found that in series, the killer more often bound his victims. Binding is used by killers in only 4.0% of all murder cases, and in only 2.0% of all child murder cases. But in child abduction murder, the binding of the victim is present in 24.0% of the cases. In non-series cases, binding is used on 21.2% of the victims, but in a much larger 38.9% of the serial murders of abducted children. Clearly, the binding of child victims may be a useful indicator of a serial killer at work.

SUMMARY AND CONCLUSIONS

Introduction

The murder of an abducted child, particularly by a stranger, is a rare event. There are estimated to be about 100 such incidents in the United States each year. The victims are typically "average" children, leading normal lives, and growing up in normal families. The vast majority of them are girls, with the average age between 11–12 years of age. In most cases, the initial contact between the victim and killer is within one-fourth mile of the victim's residence.

These cases are typically reported to a law enforcement agency as a "missing child." Often there is no initial indication of foul play, just a report that the child is unaccounted for. This is a difficult time for the investigator, not knowing whether the "missing child" is simply late in returning home, is the victim of foul play, or has been abducted. Any report to the police of a missing child should be taken seriously. As many facts as possible surrounding the missing child occurrence should be obtained as quickly as possible. An assessment of the nature of the case made should be made expeditiously. Factors to consider in assessing the case should include the age and gender of the child, the circumstances surrounding the child's missing status, and the history of the child.

Immediate action is dictated by two facts, 1) there is typically over a two hour delay in making the initial missing child report, and 2) the vast majority of the abducted children *who are murdered* are dead within three hours of the abduction. Because of these critical time features, there is a need to respond quickly in a comprehensive, labor intensive investigation. Over half of the child abduction murders are committed by a killer who is a total stranger to the victim. However, the relationship between the victim and the killer varies with the gender and age of the victim. The youngest females, 1–5 years old, tend to be killed by friends or acquaintances, while the oldest females, 16–17 years old, tend to be killed by strangers. But both the youngest and oldest male victims are likely to be killed by strangers.

The average age of killers of abducted children is around 27 years old. They are predominantly unmarried, and half of them either live alone or with their parents. Half of them are unemployed, and those that are employed work in unskilled or semi-skilled labor occupations. The killers can generally be characterized as "social marginals".

Almost two-thirds of the killers had prior arrests for violent crimes, with slightly more than half of those prior crimes committed against children. The most frequent prior crimes against children were rape and other types of sexual assaults. Most of the child abduction murderers' prior crimes were similar in MO to the murder that was committed by the same killer.

Commonly, the killers are at the initial victim-killer contact site for a legitimate reason. They either lived in the area or were engaging in some normal activity. Most of the victims of child abduction murder are victims of opportunity. Seldom did the killer choose his victim because of some physical characteristic of the victim. The primary motivation for the child abduction killer is sexual assault.

A unique pattern of distance relationships exists in child abduction murders. Often, the initial contact site is located very close to the victim's last known location. Conversely, the distance between the Initial Contact Site and the Murder Site increases to distances greater than 1/4 mile. The distance from the Murder Site to the Body Recovery Site again decreases, to less than 200 feet in the vast majority of cases.

There are investigative implications of these spatial relationships. If the Initial Contact Site is not identified by the police, the clearance rate drops drastically, and vice versa. The close proximity between the Initial Contact Site and the Victim's Last Seen Site suggests thorough neighborhood canvass and area searches be completed to locate the initial contact site. The Murder Site is second only to the body of the victim as a source of physical evidence that can be connected with the killer. Its close proximity to the Body Recovery Site suggests that a thorough search be completed to locate it.

It was discovered that once the murder investigation has begun, *the name of the killer* is likely to be in the investigative file *within the first week*. This provides an opportunity for investigators who may have run out of viable leads to regroup and review everyone whose name has been uncovered during the investigation. Similarly, it is not uncommon for the police to have actual contact with the killer before he becomes a primary suspect, for example, during the initial neighborhood canvass. Also, while at times the media seem to "get in the way," in the end they are much more likely to have a positive effect on the investigation than a negative one. In short, the media are more likely to bring witnesses forward than to aid the killer in his escape.

How Can We Protect Our Children?

One question answered by this research is: What can we tell parents to help them protect their children? Even though child abduction murders are rare events, the thing for parents to do is to eliminate, or minimize, the opportunity for their children to become victims. The first step is to be aware that children are not immune from abduction because they are close to home. In fact, well over half of these abductions that led to murder took place within three city blocks of the victim's home and approximately one-third of the abductions occurred within one-half block. Perhaps the most important single thing we can do as parents to protect our children is to be certain that our children are supervised, even if they are in their own front yard or neighborhood street.

"Stranger Danger" has become a common warning issued by American parents to children. There has been extensive publicity about educating children to avoid abduction by "not speaking to strangers" and "not getting into cars with strangers." We should carry those precautions one step further. Our children should be taught *not to even approach* a car, *whether the occupant of the car is a stranger or not,* no matter what they tell or ask them

Citizens need to be aware of strangers and *unusual* behavior in their neighborhood. They need to have the presence of mind to observe and to write down descriptions of people, vehicles, and license numbers. Many child abductions are witnessed by people who do not realize that a crime is being committed. For example, when a citizen observes an adult pulling a struggling child in a public place, it is easy to interpret the event as a guardian taking control of an unruly child. In most instances, that is exactly what it is. However, nothing prevents a citizen from evaluating the circumstances, intervening, and, certainly, from noting descriptions and license numbers, because it may be a person with criminal intentions. Finally, we need to remind parents that if their child is missing, *call the police immediately*. An immediate response to a missing or abducted child may be the difference between life and death for the child.

REFERENCES

Baker, T., Burgess, A., Rabun, J., & Nahirny, C. (2002). Abductor violence in nonfamily infant kidnapping. *Journal of Interpersonal Violence, 17*(11), 1218-1233.

Boudreaux, M.C., Lord, W.D., & Dutra, R.L. (1999). Child abduction: Aged-based analysis of offender, victim and offense characteristics in 550 cases of alleged child disappearance. *Journal of Forensic Sciences, 44*(3), 539-553.

Boudreaux, M.C., Lord, W.D., & Etter, S.E. (2000). Child abduction: An overview of current and historical perspectives. *Child Maltreatment, 5*(1), 63-387.

Boudreaux, M.C., Lord, W.D., & Jarvis, J. (2001). Behavioral perspectives on child homicide. *Journal of Trauma, Violence, & Abuse, 2*(1), 56-78.

Brown, K.M., Keppel, R.D., Weis, J.G. & Skeen, M. (2006). *Investigative case management for missing children homicides: Report II.* (Cooperative Agreement 93-MC-CX-K006). Olympia, WA: Attorney General of Washington

Bureau of Justice Statistics. (1999). Homicide trends in the United States. *Crime Data Brief* (NCJ Publication No. 173956, pp. 1-4). Washington, DC: U.S. Department of Justice.

Bureau of Justice Statistics. (2000). Homicide trends in the United States: 1988 update. *Crime Data Brief.* (NCJ Publication No. 179767, pp. 1-4). Washington, DC: U.S. Department of Justice.

Bureau of Justice Statistics. (2003). Homicide trends in the United States: 2000 update. *Crime Data Brief.* (NCJ Publication No. 197471, pp. 1-4). Washington, DC: U.S. Department of Justice.

Fass, P.S. (1999). *Kidnapped: Child abduction in America.* Cambridge, MA: Harvard University Press.

Finklehor, D., Hotaling, G.T., & Sedlak, A.J. (1992). The abduction of children by strangers and nonfamily members: Estimating the incidence using multiple methods. *Journal of Interpersonal Violence, 7*(2), 226-243.

Forst, M.L., & Blomquist, M.E. (1991). *Missing children: Rhetoric and reality*. Lexington, MA: Lexington Books.

Hanfland, K.A., Keppel, R.D., & Weis, J.G. (1997). *Investigative case management for missing children homicides*. (Cooperative Agreement 93-MC-CX-K006). Olympia, WA: Attorney General of Washington.

Keppel, R.D. (1992). An analysis of the effect of time and distance relationships in murder investigations (Doctoral dissertation, University of Washington, 1992). *Dissertation Abstracts International, 53*(03A), 933.

Keppel, R.D., & Weis, J. (1993). Time and distance as solvability factors in murder cases. *Journal of Forensic Sciences, 39*(2), 286-401.

Lanning, K.V. (1995). Sexual homicide of children. *APSAC Advisor, 7*(4), 40-44.

National Center for Missing & Exploited Children. (2000). *Missing and abducted children: A law-enforcement guide to case investigation and program management*. Alexandria, VA: Author.

National Incidence Studies of Missing, Abducted, Runaway, and Thrownaway Children in America (NISMART). (2002). *National estimates of missing children: An overview*. Washington, DC: U.S. Department of Justice, Office of Juvenile Justice Programs, Office of Juvenile Justice and Delinquency Prevention.

Katherine M. Brown, Robert D. Keppel, Joseph G. Weiss and Marvin E. Skeen, *"Investigative case management for missing children homicides: Report II."* May 2006. Cooperative Agreement 93-MC-CX-K006. Office of the Attorney General, State of Washington, and U.S. Department of Justice's Office of Juvenile Justice and Delinquency Prevention.

THE NATURE OF EXPRESSIVENESS AND INSTRUMENTALITY IN HOMICIDE

Implications for Offender Profiling

C. GABRIELLE SALFATI

University of Liverpool

CHAPTER

18

One of the main areas of concern regarding offender profiling has been the general lack of extensive empirical studies on the psychological processes underpinning this process. This study aimed to investigate the possibility of establishing a model of homicide behaviors that could be used as a basis for evaluating the scientific validity of offender profiling. A sample of 247 British single offender–single victim solved homicide cases was analyzed using a nonmetric multidimensional scaling procedure known as Smallest Space Analysis. The results indicated that homicide crime scenes could most readily be differentiated in terms of the expressive and instrumental role the victim had to the offender. The backgrounds of the offenders could similarly be differentiated by an expressive/instrumental thematic split. However, when these two elements were combined, there was a substantial mix between crime scene themes and themes of background characteristics. The results are discussed in terms of the validity of classifying homicide into a expressive/ instrumental dichotomy and the implications this classification may have for offender profiling.

There is considerable evidence favoring the proposition that individual differences in antisocial and criminal behavior emerge in childhood and remain stable across the life course (e.g., Gottfredson & Hirschi, 1990; Huesmann, Eron, Lefkowitz, & Walder, 1984). Although specific antisocial behaviors in childhood might not predict phenotypically similar behaviors (i.e., the way the behaviors are manifested) in later adulthood, they may still be associated with behaviors that are conceptually consistent with those earlier behaviors (Caspi & Moffitt, 1995).

Gottfredson and Hirschi (1990) invoke a similar idea when they refer to adult behaviors "analogous" to crime, such as accidents, smoking, and sexual promiscuity that are hypothesized to result from a common factor: lack of control. Caspi and Bem (1990) define this phenomenon as heterotypic continuity. The essence of heterotypic continuity is that the individual's characteristics in childhood (such as ill-tempered behavior) will not only appear across time but will be manifested in a number of diverse situations. Hagan and Palloni (1988) suggest that we need to examine how delinquent and criminal events mediate broader life trajectories, both criminal and noncriminal. Furthermore, the generality of these behaviors needs to be investigated so that specific behaviors in an offender's background can be linked to general behavioral themes of an offender's criminal behavior, and vice versa. In this way, links between an offender's crime scene behaviors and characteristics can be established and used as an investigative profiling tool by the police to focus their investigations and suspect selection.

UNDERSTANDING HOMICIDE

Silverman and Mukherjee (1987) suggest that most homicides can be best characterized as a social event in which there are at least two actors and a social relationship that plays a dynamic role in the way that the homicide unfolds. The social relationship between offender and victim, they suggest, should be a key component in the analysis of homicide. In particular, they hypothesize that the intensity levels associated with intimate relationships will be associated with the type of homicide that occurs.

Much of the literature on crime in general and violent crime in particular has focused on the influence of the interpersonal relationship between the offender and the victim (e.g., Canter, 1994; Wolfgang, 1958). Fesbach (1964) suggested that aggression is the basic ingredient in violent crime, and proposed two types of aggression: hostile (expressive) and instrumental aggression, which are distinguished by their goals or the rewards that they offer the perpetrator. The expressive type of aggression occurs in response to anger-inducing conditions such as insults, physical attack, or personal failures. The goal is to make the victim (the person) suffer. Most homicides, rapes, and other violent crimes are directed at harming the victim and are precipitated by hostile aggression and anger. The instrumental type of aggression comes from the desire for objects or the status possessed by another person, such as jewelry, money, or territory. Here the offender tries to obtain the desired object regardless of the cost. Usually there is no premeditated intent to harm anyone, although if someone interferes with the thief's objective, the offender may feel forced to harm that person or risk losing the desired goal.

These two types of aggression are very similar to Toch's (1969) self-preserving and needs-promoting dichotomy, which focuses on the functional use of violence in interpersonal relations. Toch suggested that most violent episodes can be traced to well-learned, systematic strategies of violence that some people have found effective in dealing with conflictual interpersonal relationships. Violence becomes not only an impulse but also a learned habitual response. Indeed, Toch postulated that if the histories of violent persons are examined, surprising consistency in their approaches to interpersonal relationships would be discovered. They learned, probably in childhood, that violence works for them. They used violent responses effectively to obtain positive and avoid negative reinforcement. They got what they wanted or avoided unpleasant situations by being violent. Toch posited that humiliating threats to reputation and status are major contributing factors to violence. A blow to the self-esteem of the person who has few skills for resolving disputes and conflicts (such as verbal skills) may precipitate violence. This is especially true if the person's subculture (see Wolfgang, 1958) advocates that disputes be settled through physical aggression.'

Behavioral Classification Systems

Behaviors should be the focus of this investigation because, first and foremost, they are what are observable at the crime scene. As an observable unit of analysis they are more objective at the first stage of interpretation. Second, using observable data at the crime scene will produce a more readily applicable model for police investigators who will be able to more directly use the results of the research in investigations of murder.

Investigators from the Federal Bureau of Investigation (FBI) in the United States (e.g., Ressler, Burgess, & Douglas, 1988) were among the first to seriously analyze the behaviors of offenders from the crime scene and to deduce the different types of offenders responsible for this evidence. However, there are inherent difficulties with this pilot work (see Salfati, 1998), and as some authors admit, "at present there have been no systematic efforts to validate these profile-derived classifications" (Douglas, Burgess, Burgess, & Ressler, 1992, p. 22). What the FBI's work does draw attention to is the possibility of using crime scene behaviors as a unit for analysis in the classification of homicide. They stress that behavioral clues that are the result of certain actions of the offender can be used to interpret the style of the offender. Indeed, much of the FBI's work is reminiscent of the expressive/instrumental aggression dichotomy advocated by Toch (1969) and Fesbach (1964). Both authors dealt with the way individuals interact with the victim in terms of their motivation and the way they would express this during the violent episode. Essentially, the FBI takes an operational approach to the issues examined by Toch (1969), Fesbach (1964), and other aggression theorists.

Salfati and Canter (1999) have built on this original work and proposed that different forms of interpersonal transaction, and thus variations in murders, will be reflected in the murder crime scene itself through the victim the offender chooses and the behaviors engaged in with the victim. Given the assumption that there is a consistency between the way offenders act in the present and their past behaviors, manifestations of behavior that are left at a homicide crime scene can then be analyzed to help us understand different styles of homicide and the kind of person responsible.

The different meanings aggressive actions have to the offender in a violent assault can be distilled into the idea of a victim being either a person onto whom the aggression is impulsively and expressively vented or a target secondary to the offender's instrumental motivations of ulterior criminal actions (Fesbach, 1964; Megargee, 1966; Toch, 1969; Zillman, 1979). It has been argued that this differentiation would be indicated through investigating particular subsets of actions that could be identified at the crime scene. Furthermore, it has been proposed that the processes that give rise to these differences would also be evident in the characteristics of the offender (Canter, 1994; Salfati & Canter, 1999).

In investigative terms, using behaviors at the crime scene as the origin of the analysis may also be a more fruitful path in classifying different types of homicides. If patterns or themes in these crime scene behaviors can be established, and in turn be used to identify the characteristics of the offender, then the science of psychological profiling can be said to be a valid and reliable technique for the identification of offenders from their crime scene themes.

A question that is pertinent to the study of the psychological profiling of offenders' actions at crime scenes is whether, at present, the process that leads to the classification of these behaviors is clear and stable enough for application in investigations. This first question is inextricably linked to the question of whether the information contained in police files is clear and concise enough to reveal more on homicide as a psychological process. Indeed, the exact nature of what information can be used from the crime scene and exactly how this links to characteristics of offenders are important steps to establish.

The Psychological Challenge at the Heart of the Profiling of Homicide

It has been suggested that psychological profiling is not only possible but that it is a psychologically straightforward process (see Ressler et al., 1988). However, as Copson (1995) concluded after having reviewed the usefulness of the information provided by 29 profilers,

> The most compelling recommendation arising from this study concerns the need for further action to be taken to educate police on the potential value and limitations of offender profiling so there is a clearer understanding of what can be expected from it, what kind of expertise is most appropriate for different situations, and in what circumstances operational profiling advice should not be commissioned. (p. vi)

These cautions raise questions about the possibility of a psychological contribution to police investigation. As Pinizzotto and Finkel (1990) have concluded, psychological profiling is much more complex than just a "multilevel series of attributions, correlations and predictions" (p. 230). Pinizzotto and Finkel go on to point out that much of the psychological profiling used in investigations to date has been guesswork based on hunches and anecdotal information accumulated through years of experience, which is consequently full of error and misinterpretation. Indeed, to date, much of the psychological profiling that has been done related to homicide investigations has been linked to individuals rather than specific tested and established scientific methods. However, as has been shown through the previous highlighted literature, establishing a classification system of homicide crime scenes and related offenders can go beyond mere experience by making use of a more rigorous scientific approach and studying the principles that underpin this system. In so doing, the previously shrouded process that has been called psychological profiling can be demystified.

The Present Study: Hypotheses

The first aim of the present study was to investigate and evaluate the hypothesis that consistencies would be found in the way offenders act during homicide. This would be evident in homicide crime scenes being classified into separate thematic types. These types, in turn, would reflect different styles of the offender interacting with the victim, such as the offender exhibiting an expressive or instrumental style.

The second hypothesis of the study postulates that these styles would not only be specific to the homicide situation, but would also reflect general interpersonal strategies that would be mirrored in an offender's past interactions with the environment. It was hypothesized that these would also reflect a dominant expressive or instrumental trend.

The third aim of the study sought to evaluate the nature of the links between an offender's crime scene style and background style. The hypothesis was that there would be some thematic relationship between the way in which the offender acted at the crime scene and the way that he or she had previously interacted with the environment. Furthermore, it was hypothesized that the establishment and evaluation of the link between the way an offender commits homicide and the previous behavioral style would ultimately form a valid and reliable scientific basis for offender profiling.

METHOD

Sample

A sample of 247 British single offender–single victim solved homicide cases dating from the early 1970s to the present were collected from various British police forces and the Crown Prosecution Service (CPS). Cases prior to 1970 were not included in the study due to the influence of different cultural norms and police recording methods, as well as differences in forensic evidence available. A thorough randomization of cases was not possible due to the nature of the data and issues of availability and access. However, the data did include cases from many areas of England and Wales throughout the time period investigated.

To examine aspects of aggressive behavior, cases selected for the study included all homicide cases regardless of the sentence outcome (i.e., whether the offender was sentenced for manslaughter or murder), as it was felt that these legal classifications do not reflect psychological patterns of behavior but depend on the ad hoc legal court procedures used to establish the moral guilt of the offender by the defense to diminish the sentence length. For this reason, the collected sample contains cases classified as domestic (i.e., where the offender killed a family member or spouse/partner) and stranger (i.e., where the police at the time of the discovery of the crime did not have an idea as to the identity of the offender). Although due to the nature of these cases some pose more of a problem to police investigators (e.g., cases where the offenders killed someone they did not know and as such had no previous links with the victim), it was felt that the study needed to go beyond just stranger killings to understand the interpersonal dynamics inherent in many different types of offender-victim relationships.

The present sample was limited to cases involving only one offender and one victim. No cases of multiple homicides (i.e., where there was more than one offender and/or more than one victim) were included in the sample under study, as the study concentrated specifically on aggression as exhibited by the individual offender, irrespective of any interaction with a fellow offender. This avoids any interference with regard to issues of group influences.

Moreover, to ensure that the offender's intention of using extreme force was taken into account, all cases involved situations where the victim had died at the crime scene. Consequently, outside forces such as the use of emergency services did not influence the difference between legal definitions of attempted homicide and homicide.

Most of the offenders were 17 years of age or older at the time the crime was committed, and as such were considered to be adults as defined by the courts. In a handful of cases, 16-year- old offenders were included because their 17th birthday was so close to the time of the crime that they were handled as adults by the courts.

There were two primary reasons for excluding younger offenders from the sample. First, it was felt that not enough recorded life experiences (i.e., offender characteristics) would be present in these files, and so analysis with regard to the consistency between their past experiences and their present homicide crime scene behaviors would be tenuous at best. Second, files on young offenders are difficult to access due to the issue of the protection of young offenders by the court system. Most files of young offenders will be kept separately and cannot be accessed for reasons of confidentiality. Although certain cases were excluded from this study, it must be stated here that it was not because of the lack of value in their analysis, but because the present analysis specifically focused on the criteria outlined above.[1]

Analysis

The data were analyzed using a nonmetric multidimensional scaling procedure known as Smallest Space Analysis (SSA; see Lingoes, 1973). SSA is based on the assumption that any underlying

---

[1] The excluded homicides involved cases of death by reckless driving, professional assassination, and euthanasia. Cases of reckless driving were not analyzed because this type of homicide did not explicitly deal with the interpersonal relationships between the offender and the victim. Nor were cases included that very clearly involved professional hit men, as it was felt that the professional aspect of these crimes would interfere with the issues being examined. Cases that were clearly defined as euthanasia, where the offender was deemed legally sane when the life of the victim was taken and where the victim was killed as an act of mercy rather than as an explicit act of aggression, were also excluded. Cases where offenders killed family members for what was rationalized as an altruistic purpose were included in the sample only if the offender was diagnosed as mentally ill or not legally sane at the time of the offense.

structure or common theme in behavior will be most readily appreciated by examining the relationship each variable has with every other variable. These relationships are measured using association coefficients, the rank order of which is visually represented as distances in geometric space. The representation is such that the higher the association between any two variables, the closer together the points representing them will appear on the spatial plot. In this way, any variables that occur frequently together at the crime scene will be represented geometrically close together on the results plot. The resulting pattern of points (regions) can hence be examined and thematic differentiations between the regions delineated.

The hypotheses of this study were built on the assumption that actions with similar underlying themes will be more likely to co-occur than those that imply divergent themes. These similarly themed actions will coincide in the same region of the plot. This regional hypothesis has previously been viewed as an appropriate way of interpreting co-occurrences of behaviors, and has successfully been used to interpret both studies of emotion and personality (Plutchik & Conte, 1997) and crimes such as homicide (Salfati & Canter, 1999).

The coefficient of alienation (Borg & Lingoes, 1987) is used in the analysis as an indication of how well the spatial representation fits the co-occurrences as represented in the matrix.[2] This measure is interpreted in such a way that the smaller the value of the coefficient of alienation, the better the fit (i.e., the fit of the plot to the original matrix).

RESULTS

Classifying Homicide Crime Scenes

Figure 18.1 shows the distribution of 36 crime scene behaviors for the 247 cases of homicide on the 1 by 2 projection of the three-dimensional SSA. The coefficient of alienation of this analysis was 0.17224, showing a good fit of the spatial representation of the co-occurrences of the behaviors. The regional hypothesis states that items that have a common theme will be found in the same region of the SSA space. To test the hypothesized framework of homicide crime scene behaviors, it was therefore necessary to examine the SSA configuration to establish whether different themes of offender-victim crime scene interaction could be identified.

As can be seen in Figure 18.1, visual examination of the SSA plot confirmed that the sample of homicide crime scenes could most readily be differentiated in terms of the expressive and instrumental role the victim had to the offender. Behaviors that co-occurr at the bottom of the plot all reflect a common expressive theme, and behaviors at the top of the plot all reflect an instrumental theme. Based on this careful examination of the patterns and meanings of the behavioral co-occurrences, a linear division was superimposed onto the plot to reflect this thematic difference.

The expressive theme was composed of behaviors that centered on the victim as a specific person. Comparatively, behaviors in the instrumental region were more focused on the benefits they had for the offender. Here the offender treated the victim as an object or a hindrance to his or her ulterior motive, which looked to be either sexual or material gain.

A number of behaviors occurred in the majority (50% and above) of all the cases, and were thus not used to discriminate between cases (see Figure 18.1). These behaviors included the

---

[2] All Smallest Space Analyses (SSAs) were analyzed using Jaccard's correlation coefficient.

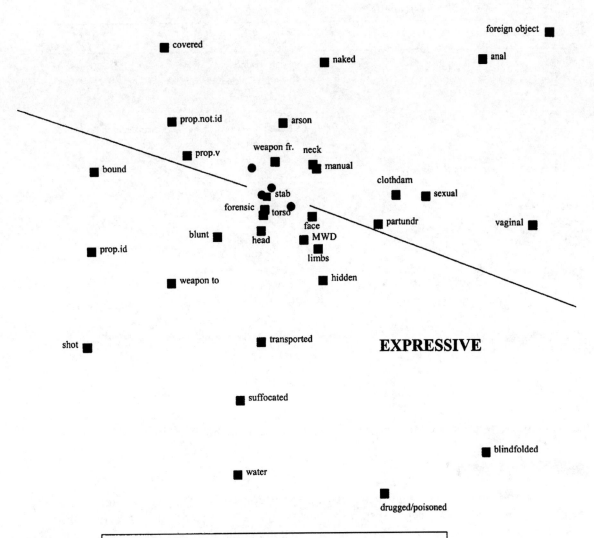

INSTRUMENTAL

EXPRESSIVE

Core high-frequency behaviors
(indicated by the dots in the middle of the plot):
1. Victim's face not having been hidden at the crime scene (88%)
2. Victim being found at the same crime scene where they had been killed (79%)
3. Victim having been found where they fell (61%)
4. Offender inflicting multiple wounds to the victim (52%)

Coefficient of Alienation = 0.17224

FIGURE 18.1

1 by 2 Projection of Three-Dimensional Smallest Space Analysis: Crime Scene Action Themes

NOTE: prop.not.id = property stolen (not identifiable), prop.v = property stolen (of value), weapon fr. = weapon from the scene used, clothdam = victim's clothing damaged, partundr = victim found partially undressed, MWD = multiple wounds distributed over victim's body, prop.id = property stolen (identifiable).

TABLE 18.1   EXPRESSIVE CRIME SCENE ACTIONS

Occurrence Percentage	Crime Scene Action
30 to 50	Face wounds
	Head wounds
	Torso wounds
	Stab wounds
	Multiple wounds distributed over victim's body
	Offender forensically aware
10 to 30	Wounds to limbs
	Weapon brought to scene
	Blunt instrument
Less than 10	Victim shot
	Victim bound
	Victim blindfolded
	Victim suffocated
	Victim drugged/poisoned
	Body of victim hidden
	Body of victim transported away from original crime scene
	Body of victim found in water
	Property stolen (identifiable)

victim's face not having been hidden at the crime scene (88%), the victim being found at the same crime scene where she had been killed (79%), the victim having been found where she fell (61%), and the offender inflicting multiple wounds to the victim (52%).

Expressive Acts

A description of actions at the scene of expressive crimes is displayed in Table 18.1. With expressive homicides, the victim sustained injuries (through stabbing, shooting, or beating) to the torso, head, and/or limbs (and very often to a combination of these body parts), suggesting an extreme physical attack. These woundings further included injuries to the limbs (usually described as defense wounds). Additionally, bringing a weapon to the scene suggests that the offender may have been anticipating a confrontation with the victim and/or had previous experience relating to violent confrontations. After the murder, the offender in many cases transported the body away from the scene of the crime and/or hid the body. Moreover, these behaviors, when looked at together, are suggestive of actions centered on the need to separate themselves from the victim and the crime scene, as these elements might have aided the identification of the killer. All of these behaviors suggest a prior relationship between the two parties, or at least suggest that the offender knew the victim to some extent. The offender's leaving no forensic evidence or removing forensic evidence further points to offenders who need to remove evidence that can link them to the victim, which in turn may indicate that they may not have been strangers.

The more infrequent behaviors, such as suffocating, drugging or poisoning the victim, and/or blindfolding them, are all indirect ways of dealing with a victim. Blindfolding will allow the

TABLE 18.2	INSTRUMENTAL CRIME SCENE ACTIONS	
Occurrence Percentage		**Crime Scene Action**
30 to 50		Neck wounds
		Manual wounding
		Weapon from the scene used
10 to 30		Property stolen (not identifiable)
		Property stolen (of value)
		Victim found partially undressed
		Sexual activity at crime scene
Less than 10		Anal penetration
		Vaginal penetration
		Foreign object used to penetrate
		Victim's clothing damaged
		Victim found naked
		Body of victim found covered
		Arson committed at crime scene

offender to depersonalize the victim to a certain extent so that he or she may complete the crime. Suffocating or drugging/poisoning the victim may be seen as indirect ways of killing someone to whom the offender may be too emotionally attached. In some cases these methods of killing the victim might indicate very vulnerable victims, such as children or the elderly.

Instrumental Acts

Actions in the instrumental theme, shown in Table 18.2, suggest that behaviors at the crime scene were not singularly directed at the victim as a person. Rather, the actions were part of a larger theme of the offender's using the victim to further attain an ulterior aim, such as sex or money. The offender's in many cases did not come prepared for a personal confrontation, so when the offender's killed the victim they used a weapon taken from the scene and/or manually (e.g., strangling, hitting, kicking) attacked the victim. If property was stolen, it typically had some financial value. This could indicate that the offender may have had an ulterior motive for the homicide, such as burglary, or that the offender decided to steal from the victim after the homicide took place, consequently turning the crime into something much more financially profitable. Indeed, it may be that a subsection of these crimes is what the police term "burglaries gone wrong."

Low-frequency behaviors within the instrumental crime scene region included a sexual subset. These behaviors consisted of the offender's anally and/or vaginally penetrating the victim, penetrating with a foreign object, leaving other sexual evidence (e.g., semen), damaging the victim's clothing, and leaving the victim partially undressed or naked. When taken together, these actions suggest a behavioral theme in which the offenders regarded the victim not as a person with whom they were personally interacting, but as an object ultimately to be used for personal gain.

In some cases, the victims were found inside their own homes, covered by a blanket or some similar item. This behavior is thematically distinct from the expressive behavior of hiding the body, in that it is more suggestive of a gesture of shame, implying that the action of murdering or raping the victim did not fit the offender's personal narrative of a "thieving" criminal. It could be hypothesized that this same reason would in some cases lead the offender to set fire to the body and/or the place where the crime took place.

Summary of Classification of Crime Scene Actions

Fesbach (1964) and Toch (1969) both distinguished between expressive and instrumental aggression, specifying that the goal of the first kind was to make the victim or a specific person suffer, whereas the second kind was centered on attaining an ulterior goal such as material goods. On distinguishing between aggressive acts, these authors have described the event and defined it as fitting a certain crime such as theft, robbery, or homicide. The present analysis of homicide crime scene behaviors has shown that not only can expressiveness and instrumentality be evidenced in the actual actions by the offender at the crime scene, but can also distinguish between these actions within the crime of homicide.

Through the analysis of the co-occurrences of the actual behaviors used by offenders at homicide crime scenes, the present study brings attention to the behavioral components that make up different themes of homicide, such as expressive and instrumental crime scenes. These behavioral components suggest that there are certain behaviors that taken singularly and out of context of the other behaviors could be interpreted much differently. However, by interpreting the actual meaning of these behaviors in relation to other behaviors with which they coincide, the thematic meaning of not only the behavior but also the two subgroups (expressive and instrumental) procures a more subtle definition than previously suggested.

The behaviors of transporting the victim away from the crime scene and hiding the victim outside occurred simultaneously with other behaviors within the expressive theme of homicide crime scene actions. These two behaviors in particular have previously been alluded to as suggesting offenders who are organized (Ressler et al., 1988) or cold-blooded, and as such instrumental in nature. However, when the occurrence of these behaviors is interpreted within the context of other behaviors associated with the offense, it can be seen that they tend to coincide with behaviors that are expressive and person oriented in nature. Transporting the victim and hiding the body can be understood as actions that are organized and more specific, but which are so designated because of who the victim is in relation to the offender. Because the offender knows the victim or can somehow be associated with the victim or the actual crime scene (e.g., the home of the victim or the offender), there is a need to remove the victim from the crime scene and hide the body so as to avoid detection. Again, it is the importance of the victim and the relationship between the offender and the victim that are important in these expressive homicides, and which define the actions that are carried out within them.

In the same way that certain expressive behaviors taken out of context can have an instrumental interpretation, there were certain instrumental behaviors that taken out of the context of the other behaviors with which they co-occurred could be interpreted as having a dominantly expressive meaning. These particular behaviors dealt with the sexual component of the homicides. Here the offender violated the person by sexually assaulting her and invading her physically. However, when understood in the context of other co-occurring instrumental behaviors, the theme of these sexual actions was consistent with the offender "stealing" such things as sex or property from the victim. Although the actual victim was violated in these cases, in many cases it was not the actual person who was targeted for the ulterior motivation of sexual gratification.

The behavioral components of expressive and instrumental homicides can thus be understood through a more subtle analysis and interpretation than previously put forward. Consequently, expressiveness and instrumentality are reinterpreted to be not only more behaviorally subtle but also more thematically specific.

Classifying the Backgrounds of Offenders

Figure 18.2 shows the distribution of the 17 offender characteristics for the 247 cases of homicide on the 1 by 2 projection of the three-dimensional SSA. The coefficient of alienation of this analysis was 0.11176, showing a very good fit of the spatial representation of the co-occurrences of offender characteristics.

Visual examination of the SSA plot shown in Figure 18.2 revealed that the background characteristics could be differentiated by the same expressive/instrumental thematic split, this time illustrating the way the offender had previously dealt with situations and people.[3] Behaviors that co-occurred on the left-hand side of the plot all reflect a common expressive theme, and behaviors on the right-hand side of the plot all reflect an instrumental theme. Based on this careful examination of the patterns and meanings of the behavioral co-occurrences, a linear division was superimposed onto the plot to reflect this thematic difference.

The behaviors in the instrumental theme were composed of characteristics reflecting how the offender had previously dealt with situations, in particular with reference to his or her previous criminal activity. On the other hand, characteristics in the expressive theme were thematically very distinct from those that fell into the instrumental theme, reflecting specifically how the offender had previously dealt with intimate relationships and how significant the relationship was with the victim.

Expressive Background Characteristics

As shown in Table 18.3, characteristics that co-occurred in this theme related to personal relationships and emotional issues. The relationship the offender had with the victim is paramount to the structure of this theme. The offender who kills a partner or an ex-partner or kills a blood relative can be seen to often have other thematically consistent characteristics in his or her background, such as previously having abused the partner either sexually or physically, or having previous psychological/psychiatric problems. Killing relatives is often considered mad or psychologically unstable in the literature due to the illogical act of killing close kin in whom many sociobiological resources have been invested (Daly & Wilson, 1988).

The expressive theme reflects offenders who deal with other people and situations as having direct emotional impact on them. It is important to offenders in this theme that the victim is a specific person, not just a body or a representative of a person significant to the offender.

Instrumental Background Characteristics

Offender characteristics that co-occurred in the instrumental theme were thematically distinguishable from the characteristics in the expressive theme of the plot. These

---

[3] It should be remembered that the offender background variables available for analysis were limited, and as such may have implications for the results.

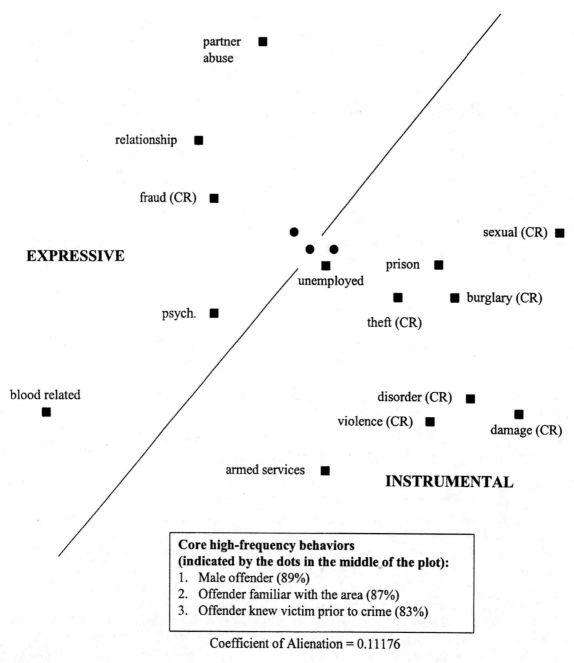

partner abuse ■

relationship ■

fraud (CR) ■

EXPRESSIVE

sexual (CR) ■

● ● ●

■

prison ■

unemployed

■ burglary (CR) ■

theft (CR)

psych. ■

blood related

■

disorder (CR) ■

violence (CR) ■

damage (CR) ■

armed services ■

INSTRUMENTAL

> **Core high-frequency behaviors**
> **(indicated by the dots in the middle of the plot):**
> 1. Male offender (89%)
> 2. Offender familiar with the area (87%)
> 3. Offender knew victim prior to crime (83%)

Coefficient of Alienation = 0.11176

FIGURE 18.2

1 by 2 Projection of Three-Dimensional Smallest Space Analysis: Offender Background Themes

NOTE: CR = offenses recorded in offender's criminal record, psych. = previous psychological/ psychiatric problems.

instrumental variables, shown in Table 18.4, almost exclusively dealt with the offender's previous criminal record. They included previous convictions for theft and burglary and an indicator of the offender's lack of employment. The fact that these particular variables

TABLE 18.3	EXPRESSIVE OFFENDER CHARACTERISTICS
Percentage Range	**Offender Characteristic**
30 to 50	Previous/current intimate relationships with victim
	Previous psychological/psychiatric problems
	Fraud (CR)
10 to 30	Past abuse to partner

NOTE: CR = offenses recorded in offender's criminal record.

occurred simultaneously across these homicide cases is not surprising, as offenders who are unemployed may be prone to commit financial gain crimes such as burglary and theft.

Also co-occurring with these variables was an indicator of previous imprisonment, which is suggestive of a seasoned offender with a substantial criminal history. A prior history of sexual offenses also co-occurred with the variables in the instrumental theme. This could be hypothesized to be due to the fact that, like theft and burglary, sex offenses are invasive on the victim and the offender stands to gain instrumentally from the crime. This association has been found in an earlier study (see Salfati & Canter, 1999).

The instrumental theme also contained previous criminal record variables that have a connection to aggressive actions, such as previous convictions for public disorder, damage, or violent offenses. Prior involvement in the armed services also occurred simultaneously with the criminal antecedent variables, which again is thematically consistent in that it broadly deals with the same theme of violence against people.

TABLE 18.4	INSTRUMENTAL OFFENDER CHARACTERISTICS
Percentage Range	**Offender Characteristic**
30 to 50	Unemployed
	Theft (CR)
	Burglary (CR)
	Prison
10 to 30	Violence (CR)
	Disorder (CR)
	Damage (CR)
	Armed services
Less than 10	Sexual offenses (CR)

NOTE: CR = offenses recorded in offender's criminal record.

Summary of Classification of Offender Background Characteristics

The co-occurrences of the 17 variables chosen for the SSA of offender background character-istics could be seen to divide into two themes of expressive and instrumental background characteristics. When looking at the pattern of the distribution of the variables across the two themes, it is important to note that the instrumental variables, particularly those relating to the offender's criminal record, occurred in a very close cluster in the SSA plot. This suggests that not only do criminals often have a variety of different prior offenses in their background, that these individuals apparently lead a very criminal lifestyle. In contrast to the instrumental theme, the variables in the expressive theme were much more dispersed in the SSA plot, suggesting a much greater variety of background characteristics that are not necessarily as closely linked to one another.

Relating Crime Scene Styles to Offender Characteristics

To validate the model and test the hypothesis that offenders behave consistently across time and situations, the final step of the research aimed to investigate the relationship between an offender's scene theme and background theme. The hypothesis sought to test the supposition that offenders exhibiting a specific theme (e.g., expressive) at the crime scene would exhibit that same theme in their background characteristics.

Any indication of association between an offender's behaviors at the crime scene and his or her personal characteristics would help validate the profiling process. However, it is important to state that this segment of the analysis is not looking at offenders who belong exclusively to one theme, as it is unlikely that individuals have only characteristics in accord-ance with either expressive or instrumental behavior patterns. Rather, this segment will look at the predominant theme that an offender exhibits. As Berkowitz (1993) suggests, violent offenders do not always fall neatly into one of the two categories in the expressive/instrumen-tal dichotomy. As well, Block (1977) stresses that the expressive/ instrumental typology is not so rigid as to suggest that instrumental killings are always coldly calculated and entirely deliberate. As an example, robbery deaths can be seen to most likely occur when victims resist armed assailants.

Each of the 247 offenses in the data set was individually examined to ascertain whether it could be assigned to a particular crime scene theme on the basis of the variables that occurred during the incident. Every offense was given a percentage score for each of the two crime scene themes, reflecting the proportion of expressive or instrumental variables that occurred during the crime. By using stringent criteria (to be categorized as belonging to one theme, the case needed to have twice the occurrence in one theme as compared to the other theme), cases were classified as being either an expressive or an instrumental scene. This same procedure was followed for offender background characteristics. For example, in the third crime scene in the data set, 16.67% of the variables occurred in the expressive theme and 7.14% in the instrumental theme, thus making it a predominantly expressive theme. The percentage of intratheme occurrences was used rather than the actual number of occurrences, because the actual total number of behaviors in each theme varied. Nor were the four core high-frequency behaviors mentioned previously included in the distribution analysis, as they occurred in almost all of the cases and as such defined the sample rather than aiding in the differentiation of the different styles of offending. A case was categorized as a hybrid case if it had an equal number of behaviors present in each of the two themes.

TABLE
18.5 **DISTRIBUTION OF CASES ACROSS CRIME SCENE THEMES**

Theme	Percentage Distribution
Expressive	38
Instrumental	24
Hybrid	30
Nonclassifiable	8

Distribution of Cases Across Crime Scene Themes

Table 18.5 shows that by using the stringent classification method, 38% of the cases could be classified as expressive and 24% could be classified as instrumental, so that a total of 62% of the cases exhibited a majority of the crime scene characteristics in a single theme.[4] Chi-square analysis showed a significant difference ($\chi^2 = 15.1$, $p < .001$) between the proportion of cases falling into either of the two themes (expressive or instrumental) and those falling into either of the two remaining categories (hybrid or nonclassifiable). Chi-square analysis also shows that there was a significant difference ($\chi^2 = 8.4$, $p < .01$) between those cases that were dominantly expressive and those that were instrumental. These results suggest that there are consistencies in the way offenders use certain behavioral strategies at homicide crime scenes. However, nearly one third of the cases were classified as hybrid, suggesting that a considerable portion of the crime scenes had a similar number of behaviors from each style. This poses an interesting question about the nature of the hybrid crimes: What behaviors are consistent to the person and what behaviors that were may be the result of situational factors?

Distribution of Cases Across Offender Background Themes

Having established the thematic split of the 247 crime scenes, the next step was to determine the pattern of the expressive/ instrumental thematic split in the backgrounds of the 247 offenders. As can be seen in Table 18.6, slightly less than three quarters (74%) of all offenders could be classified as either expressive or instrumental. Comparatively, only 4% of the cases were classified as being hybrid, that is, exhibiting an equal percentage of behaviors in each group.

TABLE
18.6 **DISTRIBUTION OF OFFENDERS ACROSS BACKGROUND CHARACTERISTIC THEMES**

Theme	Percentage Distribution
Expressive	31
Instrumental	43
Hybrid	4
Nonclassifiable	21

---

[4] All figures were rounded up/down to the nearest whole number.

TABLE 18.7	DISTRIBUTION OF CASES ACROSS COMBINED CRIME SCENE AND OFFENDER CHARACTERISTICS THEMES

Theme	Percentage Distribution
Expressive	30
Instrumental	25
Hybrid	25
Nonclassifiable	20

However, a relatively large percentage of cases (21%) could not be classified.[5] Chi-square analysis showed a statistically significant difference ($\chi^2 = 59.3, p < .001$) between the proportion of cases falling into either of the two themes (expressive or instrumental) and those falling into either of the two remaining categories (hybrid or nonclassifiable). Chi-square analysis also shows that there was a statistically significant difference ($\chi^2 = 4.9, p < .05$) between those cases that were dominantly expressive and those that were instrumental.

Despite the fact that the literature points out that people usually have a mix of both expressive and instrumental characteristics, nearly three quarters (74%) of the offenders could be classified into one of the two substantive themes. This goes some way toward validating the classification system of the instrumental/ expressive dichotomy in the themes of offender background characteristics, and additionally adds to the scientific understanding of a process that may lead to a more reliable basis for offender profiling.

Distribution of Cases with the Same Theme in Scene Behavior and Background

The same criteria were used to establish the number of offenders who had the same theme in their crime scene behaviors and their background characteristics. The results are presented in Table 18.7, where it can be seen that more than half (55%) of all the 247 cases exhibited the same theme in their crime scene actions and background characteristics. Although chi-square analysis did not show a significant difference between the proportion of cases falling into either of the two themes (expressive or instrumental) and those falling into either of the two remaining categories (hybrid or nonclassifiable; $\chi^2 = 2.5$, n.s.), the figures nonetheless go some way toward supporting the idea that a link can be made between the way an offender acts at the crime scene and his or her general background characteristics.

At the same time, a significant proportion of cases (25%) displayed a pattern where there was a mixture of themes. Indeed, a number of authors have suggested that although individuals may exhibit a particular theme in their offending behavior, they may not always have exclusively that theme in their background characteristics (Berkowitz, 1993; Block, 1977; Cornell et al., 1996). However, as yet there has not been much in the literature to suggest why this may be the case, nor what underlying pattern there may be in the cross-theme link between an offender's actions and previous characteristics. As a consequence, a more detailed examination of those

---

[5] Interestingly, within this group there were 13 cases that had none of the 14 background variables present in either theme. Although in some cases this was due to a lack of information in the case files, there were cases in which there really was no evidence of these variables.

TABLE 18.8	DISTRIBUTION OF COMBINATIONS OF CRIME SCENE AND OFFENDER BACKGROUND THEMES	
	Background Theme	
Crime Scene Theme	**Expressive (n = 48)**	**Instrumental (n = 68)**
Expressive (N = 72)	30 (26%)	42 (36%)
Instrumental (N = 44)	18 (16%)	26 (22%)

cases in the present study that could be classified as having the same dominant theme in their crime scene and background characteristics was undertaken. Table 18.8 shows the associations between the 116 (47%) cases that could be classified as having a predominant crime scene theme and background characteristics theme.

As can be seen from Table 18.8, the majority of the 116 offenders who had classifiable crime scene themes and classifiable background characteristics themes committed a majority of expressive actions at the crime scene (62%, $n = 72$, $\chi^2 = 8.4$, $p < .01$), yet the majority had instrumental background characteristics (59%, $n = 68$, $\chi^2 = 4.9$, $p < .05$). When looking at the relationship between an offender's crime scene and his or her background theme, it could be seen that 36% ($n = 42$) of the cases had an expressive crime scene theme and were committed by offenders with an instrumental background. Comparatively, only 26% ($n = 30$) of the cases had an expressive crime scene asnd were committed by offenders with an expressive background. Comparatively, Table 18.8 also shows that the 44 crime scenes that could be classified as instrumental include 16% ($n = 18$) committed by offenders with an expressive background and 22% ($n = 26$) by offenders with an instrumental background.

Although these differences were not significant, they do go some way toward explaining the relationship between offenders' crime scene themes and their background themes, suggesting that irrespective of the crime scene theme, offenders were more likely to have instrumental background characteristics as defined by the background characteristics of the study. As the instrumental background theme is largely defined by the presence of previous convictions, this suggests that most homicide offenders committed homicide as part of their general criminal career.

Summary

Having established that 55% of cases could be classified as exhibiting either a dominant expressive or dominant instrumental combined crime scene and offender characteristics theme, the current analysis has highlighted that this is still lower than when cases are classified purely on crime scene actions or purely on offender characteristics. This may be due to the fact that although offenders are predominantly thematically consistent in the way they commit crimes and in their characteristics, there are certain psychological processes present that complicate the actions-to-characteristics association (see Berkowitz, 1993; Block, 1977).

Results confirm that there is a substantial mix between crime scene themes and themes of background characteristics. Homicide is essentially an expressive crime, and this explains why offenders with expressive and offenders with instrumental backgrounds primarily commit expressive homicides. However, it should be remembered that homicides tend to be committed by people who have, to a large extent, an extensive criminal history. This explains why most homicides, and especially expressive homicides, are committed by offenders with instrumental backgrounds. At present, because of this cross-theme mix, there may be some limitations in the application of the expressive/instrumental dichotomy to offender profiling.

In reviewing the evidence in support of distinguishing between expressive and instrumental aggression, Berkowitz (1993) concluded that violent offenders do not always fall neatly into the two categories. He suggested that some persons are highly aggressive because they are emotionally reactive—often hot- tempered, easily enraged, and quick to "shift into overdrive." However, these hot-tempered people sometimes attack others because they believe that their aggression will pay off. Conversely, other aggressors can be viewed as more instrumentally oriented, because their aggression is more frequently carried out in the service of other desires—to satisfy their urges to achieve power, status, monetary gain, and so forth. Berkowitz goes on to state that these people can, on occasion, strike out at someone in rage.

Although many studies have found that there are differences in an individual's actions during a crime in terms of instrumentality and expressiveness, there appears to be a difficulty in associating these different types of crime scene behaviors directly with similarly themed previous behaviors in an offender's background. One of the critical problems in distinguishing instrumental and reactive violence in a group of adult violent offenders is that many violent offenders have a history of both instrumental and reactive violent offenses (Cornell et al., 1996). In addition, an offender who is actually committing an otherwise instrumental crime may become angry with the victim and engage in reactive (expressive) aggression.

Cornell et al. (1996), in an attempt to clarify this problem, set up a study proposing a modified group distinction based on 106 male inmates incarcerated for various offenses.[6] The subjects were allocated to one of three groups: nonviolent offenders (where there was no indication of known violent criminal or social history), reactive violent offenders, and instrumental violent offenders (where there was at least one instrumental crime in the offenders' record, regardless of how many reactive crimes they had convictions for). The results of their study again emphasized that criminal offenders need not be exclusively instrumental or reactive in their violent offenses. Expressive violence appears to be the more pervasive form of violent crime, with instrumental violence characterizing a smaller subgroup. Perhaps expressive violence should be considered the most basic form of aggression among criminal offenders, and instrumental violence should be considered a marker of a more pathological development in the ability to use aggression for goal-directed purposes.

Future Research

Although this study highlights that there is evidence of consistencies in offender behavior that may be used for offender profiling, it also highlights that we are essentially just beginning to understand these processes. The first step has been to show that valid classification systems of offender behavior can be established. However, more detailed systems must be developed encompassing valid and reliable variables that have been shown to be useful for understanding criminal behavior and for offender profiling. In particular, a more in-depth understanding and examination of the relationship between crime scene behaviors and an offender's background and personality is needed. Indeed, a valid method needs to be developed to link the scene to the offender. The present study has used a stringent yet very simple linking mechanism in that it was

---

[6] These offenses included homicide ($n = 29$), assault ($n = 19$), robbery ($n = 12$), theft or burglary ($n = 26$), fraud ($n = 9$), drug offenses ($n = 15$), parole violation ($n = 5$), and miscellaneous other offenses ($n = 10$).

only possible to look at the quantity of variables present for each case in each theme. It is likely the case that it is not only the quantity but the quality of variables that is important in this linking. Similarly, just as with personality tests, it may prove useful to look at combinations of particular thematic groups of behaviors and administer a score for each offender based on these. For offender profiling to become a valid and reliable method, this distinction must be looked at and integrated into any model on which profiling is based.

IMPLICATIONS OF THE STUDY

The results from this study are discussed in relation to two major issues. First, results are discussed in terms of classifying homicide into the categories of expressiveness and instrumentality. Second, the results are discussed in terms of the implications they have for offender profiling.

Expressive/Instrumental Classification

Although the concepts of expressiveness and instrumentality have been widely used to classify aggressive events and situations, the specifics of these two types of aggression have never been defined in any great detail. In particular, no descriptions have previously been put forward as to how expressiveness and instrumentality are exhibited during an event through specific description of the behavioral makeup of these events. In light of the results from the present study through its analysis of the co-occurrences of the actual behaviors used by offenders at homicide crime scenes, attention has been brought to the behavioral components that make up different themes of homicide such as expressive and instrumental crime scenes. Through understanding the individual behaviors in the context of other behaviors with which they co-occurred, our understanding not only of what expressiveness and instrumentality signify but also what behaviors during homicide are considered expressive or instrumental (and why) have been questioned. Further work must be developed to test these results and integrate them into a more reliable theory of the nature of expressiveness and instrumentality in homicide.

Profiling

As mentioned previously, one of the main areas of concern regarding offender profiling has been the general lack of extensive empirical studies on the psychological processes underpinning this process. The lack of any robust empirical studies has led to a lack in the validity and reliability of current methods used in the area of investigative profiling.

The results from this empirical study of actions and characteristics of homicide offenders have aided to establish a classification system of homicide crime scenes and related offenders that goes beyond the mere experience and expertise of the profiler. It has been possible to establish the foundations for a scientific approach of the study into the principles and limitations that underpin this system, and in turn has led to a more informed conception of what can be expected from this process and what issues still need to be resolved. Future research must now develop this further and more fully explore the possibilities and limitations of offender profiling as a valid and reliable method.

REFERENCES

Berkowitz, L. (1993). *Aggression: Its causes, consequences, and control.* New York: McGraw-Hill.

Block, R. (1977). *Violent crime.* Lexington, MA: Lexington.

Borg, I., & Lingoes, J.C. (1987). *Facet theory: Form and content.* New York: Springer-Verlag.

Canter, D. (1994). *Criminal shadows.* London: HarperCollins.

Caspi, A., & Bem, D. (1990). Personality continuity and change across the life course. In L. A. Pervin (Eds.), *Handbook of personality: Theory and research* (pp. 549-575). New York: Guilford.

Caspi, A., & Moffitt, T.E. (1995). The continuity of maladaptive behavior: From description to understanding in the study of antisocial behavior. In D. Cicchetti & D. J. Cohen (Eds.), *Development psychopathology: Volume 2. Risk, disorder, and adaption* (pp. 472-511). New York: Wiley.

Copson, G. (1995). *Coals to Newcastle? Part 1: A study of offender profiling* (Police Research Group Special Interests Series: Paper No. 7). London: Home Office Police Department.

Cornell, D.G., Warren, J., Hawk, G., Stafford, E., Oram, G., & Pine, D. (1996). Psychopathy in instrumental and reactive violent offenders. *Journal of Consulting and Clinical Psychology, 64,* 783-790.

Daly, M., & Wilson, M. (1988). *Homicide.* New York: Aldine de Gruyter.

Douglas, J.E., Burgess, A.W., Burgess, A.G., & Ressler, R.K. (1992). *Crime classification manual: Astandard system for investigating and classifying violent crimes.* New York: Lexington.

Fesbach, S. (1964). The function of aggression and the regulation of aggressive drive. *Psychological Review, 71,* 257-272.

Gottfredson, M., & Hirschi, T. (1990). *A general theory of crime.* Stanford, CA: Stanford University Press.

Hagan, J., & Palloni, A. (1988) Crimes as social events in the life course: Reconceiving a criminological controversy. *Criminology, 26,* 87-100.

Huesmann, L.R., Eron, L.D., Lefkowitz, M.M., & Walder, L.O. (1984). The stability of aggression over time and generations. *Developmental Psychology, 20,* 1120-1134.

Lingoes, J.C. (1973). *The Guttman Lingoes nonmetric program series.* Ann Arbor, MI: Mathesis.

Megargee, E.I. (1966). Undercontrolled and overcontrolled personality types in extreme antisocial aggression. *Psychological Monographs, 80*(3), 1-29.

Pinizzotto, A.J., & Finkel, N.J. (1990). Criminal personality profiling—an outcome and process study. *Law and Human Behavior, 14,* 215-232.

Plutchik, R., & Conte, H. R. (1997). *Circumplex models of personality and emotions.* Washing-ton, DC: American Psychological Association.

Ressler, R.K., Burgess, A.W., & Douglas, J. E. (1988). *Sexual homicide: Patterns and motives.* Lexington, MA: Lexington.

Salfati, C.G. (1998). *Homicide: A behavioral analysis of crimescene actions and associated offender characteristics.* Unpublished doctoral dissertation, University of Liverpool, UK.

Salfati, C.G., & Canter D.V. (1999). Differentiating stranger murders: Profiling offender characteristics from behavioral styles. *Behavioral Sciences and the Law, 17,* 391-406.

Silverman, R.A., & Mukherjee, S.K. (1987). Intimate homicide: An analysis of violent social relationships. *Behavioral Sciences and the Law, 5,* 37-47.

Toch, H. (1969). *Violent men: An inquiry into the psychology of violence.* Chicago: Aldine.

Wolfgang, M.E. (1958). *Patterns in criminal homicide*. Philadelphia: University of Pennsylvania Press.

Zillman, D. (1979). *Hostility and aggression*. Hillsdale, NJ: Erlbaum.

C. Gabrielle Salfati is a lecturer at the Centre for Investigative Psychology at the University of Liverpool, England, and the course leader for the Diploma/MSc in forensic behavioral science. Her main area of expertise is profiling, homicide, and criminal consistency. She has presented widely both nationally and internationally on homicide crime scene pattern analysis and has assisted the police in several homicide investigations. Other research interests include sexual crimes, domestic violence, and linking serial crime.

Gabrielle Salfati, *Homicide Studies*, vol. 4, no. 3, August 2000, pp. 265-293. ©2000 by Sage Publications, Inc. Reprinted by Permission of Sage Publications, Inc.

Psychological Aspects of Crime Scene Profiling

Validity Research

ROBERT J. HOMANT AND DANIEL B. KENNEDY

University of Detroit Mercy

Crime scene profiling is distinguished from psychological profiling and offender profiling, and the profiling process is described. A review of the literature on offender types indicates that it may be possible to generalize from various behavioral aspects of a crime scene to some characteristics of the perpetrator. There is some evidence that it may be possible to type offenders and crime scenes as organized or disorganized, and that this categorization may be related to certain aspects of offender personality. There is also some evidence that those who are FBI trained in profiling may perform better at the task. At this time, however, the evidence for the validity of profiles is weak, and it is recommended that profiling not be relied on to the exclusion of other alternatives. There is a need for more specific validity research, especially when profiling is generalized beyond its original purpose of providing leads and focusing investigations.

T hrough movies such as *Silence of the Lambs* and television series such as *Millennium* and *Profiler*, crime scene profiling has come to the attention of the general public. According to Douglas, Ressler, Burgess, and Hartman (1986), profiling may be defined as "a technique for identifying the major personality and behavioral characteristics of an individual based upon an analysis of the crimes he or she has committed" (p. 405). Numerous books and articles have described the origins of the FBI's efforts to develop and implement a formal process for crime scene profiling, which began systematically in 1978 (Annon, 1995; Dietz, 1985; Douglas & Olshaker, 1995, 1997; Geberth, 1990; Hickey, 1997; McCann, 1992; Pinizzotto, 1984; Ressler & Schachtman, 1992).

These accounts, together with the following literature that we will cite, represent a mixture of journalistic, autobiographical, and more empirically based information on profiling. Furthermore, much of the empirical literature directly relating to profiling has been published without being subjected to peer review. For the most part, these sources give a highly positive impression of the effectiveness of crime scene profiling.

Although a few critics have raised cautioning voices (Hickey, 1997; Keppel, 1995), not only does the utility of such profiling seem to be generally accepted, but it is being extended into areas far beyond its original design. The FBI currently has 12 full-time profilers who collectively are involved in about 1,000 cases per year (Witkin, 1996). In addition, many state and local police, typically

AUTHORS' NOTE: Correspondence concerning this article should be addressed to Robert J. Homant, Department of Criminal Justice, University of Detroit Mercy, P.O. Box 19900, Detroit, MI 48219-0900; e-mail: homantr@udmercy.edu.

FBI-trained, apply profiling to some unknown number of cases. With some slight differences in approach, profiling has also gained a hold in Canada (Rossmo, 1995b), Great Britain (Davies & Dale, 1995), and the Netherlands (Jackson, van den Eshof, & de Kleuver, 1994).

The purpose of this article is to review the theoretical underpinning of profiling; to examine the existing studies of its reliability and validity, especially as practiced by the FBI and FBI-trained profilers; and to comment on the application of profiling to various problem areas. We will begin with a general description of the profiling process and distinguish it from certain related attempts at prediction.

DISTINGUISHING CRIME SCENE PROFILING

The Process of Crime Scene Profiling

Profiling is referred to by various terms in the literature: psychological profiling, criminal personality profiling or assessment, criminal behavior profiling, offender profiling, criminal profiling, and investigative profiling (Annon, 1995). Currently, the official FBI term is *criminal investigative analysis*. The authors believe that, for better or worse, the term *profiling* has become too well established to change. In this article, therefore, we will use the term *crime scene profiling* to help focus on exactly what is being attempted and to help distinguish the area from related efforts that are also referred to as profiling.

Crime scene profiling is specifically based on the techniques developed by the FBI's Behavioral Science Unit, which has evolved into the Profiling and Behavioral Assessment Unit. The process was developed particularly to deal with cases of serial homicide and/or serial rape. Because of the typically chance connection between perpetrator and victim in these kinds of crime, and because a perpetrator frequently commits crimes across various jurisdictions, such cases are especially troublesome to local law enforcement.

The how-to of profiling is set out especially well by Dietz (1985), Douglas et al. (1986), and Geberth (1990). The profiler typically begins with complete photographs and descriptions of the crime scene. This includes information about the general character of the location, including traffic patterns and ease of access for various types of individuals. If the crime is a homicide, an autopsy of the victim is required to assist in reconstructing the sequence of the crime; if a rape, it is hoped that the victim can reconstruct all interactions with the rapist, especially including all the verbal and nonverbal techniques used by the offender to gain control. The profiler also requires a complete victim profile, including general lifestyle and a detailed account of behaviors prior to the victimization. All physical evidence is expected to be at the disposal of the profiler. This includes such classic clues as footprints, blood spatters, and tools or paraphernalia used. Such evidence is typically given even more weight than psychological speculation. In addition, any knowledge of the perpetrator's pre- and postoffense behavior is sought, as well as all information from other crimes that may be linked to the same perpetrator by physical or behavioral evidence.

The profiler then attempts to give as complete a description of the perpetrator as possible. This might include gender, age, race or ethnicity, level of intelligence or schooling, military service status, job status, living circumstances, nature of interpersonal relationships, and even the make and color of the perpetrator's car. The numerous descriptive statements are seen as hypotheses, and it is not expected that all will prove correct.

Many of the hypotheses are simply generalizations based on the profiler's experience and training. Other hypotheses are arrived at much more intuitively, by mentally reenacting the crime and imagining what sort of person would be involved. Profilers as a group are not clear as to whether they are trying to construct the personality of the offender or merely to generate a loosely related series of descriptive statements. There does not seem to be any particular personality theory, psychodynamic or otherwise, that guides the FBI-trained profilers. When profilers refer to the personality of the offender, then, we take them to be speaking loosely, in more or less layperson's terms, both about the interpersonal style and the underlying motives of the individual.

Dietz (1985) treats profiling as a systematic, five-step process, in which various levels of hypotheses are continuously checked against the data to arrive at a more or less final set of attributional hypotheses or reasonably specific, descriptive statements about the offender. Other writers (Douglas & Olshaker, 1995; Ressler & Schachtman, 1992) describe the process as being more intuitive. The final profile that emerges may range from a paragraph to several pages, depending partly on the amount of input data and partly on how thoroughly the profiler explains his or her deductions through references to case materials. An early example of a brief, largely unexplained profile is provided by Hazelwood, Dietz, and Burgess (1982); for an example of a more extensive profile, see Douglas et al. (1986).

Goals of Profiling

Profiling was originally intended to help law enforcement discover who the criminal is—either by narrowing an overwhelming list of suspects to a small subgroup or by providing new avenues of inquiry. Other uses were quickly found, however. Thus, case histories (e.g., Douglas & Olshaker, 1995) document the use of profiles to give police advice on how best to interrogate a suspect and to tell prosecutors the approach to cross examination most likely to break down a defendant. Profiling has been used to help set traps to flush out the offender, for example, by planting information in the media. It has been used to predict dangerousness as a factor in sentencing or at a parole hearing or to determine whether a threatening note should be taken seriously.

Proponents of profiling are normally cautious in their claims, stressing, for example, that the process is more of an art than a science and suggesting that profiling should be limited to cases that show severe psychopathology (Geberth, 1990, p. 492; McCann, 1992, p. 476; Pinizzotto, 1984, p. 33) and for which there is a sufficient database of known offenders from previous similar cases. This caution would seem to limit profiling mostly to serial rapes and serial murders; at other times, however, profiling seems to be extended to cases of single rape or murder, as well as to arson, bombing, and threats of various types. Profilers have also applied their efforts to distinguishing accidental, autoerotic asphyxiation from suicide or homicide to hostage negotiations, stalking, and even bank robbery—not all of which necessarily involve significant psychopathology.

The Validity Issue

The issue of the validity of crime scene profiling takes different forms depending on the context. From a law enforcement point of view, there is no need to wait for assurances that profiling in general is a valid process, as long as there are not any more promising alternatives and as long as the process is used cautiously. For example, a promising lead should not be abandoned just because it does not fit a profile, and no lead should be focused on too narrowly. From a forensic point of view, when profiling becomes courtroom evidence that is used to link cases, for example, it is important that such evidence that is be seen as probabilistic, and even though conclusions are based on an "art," it is still important that the profiler be able to articulate the basis for various inferences. Finally, from a social scientific point of view, there is a need to validate profiling not just for each of the individual purposes for which it is used (e.g., identifying suspects, predicting dangerousness) but also for each type of crime (e.g., homicide, rape, arson). As a research strategy, of course, one might begin by trying to establish the validity of the process for its principal use and then focus later on its extended uses.

As far as we can determine, no one has attempted to assess the validity of crime scene profiling in real-life situations. Such a study would present some unique problems. The main problem is the lack of an objective criterion against which to test a sample of actual profiles. Holmes (1989) reported that less than half of profiled cases had been solved. Even when the identity of the offender is unambiguously determined, there is still a large subjective element in deciding how well the person fits the profile. Ideally, the profile should also be compared to any cleared suspects in the case to guard against taking advantage of general statements that might fit most potential offenders. It may also be that if a profile is reasonably accurate, it is more likely to lead to an arrest, creating a spuriously positive impression of profiling accuracy for those profiles that can be evaluated.

The research strategy for examining profiling has been to use a more piecemeal approach, for example, looking at the relationships between types of known offenders and their crime scenes. A major problem here is that the pool of suitable and cooperative known serial killers, rapists, and arsonists is relatively small and possibly not very representative of the population of such offenders (Godwin, in press). Many of the studies that we are about to review appear to rely on the same pool of subjects, although not in any clearly defined way. Because the intensive study of a relatively small sample is likely to take advantage of chance relationships among the numerous variables, cross validation of findings is clearly called for, although, practically speaking, seldom feasible.

Other Types of Profiling

To evaluate crime scene profiling, it is important to distinguish it from two related processes: psychological profiling and offender profiling. Although the literature on profiling uses all three terms more or less interchangeably, we believe that more precise terminology is critical if we are to fully appreciate the validity issues involved. Two other procedures, geographic profiling and equivocal death analysis, are blends of the three basic types and also need to be distinguished.

Psychological profiling

By psychological profiling, we mean the interviewing and testing of an individual to determine whether his personality matches the established personality characteristics of a certain class of offenders. This procedure has been most developed in the area of child sexual abusers, where such profiles are sometimes called on to lend supporting evidence that a particular offender was more or less likely to be guilty of such a crime

Murphy and Peters (1992) have reviewed the literature on the profiling of child sexual abusers. In general, the results of studies of this type of profiling were unimpressive. Standardized personality testing could not distinguish child sexual abusers from other deviant groups (such as rapists, murderers, or arsonists). Penile plethysmography, a behavioral method that directly measures deviant arousal, showed more promising results. The positive results, however, were based on subjects voluntarily in treatment; there was fairly good evidence that involuntary participants could suppress sexual arousal, thus appearing normal.

Crime scene profiling and psychological profiling have in common the attempt to understand and make predictable the behavior of psychologically deviant individuals. In contrast to psychological profiling, however, crime scene profiling starts with known behavior (the crime, as witnessed or reconstructed from the scene) and infers characteristics of the offender; in psychological profiling, the profiler starts with a known individual (who can be tested and interviewed in depth) and tries to project to behavior.

Offender profiling

What we term offender profiling is strictly an empirical procedure, in which no assumptions about the motivation or personality of the offender are necessary. Simply by gathering a large amount of data, either systematically or by more loosely collected anecdotal information, law enforcement agents construct a description of the type of person most commonly involved in a certain type of offense. For example, someone driving at a certain speed, at a certain time of day, in a certain type of car, and of a certain general appearance may fit the profile of a drug courier and be stopped for a search. This type of profiling has been credited with reducing some types of criminal behavior, but it raises legal and ethical problems when ethnicity, gender, and age are part of the profile (DeGeneste & Sullivan, 1994; Easteal & Wilson, 1991).

Crime scene profiling shares with offender profiling the use of empirical data from previous similar offenses. But although offender profiling stops with generalizations about a class of offenders, crime scene profiling is only useful insofar as it can distinguish a particular offender from a general type. Also, rather than being limited to a participant's reasonably observable features, crime scene profiling attempts to extrapolate to the entire lifestyle of the offender.

Equivocal death analysis

Equivocal death analysis drew professional attention when the FBI was asked by the Navy to investigate the cause of an explosion aboard the *USS Iowa* that killed 47 sailors in 1989. Briefly put, the FBI concluded that the explosion was the result of a murder-suicide, committed by a spurned homosexual gunnery officer. Discontent with this conclusion led to a congressional investigation, which commissioned a panel of 14 prominent psychologists and psychiatrists to review the FBI procedures (Jeffers, 1991; Poythress, Otto, Darkes, & Starr, 1993). A clear majority of the panel were critical of the FBI procedures and conclusions, mainly on the grounds that there was no scientific basis for them.

The FBI agents involved in the process (and testifying before Congress) viewed equivocal death analysis as an extension of crime scene profiling. Poythress et al. (1993). specifically noted the lack of concern on the part of one of these agents for the issue of validity and also noted the total absence of any meaningful studies of the validity of equivocal death analysis. However, Poythress et al. view equivocal death analysis as much more closely related to psychological autopsy (which attempts to clarify the motivation of a known individual who engaged in a particular act—suicide or accidental death) than to crime scene profiling. We agree, and we consider equivocal death analysis as more akin to psychological than to crime scene profiling—except that the known individual's personality must be reconstructed without his or her cooperation. The lack of concern for validity and the unwarranted degree of certainty displayed by the FBI agents in the *USS Iowa* incident certainly raise a caution flag over other work done by FBI profilers.

Geographic profiling

Developed as part of his doctoral dissertation at Simon Fraser University by Detective Inspector Kim Rossmo of the Vancouver Police Department (1995a, 1995b), geographic profiling blends the insights of modern geography with the contributions of environmental criminology (Brantingham & Brantingham, 1981; see also Kennedy, 1990). It is clearly allied to crime scene profiling, in that it attempts to generalize from linked crime scene locations to the probable residence or base of operations of an unknown offender. Although primarily empirical (taking into account such variables as bus routes and travel time), geographic profiling does employ the concept of a mental map and tries to reconstruct a psychological representation of the crime-relevant areas in which the offender feels comfortable. A related approach used by Godwin and Canter (1997) also attempts to construct a social psychological portrait of the offender.

Rossmo (personal communication, June 19, 1997) considers geographic profiling as a distinct step in a criminal investigation, one that would normally follow after the construction of a crime scene profile, which might be used in helping to formulate the mental map. The geographic profile can then be used to further refine the crime scene profile. Rossmo sees geographic and crime scene profiling as enhancing each other in more than a merely additive way. Regarding validity, Rossmo (1995a) found that with serial killers, the use of geographic profiling was able to narrow the search for the residence, on average, to about 6% of the potential area of interest—depending primarily on the number of crime sites available to the profiler.

To summarize, the five types of profiling that we have differentiated all have in common the goal of making some sort of inference about an individual's personality or behavior. All are, to some extent, dependent on a model that portrays human behavior as having a good deal of consistency. The inferential burden seems to us to be by far the greatest in crime scene profiling: Not only must the personality of an unknown individual be assembled from behavioral clues, but that hypothesized personality must then be used to generate further attributions about the individual. Because trait theory and the concept of offender types is central to this process, we will briefly review some of the key studies in these areas before turning our attention to studies directly involved with the validity of crime scene profiling.

THE THEORETICAL BASIS FOR PROFILING

Trait Theory and Profiling

Crime scene profiling rests on the assumption that at least certain offenders have consistent behavioral traits. This consistency is thought to persist from crime to crime and also to affect various non-criminal aspects of their personality and lifestyle, thus making them, to some extent, identifiable.

In the field of psychology, trait theory has had a somewhat checkered past, with many researchers finding little consistency of particular traits across time and situations, let alone any pattern of personality across different traits (Kendrick & Funder, 1988). Trait theorists have responded by shifting to measures that combine data from a large number of observations across situations. Hartup and van Lieshout (1995) also suggest that antisocial behavior might be an especially stable behavior trait for aggressive persons—whether because their personalities do not change much, the genetic contribution remains constant, or they tend to remain in aggression-fostering environments.

Caspi and Moffitt (1995) cite a number of studies that, taken together, support the theory that a relatively small group of adolescents engage in life-course persistent antisocial behavior. This form of antisocial behavior has been found to correlate with various genetic, environmental, and personality variables that help account for its persistence. Presumably, individuals who display life-course persistent antisocial behavior make up the bulk of the adult incarcerated offender population. A much smaller subset of this group, in turn, would be representative of the type of offender for whom profiling is thought to be appropriate. Various research studies have attempted to identify these offender subtypes.

Offender Types

Crime scene profiling is based on the assumption that a portrait of an individual offender can be drawn that will distinguish that person from what is known about a class of offenders in general. A particular serial rapist, for example, needs to be distinguishable from the generalized picture that could be obtained by simply using modal values of known serial rapists. Although not absolutely necessary in a logical sense, the existence of reliably identifiable subtypes within any class of offenders at least supports the claim that such narrowing of the field is possible. Furthermore, much of the research work on profiling has involved the attempt to identify such subtypes of offenders.

One of the most frequent areas for developing offender typologies concerns sex offenders, particularly rapists. This research has been reviewed by Prentky and Knight (1991; see also Knight & Prentky, 1990) in the context of developing their own nine-category typology of rapists for the Massachusetts Treatment Center. Prentky and Knight identified several variables that reliably distinguished certain aspects of rapists' behavior. Perhaps most relevant to the area of crime scene profiling is the finding that lifestyle impulsivity and the presence of sexual fantasies are important predictors of recidivism (and therefore are relevant to serial rape). Other variables, such as irrational attitudes, dominance, sadism, history of child sexual abuse, social competence, aggression, and alcohol use have also been found to be of varying usefulness in distinguishing among rapists. Whether these separate variables can be combined into an empirically valid, practically useful typology, such as that proposed by Knight and Prentky, remains to be demonstrated.

Groth, Burgess, and Holmstrom (1977) proposed a simple typology of rapists that was based on two main types, each divided into two subtypes. According to Groth et al., power, anger, and sexual motives are present in all rapes, with either power or anger predominating. Rape is seen as a pseudosexual act, meaning that the sexuality involved is merely instrumental to gratifying the dominant motives of power or anger. The authors examined 225 rapes, based on reports of 133 convicted rapists and an unrelated sample of 92 rape victims. The rapes were found to be classifiable as either power-assertive (44%), power-reassurance (21%), anger-retaliation (30%), or anger-excitement (5%). Although many descriptive data were given for the four types of rapists, no data were given as to how reliably a given rape or rapist could be classified as one of the four types (or whether a person might change from one type of rapist to another).

The theorizing of Groth et al. (1977), as modified somewhat by Hazelwood and Burgess (1987), became central to the FBI's efforts to profile serial rapists. In-depth interviews were conducted with 41 incarcerated serial rapists (Hazelwood & Warren, 1989a, 1989b, 1990). In one study of these rapists, Hazelwood, Reboussin, and Warren (1989) identified a subgroup of serial rapists whom they termed "increasers." Unlike the majority ($n = 31$) of the serial rapists, the increasers ($n = 10$) escalated their use of force with succeeding rapes. They also differed in that they raped more frequently and engaged in more sadistic acts. However, no developmental differences were found between the two subgroups, so it is not clear how a profiler might use the information that a particular series of linked rapes was probably committed by an increaser. Furthermore, in this particular study, all coding disagreements between interviewers were resolved "through an assessment of all available information" (p. 69). Thus, we do not know how reliable any attempt would be to classify someone as an increaser, even based on direct interviews with the individual.

A second study using these same 41 serial rapists dealt with the accuracy of using various scales to classify serial rapists and rape crime scenes (Warren, Reboussin, Hazelwood, & Wright, 1991). Although this study produced some seemingly impressive agreements in classifying rapists and rape incidents in terms of Groth et al.'s (1997) four-category system, as well as distinguishing increasers and nonincreasers, there was a serious methodological problem. The same information that was used by the researchers to classify a rape as, say, power-reassurance, was also used to score the various scales (e.g., did the rapist reassure the victim of no intent to harm?). About all that the results mean, then, is that a set of scales can be applied consistently to both crime scenes and rapists. If a technique can be developed to independently rate both crime scenes and the rapists involved (without relying on information common to both), and if a good fit is found between the two, then a lot will have been done to establish some theoretical underpinning for profiling.

Other studies of offender types were more exploratory, looking for patterns of behavior among distinctive samples of offenders. Dietz, Hazelwood, and Warren (1990) examined the case histories of 30 "sexually sadistic criminals" that had been submitted to the National Center for the Analysis of Violent Crime. A representative finding was that 53% of the offenders kept detailed records of their crimes, and 93% showed careful planning of those crimes. This was seen as indicating the sadist's tremendous need for control and dominance. (See also Warren, Hazelwood, & Dietz, 1996, for an overlapping study.)

Ressler, Burgess, Douglas, Hartman, and McCormack (1986) studied the case histories of 28 sexual murderers. The murderers were categorized into two groups based on presence or absence of self-reported childhood sexual abuse. Numerous differences between the two groups were found, although most were only marginally significant because of the small sample size. As expected, all of the dependent variable differences (e.g., in nightmares, cruelty to animals, assaultiveness) were associated with higher levels of pathology in the abused subgroup. More important for the area of profiling, at least one crime scene difference did emerge: 78% of the abused group mutilated their victims, compared to 42% of the nonabused group ($p = .07$).

To summarize this section on offender types, several studies of extreme groups of rapists and murderers have found that some personality and behavioral distinctions can be made within these groups and that there is some reliability in making these distinctions. There is also some evidence linking these distinctions to differences in how offenders carry out their crimes. In many respects, however, these studies are closer to psychological rather than crime scene profiling, in that they typically begin with a sample of known offenders. In the next section, we will look at those studies that bear even more directly on the reliability and validity of crime scene profiling.

DIRECT STUDIES OF CRIME SCENE PROFILING

Crime Scene Classification Variables

Before looking at specific studies of the profiling process, it will be necessary to clarify the distinction between organized and disorganized crime scenes and offenders. This distinction is fairly well described in the profiling literature. Ressler and Burgess (1985) list some 25 variables that distinguish the personality, socioeconomic background, and crime scene behavior involved in the two types of offender. Compared to disorganized offenders, organized offenders are described as more intelligent, more socially competent, more likely to be responding to some precipitating situational stressor, and more likely to show care, planning, and control in the criminal act. Because of these factors, organized offenders are viewed as more difficult to catch.

The classification is complicated somewhat by the use of a mixed type. Exactly how much overlap of elements is needed before a crime scene should be called mixed is not clear; probably most crime scenes could be classified as mixed. Also, because the FBI profiler is more likely to be called in on the tougher cases, profiling is more likely to be attempted on relatively organized crime scenes, so that any statement about the distribution of the crime scene classification variable would be misleading. Some points that are not clear in the literature include whether the mixed category should be applied only to the crime scene or also to the offender, and whether and how offenders might change or evolve during their career from organized to disorganized and vice versa.

The difference between organized and disorganized offenders is further complicated by three distinctions that profilers make about the crime scene: the MO (modus operandi), the signature, and (possible) staging (Douglas & Munn, 1992; Geberth, 1995). The MO refers to the method used by the offender to accomplish the crime; it is essentially learned and changeable behavior. The signature refers to behaviors that are related to the offender's personality—specifically, the unique fantasies—and that go beyond what is needed to accomplish the crime. Although it is described as "never changing" (Douglas & Munn, 1992, p. 3), it is also possible for the signature to "evolve" from crime to crime. Profilers typically argue that the signature is more important than the MO, both for linking crimes and for deriving an offender profile. Finally, staging refers to deliberate efforts by the offender (or others) to alter the crime scene so as to mislead investigators. The presence of staging may be detected by "inconsistencies in the forensic findings and in the overall 'big picture' of the crime scene" (Douglas & Munn, 1992, p. 7). Douglas and Olshaker (1995) see staging as an aspect of MO in that it is part of the criminal's basic plan for getting away with the crime. Sometimes, however, the alteration in the crime scene can represent posing—for example, using the victim as a sort of prop to communicate a symbolic message—and thus can be a part of the signature (Douglas & Olshaker, 1995). Exactly how the profiler can determine whether some aspect of a particular crime scene represents posing as opposed to staging is not clear.

It would seem from these definitions that the categories organized/disorganized apply partly to the signature aspect and partly to the MO. On one hand, the degree of organization is seen as reflective of the criminal's personality (Ressler, Burgess, Douglas, Hartman, & D'Agostino, 1986) and therefore related to signature. On the other hand, the fact that some offenders may learn from their early crimes and become more careful offenders seems more characteristic of the MO aspect of the crime. In any event, the interrelationships of these concepts need more clarification.

Organized Versus Disorganized Killers

Ressler, Burgess, Douglas, Hartman, and D'Agostino (1986) compared 24 organized with 12 disorganized sexual killers on a wide variety of variables. The authors assume that the 36 sexual killers have been accurately classified as organized or disorganized. Although a citation is given to research that describes the basis for this classification, that source (Ressler & Burgess, 1985) only states that the interviewers made such a distinction. The troubling aspect of this is that it seems highly likely that the classification was made on the basis of information both about the offender and about the crime scenes involved. Thus, a subsequent discovery that the classification leads to significant differences on a number of crime scene variables would be essentially circular.

In addition to data on the 36 offenders themselves, data were available for 118 of their crime scenes and victims. These data were scored according to 357 variables, divided into four categories: background of offender, nature of the offense (primarily offender behavior), nature of the victim, and crime scene (primarily observable physical evidence). Numerous statistically significant differences were found in these variables when comparing organized and disorganized offenders. Besides finding consistent (though overlapping) differences in the crime scenes, the researchers found numerous variables that could be used in a profile to "identify the subject as an individual" (Ressler, Burgess, Douglas, Hartman & D'Agostino, 1986, p. 297).

Twenty-four of these variables are identified as statistically significant. However, as many as 15 of these significant findings can be attributed to chance because it appears that as many as 300 of the original 357 variables may have qualified as potential profile variables. Furthermore, some of the significant findings do not seem particularly compelling. For example, the organized offender is described as "likely to change jobs or leave town" (Ressler, Burgess, Douglas, Hartman & D'Agostino, 1986, p. 300). An inspection of the data, however, shows that although no disorganized offender did these things (out of a possible 21 homicides), organized offenders left town only 11 out of 97 possible times and changed jobs 8 times (and probably these 8 are included in the 11 who left town). A profiler who deduced that an organized offender was likely to change jobs or leave town would be wrong 89% of the time—even presuming the offender was accurately classified as organized based on the crime scene. Nevertheless, to the extent that the offenders could have been classified as organized versus disorganized based strictly on observable crime scene variables, the overall number of significant findings does represent an important beginning for showing a link between crime scene and personality/background variables.

Reliability of Crime Scene Classification

The extent to which crime scenes could be reliably classified as organized/disorganized was the subject of a study by Ressler and Burgess (1985). Sixty-four cases were taken from FBI files. An agent familiar with the case presented all relevant crime scene information to five other agents of varying experience. The measure of reliability was the percentage of agreement by the five listeners with the classification of the presenting agent. The bulk of the classifications was into the categories organized or disorganized, although the categories mixed and unknown were also used (making agreement by chance somewhat less likely). The obtained agreement was 74.1%; that is, about three fourths of the time, the agents listening to the presenter's details agreed with the presenter's classification of the crime scene. Between any two agents, across all 64 crime scenes, the agreements ranged from 45% to 89%, with experienced agents achieving at least 62% agreement.

Significance levels for the percentages are not given, and kappa coefficient would have been the appropriate statistic for measuring reliability here. Although Ressler and Burgess (1985) report the results as a positive finding, the results also show a good deal of disagreement, especially for colleagues listening to the same presenter's summary of the various crime scenes. For example, even though 48.4% of the time the right answer was "organized," one agent only got 51.7% of his answers correct, and even two trained agents agreed with each other only 62% of the time—not much better than guessing.

The Role of Fantasy

Prentky et al. (1989) based a study of fantasy in serial sexual homicide directly on the research on crime scene classification and provide some evidence relevant to the validity of that process. Prentky et al. compared 25 serial sexual murderers with 17 single sexual murderers (32 of the cases taken from the same 36 FBI cases studied by Ressler, Burgess, Douglas, Hartman & D'Agostino, 1986). They hypothesized that the serial murderers would evidence a higher degree of fantasy in their motivation and that this fantasy, via rehearsal, would result in more organized crime scenes. Crime scenes were categorized independently by FBI profilers. As hypothesized, the first murder committed by the serial killers was more likely to be organized: 68% versus only 24% for the single murderers. Also, as hypothesized, the serial murderers were much more likely to have been acting out conscious fantasies (86% vs. 23%) in their homicides. The relationship between fantasy and crime scene organization is not reported directly, but given the respective percentages, there would have to be a strong relationship. One null result was that the serial killers were no more likely to have exhibited planning prior to the crime (42% vs. 41%), although the authors report some problems with the measurement of the planning variable.

The study suffers from a serious flaw in its sampling, in that the serial killers all came from FBI files, whereas most of the single killers were taken from Massachusetts Treatment Center records. If the thoroughness or focus of the records varied by source, which is not unlikely, then the difference in the presence of fantasy as well as the categorization of the offenders as organized or disorganized may be simply an artifact of the data source. It should also be pointed out that it is the very disorganization of the crime scene that may have resulted in the single killers being caught before they could progress to become serial killers. At most, then, we can say that the findings of this study are supportive of some aspects of profiling but are in need of more methodologically rigorous replication.

The Process of Profiling

Although many methodological weaknesses need to be addressed, the studies reviewed to this point offer some support for the claim that experienced profilers can classify crime scenes with some reliability and that this classification can be related to identifiable features of the offender. What remains to be determined is whether profilers do anything more than would experienced investigators applying old-fashioned deduction. In the Prentky et al. (1989) study, for example, 58% of the serial killers had IQs above 110, compared to 29% of the single killers. This intelligence variable might account for both the organization in the crime scene and the greater use of conscious fantasy rehearsal. Perhaps any experienced investigator would be able to distinguish a relatively planned, organized crime from an impulsive, disorganized one and make a generalization about the offender's probable intelligence (and, therefore, school achievement, job level, and social adaptation).

To test the effectiveness of trained crime scene profilers as opposed to other criminal investigators, Pinizzotto and Finkel (1990) compared five groups of participants on two profiling tasks. The five groups consisted of four FBI profiling experts, six police detectives specially trained in profiling by the FBI, six experienced but not trained police detectives, six clinical psychologists, and six inexperienced undergraduate students. Each group received extensive case materials from two actual closed cases: a homicide and a rape. Participants were instructed to write detailed profiles about the probable offender based on the case materials and were asked a series of objective questions about the offender (with the correct answers based on the actual convicted offenders). Results are complicated both by the number of variables on which the groups were compared and by the fact that the FBI experts did not participate in all phases of the study.

Six findings seem especially relevant here. (a) The FBI-trained detectives wrote much longer, more detailed profiles (the FBI experts were not included in this comparison). (b) Five police detectives (not part of the five participating groups) rated the FBI-expert or FBI-trained profiles as the most helpful. (c) FBI-trained detectives scored more objectively correct responses on the sex offender case than other groups (FBI experts not given). However, the FBI-trained group had the poorest score on the homicide case. Group differences were generally small—one or two points on a 15-point scale. (d) Subjects were asked to identify the correct offender from a lineup consisting of five written descriptions of possible suspects. In the sex offense case, all six FBI experts and five of six FBI-trained detectives were correct, trailed by experienced detectives (four of six) and psychologists (three of six). Only one of six students was correct. Results are not given for the homicide case, except to report that the two profiler groups were no longer superior, and all groups did poorer than with the rape case (which must have been difficult for the student group). (e) The FBI-trained detectives recalled more details of the homicide case but were edged out by the experienced detectives on the sex offense case (FBI experts not given). (f) FBI-trained detectives cited more details as important for both cases. Groups did not differ in how they processed the case details (i.e., in whether they used specific vs. global details to make attributions).

The authors felt that the generally higher accuracy of the profiles in the rape case may have occurred because that case had more details available (thanks to the victim's report). Furthermore, too many details had to be eliminated from the cases because of privacy issues—which hurt the homicide case more because of the generally lower level of information. In any event, the Pinizzotto and Finkel (1990) study gives only limited support to the claim that profiling adds a significant degree of expertise to what is normally done by experienced detectives. However, insofar as profiling originated as an attempt to deal with serial offenses, where much more information would be available across crime scenes, this study may not be a fair test of profiling.

Satisfaction with Profiling

Two other studies of profiling may be termed *user satisfaction studies*. The first of these was conducted by the FBI itself in 1981, when profiling had barely begun as an organized process (Holmes, 1989; Pinizzotto, 1984). Beginning with FBI files on 192 profiled cases, it was determined that 88 of them had been solved. Of these 88, in 15 cases (17%), a profile helped in the identification of a suspect. In a number of other cases, the responding agencies reported that profiling helped to focus the investigation or to locate or prosecute a suspect. In only 17% of the cases were the profiles deemed to be of no assistance. Thus, the data can be read in two radically different ways. In 62% of the 192 cases where profiling was tried, it was of no known assistance. On the other hand, the profiles may have been highly accurate in the unsolved cases. If we limit our attention to cases where the outcome was known, profiling was at least of some help 83% of the time.

More recently, in 1994, Bartol (1996) conducted a survey of 152 police psychologists. Overall, 70% of the police psychologists did not feel comfortable with profiling and seriously questioned its validity and usefulness. Before giving too much weight to this study, it would be important to have more details on how much experience the respondents actually had with professionally done crime scene profiles. Nevertheless, the Bartol study does raise a cautionary note.

Summary of Relevant Findings

In summary, there is enough research to suggest that crime scene profiling may have sufficient reliability and validity to be useful for some purposes. The literature suggests that the concept of behavioral traits and consistency across situations is respectable, if measured in broad contexts. Some antisocial behavior, especially if based on underlying psychopathology, may have a high degree of consistency. Within the narrow category of sexual offenders and murderers, some theoretically reasonable and reliable distinctions can be made. Crime scenes can be categorized with some degree of reliability and have been found to correlate with some offender characteristics. Those trained in profiling have been found to produce longer, more detailed reports, possibly with increased accuracy, and field agencies have been generally positive in their feedback.

At the same time, all of the supporting data seem somewhat tentative, and much of the research is in-house and done on the same common core of offenders. Inaccurate profiles often seem to be ignored or forgotten (Jenkins, 1994; Porter, 1983; Rosenbaum, 1993). Although all profilers caution that profiling is an art and that mistakes can be made, the occasional dramatic success tends to encourage pushing the envelope to new applications. Keppel (1995) has observed that many FBI profiles are generalizations about what is known of serial killers and are not helpful for narrowing suspect lists.

IMPLICATIONS FOR THE USE OF PROFILING

Our take on the evidence at this point is that it is important to expect that a significant number of mistakes will occur with profiling. Where these mistakes can be guarded against, there is no reason not to use it. For example, in the area of criminal investigation, certainly no significant leads should be overlooked simply because someone does not fit a profile, and no particular suspect should be focused on without other supporting evidence.

In other situations, advice is harder to give. An interviewer may only get one chance to break a suspect in an interrogation or, even more so, during a courtroom cross-examination. In such situations, if a particular profiler has developed a track record of credibility and has specific advice as to how to proceed, one would need to have strong reasons to ignore the advice. Or, in dealing with a hostage taker where lives are at stake and one or another strategy must be followed, again the experienced profiler's advice, backed by soundly articulated reasoning, should be given some weight.

Suggested Research

Research on the validity of crime scene profiling suffers especially from two limitations. One is the lack of access for neutral researchers to a representative sample of actual profiles. The second problem concerns the criterion: The accuracy of a profile can only be determined in cases where the criminal has been clearly identified. This second problem is compounded by the possibility that accurate profiles may be more likely to result in solved cases; thus, inaccurate profiles may be less likely to come to light.

The practical issue with profiling is whether it leads to an increase in successful police investigations. In this sense, even an inaccurate profile may be useful, for example, by stimulating a line of inquiry. Probably the only way that this practical validity (or utility) could be determined would be by a truly randomized experiment in which profiling was withheld from some otherwise suitable cases. We do not seriously propose that such a study be done, of course, on the grounds that no method that has promise should be withheld from the types of cases with which profilers typically deal.

A more limited study that might be possible would be to make available all profiles from solved cases. This would at least permit researchers to make more or less objective judgments about the accuracy of the various elements of the profile. One limitation that we foresee in such a study is that profilers often do not clarify the basis for their predictions. Thus, a piece of physical evidence that leads to a straightforward conclusion may make the profile sound much more intuitive than it really is. There may also be legitimate policy reasons to deny neutral researchers access to FBI files. One obvious concern has to do with the privacy needs of victims and their families. A less obvious problem might be the publication of too much information that could be useful to offenders who stage crime scenes. Nevertheless, until neutral researchers have some way of determining the accuracy of the various elements of a representative sample of profiles, compared against some meaningful baseline data, the validity of the entire process has to remain in a great deal of doubt.

In the meantime, we recommend that more attention be paid to the specific concepts used by profilers. For example, objective scales for categorizing crime scenes could be developed. MO, signature, staging, and posing need to be more carefully operationalized and distinguished. Relationships between crime scenes and offender characteristics, when known, should be cross-validated on new samples of offenders.

On a larger scale, more objectively gathered qualitative data on experiences with profiles should be obtained. This would involve a more careful tracking of profiles that are generated and a comparison with actual offenders when outcomes are known. How exactly did the profile lead or not lead to the offender? How many of the elements of the profile fit the offender? Although some of this information is available anecdotally in biographical material (Douglas & Olshaker, 1995, 1997; Ressler & Schachtman, 1992), it does not seem to have been gathered systematically (e.g., to permit failures to be more carefully scrutinized).

Finally, more attention should be paid to the various uses to which profiling is being put—from various types of crimes, to interrogation advice, to predictions in negligent security cases (Kennedy & Homant, 1997). It is important that a halo effect not be created, whereby a finding of profiling success in one area might be taken as indicative of all possible uses.

REFERENCES

Annon, J.S. (1995). Investigative profiling: A behavioral analysis of the crime scene. *American Journal of Forensic Psychology, 13,* 67-75.

Bartol, C. (1996). Police psychology: Then, now, and beyond. *Criminal Justice and Behavior, 23,* 70-89.

Brantingham, P.J., & Brantingham, P.L. (Eds.)(1981). *Environmental criminology.* Beverly Hills, CA: Sage.

Caspi, A., & Moffitt, T.E. (1995). The continuity of maladaptive behavior: From description to understanding in the study of antisocial behavior. In D. Cicchetti & D. J. Cohen (Eds.), *Developmental psychology* (Vol. 2, pp. 472-511). New York: John Wiley.

Davies, A., & Dale, A. (1995). *Locating the stranger rapist* (Special Interest Series: Paper 3). London: Police Research Group, Home Office Police Department.

DeGeneste, H.I., & Sullivan, J.P. (1994). *Policing transportation facilities.* Springfield, IL: Charles C Thomas.

Dietz, P.E. (1985). Sex offender profiling by the FBI: A preliminary conceptual model. In M.H. Ben-Aron, S.J. Hucker, & C.D. Webster (Eds.), *Clinical criminology: The assessment and treatment of criminal behavior* (pp. 207-219). Toronto: Clarke Institute of Psychiatry.

Dietz, P.E., Hazelwood, R., & Warren, J. (1990). The sexually sadistic criminal and his offenses. *Bulletin of the American Academy of Psychiatry and Law, 18,* 163-178.

Douglas, J.E., & Munn, C. (1992, February). Violent crime scene analysis: Modus operandi, signature, and staging. *FBI Law Enforcement Bulletin,* pp. 1-20.

Douglas, J., & Olshaker, M. (1995). *Mind hunter: Inside the FBI's elite serial crime unit.* New York: Star.

Douglas, J., & Olshaker, M. (1997). *Journey into darkness.* New York: Scribner.

Douglas, J.E., Ressler, R.K., Burgess, A.W., & Hartman, C.R. (1986). Criminal profiling from crime scene analysis. *Behavioral Sciences and the Law, 4,* 401-421.

Easteal, P.W., & Wilson, P. (1991). *Preventing crime on transport: Rail, buses, taxis, planes.* Canberra: Australian Institute of Criminology.

Geberth, V.J. (1990). *Practical homicide investigation: Tactics, procedures, and forensic techniques*(2nd ed.). Boca Raton, FL: CRC Press.

Geberth, V.J. (1995). Criminal personality profiling: The signature aspect in criminal investigation. *Law and Order, 43*, 45-49.

Godwin, M. (in press). *Profiling serial killers: A theoretical analysis of motivational classifications*. Liverpool, UK: University of Liverpool.

Godwin, M., & Canter, D. (1997). Encounter and death: The spatial behavior of U.S. serial killers. *Policing: An International Journal of Police Strategy and Management, 20*(1), 24-38.

Groth, N., Burgess, A.W., & Holmstrom, L.L. (1977). Rape: Power, anger, and sexuality. *American Journal of Psychiatry, 134*, 1239-1243.

Hartup, W.W., & van Lieshout, C.F.M. (1995). Personality development in social context. *Annual Review of Psychology, 46*, 655-687.

Hazelwood, R., & Burgess, A. (Eds.) (1987). *Practical aspects of rape investigation: A multi-disciplinary approach*. New York: Elsevier North-Holland.

Hazelwood, R.R., Dietz, P.E., & Burgess, R.N. (1982). Sexual fatalities: Behavioral reconstruction in equivocal cases. *Journal of Forensic Science, 27*, 763-773.

Hazelwood, R.P., Reboussin, R., & Warren, J.I. (1989). Serial rape: Correlates of increased aggression and the relationship of offender pleasure to victim resistance. *Journal of Interpersonal Violence, 4*, 65-78.

Hazelwood, R.R., & Warren, J.W. (1989a, January). The serial rapist: His characteristics and victims (Part 1). *FBI Law Enforcement Bulletin*, pp. 10-17.

Hazelwood, R.R., & Warren, J.W. (1989b, February). The serial rapist: His characteristics and victims (Conclusion). *FBI Law Enforcement Bulletin*, pp. 18-25.

Hazelwood, R.R., & Warren, J.W. (1990, February). The criminal behavior of the serial rapist. *FBI Law Enforcement Bulletin*, pp. 11-16.

Hickey, E.W. (1997). *Serial murderers and their victims*(2nd ed.). Belmont, CA: Wadsworth.

Holmes, R. (1989). *Profiling violent crimes: An investigative tool*. Newbury Park, CA: Sage.

Jackson, J.L., van den Eshof, P., & de Kleuver, E.E. (1994). *Offender profiling in the Netherlands* (Report NSCR WD94-03). Leiden, the Netherlands: The Netherlands Institute for the Study of Criminality and Law Enforcement.

Jeffers, H.P. (1991). *Who killed precious* Chicago: Congdon and Weed.

Jenkins, P. (1994). *Using murder: The social construction of homicide*. New York: Aldine.

Kendrick, D.T., & Funder, D.C. (1988). Profiting from controversy: Lessons from the person-situation debate. *American Psychologist, 43*, 23-34.

Kennedy, D.B. (1990). Facility site selection and analysis through environmental criminology. *Journal of Criminal Justice, 18*, 239-252.

Kennedy, D.B., & Homant, R.J. (1997). Problems with the use of criminal profiling in negligent security tort litigation. *Trial Diplomacy Journal, 20*, 223-229.

Keppel, R.D. (1995). *The riverman*. New York: Pocket.

Knight, R.A., & Prentky, R.A. (1990). Classifying sexual offenders: The development and corroboration of taxonomic models. In W.L. Marshall, D.R. Laws, & H.E. Barbaree (Eds.), *The handbook of sexual assault: Issues, theories, and treatment of the offender* (pp. 23-52). New York: Plenum.

McCann, J.T. (1992). Criminal personality profiling in the investigation of violent crime: Recent advances and future directions. *Behavioral Sciences and the Law, 10*, 475-481.

Murphy, D.W., & Peters, J.M. (1992). Profiling child sexual abusers: Psychological considerations. *Criminal Justice and Behavior, 19*, 24-37.

Pinizzotto, A.J. (1984). Forensic psychology: Criminal personality profiling. *Journal of Police Science and Administration, 12*, 32-40.

Pinizzotto, A.J., & Finkel, N.J. (1990). Criminal personality profiling: An outcome and process study. *Law and Human Behavior, 14*, pp. 215-233.

Porter, B. (1983, April). Mind hunters. *Psychology Today*, pp. 44-52.

Poythress, N., Otto, R.K., Darkes, J., & Starr, L. (1993). APA's expert panel in the congressional review of the USS Iowa incident. *American Psychologist, 48*, 8-15.

Prentky, A.P., Burgess, A.W., Rokous, B.A., Lee, A., Hartman, C., Ressler, R., & Douglas, J. (1989). The presumptive role of fantasy in serial sexual homicide. *American Journal of Psychiatry, 146*, 887-891.

Prentky, R.A., & Knight, R.A. (1991). Identifying critical dimensions for discriminating among rapists. *Journal of Consulting and Clinical Psychology, 59*, 643-661.

Ressler, R.K., & Burgess, A.W. (1985, August). Violent crime. *FBI Law Enforcement Bulletin*, pp. 1-32.

Ressler, R.K., Burgess, A.W., Douglas, J.E., Hartman, C.R., & D'Agostino, R.B. (1986). Sexual killers and their victims: Identifying patterns through crime scene analysis. *Journal of Interpersonal Violence, 1*, 288-308.

Ressler, R.K., Burgess, A.W., Douglas, J.E., Hartman, C.R., & McCormack, A. (1986). Murderers who rape and mutilate. *Journal of Interpersonal Violence, 1*, 273-287.

Ressler, R.K., & Schachtman, T. (1992). *Whoever fights monsters*. New York: Simon & Schuster.

Rosenbaum, R. (1993, April). The FBI's agent provocateur. *Vanity Fair*, pp. 122-136.

Rossmo, D.K. (1995a). *Geographic profiling: Target patterns of serial murderers*. Doctoral dissertation, Simon Fraser University, Burnaby, British Columbia, Canada.

Rossmo, D.K. (1995b). Place, space, and police investigations: Hunting serial violent criminals. In J.E. Eck & D. Weisburd (Eds.), *Crime and place: Crime prevention studies* (Vol. 4, pp. 217-235). Monsey, NY: Criminal Justice Press.

Warren, J.I., Hazelwood, R.R., & Dietz, P.E. (1996). The sexually sadistic serial killer. *Journal of Forensic Sciences, 41*, 970-974.

Warren, J.I., Reboussin, R., Hazelwood, R.R., & Wright, J.A. (1991). Prediction of rapist type and violence from verbal, physical and sexual scales. *Journal of Interpersonal Violence, 6*, 55-67.

Wikin, G. (1996, April22). How the FBI paints portraits of the nation's most wanted. *U.S. News & World Report*, 32.

Robert Homant and Daniel Kennedy, *Journal of Contemporary Criminal Justice*, Vol. 15, No. 3, August 1999, pp. 242-261.

COALS TO NEWCASTLE: POLICE USE OF OFFENDER PROFILING

GARY COPSON

INTRODUCTION

Background

Offender profiling's is a term originally coined in the United States of America, for an approach to police investigations whereby an attempt is made to deduce a description of an unknown offender based on evaluating minute details of the crime scene, the victim, and other available evidence. Sometimes other labels are used to describe what are essentially the same range of activities. These include psychological profiling, criminal profiling, and personality profiling, while the Federal Bureau of Investigation (FBI) now use the term criminal investigative analysis to cover the range of operational support activities offered within their Behavioural Science Unit.

Following some reported successes through the use of psychologists or psychiatrists in particular investigations, this approach was placed on a more systematic footing by a group of FBI agents in the late 1970s. Its introduction in the UK also began, in the early 1980s, with isolated reported successes, but has not led to the same kind of systematisation. Rather, its development has been characterised by individual approaches which have led to arguments about the nature of the process, including the extent to which the American system is valid when applied in a different culture. Opinions vary on how far profiling is, or can be developed as, a science. A review of the literature invites the conclusion that profiling is not yet proven as a science.

It is generally accepted that the underlying principle of profiling is, the inference of offender characteristics from offence characteristics, but there are a number of different approaches, each of which advocates a different basis for this process. These approaches rely, to varying degrees, on three strands of expertise: statistical analysis of crime data, behavioural science and detective expertise.

Over the last decade there have been more than two hundred British police investigations in which offender profiling is known to have been used in its various guises, but no truly independent scientific assessment has been conducted to evaluate its usefulness.

There is no governing body for the regulation of professional or ethical standards in offender profiling. Notwithstanding several postgraduate psychology courses which incorporate some study of it, there is no academic qualification for offender profiling, and there is very little academic literature which deals directly with either the principles or the validity of offender profiling. There used to be an eleven month course run by the FBI, which was open to law enforcement officers from anywhere in the world to learn their profiling system, but even this was closed at the end of 1991 as part of a restructuring and cost saving exercise. There is no official forum for learning and development of profiling skills, no mutual support network, and precious little evidence of any feedback by which profilers can be made aware of their strengths and weaknesses.

Those wishing to know more of the history and origins of offender profiling are referred to the bibliography. The following articles offer accessible accounts of the state of offender profiling in Britain at the time of writing this report: Oldfield (1994), Wessely (1993), Pile (1994), and Davies (1994). For detailed accounts of the development of offender profiling in the United States of America, the following books are recommended: Hazelwood and Burgess (1987), Ressler et al (1988), Ressler and Schactman (1992). A personal account of profiling experiences and scientific principles to do with profiling can be found in Canter (1994).

Context

The research which gives rise to this paper is part of a wider programme of offender profiling research which emerged from the recommendations of a review designed to take stock of British initiatives in offender profiling (Britton, 1992). Conducted within the Home Office Police Research Group (PRG), on behalf of the British Police Service, it carries the mandate of the Association of Chief Police Officers (ACPO) Crime Sub-Crnnmittee on Offender Profiling.

The objectives of the PRG research programme are twofold:

- to establish whether offender profiling can significantly enhance the investigative proficiency of the experienced detective; and

- try manage the development of an appropriate mechanism to deliver any benefits of offender profiling to the police service.

Terms of Reference

The initial terms of reference for this project, which formed part of the PRG programme, were to provide a means by which investigating officers (SIOs) could obtain objective advice on the operational use of offender profiling, pending the completion of the programme. These were to be met in three parts:

i. by establishing a procedure to evaluate operational offender profiling in a manner that was useful to SIOs and acceptable to the Home Office, ACPO, and the profilers themselves;

ii. by collating and evaluating all British profiles that had been produced to date; and

iii. by managing the implementation of an interim system to provide objective advice to SIOs on operational offender profiling, pending the delivery of a long term solution on completion of the programme.

In January 1993 the project was developed and combined with a Metropolitan Police Scholarship founded to investigate the operational usefulness of offender profiling. This was partly a union defined by pragmatism, but also a response to the unexpected size and weight of the problem. It had been initially assumed that offender profiling had been used operationally in Britain not many more than a hundred times, involving perhaps ten or a dozen individuals. It was quite quickly recognised, however, that there were at least 200 instances and at least 30 profilers. What was conceived as a short data collection and analysis exercise therefore emerged as a much more significant study, in two parts.

This report deals with the first part of the study, a survey of police users of operational offender profiling advice. A content analysis of collected examples of profiling advice and, where possible, comparison of predictions and outcomes, will follow.

The question posed in the title "Coals to Newcastle?" is a reflection of a common criticism of operational offender profiling advice: that it tells the investigating officer only what he or she already knows. Little previous effort has been made to establish whether this is true, or even justified to any extent.

Definition of Offender Profiling

There is no universally accepted definition of the term offender profiling. As defined for the purposes of this study, it is a term of convenience which is applied to a range of approaches to criminal investigation, in which the behaviour exhibited in a crime, or a series of similar crimes, is studied and inferences are drawn about the offender.

In the first instance the inferences drawn from such a study of a criminal's behaviour may focus on predicted characteristics of the offender, such as domestic and social circumstances, domestic and criminal histories, education and employment records; they may go further, for example, postulating mental health or sexual preferences and dysfunctions. This inferred picture of the offender can then be used as a basis for a range of observations, predictions, and recommendations.

An offender might be implicated in previous unsolved crimes, and a pattern of expected further offending may be suggested. In an extortion case an assessment could be made of the likelihood of any threat being enacted, and responses to publicity might be predicted. Interrogation strategies are sometimes recommended. Advice based upon inferred characteristics should be regarded as offender profiling just as much as the list of characteristics itself.

Definition of Offender Profiler

An offender profiler, for the purposes of this study, is a person who offers advice to a police investigation based on having collected data on past crimes, or on relevant professional expertise, typically as a psychologist or psychiatrist. This may include people working inside as well as outside the police service, but only where they are acting as an appointed consultant to an investigation, rather than where they are operating some form of innovative interventionary intelligence system. The study is concerned, therefore, with reactive rather than proactive profiling, and with those who present themselves as having some kind of relevant expertise.

REVIEW OF PREVIOUS EVALUATIONS OF OPERATIONAL PROFILING

Only four studies were identified which deal with evaluation of operational profiling: Douglas (1981); Britton (1992); Goldblatt (1992); and Jackson et al, (1993a). Only one of them, Jackson's, has been published. Two further published studies, Pinizzotto and Finkel (1990) and Jackson et al (1993b) are each concerned with comparing the approaches of profilers and non-profilers in analysing given case material, with the object of identifying characteristics of the profiling process.

The FBI Evaluation (Douglas, 1981)

In 1981 John Douglas, then Special Agent on the Investigative Support Unit, now Unit Chief, conducted an internal review as a cost-benefit study to determine the value of profiling services which had been made available to all law enforcement agencies since 1978. It was specifically concerned with two questions: the nature and extent of any assistance provided by psychological profiling; and the actual results of utilising a psychological profile in terms of offender identification and/or savings in investigative agent days. In a discussion of the chosen methodology the difficulties are acknowledged of isolating the effect of profiling from the "infinite number of potentially decisive factors impacting upon an investigation," and a qualitative evaluation, based on a questionnaire survey, is chosen above a quantitative one.

Douglas' study is sometimes mistakenly attributed to Pinizzotto, because its widest circulation is as a series of quotes in "Forensic psychology: criminal personality profiling" (Pinizzotto, 1984). Pinizzotto offers a number of Douglas' findings, but the evaluation is best understood by direct reference to its own executive summary:

> "Based upon the findings of this research the use of psychological profiling can be of definite value in an investigation. While probably most useful in the investigation of murder, the procedure has also been of significant assistance solving other types of crimes. In the 192 cases examined, psychological profiling helped focus the investigation in 77% of those cases where the perpetrator was identified and actually identified the subject in 15 instances. Even in cases where the suspect has not been identified psychological profiling was helpful. According to detectives, the procedure was often helpful in that it ensured that a complete investigation was conducted. All in all, investigators suggested psychological profiling had saved an estimated 594 investigative man days and all users overwhelmingly agreed that the service should be continued."

The Britton Review (Britton, 1992)

This review was funded by the Home Office for ACPO and conducted by Paul Britton, head of Trent Region Forensic Psychology Service, a consultant clinical and forensic psychologist with wide experience as a profiler. It was concerned with evaluating existing British initiatives in offender profiling and the potential for further development.

Britton's examination of operational profiling was conducted by means of a questionnaire to Heads of CID, asking about their force's use of psychologists to advise on crime investigations. This aspect of the study was conducted on Britton's behalf by two police Superintendents, one of whom later wrote an annexe to the review, in which he evaluated Britton's operational profiling. The focus of the questionnaire was on identifying profilers and establishing how far, in the eyes of the respondents, profiling advice had led to the arrest of suspects. Judged on this stark criterion, and contrary to popular perception, little evidence was offered that profiles were either accurate or had contributed to any arrest. Nevertheless there was deemed to be sufficient potential in the various strands of profiling research for the review to conclude that offender profiling in Britain should be regarded as viable, and that the British offender profiling initiative should proceed, albeit with some degree of caution.

The review recommendations were presented in a confidential report to the ACPO subcommittee in July 1992 and all 26 were accepted. It is those recommendations which were taken as the starting point for the PRG Offender Profiling Research Programme.

Goldblatt's Review (Goldblatt, 1992)

The Goldblatt review took the form of an undergraduate placement essay written by Philip Gold-blatt, a psychology student from the University of Hertfordshire. It was focused on the work of the Psychological Offender Profiling Unit at the University of Surrey. The unit was founded by David Canter, a professor of psychology now at Liverpool University, who headed a group of students, several of them police officers, concerned with developing offender profiling data sets and operational advice.

The review, based upon information given to Goldblatt by Canter, finds that of 57 profiles then submitted by the unit, a suspect had been charged in "at least 12 cases." The observation was added that "unfortunately, it is not a simple matter to establish to what extent the enquiry procedure was aided by the introduction of a profile," and later "undoubtedly, those caught up in the investigative process are perhaps the best to judge the profile's effectiveness."

Goldblatt's review is partly based on feedback attributed to officers in the 12 solved cases, which allowed the profiles to be compared with information provided by police about the persons charged. He observes that "These comments, both positive and negative,...speak for themselves as an assessment of the unit's work." His analysis of those 12 cases concludes that "out of 114 pieces of information suggested by the profiles, 72% (82 pieces) were correct, 19% (22) were incorrect and 9% (10) needed more information to determine their accuracy." In two of the twelve cases, it is reported, the profile was prepared after the suspect was charged, but overall the operation of the unit was declared a success.

The Dutch Consumer Satisfaction Survey (Jackson et al, 1993a)

The Dutch consumer satisfaction survey, conducted in 1993 by researchers from the Netherlands Institute for the Study of Criminality And Law Enforcement (NISCALE) research institute, was designed to evaluate the product of a Scientific Research Advisory Unit set up within the Dutch National Criminal Intelligence Division (CRI). It was based on twenty cases over a two year period in which the unit had offered advice and where sufficient time had elapsed to enable it to be acted upon. In only six of the twenty cases did the advice amount to a formal offender profile, that is to say a list of characteristics predicted to be found in an unknown offender. Given the relatively small consumer group the researchers were able to interview respondents personally rather than send a questionnaire.

The broad conclusion drawn from the officers' ratings of the advice they received was that the majority of detectives interviewed could be viewed as satisfied customers. It was apparent, however, that it was not simply profiling that left them satisfied customers. Indeed, "a large percentage of those interviewed spontaneously said how much they had learned from the experience of discussing the case with the profiler; how many new ideas they had acquired and how useful these would be for future investigations." "This," the researchers add, "is the type of success that is very important but is also very hard to measure and this report makes no attempt to do so.

Conclusions to Be Drawn on Relevant Past Studies

What each of the four previous studies has in common is that they all rely to a large extent on the opinions of detectives who have used offender profiling advice in live investigations. All four studies offer some measure of approval for the potential of offender profiling, while three of the four go further, applauding the contribution of profiling to the cases under their consideration. None of the four, however, can be regarded as definitive.

The FBI study scans a substantial range of cases but little of substance is revealed from the questionnaires collected. The Dutch study offers substantial detail, but from a very limited range of cases. That aspect of the Britton review which is of direct concern here must of necessity be treated with caution since not only is the author's own work as a profiler quite properly excluded from his evaluation, but as a profiler himself he might be considered to have been placed in a somewhat invidious position by being required to pass judgement on others active in the field. The Goldblatt review, meanwhile, looks only at the work of Canter and his students, and was; by design, limited in scope.

Nonetheless, it is possible to extract some very useful pointers for this study. Douglas highlights the care which must be taken in pursuit of quantitative measures of usefulness if apparent precision is not to be misleading. Britton, in stating the limitations of operational profiling when judged solely in terms of the identification of offenders, while still endorsing the viability of profiling as a potential aid to police investigations, encourages the search for other measures of usefulness, while Jackson offers some such alternatives. Goldblatt echoes Douglas (apparently without having had the opportunity of reading his review) in warning of the difficulties of isolating the impact of a profile from the complex dynamics of a police investigation, and offers the investigator as the best arbiter of usefulness.

APPROACH TO THE STUDY

Development of the Methodology

The methodology chosen for this project evolved out of a process of wide consultation: within PRG, within the ACPO sub-committee, with interested psychologists, both academics and profiling practitioners, and—perhaps most significantly—amongst a range of contacts in the CID from a number of British forces: users and potential users of offender profiling. What follows in this section is a summary of methodological considerations: a more detailed account is available on application to the author.

Measuring Operational Usefulness

The starting point was the realisation that very little had been demonstrated outside the FBI Academy of the process of offender profiling, and that next to nothing had been demonstrated anywhere of its validity. In order to measure the usefulness of profiling, it would be necessary first to gather examples of operational profiling advice and analyse them to see what they consist of.

Next came the most important working assumption, that the process of profiling could well carry some benefits for investigators independent of the product: in other words, that accuracy was unlikely to be the sole reliable measure of usefulness. And while accuracy could seemingly be established quite simply by comparison of predictions with the outcomes of solved cases, understanding other dimensions of usefulness could only be achieved by reference to the users.

It followed that wider consideration of the profiler's role was necessary. Rather than seeing the profiler simply as an impersonal source of advice, it became necessary to look at aspects of communication: particularly at what in respect of medical practitioners might be termed "bedside manner." So the project was effectively divided into two parts. What was under consideration in exploring the users' judgements of offender profiling advice was not so much the science—if science it be—but the service. That is the principal subject of this report on the first part of the project. The approach to the second part of the project will be discussed in a separate report, in due course.

Constructing a Register of Cases

At the commencement of this project no official register existed of British cases in which profiling had been used. It was necessary then to create one. In constructing a register, every potential source of useful information was pursued. Letters were sent to every Chief Constable, seeking endorsement, then to every Head of CID, seeking support and assistance. At the same time letters were sent to every known profiler, explaining the intended course of research and seeking not just co-operation but also observations on the nature of the work.

Scoping and Sampling

It was decided to set the broadest parameters for the project. As, well as having adopted a definition of offender profiling which included a wide range of 'expert' advice to investigators, contributors were encouraged to nominate any advice which they thought counted as profiling. All types of crime were included, and no time limits were imposed. All degrees of involvement were included, from a single telephone conversation seeking general advice to appointment of the profiler as a consultant member of the investigative management team. Some commentators, including Jackson (private communication) have serious doubts about accepting the notion that such casual advice could be considered profiling at all, but it is included here as it conforms to the project definition in that it is based on inferred characteristics of an unknown offender and offered on the basis of relevant professional expertise. The aim of setting such wide parameters was simply to try to discover every British example it was possible to trace.

Co-operation by Profilers

Almost all active profilers expressed their support for the project, and many offered information about additional cases. Several sent copies of written advice they had offered to investigations, while some offered advice on the construction of the project. A number of other profilers, no longer active in the field, also assisted in these regards. Only one profiler declined to co-operate, questioning the usefulness and validity of the project.

Devising a Questionnaire

Investigating officers in all the cases identified were consulted by means of a questionnaire. The logistics of interviewing a large number were deemed too great an obstacle within the context of the project, despite the potential advantages in terms of the quality of information on offer. It was also considered that the impersonal use of a questionnaire would minimise the risk of any bias being introduced to influence officers' responses.

A first draft questionnaire was formulated to reflect the themes which arose in January 1993 in a meeting of a user group panel nominated by ACPO sub-committee members. The group was unanimous that an open review process was necessary to measure operational profiling objectively and to determine the effectiveness of individual profilers. Subsequent drafts came about by incorporating advice from involved and interested parties. An explanatory letter was written to accompany the questionnaire, and it was tested in a pilot project.

Conduct of the Pilot Project

Twelve cases were chosen, to reflect a blend which offered something of every variable which could be anticipated. Questionnaires were sent to the officers in charge of investigating these cases with letters explaining the purpose of the exercise and asking not just for the questionnaire to be completed, but for other relevant documentation, in preparation for part two of the study.

The Result of the Pilot Project

1. The target group co-operated beyond expectations. It had been anticipated that there would be a generally good response, but the pilot project appeared to demonstrate real enthusiasm for the exercise.

2. A good volume of quality information was captured, which would be amenable to appropriate statistical analysis.

3. It appeared that the information captured would be sufficient for both parts of the study.

The lessons of the pilot project were incorporated into minor revisions of the questionnaire and the accompanying letter, and the full data collection exercise was commenced. Copies of the final versions of the questionnaire and accompanying letter may be obtained on application to the author. Also available is an expanded version of the questionnaire showing the aggregate responses to each question.

Limitations of the Methodology

An historical questionnaire based survey is limited. There may, for example, be difficulties of involuntary, or even deliberate, bias. Reference was made to Hawkins and Hastie (1990) in considering the potential for involuntary bias. Accepting the difficulty of detecting deliberate bias, no evidence of it was observed.

The Nature of Opinion

The responses gathered in the questionnaires are clearly respondents' opinions, and factors such as pride, prejudice, ignorance and misconception can all contribute to the formation of opinion. What was being sought, however, was not personal opinions of like or dislike, but professional judgements on the service rendered. Great care has been taken throughout the course of this project that it should not be contaminated by the opinions, personal or professional, of the researcher, nor by those of any advisor.

SOME CHARACTERISTICS OF THE DATA COLLECTED

Nominated Cases

Up to 1 December 1994, the cut off date for data collection for this report, 296 instances of profiling had been nominated. There was no way of telling how this number compared with the true number of cases in which offender profiling advice has been commissioned but, based on reactions from around the country in the course of gathering information, it seemed reasonable to suppose that the true number would not have exceeded 400.

Rate of Response

Table 20.1 shows how the target for data collection (the target data set) of 242 instances was broken down, and how the response rate of 81% was arrived at by comparing the maximum possible response with the actual response. 162 questionnaires (71.4% of the possible responses) were returned without any form of reminder, while of the 43 instances for which no response had been elicited by the closing date for this data set, 14 had been received by the time of reporting, too late for inclusion.

Table 20.1 also shows the reasons why 54 nominated instances of profiling were deleted from the survey. Most commonly this was because the advice turned out not to fit within the adopted definition of profiling. Instances of this included hypnosis to try to enhance the memory of witnesses, and traumatic stress counselling. In the 14 instances in which the officer expressed no recollection of receiving advice, none of the advice had been delivered in writing. It is inferred from this that verbal advice, especially over the telephone, is less likely to have any significant impact upon either the officer or the enquiry, and may be easily forgotten.

Police forces represented in the sample

Of 56 police forces in Britain, 48 were represented in the nominated case register. Four forces returned a double figure number of questionnaires: the Metropolitan Police (28), West Yorkshire (15), Thames Valley (10) and Hampshire (10). There seems to be no clear link between crime rates or force sizes and the tendency to take profiling advice.

Case Types

Table 20.2 shows a breakdown of the types of cases and the established outcomes of the investigations in the returned data set: at 61.4%, the set is dominated by murder investigations.

TABLE 20.1 INSTANCES OF PROFILING NOMINATED FOR THE PROJECT

Nominated	296
Deleted, not relevant*	54
Target data set	242
Too early for a response	15
Possible response	227
Actual response (returned data set)	184
= > Return. Rate	81
* Reasons for deletions	
Advice deemed outside definition	22
Profiler failed to deliver any advice	4
Case solved before advice delivered	4
Officer withdrew request for advice	2
Officer had no recollection of the advice	14
No trace—Officers all retired	7
Papers lost	1
Total	54

| TABLE 20.2 | RETURNED DATA SET: CASE TYPES—PROPORTION SOLVED AND UNSOLVED |

Case Type	Number of Cases	Solved Cases		Unsolved Cases	
Murder	113	59	(52.2%)	54	(47.8%)
Fire and arson	4	4	(100%)	0	(0%)
Rape	40	23	(57.5%)	17	(42.5%)
Other sexual	10	7	(70%)	3	(30%)
Threatening telephone calls	2	1	(50%)	1	(50%)
Extortion	12	8	(66.7%)	4	(33.3%)
Abduction	3	3	(100%)	0	(0%)

N = 184 (Solved 105, Unsolved 79)
n.b. the terms "solved" and "unsolved" are used in the police accounting sense of whether the case can be shown as cleared up or not.

Prevalence of Non-Sexual Murders as the Subject of Profiling

To learn more about the precise nature of police requirements, some effort was made to see what proportion of those murder cases were the result of a sexual attack on a female victim. Because it proved difficult to identify where sex was the motive—for example, multiple stab wounds could, but would not necessarily, indicate some kind of auto-erotic manic fixation—no precise figure can be reliably offered. It is apparent, however, that at least 60% were not sexually motivated, a finding which might concern those who advocate profiling on the basis of the development and analysis of a crime data set, since little relevant developed data exists. Only the work of Rick Holden, a former police officer who studied under David Canter, has been concerned with compiling a data set of murder cases. And Holden's system, while prompting some good reports from officers who have taken advice based upon it, was founded on details of only 62 cases—a small sample upon which to place such a large burden.

Temporal Analysis

Table 20.3 shows a temporal analysis of the target data set, showing a rapid increase in demand in recent years, from 21 nominated cases in 1990 to 45 in 1993, and 75 in 1994.

Table 20.4 shows a similar analysis of the returned data set, but also shows the pattern of demand for different types of adviice. A steady general rise in demand can be observed for all types of advice, and a particular rise in demand for an understanding of offender behaviour. A single instance can contain several different types of advice, for example offering a list of predicted offender characteristics and also advice on interviewing the alleged offender on arrest, so the numbers in Table 20.4 will add up to more than 184.

Direct Dealings With the Profiler

There were 53 respondents (28.8%) who did not themselves deal directly with the profiler. This may have been because the SIO delegated direct dealings to a junior officer but nevertheless retained responsibility for deciding whether and how to make use of the advice, or it may have been because the officer who did have direct dealings with the profiler had retired and so was unavailable to complete the questionnaire.

TABLE 20.3 TARGET DATA SET: TEMPORAL ANALYSIS

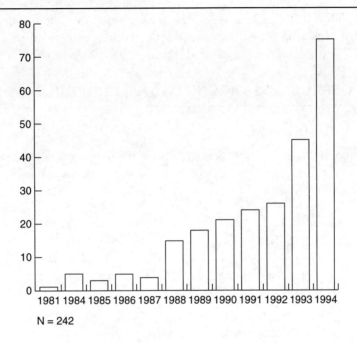

N = 242

Provision of Supplementary Information

In 168 instances brief facts of the case were supplied, in 122 instances a proper account of the profiler's advice was supplied—either a copy of written advice or a copy of notes of verbal advice—and in 6 further instances some brief details of the profiler's advice were supplied. This information will be used in part two of the study, and is mentioned here as an indication of the degree of co-operation elicited.

TABLE 20.4 RETURNED DATA SET: TYPE OF ADVICE SOUGHT EACH YEAR

Type of Advice	1981	1984	1985	1986	1987	1988	1989	1990	1991	1992	1993	1994	TOT.
Linking a series of crimes		1	2		1	5	5	3	6	5	7	12	47
Predictive profile	1	1	2	3	2	10	9	12	16	19	18	23	116
Interview strategy		1			1	5	5	4	4	7	12	12	51
News media strategy								2	1		1	2	6
Evaluation of confession		1		1			1	1	1		1	2	8
Evaluation of witness	1	1			1		2	3	2	2	5	8	25
Understanding of behavior	1	4	2	3	3	7	8	13	10	10	23	28	112
Analysis of text					1	1	1	1	1	2	2	2	11
Assessment of suspect							1	1				1	3

Profilers Identified

The profilers identified in this survey, and the number of cases in the returned data set on which they have advised, are shown in Table 20.5. It reveals 29 separate sources of profiling advice, 12 of which feature only once each. The set is dominated by the work of two individuals, who between them advised on 47.8% of the instances considered. Profilers will not be named in this report.

THE USE AND USEFULNESS OF OFFENDER PROFILING

Use of Offender Profiling

Aspects of use considered in this section are the nature of advice requested, officers' expectations of that advice, the stage of the enquiry when advice was requested, the cost of advice, and material requested by and supplied to the profilers.

TABLE 20.5 **PROFILES FEATURED IN THE RETURNED DATA SET**

Profiler	Nature of Expertise	Data	Count
1	Clinical Psychiatrist	no	1
2	Forensic Psychiatrist	no	6
3	Clinical Psychologist	no	1
4	Forensic Psychologist	no	1
5	Clinical Psychologist	no	10
6	Clinical Psychologist	no	1
7	Academic Psychologist	no	8
8	Forensic Psychologist	no	43
9	Academic Psychologist	yes	45
10	Police to System	yes	7
11	Police Officer	no	1
12	Police Scientist	yes	2
13	Law Enforcement Unit	no	6
14	Unknown	no	1
15	Forensic Psychologist	no	4
16	Forensic Psychiatrist	no	1
17	Unknown	no	1
18	Forensic Psychologist	no	8
19	Forensic Psychiatrist	no	3
20	Police Officer	yes	11
21	Police Officer	yes	6
22	Police Officer	yes	1
23	Academic Psychologist	no	1
24	Unknown	no	1
25	Academic Psychologist	no	5
26	Forensic Psychologist	no	2
27	Forensic Psychologist	no	2
28	Forensic Psychiatrist	no	1
29	Consultant Therapist	no	4

NB: 'DATA' refers to British police data collected and organised for the purposes of profiling

What Did the Officers Ask For?

There were six kinds of advice for which requests reached double figures (Table 20.4). The most common requests were for predictive profiles and for information which would further SIO's understanding of the offender's behaviour or future level of threat.

What Did the Officers Expect to Gain?

The responses to the question "what did the officers expect to gain?" suggest that many officers did not know what to expect from the advice they requested. Analysis shows that nine officers even expected to benefit from established research data when taking advice from profilers who had no access to such data.

At What Stage of the Enquiry Was the Advice Requested?

Table 20.6 shows the stage of the enquiry at which advice was requested. Respondents were left to judge within the context of their own investigation what amounted to "an early stage." It would not have been meaningful to ask for the number of days or weeks which had elapsed. In the older cases this would probably have been sheer guesswork, and even in the more recent cases a given number of weeks might reflect several different stages of an investigation. It will be seen from Table 20.6 that in recent years there seems to have been a growing trend to call in profilers earlier.

What Did the Advice Cost?

In only 28 instances was a fee charged for profiling advice, varying from a few hundred to a few thousand pounds. In only 19 instances were any expenses claimed. The rest came free and, for those concerned about hidden costs, a number of possible reasons suggest themselves. It might have been

TABLE 20.6 AT WHAT STAGE OF THE ENQUIRY WAS THE ADVICE REQUESTED:, YEAR BY YEAR

Year	At the Outset	At an Early Stage	After Direction Of Enquiry Established	After Initial Leads Exhausted	After Arrest	Not Specified
1981		1				
1984		1	2	1		1
1985				2		
1986			3			
1987			2	1		
1988	1	5	1	4	2	
1989	1	5	6	2		
1990		4	7	4	1	
1991	1	10	9	3		
1992	3	9	6	6		
1993	3	14	12	6		
1994	5	22	14	3	1	
TOTAL	14	71	62	32	4	1

N=184

out of a sense of public responsibility, it might have been because the prestige, even the thrill, of being involved seemed payment enough. It might also have been, particularly for those involved in the mental health field, because involvement in a police investigation afforded an insight into their own profession which they would otherwise rarely, if ever, have got to see—it will have informed their professional judgment and sharpened their skills. For those who deal in data analysis, every new case adds to their data set and, moreover, for all behavioural scientists, their involvement will have brought some prospect of access to an exceptionally rich field of co-operative research.

What Material Were Officers Asked to Supply?

A high degree of consistency was found between profilers in the material they required to conduct their analyses. The basic sources of material were facts of the case, Witness statements, scene photographs and maps. There is no incidence in this data of profilers asking for material and being refused it. On the contrary, it seems more information was supplied than was asked for.

Usefulness of Offender Profiling

As well as discussing different ways in which profiling advice has been perceived to be useful, this section will consider whether the profiling process has added value to information supplied and the perceived contribution of the advice to the solving of cases. Reported usefulness will be considered in relation to some variable features of the cases under consideration.

Coals to Newcastle?

Table 20.7 reveals what, at first sight, appears to be a series of contradictory findings. Only 14.1% of respondents reported that profiling advice had assisted them in solving a case (which amounts to only 21.7% of the solved cases in the sample). Only 16.3% of respondents reported that profiling advice had opened new lines of enquiry. Responses to the fundamental question of whether profiling advice told police anything they did not already know refute the common criticism that it does not, but hardly overwhelmingly, with those saying value was added outnumbering those saying it was not by 53.8% to 38.6% (7.6% chose not to answer this question). These findings—seemingly lukewarm endorsements at best—are then defied by the fact that 82.6% of respondents reported having found the advice they received operationally useful.

Aspects of Operational Usefulness

It is clear from this disparity that substantial benefits must have been perceived to lie elsewhere than in the identification of offenders and the solving of cases. Table 20.8 shows where.

TABLE 20.7   Effect of Advice

Did the advice...	Yes	No
assist in solving the case?	14.1%	78.3%
open new lines of enquiry?	16.3%	82.1%
add anything to information supplied?	53.8%	38.6%
prove operationally useful?	82.6%	17.4%

TABLE
20.8 **HOW WAS THE ADVICE OPERATIONALLY USEFUL?**

Aspects of usefulness:

Led to identification of offender	5	(2.7%)
Furthered understanding of case/ offender	112	(60.9%)
Expert opinion reassured own judgement	95	(51.6%)
Offered structure for interviewing	10	(5.4%)
Other	17	(2.3%)*
Not useful	32	(17.4%)

N = 184
*This percentage is not consistent with the others in this table as the 17 instances of unspecified usefulness were from a possible total of 736 not 184.

Overwhelmingly, the most commonly reported aspects of operational usefulness were furthering of the officer's understanding of the case or the offender (60.9%), and providing the reassurance of having expert opinion confirm the officer's own judgement (51.6'%). It is inferred from this that the most important contribution of profiling, as it has been practised in this country to date, is its part in developing the investigating officer's thinking on the case.

Analysis of reported usefulness in relation to the stage at which advice was requested revealed no significant differences. Neither did comparing responses of officers who dealt directly themselves with the profiler and those who did not reveal any meaningful differences in satisfaction with the advice. Some interesting differences were found, however, and these are featured in Table 20.9.

Respondents from police forces represented at ACPO level on the ACPO sub-committee were much more likely than those from other forces to report having found profiling advice not useful (26.7% against 12.9%). Analysis shows that this difference cannot be accounted for by any difference in the type of case, the kind of advice sought, or the profiler commissioned, and two possible explanations present themselves. These officers could have higher expectations as a result of having a better understanding. Or they could have been ordered to take profiling advice they did not really

TABLE
20.9 **THE EFFECT OF SOME VARIABLE CASE FEATURES ON JUDGEMENTS OF OPERATIONAL USEFULNESS**

Aspects of usefulness in relation to other variables	% reporting not useful	
'ACPO force' investigating	26.7%	(16/60)
Non 'ACPO force' investigating	12.9%	(12/124)
Solved investigations	15.2%	(16/105)
Unsolved investigations	20.3%	(16/79)
"Clinical" profilers	12.5%	(14/112)
"Statistical" profilers	25%	(18/72)

N = 184
For the purpose of these comparisons the following definitions apply:
"ACPO force" = one which is represented at ACPO level on the ACPO offender profiling sub committee "solved" and "unsolved" are used in the police accounting sense of whether or not the crime could be shown to be cleared up.
A "statistical profiler" is taken to be one who holds a British police data set, while a "clinical profiler" is taken to be one who does not.

want, and which they were predisposed to finding not useful. Indications encountered in. the process of collecting and discussing information point to the second interpretation as much the more likely. This impression is reinforced by a number of officers who did not return questionnaires having implied that they had been instructed to take the advice and had not used it.

Respondents whose cases were unsolved were much more likely than those whose cases were solved, using those terms in the police accounting sense of whether it can be shown as cleared up or not, to report having found profiling advice not useful (20.3% against 15.2%). Even allowing that some might be more disposed to generosity in reflecting on a solved case, this suggests a body of officers who see the usefulness of profiling advice only in terms of solving a case. They are, however, heavily outnumbered by those who could still find profiling useful in a case which was not solved. Examining the most commonly reported aspects of usefulness—further understanding and reassurance—reveals no marked difference in reported rates of usefulness between solved and unsolved cases. This would appear to bear out Douglas (1981) in his suggestion that "Even in cases where the suspect has not been identified psychological profiling was helpful. According to detectives, the procedure was often helpful in that it ensured that a complete investigation was conducted."

Respondents who had taken advice from profilers who keep a police data set (referred to here as "statistical" profilers) were much more likely than those who had taken advice from profilers without such data (referred to here as "clinical" profilers) to report having found profiling advice not useful (25% against 12.5%). The possibility was raised that this result was a reflection of the 'ACPO'/'non ACPO' finding but is rejected as officers in 'ACPO' forces took more advice from "clinical" profilers than "statistical" profilers. More information would be required to offer a full explanation, but it might be accounted for either by poor use of data or by instances of "statistical" profilers advising on types of cases for which they hold no data. One respondent reported unambiguously that he had asked for advice on a murder case on the understanding that the profiler held relevant data and discovered after receiving advice which he found unhelpful that the bulk of the data held related to rape. It is assumed for the purposes of this Study that those who keep police data use it to inform their inferential judgement.

Differences between Profilers

This research has revealed that the most significant variable affecting officers' perceptions of usefulness—also their satisfaction with the profiling service provided—is the identity of the profiler giving the advice. Discussion of the individual performances of profilers is beyond the scope of this paper, but the importance of the profiler's identity is demonstrated by the anonymised data contained in Table 20.10.

It can be seen from Table 20.10 that advice from profilers 'H' and 'E' was reported to have furthered understanding in respectively only half and fewer than half of the cases on which they advised. Advice from profilers 'B' and 'E' was reported not to have been useful at all in 40% and 33% of cases respectively, while advice from profilers 'A', 'C', and 'F' was reported to have been useful on every occasion.

Levels of Satisfaction

Table 20.11 shows that 126 respondents (68.5°/,) reported that they definitely would seek profiling advice again in similar circumstances, though only 91 (49.5%) reported that they would definitely use the same profiler in similar circumstances.

Table 20.12 shows how the identity of the profiler is of crucial importance in determining officers' satisfaction with the service they received. Indeed the research suggests that, at this stage

TABLE 20.10 WAS THE ADVICE OPERATIONALLY USEFUL?—ANONYMOUS COMPARISON OF PROFILERS' RATINGS

How Advice Was Useful	A	B	C	D	E	F	G	H	I	J	THE REST
Led to the identification of the offender		10%	12.5%	4.65%					9.1%		
Furthered understanding of case/offender	66.7%	60%	87.5%	60.5%	44.4%	57.1%	83.3%	50%	81.8%	50%	70.6%
Expert opinion reassured own judgment	83.3%	20%	62.5%	55.8%	33.3%	57.1%	50%	62.5%	54.5%	50%	67.6%
Other	3.3%	4%	2.5%	5.1%	1.3%	11.4%		5%	1.8%		1.2%
No, advice was not useful		40.%		11.6%	33.3%		16.7%	25%	18.2%	16.7%	5.9%

NB% figures shown are the proportion of the total number of cases on which each profiler advised: the columns total more than 100% as many officers found advice useful in more than one way.

Profilers A to J are those in respect of whom six or more questionnaires have been completed. The range runs from 6 questionnaires to 45.

*1: Pearson Chi Square Value = 17.14, Degrees Freedom = 10, P = 0.07

*2: Pearson Chi Square Value = 20.4, Degrees Freedom = 10, P = 0.03

of the development of profiling in Britain, approaches to profiling are so idiosyncratic as to be indivisible from the identity of the profiler.

It can be seen from Table 20.12 that three profilers, identified here as 'A', 'C', and 'F' were rated most highly, while three others, 'B', 'E' and 'G' were rated least highly.

Respondents expressing dissatisfaction were asked to give reasons, and 38 out of the 45 who said they would not, or would probably not, use the same profiler again, did so. These reasons help to put the rates of dissatisfaction into perspective, and it is very clear from them that most of the officers' verdicts were not simple expressions of like or dislike, but were considered professional criticisms of the service rendered. One profiler was felt by several officers to be carrying too heavy a workload to be able to concentrate on their case, while another was felt to be using police to further his own knowledge rather than theirs.

A few respondents reported that they would not use particular profilers again because their advice was wrong, but in a preliminary content analysis exercise it was found that, while sometimes this advice

TABLE 20.11 WOULD YOU SEEK PROFILING ADVICE/USE THE SAME PROFILER AGAIN?

	Seek Profiling Advice Again?		Use the Same Profiler Again?	
Yes definitely	126	(68.5%)	91	(49.5%)
Yes probably	44	(23.9%)	48	(26.1%)
Probably not	10	(5.4%)	32	(17.4%)
No	4	(2.2%)	13	(7.1%)

TABLE 20.12											
WOULD YOU USE THE SAME PROFILER AGAIN?—ANONYMOUS COMPARISON OF PROFILERS' RATINGS											
Use Same Profiler Again?	A	B	C	D	E	F	G	H	I	J	THE REST
Yes, definitely	83.3%	55.6%	100%	60.5%	17.8%	71.4%	50%	50%	72.7%	66.7%	41.2%
Yes, probably	16.7%			20.9%	46.7%	28.6%		37.5%	9.1%	16.7%	29.4%
Probably not		22.2%		16.3%	28.8%		16.7%		18.2%	16.7%	17.6%
No		22.2%		2.3%	6.4%		33.3%	12.5%		11.8%	

Profilers A to J are those in respect of whom six or more questionnaires have been completed. The range runs from 6 questionnaires to 45.
*The 100% record for profiler 'C' is based on a relatively small number of questionnaires and should therefore be treated with caution.
Pearson Chi Square Value = 57.07, Degrees Freedom = 30, P = 0.002

had been wrong, in one instance the respondent had misread the advice, which had later been proven correct. There appears to be a lesson here about clarity of presentation, and also about the need for officers to ensure that they have carefully studied and understood the advice they have been offered. Officers' interpretation of advice will be considered in more detail in part two of this project.

Profiling as an Issue in Court

Of the 90 instances of profiling in cases which have been to court, there were only six reports that profiling had been at issue in the proceedings. In 20 instances it was reported that the advice had been disclosed to the defence, and in 20 others it was reported that it had been revealed to the Grown Prosecution Service. There were only two reports of the profiler being required to give evidence. While there was great concern in police circles at the outset of this project about potential difficulties over disclosing profiling advice prior to trial, these responses suggest that in reality those fears have as yet come to nothing:

In the course of conducting the project no evidence was found to suggest that disclosure of profiling advice had had an adverse effect on the prosecution of any case. Even widely reported criticism both of police and of the profiler concerned in the case of Colin Stagg, who was tried and acquitted in October 1994 of the murder of Rachel Nickell, tended to obscure the point that that case turned on substantially different issues. It was the adjudged unfairness of aspects of an undercover police operation which led to the dismissal of the prosecution case, before those aspects which were more directly concerned with offender profiling even came to be argued. The judge's ruling in that case nevertheless does encompass some discussion of profiling and, while it is made abundantly clear that there are great and potentially insurmountable difficulties in introducing profiling as evidence in British courts, nothing is said to undermine its use as a basis for investigative decision making (Ognall, 1994).

RESULTS AND CONCLUSIONS

Conclusions based on the results of analysis of the questionnaire data presented here need to be carefully drawn; given the nature of historical questionnaire based surveys, as discussed in section 3 of this report. They do, however, offer insights into police attitudes to offender profiling that have not previously been reported.

The following summarises the findings:

1. Police expectations of offender profiling are not always clear.

2. The great majority of officers who have taken profiling advice report having found it beneficial.

3. What officers report finding most useful is information which furthers their understanding of a case or an offender, or which reassures them by confirming their own judgements.

4. The reported benefits of profiling do not to any significant degree include the identification of the offender.

5. It appears that few officers have acted directly on the advice they have received.

6. There are signs that there is little point in instructing a reluctant officer to take profiling advice.

7. Some officers seem to have commissioned profiling advice without the intention of actually using it.

8. Casual, verbal advice appears to make little impact and to be easily forgotten.

9. It appears that not all profilers are equally well regarded.

10. It appears that, at this stage of the development of profiling in Britain, approaches to profiling are so idiosyncratic as to be indivisible from the identity of the profiler.

11. It appears that advice from "statistical" profilers (those who keep a police data set) was less well appreciated by investigators than advice from "clinical" profilers (those without such data).

12. The disclosure of profiling advice, whether or not it is borne out in its predictions, has not to date jeopardised a prosecution case.

This project has also created:

• A procedure to evaluate operational profiling in a manner which promises to be useful to SIOs. It has so far proved acceptable to the Home Office and to ACPO, and to most of the profilers themselves. Reactions to this report, of course, will be the clearest guide to acceptability.

• A register of British cases in which offender profiling advice has been commissioned, and a bank of detailed information concerning its use in approaching 200 of those cases.

• A system to provide objective advice on operational profiling to SIOs.

• A system to provide objective and constructive feedback to profilers.

Interpreting the Findings

The findings of this survey reflect some degree of confusion amongst police users of profiling advice. There are clear indications that many officers who really want to use profiling are unsure of what to expect from it, beyond a vague faith that they will be dealing with some kind of expert. There are equally clear signs that some of the officers who have commissioned profiling advice did not really intend to use it.

It is clear, however, that profiling advice has made little impact on the courts. Offender profiling, after all, is not evidence one way or the other. As set out in the ACPO policy at appendix 1, it is about informing investigators, to help them in decisions concerned with the management of investigative options and resources in pursuit of admissible evidence. A profile which fits the accused is no more evidence of guilt than one which does not is evidence of innocence: neither proposition is realistic.

If operational profiling is to add anything to detective expertise then it seems reasonable to suppose that it will do so because it helps to make an investigation more efficient or more effective, or else because it will reassure the officer that no obvious avenue of enquiry has been neglected. There are clear signs that it does so, with 82.6% of respondents reporting that they found the advice they received useful in one way or another. But the detectives in this survey do not appear to perceive any particular benefit from the inference of offender characteristics. Instead, they perceive the benefits of operational profiling as being to do with the introduction of new thoughts, arising from an intelligent second opinion, and the development of investigative philosophy—formulating and testing theories about the case and the offender—through the process of consultation and debate with the profiler.

This backs up Simon Wessely's observation that "the simple act of obtaining advice from a well informed professional may help police take a fresh look at information they already have" (Wessely, 1993). It Supports Janet Jackson's conclusion that "By taking an independent stance, not bogged down with the inconsequential details that a detective actively working on a case has to contend with, the professional profiler can offer directions and advice that can result in the team achieving success in apprehending the culprit" (Jackson et al, 1993a). And it bears out Inspector Finney of the New York Police, (Brussel, 1968): "Sometimes the difference between failure and success is a new thought."

It can be said then, that operational profiling works as a service, albeit one which is more likely to assist indirectly than directly in the solving of a case. But the premise underlying offender profiling is that offender characteristics can be inferred from offence characteristics. If, therefore, profiling is to be judged valid on its own terms then its success ought to be based upon telling officers something of the type of person who has committed the offence under consideration, so that the conduct of the investigation—and its outcome—might be influenced by advice based on those inferences. The respondents in this survey perceive that profiling does not succeed on those terms. This may be because:

a. it is unrealistic for profilers to accurately predict offender characteristics;

b. though it is realistic for profilers to accurately predict offender characteristics, they most often fail to do so;

c. officers lack the conviction to act upon profilers' predictions;

d. although officers do act upon profilers' predictions, they fail to recognise or to acknowledge that they have done so.

The second part of this project will go some way to clarifying this important issue. It is concerned with content analysis of operational profiling advice collected from amongst the officers involved in this survey and, where possible, will compare profilers' predictions with the outcomes of investigations. This will give an indication of how reliable such predictions are, and therefore how safely they can be acted upon. It might also help to distinguish more clearly between police satisfaction with a profiler's contribution and the real potential value of it: in other words, between the service and the science.

RECOMMENDATIONS

The recommendations made here are based on the outcome of part one of this project, and also on some very clear impressions gained in the conduct of it.

Further action should be taken to educate police on the potential value and limitations of operational profiling so there is a clearer understanding of what can be expected from it, what kind of expertise is must appropriate for different situations, and in what circumstances operational profiling advice should and should not be commissioned. Offender profiling should be more clearly defined in detective training, and the ACPO policy on offender profiling should be the key to that training.

Police officers should not commission operational profiling advice unless they actually want to consider using it.

- Police officers commissioning operational profiling advice should make use of the register of profiled cases to communicate with other officers who have used the same profiler, or who have used profiling in similar circumstances, to help them to make best use of the advice they receive.

- Police officers commissioning operational profiling advice should agree in advance what it might cost and when and how it is to be delivered.

- Police officers commissioning operational profiling advice should consider offering a reasonable fee for it, so they can be in a position to state their own requirements.

- Police officers commissioning operational profiling advice should ask for predictions, recommendations and significant observations to be expressed clearly in writing.

- Police officers should take steps to ensure that they understand the meaning of operational profiling advice they have received. Where any doubt exists as to the exact meaning of any, piece of advice they should ask the profiler to clarify it.

- Where interrogation strategies are offered, detectives should treat them with caution as they are not always founded on a proper understanding of the legal and ethical framework within which police interviews with suspects must be conducted.

- Police officers who commission offender profiling advice should continue to receive questionnaires for the information of the police service, through the responsible ACPO committee. By collecting information as soon as it is available the exercise would not only be liable to reap more accurate information, but by taking on some of the characteristics of a prospective (contemporaneous) study, would eliminate the problems associated with hindsight bias.

- When sufficient numbers of questionnaires have been collected, analysis should be conducted to assess the levels of satisfaction with active profilers, and the results of this analysis should be used to inform officers who would commission operational profiling advice for live investigations.

- A comprehensive good practice guide for police officers seeking and using operational profiling advice should be produced on the completion of part two of this project.

- Profilers should be given clear guidance on police requirements, and a guide for responsible operational profiling should be produced on the completion of part two of this project.

Gary Copson, "Coals to Newcastle: Police Use of Offender Profiling," Home Office Police Research Group, 50 Queen Anne's Gate, London SW1149AT, 1995.

STATISTICAL AND GEOGRAPHICAL PROFILING AND LAW ENFORCEMENT DATA BASES

Investigators and officers often find themselves facing seemingly overwhelming cases, with limited resources, and pressures of time. It is the duty and responsibility of every investigator to stay current with the research in the field. Quantitative research and studies provide a knowledge base that can significantly improve investigations and case management. Empirical research often has meaningful information for law enforcement and offers opportunities to improve strategies for dealing with crimes.

The articles in *Section VII: Statistical and Geographical Profiling and Law Enforcement Data Bases* have serious implications for the investigations of violent crimes. They exemplify the various strategies and the knowledge base required of law enforcement to effectively and efficiently develop strategies for conducting investigations. The following articles are excellent examples of the types of statistical analyses at the forefront of profiling research. They illustrate the important information that can be gained through empirical study.

Keppel and Weis (1993) illustrate the need for effective systems to manage and coordinate information *in Improving the Investigation of Violent Crime: The Homicide Investigation Tracking System (HITS).* Today's complex society with its various law enforcement needs relies on identifying, accessing, and sharing information. Recognizing this fact, the authors research the effectiveness of computerized programs to organize and analyze relevant information to successfully link and solve cases. Using HITS as an example, the authors show the increasing need for access to a coordinated and organized flow of information for the efficient and effective investigation of violent crimes.

HITS is a computerized murder and sexual assault program developed in Washington State that collects and analyze information about serious criminal offenses. Officers submit information to HITS on murder, attempted murders, missing persons, sexual assaults, and unidentified persons believed to be murder victims. This information can be accessed by investigators to develop leads and solve cases. Keppel and Weis, detail how HITS can be used, the resources it provides to investigators, and the various benefits of HITS. The underlying theme of the article emphasizes the power of computerized programs, such as HITS, as a resource and tool in criminal investigations.

The final article, *Crime Scene and Distance Correlates of Serial Rape* delves into the research on serial rapists and their patterns of offending. This research focuses on distance correlates between incident location and victim choice, home location of the offender, demographics of the offender, prior criminal history, and crime scene behaviors. The authors address the decision-making process of the serial rapists as it relates to victim choice and location choices. Evidence suggests the serial rapist's first rape incident site is strongly correlated to his home location. Basically, serial rapists begin with what is familiar to them and in their own comfort zone. Analysis of serial rape offenses reveals that earlier offenses are clustered close to the offender's home or workplace, spiraling outward over time.

This research evolved out of criminal investigative analysis, theories of environmental criminology, ethnographic geography, journey to crime literature, and geographic profiling. The study utilized a non random sample of 565 rape offenses and sought to correlate crime scene behavior with decisions about crime site selection. Analysis of the offenses show that serial rapists travel on average 3.41 miles to commit the rape and more significantly, roughly half of the serial rapists in the study committed at least one rape within .5 mile of their homes. The research suggests correlations between the offenders' demographics and the distance traveled to commit the offense. In addition, the authors found that ritualistic behavior and the use of restraints corresponded to greater distances traveled by the offender. The various distance correlates detailed by the authors have serious implications for how investigators should respond and investigate serial rape cases.

IMPROVING THE INVESTIGATION OF VIOLENT CRIME: THE HOMICIDE INVESTIGATION AND TRACKING SYSTEM

ROBERT D. KEPPEL, Ph.D., AND JOSEPH G. WEIS, Ph.D

I n conducting investigations, detectives need methods and tools that will help them do their jobs as effectively and efficiently as possible. Ready access to information about the crimes being investigated is one of their needs. Armed with such information, detectives will be better able to develop good leads and in turn to solve the cases. The Homicide Investigation and Tracking System (HITS), a program that began in Washington State, is helping investigators work better by allowing them access via computer to a wide range of information about serious crimes and to resources that can help solve them.

HITS is a computerized murder and sexual assault investigation program that collects and analyzes information pertaining to specific serious criminal offenses. The system relies on law enforcement agencies in Washington State to voluntarily submit information to HITS investigators on murders, attempted murders, missing persons cases in which foul play is suspected, unidentified persons believed to be murder victims, and predatory sex offenses.[1] The information is stored in the seven data files that compose the HITS system.

HITS provides three major services to law enforcement agencies. First, it supplies information related to a murder or predatory sexual assault case, including the following:

- Incidents with similar characteristics involving murder, attempted murder, suspected murder, or predatory sexual assault and persons missing as a result of suspected foul play.

- Evidence, victimology, offender characteristics, offender's method of operation, associates, geographic location of the case, weapons, and vehicles.

- Identification of known murderers and sex offenders living in a particular community.

- Second, HITS permits analysis of murder cases to identify:

- Factors that may help solve a particular murder case.

- Possible links between a single victim, offender, or case and other incidents of violence.

---

[1] Predatory sex offenses are those in which the victim is a stranger to the assailant.

For years police investigators working in different jurisdictions on similar cases have worked independently of one another. They did not have access to the information available elsewhere that could speed and enhance investigations in their own jurisdiction. For example, although investigators knew that similar crimes were being committed in jurisdictions across the country, they sometimes had difficulty finding out what types of victims had been singled out, what methods of operation had been repeatedly used, or which suspects were under investigation.

Innovations such as Washington State's Homicide Investigation and Tracking System (HITS) have changed all that. HITS compiles all that is known in its participating jurisdictions about serious crimes—rape, murder, and gang-related crime—into integrated data bases that are rapidly expanding beyond Washington State to include California, Oregon, and Canada. By filling out a simple form that takes less than 30 minutes, investigators save countless hours on the phone or on their feet searching for information that the HITS system locates for

them. This Research in Brief highlights how HITS works and some of its benefits.

The National Institute of Justice (NIJ), the research arm of the Department of Justice, played a key role in developing this project. NIJ provided seed money that enabled a model system to be designed and implemented using state-of-the-art computer technology. After the research phase was completed in 1986, the Washington State Legislature was so impressed by HITS' record of achievement that it has continued to fund both the project and its expansion.

Integrating police investigations with computer technology is one of the most exciting advancements in law enforcement today. The opportunity to coordinate field investigations among officers working in local, State, and Federal jurisdictions promises to increase public safety and make the criminal justice system more effective.

Michael J. Russell
Acting Director
National Institute of Justice

- Verification of statements provided by informants, offenders, or both, in which the information relating to an alleged murder is incomplete or questionable.

Third, HITS provides investigators with the following resources:

- Names of experts who can assist with a murder or sexual assault investigation.

- Advice and technical assistance on the various steps to be followed in a murder or sexual assault investigation.

Prior to HITS' use in Washington State, the only way to obtain this type of crime information was through time-consuming, labor-intensive personal visits, interviews, telephone calls, teletypes, and letters.

Most cases listed in HITS occurred from 1981 through 1986, and data on these cases were compiled under a 1987 National Institute of Justice (NIJ) grant. Subsequently, HITS has been funded through the Washington State attorney general's office, and some agencies have begun adding murder and rape incidents reported prior to 1981 to the system.

SETTING UP THE SYSTEM

As part of the NIJ project, researchers first wanted to determine the number of murders that occurred in Washington State from 1981 to 1986. Each of the following agencies were contacted for information:

- Police and sheriffs' departments covering 273 jurisdictions.

- Medical examiners' and coroners' offices in 39 counties.

- Prosecuting attorneys' offices in 39 counties.

- Washington State Department of Vital Statistics.

- Uniform Crime Report unit of the Washington Association of Sheriffs and Police Chiefs.

To date, every police and sheriff's department in Washington State has cooperated in developing the HITS system.

Initially, more than 1,300 murder files were located in police agencies across the State. Virtually every department had investigated one or more murders in the 1981–1986 period. After all known cases had been identified by name, case number, and investigating jurisdiction, each police and sheriff's department was asked to voluntarily complete the HITS data collection instrument, a 54-page form containing 467 fields of information, for each murder file. In addition to salient characteristics about the murder event, victim(s), and offender(s), the HITS form also asked questions about the quality of the murder investigation and its solvability. Investigators spent an average of 2.3 hours completing each form.

After 1986, a shorter version of the HITS form, containing 250 fields of information, was developed. This form asks much of the same information as the original form, but omits questions related to the NIJ research project. The shorter form takes approximately 30 minutes to complete.

The short version of the HITS form has been evaluated by homicide investigators in all the larger police and sheriffs' departments in Washington State as well as by investigators in Arizona, California, Florida, Georgia, Iowa, New York, Oregon, and Texas. They concluded that it is the most comprehensive application of homicide information for investigative purposes ever developed.

USING THE HITS PROGRAM

The HITS program uses a relational-based data management system to manage the data files.[2] The most important feature of HITS for murder and rape investigations is its interactive search capability.[3] By choosing among 250 fields of information, HITS analysts can ask for single-or multiple-field information in any order or combination.

For example, if a detective were investigating the rape and murder of a white female prostitute, he or she could use HITS to discover whether similar crimes had been committed in the previous 2 years. Using information provided by the detective, a HITS analyst could query the data base for any combination of data: victim's gender, race, or lifestyle; date and cause of death; location of the body; presence or absence of clothing; concealment of the body; or date of body discovery. In this way, the analyst could identify other cases with common elements and supply the detective with the names of victims murdered in

---

[2] This system allows information in any file to be associated with related information in any other file.

[3] A system with this capability allows the user to "talk" to the computer and receive an immediate response.

21.2   *HITS Staff*

Located in Seattle in the State attorney general's criminal division, the HITS unit is staffed by the following:

- One manager.
- Five investigators/analysts.
- One violent crime analyst.
- Two computer programmers.
- One secretary.
- One data entry operator.

The manager coordinates all HITS activities, including training, data collection, and analyses for police investigators statewide. The unit is supervised by the chief investigator of the attorney general's criminal division, who also conceptualized the HITS project. The chief investigator also analyzes major cases and consults with local law enforcement agencies.

---

similar ways, date of body discovery, investigating agencies, case numbers, and primary investigators' names and telephone numbers. This type of search would take only a few minutes to perform.

DATA ORGANIZATION

The HITS program contains information from at least six sources and is stored in seven different data files: murder, sexual assault, preliminary information, Department of Corrections, gang-related crimes, Violent Criminal Apprehension Program (VICAP), and timeline. Because of the diversity of sources, three master data files were constructed to aggregate information about persons, addresses, and vehicles so that any one query could search all seven data bases at the same time. The fields available for analysis range from 20 to more than 250.

HITS Murder File

The data base created with the NIJ grant is the HITS murder file, which contains information about victims, offenders, and methods of operation for more than 4,000 murder investigations (table 21.1). When a murder is committed, law enforcement officers complete the HITS murder form, which is then keyed into the murder file.

TABLE 21.1   RECORDS IN THE HITS MURDER AND SEXUAL ASSAULT FILES (JANUARY 1981 THROUGH JANUARY 1993)

Type	Number of Records in Murder File	Number of Records in Sexual Assault File
Victims	4,086	2,692
Incidents	3,733	2,345
Offenders	4,312	2,563

Source: Homicide Investigation and Tracking System, 1993

TABLE 21.2 ADDITIONAL HITS FILES AND RECORDS USED FOR ANALYSIS (JANUARY 1989 THROUGH JANUARY 1993)	
Files	**Number of Records**
Green River murders task force (in murder file)	57,538
Department of Corrections	189,960
Gang-related crimes	76,150

Source: Homicide Investigation and Tracking System, 1993

The murder file also includes information on 49 cases from the Green River Task Force (table 21.2). A series of murders involving prostitutes in the Seattle/Tacoma area, the Green River murders began in July 1982 and ended in March 1984. To date the Green River murder count is 41 dead and 8 missing.

The following three cases demonstrate how HITS has helped Washington's law enforcement agencies in their murder investigations. For these and other cases discussed in this report, names, locations, and related facts have been withheld in cases where investigations are ongoing.

Random railroad killings

A Spokane detective filed a HITS form for the murder of a male vagrant found stabbed to death in a railroad yard. When analysts checked the HITS system, a similar case involving a male vagrant in Cowlitz County was identified. The HITS investigation revealed that a person previously considered a possible witness in the Spokane case was listed as a suspect in the Cowlitz County case. When HITS information was communicated to other law enforcement agencies, investigators from Thurston County reported a third case involving a male vagrant to Hits. The witness is now listed as a suspect in a Midwestern State for a similar murder.

Double murder

When a Federal undercover agent overheard someone bragging about killing two people in Washington State and being enroute to the Western United States to kill someone else, the agent requested information on double murders in Washington State. The agent was referred to a law enforcement agency in Washington that had cases similar to those mentioned by the potential suspect. The suspect is currently under investigation.

Victim location

A police informant from the Eastern United States told a police detective in Western Washington that an acquaintance had murdered two people in the same area—one victim from the detective's own jurisdiction and another from an unknown location. After spending 4 days contacting numerous police agencies trying unsuccessfully to locate the second victim and coordinate investigations, the detective called HITS and was given the information needed within seconds.

HITS sexual assault file

The HITS sexual assault data file contains information about victims, offenders, and methods of operation for more than 2,000 rape investigations (table 21.1). The HITS sexual assault file form asks investigators to provide data on serial rapists, stranger rapists, and predatory sex offenders.

Two cases show how HITS data have helped detectives solve sexual assault investigations.

TABLE
21.3   RECORDS IN THE HITS PRELIMINARY INFORMATION FILE (JANUARY 1986 THROUGH JANUARY 1993)

Incident Classification	Number
Murder	2,150
Sex offense	7,785
Robbery	2,052
Arson	220
Total	**12,207**

Source: Homicide Investigation and Tracking System, 1993

Tracking known sexual offenders

After an extremely brutal rape and attempted murder, the investigating detective requested HITS information about offenders with a particular physical description and method of operation. HITS staff provided the detective with a list of known sexual offenders who had been released from prison during the past 5 years and the areas to which they had been released. The detective was also provided photographs of suspects, one of whom was immediately identified by the victim as her assailant.

Victim identification

A western Washington police agency was trying to identify a female victim who had been raped and murdered at an unknown location east of the Cascade Mountains about 5 years earlier. The HITS unit provided the name of the victim and the investigating officer to the inquiring agency.

Hits preliminary information file

The preliminary information file stores information about crime classification, chronology, victims, offenders, methods of operation, weapons, vehicles, geographic locations, and other pertinent information (table 21.3). The file also contains more than 4,600 sex-offender registrations. Information for the file is gathered from the following sources:

- Teletypes.
- Newspapers.
- Crime bulletins.
- Sex-offender registration files.
- Requests for information from investigators.

Violent crime information transmitted via teletype through the Washington State Patrol's access system is automatically entered into HITS' preliminary information file. No other State system stores this type of data for retrieval and use in investigations. In addition, every week a clipping service provides newspaper articles containing information about murders and rapes that have occurred in Washington State. This information is also entered into the file. The teletype and newspaper data are particularly valuable because they are usually the first information given to HITS about the occurrence of a violent crime.

Every inquiry from a police investigator, whether it receives a response or not, is stored in the preliminary information file. This allows investigators to keep their inquiries active in the event that information becomes available in the future. For example, if an investigator asks whether an adult male named Joe Smith has been found murdered, a negative answer might be given, but the inquiry is stored in the file. Later, if another investigator reports Joe Smith as a murder victim, the two items are matched and the appropriate authorities informed of their mutual interest in the case.

The preliminary information file stores data about murder and sexual assault cases only until completed HITS reports have been submitted by the investigating agency. The following case illustrates how this file has been used in the field.

Suspect analysis

During an investigation of a rape, the victim described the suspect's appearance and vehicle, which matched those of someone the investigating officer had stopped only minutes before being detailed to the rape case. The officer notified other agencies by teletype to be on the lookout for the suspect. When the teletyped information was entered into the HITS preliminary information file, another teletype was found describing a similar rape that had occurred in another jurisdiction several months earlier. Both the physical description and the method of operation matched, and the prior address of the suspect was located in the same city as the agency that had issued the earlier teletype. HITS staff notified both police agencies that they both had cases involving a similar method of operation and known offender.

Department of Corrections file

The more than 189,000 records stored in the Department of Corrections data file (table 21.2) offer immediate access to the identification of current and former inmates who have been convicted of murder or sexual assault. Updated bimonthly, the file can be used to check the physical description of a convicted felon against the description of an unknown suspect in investigations involving sexual assault. The following case illustrates how the file has been used.

Suspect and method of operation

When HITS received a teletype summarizing a second-degree rape incident, physical description of the suspect, and method of operation, HITS staff identified a convicted rapist with a comparable physical description and method of operation who had been released from prison in the previous 3 months. The subject was living only a few blocks from the location of the rape. HITS released all of the information to the investigating detective.

Gang-related crime file

A separate data file for gang-related crimes and driveby shootings contains more than 76,000 records from the Los Angeles County sheriff's department and police agencies within Washington State (table 21.2). The data from Los Angeles were received after investigators discovered that numerous gang members had migrated from California and had committed crimes in Washington. The file is routinely used to search for aliases or nicknames and physical descriptions of potential offenders.

VICAP file

Prior to implementation of the HITS system, the State attorney general's office helped local police agencies participate in VICAP, a national serial murder tracking program run by the Federal Bureau of Investigation (FBI). Approximately 350 of the State's murder cases, entered into the VICAP system before HITS was created, have subsequently been merged into the HITS murder file. Now, when data from a HITS form are entered into the HITS system, the computer automatically reformats the information and creates a report to be submitted to VICAP.

Timeline file

Another data file used for analysis is a timeline file that records chronological activities of known murderers. The file contains information about times and places of offenders' movements. As of January 1993, the file had information on 9,083 locations for 73 known murderers.

Data for the file are gleaned from employment records, arrest records, banking records, traffic tickets, and any other record collected during a murder investigation that reveals the location of a possible offender. These times and places can be cross-checked against the dates and locations of murders. The file is another way to determine if a known murderer could have been the perpetrator in other murders. The following two cases illustrate how detectives have made use of the timeline file.

Travel pattern analysis

When an alleged serial killer from Minnesota was arrested in Texas, his travel pattern was examined, and investigators determined that he had spent a considerable amount of time in Washington State. Minnesota authorities contacted the HITS unit, and an analysis was conducted by HITS staff. A murder case involving a woman who had been beaten, strangled, and raped was located in the files. Further investigation revealed that the suspect had been released from a jail in Western Washington the day before the murder and had hitchhiked along the same thoroughfare where the body was discovered. The case is under continuing investigation.

Methods of operation

A Kansas detective contacted the HITS unit when he discovered that an identified multiple murderer from Kansas was known to have visited Washington State. The detective described in detail what the killer did to his victims and how he disposed of their bodies. When a similar case was found in the files. HITS analysts contacted the police agency that had reported the case. Currently the suspect is under investigation.

COST OF HITS

Since 1986, after initial NIJ support, ongoing operational costs have been borne by the Washington State Legislature, which in 1990 awarded $1.2 million for the 11-member HITS staff in the attorney general's office to operate the program for 2 years.

The only cost to local agencies has been the 30 minutes it takes an investigator to fill out the HITS form. This is negligible compared to the time an investigator would spend trying to obtain information that HITS can supply in a matter of minutes.

TABLE 21.4	TYPES OF REQUESTS FOR ASSISTANCE (JANUARY 1989 THROUGH JANUARY 1993)		
Types of Requests		Number of Requests	Information Provided
Name searches		169	87
Investigation analysis to develop leads		51	48
Inquiries concerning details of individual case		67	52
Checks of offenders' methods of operation and other characteristics against cases in data base		159	98
Inquiries about best way to pursue particular leads		24	20
Responses to HITS confidential bulletins		142	81
Requests for statistical information *		13	13
Requests for names of experts or other resources to help with investigations		95	73
Requests for HITS bulletins		67	60
Requests for verification of informant information		20	11
Subtotal		**807**	**543**
Connections made as a result of independent HITS analysis of incoming cases			388
Total connections or "HITS"			**881**

*Includes specific interests such as numbers of child victims or prostitutes in the data base.

Source: Homicide Investigation and Tracking System, 1993

Time is also saved by the automatic integration of HITS with VICAP. Investigators are not required to complete two questionnaires because the HITS computer automatically generates VICAP data from the HITS form. HITS staff also routinely verify leads, telephone contacts, and other information that VICAP requires concerning a murder.

SIGNS OF SUCCESS

As of January 1993, HITS staff had received more than 800 requests for investigative assistance in violent crime cases. Most of these requests had been received since 1988, when the Washington State attorney general announced that the HITS system contained investigative information on more than 1,600 murder cases. The rate of response to requests has been extremely high: assistance has been provided in more than 850 murder and rape investigations (table 21.4).

A 1990 survey of 495 police chiefs, sheriffs, and homicide investigators indicated that 90 percent of respondents had heard of HITS and that 86 percent of respondents who had used the system found it ranged from "somewhat useful" to "extremely useful" in their investigations.

National recognition

HITS is known as a computerized information system that is used in the field as an effective investigative tool. Recently HITS won two national awards for outstanding achievement—one from the Council of State Governments and another from the National Association of State Information Resource Executives.

EXPANSION BEYOND WASHINGTON

Offenders recognize no State boundaries. With that in mind, in October 1991 Kenneth Eikenberry, then Washington State attorney general, and Reginald Madsen, superintendent of the Oregon State Police, signed an agreement to allow Oregon access to the HITS system. Oregon State investigators can now electronically transfer information about violent crimes committed in their jurisdictions into the HITS computer. As of January 1993, data from more than 700 murders committed in Oregon in the past 6 years have been entered into the HITS program. As a result, police and sheriffs' investigators have violent crime information from two States readily accessible for use in their own investigations. In addition, law enforcement officer from California, Idaho, Kansas, and Canada have submitted information about selected violent crimes to HITS for analysis.

BENEFITS OF HITS

Small law enforcement agencies that do not encounter murder cases frequently or that have investigators inexperienced in specialized murder investigation techniques have found the HITS program to be especially beneficial. HITS analysts can offer guidance, based upon years of experience, on how to organize a murder investigation and provide access to information not available in any one department's files. Other benefits include the following.

HITS' prioritization of solvability factors helps investigators identify avenues of proper and logical followup

Through HITS, analysts have discovered that different types of murder cases reflect critical solvability factors—such as the likelihood that a friend, lover, or spouse committed the crime—unique to each category of murder. Such information is particularly useful to a detective in a small jurisdiction where there are few murder cases to be investigated.

HITS' methods improve the criminal justice training curriculum for law enforcement investigators

For example, the Washington State Criminal Justice Training Commission has redesigned its basic homicide investigators training curriculum to reflect changes initiated because of HITS.

HITS complements Federal research and programs against violent crime

In addition to the automatic link between HITS and VICAP, the data collected on homicides in Washington State are useful for the FBI's Uniform Crime Reporting Program. But because the information collected by HITS is more comprehensive and richer in detail, it is even more valuable in answering questions from legislators, elected officials, and government staff about the characteristics of victims, offenders, and murder incidents.

The information HITS provides enables other government agencies to better understand the complex process of murder investigation and its accompanying costs

Using data from HITS files, law enforcement agencies can help educate other government bodies about the needs that must be addressed in agency budgets.

HITS is a model that other States can replicate and adapt to their own needs. The creation of computer programs and methods for data collection and routine analyses could assist other jurisdictions in coordinating and sharing violent crime investigation information.

Findings and conclusions of the research reported here are those of the authors and do not necessarily reflect the official position or policies of the U.S. Department of Justice.

Robert D. Keppel, Ph.D., is chief investigator, Criminal Division, Office of the Washington Attorney General. Joseph G. Weis, Ph.D., is professor of sociology and director of the Center for Law and Justice at the University of Washington. The initial HITS project was supported by NIJ grant 87-IJ-CX-0026. A two-volume final report (NCJ 138618) is available. Call the National Criminal Justice Reference Service at 800–851–3420. For further information about the HITS program, contact Dr. Keppel at 800–345–2793 or 206–464–6430.

Joseph G. Weis and Robert D. Keppel, "Improving the Investigation of Violent Crime." *National Institute of Justice Research in Action,* 1993

CRIME SCENE AND DISTANCE CORRELATES OF SERIAL RAPE

JANET WARREN,[1,7] ROLAND REBOUSSIN,[2] ROBERT R. HAZELWOOD,[3] ANDREA CUMMINGS,[4] NATALIE GIBBS,[5] AND SUSAN TRUMBETTA[6]

This study, derived from a sample of 108 serial rapists (rapes = 565), examines the relationship between demographic, crime scene, and criminal history variables and the distance traveled by serial rapists in order to offend. The pattern of offenses perpetrated by each of the 108 serial offenders as it relates to his place of residence is also analyzed in terms of known characteristics of the offender and his offenses. The theoretical focus of the study integrates premises derived from criminal investigative analysis, environmental criminology, ethnographic geography, journey to crime research, and criminal geographic targeting to explore the cognitive symmetry between the "how" and the "where" of serial sexual offenses. These components or dimensions of serial crime are explored in an attempt to aid law enforcement in their investigation of hard-to-solve serial crimes.

INTRODUCTION

Research demonstrates that a large number of sexual crimes against strangers are committed by a relatively small number of serial offenders (Abel *et al.*, 1987; Hazelwood and Warren, 1990; Grubin and Gunn, 1990; Jackson *et al.*, 1995). This observation, coupled with the potential for studying patterns of events in terms of their usefulness in predicting future events, has given rise to a growing interest in studying the behavior of serial or career criminals. The patterning of their criminal behavior over time in terms of the types of crime perpetrated, the modus operandi manifest in categorically similar crimes, and the temporal and geographical constellations created by a crime series allows for empirical and investigative inquiry not possible with crimes that are studied either individually or in the conglomerate.

[1]Institute of Law, Psychiatry and Public Policy, Box 100, Blue Ridge Hospital, University of Virginia, Charlottesville, Virginia 22901.
[2]Behavioral Science Unit (Retired), FBI Academy, Quantico, Virginia 22135.
[3]The Academy Group, Manassas, Virginia 22110.
[4]Weil, Gotshal & Manges, Dallas, Texas 75201.
[5]Department of Medicine, University of North Carolina, Chapel Hill, North Carolina 27599.
[6]Department of Psychiatry, Dartmouth Medical School, Concord, New Hampshire 03301.
[7]To whom correspondence should be addressed.

One area of inquiry that has evolved out of this perspective involves the behavior of the serial rapist. Known to offend primarily against strangers (Hazelwood and Warren, 1990), the serial rapist's involvement in rather startling numbers of sexual assaults has led to study of this phenomenon by law enforcement in the United States and elsewhere (Davies and Dale, 1995; Jackson *et al.*, 1995). Hazelwood and Warren (1990) reported on the study of 41 serial rapists who were responsible for 837 rapes and 400 attempted rapes. Further research using this same data set indicated that the behavior of the serial rapists could be quantified using behavioral scales that summarized the interaction between the rapist and his victim during each of his successive rapes. The behavior demonstrated during the first rape was found to be useful in determining which of the rapists in that particular data set would escalate in violence and the motivational type that they would manifest over the course of their series of offenses (Warren *et al.*, 1991). These findings motivated the current study of serial rape that sought to explore the relationship between this quantifiable crime scene behavior (i.e., what the rapist did and said to the victim during the rape) and the geographical sequencing of successive rapes by the same offender (i.e., the distance traveled to offend and the location of the rapist's residence in relation to his series of crimes).

Intrinsic to this type of inquiry was the attempt to define the cognitive decision-making that determined these disparate aspects of serial sexual crime (i.e., the where, when, and why of the criminal behavior) and to determine if one known component of it (i.e., the crime scene behavior of the rapist as described by the victim) could be used to determine a yet unknown component of the offender's crime behavior (i.e., the locations in which the offender might live or reoffend). This conceptual framework hypothesizes that serial rapists may rape different types of victims, for different reasons, and that these differences might manifest in differing search patterns for victims in relation to the offender's place of residence. The applied value of this type of inquiry lies in its potential predictive and investigatory relevance to law enforcement in its attempts to apprehend serial sexual offenders.

The origins of the current study lie in the development by the FBI of an investigative adjunct termed criminal investigative analysis (CIA). Criminal investigative analysis or "profiling" was developed by the FBI in the late seventies to aid local law enforcement in the investigation of hard-to-solve, serial violent crimes. Originally evolving out of the investigatory experience of a handful of individuals, over the past 5 years it has become the focus of empirical study in Canada, England, The Netherlands, and the United States. One of these areas of inquiry has focused on the geographical patternings of offenses by a single offender and has, in its development, looked to preexistent bodies of theory and research contained in environmental criminology, geographical ethnography, journey to crime literature, and geographical profiling or targeting. Unique to the current research is the use of detailed crime scene information in the individualized study of the "hunting patterns" (Rossmo, 1995b) of a large sample of serial sexual offenders.

Criminal Investigative Analysis

Ault and Reese (1980), in the first written piece on offender profiling, define profiling as a process designed to identify and interpret certain items of evidence at the crime scene as it may inform a description of the personality type or motivation of the perpetrator. Douglas *et al,* (1986) subsequently described "criminal profiling" as a six-stage process that ideally results in the apprehension of a serial criminal. Stage 1, the profiling input stage, involves the careful review of all pertinent case information, including a complete description of the crime and the crime scene, the background of the victim, forensic information pertaining to all aspects of the crime, photographs of the crime, and autopsy reports if relevant. Stage 2, the decision process stage, involves the arranging of the information into meaningful patterns. These patterns involve the type of murder (e.g., mass, spree, and serial) or rape (e.g., power-reassurance or power-assertive), victim risk factors, offense risk level, the potential for escalation, the timing of different aspects of the crime, and location characteristics. Stage 3, the criminal assessment stage, involves the possible reconstruction of the sequence of events and behaviors occurring between the victim and the perpetrator and the motivation as best estimated from the constellation of crime scene dynamics. Stage 4, the criminal profile stage, involves an assessment of the type of person likely to have committed the crime given the motivation themes derived from the previous analysis of the crime scene. In stage 5, the investigation stage, suspects fitting the general profile are evaluated and further information generated regarding them, while in stage 6, the perpetrator is identified and apprehended.

Following case descriptions of the process by Hazelwood et al. (1987) and an outline for a profiling interview to be used with victims of rape by Hazelwood and Burgess (1987), Pinizzotto and Finkel (1990) undertook an empirical study of the process as performed by profilers, detectives and psychologists. Finding the profilers able to create a richer, more comprehensive description of the perpetrator in the case of rape, Pinizzotto and Finkel comment on the complexity of the profiling process and suggest that it is not simply an unilevel process that links the what, why, and who of a crime in a linear fashion but, rather, a complex multilevel series of attributions, correlations, and predictions that encompass the "what"-to-"who" loop. In 1992, Douglas and Munn described three aspects of a sexual crime: the modus operandi (i.e., the means of locating a victim, perpetrating the crime and escaping without being apprehended), the signature (i.e., aspects of the sexual encounter that convey the sexual fantasy underlying the crime), and the staging of the crime (i.e., altering of evidence at the scene of the crime) and suggest that these three aspects have different developmental processes and hence different significance in linking offenses by the same offender. Most recently, Jackson et al. (1995) examined the process of creating profiles using an expert/novice paradigm and found that a profiler, compared to an experienced detective, used more probabilistic thinking and reasoning processes that evolved out of the extensive study of a large number of solved crimes of a similar type.

This set of writings seeks to provide conceptual and, more recently, empirical substance to a subjective process of investigation that has been found useful in the apprehension of particularly violent, serial offenders. The present study, building on this applied foundation, attempts to inform this process regarding suppositions about the location of the offender as potentially implied by his behavior in the context of his actual crimes.

Environmental Criminology

Brantingham and Brantingham (1984) were the first to develop the concepts of "cognitive mapping" and "opportunity space" as they apply to criminal behavior. Citing the work of Tolman (1948), they defined cognitive mapping as "the process by which individuals learn about, remember and use knowledge about an area" (p. 358). They observe that an individual's cognitive map has many dimensions (i.e., color, sounds, and symbols) and reflects the individual's (or in this particular case, the offender's) "overall geographic ... knowledge of an area." In defining the concept of "opportunity space," they suggest that potential crime victims are not distributed uniformly in space. Rather, it is "the interaction of the location of potential targets and the perpetrator's awareness or activity space that culminates in particular patterns of crime occurrence" (p. 362). From this perspective, Brantingham and Brantingham emphasize that crime occurrence in a city is highly patterned and can be understood only if the "subjective environment" of the perpetrator is appreciated. They emphasized that "potential criminals do not search through a whole city for targets, they look for targets within their more restricted awareness space" (p. 365).

Of relevance to law enforcement is the Brantinghams' (1981) conception of a buffer around the offender's place of residence; as they hypothesize, "While criminals know more of the area close to home and are more likely to locate a target easily, they are also more likely to *be* known and increase their risks close to home. One would expect that there would be an area right around the home base where offenses would become less likely" (p. 32). In developing this search model, Brantingham and Brantingham reference research by Turner (1969), who used a distance decay model to explore burglaries perpetrated by Philadelphia delinquents. He found a peak in burglaries approximately a block distant from the offender's home, with little delinquent activity in the intervening block area.

Brantingham (1978) and Brantingham and Brantingham (1981) also discuss the cognitive processing which accompanies the offender's decisions regarding crime site selection. They suggest that offenders learn through experience or social transmission cues or clusters of cues that are associated with "good" victims or targets. These cues constitute a template against which potential targets are evaluated and, as such, represents a "search process [which] may be consciously conducted, or ... [which] may occur in an unconscious, cybernetic fashion so that the individual cannot articulate how [it is] done" (Brantingham and Brantingham, 1981, p. 29). Bran-tingham and Brantingham postulate that once this template is formulated, it becomes relatively fixed and eventually self-reinforcing.

These tenets of environmental criminology provide probabilistic assumptions that combine the offender with his potential criminal targets according to basic premises of human behavior. As such, they provide a theoretical basis for the consistency and predictability in the offender/ victim/ environment paradigm that constitutes the basis of the geographical analysis underlying this extension of criminal investigative analysis.

Ethnographic Geography

Coucelis *et al*. (1987) examined various templates of cognitive space and the role of certain points in organizing spatial cognitive information and structuring mental maps. Highlighting the potential significance of particular "anchor points" in a person's life and movement, they discuss the perceptual or symbolic salience of these locations; their rational-spatial properties, such as location within daily activity space; and relational-nonspatial properties, such as their actual or potential significance in a person's life. Reporting on the mental maps of 57 subjects in Goleta, California, the authors note that major anchor points tend to define associated regions of the mental map and that "cues associated with a particular anchor point will be displaced (distorted) in the same direction as the anchor point itself, so that the whole corresponding region will 'move' in piece, relative to the regions defined by the other anchor points" (p. 107).

In a final report submitted to the U.S. Department of Justice, Rengert and Wasilchick (1990) examined six statistical models that define the spatial patterns of individual burglars. Developing the models based in part upon the work of Huff (1984) and Coucelis *et al*. (1987), they commented upon the ubiquitousness of criminal opportunities, a "distance bias," which motivates a burglar to stay close to important "anchor points," and a "directional preference," wherein a burglar tends to operate in "more familiar rather than less familiar areas" (p. 50). Taking into consideration these factors as well as the behavior of the drug-free and drug-dependent burglar, they proposed six resultant patterns of offending but found that one or two models generally resulted in the most correct predictions for each burglar, suggesting that burglars tend to follow replicable decision-rules as they choreograph offenses.

Journey-to-Crime Literature

Journey-to-crime studies indicate that the distances traveled by offenders to commit offenses vary according to demographic characteristics of the offender such as age (Nichols, 1980), sex (Rengert, 1975), and race (Petti-way, 1982), The nature of the crime itself also influencesthis distance factor. Pyle (1974) found that rapists in Akron, Ohio, traveled shorter distances than did robbers and burglars, a finding confirmed a few years later by Rhodes and Conly (1981) in Washington, DC. These authors also found that rape tended to occur in areas characterized by construction, urban renewal, and temporary lodgings.

In a study that looked specifically at rapes over a 4-year period, LeBeau (1985) found that serial offenders tended to "use repeatedly the same geographic and ecological space" (p. 397). He reported that this geographically specific pattern of offending contributed significantly to changes in the numerical, geographical, and ecological descriptions of rape from one year to the next in various areas throughout San Diego. In subsequent research, LeBeau (1987a) attempted to differentiate among single, serial, and open (unapprehended) rapists. LeBeau found that while serial rapists tended to vary in the distance that they traveled from home to rape, they consistently seemed to restrict their attacks to within one-half mile of their previous attacks.

Five years later, LeBeau (1993) presented four case studies from the same sample that looked at the "spatial-temporal analysis of serial rapists." Focusing on the patterning of offenses in terms of both their geographical patterning and their temporal sequencing, he suggests that the choice of crime location evolves out of four distinct factors: spatial knowledge, time, distance, and type of area. In reviewing his four cases, LeBeau descriptively outlines the relative importance of these factors in producing the different spatial patterns created by four serial rapists of different ages and ethnic backgrounds. In so doing, he identifies a pattern by which each of the rapists eventually backtracked to the area of an earlier offense. Hypothesizing that this tendency may derive from time pressures, rewarding memories, or the exhaustion of spatial knowledge, he emphasizes the need for further study of this pattern in order to facilitate the investigation of unapprehended offenders.

Drawing upon the work of Brantingham and Brantingham (1981) and Rengert and Wasilchick (1985), Canter and Larkin (1993) explored the spatial activity of 45 British offenders charged with two or more sexual offenses. They hypothesized that two general models could be used to describe the relationship between an offender's area of offending and his home base. The "commuter model" assumes that the offender travels away from his home to perpetrate his crimes, with his "criminal range" being independent of and an appreciable distance from his home base. The "marauder model" assumes a closer relationship between an offender's home and his criminal range and hypothesizes that the offender moves out in a random pattern from his home base to commit crimes.

In examining the spatial activity of these 45 sexual offenders who were responsible for 251 sexual offenses, Canter and Larkin found that 91% of the offenders did, in fact, have their crimes located within a precise, circular region and that 87% of the offenders lived within the circular area. According to Canter and Larkin, further analysis revealed that the offenders maintained a "safe area" of at least 0.61 mi around their home, with the average minimum distance from crime to home being 1.53 mi. In discussing these findings, Canter and Larkin (1993) suggested that "the clarity of these mathematical results is a little short of remarkable for what is regarded as an impetuous, emotional violent crime ..." (p. 18). They emphasize that "whatever the rapist's experience of committing the crime, there is a basis to his choice of location that can be modeled from relatively logical environmental psychology principles" (p. 18). In a subsequent set of analyses, Canter and Gregory (1994) examined certain offender and offense characteristics to see if they could be used to reduce the area covered by their circle hypothesis. They computed chi-squares on four variables: race, venue (indoors or outdoors), day of the week, and age at arrest. Race and venue were significant. Black offenders offended closer to their residence than white offenders and those offenders who raped out of doors traveled 2.7 times farther than those who raped indoors.

Davies and Dale (1995) studied the distances traveled by 111 serial rapists using information obtained from the national identification records maintained by police departments throughout Britain. They observed that 22% of the offenders "were known to be itinerant to a greater or less extent" and referenced Farrington's (1993) observation that "convicted offenders move home more often than non-offenders" (p. 6). Regarding the distanced traveled by the rapist, Davies and Dale report that 29% of 299 rapes occurred within a mile of the rapist's residence, 51% within 2 mi of the rapist's residence, and 76% within 5 mi (Table 22.1, p. 8). The authors found "no evidence" (p. 8) of the buffer zone discussed by Brantingham and Brantingham (1984), Canter and Larkin (1993), and Rossmo (1995a); they observe, however, that many of their cases were from the densely populated London area and that a buffer zone might not be observable given the 0.5 mi intervals used in their research (Table 22.1, p. 8).

These studies offer empirical support to the theoretical premisesdis-cussed above, specifically that rapists manifest distinct travel patterns in their search for victims, that these appear to be relatively consistent over time, and that different patterned relationships between the cluster of the offenses and the offender's home can be observed for groups of offenders.

TABLE 22.1 DISTANCES TRAVELED BY SERIAL RAPISTS: COMPLETE SAMPLE AND LOCALLY-BASED RAPISTS

Distance		N	Mean	SD	Range
1.	Closest distance				
	Complete	99	8.18	31.16	0-242.48
	Local	83	1.66	0.48	0-13.90
2.	Mean distance				
	Complete	99	14.54	43.88	0.03-310.24
	Local	83	3.14	3.04	0.03-16.40
3.	Farthest distance				
	Complete	99	22.03	70.69	0.05-620.22
	Local	83	4.93	4.22	0.05-18.40
4.	Area				
	Complete	76	55.38	227.00	0-1628.60
	Local	64	9.27	26.71	0-192.50

Criminal Geographical Targeting/Profiling

Rossmo (1995b) defines geographical profiling as the process through which target location patterns of serial violent offenders are used to determine spatial information about the offender, most often the location of future offenses or the offender's residence. In discussing the implement-ation of this type of process, Rossmo suggests that it is best undertaken after a criminal investigative profile has been completed both to inform investigators about the personality and lifestyle of the offender and to inform decision-making about whether a series of offenses have been perpetrated by the same offender.

Drawing from the Brantingham and Brantingham model for crime selection (1981) and the routine activities approach of Felson (1986), Rossmo developed an applied system of spatial analysis which integrates target backdrop information with crime location characteristics. Used with cases of serial murder, arson, and rape, the "criminal geographical targeting model" derives from a four-step process: (1) a delineation of the offender's hunting area calculated from the offender's crime locations; (2) the calculation of "Manhattan"[8] distances from every point on the map to each crime location; (3) the use of the Manhattan distance in a function that assigns each point a value based upon a distance-decay assessment of whether or not the point lies inside a buffer safety zone; and (4) the addition of these multiple values to create a score for each map grid wherein the higher the resultant score, the greater the probability that the grid contains the offender's home or workplace. The derivation of these values creates a three-dimensional probability surface that can be overlaid on a city map to direct investigatory efforts as they relate to suspect prioritization, patrol saturation, alternative information system access (e.g., postal code access), and Task Force integration.

Criminal geographical targeting represents the first attempt to apply many of the theoretical tenets of environmental criminology to the actual investigation of violent serial offenders. Its success is encouraging and supports further inquiry into detailed information on the travel patterns of serial offenders in order to add specificity to this deductive, applied process.

The present study builds upon these theoretical tenets and empirical bodies of research to further explore the cognitive symmetry that combines crime scene behavior with decisions about crime site selection. Drawing on the FBI's format for "profiling" cases of serial crime, the current study uses variables describing the offender and his modus operandi to explore correlational or predictive relationships with the distance and directionality the offender travels in order to offend. As such, it examines the relationship between the "how" and the "where" of the criminal behavior manifested by a single offender in a way that is designed to inform the investigative efforts of law enforcement. Implicit to this inquiry is the assumption that some kind of cognitive symmetry can be determined in the offense decision making of an offender, so that one known parameter of a rapist's offending (i.e., how he commits his offenses) can be used to better predict or estimate a yet unascertained component of his activity (i.e., the offender's location).

In so doing, the study will contribute to the journey to crime literature as it pertains to the behavior of serial rapists while also informing certain tenets of environmental criminology. While environmental criminology posits that crime occurs when a potential offender interacts with a potential victim in a situation that makes a crime profitable and easy, the current study suggests that racial, motivational, and historical characteristics of the individual offender also interact with these tenets to create identifiable spatial patterns of crime that are determined, to some extent, by the anchor point of the offender's residence. As such, the results can be used to refine further the

---

[8] The Manhattan distance is the actual distance traveled between points using the street grid, as opposed to the straight-line distance.

estimative accuracy of the travel predictions utilized when these premises are translated into criminal geographical targeting. Finally, the current study explores the concept of a buffer zone presented by Brantingham and Brantingham (1984), and referenced by Canter and Larkin (1993), Rossmo (1995a), and Davies and Dale (1995), and offers empirical support for this theoretical proposition.

METHOD

The study involves a nonrandom sample of 565 rapes perpetrated bty 108 serial rapists. The cases were collected from participants in a course offered four times a year to middle-management police officers from around the country by the FBI. The participants obtained these cases in most instances from their own departments, although, on occasion, they procured a case from a neighboringjurisdiction. Included in the submission of these cases were (1) a detailed victim statement for each rape, (2) the police report detailing the series of crimes, and (3) a map showing the location of each rape as well as the home and place of employment of the rapist. This resulted in the identification of 108 serial rapists with a mean of 5.3 rapes (SD = 3.5) and a range of 2-17 rapes.

The crime scene behavior manifest during each of the 565 rapes was quantified by two coders using a 30-page protocol developed by the authors. Part A of the protocol contained 52 multiple-choice items which described the relationship of the victim to the offender; the encounter, rape contact and dropoff locations; the type of approach used by the rapist to gain proximity to the victim; the use or presence of bindings, weapons, and fetishistic items; the use of alcohol and drugs by the rapist; the sexual acts performed and sexual dysfunctions displayed; victim characteristics; the presence or use of a vehicle; and the types of articles removed from the rape site by the perpetrator. Many of these items included subparts and, when coded, produced 123 variables. Modal variables were also created to describe the behavior manifest by an offender across his series of offenses and were used in many of the analyses reported below.

Part B of the protocol contained 58 5-point scales that described the verbal, sexual, and physical interactions that occurred between the rapist and his victim during the rape. Of these, 49 were revisions and expansions of a previous set of scales, described by Warren *et al.* (1991). The remaining nine scales were retained from the previous study (Warren *et al.*, 1991) in their identical form.

Reliability coding was obtained for 100 of the rapes over the course of the coding. On the first section of the protocol, which contained the multiple-choice items describing the rape and its context, κ'scould be computed for 106 of the 123 variables. The mean κ was 0.78; for the 10 κ'S below 0.40, the median percentage agreement was 95. For the behavioral scales, the second section of the protocol, the median of the correlations was 0.76; the median percentage agreement for the 10lowest correlations (0.57 and below) was 79.

The geographical data were generated using MapInfo software. The geocoding included, for every case, the latitudes and longitudes of each of the rape incidents, the rapist's residence, and his place of employment (if the rapist was employed). When the rapist had lived at several locations during the case, all of the residences were entered into the geographical database and later analyzed according to the temporally determined rape-residence spatial relationship. In these cases with multiple residences, only the rape-residence pattern with the largest number of rapes was included in the larger data set.

The geographical database was subsequently integrated with the crime scene database that summarized the rapist's behavior on each of the rapes for which there was geographical data.

Sixteen cases were removed from the main data analyses, as they involved rapes occurring over 20 mi (i.e., 21 to 620 mi) from the rapist's residence; these cases represented travel patterns between cities or across states that were thought to confound the local patterns being explored in the current study. Two distance variables were computed in addition to the mean (i.e., closest and farthest distance). The closest (shortest) distance represented the distance from the rapist's residence to the rape closest to the residence regardless of its placement in the sequence of rapes. Similarly, the farthest distance represented the longest distance the offender traveled to commit an offense. These were computed to estimate the extent of the search behavior manifested by serial offenders.

Two shapes were also designed to examine the relational patternings of the crimes to the residence: the convex hull polygon (CHP) and the Marauder/Commuter model. The area of the convex hull polygon was determined by drawing a boundary around the outermost rape points in each case so as to include all of the rape points in that particular case. The Marauder/Commuter model (Canter and Larkin, 1993) was drawn by joining as the diameter the two rapes that were the farthest distance from each other in each case and determining whether the residence of the offender lay inside or outside the area. The offenders whose residence lay inside the circle were designated Marauders, and those outside, Commuters. These shapes were used to explore the relationship between the offenses and the location of the offender's residence.

RESULTS

As summarized in Table 22.1, the 83 local serial rapists (i.e., those rapists who traveled less than 20 mi) in this sample traveled, on average, 3.14 mi to commit their rapes. Their closest distance was, on average, 1.7 mi, while their farthest distance traveled was, on average, 4.9 mi. Interestingly, while the mean closest distance was 1.7 mi, almost one-half (40 rapists) of the rapists raped at least once within 0.5 mi of their home.

Given the frequency at which offenders raped within 0.5 mi of their home, an attempt was made to explore the applicability of the buffer zone discussed in the environmental criminology literature referenced above. Data relevant to this inquiry are summarized in Figs. 22.1 and 22.2. Figure 22.1 contains data on the absolute distance traveled by each of the local rapists with three or more rapes. Figure 22.2 contains data for each case with five or more rapes, standardized relative to the mean of that case.[9] Five or more rapes were used in the configuration of Fig. 22.2 to provide a more continuous distribution for each case. The data in Fig. 22.1 suggest a fairly consistent distance decay function with the exception of the first distance interval, which contains 8% ($n = 34$), in contrast to 13% ($n = 52$), of the overall rapes which are contained in the second distance interval.[10] The relatively small distance encapsulated in these two distance intervals (approximately 0.4 mi) suggests that a significant number of rapes (over 20%) occur in areas that have a rather striking proximity to the offender's home. Following this interval, the expected distance decay function is demonstrated.

A more explicit pattern is seen in the context of the standardized distances (interval = 0.075) displayed in Fig. 22.2. As demonstrated, there is no interval around the home where no rapes occur. In the first interval of 0.075 of the mean distance traveled, 6 (1.8%) rapes are recorded.

---

[9] Distances were standardized to take into account differences in local geography and offender perceptions of distance.

[10] In part, the relatively small number of cases in the first interval may be an artifact since there are fewer targets between 0 and 0.2 mi from home than between 1.0 and 1.2 mi from home. Because of street grids and the Manhattan distance, this relationship is not quadratic (Larson, 1972).

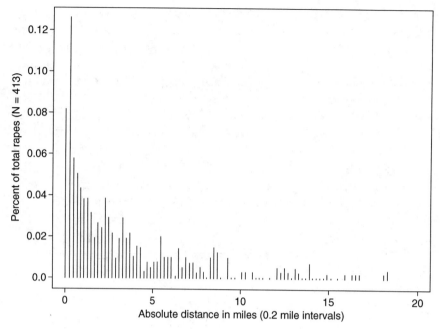

FIGURE 22.1

Proportion of rapes by distance from resisdence to rape location.

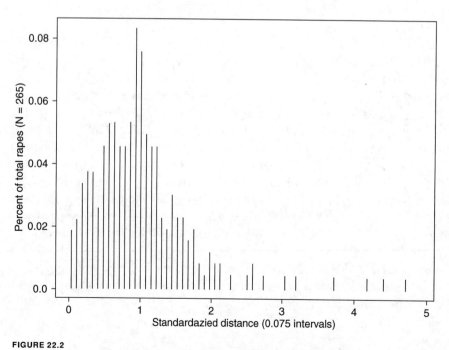

FIGURE 22.2

Proportion of rapes by standardized distance from residence to rape location. Cases with five or more rapes.

Brantingham and Brantingham (1984), however, define their concept of the buffer zone as representing the part of the individual's journey to crime distribution that does not follow a distance decay function. This construct, represented by the modal crime trip distance, equals 0.975 in the current study, onlyslightly less than the mean distance.

In an attempt to explore these travel patterns further, the relationship of the distance traveled to the demographic characteristics of the offender, his crime scene behavior, and his criminal history was explored. The shortest, mean, and farthest distance traveled as well as the area covered by the polygon created by the cluster of each offender's rapes are presented in Table 22.2. Mean distances and confidence intervals for variables that obtained the 0.10 level of significance are shown in Fig. 22.3. Median areas of the polygons created by the cluster of each offender's rapes, with interquartile ranges, are shown in Fig. 22.4 (the interquartile ranges were used to avoid having to show negative values for the standard deviations, which were produced by the skewed distributions). This manner of presenting the data was chosen for two reasons. First, the nonrepresentative nature of the data diminishes the meaningfulness of significance levels. Second, the applied purpose of the paper heightened the need to present the data in a visually clear and practically interpretable form. Distance was found to vary with the demographic characteristics of the offender as well as certain "signature" and "modus operandi" aspects of his crime scene behavior. Elements of his criminal history also showed consistent variability with hisjourney to crime behavior.

As shown in Table 22.2, white rapists traveled farther than their minority counterparts, as did minority rapists who raped white women (the rate of racial crossover was 2% for white rapists and 69% for minority offenders). White rapists had larger shortest (2.70 mi compared to 1.23 mi), mean (4.32 mi compared to 2.46 mi), and farthest (6.24 mi compared to 3.97 mi) distances. As illustrated in Fig. 22.3, the minority rapists showed less variability in mean distance traveled, with 98% of the minority rapists raping within a mean distance of 4.75 mi from their home. Alternatively,rapists who traveled more than a mean of 4.75 mi were almost always white in the current sample. Older rapists also traveled farther than younger rapists. As summarized in Table 22.2, the shortest (P = 0.09), mean (P = 0.09), and farthest (P = 0.10) distance traveled varied across the three age categories. As illustrated in Fig. 22.3, unlike their older counterparts, 98% of the rapists under the age of 20 years raped within a mean of 2.75 mi of their homes.

As referenced earlier in the paper, Douglas and Munn (1992) describe certain "signature" aspects of sexual crimes that contain the fantasy substrate of the sexual crime and which, as a result, are expected to remain fairly consistent over a series of sexual assaults. As indicated in Table 22.2, three of these signature components vary significantly with the distance traveled by the offender (i.e., the presence of ritual in the majority of the rapes, the use of bindings in the majority of the rapes, and the manner in which the bindings were obtained for the majority of the rapes). As shown in Table 22.2, rapists who demonstrated a "ritualized" behavior in the majority of their offenses tended, on average, to travel farther than rapists who did not (on average 3.64 mi, as contrasted to 2.30 mi; P<0.05). In the current study, "ritual" was coded if the rape included verbal or behavioral scripting, sexual bondage, or any type of fantasy-based behavior that was not directly concerned with obtaining a victim, protecting the rapist's identity, and/or facilitating the rapist's escape. Similarly, rapists who used bindings or restraints in the context of their offenses tended to travel farther (on average 4.63 mi, as contrasted to 2.61 mi; P < 0.01) and raped over a significantly larger area than those who did not (20.39 mi^2, as contrasted to 4.57 mi^2; P < 0.05). These two variables may be capturing the same behavior or different gradations of the use of restraints in enacting sexual bondage.

As indicated in Table 22.2, the *manner* in which the restraints were obtained also was related to the mean distance traveled by the offender. Those who brought restraints to the scene of their rapes traveled, on average, 2.39 mi, while those who obtained their restraints at the scene of the

TABLE

22.2 DISTANCE TRAVELED (MI) AND AREA COVERED BY MODAL DEMOGRAPHIC, CRIMINAL HISTORY, CRIME SCENE BEHAVIOR, AND GEOGRAPHICAL PATTERN OF SERIAL RAPISTS

Factors		N	Shortest	Mean	Farthest	N	Area of polygon
1.	Rapist's race						
	White	26	2.70**	4.32***	6.24**	20	9.52*
	Other	43	1.24	2.46	3.97	32	3.45
	Unknown	14	—	—	—	—	—
2.	Clinical type						
	Type 1	33	2.16	3.36	4.81	29	7.06
	Type 2	42	1.43	3.17	5.32	30	12.67
	Types 3 & 4	8	0.83	2.12	3.37	5	1.63
3.	Increaser status						
	Increaser	21	0.81*	2.59	5.10	18	5.45
	Nonincreaser	62	1 95	3.33	4.86	46	10.76
4.	Indoors/outdoors						
	Indoors	49	1.61	3.38	5.44	43	11.91
	Outdoors	29	1.55	2.69	4.22	19	4.20
5.	Victim race						
	White	60	1.91	3.61**	5.55**	46	11.61
	Other	23	1.00	1.93	3.31	18	3.28
6.	Approach						
	Con	11	1.05	2.49	3.96	7	2.10
	Surprise	59	1.55	3.20	5.20	52	10.86
7.	Ritual						
	No	31	1.27	2.30**	3.90*	24	4.78
	Yes	52	1.89	3.64	5.54	40	11.96
8.	Restraints						
	No	61	1.31**	2.61***	4.22***	45	4.57**
	Yes	22	2.62	4.63	6.89	19	20.39
9.	Bindings obtained						
	At scene	10	2.35	5.37**	0.82*	9	38.26
	Brought	8	0.99	2.39	4.41	6	6.22
10.	Gun presence or use						
	No	73	1.74	3.17	4.80	56	9.84
	Yes	10	1.08	2.93	5.84	8	5.22
11.	Knife presence or use						
	No	37	1.75	3.38	5.31	32	11.79
	Yes	46	1.59	2.95	4.62	32	6.75
12.	Day or night						
	Daytime	11	3.12**	3.88	4.86	8	0.80
	Nighttime	65	1.44	3.09	5.11	53	10.85
13.	Time of week						
	Weekdays	46	1.74*	2.87	4.31	32	3.82
	Weekend	23	0.86	2.85	5.49	21	15.37

14.	Victim					
	Child	5	2.86	3.90	5.18	5	1.31
	Adult	61	1.66	3.21	5.09	49	9.64
	Aged	5	0.85	2.05	3.96	4	1.94
15.	Offender age					
	<20	11	0.59*	1.61*	2.64*	5	1.25
	20-29	53	1.55	3.10	5.01	46	11.22
	>29	19	2.58	4,13	6.02	13	5.43
16.	Community					
	Rural	2	2.88	3.34	4.19	1	1.51
	Suburban	55	1.97	3.58	5.33	44	11.75
	Urban	13	0.67	1.49	3.72	12	4.06
17.	Entry					
	Not forced	46	1.67	3.04	4.70	31	3.97
	Forced	37	1.64	3.26	5.21	33	14.24
18.	Sexual dysfunction					
	No	65	1.49	2.96	4.76	53	9.13
	Yes	18	2.27	3.78	5.53	11	9.92
19.	Substance abuse					
	No	73	1.76	3.21	5.00	58	10.19
	Yes	10	0.92	2.61	4.39	6	0.33
20.	Burglary					
	No	40	1.36	2.54*	4.02**	30	2.49*
	Yes	42	1.96	3.73	5.82	34	15.24
21.	Presence of other person					
	No	73	1.67	3.11	4.88	59	9.12
	Yes	10	1.60	3.39	5.30	5	11.01
22.	Convex hull polygon					
	Res./inside	16	1.08	3.20	5.51	16	23.54***
	Res./outside	48	1.66	3.06	4.92	48	4.51
23.	Marauder/commuter					
	Marauder	36	0.74***	2.36**	4.55	36	7.62
	Commuter	28	2.51	4.03	5.73	28	11.38

*P<0.10.
**P<0.05.
***P<0.01.
****P<0.00l.

crime traveled, on average, 5.37 mi (P < 0.05). The use of restraints was also related to whether the offender's first or last rape was closest to his home. Those rapist's whose first rape was closest to home tended to use bindings significantly more often than those whose latter offenses were closest to home. These variables, as illustrated in Fig. 22.3, suggest that 98% of these rapists who did not manifest a ritualized type of rape behavior, who did not use restraints, and/or who did not fashion restraints at the scene of the crime tended to offend on average no farther than 4 to 4.5 mi from their residences. Those who manifest the more ritualized aspects of rape behavior showed greater variability and tended as a group to travel, on average, longer distances to locate their victim. This pattern may reflect greater specificity in terms of the type of victim being sought or alternatively

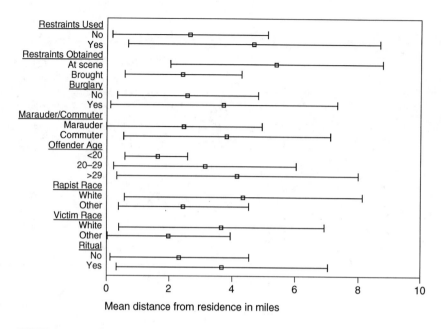

FIGURE 22.3

Mean distance from residence. Confidence interval (2 SD).

more complex, methodical behavior patterns in general. The aspects of the offender's modus operandi (i.e., the means of locating a victim, perpetrating the crime, and escaping without detection) that varied with the distance traveled focused on the timing of the offense and the association between the rape and the burglarizing of the victim. As shown in Table 22.2, the

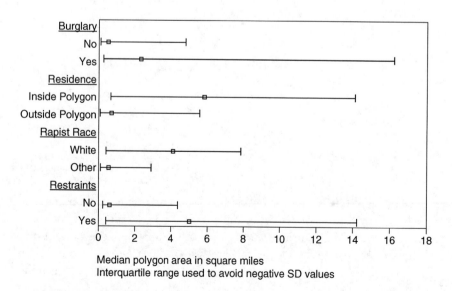

FIGURE 22.4

Median area of polygon. Lines show interquartile range.

shortest distance traveled is longer for rapists who rape predominantly during the day than for those who rape predominantly at night (3.12 mi, as contrasted to 1.44 mi; $P < 0.05$). Burglarizing victims in the majority of the rapes was also related to the offender's mean ($P < 0.08$) and farthest distance $P < 0.05$) traveled as well as the overall area covered ($P < 0.06$). These components of the crime suggest that the offender has had experience with other types of property crime and that his motivation for the crime encompasses both a sexual and a nonsexual component. This hypothesis was confirmed with subsequent analysis of the criminal history information obtained for each offender. This analysis showed significant positive correlations among the size of the nonoffending area, the average distance traveled, the general area covered by the rapist, and the number of property crimes contained in the rapist's computerized criminal history. The number of previous rapes reported on the rapist's computerized criminal history also correlated with the area variable, suggesting that rapists who have been convicted of previous rapes tend to travel farther when implementing a subsequent series of sexual assaults.

Finally, the overall geographical pattern of rapes manifested by each rapist appears to be related to the distance traveled by the rapist. Specifically, the area of the rapes perpetrated by those rapists whose residences liewithin the convex hull polygon is significantly larger ($P < 0.05$) than the area of rapists who residences lie outside the convex hull polygon (23.53 mi^2, as contrasted to 4.51 mi^2). This finding, if replicated, may prove useful in determining location of a serial offender's residence (i.e., if the area of a rapist's offenses is less than 4 mi^2, the probability is greatest that he lives somewhere outside the pattern created by his crimes). In contrast, if the area of the offenses is greater than 5 or 6 mi^2, the probability is greater that the offender lives inside the pattern created by his offenses. The variables related to the polygon area at a significance level of 0.10 or less are summarized in Fig. 22.4. As indicated, the race of the rapist and whether he burglarized hisvictims and/or used restraints were all related to a larger area covered. Interestingly, a larger polygon area did not necessarily reflect larger distances traveled but, in may cases, represented more multidirectional search patterns. Marauders as defined by Canter and Larkin (1993), rapists whose residence lay within the circle formed by the two distances in their series that are a greatest distance from each other, were also found to travel, on average, less distance than Commuters, whose residence lay outside the cluster of their offenses. The shortest distance traveled was also significantly different for the two groups ($P < 0.01$). For Marauders, the shortest distance traveled was 0.74 mi, while for Commuters, it was 2.51 mi. Interestingly, the area covered by the two groups over the course of their rapes was not substantially different, suggesting that different conceptualizations of space rather than size of space defines the victim search pattern of these two groups.

To assess the relative importance of the variables found to be significantly related to the distances traveled by the serial rapists in the current study, a multiple regression was run for each of the distance variables described above (see Table 22.3). The offender's race, the victim's race, the presence or absence of "ritual," the use or nonuse of restraints, whether the rapist escalated in violence over the course of his rape career (i.e., increaser/ nonincreaser status), the presence or absence of forced entry, the coocurrence of burglary, the offender's age, the timing of the rape, the weekday/weekend designation of the rape, and whether the residence was inside or outside the convex hull and the Marauder/Commuter model were entered (stepwise) as the dependent variables. Each of these variables was found to be significant or close to significant in the bivariate analysis and reflect either demographic or crime scene information believed by criminal investigative analysts to be relevant in the investigation of serial crime. Significant models were obtained for the shortest and average distance. A correlation matrix revealed no problems of multicollinearity in the data. The highest correlation in the matrix was 0.53 (reflecting the tending

<table>
TABLE
22.3

MULTIPLE REGRESSION OF DISTANCES TRAVELED AND AREA COVERED BY DEMOGRAPHIC, CRIME SCENE BEHAVIOR, AND GEOGRAPHICAL PATTERNS OF SERIAL RAPE
</table>

Dependent variable	Close distance	Average distance	Farthest distances	Area
1. Offender race	0.07	0.05	−0.02	−0.004
2. Offender age	0.21	0.22	0.22	0.02
3. Victim race	0.04	−0,06	−0.10	0.09
4. Ritual	0.04	0.12	0.10	−0.02
5. Restraints	0.35	0.31	0.28	0.29
6. Increaser status	−0.22	−0.14*	0.005	−0.06
7. Forced entry	0.03	−0.02	−0.004	0.08
8. Burglary	0.06	0.13	0.15	0.19
9. Day/night	0.01	0.09	0.10	0.04
10. Day of week	0.12	0.11	0.08	0.25
11. Convex hull	−0.10	−0.04	0.04	0.35*
12. Commuter/Marauder	0.46**	0.28	0.08	0.03
R^2	0.30	0.18	0.06	0.15
F value	2.93**	1.99*	1.29	1.78

*$P < 0.05$.
**$P < 0.01$.

of whites to use restraints more than blacks), wellbelow the 0.70 levelat which Tabachnik and Fidell (1989, p. 87) admonish the analyst to "think carefully" before including both variables in the analysis.

The model for shortest distance ($P < 0.01$) accounted for 30% of the variance; the only significant variable was Marauder/Commuter status ($P < 0.01$); as illustrated in Table 22.2 and Fig. 22.3, Marauders rape closer to home than do Commuters. The model for average distance ($P < 0.05$) explained 18% of the variance; those rapists who escalated in violence tended to travel shorter mean distances than those rapists who did not escalate in violence.

DISCUSSION

The results of the current study must be considered in terms of the nonrandom nature of the sample. The cases analyzed represent a sample of solved cases that may be overrepresentative of the more "interesting" cases investigated by various departments across the country. Less "interesting" or complex series of rapes might not have been included in this sample and thus biased the sample in terms of larger geographical dispersion. Unsolved cases might also involve more complex victim selection or travel patterns that contribute to the difficulty investigators have in identifying and apprehending the offender.

Of relevance to journey-to-crime literature is the finding that local serial rapists travel on average 3.14 mi to rape but that the average shortest/closest distance is 1.66 mi. More important to investigators was the finding that half of the serial rapists in the study raped at least once within 0.5 mi from their residence. This suggests that rapists tend, at least on occasion, to rape in areas that seem to put them at risk because of the proximity of their offense behavior to their home. As shown in Figs. 22.1 and 22.2, there does, however, also appear to be an area around the important anchor point of the offender's home that contains a lower probability of rape behavior.

In terms of the Brantinghams' (1984) conceptualization of the buffer zone (i.e., the space over which offending becomes more probable as the distance from home increases), this distance for the current sample of serial rapists was 0.975 of their mean crime trip distance. This finding suggests that the factors pertinent to defining the individual search patterns of these serial rapists vary in their individual and cumulative effect as the distance from home varies. The small number of rapes in the intervals most proximate to the homes of the offenders suggest that the wish to avoid recognition supersedes, significantly, the wish to procure a victim with the least temporal and geographical effort. This wish is not as absolute as one might expect, however, as at least a small number of rapes occur in the same complex as the offender's residence. It seems likely that the travel patterns away from home also allow the offenders increased access to an ever-widening pool of potential victims and, for some offenders, reflect movement toward other significant anchor points (e.g., place of work, red light district, etc.).

As theorized by the Brantinghams, this centrifugal movement, however, eventually begins to wane; the offender's apparent wish to avoid recognition and find an ever-widening pool of potential targets diminishes and the distance decay function that determines many aspects of human spatial behavior begins to dominate. Brantingham and Brantingham (1984, p. 344) observe, "People interact more with people and things that are close to their home location than with people and things that are far away." They ascribe this tendency to the costs of farther travel as well spatial familiarity with the area proximate to a person's home. The pervasiveness of this pattern is quite remarkable given that it clearly contradicts the objective reality of their being an increasing pool of targets as the radius of the offender's crime pattern increases. This increase is, however, further influenced and/or diminished by the realities of actual travel time.

The results further suggest that the rapist's geographical decisions in terms of the distance he travels to rape vary systematically with certain of his demographic characteristics, his crime scene behaviors, and aspects of his criminal history. This suggests some degree of cognitive symmetry that may be of value in the investigation of serial crime. Of particular importance to investigation is the finding that white rapists travel on average farther than minority rapists, as may older offenders, to locate their victims. The finding regarding race is similar to that found by Canter and Gregory (1994) in their study of 45 British offenders charged with sexual assault. In the current sample, these racial differences may reflect class distinctions and therefore lesser and greater mobility, the smaller area covered byexclusively minority neighborhoods, or cultural differences in the cognitive structuring of space. The differences in the distance traveled by younger and older rapists may reflect greater impulsivityin the offense behavior of younger offenders, greater access to vehicles by older offenders, or, as mentioned above, differences in age-related development of geographically determined cognitive space.

Somewhat more unexpected was the relationship between ritualized behavior and the use of restraints and the distance traveled by the rapist. It appears that the rapist who is enacting a more scripted, ritualized type of rape tends to travel farther to find his victim. The manifestation of ritualized behavior and the use of restraints have been associated with specific sexual fantasies that are driving the sexual assault and, as such, may also be associated with the choice of a more specific victim and/or more sophisticated cognitive processing of all aspects of the crime.

The distance characteristics of the rapes were also found to vary with the criminal history of the rapist and the means he used in gaining access to the victim within her home. Rapists who had more extensive criminal histories, who used forced entry, and who burglarized the victim during the rape tended to travel farther to rape. This seems to reflect both a more generalized criminal motivation for the crime and more experience in perpetuating nonsexual crimes.

Of particular investigative relevance is the significant difference in the area covered by rapists who live inside the convex hull polygon formed by their offenses as contrasted to those who live outside the convex hull polygon. As indicated in Table 22.2 and Fig. 22.3, those who reside inside the convex hull polygon cover on average 23.5 mi^2, as contrasted with those who live outside the convex hull polygon, who cover on average 4.5 mi^2. This pattern is manifest regardless of the fact that the two groups show no differences in the closest, average, or farthest distance traveled, demonstrating that the difference lies in the patterning of the offenses in relationship to the residence rather than the actual distance traveled. This finding might be used by investigators to inform their prediction of whether or not any particular offender lives inside the polygon (i.e., the area covered is equal to or less than 4.5 mi). This patterning may emanate from the fact that rapists who rape in the area around their home have a more intimate knowledge of a broader area than those who commute to a more unknown area. Conversely, those rapists who commute may also be targeting a particular, specific type of victim or situation that is contained in a more precise geographical locale.

These findings are obviously not conclusive given the nonrandom nature of the sampling. However, the relationships discussed above do point toward some degree of cognitive symmetry between what the rapist does during his rape and the decisions he makes regarding the means he uses to locate his victims. This manifestation of cognitive symmetry is not surprising given other aspects of human decision-making. This symmetry may not, however, be part of the offender's conscious decision-making. It may represent an unconscious synthesis of cues that are not apparent to the perpetrator and, in fact, represent a geographical fingerprint which he inadvertently leaves behind as he perpetrates his crimes.

Obviously, further study of and replication of these findings could be of great value to the investigator or criminal investigative analyst. For example, the current data suggest that younger rapists will be living closer to their offenses than older rapists; alternatively, those who manifest a more complex, ritualized form of crime scene behavior are more likely to have traveled farther to locate their victims. These findings may also serve to help structure empirical attempts to determine the most probable location of the rapist's residence. Even in this preliminary form, they can help to inform the deductive reasoning that lies at the heart of criminal targeting analysis (Rossmo, 1995). Already being introduced into standardized software, this technique makes use of general journey to crime estimates of the travel patterns of different types of offenders. More detailed estimates of travel patterns related to observable crime scene behavior and demographics of offenders can only help to increase the predictability and applicability of these evolving spatially oriented investigative processes.

ACKNOWLEDGEMENTS

This research was supported by transfer of funds 91-IJ-R027 awarded by the National Institute of Justice, Office of Justice Programs, U.S. Department of Justice, to the Federal Bureau of Investigation. Points of view in this document are those of the authors and do not necessarily represent the official position or policies of the U.S. Department of Justice. The authors wish to thank Dr. David Reboussin for statistical assistance and many useful comments in the preparation of the manuscript and our anonymous reviewers for their invaluable suggestions.

REFERENCES

Abel, G., Becker, J., Cunningham-Rathner, J., Mittelman, M., Rouleau, J., & Murphy, W. (1987). Self-reported sex crimes of nonincarcerated paraphiliacs. *J. Interpers. Violence* 2(6): 3-25.

Ault, R.L., & Reese, J.T. (1980). A psychological assessment of crime profiling. *FBI Law Enforce. Bull.* 49(3): 22-25.

Brantingham, P.J. (1978). A theoretical model of crime site selection. In Kuohn, M., and Akers, R. L. (Eds.), *Crime, Law and Sanction*, Sage, Beverly Hills, CA, pp. 105-118.

Brantingham, P., & Brantingham, P. (1981). *Environmental Criminology*, Sage, BeverlyHills, CA.

Brantingham, P., & Brantingham, P. (1984). *Patterns in Crime*, New York: Macmillan.

Canter, D., & Gregory, P. (1994). Identifying the residential location of rapists. *J. Forens. Sci. Soc.* 34: 169-175.

Canter, D., & Larkin, P. (1993). The environmental range of serial rapists. *J. Environ. Psychol.* 13:63-69.

Coucelis, H., Golledge, R., Gale, N., & Tobler, W. (1987). Exploring the anchor point hypothesis of spatial cognition. *J. Environ. Psychol.* 7: 99-122.

Davies, A., & Dale, A. (1995). *Locating the Stranger Rapist*, Police Research Group Special Interest Series: Paper 3, Home Office Police Department, London.

Douglas, J.E., & Munn, C. (1992). Violent crime scene analysis: Modus operandi, signature, and staging. *FBI Law Enforce. Bull.* Feb.: 1-10.

Douglas, J.E., Ressler, R.K., Burgess, A.W., & Hartman, C.R. (1986). Criminal profiling from crime scene analysis. Special issue: Psychology in Law Enforcement. *Behav. Sci. Law 4*: 401-421.

Farrington, D. (1993). Have any individual, family, or neighbourhood influences on offending been demonstrated conclusively. In Farrington, D., Sampson, R., and Wikstrom, P. (Eds.), *Integrating Individual and Ecological Aspects of Crime*, Sweden: National Council for Crime Prevention, .

Felson, M. (1986). Routine activities and crime prevention in the developing metropolis. *Criminology 25*: 911-931.

Grubin, D., & Gunn, J. (1990). *The Imprisoned Rapist and Rape*, London: Institute of Psychiatry, Department of Forensic Psychiatry, .

Hazelwood, R., & Burgess, A.W. (1987). *Practical Aspects of Rape Investigation: A Multidisciplinary Approach*, New York: Elsevier.

Hazelwood, R., & Warren, J. (1990). The criminal behavior of the serial rapist. *FBI Law Enforce. Bull* Feb.: 11-17.

Hazelwood, R., Ressler, R.K., Depue, R.L., & Douglas, J.E. (1987). Criminal personality profiling: An overview. In Hazelwood, R., and Burgess, A.W. (Eds.), *Practical Aspects of Rape Investigation: A Multidisciplinary Approach*, New York: Elsevier, pp. 137-150.

Huff, J. (1984). Spatial aspects of residential search. In Clark, W. (Eds.), *Modelling Housing Market Search*, New York: St. Martin's Press, pp. 169-199.

Jackson, J., Van den Eshof, P., & De Kleuver, E. (1995). In Bekerian, D., and Dennett, J. (Eds.), *Offender Profiling—Apprehending the Serial Criminal*, Chichester: John Wiley & Sons.

Larson, R.C. (1972). *Urban Police Patrol Analysis*, Cambridge, MA: MIT Press.

LeBeau, J. (1985). Some problems with measuring and describing rape presented by the serial offender. *Just. Q.* 2: 385-398.

LeBeau, J. (1987). Patterns of stranger and serial rape offending: Factors distinguishing apprehended and at large offenders. *J. Crim. Law Criminol.* 78: 309-326.

LeBeau, J. (1993). Four case studies illustrating the spatial-temporal analysis of serial rapists. *Police Stud. 15*(3): 124-145.

Nichols, W. (1980). Mental maps, social characteristics and criminal mobility. In Georges-Abeyie, D., & Harries, K. (Eds.), *Crime, a Spatial Perspective*, New York: Columbia University Press, pp. 156-166.

Pettiway, L. (1982). Mobility of robbery and burglary offenders: Ghetto and nonghetto spaces. *Urban Affairs Q. 18*: 255-270.

Pinizotto, A.J., & Finkel, N.J. (1990). Criminal personality profiling: An outcome and process study. *Law Hum. Behav. 14*(3): 215-233.

Pyle, G. (1974). *The spatial dynamic of crime* (Research Paper No. 159), Department of Geography, University of Chicago, Chicago.

Rengert, G. (1975). Some effects of being female on criminal spatial behavior. *Pa. Geographer 13*(2): 10-18.

Rengert, G., & Wasilchick, J. (1985). *Suburban Burglary: A Time and Placefor Everything*, Charles C Thomas, Springfield. II.

Rengert, G., & Wasilchick, J. (1990). *Space, time and crime: Ethnographic insights into residential burglary*. Report submitted to U.S. Department of Justice, National Institute of Justice, Office of Justice Programs.

Rhodes, W., & Conly, C. (1981). Crime and mobility: An empirical study. In Brantingham, P., and Brantingham, P. (Eds.), *Environmental Criminology*, Sage, Beverly Hills, CA, pp. 167-188.

Rossmo, D. (1995a). Overview: Multivariate spatial profiles as a tool in crime investigation. In Block, C.R., Dabdoub, M., & Fregley, S. (Eds.), *Crime Analysis Through Computer Mapping*, Washington, DC: Police Executive Research Forum,pp. 65-97.

Rossmo, D. (1995b). Place, space, and police investigations: Hunting serial violent criminals. In Eck, J.E., & Weisburd, D. (Eds.). *Crime and Place*, New York: Criminal Justice Press, pp. 217-235.

Tabachnik, B.G., & Fidel, L.S. (1989). *Using Multivariate Statistics*, 2nd ed., New York: Harper Collins, .

Tolman, E.C. (1948). Cognitive maps in rats and man. *Psychol. Rev. 55*: 189-208.

Turner, S. (1969). Delinquency and distance. In Wolfgang, M.E., and Sevin, T. (Eds.), *Delinquency: Selected Studies*, New York: John Wiley.

Warren, J., Reboussin, R., Hazelwood, R., & Wright, J. (1991). Prediction of rape type and violence from verbal, physical and sexual scales. *J. Interpers. Violence 6*(1): 55-67.

Janet Warren et al., "Crime Scene and Distance Correlates of Serial Rape" in *Journal of Quantitative Criminology*, vol. *14*, no. 1, 1998, pp. 35-59. 1998 by Kluwer Academic Publishers. Reproduced by permission of Springer Science Business Media B.V., Formerly Kluwer Academic Publishers B.V.

SECTION

VIII

ETHICAL CONSIDERATIONS IN PROFILING

Section VIII: Ethical Considerations reflects professional, legal and ethical issues in offender profiling practices. These considerations are as important to the development and use of profiling practices, as the empirical studies and research upon which profiling methods are based. As professionals, investigators, consulting detectives, and expert witnesses are bound to uphold professional standards and codes of ethics. The outcome and influence of profiling practices in investigations and profiling testimony in criminal court cases demand that they adhere to professional and ethical guidelines. When using profiling techniques, investigators should conduct themselves carefully and thoughtfully always mindful of these guidelines. As illustrated in the following articles, serious consideration of professional, legal, and ethical issues surrounding the use of profiling methods for criminal investigation and expert witness testimony is required by those in the field.

Laurence Allison and David Canter (1999) summarize the basic professional, legal, and ethical issues associated with profiling. As illustrated in *Professional, Legal, and Ethical Considerations*, there are generally two approaches to offender profiling. One approach relies on researchers and profilers experience with criminals and the other on the scientific method to systematically explore the psychological contributions to criminal investigation. Since many contemporary efforts of profiling are not validated through systematic and scientific study, the profiles that are generated must be treated cautiously and skeptically. Allison and Canter argue that investigators offender profiling should develop through scientific study, rather than relying solely on the investigators personal experience with crime and criminals.

Allison and Canter (1999) contend that professionalism in the use of offender profiling requires extensive training, credentials, and qualifications. Reasoning errors, biases, and distortions commonly associated with human decision making point to the need for scientific methods over personal experiences and opinions. The use of scientific methods is at the heart of professionalism in offender profiling. As shown by Allison and Canter, scientific methods help reduce the effects of bias and allows for hypothesis testing in research, investigation, and findings. This also assists in ensuring that correlations between crime scene behaviors and offender characteristics are empirically based rather than illusory correlations influenced by investigators prior beliefs.

Allison and Canter illustrate the influence of the expert and the implications of profiling testimony in criminal cases. Serious legal issues are raised on the nature and basis of profiling practices. In addition, Allison and Canter emphasize how psychologists and investigators that provide profiling input into investigations must value integrity, impartiality, and respect, and adhere to professional and ethical codes due to the potential influence of the profile on the investigation.

In *Criminal Profiling: Trial by Judge and Jury, not Criminal Psychologist*, author David Ormerod discusses the various difficulties in introducing profiling evidence and testimony into criminal cases at trial. He argues that the introduction of profiles often conflicts with basic rules of evidence. He addresses the legal hurdles facing the prosecution and defense concerning the admissibility of profiles, and the resulting implications for expert witnesses. The goal of the article is to address legal concerns and issues, to assist psychologists in handling requests for profiles.

The *APA's Expert Panel in the Congressional Review of the USS Iowa Incident* by Poythress, Otto, Darkes, and Starr (1993), is a perfect example of the professional, legal, and ethical issues that arise in profiling. The case study focuses on a 1989 explosion that took place aboard the USS Iowa. What first appeared to be an accident was later investigated as a murder suicide by Gunners Mate Clayton Hartwig. The resulting investigation led to an Equivocal Death Analysis by the FBI. Evidence suggests that the analysis lacked reliability and validity.

This case illustrated the need for the scientific method in profiling that relies on empirical evidence rather than the profiler's personal experience, beliefs, and biases. In this case, the profile created was developed out of pre-existing biases and beliefs, rather than crime scene evidence. It was handled with questionable professionalism and ethics. As seen in the conclusions and statements of the House Armed Services Committee, lack of scientific methods and professionalism creates serious legal concerns, as well as raises questions about the validity of all profiles and the ethics of those generating them. This can have serious implications for offender profiling, as it only takes a few inadequate, incorrect, and/or invalid profiles to overshadow the success stories and utility of offender profiling in criminal investigations.

CHAPTER 23

Professional, Legal and Ethical Issues in Offender Profiling

Laurence Alison and David Canter

This chapter addresses a neglected area of offender profiling, namely ethical and professional issues. Through a consideration of the general standards of practice deemed appropriate by the British Psychological Society we outline how many profiling standards fall short of these recommendations. In doing so we highlight the importance of processes over outcome and note how endemic unprofessional and unethical practices are maintained by the failing to consider appropriate procedures. We do not promote this as the definitive set of regulations but rather wish to open up debate about standards where, previously, such discussion has been entirely absent.

> "I am afraid that this behaviour betrays not merely an excess of zeal but a substantial attempt to incriminate a suspect by positive and deceptive conduct of the grossest kind."
>
> The Honourable Mr Justice Ognall from Regina v Colin Stagg

Although the data is not clear there is some evidence that contributions from psychologists to police investigations have been steadily increasing (Copson 1995). Commonly, this has been for the defence (Haward 1985) but more recently psychology has been used to provide advice to investigators by drawing up 'psychological profiles' of offenders in order to narrow the parameters of a suspect search (Canter 1989, Canter and Alison 1997). Despite concerns about the use of experts outside the police to guide enquiries that date back to the 1920s' Royal Commission reports, it has only been recently, and in a select few fields, that ethical and professional guidelines for these activities have been considered by psychologists.

For example, contributions have been made to interviewing strategies for many years from the study of memory recall (Fisher and Geiselman 1987); deception (Ekman 1991, Kohnken 1987) and the psychology of suggestibility (Gudjonsson 1992) but Shepherd (1991) is one of the few people to propose ethical guidelines. In the relatively new area of 'offender profiling', psychologists have remained silent.

The purpose of this chapter is to break that silence by outlining some of the professional, legal and ethical issues associated with profiling and, in particular, the implications of expert opinion in investigations and in the courtroom.

Offender Profiling and Psychology

Origins of Profiling

> Let me have men about me that are fat; Sleek headed men and such as sleep o'nights; Yond Cassius has a lean and hungry look; He thinks too much: such men are dangerous.
>
> Shakespeare (from Julius Caesar)

Associating idiosyncratic features with particular forms of behaviour has been a common theme throughout history and literature. Whilst the FBI have staked a claim to the genesis of 'offender profiling', the notion of inferring offender characteristics from actions has its origins as far back as Biblical references (Canter and Alison 1997).

For many years, a variety of different sorts of people, with many different types of experience to draw upon, have always been prepared to give advice to the police about the type of person who has committed an unsolved crime. Over one hundred year ago, for example, Dr Thomas Bond described the characteristics of 'Jack the Ripper' by using his clinical experience to make inferences from the ways in which the Ripper's victims had been killed. During World War II, William Langer, a psychiatrist, was commissioned by the United States Office of Strategic Services to provide a profile of Adolf Hitler. Langer was correct about Hitler's determination to fight to the end, his worsening mental condition and, ultimately, his suicide.

The technique rose to prominence after James A. Brussel's profile of the 'Mad Bomber of New York' and in particular during the 1960s and 1970s with the increasing trend in serial killing which led to the development of a 'profiling' unit at the FBI Academy at Quantico in Virginia who defined the process of profiling as one of:

> Identifying the gross psychological characteristics of an individual based upon an analysis of the crimes he or she committed and providing a general description of that person.
>
> Ressler, Burgess and Depue 1985

Since the FBI gave publicity to profiling a number of people around the world have come forward to offer opinions based on their own personal experience, typically of offenders in therapy. The claims of these individuals have often been little more than anecdotal accounts, on par with the claims of psychics and astrologers (although not usually so clearly based on any specific process!). There have been, and still are, a variety of people and a variety of methods employed to give advice to investigations. This situation is likely to remain so long as there are people prepared to give advice and there are investigators who are prepared to listen.

Approaches to Profiling

> I knew how this killer functioned; I knew what drove him, because I had seen the same impulse in other people I'd interviewed and treated over the years. Paul Britton (from 'Inside the mind of Rachel's killer - The Mail on Sunday, December 1, 1996)

> Consider one example of the need for research: the seemingly obvious conclusion that Duffy was out of a job because he attacked during working hours. A general analysis of solved cases to see if offenders with jobs tend to attack at different times from those without would be one step in testing the robustness of even such an 'obvious' inference. That type of test is the cornerstone of turning profiling into a science.
>
> David Canter (p. 90, from 'Criminal Shadows' 1994)

In terms of processes of generating profiles, the procedure of Offender Profiling has taken on two rather different meanings. One is as the presentation of the personal opinion of an individual who has some experience of criminals through interviewing them as part of his or her professional activity. The second is as the development of the area of applied, scientific psychology known as 'Investigative Psychology'.

It has only been in the last few years that any attempts have been made to set up a structured, systematic approach directly to explore psychological contributions to the investigation of crime. Even those adopting the clinical approach have recently come to the conclusion that a systematic framework is important for contributing to enquiries (Britton 1997) though for many years this has not been the case. Indeed, the FBI conceded in relation to their own work that:

> ... At present there have been no systematic efforts to validate these profile derived classifications.
>
> Ressler, Douglas, Burgess and Burgess (1993)

However, David Canter has coined the term 'Investigative Psychology' to summarise a growing discipline that examines broadly three areas - (i) criminal behaviour, (ii) information and evidence and (iii) investigative decision making (Canter and Alison, 1997). These areas are seen as closely intertwined components of the investigative process. However, he and his colleagues at the University of Liverpool are well aware that such a discipline must draw upon established principles and the methods that have been the backbone of scientific research in the development of psychological understanding of human behaviour in other areas. In this respect Investigative Psychology is not a new discipline at all but rather a term that encapsulates and focuses upon those areas of psychological research that connect directly with processes in investigations. Investigative psychology is not a new approach or an 'angle' on examining criminal behaviour but rather a term that encapsulates a wide range of procedures centring around a scientific framework.

In a recent edited review of psychological examinations of aspects of investigation Canter and Alison (1997) have made this clear by drawing upon a number of texts of historical scientific interest - many of which illustrate that the process of inferring general characteristics of offenders is not new. For example, Bowlby (1949) compared the characteristics of 44 serious juvenile offenders with a group referred to a Child Guidance Clinic who did not steal. He established that children given less affection at an early age were significantly more delinquent than the control group, were more likely to have mentally disordered parents or were separated from their parents or they had parents that openly displayed their hostility. Burt, in the same year, provided similar explanations of delinquency:

> Judged by the coefficients, the following proves to be the order of importance of the various conditions we have reviewed:
> (1) Defective discipline (2) specific instinct (3) general emotional instability (4) morbid emotional conditions, mild rather than grave, generating or generated by so called complexes (5) a family history of vice or crime (6) intellectual disabilities such as backwardness or dullness (7) detrimental interests such as passion for adventure...

These conclusions by Burt and Bowlby could be used as 'profiles' of the typical delinquents of their day and could certainly have been used to focus a police enquiry.

The common ground between the two pieces of research was that they were attempts to set conclusions and processes of investigation within the context of a scientific approach. The defining components of such a discipline involve the making of observations (empirical/factual component) and the systematic attempt to explain these facts (theoretical component). Early on in the observation phase of a given domain, hypotheses are necessarily quite general. With increasing knowledge of the area such hypotheses can be developed and refined. Hypotheses are devices used by scientists to force between selections in the hope of generating increasingly precise explanations for behaviour - those that survive the rigours of scientific debate become 'laws' - those that are rejected on the basis of discoveries are abandoned.

According to Hull (1943) the core of the scientific method is the generation of a theory to help explain a given area of observable interest:

> A theory is a systematic deductive derivation of the secondary principles of observable phenomena from a relatively small number of primary principles or postulates, much as the secondary principles or theorems of geometry are all ultimately derived as a logical hierarchy from a few original definitions and primary principles called axioms. In science an observed event is said to be explained when the proposition expressing it has been logically derived from a set of definitions and postulates coupled with certain observed conditions antecedent to the event. This, in brief is the nature of scientific theory.
>
> C. L. Hull (1943)

Thus the starting point for the scientific method is a definition of the given domain of interest followed by a theoretical stance on explaining the phenomenon and finally the empirical testing of this theoretical standpoint.

Curiously, offender profiling has developed the tendency for these principles to be ignored in favour of quick answers based on experience rather than any systematic cumulative study. In part, this may have been influenced by expectations based on unrealistic, fictional media portrayals (Gerbner, Gross, Morgan and Signorielli 1994). If a senior investigator has such an unrealistic perspective s/he may ask for advice from a psychologist that cannot be scientifically provided and is only speculative opinion. At the moment, there is no professional qualification of 'offender profiler'. As stated, there are different approaches used by a variety of different individuals. Outlined below are a number of concerns related to this lack of formalisation of 'advice giving' and in particular a number of concerns in relation to the lack of a systematic scientific procedure. The general tenet, then, is that profiling as an art form or 'craft' is not ethically or professionally acceptable.

TRAINING AND CREDENTIALS IN OFFENDER PROFILING

It would be intriguing to know why demands made upon occupational and clinical psychologists in terms of specific training in these areas are not similarly applied to individuals giving a consultancy service as an offender profiler to police investigations - an area in which there has been hardly any special training. It is doubtful that a senior officer would neglect to examine the credetials and training of a financial advisor and yet it does not appear to be the case that similar considerations are given to the background and training of an individual who claims to have special expertise in offender profiling. By definition there cannot have been any special consideration because, as stated, there *is* very little training in offender profiling.

The Crime Faculty based at the police staff training college has drawn up a list of people who may act as 'profilers' to police investigations. But that list was not based on any professionally agreed criteria, but on police assessment of the self-reports of people who wished to be on the list.

Whilst the FBI had a behavioural science unit the qualifications it gave were provided as credits to the local university. People who completed a course of study at Quantico were still required to keep in touch with the 'masters' at the BSU until it was felt they had amassed enough experience to go it alone. Thus, despite the possibility that such individuals may have developed experiential skills as profilers, with the retirement of these masters it is unclear how future generations can gain recognised accreditation.

Similarly, although The Investigative Psychology Unit at Liverpool University runs a variety of courses in psychological contributions to police investigations, including a one year MSc course and PhD related training in specific areas of research including homicide, arson and rape, the focus on profiling is minimal and is seen as a small part of a much broader perspective on understanding, exploring, explaining and aiding police enquiries. In other words the course does not advocate the use of or seek to 'produce' profilers. In fact, 'profiling' is seen as a somewhat redundant area of activity that is more of a media promoted anachronism than a developing field. More fundamental concerns such as systematising information in a format that can be used as data, in developing prioritisation systems, in aiding police interviewing and in examining detective decision making are seen as priorities. Thus profiling plays a relatively minor role in the academic syllabus.

THE FRAILTIES OF HUMAN THINKING

Without recourse to a cumulative systematic research based approach, inferences made on the basis of experience and opinion are subject to a number of distortions, biases and shortcomings that are associated with the frailties of human decision making.

The phenomenon known as 'hindsight bias' (Fischhoff 1975) is a particularly apposite example - where an individual underestimates how much they have learned, claiming that they knew all along the outcome of a situation. For example, Wiseman, West and Stemman (1996) established that where psychics had contributed to police enquiries the psychics and the police they advised were only likely to remember those aspects of the case they were correct about and forgot a considerable number of assertions that were totally incorrect. Similarly, Rowe (1993) noted the fact that vague predictions were later made to fit the facts of the case. If psychics are able to convince themselves and police officers that they made successful contributions (as Wiseman et al 1996 show) then similar processes may lead to apparently convincing contributions from 'expert' profilers.

Canter (1994) takes this comparison head on:

> For some detectives the idea of approaching a psychologist for help hardly differs from
> approaching a psychic or astrologer. It might work so where's the harm in trying? To my mind,
> the harm comes if there is no accumulation of tested and proven logic.
>
> From 'Criminal Shadows' (p. 79)

Thus the approach does not rely on intuition or experience. 'Success' is not measured on the basis of how many 'correct hits' have apparently been made but rather on developing, in accordance with the scientific process, appropriate strategies for researching criminal actions and the characteristics associated with those actions. Concern lies within the slow, steady accumulation of knowledge based on the foundations of psychology and the scientific process. It is to the professional, legal and ethical considerations associated with this approach that we now turn.

PROFESSIONAL ISSUES

A psychological approach to aiding criminal investigations represents an example of a scientific mode of thinking set against and tested by a variety of statistical procedures. Such a mode of thinking involves the testing of hypotheses where evidence comes from scientific observation.

As with all modes of thinking (such as diagnosis, insight, and reflection) good thinking is represented by a thorough search for alternatives without favouring what one already has in mind. Poor thinking involves missing something in the search and/or seeking evidence that prevents the scientist from choosing between alternatives.

Avoiding Bias

A powerful argument for relying heavily on the scientific mode of thinking is to counter the frailties of poor thinking. For example, explorations of accuracy of probability judgements show that there is a normal human tendency to underestimate high frequencies and overestimate very low ones. This inappropriate heuristic could be counteracted through statistical observations but is potentially dangerous if a profiler is relying on experience to compare similar cases. Moreover, if bound by normal human reasoning the profiler is likely to be overconfident in his predictions because as Fischhoff, Slovic and Lichtenstein (1977) have suggested it is not usual for people to have a clear perception of what probability means. For example whilst degrees of certainty are often used in everyday language they are rarely expressed numerically. Employing statistical procedures can help to prevent such errors. Thus when a person offers the opinion that there is a high probability that the offender is white it may be assumed by many police officers that the offender must be white, although the statistical probability may be only 65%.

For example, in reference to the profile in the Wimbeldon Common enquiry the comment by Britton that the probability of the offender having particular characteristics was 'vanishingly' rare is an indication of a confused view of the probabilities involved - particularly given that in reference to the features of the profile that Britton mentions, some studies indicate the alleged characteristics are prevalent in at least 10% of the population (Comfort 1987, Leitenberg and Henning 1995; Alison and Lee 1999).

Inappropriate Heuristics

As well as problems associated with estimating probabilities, it is part of human nature to use inappropriate heuristics in decision making. Tversky and Kahneman (1982) have highlighted a number of these.

Perhaps the most relevant to this area is the availability heuristic (Tversky and Kahneman 1973) where the individual makes judgements on a probability by thinking of examples that are easily accessible to memory whilst less salient counter examples are forgotten. Individuals are more likely to remember their own point of view more vividly thus resulting in a bias in the recall of information. Ross and Silcoly (1979) for example established that in asking husbands and wives their share of responsibilities they were only likely to be able to recall their own share rather than that of their partner - they were also more likely to remember instances when they had shirked their responsibility than similar instances when their partner had done so. Thus a profiler may remember more clearly offenders that had a significant impact on him than those, that for whatever multitude of reasons, are not so accessible to memory.

Anchoring and Adjustment

Further biases include anchoring and adjustment (Tversky and Kahneman 1974) where individuals will base a decision on what they have already been told - even if what they have been told is irrelevant to making an accurate assessment. For example, simply spinning a wheel with probabilities ranging from 1–100% will result in a probabilistic prediction being biased by the position the arrow lands on. So, for example, if asked the probability of rain, individuals will be influenced in their decision by a random probabilistic guess - i.e. given a prior random probability of 95% as opposed to 20% will result in the individual making a higher prediction of rain. In simple terms we tend to be biased by our 'starting point' beliefs - even if they are irrelevant to the case at hand. So if investigators mention a possible culprit to the profiler this may bias his approach to the case even if the suspect is later excluded from the investigations.

The frequently reported police assumption that a suspect is lying is also a good illustration of the anchor belief of the person being a suspect having a biasing influence.

Hypothesis Testing

Search inference processes in hypothesis testing are also prone to these type of problems. The simplest form of hypothesis testing is to imagine some result that would be definitely obtained if the hypothesis is true and then look for that result. An obvious danger with this is that there may be alternative explanations, which have not been considered. A second danger is that a hypothesis will be falsely rejected because of poor experimentation. The tendency to look for confirmation of a hypothesis is demonstrated by Wason's (1960) experiment of asking subjects to find the rule behind the sequence 2, 4, 6. If individuals first 'rule' to test this sequence was, "increase the digits by two" then they would not search for an alternative hypothesis - such as the more parsimonious alternative, "increase the number" - i.e. 2, 4, 6, 9, 167, 2204. This is an elegant example of confirmation bias - the tendency to look for information to support a theory rather than discount it. This process can explain a number of miscarriages of justice. Having decided who was guilty evidence was sought to support that and contradictory evidence was reinterpreted.

Illusory Correlation

Another curious feature of human thinking is to find associations between variables where there are none. Smedslund (1963) for example presented nurses with a random correlation between a symptom and disease. Despite no association 85% of nurses said there was a relationship. This is probably because individuals are more likely to examine present/present cells of a contingency table than absent / present and absent / absent cells. In this case the nurses only examined cases where the disease and the symptoms were present. Illusory correlation is also influenced by prior beliefs. For example, Chapman (1967) questioned why clinicians used 'Draw-a-person' tests even though they proved diagnostically useless. The reason it seemed was that the clinicians had already convinced them that there must be some evidence of usefulness in the test despite evidence proving otherwise. The clinicians were also likely to have only been attending to cases where results did tie in with characteristics. This effect of attention bias can be increased by prior belief - when prior belief is present one tends to focus on evidence that supports it and ignore evidence against it.

Illusory correlation and attention bias distort perceptions of the evidence available. It appears to be human nature to think that evidence weighs more heavily on the side of beliefs we already hold than it actually does.

In a criminal investigation many processes, including what the media give emphasis to may feed such illusory correlations. So it may be assumed that many violent offenders are insane, even though people diagnosed as mentally ill are no more likely to commit violent crimes than anyone else. A profiler brought in because he has treated mentally ill people may be especially prone to such an illusion, supported by an attention bias.

Irrelevant Information and Belief Persistence

Other seemingly innocuous and irrelevant factors can also effect judgements. An example would include the 'ordering effect' - i.e. when the order in which information is gained is not relevant the order should not be considered as significant. An example of a primacy ordering effect would be Asch's (1946) use of reordering adjectives to describe a person. When the first adjective used to describe a person was negative (for example 'mean') this tended to colour perceptions of more positive adjectives that came later in the list. However, if the order was reversed and the negative came at the end of the description the more positive adjectives were not tainted by the negative starting point. In simple terms such distortions occur because of an initial commitment to a prior belief. Dailey (1952) for example, found that subjects were less sensitive to new information when they answered inferential questions after receiving early evidence in an impression formation task. Similar processes occur even in perceptual experiments - Bruner and Potter (1964) discovered that the initial hypothesis in identifying an out of focus image inhibited recognition when the picture came into focus.

A case where a particular type of individual or a specific individual has been focused on may represent an example where the profiler could be prone to look for confirmation of the assertion rather than evidence to challenge it. This is a common phenomenon, examples of which are exemplified by 'Ripperologists' (individuals who have theories as to the identity of Jack the Ripper). Ripperologists tend to cite a specific individual as a possibility for the crimes and then seek out evidence to support their claim rather than seeking to disconfirm their evidence through a search for alternatives.

As well as the inappropriateness of adhering to an initial incorrect belief after contrary evidence there is a tendency for individuals to strengthen their beliefs with neutral information - i.e. information that is consistent with the belief and its converse. Lord, Ross and Leper (1979) selected people on the basis of whether they were for or against capital punishment. Each person was then presented with mixed evidence on the effectiveness of capital punishment. People more easily found flaws in the reports that went against their belief whilst using pro-belief neutral evidence in a far more glowing light than it should have been given credit for. This phenomena is particularly pernicious in unscientific profiling because much of the material drawn upon will have no known validity and is likely, in effect, to be neutral with regard to the offence. For example, a suspect may have had a minor conviction as a teenager for indecent exposure because someone complained that he urinated on their fence. This could then be treated as if it were a chronic history of sexually related offending that is in accord with the putative profile.

Furnham and Alison (1994) have established that there are a number of beliefs that police officers may hold in relation to juror bias. Bias in this context was measured by a Juror Bias Scale (Kassin and Wrightsman 1983) which measures the degree to which an individual is biased towards a prosecution or defence standpoint in the face of neutral evidence. Furnham and Alison found that the police were more likely than a control group to believe a suspect is guilty on the basis of neutral information. According to theories of irrational belief persistence, given this biased view, officers would be more inclined to look for examples to support presumed guilt, be less able to search for evidence to counter these beliefs and to view neutral information as proof of guilt. As Furnham and Alison suggested it may be that one's role has some influence on the information to which one attends. In the case of a police officer one may reasonably assume that the number of cases on which individuals are not tried and convicted for crimes, where the officer was convinced of guilt, would become more salient than those where the individual was correctly convicted.

Cultural and Group Effects.

In terms of the promulgation of poor thinking through cultural norms, institutions where defence of one's beliefs is a virtue and questioning a vice are the ones most likely to overcome challenges from the outside. However this does not necessarily make for good decision making. It is possible that the strong cultural identity of the police force to some extent condones such a way of thinking and so may be particularly susceptible to biases. Furthermore, when such beliefs are challenged the first instinct is to bolster them (Janis and Mann 1977). Accompanying factors such as stress, where excessive levels can lead to hypervigilance in which the decision maker considers one option after another with little search for evidence (Keinan 1987) creates a decision context fertile for distortions if not closely monitored.

Finally, there are group effects that could contribute to ineffective decisions. Studies carried out extensively by Janis (1982) identified the following major causes of inappropriate decisions on the basis of inefficient group processes. Many of these bear similarities to problems known to exist within management circles and organisations (Blau and Scott 1963).

Overestimation of the group This involves what Janis has termed 'The Illusion of invulnerability' - often fostered by past success where there is a belief in the inherent morality of the group - in which immoral means are used to obtain supposedly moral ends. This is a similar process to the identification of 'Bottom line mentality' in organisations where a financial success is believed to be the only value worthy of consideration even at the expense of long-term finances.

Closed mindedness Involves collective rationalisation - where members convince themselves and others that they do not have to consider other information or alternatives.

Stereotypes of out groups The tendency to believe that the group's opponents are weak, foolish and immoral - therefore underestimating them. Again a similar process - 'Exploitative mentality' has been examined in organisations and concerns the promotion of stereotypes thereby undermining empathy.

Pressures towards uniformity The use of self censorship where members hold back from expressing inconsistent views in order to conform.

Illusion of unanimity Related to the above the use of self-censorship is reinforcing because it creates an illusion of unanimity.

Direct pressure on dissenters Occurs where 'self-appointed mind guards' in the group take it upon themselves to keep others in line with the supposed consensus viewpoints. 'Madison Avenue Mentality' conforms to such a process where the group is happy with the belief that anything is right if the public can be made to believe so. Such a belief system, as well as being ethically unsound, are professionally inefficient and, therefore, very rarely financially beneficial in the long run.

Thus, a fundamental proposition is that without recourse to a scientific mode of thinking and the establishment of an approach based on cumulative knowledge which can be challenged and reworked, investigative 'expertise' is subject to all the frailties of human thinking whether the individual is a profiler or an experienced Detective.

THE INFLUENCE OF THE EXPERT

The profiler, however, may present a danger that is more invidious than an experienced detective if he or she is considered to be an informed 'expert'. Much of the literature on persuasion demonstrates that the perceived authority of the information source is crucial in determining the impact of the opinion offered (Milgram 1974, Arendt 1963, Comfort 1950). The notorious Milgram experiments also serve to illustrate how much power apparently neutral 'scientists' can wield. The proneness of experienced investigators to these influences has certainly been demonstrated both in the Yorkshire Ripper enquiry and in the enquiry into the murder of Rachel Nickell. The danger then is that the profiler brings in many biases that are masked by the belief in his/her neutral expertise and that these are further confused by the investigating officer's own biases. The consequence, clearly demonstrated with 'psychic Detectives' (Wiseman et al 1997) is that both the police and the advisors believe their interaction is much more fruitful than it actually is. The profiler mistakenly believes he/she has made a real contribution, the investigating officers' believing the profiler has strengthened the views they had already formulated. Indeed the prevalence of this process is strongly supported by the findings of Copson's (1995) survey of police officers' opinions of the profiling services they had obtained.

LEGAL ISSUES

> The notion that a psychological profile is in any circumstances admissible in proof of identity is to my mind redolent with considerable danger.
>
> The Honourable Mr Justice Ognall (1994) from Regina v Colin Stagg

Definitional Problems

Despite the FBI's broad classification (noted under the section 'Origins of Profiling') there is no commonly agreed definition of what constitutes a profile or how one may be constructed. Lack of clear definition regarding the contents or process of constructing a profile is therefore the first stumbling block in terms of its relevance (or irrelevance) in the courts. One generally agreed principle is that it involves inferring *characteristics* of the offender from *actions* at the scene of the crime. The definitional problem lies in what constitutes an action or characteristic and how best the process of associating one with the other may be carried out.

Because there is at present no established discipline of profiling or widely published scientific literature, each person who provides a profile does so by drawing upon his or her own particular predilections. Some, for example, may give emphasis to the criminal background, whilst others may give special emphasis to the criminal background, whilst others may give special emphasis to the thoughts and wishes (sometimes called 'fantasies') of the offender. Thus, as well as differentiation amongst profilers in their use of different criminal actions to analyse (varying from crime scene reports to witness statements) their generation of criminal characteristics can also vary - from demographic features such as the age or approximate residential location of the offender to the nature of his sexual fantasies.

The Myth of the Expert

Aside from the number of concerns highlighted, there is the question of what an offender profiler's field of expertise actually is and how this relates to the problem of interpreting characteristics from actions. In other words, what special credentials does an offender profiler claim to have over, for example, a police officer in the interpretation of criminal actions?

There is no evidence to suggest that clinicians or experienced detectives have any special skills in constructing offender profiles. In fact, the limited research that does exist suggests that there is little difference between 'professional' profilers, detectives, psychologists and college students (Pinizotto and Finkel 1990). Indeed, there are some studies on other fields where there may be a presumed correlation between experience and expertise that in issues of detecting deception police officers can actually perform more poorly than other groups (Kohnken 1987). Furthermore, the studies by Wilson et al (1997) on the ability of police officers to link rapes validly to a common offender found that experienced rape investigators were no better than inexperienced ones. Clearly, we are not suggesting that experience is a handicap in generating possible suspect characteristics. Indeed, the Investigative Psychology Unit strongly promotes links with the police force precisely for the wealth of investigative acumen that they possess regarding previous cases. We are merely pointing out that one must check and treat with caution all opinions and not simply assume that because it is said with great conviction by someone with experience that it must be true.

There is also of course a fundamental problem of whether a 'profiler' can ever be objectively evaluated anyway. As Ormerod (1996) has pointed out claims to success rates in profiling are

> ... open to attack given the impossibility of an objective assessment of reliability. Given the nature of the exercise, a controlled experiment is out of the question. Similarly, practical difficulties would be encountered in any retrospective evaluation of trial outcomes. It would simply not be possible to disentangle from the ultimate profile what information came from guesswork, what was 'forensic' input, etc.

p. 870

There must therefore be real doubt as to whether investigating officers are necessarily the best judges of what is useful to their enquiry in terms of profiles or profilers. They may be unaware of what constitutes the scientific rationale behind a profile, unable to implement or put to use any of the statements made within it and unable to question certain aspects of accuracy or process. If they cannot evaluate 'profiles' and there is unlikely to be any in depth objective assessment of them, in what sense can they be regarded as a product of expertise?

Profiling as a Discrete Discipline?

Poythress, Otto, Darkes and Starr (1993) examined the FBI agents' use of psychological autopsy produced to explain the explosion on USS Iowa. These agents formed the opinion that based on their experience in criminal investigation that the explosion was the result of a suicide. After the American Psychological Association examined the case more thoroughly they established that the FBI's analysis was invalid and further evidence came to light that suggested the explosion was the result of an accident.

Poythress et al point out that though it may be tempting to make inferences from crime scene details on the basis of experience there are a number of considerations that may bias and distort these conclusions - not least of which is the nature of the information itself. In other words, if the collection process and the type of information is impoverished then what Poythress et al call "reconstructive evaluations" (by which they mean offender profiles and psychological autopsies) are going to be similarly impoverished, unreliable and invalid. Therefore, a number of research groups around the world (including units set up within police forces) are now following the lead of the IPU research aimed at building up a cumulative scientific discipline that may be drawn upon by the police themselves rather than emphasising 'hands on' advice to ongoing enquiries. Obviously of central concern is the information collection process - distortions in which present similar problems for any scientifically based study. Thus if the information employed to construct hypotheses is distorted the results and conclusions are likely to suffer from such misrepresentative material. An early concern of the investigative psychology approach concerns improving these early stages of information collection.

The fact that the IPU is sceptical of 'profiling expertise' is backed up by other areas of research. Even in more 'conventional' investigative domains both Ekman's (1991) and Kohnken's work (1987) suggests that there is nothing 'special' about Detective or clinical expertise. As mentioned, in detecting deception both studies point to the same conclusion - i.e. that experience is *not* associated with better performance. In fact in Kohnken's study it was found that accuracy was *negatively* correlated with length of on-the-job experience. There is no reason to assume that offender profiling is an exceptional field where experience is associated with increased accuracy. In mind of these early warning signals, the investigator should seriously consider exactly why s/he needs to employ the use of an 'expert' external to the enquiry and if so in what ways can they justifiably, professionally and ethically be employed.

Profiling in Investigations and Profiling in Court

A number of individuals, from a variety of professions have proposed that there is little problem associated with viewing profiling as an investigative tool. For example as Ormerod, Ognall and Canter state:

> Statistics show that the police have used psychological profiling to focus their investigations, identify and locate possible suspects, and to assist in prosecution.
>
> Ormerod (1996) p. 866

> Nobody questions that in certain cases the assistance of a psychologist of that kind can prove a very useful investigative tool.
>
> The Honourable Mr Justice Ognall (1994) from Regina v Colin Stagg

> Changes in the demands made on police forces around the world mean that they are increasingly in need of such help. The lone detective, so popular in fiction, has given way to organized teams which require systematic guidance.
>
> Canter (1994) from Criminal Shadows (p. 4)

However, the dangers to the investigation are greatly magnified when attempts are made to use profiles to single out individuals as probative proof of identity in the courtroom. For example Boon and Davies have highlighted potential problems with the technique:

> ... it should never be forgotten that its [profiling] contribution to any investigation can only be supportive rather than substantive. Furthermore, it must also be borne in mind that no matter how much research is conducted profiles can be inaccurate and that this can have seriously misleading effects upon an enquiry.
>
> Boon and Davies (1991)

This viewpoint is further extended by Ormerod (1996) in a discussion of the evidential implications of profiling:

> ... it has been acknowledged that some profiles are 'so vague as to point to practically anyone' and can 'severely hamper an investigation by sending the police off in the wrong direction'.
>
> Ormerod (1996)

Thus, whilst some cases have raised the prestige of profiling (cf. Ormerod 1996) others which have failed have resulted in doubts and scepticism. Not all profiling attempts have been as impressive as those of Langer and Brussel and even those appeared to have no influence at all on the actual police investigation. There are some very clear examples of profiles being outstandingly incorrect:

> In one case, for example, a profile on a criminal suspect told investigators that the man they were looking for came from a broken home, was a high school drop out, held a marginal job, hung out in 'honky tonk' bars and lived far from the scene of the crime. When the attacker was finally caught, it was learned that the psychological assessment was 100% wrong. He had not come from a broken home, he had a college degree, held an executive position with a respected financial institution, did not use alcohol and lived near the scene of the crime.
>
> Goodroe (1987)

The authors also have experience of providing totally incorrect profiles. For example, in one of the earliest profiles from the Unit, in the brutal slaying of a teenager the profile suggested a white male between 20 and 30 years old - based purely on the statistical probablity of such offences as carried out in previous similar crimes. The offender was, in fact, a 12 year old black girl. Thus in terms of the actual content of a profile (regardless of the appropriateness or otherwise of the means by which it was constructed), evaluation and the use of the profile can be seriously misleading. In the cases mentioned above, for example, the means by which the profile was obtained may have been scientifically sound but the actual case statistically anomalous. Therefore, even casting aside difficulties of evaluation it is still possible for profiles to present problems for an enquiry team unless they are very carefully considered.

It is hardly surprising then that profiling has never been used in a British court of law. For example, from the concerns highlighted so far - which include (i) definitional problems, (ii) lack of evidence to suggest expertise, (iii) the question of whether profiling is in fact a systematic discipline and (iv) the agreement by a variety of professionals as to its lack of usefulness in identifying and individual it is evident that the use of a profile in court is redolent with danger. Aside from these important issues there are two major hurdles that would have to be overcome by the party relying on the profile. These are the concepts of relevance and admissibility (Ormerod 1996). As Sheldon and MacLeod (1991) have noted in relation to 'statistical profiling' (i.e. profiling based on examinations of the offence behaviours of a number of cases):

> Normative data ... is of little use to the courts. The courts are concerned to determine the past behaviour of accused individuals, and in carrying out that function, information about the past behaviour of other individuals is wholly irrelevant.
>
> p. 814

The probative guilt of the accused (or probative innocence - profilers have been asked by defence barristers to present information that suggests their client *did not* commit an offence but so far these opinions have not found their way into the courts) cannot be established by such research or opinion based profiles. Because opinions of clinicians are based upon experience of allegedly similar cases and statistical research is based on purportedly relevant data sets neither connects directly with the specific case at hand. The central problem for the courts lies in the potential for extreme prejudice against the defendant who, by definition, being an individual, does not fit the criteria for a system based on generalities - whether they are based on opinion or research.

Furthermore, as Ormerod (1996) argues very cogently, there are strong legal barriers as to the admissibility of profiles both because they would be legally regarded as based on unacceptable hearsay, and because they would introduce prejudice into the evidence. These are high barriers in English law but may not be so strict in other jurisdictions (Canter 1997).

ETHICAL ISSUES

> In all their work psychologists shall value integrity, impartiality and respect for persons and evidence and shall seek to establish the highest ethical standards in their work.
>
> BPS Codes of Conduct 1991

The above statement comes from the BPS's fundamental and general principle section. It encapsulates rather well the elements of concern to psychologists contributing to police enquiries with the emphasis on integrity, impartiality and respect. To illustrate how these principles may be maintained, a detailed account is given below of how the psychologist may adhere professionally and ethically to the codes of conduct through keeping detailed documents, outlining sources of the inferences, allowing for peer review of work, searching for alternative explanations through an impartial, objective approach and maintaining a concern and respect for the individuals who s/he may influence through his/her input.

Keeping Detailed Documents

It is essential to keep as full an ongoing account of one's work as possible because (a) crucial details may be forgotten or wrongly interpreted with hindsight and (b) so that others may challenge the steps and assertions after the work has been carried out. If these steps are not open to scrutiny they cannot be challenged or explored. Moreover, the psychologist is laying himself open to the challenge that inferences were made *after* the discovery of certain pieces of evidence. For example, if a profile is constructed and no details of it are recorded, it is feasible that the psychologist could have constructed the profile *after* a suspect became the focus of police attention.

The psychologist should therefore have a dated copy of all information given to the police. Word of mouth is not acceptable - nor is it adequate to sketch out ideas or write them on blackboards later to be removed. The investigating team and the psychologist should have duplicates of every piece of information passed between them.

Sources of the Inferences

The psychologist should always be able to cite where possible what the bases are for his/her inferences. For example, if his/her psychological framework is psychoanalytic, cognitive or behavioural this should be explicitly stated with reference to the appropriate literature. Similarly, the psychologist should be able to give an account of what work s/he has drawn upon with respect to the inferences made. This allows the psychologist (a) to be able to give advice on the strength of the inference (i.e. is the work referred to preliminary or well established?) and (b) to be challenged about his/her assertions. Moreover, the psychologist should provide a definitional system for the given domain of interest. For example, the psychologist may on the basis of the pattern of the stab wounds suggest that the offender knew the victim. If this is based on two clinical cases that the psychologist has previously come across then this inference can be made with less certainty than if the psychologist has been working specifically on the analysis of stab wound patterning and established that in the 400 crimes with similar patterning only three did not involve someone who was known to the victim. In both cases the psychologist would need to define precisely what s/he is looking for in the patterns and why this is relevant.

Peer Review

In a scientific context it is expected that any assertions or inferences are open to challenge and review. This commonly involves the following:

Publication of work in journals;

Having internal documents that can be open to scrutiny if required;

In house reviews of material by other colleagues;

Invitations to external reviewers to oversee the work (this may involve the presentation of material at academic conferences).

From the previous 'stab wound' example both psychologists should be able to direct the appropriate authorities to the work that they refer to - the clinical psychologist should have some documentation on the previous two cases that s/he has come across and the psychologist whose area of speciality lies in the analysis of 'stab wounds' should be able to produce the evidence of his/her results (even if this is only an internal document).

In light of this and in relation to the biases mentioned so far there are a number of measures that may help to prevent distortions in the handling and collection of information:

All the facts The psychologist should inform the investigative team that they should present *all of the facts* known about the case - suspicions, intuitions and 'gut feelings' are not relevant and may bias the research.

Presentation of the facts It may be beneficial for an individual *not* directly involved in the case to present the psychologist with the material - i.e. if possible, someone who has no suspicions about particular suspects. Therefore it may not be necessary and in fact may be detrimental to the inquiry for the most senior individual to present the information.

The irrelevance of suspicions The psychologist should state that under no circumstances should any information be given about a likely suspect. If an offender profile is to be drawn up it should be without the 'benefit' of a possible suspect. It is the Investigative Psychology Unit's experience that both police officers and members of the legal profession are often inappropriately keen to get involved with who the offender may or may not be. This makes it more difficult for the psychologist to approach the problem with an open mind. Indeed, both authors have experienced the process of being unable to avoid picking up certain cues from the investigating officers as to those officers' likely suspicions. This transference is unlikely to be deliberate on the part of the officer but is simply an unavoidable product of having an opinion on the case. Obviously it would be impossible not to have some preferred account of the possible sequence of events and in the case of experienced Detectives these may be well founded. The profiler may, therefore, simply be picking up on and gaining the benefits of that officers' correct assumptions. Similarly, if the officer is wrong then similar incorrect assumptions could be made by the profiler.

Keeping a record It may be useful to tape exchanges between psychologist and investigating team so that any potential for biasing opinions can be examined.

Respect for Persons

'Respect': Deferential regard or esteem felt or shown towards another person or thing; the condition or state of being esteemed or honoured; rank standing or station in life.
The Shorter Oxford English Dictionary 3rd Ed. 1986

As with ethical concerns regarding the laboratory and fieldwork of psychologist's attention should be paid to the possible consequences that psychological input might have to police enquiries.

In such instances psychologists should be concerned in any advice they are giving to undercover operations or interviews with respect both to the possible future implications for the suspect and the officers involved. In other words, the psychologist should not be cajoled into advocating behaviour that may put the suspect (or the officers involved in the operation) at risk psychologically or physically. Therefore, at the *outset* of any advice on undercover operations the psychologist should have full documentation regarding the likely outcomes of the operation - this would include psychological and physical implications both for the suspect and the undercover officer.

Competence

'Competence': "A sufficiency of; sufficiency of qualification, capacity, esp. legal capacity; adequacy."

The Shorter Oxford English Dictionary 3rd Ed. 1986

The British Psychological Society's codes of conduct states that psychologists should endeavour to work within their professional limits and to identify factors which restrict it - in particular recognising the boundaries of their competence. Therefore there are questions as to levels of competence in having the sufficient skills and ability to advise on profiles and give guidance to investigations.

As stated, given that there is no evidence to support any special skill in profiling it is questionable whether psychologists should be used in this way without a careful consideration of their credentials and work. However, as well as the competencies involved in the construction of the profile, there should be additional questions when the psychologist is asked to contribute to other areas of the enquiry. For example, whilst a 'profiler' may give information relating to the characteristics of the offender, s/he should not be concerned with aiding in the interview process when a suspect is called in unless s/he is competent to advise on the interviewing process. Similarly, if the suspect were mentally ill, unless the profiler had the relevant skills as a clinician s/he should not advise with respect to dealing with the peculiarities of the suspect's presumed diagnosis. The number of disciplines that may be called in for relevant expert advise may therefore range from interviewing skills to psycholinguistics to diagnoses of neurological damage.

Competence is a particularly difficult issue for psychologists contributing to enquiries as 'profilers' to assess. As stated, there is no formally agreed discipline or profession, exclusively as a profiler. Therefore police investigators should be extremely cautious of an individual who claims a professional status solely as a 'profiler'. Competence can only really be gauged then in reference to other professionally recognised disciplines and even then it is questionable whether these connect sufficiently closely with the profiling domain.

Impartiality

Impartiality: "The quality of being impartial; freedom from prejudice orbias; fairness. Impartial - not partial; not favouring one more than another; unprejudiced; unbiased, fair, just, equitable."
The Shorter Oxford English Dictionary 3rd Ed. 1986

As stated, profilers may be prone to use inappropriate heuristics where there is no scientific rational for making the assertions and where there is no external monitoring of the enquiry. Further, many of the heuristics outlined may distort views and create biases amongst those profilers who base their assertions with total conviction solely on experience. For example, they may make inferences on the basis of only the most salient cases, only generate information consistent with a prior belief, and neglect to look for alternative explanations and be overconfident in their assertions. Moreover, they may be susceptible to some of the features outlined that relate to stress and distortions through group processes.

We realise that the recommendations here are a counsel of perfection that are very difficult to achieve in the far from ideal pressure and haste of police investigations. We are also aware of the attractions (indeed seductions) in giving immediate and confident answers to police officers involved in nationally important cases. But unless serious attempts are made to reach for the ideals then there is a grave risk of the potential for contributions from experts being lost, or worse, actually resulting in miscarriages of justice.

IN THE FINAL ANALYSIS

In summary there are some fundamental questions about offender profiling that need to be addressed:

Why use a profiler? The contribution of an outside expert offering opinions to a very select and particular area needs to be reconsidered. It is not appropriate to generate profiles on the basis of inappropriate information. In other words, unless the means of collecting information is adequate the bases on which characteristics are inferred from actions may be unsound. Crime scene reports may not be entirely appropriate for psychologists to work with. But once that information has been more effectively collected it may not need any very specialist knowledge to make inferences from it. In other words, as the process of Investigative psychology becomes more established within police practice there will be less need to bring in an outside expert, as developments in a number of police forces are revealing (see Lee and Alison 1997).

When are psychological contributions inappropriate? Contributions are inappropriate when the individual(s) concerned cannot demonstrate clearly that their area of expertise is relevant to the area under investigation. In the same way that it would be inappropriate for a psychologist whose speciality is the study of optical illusions to be exploring speech impediments, it is also inappropriate for a psychologist whose speciality is the fitness of a patient to plead in court to be giving advice on how to carry out an undercover police operation.

Who is giving the advice and what are their competencies? Related to the last point, the investigative team need to know the boundaries within which their 'expert' can operate. They need documents that outline clearly what the psychologist's field of expertise is, what his/her formal qualifications are, what tests his/her expertise has undergone, what papers he/she has written or presentations he/she has made and what internal documents he/she has produced. As our review of the room for bias has demonstrated accounts of previous cases may not be the best gauge of competence.

Art is not enough The central principle underlying this area, as with any other approach to science, should be one of impartiality. In the case of profiling, a subjective, intuitive, biased or gut feeling is inadequate, unprofessional and ethically and legally unsound. The recommendation is that an objective systematic framework should be drawn up in which the contribution to investigations is through a cumulative scientific approach rather than one based on personal expert opinion.

It is worth emphasising that there are parallels here to the role of clinical experience versus scientific inference in the therapeutic activities of clinical psychologists. Over three decades ago studies demonstrated clearly the power of science (Meehl 1954). It may be that this debate will need to be revisited in this new area of applied psychology.

Thus, whilst we remain optimistic on the contributions that psychology can make to inquiries, caution must be observed. Unless combined with an ongoing concern with the professional, legal and ethical issues, investigators and psychologists will continue to be blessed one minute and cursed the next by the peaks and troughs of individual successes and failures. As Ormerod (1996) has stated, "...just as these successes [in profiling] herald psychological profiling as a powerful new weapon to combat serious crime, cases which have spectacularly failed, such as *Stagg*, generate doubts and concerns". Since profiling and police work constantly attracts media attention it is evident that to secure foundations for a discipline that can genuinely contribute to dealing with crime individuals employed in the area should put professional, legal and ethical concerns at the forefront of its development. The concern should not simply be with profiling criminals. If that is the only consideration then it is the public 'profile' of these professionals that will gradually fall into disrepute and decline. Again, the BPS codes carry a particularly apposite warning:

> Psychologists shall conduct themselves in their professional activities in a way that does not damage the interest of the recipients of their services or participants in their research and does not undermine public confidence in their ability to carry out professional duties.
>
> From the BPS Codes of Conduct 1991

FUTURE RESEARCH

One final, scientific point is worth emphasising. There have been very few studies of investigative decision making and only a handful of in depth analyses of how police officers incorporate psychologists, or psychological thinking into their detective work. This chapter can therefore be looked on as a research agenda, outlining hypotheses about the cognitive biases and procedural confusions that may be inherent in the complex and difficult task of solving a crime. Indeed, this is a much-neglected area that connects directly with the structural and professional standards of the police environment itself. Caution must be observed if an individual professing to be a 'profiler' seems unconcerned or has neglected to consider these important aspects of the way in which s/he interacts with the chosen profession that s/he has sought to liaise with.

REFERENCES

Alison, L.J., & Lee, J. (1999). The feasibility of profiling from sexual fantasies. In D. V. Canter and L. J. Alison (eds.) (1999). *Profiling Rape and Murder*. Offender Profiling. Series III. Aldershot: Dartmouth.

American Psychological Association (1992). Ethical Principles of Psychologists and Code of Conduct *American Psychologist 47* (12).

Asch, S.E. (1946). Forming impressions of personality. *Journal of Abnormal and Social Psychology*, *41*, 258-290.

Baron, J. (1994). *Thinking and Deciding*. Cambridge University Press.

Bowlby, E.J.M. (1949). Forty four juvenile thieves: Their characteristics and home life, conclusions and summary. *Baillere London* 53-55.

British Psychological Society (1991). *Codes of Conduct, Ethical Principles and Guidelines,* Leicester: BPS.

Britton, P. (1997). Inside the mind of Rachel's killer. Extract from *The Mail on Sunday. December 1st* 1997.

Britton, P. (1997). *The Jigsaw Man.* London: Bantam Press.

Bruner, J.S., & Potter, M.C. (1964) Interference in visual recognition. *Science, 144,* p. 424-425.

Burt, C. (1949). *The young delinquent. Conclusion.* University of London Press p. 599-614.

Canter, D.V. (1989). Offender Profiles. In *The Psychologist* 2(1) 1989, p. 12-16.

Canter, D.V. (1994). *Criminal Shadows.* London: Harper Collins.

Canter, D.V. (1995). The psychology of offender profiling. In T. H. Blau (eds.) *Psychological Services for Law Enforcement.* John Wiley and Sons, Inc. p. 261-274.

Canter, D.V. (1997). New Forms of Expertise. *Forensic Update.*

Canter, D.V., & Alison, L.J. (1997). *Criminal Detection and the Psychology of Crime.* Aldershot: Dartmouth.

Chapman, L.J., & Chapman, J.P. (1967). Genesis of popular but erroneous psychodiagnostic observations. *Journal of Abnormal Psychology, 72,* p. 193-204.

Copson, G. (1995). Coals to Newcastle? Part 1: A study of offender profiling. Police Research Group. *Special Interest Series: Paper 7.*

Dailey, C.A. (1952). The effects of premature conclusions upon the acquisition of understanding a person. *Journal of Psychology, 33,* p. 133-152.

Ekman, P. (1991). "Who Can Catch a Liar?" *American Psychologist, 46*(9), p. 913-920.

Fischhoff, B. (1975). Hindsight and foresight: The effect of outcome knowledge on judgement under uncertainty. *Journal of Experimental Psychology: Human Perception and Performance, I,* p. 288-299.

Fischhoff, B. Slovic, P., & Lichenstein, S. (1977). Knowing with certainty: The appropriateness of extreme confidence. *Journal of Experimental Psychology: Human Perception and Performance,* 3, p. 552-564.

Fisher, R.P., Geiselman, R.E., Raymond, D.S., Jurkevich, L.M., & Warhafting, M.L. (1987). Enhancing eyewitness memory: Refining the cognitive interview. *Journal of Police Science and Administration, 15* (4), p. 292-297.

Furnham, A., & Alison, L.J. (1994). Theories of crime, attitudes to punishment and juror bias amongst police, offenders and the general public. *Personality and Individual Differences 17*(1) p. 35-48.

Gerbner, G. Gross, L. Morgan M., & Signorielli (1985). Growing up with television: The cultivation perspective. In J. Bryant and D. Zillman (eds.) *Media Effects: Advances in Theory and Research,* p. 17-41. Hillsdale, N.J. Lawrence Erlbaum.

Gudjonsson, G. (1992). *The Psychology of Confessions and Testimony.* England: John Wiley and Sons Ltd.

Haward, L. (1985). Forensic Psychology in S. and D. Canter (eds.). *Psychology in Practice.* Chichester: Wiley

Hsu B., Kling A., Kessler K., & Diefenbach, P. & Elias, J. (1994). "Gender Differences in Sexual Fantasy and Behaviour in a College Population: A Ten Year Replication" Journal of Sex and Marital Therapy vol. *20,* No 2.

Hull, (1943). *Methods of Observation.* in R. A. King (1961). Readings for an introduction to psychology. New York: McGraw-Hill Book Company, Inc.

Janis, I.L. (1982). *Groupthink; Psychological studies of policy decisions and fiascos* (Revised edition of *Victims of groupthink: A psychological study of foreign-policy decisions and fiascos*, 1972) Boston: Houghton-Mifflin .

Janis, I.L., & Mann, L. (1977). *Decision Making: A psychological analysis of conflict, choice and commitment*, New York: Free Press.

Kassin, S.M., & Wrightsman, L.S. (1983). The construction and validation of a juror bias scale. *Journal of Research in Personality, 17*, p. 423-442.

Keinan, G. (1987). Decision making under stress: Scanning of alternatives under controllable and uncontrollable threats. *Journal of Personality and Social Psychology, 52*, p. 639-644.

Kohnken, G. (1987). Training police officers to detect deceptive eyewitness statements: Does it work?" *Social Behaviour, 2*, p. 1-17.

Lee, J., & Alison, L.J. (1997). Beyond Cracker. *Police Review 19, 16th May.*

Lieberman, D. (1990). *Learning, Behaviour and Cognition.* Wadsworth Publishing Company.

Lombroso, C. (1911). *Crime: Its Causes and Remedies.* Boston: Little, Brown.

Lord, C.G., Ross L., & Lepper, M.R. (1979). Biased assimilation and attitude polarisation: The effects of prior theories on subsequently considered evidence. *Journal of Personality and Social Psychology, 37*, p. 2098-2109.

Malamuth, N.M., & Check J.V. (1983). Sexual arousal to rape depictions: Individual differences. *Journal of Abnormal Psychology, 92*(1).

Meehl, P.E. (1954). *Clinical versus statistical prediction: A theoretical analysis and a look at the evidence.* Minneapolis: University of Minnesota Press.

Ormerod, D.C. (1996). The evidential implications of Psychological profiling. *Criminal Law Review, 717.* p. 863-877.

Ormerod, D.C. (1996). Psychological profiling. *The Journal of Forensic Psychiatry 7*(2) p. 341-352.

Poythress, N., Otto, R.K., Darkes, J., & Starr, L. (1993). APA's expert panel in the congressional review of the USS Iowa incident. *American Psychologist Jan* p. 8-15.

Pinizzotto, A.J., & Finkel N.J. (1990). Criminal personality profiling: An outcome and process study. *Law and Human Behaviour, 14*(3), p. 215-233.

Rachman, S. & Hodgson, R. (1968). Experimentally induced 'sexual fetishism: replication and development' *Psychological Record 18.*

Ressler, R.K., Burgess, A.G., Douglas, J.E., & Depue, R.L. (1985). Violent Crime. *FBI Law Enforcement Bulletin, 54*, no. 8.

Ressler, R.K., Douglas, J.E., Burgess, A.W., & Burgess A.G. (1993). *Crime Classification Manual: The Standard System for Investigating and Classifying Violent Crimes.* London: Simon and Schuster.

Ross, M., & Silcoly, F. (1979). Egocentric bias in availability and attribution. *Journal of Personality and Social Psychology, 37*, p. 322-336.

Rowe, W.F. (1993). Psychic detectives: A critical examination. *Skeptical Inquirer Vol. 17* (2), p. 159-165.

Royal Commission (1929). *Duties of police in investigation of crimes and offences.* Report of the Royal Commission on Police Powers and Procedures.

Royal Commission on Criminal Justice (1993). Report Cmnd 2263. London: HMSO.

Shepherd, E. (1991). Ethical interviewing: Aspects of police interviewing. *Criminological and Legal Psychology 18* p. 46-59.

Smedslund, J. (1963). The concept of correlation in adults. *Scandanavian Journal of Psychology, 4*, p. 165-173.

Tversky, A., & Kahneman, D. (1973). Availability: A heuristic for judging frequency and probability. *Cognitive Psychology, 5*, p. 207-232.

Tversky, A., & Kahneman, D. (1974). Judgement under uncertainty: Heuristics and biases. *Science*, *185*, p. 1124-1131.

Wason, P.C. (1960). On the failure to eliminate hypotheses in a conceptual task. *Quarterly Journal of Experimental Psychology*, *12*, p. 129-140.

Wilson, C., & Odell, R. (1991). *The Complete Jack the Ripper*. Penguin Books.

Wiseman, R., West D. and Stemman, R. (1996). Psychic crime detectives: A new test for measuring their successes and failures. *Skeptical Inquirer Jan* p. 38-40.

Laurence John Alison *is currently employed as a lecturer at the Centre for Investigative Psychology at the University of Liverpool. Dr Alison is developing models to explain the processes of manipulation, influence and deception that are features of criminal investigations. His research interests focus upon developing rhetorical perspectives in relation to the investigative process and he has presented many lectures both nationally and internationally to a range of academics and police officers on the problems associated with offender profiling. He is currently working on false allegations of sexual assault and false memory. He is affiliated with The Psychologists at Law Group - a forensic service specialising in providing advice to the courts, legal professions, police service, charities and public bodies.*

David Canter *is Director of the Centre for Investigative Psychology at the University of Liverpool. He has published widely in Environmental and Investigative Psychology as well as many areas of Applied Social Psychology. His most recent books since his award winning* "Criminal Shadows" *have been* "Psychology in Action" *and with Laurence Alison* "Criminal Detection and the Psychology of Crime".

CRIMINAL PROFILING: TRIAL BY JUDGE AND JURY, NOT CRIMINAL PSYCHOLOGIST

DAVID ORMEROD[1]

This chapter examines the numerous difficulties facing any party seeking to adduce an offender profile in a criminal trial in England. An offender profile is likely to conflict with some of the most fundamental rules of the law of evidence such as the rules of legal relevance, opinion, hearsay, and the rules guarding against prejudicial evidence. This chapter explains these rules and how they would affect the admissibility of the profile, whether adduced by the prosecution or the defence. It identifies the dangers in criminal psychologists being treated as expert witnesses and the legal hurdle profiles would face if they sought to rely on earlier research to support a particular profile. By providing an explanation of the relevant rules of the law of evidence and how they impinge on the admissibility of the profile, the aim is for psychologists to be better equipped to address requests from the investigating authorities for profiles.

INTRODUCTION

R v Colin Stagg remains the only English criminal case in which psychological profiling has been considered directly.[2] In that notorious case the trial judge, Ognall J, not only rejected the prosecution evidence but also made notably pessimistic statements about the use of profiles as evidence. His lordship was not wholly dismissive of the work of the criminal psychologist, acknowledging that "in certain cases the assistance of a psychologist of that kind can prove a very useful investigative tool".[3] But, the idea that this material could be put in evidence in a criminal trial met with a much colder reception. His lordship stressed that the court "[w]ould not wish to give encouragement either to investigating or prosecuting authorities to construct or seek to supplement their cases on this kind of basis".[4]

Is the picture necessarily so bleak? Is the criminal psychologist restricted to helping police with their inquiries or may he also have his say in court? Despite the decision in *R v Stagg*, and the negative comments made, the admissibility of criminal profile evidence is, for a number of reasons,

---

[1] I am grateful to Ms T.K. Baxter for her excellent research assistance.

[2] (1994) Central Criminal Court 14th September. See Grubin, D., "Offender Profiling" (1995) 6(2) Journal of Forensic Psychiatry 259. See also Britton, P., The Jigsaw Man (1997) Bantam Press: London.

[3] Transcript p.29.

[4] *Ibid.*

still open for the courts to decide. First, the decision in *R v Stagg* is that of a Crown Court, not one of the appellate courts. The binding precedent of Crown Court decisions on any future court is very limited.[5] Furthermore, the evidence against Stagg was rejected by Ognall J on grounds unrelated to the admissibility of the profile: that the investigation was conducted in such a manner as to render the evidence unreliable. Mr Justice Ognall's statements concerning the admissibility of the profile evidence were merely asides, or *obiter dicta*, that do not bind any future court. Moreover, Ognall J's *dicta* are less persuasive because they are expressed in such broad terms. That is not to criticise the decision of that judge, who was faced with an appalling case in which the abuse of the profile technique was blatant. The case was described as "so bad even a moron in a hurry could see it could never stand up".[6] Mr Justice Ognall was, quite understandably in that context, erring on the side of caution.

If the issue is still open for decision, as it appears it must be, is a court ever likely to accept the evidence of the criminal psychologist in the future? This chapter tries to identify the many reasons which prevent a court relying on the evidence of the criminal psychologist. The aim is to paint a positive, yet realistic picture, including an attempt to identify the very rare circumstances in which the evidence could be admitted.

It has been argued elsewhere that the admissibility in a criminal trial of a profile would be unlikely, largely because of a number of rules of evidence.[7] The specific goals of this chapter are, first, to assist the psychologist in understanding these rules of criminal evidence. Unravelling some of the complexities of the rule will at least provide the psychologists with an idea of the law's major concerns and expectation. In this way, psychologists will be better equipped to address requests to testify from investigating authorities. In addition, by drawing on the experience of the use of DNA profiling in the criminal courts, it will be possible to highlight analogous dangers and how some of them may be avoided in the unlikely event that the profiler testifies in court. Given the (understandably) negative judicial attitude following *R v Stagg*, the criminal psychologist must be as well prepared as possible for any further attempts to rely on his work in court. The further goal is then that when a future criminal trial presents an opportunity to admit such evidence, there will be a greater likelihood that the psychologist will have generated the sorts of evidence to which the courts will be receptive.

REASONS FOR REJECTING THE PROFILE AS EVIDENCE IN COURT

One reason that the concept of a criminal profile is so attractive in both fact and fiction,[8] is the idea that from the seemingly few clues it is possible to create a *complete* picture of the offender. This not only makes profiles potentially powerful in the fight against crime, but also gives them an air of mystique.[9] The long and varied list of characteristics which it is claimed will be catalogued reinforce this belief. Thus, a "typical profile will include most, or all, of the following descriptive criteria: age, race, occupational level, marital status, intelligence, education level, arrest history, military history,

---

[5] See further Ashworth, A., "The Binding Effect of Crown Court Decisions" [1980] Crim. L.R. 402.

[6] Mark Stephens, leading criminal solicitor, quoted in *The Independent on Sunday* 18 September 1994 p.15.

[7] See Ormerod, D.C., "The Evidential Implications of Psychological Profiling" [1996] Crim. L.R. 863. This chapter draws upon and develops many of the issues raised therein.

[8] See Holmes, R.M., and Holmes, S.M., *Profiling Violent Crimes: an investigative tool.* (1996) New York: Sage Publications, Ch.2.

[9] See the discussions of the famous Brussel profile of the Mad Bomber of New York: Porter, B., "Mind Hunters" (1993) (April) Psychology Today 44, p.46; Boon, J., and Davies, G., "Criminal Profiling" (1993) Policing 218.

family background, social interests, socio-economic level, residence in relation to crime and with whom residing, personality characteristics (rigid, passive, manipulative, aggressive), colour, age, and description of vehicle, suggested interview technique for offender".[10] This almost exhaustive detail about the offender can be seen in Professor Canter's extremely successful profile of the Railway Murderer - Duffy. Out of the seventeen pointers Canter put forward, thirteen were accurate.[11]

"The Profile (M denotes the Murderer)	*The Match*
M lived in the Kilburn or Cricklewood area of London.	Duffy lived in Kilburn.
M was married but had no children.	Duffy was married, and a low sperm count meant he was infertile.
The marriage was in serious trouble.	Duffy was separated from his wife.
M was a loner with few friends.	Duffy had only two male friends.
M was a physically small man who felt himself to be unattractive.	Duffy was five feet four inches tall, and had acne.
M was interested in martial arts or body building.	Duffy spent much of his time at a martial arts club.
M felt the need to dominate women.	Duffy was a violent man who had already attacked his wife.
M fantasized about rape and enjoyed bondage.	Duffy liked tying his wife up before intercourse.
M had a fascination for weapons, particularly knives and swords.	Duffy had many 'Kung Fu' style weapons in his home.
M indulged his fantasies of sex and violence with videos and magazines.	Duffy collected hard-core porn and martial arts videos.
M was a man who kept some sort of souvenir of his crimes.	Duffy had 33 door keys, each taken from a victim as a souvenir.
M had a semi-skilled job as a plumber, carpenter, or similar.	Duffy trained as a carpenter with British Rail.
M was in the age range 20 to 30.	Duffy was 28 when arrested and had been a rapist for four years".[12]

It will be useful to return to this profile, which proved successful, to illustrate various points throughout the ensuing discussion of the numerous reasons why the court should reject evidence of this kind in a criminal trial.

---

[10] Vorpagel, R.E., "Painting Psychological Profiles: Charlatanism, Coincidence, Charisma, Chance or a New Science" (1982) The Police Chief 157, p.159.

[11] Canter, D., *Criminal Shadows* (1994) Harper Collins: London, Ch.2. See pp. 84–87 in Stevens, J.A. (1997) Standard Investigatory Tools and Offender Profiling. in Jackson, J.L. and Bekerian, D.A. (eds) *Offender Profiling: Theory, Research and Practice*. Wiley: Chichester, UK.

[12] As tabulated in Smith, C., "Psychological Offender Profiling" (1993) The Criminologist 244. See also Canter, D., *op cit*. n11.

INTUITION

Although many aspects of a profile will be based on scientific data, the gaps are filled, to varying degrees,[13] with intuition to give a fuller picture. As once commentator put it this "lend[s] to the colour, hue and tint" of the portrait of the offender.[14] The completeness of this picture which at first makes the profile so attractive is also what leads to its rejection as a piece of evidence as a whole. The court is not prepared to hear testimony from any person, no matter how well qualified or experienced, that he has an intuition that the offender will have a certain characteristic. It is for this reason that the courts would refuse to hear the evidence of say an astrologer (unless of course he were testifying about the customs and activities of astrologers should that be relevant to the trial).

LEGAL RELEVANCE

Relevance Explained

Every criminal trail involves an attempt to reconstruct and analyse a past event. One function of the rules of evidence is to regulate how much information should be admitted in attempting this reconstruction. This is not merely to ensure that the trial does not go on for an unduly protracted period, but also that the trier of fact (the jury or magistrate) are not distracted from their central enquiry by a limitless clutter of material. The first concern with any potential item of evidence is to ensure that it is "legally relevant". This term has taken on a particular meaning in the law of evidence, but it is essentially one of common sense. Stephen's classic definition of relevance from the last century is widely adopted: "any two facts to which it is applied are so related to each other that according to the common course of events one either taken by itself or in connection with other facts proves or renders probable the past, present, or future existence or non-existence of the other".[15] This definition is not restricted to English law, and can be found in the American Federal Rules of Evidence r.401: Relevant evidence is "evidence having any tendency to make the existence of any fact that is of consequence to the determination of the action more probable or less probable than it would be without the evidence".

The definition is clear enough, but it begs the obvious question: relevant to what? In any criminal trial, the issues which must be proved by the prosecution (or in some rare instances, as in a case of insanity, by the defence) to succeed can be labelled the "facts in issue". This is the agenda for the trial, but it is never a fixed agenda. If the elements of murder which the prosecution must prove include an intentional unlawful killing of a person, those issues are all on the agenda; facts in issue. If the defendant, at trial, pleads that he killed intentionally, but that he was provoked into doing so, all the issues on the original agenda are redundant, and the new agenda is whether he

---

[13] Canter, *op cit.* n11, p.65; Pinizzotto, A.J., "Forensic Psychology: Criminal Personality Profiling" (1984) 12(1) Journal of Police Science and Administration 32, p.39.; Boon J., andDavies, G., *op cit.* n9, p.224. Many different methods of profiling have been described. See McCann, J., "Criminal Personality Profiling in the Investigation of Violent Crime" (1992) 10 Behavioural Sciences and the Law 475, p.478; Turco, R.N., "Psychological Profiling" (1990) International Journal of Offender Therapy and Comparative Criminology 147 and Holmes and Holmes, *op cit.* n8, Ch.3.

[14] Vorpagel, *op cit.* n10, p.156.

[15] See Tapper C., *Cross and Tapper on Evidence* (8th ed 1995) : Butterworths: London, p.56; Stephen, J.F.J., *Digest of Law of Evidence* (12 ed 1948) MacMillan: London, Art 1. See also *R v Kilbourne* [1973] A.C. 729 "...relevant (i.e. logical probative or disprobative) evidence is evidence which makes the matter which requires proof more of less probable" *per* Lord Simon of Glaisdale, p.756.

satisfies the legal requirements of the defence of provocation. It will be noticed that the "facts in issue" in any case are derived not from the procedural rules of evidence but from the substantive criminal law; that is the law defining offences and defences, not procedure. From all of this, it becomes obvious that the answer to the question posed above, "relevant to what?" is simply "relevant to the facts in issue".

One further aspect of the rules about relevance can be best explained by way of an example. If D is charged with the murder of V, it is clear from the discussion above, that the facts in issue will be whether he intentionally killed. Using Stephen's definition, any fact which makes it more likely (or less likely) that these facts in issue occurred (i.e. that D intentionally killed V) is a relevant fact. This would include, for example, D's fingerprints on a weapon with V's blood on it. Common sense dictates that a court inquiring into this charge would also want to hear about the fact that an eyewitness, W, has very poor eyesight. That fact is neither a fact in issue, nor a relevant fact: W's poor eyesight does not make it more likely or less likely that D stabbed V. Another example would be the reliability of a computer that processed information relevant to an investigation. Such facts are acknowledged to be relevant, and are labelled "collateral facts" and will often be relevant only to credit (i.e. the credibility of a witness) rather than relevant to the issue (i.e. relevant directly to guilt).

In addition to taking a strict stance on what constitutes legal relevance, the courts will reject as insufficiently relevant evidence likely to lead to the trier of fact being distracted.[16] In the context of the criminal profile, this could give rise to significant problems. If the criminal psychologist wishes to testify that, for example, a certain percentage of rapes are intraracial,[17] or that the age of a rapist is likely to be between 20 and 30 (as in Duffy), this could lead into may side-issues, such as the size of sample in the study, the reliability of methodology etc. These would all distract the jury from the primary purpose of assessing the guilt of the accused on trial for this particular rape.

The courts' strict approach to the question of relevance can be seen in the course taken by the House of Lords in the leading case of *R v Blastland*.[18] Blastland was convicted of murdering a 12 year old boy. Having admitted that he had been engaged in sexual activity with the boy, Blastland claimed that they had been disturbed by a third party and that he had run away leaving the boy alive and well. The description of the third party fitted that of Mark, someone who had actually confessed to the murder but then retracted his confession. Blastland sought to rely in his defence on the fact that Mark had detailed knowledge about the murder at a time when the body had not been discovered. The House of Lords held that since there was no evidence as to how Mark might have acquired his knowledge, the evidence was "irrelevant" to Blastland's defence. This seems unduly harsh, but on strict application of Stephen's test above, it is the right decision. The fact that Mark knew about the existence of a dead body does not make it more or less likely that Blastland killed that person. Mark could have killed the boy, seen Blastland do it, or even seen a fourth party do it. What is necessary is to know how Mark came by his knowledge. As Lord Bridge said: "Mark's knowledge that [the boy] had been murdered was neither itself in issue, not was it, per se, of any relevance to the issue".[19]

---

[16] *Agassiz v London Tramway Co.* (1872) 27 L.T. 492.

[17] Such a claim is doubted by Canter, *op cit.* n11, p.188.

[18] [1986] A.C. 41. See also *R v Kearley* [1992] 2 A.C. 228; Choo, A. L.-T., "The Notion of Relevance and Defence Evidence" [1993] Crim. L.R. 114.

[19] [1986] A.C. 41, 54.

The decision has been heavily criticised for, at the very least, failing to ensure that justice is seen to be done.[20] The decision, coupled with other recent appellate court decisions in similar vein have led one commentator to suggest the term relevance is not a simple question of logic or common sense as in Stephen's definition. Professor Choo has argued that the courts have, in applying the rules of relevance, paid insufficient attention to the fundamental rights of an accused to be protected from wrongful conviction.[21] This is a powerful claim, particularly in the light of cases such as *Blastland*, but it can be countered by the equally persuasive argument from Adrian Zuckerman that "[i]n piling up evidence, albeit relevant, a point will come where any further piece of evidence may detract from rather than increase, the correctness of the final assessment".[22] It would seem that the idea of legal relevance, as applied by the courts is, first and foremost a question of logic, but also involves an assessment of other factors such as the likelihood of distraction for the trier of fact, the risk of increasing the length of trial etc. Relevance is then not simply a question of probability.[23]

Implicit within the decision about relevance are a number of questions about the sufficiency of the evidence and how appropriate it is for the jury to hear it. These are really issues of exclusion that should be tackled explicitly once the question of relevance has been resolved. The rules of evidence do go on to regulate explicitly the *admissibility* of *legally relevant* evidence. Relevant evidence will be excluded if it is unreliable, unfair, too prejudicial or privileged. Before addressing these rules of exclusion and how they affect the use of a criminal profile, it is necessary to consider whether a profile (or part thereof) is legally relevant as defined.

Relevance and the Profile

If all that a profile can do is to suggest that, in the opinion of a criminal psychologist, the perpetrator will have certain characteristics (age, residence in a certain area, etc.) that will be insufficiently relevant to be received by the court. The psychological profile, as a whole, is tendered to help prove the facts in issue. It is tendered as a relevant fact. However, before we are able to rely upon this relevant fact (the profile) to render more probable the facts in issue (killing by D) we must be satisfied that the relevant fact (the profile) is indeed a "fact" or "true". This can never be done: it is an opinion. Although the profile may well be based upon statistical data, that foundation alone will not make *the entire profile* "a fact" that is "true".

Would a part of a profile be accepted as legally relevant? If a criminal psychologist has, as a result of reliable research, concluded that, say 90% of rapes are intraracial, would that statistic be legally relevant in the trial of a white defendant for the rape of a black woman? The statistic suggests that it is less likely that the man is guilty. According to the leading American commentator, "[i]t is enough if the item [of evidence] could reasonably show that the fact is slightly more probable than it would appear without that evidence".[24] However, in view of the strict approach of the English courts, it is far from clear whether even this part-profile would be accepted as legally

---

[20] See further, Birch, D.J., "Hearsay-logic and hearsay-fiddles: *Blastland* revisited" in P.F. Smith (ed) *Criminal law: Essays in Honour of J.C. Smith* (1987) Butterworths; London: Carter, P.B., "Hearsay, relevance and admissibility: declarations as to state of mind and declarations against penal interest" (1987) 103 L.Q.R 106.

[21] Choo, A.L.-T., *op cit.* n18. A very detailed examination of the concept of evidence) Wigmore, J.H., *Evidence in Trials at Common Law (Vol 1A)*, Tillers, P., (1983 rev).

[22] *Principles of Criminal Evidence* (1989 Clarendon, Oxford: p.49.

[23] For a fascinating discussion of the relationship between these concepts see Eggleston, R., *Evidence, Proof and Probability* (2nd ed 1983) Weidenfield: London.

[24] Cleary, E.W., *McCormick on Evidence* (3rd ed 1984) St Paul: West, p.542.

relevant. The dangers of collateral issues arising (how accurate was the statistic? Was the methodology reliable? etc.) would *probably* lead a court to conclude that even this evidence was insufficiently relevant to be admitted.[25] In *R v Mohan*,[26] the Supreme Court of Canada upheld the trial judge's decision to exclude profile evidence where the defendant sought to call a psychiatrist to testify that the typical offender in the cases in question would have certain abnormal characteristics (paedophilia) and that the accused did not have these characteristics. Sopinka J stated that "there was no material in the record to support a finding that the profile of a paedophile or psychopath has been standardized to the extent that it could be said that it matched the suggested profile of the offender depicted in the charges".[27]

It has been argued that the reliance on such normative data should *never* be accepted as sufficiently relevant.

> The findings derived from empirical research are used by psychologists to formulate 'norms' of human behaviour. From observations and experiments, psychologists may conclude that in circumstance X there is a likelihood that an individual or group member will behave in manner Y. But "normative data" of this sort are of little use to the courts. The courts are concerned to determine the past behaviour of accused individuals, and in carrying out that function, information about the past behaviour of *other* individuals is wholly irrelevant. What the courts require is information, direct or circumstantial, about the alleged criminal acts or omissions of the *accused*. Such information might be termed "positive data". Such data are (or may be) legally relevant because they "attach" to the person of the individual accused. Normative data, in contrast do not "attach" to the accused because they are not relevant about that particular individual's conduct. To become legally relevant (and practically helpful), the findings from psychological research must in some way be connected to the particular case.[28]

But surely this is how all criminal trials are decided - on the basis of people making judgements founded on their experiences of life.

The profile as a whole will then be deemed legally irrelevant and thus rejected by the judge in a criminal trial,[29] but there is a slightly better chance of admitting a number of individual items of evidence, possibly generated by a number of different experts. This idea of a "profiling team", where individual members of the team would be responsible for analysing specific aspects of the crime, may be viewed more favourably by the court. It would certainly represent a move away from a single individual acting on intuition. Furthermore, it has been recognised that a more accurate report may be produced in this way: "certain profilers were more accurate and more keenly perceptive with certain tasks than they were with others. ...Since individual profilers appear to enjoy certain areas of expertise within the general field of profiling, it seems plausible that more accurate and richer profiles would result from "group profiling" than from individual profiling".[30]

---

[25] This provides an example of the exclusionary approach implicit in the question of relevance. If the defence sought to adduce the evidence and were denied, this would raise the issues Choo considers *op cit.* n18.

[26] [1994] 2 S.C.R. 9.

[27] At p.38.

[28] Sheldon, D.H., and MacLeod, M.D.,"From Normative to Positive Data: Expert Psychological Evidence Re-Examined" [1991] Crim. L.R. 811, p.815.

[29] In the absence of the jury at a *"voir dire"*.

[30] Pinizzotto, A.J., and Finkel, N.J.,"Criminal Personality profiling: An Outcome and Process Study" (1990) 14 (3) Law and Human Behaviour 215, p.230.

However, all that has been considered thus far is the most basic rule which filters out the irrelevant, it remains to consider the exclusionary rules which exclude the concededly relevant evidence. Specific rules create problems for the admissibility of a profile, and even a part profile. The most important rule, and that to be considered first, relates to the undue prejudice which may be created.

RULES OF EXCLUSION: SIMILAR FACT EVIDENCE[31]

An accused is charged with murdering a young girl by strangulation, and there is no sexual interference with the girl, nor any attempt to conceal the body. In such a case, it is surely relevant that the accused has twice previously killed in identical circumstances. Applying the test of relevance above, it is obvious that this information makes it more likely that *this* accused rather than a member of the general public selected at random committed the act.[32] The evidence creates a greater likelihood of his being convicted and as such can be described as prejudicial to the accused, as could any piece of incriminating evidence such as a fingerprint or DNA evidence. However, the evidence of the previous convictions, or other discreditable conduct not amounting to a crime, also creates in the minds of the jury more sinister prejudices: "he did it before so he deserves to be punished anyway" etc. The most important of these prejudices have recently been described as "moral prejudice" and "reasoning prejudice".[33] The first label is being used to describe the danger that the fact-finders might treat the evidence as being more probative of guilt than it really is, and the second, that it might lead them to convict the defendant without being properly satisfied that he is guilty as charged.[34] There is the potential for these prejudices to be exacerbated in two ways in the context of the criminal profile. First, the risk of moral prejudice is increased in cases involving deviant crimes[35] - and there is an argument that profiles are used more in relation to deviant crimes than others.[36] The Law Commission's research with a mock jury led to the conclusion that the prejudice created by certain types of crime was significantly greater than others. Second, the risk of reasoning prejudice is increased in cases of serial crimes, and there are many who argue that profiles are most often called upon in relation to serial activity.[37] Other well-

---

[31] This is an extremely controversial area with a wealth of literature including: Hoffman, L., "Similar facts after *Boardman*" (1975) 91 L.Q.R. 193; Cross, R., "Fourth time lucky - similar fact evidence in the House of Lords" [1975] Crim. L.R 62; Zuckerman, A.A.S., "Similar fact evidence - the unobservable rule" (1987) 104 L.Q.R. 187; Mirfield, P., "Similar facts - *Makin'* Out?" [1987] C.L.J. 83; Allan, T.R.S., "Some favourite fallacies about similar facts" (1988) 8 L.S. 35; Nair, R., "Similar Fact Evidence - prejudice and irrelevance" [1993] Crim. L.R. 432; McEwan, J., *Evidence and the Adversarial Process: The Modern Law* (1992) Blackwell: London.

[32] See *R v Straffen* [1952] 1 Q.B. 911. For an interesting account of the rule and it's relationship with probability see Eggleston *op cit.* n23, Ch.7.

[33] See Law Commission Consultation Paper No.141 *Evidence in Criminal Proceedings: Previous Misconduct of a Defendant* (1996) H.M.S.O: London and the *Report of the Royal Commission on Criminal Justice* (1993) Cmnd. 2263 H.M.S.O.: London which described this rule as "difficult to comprehend embodied as it is in a series of judgements that are not always readily reconcilable". Chapter 8 para 30.

[34] Law Commission Consultation Paper No. 141, para 9.92.

[35] "The more revolting the suggestion, the more the jury may be likely to lose sight of the fact that it may not be true." Cowen, Z., and Carter, P.B., *Essays in the Law of Evidence* (1956) Clarendon: Oxford p.146.

[36] Porter, B., *op cit.* n9, p.45; Holmes and Holmes, *op cit.* n8, p.2; McEwan.,"'Similar Fact' Evidence and Psychology: Personality and Guilt" (1994) Expert Evidence 113. See also Pinizzotto, *op cit.* n13, p.33; Smith, *op cit.* n12, p.249; Davies, A., "Editorial: Offender Profiling" 91994) 34(3) Med. Sci. Law 185.

[37] See McEwan, *op cit.* n36. See also Pinizzotto, *op cit.* n13; p.33; Smith, *op cit.* n12, p.249; Davies, A., "Editorial: Offender Profiling" (1994) 34(3) Med. Sci. Law 185.

rehearsed dangers justifying the exclusion of this type of evidence are also apparent, including the danger that the evidence of discreditable attributes leads the police to "round up the usual suspects".[38] Finally, there is a risk that evidence of previous misconduct will not only create prejudice, but might "mislead, confuse or distract the fact-finders, or cause undue waste of time."[39]

The rules of evidence provide a general safeguard against such prejudices in the rule against similar fact evidence. In the leading authority on the similar fact evidence rules (*D.P.P v P*)[40] Lord Mackay, the Lord Chancellor, said that the key was the "probative force" of the evidence. This had to be so great as to make it just to admit the evidence, *notwithstanding* the prejudice to the accused. In the case of the strangler, the proof of his previous convictions will, undoubtedly create the prejudices, but the evidence is *so* probative of guilt (without reference to such prejudice) that to exclude it would be as one distinguished Law Lord once said, "an affront to common sense".[41]

As the discussion focuses more specifically on the similar fact rule and profile evidence, it is worth bearing in mind the two elements that must be balanced. First the judge will have to be satisfied that the evidence has probative force, i.e. relevance, and then secondly, that the probative force is sufficient to outweigh the prejudicial effect on the jury.

Using Similar Facts to Identify the Offender

There is no limit to the use of similar fact evidence once it is admissible under the test. There are cases where it is used to rebut a defence or an innocent explanation raised by the defendant.[42] More importantly for profiling, similar fact evidence may be used to prove the identity of the perpetrator. This use is the most controversial, and can operate by one of two distinct methods: cumulative or sequential.[43] The sequential approach works by the prosecution first proving that the defendant performed an act A (usually a crime) before turning to the second act B. Having established that acts A and B share such peculiarity that there is no doubt they were the work of the same person, it is legitimate for the jury to conclude that this defendant performed both.[44] Unless the prejudicial effect (i.e. the jury engaging in moral or reasoning prejudice) of admitting the evidence is outweighed by its probative force (e.g. the peculiarity of the *modus operandi*) the similar fact rule will lead to the exclusion of the evidence. With the cumulative approach the prosecution must first prove that the two (or more) activities or offences are the work of the same person. This will usually depend on there being a sufficient peculiarity in the activity or manner of performance. Thereafter, the jury will be allowed to combine items of inconclusive evidence (e.g. identification) from each individual offence to prove that this defendant was the offender on both occasions.[45]

---

[38] See Zuckerman, *op cit.* n31, p.224; Law Commission, *Consultation Paper No. 141*, paras 7.36–7.41; Canter, *op cit.* n11, Ch.7.

[39] Law Commission Consultation Paper No.141, para 10.85. See McEwan, J. (1997) *Law Commission Dodges the Nettles in Consultation Paper No. 141*. Crim. L.R. 93.

[40] [1991] 2 A.C. 447.

[41] Lord Cross of Chelsea in *R v Boardman* [1975] A.C. 421, p.457. There need not be similarity e.g. where D steals from house A and then drops his swag in house B where he commits a murder, the prosecution will be allowed to reveal his conviction for the burglary at the trial for the murder, even though this reveals a criminal conviction which has no similarity whatsoever. See *R v O'Meally* [1953] V.L.R. 30.

[42] As in a famous case such as *R v Smith* (1913) 11 Cr App R 229, and *Makin v Attorney General for New South Wales* [1894] A.C. 57.

[43] See Pattenden, R., "Similar Fact Evidence and the Proof of Identity" (1996) 112 L.Q.R. 446.

[44] *Barnes* [1996] Crim L.R. 39; [1995] 2 Cr App R 491. *R v Wharton* (1998) Crim. L.R. (Sept)

[45] *Downey* [1995] Crim L.R. 414; [1995] 1 Cr App R 547.

The use of a criminal profile relies on a very different sort of reasoning from either of these accepted techniques, and yet it falls foul of the general prohibition on similar fact evidence. Reliance is on the reasoning that X% of those who commit this type of crime have a certain characteristic or trait (e.g. possession of a collection of hard-core pornography as in Duffy). The accused has that certain characteristic, therefore, he is more likely to be the perpetrator of the offence. It is simply an attempt to assist in focusing investigative attention on individuals whose personality traits match those of others who have been convicted of such crimes. This tells us nothing about *the accused* i.e. the man in the dock. It tells us that there is an X% likelihood that *the perpetrator* is of a certain type.[46] There is insufficient probative force in such evidence (irrespective of the prejudicial effect that will be considered shortly). Even if in a rape case, the statistics say that the likelihood of a rapist being between 20 and 30 years old is 80%, that does not, as noted above, have tremendous probative value in the question whether it is more likely that his accused committed this particular rape.

The danger is even more obvious where, rather than as one individual statistic, the profile is relied upon *as a whole*. The tendency then is towards ambiguity:

> Nine out of ten profiles are vapid. They play at blind man's bluff, groping in all directions in the hope of touching a sleeve. Occasionally they do, but not firmly enough to seize it, for the behaviourists producing them must necessarily deal in generalities and types. But policemen can't arrest a type. They require hard data: names, dates, none of which the psychiatrists [or others involved in creating profile evidence] can offer.[47]

For the purposes of the criminal trial, and the rules of evidence, the evidence of the criminal psychologist will usually be insufficiently relevant. They will identify a type of person likely to have committed the offence(s) in question. This is inadequate for the purposes of the criminal trial. This highlights a major distinction between the values of profiles in investigation as opposed to evidence:

> The requirements for investigation and proof are very different. The use of offender profiling can be compared with the use of screening techniques in medicine. Here the tests required for diagnosis must be far more rigorous than the tests for screening: a doctor does not rely on an abnormal mass X-ray to make an individual diagnosis of tuberculosis. The same distinction should apply between information that directs an investigation and information that proves guilt. The success of offender profiling as an investigative tool depends first on its sensitivity in identifying the characteristics of anyone capable of committing the crime in question. If people without these characteristics could also commit this crime, then use of the profile will focus the search for suspects too narrowly so that possible culprits will be missed. Also the initial scan will inevitably, as in preventive medicine, include many false positives. However, if profiling is to be used to determine guilt, specificity becomes more important than sensitivity. The profile must identify factors that are specific to those who commit he type of crime in question and are not shared by the rest of the population.[48]

This difference was recognised recently in the US Supreme Court in the context of novel techniques and expert evidence:

> ...there are important differences between the quest for truth in the courtroom and the quest for truth in the laboratory. Scientific conclusions are subject to perpetual revision. Law, on the other hand, must resolve disputes finally and quickly. The scientific project is advance by

---

[46] This distinction is crucial: see the discussion of transposing the conditional below.

[47] Holmes and Holmes *op cit*. n8, p.44.

[48] Mair, K., "Can a profile prove a sex offender guilty?" (1995) Expert Evidence 139. On investigation and profiles see also Stevens, J.A. Standard Investigatory Tools and Offender Profiling. in Jackson, J.L. and Bekerian, D.A. *op cit*. n11 and Oldfield, D. What Help Do the Police Need with their Enquiries? in Jackson, J.L. and Bekerian, D.A. *op cit*. n11

broad and wide-ranging consideration of a multitude of hypotheses, for those that are incorrect will eventually be shown to be so, and that in itself is an advance. Conjectures that are probably wrong are of little use, however, in the project of reaching a quick, final, and binding legal judgment - often of great consequence - about a particular set of events in the past. ... Rules of evidence [are] designed not for the exhaustive search for cosmic understanding but for the particularised resolution of legal disputes".[49]

The probative value of the evidence of the criminal psychologist does not weigh too heavily, and when it comes to considering the other side of the similar fact balance - the prejudicial effect - the profile fairs no better. All the hazards of the prejudices noted above can be demonstrated by reference to the successful profile of Duffy. The reception of evidence about the *accused's* collection of hard-core pornography, his violence towards his wife and collection of Kung-fu weapons would certainly create (moral and reasoning) prejudice against him in the minds of the jury: "[t]here is all the difference in the world between evidence proving that the accused is a bad man and evidence proving that he is *the* man".[50]

The other potential prejudices are all too obvious. If the police are led to believe that the offender in such cases will, on the basis of proven statistics, have an interest in martial arts, they may well simply round up the local enthusiasts. To take a different example, if the profiler relies on a statistic that, for example, rapes are usually committed by men of the same racial group as the victim and most likely of an age between 20–30, there is a risk that the police will *only* direct their enquiries towards such people, therefore leading to proportionately higher conviction rates of such people, thus feeding back into the statistical data from which we began. This is exacerbated by the accumulation of self-reports from convicted criminals to provide material from which profiles can be drawn:[51] "Offender profiling as an activity carries with it the danger of creating new, apparently scientifically-reinforced, stereotypes, hence criminalising sections of the population".[52] In addition to all of this there is the acknowledged possibility that the perpetrator may have staged the crime scene[53] (i.e. altered it to confuse investigators) or has altered his *modus operandi* if he is a repeat offender.[54] Finally, returning to the Duffy case, the evidence of facts such as the accused's violence towards his wife could give rise to collateral issues - how often, how badly, were the events proven? etc. - which could create confusion for the jury by distracting them from the central inquiry.

All in all, the similar fact rule seems to present a significant obstacle to the admissibility of both the criminal profile as a whole, and even the limited use of a single item of statistical evidence adduced by a criminal psychologist. The best that could be hoped for is that a court would accept statistical evidence such as the hypothetical intraracial rape statistic discussed above. It is submitted that even this evidence lacks sufficient probative force. But in case that opinion is wrong, and a criminal court is prepared to accept such a statistic, it remains to explain how these items will be presented to the court and to identify the host of hidden perils which might prevent the acceptance of even this limited evidence. These should make every criminal psychologist extremely wary of testifying.

---

[49] *Daubert v Merrel Dow Pharmaceutical Ltd* (1993) 1265 Led 2d 469, 485.

[50] *per* Lord Sumner in *Thompson* [1918] A.C. 221, p.234.

[51] See especially Mair *op cit.* n48, p.140; Canter, *op cit.* n11, Ch.3. See p.119 in Jackson, J.L. and Berian, D.A. Does Offender Profiling Have a Role to Play? Jackson, J.L. and Berkerian, D.A. *op cit.* n11.

[52] McEwan, *op cit.* n36, p.118. On the potential for bias in the profile(r) see also the discussion of racial bias in Higgins, M. (1997) *Looking the Part.* American Bar Association Journal p.48.

[53] See Vorpagel, *op cit.* n10, p.150; Douglas, J.E., Burgess, A.W., Burgess, A.G., and Ressler, R.K., *Crime Classification Manual* (1992) Lexington: New York, p.249. See also Smith, *op cit.* n12, p.249 and Turco, *op cit.* n13, p.150.

[54] See Smith, *op cit.* n12, p.250; McCann, *op cit.* n13, p.479.

RECEIVING THE OPINION OF THE CRIMINAL PSYCHOLOGIST

The Criminal Psychologist as an Expert

Expertise[55]

It has long been established that for a court to hear expert testimony, it must be satisfied that the expert witness is suitably qualified.[56] This question is one to be decided by the judge alone. "Qualification" in this context is not limited to formal academic qualification, but includes practical experience. This was illustrated in the recent case of *Clare*,[57] in which the Court of Appeal accepted expert evidence from a police officer who had watched a video-recording approximately 40 times. He was an expert as to the identify of those on the film although, clearly, the officer had no "formal qualification". Similarly in another recent Court of Appeal decision, an expert was allowed to testify although he had no scientific training, no formal qualification and was not affiliated to any professional body.[58] Although the Royal Commission on Criminal Justice recommended that professional bodies should maintain a register of those members who were suitably qualified to act as expert witnesses, no action has been taken to implement the suggestion.[59]

There is considerable scepticism exhibited by many towards expert evidence of criminal profiles. One commentator has stated recently that "psychiatrists or psychologists have [no] business pretending to be experts in profiling criminal suspects".[60] The flexibility of the approach seen above in *Clare* and *Stockwell* could work, in the long term, to the disadvantage of the criminal psychologist by allowing any person who claimed to have practised the "art" of profiling to testify. Such amateurs could leave a poor impression resulting in a negative attitude to all involved including the true experts. Worse still, the evidence of such amateurs could easily result in a miscarriage of justice.[61] This, coupled with the courts' acknowledged suspicion of all experts[62] and

---

[55] See generally: Hodgkinson, T., *Expert Evidence: Law and Practice* (1990) London: Sweet and Maxwell; Carson, D., "Expert Evidence in the Courts" (1992) 1 Expert Evidence 13; Gudjonsson, G.H., "The Implications of Poor Psychological Evidence in Court" (1993) 2(3) Expert Evidence 120; Freckleton, I.R., *The Trial of the Expert: A Study of Expert Evidence and Forensic Experts* (1987) OUP: Melbourne, pp.18-36; Jones, C.A.G., *Expert Witnesses: Science, Medicine and the Practice of Law* (1994) Clarendon Press: OxFord, Eggleston, *op cit.* n23, Ch.10; Haward, L.R.C., "The Psychologist as Expert Witness" in Farrington, D.P., Hawkins, K., and Lloyd-Bostock, S.M.A. (eds) *Psychology, Law and Legal Process* (1979) MacMillan: London, Roberts, P.R., "Will You Stand Up In Court? On the Admissibility of Psychiatric and Psychological Evidence." [1996] J. For. Psy. 63; American Federal Rules of Evidence r.702, and Slovenka, R., "Expert Testimony: Use and Abuse" (1993) 12 Medicine and Law 627. Gudjonsson, G.H. and Copson, G. The Role of the Expert in the Criminal Investigation. in Jackson, J.L. and Bekerian, D.A. *op cit.* n11.

[56] *R v Silverlock* [1894] 2 Q.B. 766: "is he *peritus*? is he skilled? Has he adequate knowledge?" *per* Lord Russell C.J. p.771.

[57] [1995] 2 Cr App R 333.

[58] *R v Stockwell* (2993) 97 Cr App R 260

[59] Para 9.77. "It should continue to be for the courts to assess the competence of expert witnesses. The professional bodies should, however, assist the courts in this task by maintaining a special register of their members who are suitably qualified to act as expert witnesses in particular areas of expertise." See also US Federal Rules of Evidence r.706.

[60] Park Elliot Dietz, Associate Professor University of Virginia School of Law and Medicine, cited by Porter *op cit.* n9, p.47.

[61] A number of the notorious miscarriages of justice in the last decade were due at least in part to the inadequacy of the expert evidence: *Maguire* (1992) 94 Cr App R 133, *McIllkenny* (1991) 93 Cr App R 287, *Ward* (1993) 96 Cr App R 1. See also Zuckerman, A.A.S., "Miscarriage of Justice: A Root Treatment" [1992] Crim. L.R. 323.

[62] Sir Fredrick Lawton wrote extra-judicially of there being "liars, damned liars and expert witnesses." Lawton, F., "The Limitations of Expert Scientific Evidence" (1980) 20 J. For. Sci. Soc. 237, p.238.

particularly psychologists becoming involved in the criminal trial[63] suggests that only those who are in fact specialists in criminal psychology and profile work will be likely to be permitted to give expert evidence.

The expert opinion must deal with matters beyond the jury's knowledge

Expert evidence will be admissible in any criminal trial only "to furnish the Court with ... information which is likely to be *outside the experience and knowledge of a judge or jury*".[64] This requirement has been the subject of considerable academic comment. It has recently been claimed that

> The true test of admissibility is whether the evidence that is proposed to give will be sufficiently helpful to the jury to offset any disadvantages that its admission is likely to entail, in terms of lengthening the proceedings, increasing their complexity, or diverting the jury's attention away from the main issues in the case and the proper way to evaluate them.[65]

This compares with the approach of the US Federal Rules of Evidence, r.702[66] in which the true test rests on how helpful the expert's evidence will be. Such vague tests give the courts considerable discretion, which has often been exercised against psychological evidence. However, it must be noted here that the expert in the context of this discussion would be testifying about the offender not the defendant. In most cases where expert psychological evidence has been considered by the courts, the question has been about the defendant's mental normality or otherwise.[67] Psychiatric or psychological evidence about the defendant's state of mind will be inadmissible unless he is abnormal and therefore beyond the jury's experience and understanding.

The construction of an entire profile in the sense discussed above is certainly a technique beyond the scope of the ordinary person or juror. Even if reduced to its essential elements, this must be the case:[68]

> The process used by an investigative profiler in developing a criminal profile is quite similar to that used by clinicians to make a diagnosis and treatment plan: data are collected and assessed,

---

[63] See Haward, L.R.C., "A Psychologist's Contribution to Legal Procedure" (1964) 27 M.L.R. 656, at p.657; Haward, L.R.C., "The Psychologist as Expert Witness" in Farrington, Hawkins and Lloyd-Bostock, *op cit*. n55; Clapham, B., "Introducing Psychological Evidence in the Courts: Impediments and Opportunities" in Lloyd-Bostock, S.M.A. (eds) *Psychology in Legal Contexts* (1981) MacMillan: London, Mackay, R.D., and Colman, A.M., "Excluding Expert Evidence: A Tale of Ordinary Folk and Common Experience" [1991] Crim. L.R. 800; Pattenden, R., "Conflicting Approaches to Psychiatric Evidence" [1992] Crim. L.R. 92, at p.99. See also Freckleton, *op cit*. n55, p.42.

[64] *Turner* [1975] Q.B. 834 *per* Lawton L.J. The difficulty in applying this test is well reported. See generally Mackay, R.D., and Colman, A.M., "Equivocal Rulings on Expert Psychological and Psychiatric Evidence: Turning a Muddle into a Nonsense" [1996] Crim L.R. 88; Thornton, P., "The Admissibility of Expert Psychiatric and Psychological Evidence: Judicial Training" (1995) 35 Med. Sci. Law 143; Sheldon, D.H., and MacLeod, M.D., "From Normative to Positive Data: Expert Psychological Evidence Re-Examined" [1991] Crim. L.R. 881; Pattenden, R., "Conflicting Approaches to Psychiatric Evidence in Criminal Trials: England, Canada and Australia" [1986] Crim. L.R. 92; Hodgkinson, *op cit*. n55, pp.229-232.

[65] Roberts, *op cit*. n55, p.67.

[66] See Slovenko, *op cit*. n55. See also the Canadian approach in *R v Abbey* (1982) 68 CCC (2d) 394.

[67] Psychology has been noted to be likely to fall foul of the *Turner* rule "not only because psychologists lack medical training but also by reason of the fact that psychology is a science devoted in the main to the study of normal behaviour". Mackay and Coleman, *op cit*. n64, p.801.

[68] Described as "(1) A comprehensive study of the nature of the criminal act and the type of persons who have committed this offence; (2) A thorough inspection of the specific crime scene involved in the case; (3) An in-depth examination of the background and activities of the victim(s) and any known suspects; (4) A formulation of the probable motivating factors of all parties involved; 95) The development of a description of the perpetrator based upon the overt characteristics associated with his/her probable psychological makeup. Wolbert, A., (ed) *Rape and Sexual Assault: A Research Handbook* (1985) Garland: New York, p.344.

the situation reconstructed, hypotheses formulated, a profile developed and tested, and the results reported back. Investigators traditionally have learned profiling through brainstorming, intuition and educated guesswork. Their expertise is the result of years of accumulated wisdom, extensive experience in the field, and familiarity with a large number of cases.[69]

A part-profile such as a statistic related to the likelihood of an offender bearing a specific characteristic will also, in general, lie outside the scope of the juror's knowledge. This will be a question of degree. While the average juror applying his common-sense will realise that there is a (slightly) greater likelihood of a murderer who kills in the middle of the afternoon being a shift-worker than someone who works regular office hours, the same is not true of other characteristics (e.g. a collection of pornography or interest in martial arts). Where the research and experience of the psychologist enables him to provide an opinion as to the likelihood of the offender being interested in martial arts or separated from his wife, the information is clearly beyond the scope of the jury's knowledge. There is a possible challenge even to statistics of this type being beyond the knowledge of the jury. Research in the USA by Pinizzotto and Finkel showed that, in controlled conditions, professional profilers were found not to "process material in a way *qualitatively* different"[70] from untrained psychologists, detectives and first-year psychology students.[71] All that the research shows is that at least some of the jury may be able to construct a profile. That is not to say that they have knowledge and experience of the way the particular profile before the court was constructed. That the profile is beyond the knowledge of the jury is even more clearly apparent where the crime involved is one of particular deviance, as most profiled crimes are.

Additional safeguards for novel techniques?

Ognall J. in *R v Stagg* stated that any prosecutor wishing to rely upon profile evidence would face "formidable difficulties" in proving that such a profile was in fact expert evidence. His lordship was also doubtful that the psychological profile evidence is sufficiently well established or "generally accepted" as a scientific method to be received as expert evidence.[72] He went on to suggest that such a novel technique must satisfy tests such as those developed in the USA in cases such as *Frye v US* (1923)[73] and *Daubert v Merrell Dow* (1993)[74]. Similarly, the Supreme Court of Canada ruled that "expert evidence which advances a novel scientific theory or technique is subjected to special scrutiny to determine whether it meets a basic threshold of reliability and whether it is essential in the sense that the trier of fact will be unable to come to a satisfactory conclusion without the assistance of the expert".[75]

---

[69] Douglas, J.E., Ressler, R.K., Burgess, A.W., and Hartman, C.R.,"Criminal Profiling from Crime Scene Analysis" (1986) 4(4) Behavioural Sciences and the Law 401, p.405.

[70] Pinizzotto and Finkel, *op cit.* n30, p.227; Canter, *op cit.* n11, p.150-1.

[71] The groups were provided with hypothetical cases, with known outcomes. The results showed that the profilers produced more detailed reports than the other groups, and were more accurate in profiling sexual offenders, but that they were not more accurate in profiling homicides. See also McCann, *op cit.* n 13, p.478.

[72] Vorpagel, *op cit.* n10, notes that "psychological profiles have not yet achieved the level required for probable cause to arrest, or to attain a search warrant, we feel that in the near future sufficient expertise will have been accumulated to allow a profiler to testify as an expert witness in court" p.162.

[73] *Frye v US* (1923) 293 F 1013 (D.C. Cir). See Freckleton, *op cit.* n55, p.60-67.

[74] 113 S Ct 2786; 125 L Ed 2d 469 on which see *inter alia* [1994] 84(4) J. Crim Law and Criminology especially, Allen, R.J., "Expertise and the *Daubert* Decision" [1994] 84(4) J. Crim Law and Criminology 1157; "Confronting the New Challenges of Scientific Evidence" (1995) 108 Harv. L.R. 1481-1605; Edmond, g., and Mercer, D., "Recognising Daubert. What judges need to know about falsificationism". (1997) Expert Evidence 29. See also Bernstein, D.E., "Junk Science in the United States and the Commonwealth" 91996) 21 Yale Journal of International Law 123.

[75] *per* Sopinka J at p.25.

There is no authority in English law that applies such a test.[76] The preferred English approach is well illustrated by the case of *R v Robb*[77] in which the Court of Appeal accepted evidence of techniques of voice identification, which had minority support amongst the relevant scientific community. Bingham L.J., as he then was, stated that

> Expert evidence is not ... limited to the core areas. Expert evidence of finger-printing, handwriting, and accident reconstruction is regularly given. Opinion may be given of the market value of land, ships, pictures, or rights. Expert opinions may be given of the quality of commodities, or on the literary, artistic, scientific or other merit of works alleged to be obscene ... Some of these fields are far removed from anything which could be called a formal scientific discipline. Yet while receiving this evidence the courts would not accept the evidence of an astrologer, a soothsayer, a witch-doctor[78] or an amateur psychologist and might hesitate to receive evidence of attributed authorship based on stylometric analysis.[79]

In a similar vein, in *R v Stockwell*[80], a case concerning facial-mapping, Lord Taylor C.J. approved the trial judge's statement that "[o]ne should not set one's face against fresh developments, *provided they have a proper foundation*".[81]

Daubert requires a court to consider whether the method is reliable and relevant, tried and tested, has been subjected to peer review, has a known potential error rate, and has some support in the scientific community. These factors will not be considered explicitly by English courts. Nevertheless, the English courts will be influence by a number of these factors in determining whether the method has a "proper foundation".

(i) Reliability

"Perhaps the most controversial aspect of psychological expertise...is the problem of knowing when the specialised knowledge is sufficiently reliable and valid to quality either scientifically or legally, as expertise".[82]

The reliability and source of the profile must be established. There are two points here. First, if the profile is not reliable it will not pass as "expert" evidence even under the test in *R v Robb or R v Stockwell*. Secondly, even if it is admitted as expert evidence, it will not be strong enough to withstand critical examination in court. As observed earlier, opinion evidence does not necessarily attract a great deal of weight; it is not conclusive proof of anything. The more reliable the procedure is perceived to

---

[76] See also Alldridge, O., "Novel Scientific Techniques: DNA as a Test Case" Crom. L.R. 687, p.692; Freckleton, *op cit*. n55, Ch.4. and pp.165-174; Bessner, R., "The Admissibility of Novel Scientific Techniques in Criminal Trials: Voice Spectroscopy" (1987-88) 30 Crim. L.Q. 294; Giannelli, P.C., "The Admissibility of Novel Scientific Evidence: *Frye v United States*, a Half Century Later" (1980) 80 Columbia Law Rev. 1197.

[77] (1991) 93 Cr App R 161. See also Alldridge, *op cit*. n76, p.694.

[78] With respect, even a soothsayer or an astrologer could give evidence as an expert, but only on matters relating to their beliefs or customs or that upon which they were qualified. The reason that astrologers and such like are not permitted to give expert evidence on the likelihood of guilt of an accused is that their evidence is irrelevant, as discussed above, in that it cannot be established to be reliable enough to support any proposition relating to guilt. Even a magician has been called to give evidence on the "fraudulent manipulation of coins". *Moore v Medley* (1995) *The Times* 3rd Feb as noted in Smith, J.C., *Criminal Evidence* (1995) Sweet and Maxwell: London, p.113.

[79] At p.164, referring to Kenny, A., "The Expert in Court" (1983) 99 L.Q.R. 197.

[80] (1993) 97 Cr App R 260.

[81] At p.264 (emphasis added).

[82] Goldring, S.L., "Increasing the reliability, validity and relevance of psychological expert evidence: An introduction to the special issue on expert evidence" 91992) 16 Law and Human Behaviour 253 cited in Editorial Introduction, "Some Legal Issues Affecting Novel Forms of Expert Evidence" (1992) 1 Expert Evidence 79, p.79.

be, the more weight is likely to be attached to it by the trier of fact.[83] It is arguable that the reliability issue would go to weight and not admissibility, but there must be a cut-off point below which, evidence is of such unreliability as to be of no assistance to the court, and indeed may be a positive impediment.

Both of these points indicate a need for profiling to be established as reliable. But can this ever be proved? Profiling has been under constant scrutiny for reliability for a number of years. The FBI's success rate has been put as high as 46%,[84] others have claimed success rates of up to 80%.[85] In England, Canter's Offender Profiling Research Unit was judged to be successful by detectives in "most of the 30-plus profiles thus far produced".[86] These claims are open to attack given the impossibility of an objective assessment of reliability.[87] Given the nature of the exercise, a controlled experiment is out of the question.[88] Similarly, practical difficulties would be encountered in any retrospective evaluation of trial outcomes. It would simply not be possible to disentangle from the ultimate profile what information came from guess work, what was forensic input, crime scene analysis etc. An equally cogent criticism of the claims for reliability is that many relate only to success as an investigative tool rather than as admissible evidence: profiles are usually intended to assist investigation rather than prove guilt. There is an important point behind this attack, as noted by Mair[89] and discussed above. Whereas investigation calls for sensitivity to all possible material, the criminal trial is concerned only with very specific evidence.

This inability to establish, categorically, that the procedure is reliable is problematic even for the use of part-profiles such as statistical data. If the statistic is not capable of proof as an uncontroverted fact, it could be rejected as being of insufficient relevance. A court could rule that such matters were likely to divert the attention of the tribunal into too many side issues as discussed above.[90] In one decided US case this was the basis upon which the profile evidence was rejected. In *State v Cavallo*[91] the defendant was charged with rape and sought to introduce expert evidence that he lacked the psychological traits common to rapists. The court rejected the evidence, noting that "the testimony was based on two unproven and unreliable premises: (a) rapists have particular mental characteristics, and (b) psychiatrists can, by examination, determine the presence or absence of these characteristics".[92]

Finally, there is the danger of the lack of reliability owing to the poor knowledge and/or technique of the profiler himself.[93] As Grubin has noted:

---

[83] For example, more weight attaches to finger-print evidence than to identification by facial-mapping.

[84] 88 of 192 requests led to the suspect being identified from the profile: Pinizzotto, *op cit*. n13, p.39. See further Ressler et al, *op cit*. n53, p.346. Gudjonsson, G.H. and Copson, G. The Role of the Expert in the Criminal Investigation. at p.73 in Jackson, J.L. and Bekerian, D.A. *op cit*. n11.

[85] Hazelwood, R.R., and Douglas, J.E., "The lust murderer" (1983) 49(4) FBI Law Enforcement Bulletin 18.

[86] Boon and Davies, *op cit*. n9, p.221.

[87] Grubin, D., "Offender Profiling" (1995) 6(2) Journal of Forensic Psychiatry 259, p.261; McCann *op cit*. n13, p.476. See also Editorial Introduction, *op cit*. n55, p.16.

[88] "Psychological research can seldom be of [a] strictly scientific character - 'controls' and 'subjects', with human characteristics are quite unlike chemicals, acids, atoms, electrons or neutrons." Clapham, *op cit*. n63, p.98.

[89] *op cit*. n48.

[90] See *Aggassiz v London Tramway Company* (1872) 27 L.T. 492.

[91] Slovenko, *op cit*. n55, p.636.

[92] (1982) 88 NJ 508; 443 A 2d 1021.

[93] See Gudjonsson, G.H., "The Implications of Poor Psychological Evidence in Court" (1993) 2(3) Expert Evidence 120, p.122 listing these as key problems.

An increasing number of individuals are now claiming expertise in offender profiling, and most are not shy in offering their services to the police. Their techniques are often poorly articulated, if articulated at all, with intuition and 'brainstorming' often playing a prominent role.[94]

(ii) A uniform method of profiling?

In Robb, it was not fatal to the reception of the evidence that the method used to identify voices by this particular method was different to the majority of others in that scientific community. There would seem to be no need to establish a uniform method of profiling. Nevertheless, the more scientific the approach can be made to appear, the more acceptable it is likely to be to the court; it will have greater objectivity. As noted, there are so many different approaches to creating a profile that it is difficult to discern any uniform methodology. There have been efforts to establish a uniformity of definition of types of crime: for example the publication of the Crime Classification Manual.[95] Such attempts to produce a definitive catalogue of aspects of human behaviour are never likely to result in universal acceptance. There is, for example, widespread scepticism as the reliability of the approach used in the famous Diagnostic and Statistical Manual of Mental Disorders: DSM IV.[96] In *R v Mohan* the Supreme Court of Canada excluded profile evidence precisely because of this failure to prove that the psychological characteristics listed in a profile had been "standardized" to a satisfactory extent.[97]

(iii) Profiling as a science?[98]

Once again, the English authorities are clear that expert evidence may be received on issues of art, taxation, accounting practice, stylometry[99] and even foreign law, none of which could really be described as a science. Nevertheless, the more scientific, the more objective it appears the less sceptical courts will be. It has been noted above that the profile produced as a whole may appear less scientific than a part-profile and thus be less well received. In general, profiles "... are the result of statistics. In other words, given many incidents of a similar nature, the investigators have discovered that the individuals who often committed "this particular type of offence" displayed specific characteristics or traits".[100] Material such as that in the studies conducted as the residence of rapists,[101] could not be sensibly distinguished, *in this scientific sense*, from statistical evidence about the likelihood of a voice-match for identification of the accused as in *Stockwell*. The statistical evidence will, if properly constructed, be consistent, cumulative, methodical and predictive, and as

---

[94] *op cit.* n87, p.260.

[95] Douglas, J.E., Burgess, A.W., Burgess, A.G., and Ressler, R.K. Crime Classification Manual (1992) New York: Lexington. See Jackson, J.L. and Bekerian, D.A. "Does Offender Profiling Have a Role to Play?" and Bekerian, D.A. and Jackson, J.L. "Critical Issues in Offender Profiling" in Jackson, J.L. and Bekerian, D.A. *op cit.* n11.

[96] *Diagnostic and Statistical Manual of Mental Disorder*, 4th ed, (1994) American Psychiatric Association: Washington DC, McCann *op cit.* n13, p.478. On whether psychiatry really is a science, see Kenny, *op cit.* n79.

[97] At p.38, *per* Sopinka J.

[98] See Canter, *op cit.* n11, Ch.4. See also Davies, A. "Specific Profile Analysis: A Data-based Approach to Offender Profiling" in Jackson, J.L. and Bekerian, D.A. *op cit.* n11.

[99] See Robertson, B., Vignaux, G.A., and Egerton, I. "Stylometric Evidence" [1994] Crim L.R. 645. See also Editorial Introduction, *op cit.* n82.

[100] Pinizzotto, *op cit.* n13, p.35.

[101] See Canter, D. and Gregory, A, "Identifying the residential location of rapists" (1994) 34(3) J. For. Sci. Soc. 169; Davies, A., and Dale, A., "Locating the Stranger Rapist" (1996) Med. Sci. Law 146.

such will qualify, in the view of one leading commentator, as a science.[102] The difference will lie, if at all, in the question of the legal relevance of such evidence.

(iv) Avoiding the trial by expert

One other factor which will influence the court's decision whether to receive expert testimony of profile evidence is the likelihood that the issues raised by that testimony will become the substance of a debate between competing experts. This could distract the jury, waste time and, rather than assisting the court as it is designed to do, could simply create confusion. In *Stagg*, Mr Paul Britton was the main instigator of the prosecution case, while the defence were to rely on a formidable team of experts including Gisli Gudjonsson, Glenn Wilson and David Canter to discredit the profile.[103]

Although it is not possible to address the issue of the neutral expert[104] and the dangers of trial by expert[105] in full, it is possible to highlight the particular hazard with the criminal psychologist testifying for the prosecution. Because the profiler will have helped *throughout the investigation*, bias is even more likely than in the usual case of an expert witness hired by one party to testify to their cause.[106] The psychologist may well, at the very least, be perceived to be more anxious to get a conviction because of his close involvement in the investigation and because the conviction would reflect positively on his work in general.

(v) The "ultimate issue" rule

There is a technical rule which prohibits the expert giving his opinion on the very matter on which the tribunal of fact will ultimately have to arbitrate – the "ultimate issue" – as this would be to usurp their function.[107] The rule is now regarded as a "matter of form rather than substance": *Stockwell*.[108] Nevertheless, the jury must be reminded that they are the decision-makers and are not bound by the opinion of the expert.

> Refusing to allow experts to express opinions on material questions reflects our fears that [the jury] will pay undue attention to those opinions. In effect we are saying that they may be overborne by the articulateness, the impressiveness of the jargon of the expert.[109]

---

[102] Kenny, *op cit*. n79. "[C]ourts should place confidence in social science research to the extent that the research (a) has survived the critical review of the scientific community, (b) has valid research methods, (c) is generalizable to the legal question at issue, and (d) is supported by a body of other research": Monahan, J. and Walker, L., *Social Science in Law: Cases and Materials* (2nd ed 1990) Foundation Press, New York: p.468.

[103] See Britton, *op cit*. n2.

[104] There are numerous problems with court appointed experts: When is he to be appointed? How is he to be selected? Should the prosecution or the defence have a right to object to the proposed court expert? How would the expert inform himself as to the relevant facts? Should either party be allowed to cross-examine the court expert? Should either party be allowed to call his own expert to contradict the court expert? Smith, *op cit*. n78, p.118.

[105] The advantages of court-appointed experts and the neutral expert is discussed in full in Howard, M.N., "The Neutral Expert: A Plausible Threat to Justice" [1991] Crim. L.R. 98 and Spencer, J.R., "The Neutral Expert: An Implausible Bogey" [1991] Crim. L.R. 106. See Sheldon, D.H. and MacLeod, M.D., "From Normative to Positive Data: expert psychological evidence re-examined" [1991] Crim. L.R. 811, 819. See also Freckleton, *op cit*. n55, Ch.11. See also McEwan, *op cit*. n31, p.138.

[106] Gudjonsson, *op cit*. n93, p.122 notes that this 'eagerness to please' is a major problem for expert evidence in general. See Howard *op cit*. n105, p.101 and Spencer *op cit*. n105, p.107.

[107] *R v Wright* (1821) Russ and Ry 456, 458.

[108] (1993) 97 Cr App R 260, p.265. See generally, Jackson, J.D., "The Ultimate Issue Rule: One rule too many" [1984] Crim. L.R. 74, and May, R., *Criminal Evidence* (3rd ed 1995) Sweet and Maxwell: London, para 8–04 - 8–06; Hodgkinson, *op cit*. n55, p.150.

[109] Freckleton, *op cit*. n55, p.76. "The fact that an expert witness has impressive scientific qualifications does not by that fact alone make his opinion on matters of human nature and behaviour within the limits of normality any more helpful than that of the jurors themselves; but there is a danger that the jury may think it does." *per* Lawton L.J. in *Turner* [1975] Q.B. 834, p.840.

It is a fear of the usurpation of the jury's function which results in the rule preventing an expert from testifying as to whether an accused had the requisite mental state (e.g. intention or recklessness) at the time of the commission of the offence charged. This concern, and the general rule of relevance, also lies behind the prohibition on any witness (including an expert) testifying as to the credibility of any other witness (including the accused).[110]

Finally in relation to expert evidence, it is worth noting that the *Royal Commission on Criminal Justice* Cm. 2263 (1993) and the Law Commission (*Report No 245 Evidence in Criminal Proceedings: Hearsay and Related Topics* (1997)) have both made recommendations which attempt to facilitate more reliable expert evidence which is not time-consumingly and confusingly contested at trial unless it is disputed.

From this detailed review of the current position, it would seem that a profile is the opinion[111] of an expert based on material gleaned from reports of other investigations, prosecutions and from reports of those convicted (self-reports). The mechanics of admissibility are being continually simplified by legislation.[112] Section 9 of the Criminal Justice Act 1967 permits any witness evidence, including the evidence of an expert, to be admitted subject to certain procedural formalities. Section 30 of the Criminal Justice Act 1988 renders expert reports admissible in criminal proceedings (with leave of the court required where the expert does not testify). Section 31 provides that "for the purpose of helping members of juries to understand complicated issues of fact or technical terms Crown Court rules make provision: (a) as to the furnishing of evidence in any form".[113]

Before such an opinion can be admitted as evidence, there are a number of other factors of which the criminal psychologist ought to be aware. These apply equally to expert opinion adduced by the defence or the prosecution.

OTHER PERILS FOR THE EXPERT CRIMINAL PSYCHOLOGIST[114]

Transposing the Conditional

One of the gravest sins for the expert witness whose testimony contains statistical material is to transpose the conditional. This is lesson to be learnt from the use of expert evidence on DNA.[115]

---

[110] There is a historic but largely redundant exception which allows for a witness to testify as to the "general reputation for untruthfulness" of another. This is very rarely relied upon: *Toohey v M.P.C.* [1965] A.C. 595; *R v Bogie* [1982] Crim L.R. 301. See the discussion of the Royal Newfoundland Constabulary Criminal Behaviour Analysis Unit in House, J.C. "Towards a Practical Application of Offender Profiling: The RNC's Criminal Suspect Prioritization System" in Jackson, J.L. and Bekerian, D.A. *op cit.* n11.

[111] Meaning simply an inference drawn from the facts: May, R., *Criminal Evidence* 3rd ed (1995) Sweet and Maxwell: London, p. 157.

[112] See Hodgkinson, *op cit.* n55, Part B.

[113] See Carson, *op cit.* n55; Hodgkinson, *op cit.* n55.

[114] Clapham, *op cit.*, n63; Carson, D., *Professionals and the Courts: A Handbook for Expert Witnesses* (1990) Venture Press: Birmingham.

[115] See Balding, D.J. and Donnelly, P., "The Prosecutor's Fallacy and DNA Evidence" [1994] Crim L.R. 711. On DNA see also Gill, P., and Fedor, T., "DNA Profiling: Is It Reliable?" Sol. J 3 Dec 26; McLeod, N., "English DNA Evidence Held Inadmissible" [1991] Crim. L.R. 58. The 'DNA reliability war' which rages in the USA is discussed in: Thompson, W.C., "Evaluating the Admissibility of New Genetic Identification Tests: Lessons from the 'DNA Wars' (1993) 84 J. Crim. Law and Criminology 22; Harmon, R.P., "Legal Criticisms of DNA Typing: Where's the Beef?" (1993) 84 J. Crim. Law and Criminology 175; Neufeld, P.J., "Have You No Sense of Decency" (1993) 84 J. Crim. Law and Criminology 189; Farrington, "Unacceptable Evidence" (1993) 143 N.L.J. 806, and 857; Cellmark Diagnostics (1993) 143 N.L.J. 1596; Redmayne, M., "Doubts and Burdens: DNA Evidence, Probability and the Courts" [1995] Crim. L.R. 464; Alldridge, P., "Recognising Novel Scientific Techniques: DNA as a test case" [1992] Crim. L.R. 687; Young, S.J., "DNA Evidence - Beyond Reasonable Doubt?" [1991] Crim. L.R. 264.

The courts have been so troubled by this that they have recently provided a model direction for trial judges to follow in cases involving DNA: *R v Doheny* (1996)

> Members of the jury, if you accept the scientific evidence called by the Crown, that indicates that there are probably only four or five white males in the United Kingdom from whom that semen stain could have come. The defendant is one of them. The decision you have to reach on all the evidence is whether you are sure that it was the defendant who left that stain or whether it is possible that it was one of that other small group of men who share the same DNA characteristics.[116]

The dangerous process of reasoning is to take the statements relating to the *offender* and transpose them to the *accused*. If the compiler of a profile were permitted to testify, he could only venture an opinion as to the likelihood of the offender having a specific characteristic. Under no circumstances must the opinion relate to the likelihood of the accused being guilty because he has that characteristic.

The problem usually arises when it comes to questions being put to the witness in court.[117] There are two questions with a crucial distinction:

1. What is the probability that D's profile matches the sample profile, assuming he is innocent?

2. What is the probability that D is innocent assuming that his profile matches the sample profile?

The most famous example used to demonstrate the difference is by reference to a card game with the Archbishop. What is the probability of the Archbishop dealing himself a straight-flush if he is playing honestly? (Answer: 3/216,580) What is the probability of the Archbishop playing honestly is he has dealt himself a straight-flush? (Answer: depends on the assessment of this Archbishop's morality.)[118]

The expert can answer question 1, but the court is interested in the answers to question 2. The expert is not able to answer the second question: that is a matter for the jury. Whereas question 1 assumes the innocence of the accused (as is appropriate with the presumption of innocence in a criminal trial) and asks about the likelihood of an accurate match, question 2 assumes a match and asks about the likelihood of innocence. The fact that an answer to question 1 gives a very small statistical probability does not necessarily lead to a similarly small probability in answer to question 2. The prosecutor's fallacy, as it became known in DNA cases, is for the expert to give an answer to question 1 that purports to be an answer to question 2.

A related problem in which the courts have demonstrated an equally cautionary approach to statistics, recently came into the open for the first time in England.[119] This is the argument; that all issues in a criminal trial could be processed by the jury using a mathematical formula: Bayes theorem. The Court of Appeal's rejection of this theory demonstrates a clear reluctance to have the courtroom turned into a mathematics seminar. This links in with the courts' long acknowledged worries about the use of scientific jargon by expert witnesses in general. Theories such as

---

[116] [1997] Crim. L.R. 669. See also Redmayne, M. "The DNA Database: Civil Liberty and Evidentiary Issues" [1998] Crim. L.R. 437 and Hunter, K. "A New Direction on DNA" [1998] Crim. L.R. 478, and the Criminal Evidence (Amendment) Act 1997.

[117] On the use of the hypothetical question and the expert see Jones, *op cit.* n55, pp.110-127. On hypothetical questions and the relationship to adverse trials see Carson, *op cit.* n55, p.16.

[118] Balding and Donnelly, *op cit.* n115, p.713.

[119] See *R v Adams* [1996] Crim L.R. 898; *R v Doheny* [1997] Crim L.R. 669. See also the discussion of the notorious US case *State v Collins* in Eggleston *op cit.* n23, p.142 and by Haward *op cit.* n55, p.49; Redmayne, M., "Doubts and Burdens: DNA Evidence, Probability and the Courts" [1995] Crim. L.R. 464; Robertson, B., and Vignaux, G.A., "Probability - The Law of Logic" (1993) 13 O.J.L.S. 457; Robertson, B., and Vignaux, G.A., *Interpreting Evidence: Evaluating Forensic Science in the Courtroom* (1995) Wiley: Chichester; Redmayne, M., "Science Evidence and Logic" (1996) 59 M.L.R. 747.

Bayes Theorem are ill suited to the criminal trial. The theorem requires that values for each item, "prior probabilities", be multiplied together to produce a final probability. In the recent case *R v Adams*,[120] figures were being suggested for items of evidence including "the likelihood that the perpetrator was a local man" and the "likelihood that the alibi evidence was true". It is obvious that no precise figure can be place on the accuracy of any such evidence. A further danger lies in attaching a numerical value to each item of evidence with a view to multiplying the values together to produce an overall probability. This hazardous assumption that each item of evidence is statistically independent is often labelled the "Kouskas fallacy". To take a well known example, in an armed robbery the offender drove a red sports car to escape and had a blond passenger. It is wrong to assume that the two facts were statistically independent and assign values to each to produce an overall probability: blondes may prefer red cars.

These types of objection could arise in the case of the criminal psychologist's work. Although there is no reported instance of a psychologist calculating the likelihood of an offender possessing a particular profile, there is always a danger that such a technique could be attempted in an effort to render the evidence more credible. Certainly where the evidence relates to the less-scientific evidence, the courts will object to the possibility that (as with Bayes Theorem) it could lead jurors to assume (falsely) that it was possible to represent the accuracy of an item of non-scientific evidence by a precise numerical value.

Hearsay

Any expert's testimony must be based upon facts which can themselves be proved by admissible evidence.[121]

> Before a court can assess the value of an opinion it must know the facts upon which it is based. If the expert has been misinformed about the facts or has taken irrelevant facts into consideration or has omitted to consider relevant ones, the opinion is likely to be valueless. In our judgment, counsel calling an expert should in examination-in-chief ask his witness to state the facts upon which his opinion is based.[122]

One of the major problems is to ensure that the facts upon which the opinion is based do not offend the rule against hearsay. The now accepted definition of hearsay is:

> an assertion other than one made by a person while giving evidence in the proceedings, is inadmissible as evidence of any fact asserted.[123]

This unduly technical rule has taken on a logic of its own, and it would be inappropriate to do more than attempt the briefest of outlines here. The key problem to bear in mind is that even though the information (statements made by a person otherwise than while testifying) may be the most reliable and trustworthy source of information, it will still constitute hearsay if someone seeks

---

[120] [1996] Crim. L.R. 898. See also R v Adams (No.2) [1998] 1 Cr App R 377. As Lord Bingham of Cornhill, the Lord Chief Justice noted, "in the light of previous rulings on this matter in this Court, and having had the opportunity of considering the [matter], we regard the reliance on evidence of this kind in such a case as a recipe for confusion, misunderstanding and misjudgement, possibly even among counsel, but very probably among judges and, as we conclude, almost certainly among jurors". p.384.

[121] *Per* Lawton L.J. *Turner* [1975] Q.B. 834, 840. See Freckleton, *op cit.* n55, Ch.6.

[122] *Turner* [1975] Q.B. 834, 840 per Lawton L.J.

[123] *Per* Lord Havers in *R v Sharp* [1987] 1 W.L.R. 7, p.11 approving Tapper, C., *Cross on Evidence* (6th ed 1985) Butterworths, London: p.38.

to rely on it in court.[124] It is not possible to prove such material as "true", although the expert is permitted to rely upon the material to form his opinion.[125]

How does all this bear on the expert evidence of the criminal psychologist? Canter and Kirby recently wrote that "By working with records of convicted offenders it was thus possible to ensure that the evidence for the offence had been evaluated through the legal process before being incorporated into the research."[126] This may be true, but the information (assertions made by others) in the police records or documents is still hearsay! The hearsay rule is especially problematic in relation to all data collected by self-report. It matters not that the material for the report was compiled from police sources or even from the transcripts of an earlier trial.

Further problems are created by the technical possibility of counsel insisting on all who had a hand in the preparation of a report or profile attending as a witness. If A, B and C had been working on the collation of material and statistics, and only C gave evidence, it would be hearsay for C to report anything he had not witnessed with his own eyes. The work of A and B, if conducted independently could not be relied upon unless they testified. This could, at face value, render the profile inadmissible, but the Court of Appeal has recently acknowledged that a strict application of the rule would be unworkable. In *Jackson*,[127] it was accepted that there is a widespread practice of adducing Crown expert evidence without calling each of the technicians or others involved in the creation of the report: plainly this is with a view to saving costs on uncontroversial matters. The Law Commission's recommendations in Report No. 245, *Evidence in Criminal Proceedings: Hearsay and Related Topics*[128] will, if enacted, reduce the opportunity for such pointless and time-consuming cross-examination of assistants.

The hearsay rule may be a hindrance to the expert, but it has not been allowed to create absurdity. It is well established that once the primary facts on which the expert's opinion is based have been proved by admissible evidence, the expert is entitled to draw on the work of others (i.e. published and unpublished works, articles and textbooks) as part of the process of drawing conclusions from those facts. For example, in the case of *Abadom*,[129] a forensic expert was able to refer to statistics collated by the Home Office Central Research Establishment in order to demonstrate that the refractive index of glass found in two samples was uncommon. The difficulty for the criminal psychologist is that while he will be allowed to refer to the works of others to form his opinion, that, say, the rapist resided in an area close to the attack, it will not be possible to probe the specific statistic as a fact unless he has conducted that research himself.

A much wider hearsay exception might well prove useful in many cases: section 24 of the 1988 Criminal Justice Act. This admits documents "created or received by a person in the course of a trade, business, profession or other occupation or as the holder of a paid or unpaid office; and [provided] all information contained in the document was supplied by a person (whether or not the maker of the document) who had, or who may reasonably be supposed to have had personal knowledge of the matters dealt with". There are many drafting deficiencies with the statute which

---

[124] Canter, D., and Kirby, S.,"Prior Convictions of Child Molesters" (1995) Science and Justice 73, 75. "The data is obtained from a reliable and properly documented source which is arguably more robust than relying on an individual's account." Reliability is no exception to hearsay!

[125] *Bradshaw* (1985) 82 Cr App R 79; *Turner* [1975] Q.B. 834; *Abadom* (1983) 76 Cr App R 48.

[126] Canter and Kirby, *op cit*. n124, p.75. See also Davies and Dale, *op cit*. n101.

[127] [1996] Crim. L.R. 732.

[128] (1997) H.M.S.O: London.

[129] [1983] 1 W.L.R. 126.

could cause problems, but they lie beyond the scope of this chapter, and would be removed by the Law Commission's proposed reform.[130]

There is no requirement that the document form part of a record, nor hat it be created by someone acting under a duty. Any work compiled by a criminal psychologist in the course of his business would be covered. The statement in the document will be admissible subject to the judge's discretion (under section 25 or 26) not to receive such evidence unless it is in the interests of justice to do so. The application of the section should apply to material such as the police records, which formed the basis of the Canter and Kirby study above.[131]

Computers

Computers are playing an increasingly important role[132] in the work of the criminal psychologist. In the USA, the famous VICAP programme of the FBI is the most prominent,[133] but there are many others including: the AIMS - Arson Information Management System; HALT - New York State's Homicide Assessment and Lead Tracking System; HITS - Michigan's Homicide Investigative Tracking System. Although it has been said that in the UK, "[a]ttempts to produce computerised 'M.O. indexes' at great expense [have] ... been found to be qualified failures",[134] there seems little doubt that computers will take on a greater role for the criminal psychologist here as in the USA.[135] The use of computers can be seen in a significant amount of the academic work published by criminal psychologists. Recent examples include the work of Canter on rape locations and on previous records of offenders.

Unfortunately, the rules of evidence include a provision which hinders reliance on computer generated material as evidence in a criminal trial. Section 69 of the Police and Criminal Evidence Act 1984 (PACE) requires that *all* computer evidence is admissible only where it has been shown that the computer(s) is/are, being operated properly and operating properly. Reliability may be proved by a written certificate (para 8 of Schedule 3), or, where required by the trial judge, by oral evidence (para 9 of Schedule 3). The s.69 requirements will be unnecessary where the other party consents to the admission of the evidence, but if, as in most reported cases, the issue is contested there will be a trial within a trial, where legal argument is conducted in the absence of the jury, to decide on admissibility. Furthermore, it was held in the case of *Cochrane*[136] that it is necessary to explain the function and working of the computer in all cases. The burden of proof always lies on

---

[130] See Report No. 245, *Evidence in Criminal Proceedings: Hearsay and Related Topics* (1997) H.M.S.O.: London, See Tapper, C. "Hearsay in Criminal Cases: An Overview of Law Commission Report No.245" [1997] Crim. L.R. 771.

[131] It is possible that the records, because they are police records would be classified as documents created in the course of a criminal investigation. If this is the case, the statute imposes a number of other conditions before the material can be admitted, and even then it still remains at the discretion of the judge. This would also arguably apply to all self-report statistics.

[132] Boon and Davies, *op cit*. n9.

[133] FBI's NCAVC - National Centre for the Analysis of Violent Crime and VICAP - Violent Criminal Apprehension Programme both rely heavily on computer analysis of data. This is discussed at length in Douglas, et al *op cit*. n53 and Ressler, R.K., Burgess, A.W. and Douglas, J.E., *Sexual Homicide: Patterns and Motives* (1988) New York: Lexington, pp.111-119. See Wolbert, *op cit*. n68, pp.347-9, and http://www.fbi.gov.vicap. House, J.C. "Towards a Practical Application of Offender Profiling: the RNC's Criminal Suspect Prioritization System"; Farrington, D.P. and Lambert, S. "Predicting Offender Profiles from Victims and Witness Descriptions" and Davies, A. "Specific Profile Analysis: A Data-based Approach to Offender Profiling" in Jackson, J.L. and Bekerian, D.A. *op cit*. n11.

[134] Canter, *op cit*. n11, p.237.

[135] See Pinizzotto, *op cit*. n13, p.38; Canter, *op cit*. n11, pp.12-14.

[136] [1993] Crim. L.R. 48.

the party wishing to adduce the computer evidence, and the normal criminal standard applies: beyond reasonable doubt for the prosecution, and on the balance of probabilities for the defence.

As if these undiscriminating requirements were not enough, there are many problems with the drafting of the section. Section 69(1)(b) is concerned with the accuracy of the contents of the computer evidence. Where there is an error in relation to an aspect of the information supplied to the computer, the whole will be admissible if the erroneous part has no bearing on the way the computer functions. Thus in *McKeown v D.P.P; Jones v D.P.P.*[137] the clock of an intoximeter (treated here as a computer) was operating incorrectly, yet the documentary evidence produced by that device was admissible because the accuracy of the clock had no bearing upon the accuracy of the alcohol reading. If a computer printout containing the information forming part of the criminal psychologist's expert evidence was incorrect, for example, as to the date, s.69 would not render the whole document inadmissible.

Numerous other difficulties have arisen because of the nature of computers. These include the difficulties of proving reliability where there is networking of machines. This problem has proved particularly acute where large mainframes are concerned (e.g. a bank mainframe or the police computer network). It may be difficult or even impossible to find anyone who can certify the reliability of such a complex system. As with any very complex piece of technology, it is not too difficult to raise such a doubt in the minds of the trier of fact. The effect of even the most scientifically reliable data can be severely damaged by counsel's suggestions about computer error.

One advantageous aspect of section 69 is that it applies *only* to documents *actually tendered*. In *Sophocleus v Ringer*[138] the Divisional Court held that s.69 was "wholly reserved to cases in which the prosecution choose to put before the justices, without any other evidence attached to it, a computer record or document which contains some statement". Thus where, in *Golizadeh*[139] an expert relied on evidence which has been prepared with the assistance of computers which were not subjected to s.69 scrutiny, but has not actually adduced the computer printout as evidence, the expert's opinion will be admitted.[140]

Finally it must be noted that this position may not be around to trouble the criminal profilers for too much longer. In Report No.245, *Evidence in Criminal Proceedings: Hearsay and Related Topics* (1997) the Law Commission's recommendation is to repeal s.69.

EXCLUSIONARY DISCRETION

Even if the profile(r) has jumped all these hurdles, there is still the chance that the court will exclude the evidence under its general discretion. Exclusion would be most likely to occur under this head by virtue of section 78 of PACE:

> In any proceedings the court may refuse to allow evidence on which the prosecution proposes to rely to be given if it appears to the court that, having regard to all the circumstances, including the circumstances in which the evidence was obtained, the admission of the evidence would have such an adverse effect on the fairness of the proceedings that the court ought not to admit it.

---

[137] [1997] 1 All E.R. 737.

[138] [1988] R.T.R. 52.

[139] [1995] Crim L.R. 232.

[140] This has been heavily criticised since the computer document is being put to use by the court without being subjected to the test of reliability which s.69 provides.

Section 78 focuses on unfairness in the proceedings as the criterion for exclusion.

This can include the way in which the evidence was obtained. Unfairness in the gathering of evidence could have a "knock-on" effect on the fairness of the trial. The central ruling in Stagg was that the evidence obtained by the undercover police operation would have such an adverse effect upon the fairness of the proceedings as to require its exclusion.

Ognall J reviewed the law in this area, and in particular a number of recent decisions relating evidence obtained as a result of police "entrapment".[141] The principles to be derived from the earlier cases are concerned mainly with the question of whether the police have tricked the defendant. These principles are unlikely to arise in properly conducted profiles.[142] One other principle which can be derived from the recent case law is more worthy of note, this is the fact that "public policy is in favour of the proposition that the more serious the offence, the more unusual form of investigation may be justified."[143] Since it is widely claimed that criminal profiles can generally be compiled only in relation to serious crimes, this principle is unlikely to represent a hindrance to the use of profile evidence. In the most recent pronouncement, *Latif*,[144] the House of Lords once again drew attention to this with an instruction to judges to:

> weigh in the balance the public interest in ensuring that those that are charged with grave crimes should be tried and the competing public interest in not conveying the impression that the court will adopt the approach that the end justifies the means.[145]

WOULD EVIDENCE OF THE CRIMINAL PSYCHOLOGIST EVER BE RECEIVED

There are three possible situations in which the potential for a court to receive a criminal psychologist's opinion evidence deserves special consideration.

Similar Fact Cases

In cases in which the prosecution seek to prove the identity of the offender by similar fact evidence, it might be appropriate for a criminal psychologist to testify. As discussed above, there are two distinct approaches to the proof of identity by similar facts: cumulative and sequential. In both approaches it is vital that the court is satisfied that the two acts (usually crimes) are the work of the same offender. It is submitted that there would be nothing to stop a criminal psychologist testifying as to how similar two offences are in his opinion. Normally, there would be no need to hear evidence as to the degree of similarity since it would be something which the jury could itself

---

[141] *Smurthwaite* (1994) 98 Cr App R 437; *Christou* [1992] 2 Q.B. 979; *Bryce* (1994) 95 Cr App R 320; *Bailey and Smith* [1993] 3 All E.R. 523.

[142] Ognall J described as "highly disingenuous" the prosecution's claim that the undercover operation was to afford Stagg the opportunity of eliminating himself from the enquiry. The conduct of the investigation was "thoroughly reprehensible" and displayed "not merely an excess of zeal but a substantial attempt to incriminate a suspect by positive and deceptive conduct of the grossest kind" (Transcript, p.21). In conclusion, his lordship ruled that the conduct of a fair trial demanded the exclusion of the evidence.

[143] Transcript, p.9.

[144] [1996] 1 W.L.R. 104.

[145] *Per* Lord Steyn, p.113.

perceive. However, in some cases, it would be useful for the court to hear precisely how peculiar is a particular *modus operandi*. The jury could then assess how likely it would be that the offences were committed in such a peculiar way by different people. If satisfied that the offences were the work of the same person they would be able to apply either the cumulative or sequential line of reasoning as appropriate. There is some judicial support for such evidence. In *R v Mullen*[146] evidence was received of the statistical fact that notionally, only 13 burglars used a blow torch to crack the glass windows to effect entry.[147] The criminal psychologist would simply be using his expertise to draw more clearly to the attention of the court, the particular aspects of the crime(s) in question. Care must be taken here since it will not be possible for an expert to testify that, for example, the offence in question is a "classic sadistic rape". The courts would not be prepared to accept such expert evidence unless satisfied that the classification system used was sufficiently precise and reliable. What will be permitted is evidence highlighting similarities or, for that matter discrepancies between the offences. In the Canadian case of *R v Mohan*, the Supreme Court accepted that a "psychiatrist's testimony was admissible to show that the offences alleged were *unlikely* to have been committed by the same person".[148]

As Evidence in Support of the Defence

It is not difficult to conceive of a case in which an accused wishes to rely upon a profile in an attempt to raise reasonable doubt as to his guilt. The right of the accused to meet the charge against him by all legitimate means is "fundamental to the administration of criminal justice."[149] Colin Stagg, had the case gone to full trial, would certainly have sought to introduce evidence from a criminal psychologist to rebut the prosecution profile. Specifically, the accused would wish first to identify aspects of the profile of the offender, and second to draw attention to this own personality and its incompatibility with the profile. In both instances there would be problems of admissibility.

First, the psychologist's evidence as to what constitutes a profile of the *offender* will be unlikely to be admissible for the many reasons already considered. Secondly, the psychologist's comments as to the *accused's* character would also be likely to be excluded. In so far as such evidence related to the accused's mental state, it would be inadmissible unless the accused were abnormal (thus beyond the jury's understanding and experience). Thus, in the Canadian case of *R v Mohan*,[150] the Supreme Court upheld the trial judge's decision to exclude profile evidence on which the accused proposed to rely, The charge was one of sexual assault on young women, and the evidence of the profiler was that a typical offender in such cases would be a paedophile and that the accused was not. Sopinka J stated that "such [e]vidence of an expert witness that the accused by reason of his or her mental make-up or condition of the mind, would be incapable of committing or disposed to commit the crime would be inadmissible".[151]

A more fundamental objection to the testimony on the accused's character is that the decision in *R v Rowton*[152] forbids the accused calling evidence of particular acts or witnesses' opinions at to

---

[146] [1992] Crim. L.R. 735. See Farrington, D.P. and Lambert, S. "Predicting Offender Profiles from Victims and Witness Descriptions" in Jackson, J.L. and Bekerian, D.A. *op cit*. n11.

[147] See also McCann, *op cit*. n13 for consideration of this in serial offences.

[148] [1994] 2 S.C.R. 9, at p.19 *per* Sopinka J. (emphasis added).

[149] *Per* Winncke C.J. in *R v Lavery and King* (No 3) [1992] V.R. 939, P.947.

[150] [1994] 2 S.C.R. 9.

[151] At p.27.

[152] (1865) Le & Ca 520 (CCR).

his disposition. The accused may bring only evidence of his general reputation in the neighbour-hood. Thus, if an accused is charged with a homosexual offence, this rule prevents him calling specific evidence of his heterosexuality by reference to particular incidents or by calling his female partner(s).[153] To take a further example, the rule would, if applied strictly, prevent an accused on trial for gross indecency calling a psychologist to testify that he had examined the accused and found him to be a heterosexual with a marked intolerance to homosexuality.[154] The rule seems unduly harsh and impractical, but as one commentator observes "[th]ere would appear to be five reasons for limiting evidence as to character, namely, that such evidence (a) is easy to fabricate; (b) is often irrelevant; (c) may lead to the investigation of side issues of little relevance to the case; (d) amounts frequently to evidence of opinion which is generally excluded; and (e) may create a risk that the function of the jury will be usurped".[155] The rule in *Rowton*, despite being cogently criticised,[156] still represents the law. It would prohibit an accused from relying upon a psychological profile, or any part thereof, which related to his particular disposition. It is only avoided in practice, in cases in which the courts show particular "indulgence" to an accused.[157]

Finally, it should be noted here that there is a common law rule which would prohibit a witness testifying as to the credibility of any other witnesses, including the accused.[158]

Where One of Two Accused Must Have Done It

When one defendant wishes to draw upon a profile to show that he is less likely to have committed the offence that a co-accused things become more difficult. In any case involving multiple accused, the rules of evidence have to applied with much more care.

One case which presents particular difficulty here is the decision of the Privy Council in *Lowery v R*.[159] In that case one accused, K, was permitted to adduce psychological opinion evidence to establish that he was less likely than L, his co-accused, to have committed the horrific murder with which the two were charged. This case might be taken to lend support for the use of defence profile evidence. However, there are a number of reasons why it is submitted that *Lowery* should not be held to support such a proposition. First, the case has been distinguished as being "decided on special facts".[160] The Privy Council stressed that the evidence was not being received as evidence of criminal tendency. Lord Morris of Borthy-Gest stated that the evidence "was not related to crime or criminal tendencies: it was scientific evidence as to the respective personalities of the two accused".[161] Second, as Thornton has pointed out "it may also be a decision which was fashioned by the peculiar jurisdiction of the Privy Council in which a conviction will not be quashed unless the court concludes that there is a serious likelihood of a

---

[153] See *R v Redgrave* (1981) 74 Cr App R 10. Cf Slovenko, *op cit*. n55, p.635 on the US position.

[154] Cf the Canadian case of *R v Lupien* [1970] S.C.R. 263, and see Mewett, A.W., "Character as a Fact in Issue in Criminal Cases" (1984) 27 Crim. L.Q. 29.

[155] May, *op cit*. n108, para 7.13.

[156] See e.g.. McEwan, J., *Evidence and the Adversarial Process: The Modern Law* (1992) Blackwell: London, p.154; Tapper, C., *op cit*. n15, p.353.

[157] See e.g. *R v Redgrave* 91982) 74 Cr App R 10; *R v Kinsella, Kinsella and MacFhlionn* [1995] Crim L.R. 731 and commentary.

[158] *Toohey v M.P.C.* [1965] A.C. 595. See further text accompanying n110 above.

[159] [1974] A.C. 85. See Tapper and Cross, *op cit*. n15, pp.355-356; Hodgkinson, *op cit*. n55, p.239; Freckleton, *op cit*. n55, p.47; Eggleston, *op cit*. n23, p.134. See also Elliott, D.W., "Cut-Throat Tactics: the freedom of an accused to prejudice a co-accused" [1991] Crim. L.R. 5; *R v Mohan* [1994] 2 S.C.R. 9.

[160] *Per* Lawton L.J. in *Turner* [195] Q.B. 834, p.842. See also *Neale* (1977) 65 Cr App R 304.

[161] [1974] A.C. 85, p.101.

miscarriage of justice".[162] Third, the evidence was only admitted to rebut the specific allegations of the co-accused.[163] Finally, the victim in *Lowery* was definitely killed by one of the accused (or both), and both had been subjected to the same psychological examination. The facts are very different from a situation in which a profile seeks to identify the killer from the population at large, or even to distinguish the accused from a general type of person capable of committing the crime.

In a situation such as this the court *might* be prepared to accept the profile evidence of the criminal psychologist, thought the words of Lawton L.J. in *R v Turner* (rejecting *Lowery*) should not be ignored:

> We do not consider that [Lowery] is an authority for the proposition that in all cases psychologists and psychiatrists can be called to prove the probability of the accused's veracity. If any such rule was applied in our courts, trial by psychiatrists would be likely to take the place of trial by jury ... We do not find that prospect attractive and the law does not at present provide for it.[164]

There are a number of these cases where one accused has sought to introduce evidence of the propensity of a co-accused to commit the offence with which they are both charged. The central question will be one of relevance and, as Devlin J noted in *Miller*,[165] "the character of the accused is no more relevant at the hands of a co-accused than it is at the hands of the prosecution". The question of relevance takes on a more prominent role in the cases involving the co-accused because, the court has no discretion to exclude evidence of a defendant as it does when the prosecution seek to rely on such evidence. The courts are therefore more likely to rule the evidence inadmissible on grounds of relevance.[166] *R v Neale*[167] provides a good example. N was charged with arson and sought to support his defence that he was not a participant to the attack by adducing evidence that his co-accused, B, was a known fire-raiser. This was held to be insufficiently relevant, since it did not prove that B had started this fire alone. The court interpreted *Miller*, as requiring as strict a test of relevance to defence evidence as prosecution evidence in these cases. This strict attitude is also apparent in a number of other cases,[168] but it has been doubted by academic commentators whether there ought to be such a rigid application of relevance.[169]

A more complicated scenario is one in which D is on trial for an offence, and a third person, has also been investigated by the police but not charged. The decision in *R v Blastland*[170] discussed above provides an example. If the third party, Mark, fitted a profile prepared for he police, could Blastland have relied upon it to support his claim that Mark was the murderer? The case is very easily distinguishable from *Lowery* on the basis that Mark is not a co-accused; he is not on trial. On the other hand it would bear similarity to *Lowery* provided the criminal psychologist had compared the profile to both the two people investigated. Returning to first principles of evidence, there

---

[162] Thornton, *op cit*. n64, 147.

[163] In this regard it is similar to *Bracewell* (1979) 68 Cr App R 44, in which B was entitled to rebut the suggestion that his co-accused, A, was a cool professional burglar unlikely to indulge in violence.

[164] [1975] Q.B. 834, 840.

[165] (1952) 36 Cr App R 169, p.172.

[166] See, for example, the recent case of *Kracher* [1995] Crim. L.R. 819. See also the strict approach taken in *R v Neale* (1978) 65 Cr App R 304; *R v Knutton and England* (1992) 97 Cr App R 115; *R v Nightingale* [1977] Crim. L.R. 744.

[167] (1977) 65 Cr App R 304.

[168] Ormerod, L.J. in *Bracewell* stated that "where the evidence is tendered by a co-accused the test of relevance must be applied, and applied strictly." (1979) 68 Cr App R 44, p.50; *Knutton* (1993) 97 Cr App R 114.

[169] See Andres, J.A. and Hirst, M., *Criminal Evidence* (2nd ed 1992) Sweet and Maxwell, London: para 15–06.

[170] [1986] A.C. 41.

can be no question of prejudice rendering the evidence inadmissible. Furthermore, the rule in *R v Rowton* and other exclusionary rules would appear not to apply. Thus the sole question would be one of relevance. The question can be posed as follows: Does the fact that an expert witness is of the opinion that a specific person other than the accused is more likely to be the perpetrator make it more (or less) likely that the accused committed the crime? It is submitted that, subject to the arguments about reliability above, the evidence is logically relevant. However, given the courts' recent strict approach to legal relevance,[171] the acceptance of such an opinion is by no means beyond doubt. In particular, the court would be wary of the numerous side issues which would arise. Even here it is doubtful that the criminal psychologist will have his day in court.

CONCLUSION

In *Stagg*, Ognall J made broad and perhaps unnecessary statements doubting the admissibility of psychological profile evidence in the English criminal trial. A detailed review of the rules of evidence suggests that his lordship was right to sound this more of discouragement to those traditionally involved in the investigation and prosecution of crime and to criminal psychologists who might be persuaded to become involved in any such prosecution.

The prosecutor seeking to rely on a profile (if such a thing exists) or even part of a profile will have to navigate his way through practically all of the most difficult rules of the law of evidence. The most fundamental and primary question of what relevance a profile has to the facts in issue may well be as far the legal argument gets before being rejected. This rule of relevance, although not expressly tackled by Ognall J in *Stagg*, also underpins the further difficulties facing the prosecutor: rules against the admissibility of highly prejudicial similar fact evidence, and against admitting the opinion evidence of an expert on so controversial a subject. The rules of evidence are clearly stacked against the admissibility of this material except in very rare cases. The legal argument would be equally foreboding in the case of a defence application to admit such evidence.

The rules of evidence also present difficulties for the criminal psychologist. If involved in the presentation of the case the criminal psychologist will have to face extensive questioning as to his expertise, the reliability of his methodology and working practices, the availability of alternative methodologies and their success rates. There would also be the inevitably detailed and testing questions in the light of evidence provided by the opposing party's own criminal psychologist who will have cast doubt on the methodology, the interpretations etc. In addition, the psychologist will have been constrained by the evidential rules even before setting foot in court. The hearsay rule will inhibit reliance on data even though it may be the most reliable available, the provisions of the Police and Criminal Evidence Act 1984 will also necessitate the proof of computer reliability.

In the case of a prosecution profile, the story does not end there. In the event that all of these problems are overcome by both the psychologist and the prosecutor, the court may still exclude the evidence, in its discretion, on the ground that it would be unfair to the accused.

It will be most unlikely that counsel can persuade the court of the relevance of this potentially highly prejudicial opinion. If it should happen, the opinion evidence of the psychologist will be admitted as mere circumstantial evidence. Admittedly, there is no rule preventing a conviction based on circumstantial evidence alone,[172] but in view of all the hazards addressed above, one

---

[171] See Choo, *op cit*. n18, and for a further discussion see Tapper *op cit*. n15, p.356.171.

[172] There is no rule preventing a verdict on circumstantial evidence along: cf *Onufrejczyk* [1955] Q.B. 388, in which D was convicted of murder on circumstantial evidence without a body.

question then has to be asked: was it worth it? Perhaps Ognall J saved the criminal psychologists considerable strife with his suggestion that they limit their activities to helping the police with the investigation.

On a more positive note, one of the aims stated above was to explain the rules of evidence to the psychologist, but there is also a clear need for judicial training so as to be aware of progress in science and other fields of expertise.[173]

> Psychologists and other behavioural scientists might be more usefully employed outside the witness box, assisting, not only in the earlier stages of criminal investigation and prosecution, but also in the training of lawyers and judges. This might at least ensure that not too much would be expected of them in court.[174]

INDEX OF ABBREVIATIONS USED

The style of citation adopted in this chapter is an orthodox one which will be familiar to lawyers. For a complete guide, non-legal readers are referred to Raistrick, D., *Index to Legal Citations and Abbreviations*. 2nd ed, 1993, Bowker-Saur: London. The following is a list of the more common abbreviations used:

A.C.	*Appeal Cases (Law Reports)*
All E.R.	*All England Law Reports*
C.L.J.	*Cambridge Law Journal*
Cr. App. R.	*Criminal Appeal Reports*
Crim.L.Q.	*Criminal Law Quarterly*
Crim.L.R.	*Criminal Law Review*
D.L.R.	*Dominion Law Reports*
Harv.L.R.	*Harvard Law Review*
J.For.Sci.Soc.	*Journal of the Forensic Science Society*
L.Ed	*Lawyer's Edition, United States Supreme Court Reports*
L.Q.R.	*Law Quarterly Review*
L.S.	*Legal Studies*
L.T.	*Law Times*
M.L.R.	*Modern Law Review*
Med. Sci. Law	*Medicine Science and the Law*
N.L.J.	*New Law Journal*
O.J.L.S.	*Oxford Journal of Legal Studies*

---

[173] Thornton, *op cit*. n64.

[174] Mair, *op cit*. n48, p.142.

Q.B.	*Queen's Bench (Law Reports)*
R.T.R.	*Road Traffic Reports*
S.C.R.	*Supreme Court Reports (Canada)*
V.R.	*Law Reports of Victoria (Australia)*
W.L.R.	*Weekly Law Reports*

BIBLIOGRAPHY

Allan, T.R.S. (1988). Some favourite fallacies about similar facts. *8 L.S.* 35.

Alldridge, P. (1992). Recognizing Novel Scientific Techniques: DNA as a test case. *Crim L.R.* 687.

Allen, R.J. (1994). Expertise and the *Daubert* Decision. *84(4) J. Crim Law and Criminology* 1157.

Andrews, J.A., & Hirst, M. (1992). *Criminal Evidence* (2nd ed) London: Sweet and Maxwell.

Ashworth, A. (1980). The Binding Effect of Crown Court Decisions. *Crim. L.R.* 402.

Badcock, R. (1997). Developmental and Clinical Issues in Relation to Offending in the Individual. In J.L. Jackson, & D.A. Bekerian (eds) *Offender Profiling: Theory, Research and Practice*. Chichester, UK: Wiley.

Balding, D.J., & Donnelly, P. (1994). The Prosecutor's Fallacy and DNA Evidence. *Crim. L.R.* 711.

Bernstein, D.E. (1996). Junk Science in the United States and the Commonwealth. *21 Yale Journal of International Law* 123.

Bessner, R. (1987–88). The Admissibility of Novel Scientific Techniques in Criminal Trials: Voice Spectroscopy *30 Crim. L.Q.* 294.

Birch, D.J. (1987). Hearsay-logic and hearsay-fiddles: *Blastland* revisited. In P.F. Smith (eds) *Criminal law: Essays in Honour of J.C. Smith*. London: Butterworths.

Boon, J.C.W. (1997). The Contribution of Personality Theories to Psychological Profiling. In J.L. Jackson, & D.A. Bekerian (eds) *Offender Profiling: Theory, Research and Practice*. Chichester, UK: Wiley.

Boon, J., & Davies, G. (1993). Criminal Profiling. *Policing* 218.

Britton, P. (1997). *The Jigsaw Man*. London: Bantam Press.

Canter, D. (1994). *Criminal Shadows*. London: Harper Collins.

Canter, D., & Kirby, S. (1995). Prior Convictions of Child Molesters. *Science and Justice* 73.

Canter, D., & Gregory, A. (1994) Identifying the residential location of rapists. *34(3) J. For. Sci. Soc.* 169.

Carson, D. (1990). *Professionals and the Courts: A Handbook for Expert Witnesses*. Birmingham: Venture Press.

Carson, D. (1992). Expert Evidence in the Courts. *1 Expert Evidence* 13.

Carter, P.B. (1987). Hearsay, relevance and admissibility: declarations as to state of mind and declarations against penal interest. *103 L.Q.R.* 106.

Cellmark Diagnostics (1993). *143 N.L.J.* 1596.

Choo, A.L.-T. (1993). The Notion of Relevance and Defence Evidence. *Crim. L.R.* 114.

Clapham, B. (1981). Introducing Psychological Evidence in the Courts: Impediments and Opportunities. In S.M.A. Lloyd-Bostock (eds) *Psychology in Legal Contexts*. London: Macmillan.

Cleary, E.W. (1984). *McCormick on Evidence* (3rd ed) West: St Paul.

Confronting the New Challenges of Scientific Evidence (1995). *108 Harv. L.R.* 1481-1605.

Cowen. Z., & Carter, P.B. (1956). *Essays in the Law of Evidence.* Oxford: Clarendon.

Cross, R. (1975). Fourth time lucky – similar fact evidence in the House of Lords. *Crim L.R.* 62.

Davies, A. (1994). Editorial: Offender Profiling. *34(3) Med. Sci. and Law* 185.

Davies, A. (1997). Specific Profile Analysis: A Data-based Approach to Offender Profiling. In J.L. Jackson & D.A. Bekerian (eds) *Offender Profiling: Theory, Research and Practice.* Chichester, UK: Wiley.

Davies, A., & Dale, A. (1996). Locating the Stranger Rapist. *Med. Sci. Law 146 Diagnostic and Statistical Manual of Mental Disorder,* 4th ed, (1994) American Psychiatric Association: Washington DC.

Douglas, J.E., Burgess, A.W., Burgess, A.G., & Ressler, R.K. (1992). *Crime Classification Manual.* New York: Lexington.

Douglas, J.E., Ressler, R.K., Burgess, A.W., & Hartman, C.R. (1986). Criminal Profiling from Crime Scene Analysis. *4(4) Behavioural Sciences and the Law* 401.

Editorial Introduction. (1992). Some Legal Issues Affecting Novel Firms of Expert Evidence. *1 Expert Evidence* 79.

Edmond, G., & Mercer, D. (1997). Recognising Daubert. What judges need to know about falsificationism. *Expert Evidence* 29.

Eggleston, R. (1983) *Evidence, Proof and Probability* (2nd ed). London: Weidenfield.

Farrington, D.P., & Lambert, S. (1997). Predicting Offender Profiles from Victims and Witness Descriptions. In J.L. Jackson & D.A. Bekerian (eds) *Offender Profiling: Theory, Research and Practice.* Chichester, UK: Wiley.

Farrington, L. (1993). Unacceptable Evidence. *143 N.L.J.* 806.

Freckleton, I.R. (1987). *The Trial of the Expert: A Study of Expert Evidence and Forensic Experts.* Melbourne: OUP.

Giannelli, P.C. (1980). The Admissibility of Novel Scientific Evidence: *Frye v United States,* a Half Century Later. *80 Columbia Law Rev.* 1197.

Gill, P., & Fedor, T. (1993). DNA Profiling: Is It Reliable? *Sol. J 3 Dec* 26.

Goldring, S.L. (1992). Increasing the reliability, validity and relevance of psychological expert evidence; An introduction to the special issue on expert evidence. *16 Law and Human Behaviour* 253.

Grubin, D. (1995). Offender Profiling. *6(2) Journal of Forensic Psychiatry* 259.

Gudjonsson, G.H. (1993). The Implications of Poor Psychological Evidence in Court. *2(3) Expert Evidence* 120.

Gudjonsson, G.H., & Copson, G. (1997). The Role of the Expert in the Criminal Investigation. in J.L. Jackson & D.A. Bekerian (eds) *Offender Profiling: Theory, Research and Practice.* Chichester, UK: Wiley.

Harmon, R.P. (1993). Legal Criticisms of DNA Typing: Where's the Beef? *84 J. Crim. Law and Criminology.*

Haward, L.R.C. (1964). A Psychologist's Contribution to Legal Procedure. *27 M.L.R.* 656.

Haward, L.R.C. (1979). The Psychologist as Expert Witness. In D.P. Farrington, K. Hawkins & S.M.A. Lloyd-Bostock (eds) *Psychology, Law and Legal Process.* London: MacMillan.

Hazelwood, R.R., & Douglas, J.E. (1983). The lust murderer. *49(4) FBI Law Enforcement Bulletin* 18.

Higgins, M. (1997). Looking the Part. *American Bar Association Journal.* p.48.

Hodgkinson, T. (1990). *Expert Evidence: Law and Practice.* London: Sweet and Maxwell.

Hoffman, L. (1975). Similar facts after *Boardman. 91 L.Q.R.* 193.

Holmes, R.M., & Holmes, S.M. (1996). *Profiling Violent Crimes: an investigative tool*. New York: Sage Publications.

House, J.C. (1997). Towards a Practical Application of Offender Profiling: The RNC's Criminal Suspect Prioritization System. In J.L. Jackson & D.A. Bekerian (eds) *Offender Profiling: Theory, Research and Practice*. Chichester, UK: Wiley.

Howard, M.N. (1991). The Neutral Expert: A Plausible Threat to Justice. *Crim. L.R.* 98.

Jackson, J.D. (1984). The Ultimate Issue Rule: One rule too many. *Crim. L.R.* 74.

Jackson, J.L., & Bekerian, D.A. (1997). Does Offender Profiling Have a Role to Play? In J.L. Jackson & D.A. Bekerian (eds) *Offender Profiling: Theory, Research and Practice*. Chichester, UK: Wiley.

Jackson, J.L., van den Eshof, P., & de Kleuver, E.E. (1997). A Research Approach to Offender Profiling. In J.L. Jackson & D.A. Bekerian (eds) *Offender Profiling: Theory, Research and Practice*. Chichester, UK: Wiley.

Jones, C.A.G. (1994). *Expert Witnesses: Science, Medicine and the Practice of Law*. Oxford: Clarendon Press.

Kenny, A. (1983). The Expert in Court. 99 *L.Q.R.* 197.

Law Commission, report No.245. (1997). *Evidence in Criminal Proceedings: Hearsay and Related Topics*. London: H.M.S.O.

Law Commission Consulation Paper No.141. (1996). *Evidence in Criminal Proceedings: Previous Misconduct of a Defendant*. London: H.M.S.O.

Lawton, F. (1980). The Limitations of Expert Scientific Evidence. 20 *J. For. Sci. Soc.* 237.

Mackay, R.D., & Colman, A.M. (1996). Equivocal Rulings on Expert Psychological and Psychiatric Evidence: Turning a Muddle into a Nonsense. *Crim. L.R.* 88.

Mair, K. (1995). Can profile prove a sex offender guilty? *Expert Evidence* 139.

May, R. (1995). *Criminal Evidence* (3rd ed). London: Sweet and Maxwell.

McCann, J. (1992). Criminal Personality Profiling in the Investigation of Violent Crime. *10 Behavioural Sciences and the Law* 475.

McEwan, J. (1994). 'Similar Fact' Evidence and Psychology: Personality and Guilt. *Expert Evidence* 113.

McEwan, J. (1992). *Evidence and the Adversarial Process: The Modern Law*. London: Blackwell.

McLeod, N. (1991). English DNA Evidence Held Inadmissible. *Crim. L.R.* 58.

Mewett, A.W. (1984). Character as a Fact in Issue in Criminal Cases. 27 *Crim. Law Q.* 29.

Mirfield, P. (1987). Similar facts – *Makin' Out. C.L.J.* 83.

Monahan, J., & Walker, L. (1990). *Social Science in Law; Cases and Materials* (2nd ed) Foundation Press: New York.

Nair, R. (1993). Similar Fact Evidence – prejudice and irrelevance. *Crim. L.R.* 432.

Neufeld, P.J. (1993). Have You No Sense of Decency. 84 *J. Crim. Law and Criminology* 863.

Oldfield, D. (1997). What Help Do the Police Need with their Enquiries? In J.L. Jackson & D.A. Bekerian (eds) *Offender Profiling: Theory, Research and Practice*. Chichester, UK: Wiley.

Ormerod, D.C. (1996). The Evidential Implications of Psychological Profiling. *Crim. L.R.* 863.

Pattenden, R. (1986). Conflicting Approaches to Psychiatric Evidence in Criminal Trials: England, Canada and Australia. *Crim L.R.* 92.

Pinizzotto, A.J. (1984). Forensic Psychology: Criminal Personality Profiling. *12*(1) *Journal of Police Science and Administration* 32.

Pinizzotto, A.J., & Finkel, N.J. (1990). Criminal Personality Profiling: An Outcome and Process Study. *Law and Human Behaviour* 215.

Porter, B. (1993). Mind Hunters. *Psychology Today* (April) 44.

Redmayne, M (1995). Doubts and Burdens: DNA Evidence, Probability and the Courts. *Crim. L.R.* 464.

Redmayne, M. (1996). Science, Evidence and Logic. *M.L.R.* 747.

Report of the Royal Commission on Criminal Justice (1993). Cmnd.2263 London: H.M.S.O.

Ressler, R.K., Burgess, A.W., & Douglas, J.E. (1988). *Sexual Homicide: Patterns and Motives*. New York: Lexington.

Roberts, P. (1996). Will You Stand Up In Court? On the Admissibility of Psychiatric and Psychological Evidence. *J. For. Psy.* 63.

Robertson, B., & Vignaux, G.A. (1993). Probability – The Law of Logic. *13 O.J.L.S.* 457.

Robertson, B., Vignaux, G.A., & Egerton, I. (1994). Stylometric Evidence. *Crim. L.R.* 645.

Robertson, B., Vignaux, G.A., & Egerton, I. (1995). *Interpreting Evidence: Evaluating Forensic Science in the Courtroom*. Chichester, UK: Wiley.

Rossmo, D.K. (1997). Geographic Profiling. In J.L. Jackson & D.A. Bekerian (eds) *Offender Profiling: Theory, Research and Practice*. Chichester, UK: Wiley.

Sheldon, D.H., & MacLeod, M.D. (1991). From Normative to Positive Data: Expert Psychological Evidence Re-Examined. *Crim. L.R.* 811.

Slovenko, R. (1993). Expert Testimony: Use and Abuse. *12 Med. and Law* 627.

Smith, C. (1993). Psychological Offender Profiling. *The Criminologist* 244.

Smith, J.C. (1995). *Criminal Evidence*. London: Sweet and Maxwell.

Spencer, J.R. (1991). The Neutral Expert: An Implausible Bogey. *Crim. L.R.* 106.

Stephen, J.F.J. (1948). *Digest of Law of Evidence*. (12th ed). London: MacMillan.

Stevens, J.A. (1997). Standard Investigatory Tools and Offender Profiling. In J.L. Jackson & D.A. Bekerian (eds) *Offender Profiling: Theory, Research and Practice*. Chichester, UK: Wiley.

Tapper, C. (1995). *Cross and Tapper on Evidence* (8th ed). London: Butterworths.

Thompson, W.C. (1993). Evaluating the Admissibility of New Genetic Identification Tests: Lessons from the 'DNA Wars'. *84 J. Crim. Law and Criminology* 22.

Thornton, P. (1995). The Admissibility of Expert Psychiatric and Psychological Evidence: Judicial Training. *35 Med. Sci. Law* 143.

Turco, R.N. (1990). Psychological Profiling. *International Journal of Offender Therapy and Comparative Criminology* 147.

Vorpagel, R.E. (1982). Painting Psychological Profiles: Charlatanism, Coincidence, Charisma, Chance or a New Science. *The Police Chief* 157.

Wigmore, J.H. (1983 rev). *Evidence in Trials at Common Law (Vol 1A)*. Tillers, P.

Wolbert, A. (eds) (1985). *Rape and Sexual Assault A Research Handbook*. Garland: New York.

Young, S.J. (1991). DNA Evidence – Beyond Reasonable Doubt? *Crim. L.R.* 264.

Zuckerman, A.A.S. (1987). Similar fact evidence – the unobservable rule. *104 L.Q.R.* 187.

Zuckerman, A.A.S. (1989). *Principles of Criminal Evidence*. Oxford: Clarendon.

David Ormerod read law at Essex University and lectured there before being appointed to a lectureship at the University of Nottingham in 1990. He was promoted to senior lecturer in 1998. His main research interests are Criminal law and the law of Evidence. He has written a number of articles on topics within these fields including items on expert evidence, the use of documentary evidence, computer evidence, psychological profiling, and psychiatric harm in the criminal law. In addition to his work in the Law School at Nottingham, David Ormerod has presented lectures to the legal profession, (especially the Crown Prosecution Service) and has acted as a consultant to the Law Commission and the Criminal Bar Association. He writes monthly case commentaries for the Criminal Law Review *and is a member of the Editorial Board of the* International Journal of Evidence and Proof.

APA's Expert Panel in the Congressional Review of the USS *Iowa* Incident

NORMAN POYTHRESS, RANDY K. OTTO,

JACK DARKES, AND LAURA STARR

In 1989, an explosion aboard the USS Iowa killed 47 sailors. The navy attributed the explosion to the intentional suicidal acts of Gunners Mate Clayton Hartwig, a conclusion supported primarily by an "equivocal death analysis" conducted by the Federal Bureau of Investigation (FBI). The U.S. House of Representatives Armed Services Committee (HASC) was highly critical of the FBI's report and the navy's conclusions, in part because of the peer review provided by 12 psychologists organized by the American Psychological Association (APA). This article (a) reviews the nature of equivocal death analysis and related reconstructive psychological evaluations, (b) describes the nature of APA's consultation and involvement with the HASC, (c) discusses the conclusions reached by the HASC and the influence of the APA panelists, and (d) suggests limitations on the use of equivocal death analysis and related procedures in light of scientific concerns and ethical considerations.

On April 19, 1989, an explosion occurred in Tur ret 2 of the USS *Iowa*. Five 94-pound bags of smokeless powder ignited while being loaded into the open breach of a 16-inch gun, resulting in the deaths of 47 U.S. Navy sailors. In an extensive investigation, the navy sought to uncover the causes of the explosion. Initial efforts focused on the possibility of an accidental or unintentional explosion. However, in a statement to the Committee on Armed Services of the U.S. House of Representatives on December 12, 1989, Rear Admiral Richard D. Milligan reported that, after conducting extensive tests, the navy had concluded

> that an accident did not cause this explosion. It was not caused by unstable propellant. It was not caused by a direct flame or spark. It was not caused by frictional heating, or by impact and compression. It was not caused by electrostatic discharge. It was not caused by hazards of electromagnetic radiation. It was not caused by the kind of procedural errors or negligent acts crew members might have made. (*Review of Navy Investigation*, 1990, p. 24)

Having ruled out accidental or unintentional causes, the navy's investigation of the USS *Iowa* incident ultimately attributed the explosion to the intentional acts of one sailor, Gunners Mate Clayton Hartwig, who was himself killed in the explosion. This conclusion was reached after the Naval Investigative Service (NIS) conducted interviews with Hartwig's friends, family members, and former shipmates, and had gathered additional archival information (e.g., letters, personal writings, bank account balances) offering clues to his habits, life-style, aspirations, and personality. These data were provided to agents at the National Center for the Analysis of Violent Crime, a division of the Federal Bureau of Investigation (FBI). The reconstructive psychological evaluation (termed an *equivocal death analysis* [EDA] by the FBI) conducted by the FBI resulted in an unequivocal conclusion that Clayton Hartwig had acted alone and intentionally to cause the explosion on the USS *Iowa*. The FBI report was the primary piece of evidence in support of the navy's attribution of responsibility for the incident to Clayton Hartwig.

The navy's investigation of the incident was closely scrutinized by the U.S. House of Representatives Armed Services Committee (HASC). The HASC enlisted the assistance of the American Psychological Association (APA) in reviewing the FBI's report and the navy's conclusions. In this article we (a) review the nature of EDA and related reconstructive psychological evaluations, (b) describe the nature of APA's consultation and involvement with the HASC, (c) discuss the conclusions reached by the HASC and the influence of the APA panelists, and (d) suggest limitations on the use of EDA and related procedures in light of scientific concerns and ethical considerations.

RELIABILITY AND VALIDITY OF EQUIVOCAL DEATH ANALYSIS AND RELATED TECHNIQUES

The HASC was concerned with the reliability and validity of equivocal death analysis as a clinical-investigative method. This was evident from its vigorous interrogation of the agents who wrote the FBI report (*Review of Navy Investigation*, 1990, pp. 234–268) and its request that APA provide a panel of psychologists to offer independent evaluations of the NIS data and the conclusions drawn by the FBI and the navy.

Except in the FBI's own documents and in the publications of its staff (e.g., Hazelwood, 1984) the term *equivocal death analysis* is virtually unknown in the psychological-behavioral sciences community.[1] Testimony by FBI Agents Richard Ault and Robert Hazelwood before the HASC indicated that EDA is an extension of and conceptually related to criminal profiling (*Review of Navy Investigation*, 1990, p. 234). The FBI behavioral science experts consult in cases in which a police investigation has failed to determine the manner of a death. The EDA does not involve direct data gathering by the FBI agents; rather, they use the evidence developed by the referring agency to generate a psychological analysis of the victim, leading to a conclusion regarding the manner of death. The conclusion is couched in categorical terms (indeterminate, accident, homicide, or suicide (*Review of Navy Investigation*, 1990, p. 236) and is routinely offered with absolute rather than probabilistic certainty (p. 249). The indeterminate finding is rarely an outcome; Agent Hazelwood reported to the committee that he could recall only 3 of 45 cases (7%) in which he was unable to arrive at a conclusive opinion (p. 267).

EDA is conceptually related to two other procedures—criminal personality profiling and psychological autopsy—that have some level of acceptance in behavioral science circles. An important feature of all three procedures is that each involves the imposition by the profiler of a theoretical framework on selected data from a large, complex data set; thus, the training, experience, and theoretical preferences of the profiler may be important determinants of the weights assigned to individual pieces of data and to the manner in which the data are integrated. However, EDA is distinguishable from the other two procedures in important ways.

---

[1] A review of *Psychological Abstracts* failed to reveal any citations to *equivocal death analysis*.

Criminal personality profiling has been developed primarily by the FBI (Douglas, Ressler, Burgess, & Hart-man, 1986; Geberth, 1981; Holmes, 1989; Porter, 1983; Turco, 1990). Its application is thought to be limited to cases in which the crime scene itself indicates psycho-pathology (e.g., sadistic torture in sexual assaults, postmortem slashings, ritualistic crimes, and rapes; Piniz-zotto, 1984). It is distinguished from EDA in that (a) the focus is on a (presumably) living, but unknown, perpetrator; (b) the profilers conduct their own investigation and examination of the crime scene; and (c) the objective is to develop investigative leads based on perpetrator personality traits. Identification of the suspected perpetrator is not considered helpful in criminal personality profiling. "Profiling does *not* provide the specific identity of the offender" (Douglas et al, 1986, p. 402), and "information the profiler does *not* want included in the case materials is that dealing with possible suspects. Such information may subconsciously prejudice the profiler and cause him or her to prepare a profile matching the suspect" (p. 406). In contrast, EDA rests on knowing the identity of the suspected perpetrator and then offering conclusions about likely scenarios based on this information.

Psychological autopsy is more similar to EDA in that the focus is on a deceased person and involves a reconstruction of a personality profile on the basis of interview and archival data (Ebert, 1987). This method has been associated primarily with inquiries into possible or known suicides (e.g., Brent, 1989; Litman, Curphey, Schneidman, Faberow, & Tabachnick, 1963), although conceptually it may be applied to any postmortem psychological analysis (e.g., Fowler, 1986; Selkin, 1987; Selkin & Loya, 1979). It differs from EDA in that profilers typically examine the death scene (in the case of suspected or known suicide) and conduct their own interviews rather than rely on evidence developed by a police investigation.

There has been some empirical investigation of the use of psychological autopsy by medical examiners in determinations of the manner of death (Jobes, Berman, & Josselson, 1986), although the accuracy of judgments rendered as a result of psychological autopsy has not been systematically studied (Shuman, 1986). However, some proponents of psychological autopsy recognize the need to establish the reliability and validity of medical-legal certifications of suicide (Jobes, Berman, & Josselson, 1987). Preliminary conceptual work to identify operational criteria for the determination of suicide (Rosenberg et al., 1988) and to test empirically the utility of these criteria (Jobes, Casey, Berman, & Wright, 1991) has begun.

There have been no published studies of the reliability or validity of EDA. In contrast to the general concern of the scientific community with issues of reliability and validity, and despite the preliminary efforts to investigate the reliability and validity of psychological autopsy, FBI Agent Ault spoke of these issues with disdain when questioned by members of the House committee about the validity of EDA and the integrity of the data on which EDA is based:

> I certainly appreciate that wonderful academic approach to a practical problem. It is typical of what we find when we see people who have not had the experience of investigating either crime scenes, victims, criminals and so forth in active, ongoing investigations. . . . [I]n the field of psychology and psychiatry, there are existing raging arguments about the validity of the very techniques that exist. They won't be resolved in this world. So, to ask us to provide the validity is an exercise in futility. (*Review of Navy Investigation*, 1990, p. 253)

THE ROLE OF ORGANIZED PSYCHOLOGY IN THE REVIEW

The House Armed Services Committee requested that the APA provide assistance by identifying psychological experts to conduct independent evaluations of much of the data provided by the NIS to the FBI, and to comment on the conclusions reached by the FBI and the navy on the basis of that data.[2] The APA identified psychologists with credentials and expertise in diverse areas including adolescence and young adulthood, suicidology, assessment of personality and psychopathology violence and risk assessment, forensic psychology, and peer review. From a larger pool of candidates, 12 panelists were selected "based on the amount of research and experience in their area of expertise as well as their national prominence in their respective fields" (*Review of Navy Investigation*, 1990, p. 285). Two psychiatric experts were appointed by the HASC without input from the APA.

The committee asked the panelists to comment on four basic issues:

1. The validity of the navy's conclusion (How valid is the Navy's conclusion about Hartwig based on the evidence?);

2. The adequacy of the database that was developed by NIS (How valuable are the materials for developing Hartwig's psychological profile? Was the investigation exhaustive?);

3. Hartwig's personality and tendencies (What motives or predispositions for suicide did Hartwig have, if any? And if he was suicidal, what is the likelihood that he'd commit such an act? What other conclusions, if any, would you draw from the material about Clayton Hartwig's psychological profile?); and

4. The validity of posthumous psychological profiles (What are the pitfalls of posthumous determination of suicidal tendencies and behavior?).

The 14 panelists worked independently and served on a pro bono basis. Each prepared a written report for the committee; six panelists (five psychologists, one psychiatrist) testified before the Investigations Subcommittee on December 21, 1989.[3]

CONCLUSIONS OF THE HOUSE ARMED SERVICES COMMITTEE

In rejecting the conclusion reached by the navy (that Hartwig acted alone and intentionally to cause the USS *Iowa* blast), the committee characterized the navy's effort as "an investigative failure" (*U.S.S. IOWA Tragedy*, 1990). Committee Cochair Les Aspin said "The major problem with the Navy investigation is that it fell into the trap of an excess of certitude. Thin gruel became red meat. Valid theories and hypotheses were converted into hard fact" (HASC, 1990, p. 1). The committee was particularly critical of the FBI's equivocal death analysis. This criticism appeared to be based, in part, on the results of the peer review in which the APA panelists participated. Committee Cochair Nicholas Mavroules commented,

> [T]he psychological analysis performed by the FBI for the Navy may be the real villain of this case. The Committee gathered a panel of 14 psychologists and psychiatrists to review the FBI's work. The FBI flunked this peer review. (HASC, 1990, p. 2)

---

[2] The APA psychologists did not have every item of data that had been provided to the FBI. As noted in the Report of the Investigations Subcommittee "The NIS and FBI did not keep a comprehensive inventory of the documents reviewed for the psychological profile. The subcommittee used as a baseline those documents known to have been retained by the FBI for their significance, as well as the Equivocal Death Analysis, and subcommittee staff interviews of several witnesses" (*U.S.S. IOWA Tragedy*, 1990, p. 43, Footnote 4).

[3] A transcript of the complete testimony and the reports of all 14 panelists are contained in the reports of the Joint Hearings (*Review of Navy Investigation of U.S.S. IOWA Explosion*, 1990. HASC No. 101-41. Washington, DC: U.S. Government Printing Office.)

In its final report the Investigations Subcommittee and Defense Policy Panel noted:

> Ten of the 14 experts consulted considered the FBI analysis invalid. And even those who believed the analysis to be somewhat credible were critical of procedures, methodology, and the lack of a statement of the limitations of a retrospective analysis of this nature. (*U.S.S. IOWA Tragedy*, 1990, p. 4)

We conducted a study in which independent raters used an instrument composed of Likert scales that we designed to quantify the judgments and opinions contained in the reports of the 12 psychologists and 2 psychiatrists organized by APA and the HASC (Otto, Poythress, Darkes, & Starr, 1992).[4] Twenty-four clinical psychologists and psychiatrists rated the reports of the 14 panelists and the report read verbatim by Agent Hazelwood at the HASC hearings. Each report was rated (without knowledge of who wrote it) by three subjects.

Our raters' responses indicated that the 14 panelists generally agreed that psychological autopsies designed to determine suicidal tendencies and behavior are of moderate value and utility. However, a cluster analysis of the ratings revealed clear majority and minority positions among the panelists' reports regarding the specific methods used and conclusions reached by the FBI and navy. A majority of the panelists ($n = 11$) were critical of the approach used and conclusions reached by the FBI and navy. A minority of 3 psychologists believed that the navy's report was relatively unbiased and that the conclusions were appropriately stated. All panelists agreed that additional information regarding Hartwig would have been useful. Adopting broad criteria for agreement, there was moderate agreement with respect to Hartwig's adjustment and psychological functioning. Generally, the FBI's impressions of Hartwig were more negative than those developed by the 14 panelists called by the HASC.

After the committee hearings, the investigation into the USS *Iowa* incident was reopened. Media reports indicated that additional tests conducted at Sandia National Laboratories revealed new evidence suggesting an accidental cause for the explosion (Nelson, 1990; "Test Rejects USS Iowa Sabotage," 1992).

IMPLICATIONS FOR RECONSTRUCTIVE EVALUATIONS IN PRACTICE

The EDA conducted by the FBI led the navy to conclude that Clayton Hartwig was responsible for a disastrous explosion, a conclusion with substantial implications on a number of fronts. At a personal level are the effects on Hartwig's reputation and on those friends and family members whose memories of him were affected by the controversy. The FBI-navy findings could potentially have influenced decisions regarding benefits due Hartwig's family or other beneficiaries (e.g., if his insurance policy paid differentially depending on the cause of death). The navy's findings could also potentially affect future decisions regarding benefits to families of other sailors. The Associated Press reported that 37 families of sailors killed aboard the USS *Iowa* were suing the navy for wrongful death, alleging negligence on the navy's part ("Families of USS Iowa Victims Sue," 1991). Although it may not have been intended as such, Admiral Milligan's choice of words in reporting the navy's conclusion that the explosion *"was not caused by* the kind of procedural errors or *negligent acts* crew members might have made" (*Review of Navy Investigation*, 1990, p. 24, italics added) can be read as a preemptive strike against subsequent allegations of negligence by navy personnel.

---

[4] A report of this study may be obtained from Norman Poythress.

The general conclusions of the review panel raise several questions about the status and utility of reconstructive psychological evaluations. Although most cases involving reconstructed psychological profiles will not receive as much attention as the USS *Iowa* explosion and investigation, their impact remains great. Such investigations may affect decisions about whether to pursue criminal explanations for otherwise unexplained deaths, or the kinds of benefits due to survivors of persons who die under ambiguous or mysterious circumstances. Given the potential unreliability of these procedures, should they be used? If so, for what purposes or in which situations, and what should be the limits or parameters of such procedures? What protections can or should be offered to potential consumers?

SHOULD RECONSTRUCTIVE PSYCHOLOGICAL PROCEDURES BE ALLOWED?

Certainly, good arguments can be mustered against using reconstructive psychological procedures such as criminal profiling, psychological autopsy, and EDA. Critics have expressed concerns about the reliability and validity of psychological reconstructions in other contexts, for example, in determining a person's mental state at the time of an offense—arguably a less problematic application than those considered here, given that clinicians gather their own data and have direct access to the subject of the inquiry. Criminal profiling, psychological autopsy, and EDA all require judgments about persons not available for direct assessment; in the case of EDA, the indirect assessment is done by someone other than the investigator-clinician. Furthermore, given less (or at least less desirable) data to work with, the clinician is asked to do more with it. The EDA invites the investigator to go beyond the conventional realm of his or her presumed expertise (the person's mental state) and to reach opinions and conclusions about the legally relevant act itself.

The important differences among these three reconstructive procedures provide grounds for being differentially concerned with their use. As noted earlier, criminal profiling is an attempt to glean clues about the *type* of person most likely to have been involved in particular kinds of cases. At least at the earlier stages of an investigation, such profiling is not used to identify the offender. Reliance on profile analysis may induce law enforcement officers to concentrate their investigative efforts on particular individuals. Thus, this procedure is more likely to pose an increased threat to individual liberty (in terms of investigative intrusions into a person's privacy) than to inappropriately direct the legal fact finder or usurp the fact finder's role. Although we have not found published, programmatic research on the reliability or validity of criminal profiling (see Pinizzotto & Finkel, 1990, for one such study), its utility in guiding police investigations in particularly heinous cases or cases involving suspected serial murderers may be tolerated, if not justified, in the absence of clear evidence of privacy abuses.

We have greater concerns about the use of psychological autopsy and EDA, although we decline to develop and extend earlier arguments regarding why psychologists should not (or should not in legal contexts be allowed to) engage in such practices. It is clear that these investigations are sought out of necessity to help resolve difficult questions. In the absence of a governmental or professional regulatory agency having the authority (if not the inclination) to limit the use of these procedures, the question of whether they should be allowed is a moot one. The demands of the marketplace and the necessity that some resolution be achieved in certain contexts will provide the impetus for their use. The appropriate considerations, then, deal with limiting their use in ways consistent with the limits of the expertise of the professions involved.

SCIENTIFIC CONSIDERATIONS REGARDING THE USE OF PSYCHOLOGICAL AUTOPSY AND EQUIVOCAL DEATH ANALYSIS

We suggest at least the following three limits on the clinical-legal application of reconstructive psychological procedures.[5] First, the use of these procedures should not be extended at present to nondeath situations. To date, psychological autopsy and related techniques have been used primarily to assess and describe issues related to cause of death. Logically, however, if one accepts whole-heartedly that psychologists, psychiatrists, or other social scientists can accurately reconstruct the mental state, motives, and actions of the deceased from third-party and indirect information, then the door should be open to other applications (e.g., "equivocal burglary analysis" or "equivocal kidnapping analysis"). Such extensions should be resisted at all levels, unless considerably more evidence of high reliability and validity of judgments from these procedures is in hand. There should be less political or other external pressure to resolve such events by psychological autopsy, and most nondeath events will not create the need to resolve issues of distribution of the actor's assets (e.g., insurance, will, etc.). Even with regard to equivocal death situations, however, we would discourage extended or widespread use of EDA. The FBI's record of reaching a "conclusive" opinion in 42 of 45 cases notwithstanding, we urge exceeding caution in deciding to use posthumous psychological investigations; many equivocal or unsolved death cases may simply have to remain unsolved.

Second, in legal and quasi-legal contexts, persons who conduct reconstructive psychological evaluations should not assert categorical conclusions about the precise mental state or actions suspected of the actor at the time of his or her demise. The conclusions and inferences drawn in psychological reconstructions are, at best, informed speculations or theoretical formulations and should be labeled as such (Bonnie & Slobogin, 1980; Melton, Petrila, Poythress, & Slobogin, 1987). In its report to the navy, the FBI stated unequivocally that Clayton Hartwig was responsible for the explosion on the USS *Iowa* as an act of suicide, and advised the navy of the method used to start the explosion on the basis of social history and third party interview data. The kinds of unequivocal, bottom-line statements offered by the FBI in its EDA report regarding Clayton Hartwig are not defensible within the technical limitations of our science.

Third, clinicians and social scientists should be careful not to mislead consumers about the accuracy of conclusions drawn from psychological reconstructions by offering inadequate proxies for nonexistent validation studies. It is tempting, particularly when defending one's testimony in an adversarial setting, to overstate one's position. Such efforts, however, can be confusing and misleading. The testimony of Commander Thomas Mountz before the House Armed Services Committee is illustrative. Mountz was sensitive to the limits of psychological reconstructions, as indicated by the statement in his report that "Due to the post-dictive nature of this assessment, the results should be regarded as speculative" (*Review of Navy Investigation*, 1990, p. 270). When asked about his confidence level in his findings (that Hartwig was responsible for the explosion), Mountz responded "better than 99%" (p. 277). It is not a problem that a social scientist-clinician may believe, and even be able to illustrate, that one hypothesis or theoretical formulation seems to fit the available data somewhat better than others. On the other hand, such people should also be aware of the failure of confidence to correlate highly with accuracy in other areas of psychological or personal judgment (e.g., the eyewitness identification and clinical judgment literatures) and avoid misleading consumers with what might be construed as statements of overconfidence.

---

[5] For a discussion of other uses of psychological autopsy, such as assessing the quality of care provided to a person prior to death or determining risk factors for suicide, see Clark and Horton-Deutsch (1992).

ETHICAL GUIDELINES AND IMPLICATIONS REGARDING THE USE OF PSYCHOLOGICAL AUTOPSY AND EQUIVOCAL DEATH ANALYSIS

It is clear that these types of investigations or assessments are performed out of the necessity to answer difficult and important legal questions that arise in a variety of situations.[6] Given the importance of these questions, it seems that mental health professionals should offer their assistance, if they are able to provide some information that helps the fact finder answer important questions. Mental health professionals, in determining whether and how to undertake such assessments, should take into consideration relevant ethical and professional obligations.

The 1990 Ethical Principles of Psychologists (APA, 1990) require psychologists to (a) avoid acting in ways that violate the civil rights of others (Principle 3); (b) prevent distortion or misuse of their findings (Principles 1 & 8); and (c) identify any reservations that exist regarding the validity or reliability of an assessment technique (Principle 8). The Specialty Guidelines for Forensic Psychologists (Committee on Ethical Guidelines for Forensic Psychologists, 1991) are also relevant to psychologists' involvement in psychological autopsies and related pursuits. The Specialty Guidelines, among other things, require psychologists to (a) document or make available for review all data that form the basis of their opinions; (b) ensure that data gathered by others is gathered in such a way that is professionally acceptable; and (c) note the limitations of making statements about persons who were unavailable for examination (Section VI).

Used together, these guidelines can limit whether psychologists engage in these evaluations and how they present their findings. Ethical guidelines promulgated by related organizations (e.g., American Academy of Psychiatry and Law, 1987/1991) can have a similar effect on those organizations' members.

The Standards for Educational and Psychological Testing, which are published by the American Educational Research Council (AERC), the APA, and the National Council on Measurement in Education (1985) may also be used to protect the consumer of these evaluations. Although these standards primarily apply to traditional measures of behavior, they may also be applied to "the entire range of assessment techniques" (AERC et al., 1985, p. 4). These standards obligate those using assessment techniques to (a) evaluate the validity and reliability-of their techniques (Standard 6.1) and (b) demonstrate the validity of a technique if it is used for a purpose that has not been previously validated (Standard 6.3).

Assuming these standards are applicable to psychological autopsies and similar reconstructive assessments, they require those who engage in such assessments to try to evaluate the reliability and validity of their techniques. In light of this, FBI Special Agent Ault's response to the House committee's questions about validity of EDA, "I certainly appreciate that wonderful academic approach to a practical problem. . . . So, to ask us to provide the validity [of EDA] is an exercise in futility" (Review of Navy Investigation, 1990, p. 253) is unacceptable. Similarly, simply citing customer satisfaction or gross evaluation of the general technique also fails to meet the requirements of reliability and validity established by these standards. Thus, Ault's statement that "we have done research on the amount of work we do, and the feedback has been that in probably 80 percent, well above chance, the cases we have were successful" (Review of Navy Investigation, 1990, p. 253) should be considered, like statements of subjective confidence, another example of an inadequate proxy for having validated the procedures that one uses.

---

[6] Our review of legal cases indicated that attorneys have used or attempted to use psychological autopsies to assist in testamentary, life insurance, and workers' compensation cases, as well as in criminal defenses and criminal prosecutions.

Although ethical guidelines and ancillary professional standards could protect consumers and the general public from overstated conclusions based on techniques of limited or unknown reliability, they often do not. Two principal reasons are that professionals who use these techniques disregard the tenets and their colleagues fail to hold them accountable for this, and that some persons who use these techniques are not members of the relevant professional organizations and thus do not feel bound by the relevant professional and ethical principles. More troubling are employment settings in which professionals are not answerable either to governmental regulatory agencies (e.g., licensing boards) or to professional organizations. Compounding this is the potential for these persons to be professionally isolated.[7] Professional isolation may make it difficult to keep abreast of developments in the discipline and may severely limit the opportunity or potential for quality control. In some cases, education of consumers or legal protections appear to be necessary to regulate practice, particularly when these assessments have such serious consequences and are of questionable validity. The APA's response to the House subcommittee's request for assistance in the USS *Iowa* case is one example of how the profession can serve an important public interest function.

LEGAL PROTECTIONS

The law of evidence also has the potential to protect the public from techniques that are of questionable reliability and validity. The law of evidence determines whether mental health professionals may offer courtroom testimony about their conclusions based on psychological autopsies, EDA, or profiling. Although the law varies across jurisdictions, admissibility of psychological autopsies is largely affected by either the *Frye* test (*Frye v. U.S.*, 1910) or the Federal Rules of Evidence and their state equivalents.

The *Frye* test holds: "[the scientific technique] from which the deduction is made must be sufficiently established to have gained general acceptance in the particular field in which it belongs" (*Frye* v. *U.S.*, 1910, p. 1014). Whether these reconstructive techniques can pass this test is arguable given their lack of development, questionable reliability, and unproven validity. Given the published literature that describes at least the conceptual and theoretical basis for psychological autopsy, a stronger argument for general acceptance can be made for this procedure than for EDA, which is virtually unheard of in the psychological and psychiatric community. Ultimately, of course, this test must be applied by a trial judge.

The admissibility of evidence based on these techniques might also be determined by various sections of the Federal Rules of Evidence, 1990 (or state equivalents of this rule). Rule 401 limits admissible evidence to that which is relevant. Assuming EDA and similar techniques are believed to have some validity, meeting the requirements of Rule 401 should not be difficult. Perhaps a more challenging hurdle for EDA and related techniques is Rule 403: "Although relevant, evidence may be excluded if its probative value is substantially outweighed by the danger of unfair prejudice, confusion of the issues, or misleading the jury." The law is always concerned about the possibility of the legal decision maker (i.e., judge or jury) being unduly influenced by particular evidence. Testimony or evidence which comes close to the legal decision that must be made (the "ultimate issue"; see Slobogin, 1989, for a discussion) is considered to present such a risk (e.g., Rule 704 bars mental health professionals from offering ultimate issue testimony in insanity cases). Thus, EDA or psychological autopsy might be deemed inadmissible on the grounds that the conclusions are too close to the legal decision to be made and, consequently, may overwhelm or bias the legal decision maker.

---

[7] Laudably, some organizations attempt to reduce isolation through the use of outside consultants.

The Federal Rules of Evidence (1990) concerned with expert evidence and testimony are also relevant to a discussion of the admissibility of EDA and related procedures. Rule 702 reads

> If scientific, technical, or other specialized knowledge will assist the trier of fact to understand the evidence or to determine a fact in issue, a witness qualified as an expert by knowledge, skill, experience, training, or education, may testify thereto in the form of an opinion or otherwise.

Admissibility, according to Rule 702, appears to hinge on the degree to which the technique of psychological autopsy may be considered to constitute scientific or specialized knowledge and to assist the trier of fact in understanding evidence or determining a fact at issue. Again, because psychological autopsy is relatively undeveloped, with little known about its reliability or validity, it may have difficulty passing the first requirement. The second prong appears easier to meet, insofar as mental health professionals might be able to provide the fact finder with information, hypotheses, or theoretical formulations about the individual in question, or actuarial data about populations similar to the individual, that is of some assistance in determining issues in question. Whether psychological autopsy and related techniques pass these requirements, of course, is to be decided by the trial judge.

The courts appear to be struggling with the admissibility of psychological autopsies and related techniques (Dregne, 1982; Harris, 1990). Although psychological autopsies have been admitted by a number of courts (*Brown v. Hartford Life*, 1992; *Campbell v. Young Motor Company*, 1984; *Evans v. Provident Life*, 1990, 1991; *Gaido v. Weiser*, 1988; *Harvey v. Raleigh Police Department*, 1987, 1989; *Jackson v. State*, 1989; *Lockwood v. Rolfe*, 1967; *Mache v. Mache*, 1991; *Rodriguez v. Henkle Drilling*, 1992; *Starkey v. Springfield Life*, 1975), other courts have refused to admit such testimony (*Skulina v. Boehning*, 1988, 1991; *State v. Montijo*, 1989; *Thompson v. Mayes*, 1986).

A recent, high-profile Florida case (*Jackson v. State*, 1989) is illustrative of the unusual ways in which psychological autopsies may be used in legal proceedings and demonstrates the reasoning underlying their admission into evidence. Theresa Jackson encouraged her underage daughter, Tina Mancini, to work as a nude dancer, and charged her room and board from her earnings. Tina later committed suicide. The state retained a psychiatrist, who performed a psychological autopsy on Tina. The psychiatrist concluded that "the nature of the relationship, (and) the abusive relationship with the mother, was a substantial contributing cause to Tina Mancini's suicide" (cited in Harris, 1990). The psychiatrist's approach in this case was similar to the EDA in that much of the information he reviewed was collected by third parties. Ms. Jackson was convicted of child abuse and two other related charges; she subsequently appealed, challenging the trial court's decision to admit the psychiatrist's testimony. The appellate court affirmed the trial court's decision to admit the psychiatrist's testimony and compared psychological autopsies to more accepted and well-established forensic pursuits:

> we perceive no distinction between the admission of the expert's opinion in this case and, for example, admitting psychiatric opinion evidence to establish a defendant's sanity at the time of committing an offense or to prove the competency of an individual at the time of executing a will. (*Jackson v. State*, 1989, p. 720)

Although the law in this area is still evolving, some courts are willing to accept psychological autopsies and related procedures in a variety of circumstances. This obligates mental health professionals and professional organizations alike to take steps to ensure that consumers are informed and well educated about the nature and limitations of these techniques.

CONCLUSION

As long as serious, unexpected, and seemingly unpredictable events occur, interested parties will attempt to discern why they happened in order to identify responsible persons or parties, prevent future occurrences, and attempt to make whole those persons who have suffered. When human behavior is involved, mental health professionals are likely to be approached, on the supposition that we have some expertise in matters of human behavior. Although psychologists and other mental health professionals clearly have expertise in many aspects of human behavior, this expertise has limits. We are obligated to define our expertise carefully and to note our limitations. This is particularly necessary when the stakes are so high and the effect of errors so great, as is the case with EDA, psychological autopsies, and psychological profiling. The repercussions of the USS *Iowa* explosion and investigation demonstrate this very clearly. We should tread slowly and carefully when entering such relatively uncharted waters: To do any less would be a disservice to the public and to our profession.

REFERENCES

American Academy of Psychiatry and Law. 1991. Ethical guidelines for the practice of forensic psychiatry. In Committee on Psychiatry and Law, Group for the Advancement of Psychiatry, *The mental health professional and the legal system* (pp. 156-161). New York: Brunner/ Mazel. (Original work published 1987)

American Educational Research Association, American Psychological Association, and National Council on Measurement in Education. (1985). *Standards for educational and psychological testing.* Wash-ington, DC: American Psychological Association.

American Psychological Association. (1990). Ethical principles of psychologists (Amended June 2, 1989). *American Psychologist, 45,* 390-395.

Bonnie, R., & Slobogin, C. (1980). The role of mental health professionals in the criminal process: The case for informed speculation. *Virginia Law Review, 66,* 427-522.

Brent, D.A. (1989). The psychological autopsy: Methodological issues for the study of adolescent suicide. *Suicide and Life-Threatening Behavior, 19,* 43-57.

Brown v. Hartford Life, 593 So. 2d 1376 (Ct. App. La. 1992).

Campbell v. Young Motor Company, 211 Mont. 68, 684 P.2d 1101 (1984).

Clark, D.C., & Horton-Deutsch, S.L. (1992). Assessment *in absentia:* The value of the psychological autopsy method for studying antecedents of suicides and predicting future suicides. In R. Maris, A. Berman, J. Maltsberger, & R. Yufit (Eds.), *Assessment and prediction of suicide* (pp. 499-519). New York: Guilford Press.

Committee on Ethical Guidelines for Forensic Psychologists. (1991). Specialty guidelines for forensic psychologists. *Law and Human Behavior, 15,* 655-665.

Douglas, J.E., Ressler, R.K., Burgess, A.W., & Hartman, C.R. (1986). Criminal profiling from crime scene analysis. *Behavioral Sciences & the Law, 4,* 401-421.

Dregne, N. (1982). Psychological autopsy: A new tool for criminal defense attorneys? *Arizona Law Review, 24,* 421-439.

Ebert, B.W. (1987). Guide to conducting a psychological autopsy. *Professional Psychology: Research and Practice, 18,* 52-56.

Evans v. Provident Life and Accident Insurance Company, 15 Kan. App. 2d 97, 803 P.2d 1033 (Kan. App. 1990).

Evans v. Provident Life and Accident Insurance Company, 249 Kan. 248, 815 P.2d 550 (1991).

Families of USS Iowa victims sue. (1991, April 18). *St. Petersburg Times*, p. 9.

Federal rules of evidence. (1990). 28 *United States Code Annotated*. St. Paul, MN: West.

Fowler, R. (1986, May). Howard Hughes: A psychological autopsy. *Psychology Today*, pp. 22-33.

Frye v. U.S. 293 F. 1013 (1910).

Gaido v. Weiser, 227 N.J. Super. 175, 545 A.2d 1350 (N.J. Super. 1988).

Geberth, V.J. (1981). Psychological profiling. *Law and Order*, 29(9), 46-52.

Harris, A.A. (1990). The psychological autopsy: A retrospective study of suicide. *Stetson Law Review*, 20, 289-309.

Harvey v. Raleigh Police Department, 96 N.C. App. 540, 384 S.E.2d 549 (N.C. App. 1989).

Harvey v. Raleigh Police Department, 85 N.C. App. 540, 355 S.E.2d 147 (N.C. App. 1987).

Hazelwood, R. (1984). *The behavior-oriented interview of rape victims*. Washington, DC: Federal Bureau of Investigation, Department of Justice.

Holmes, R.M. (1989). *Profiling violent crimes: An investigative tool*. Newbury Park, CA: Sage.

House Armed Services Committee. (1990, March 5). HASC releases U.S.S. IOWA investigation report [news release]. Washington, DC: Author.

Jackson v. State, 553 So.2d 719 (Fla. 4th DCA, 1989).

Jobes, D.A., Berman, A.L., & Josselson, A.R. (1986). The impact of psychological autopsies in medical examiners' determination of manner of death. *Journal of Forensic Sciences*, 31, 177-189.

Jobes, D.A., Berman, A.L., & Josselson, A.R. (1987). Improving the validity and reliability of medical-legal certifications of suicide. *Suicide and Life-Threatening Behavior*, 17, 310-325.

Jobes, D.A., Casey, J.O., Berman, A.L., & Wright, D.G. (1991). Empirical criteria for the determination of suicide manner of death. *Journal of Forensic Sciences*, 36, 244-256.

Litman, R.E., Curphey, T.J., Schneidman, E.S., Faberow, N.L., & Tabachnick, N.D . (1963). Investigations of equivocal suicides. *Journal of the American Medical Association*, 184, 924-930.

Lockwood v. Rolfe, 254 Cal. App. 309, 62 Cal. Rptr. 230 (Cal. Ct. App. 1967).

Mache v. Mache, 218 111. App. 3d 1069, 578 N.E.2d 1253 (111. App. 1991).

Melton, G., Petrila, J., Poythress, N., & Slobogin, C. (1987). *Psychological evaluations for the courts: A handbook for mental health professionals and lawyers*. New York: Guilford Press.

Nelson, R. (1990). What really happened on the IOWA? *Popular Science*, 1990(12), 84-87 & 120-121.

Otto, R.K., Poythress, N.G., Darkes, J., & Starr, L. (1992, February). *The reliability and validity of psychological autopsies: An analysis of the USS IOWA incident*. Paper presented at the 44th Annual Meeting of the American Academy of Forensic Sciences, New Orleans, LA.

Pinizzotto, A.J. (1984). Forensic psychology: Criminal personality profiling. *Journal of Police Science and Administration*, 12(1), 32-40.

Pinizzotto, A.J., & Finkel, N.J. (1990). Criminal personality profiling: An outcome and process study. *Law and Human Behavior*, 14, 215-233.

Porter, B. (1983, April). Mind hunters. *Psychology Today*, pp. 44-52.

Review of Navy Investigation of U.S.S. IOWA Explosion. (1990). Joint Hearings before the Investigations Subcommittee and the Defense Policy Panel of the Committee on Armed Services, House of Representatives, 101st Congress, 1st Session (HASC No. 101-41). Washington, DC: U.S. Government Printing Office.

Rodriguez v. Henkle Drilling, 16 Kan. App. 2d 728 (Kan. App. 1992).

Rosenberg, M.L., Davidson, L.E., Smith, J.C., Berman, A.L., Buzbee, H., Gantner, G., Gay, G.A., Moore-Lewis, B., Mills, D.H., Murray, D., O'Carroll, P.W., & Jobes, D. (1988). Operational criteria for the determination of suicide. *Journal of Forensic Sciences, 33*, 1445-1456.

Selkin, J. (1987). *Psychological autopsy in the courtroom.* Denver, CO: Author.

Selkin, J., & Loya, F. (1979). Issues in the psychological autopsy of a controversial public figure. *Professional Psychology, 10*, 87-93.

Shuman, D. (1986). *Psychiatric and psychological evidence.* Colorado Springs, CO: Shepard's/McGraw-Hill.

Skulina v. Boehning, 168 Mich. App. 704, 425 N.W.2d 135 (Mich. App. 1988).

Skulina v. Boehning, 187 Mich. App. 649, 468 N.W.2d 322 (Mich. App. 1991).

Slobogin, C. (1989). The "ultimate issue" issue. *Behavioral Science and the Law, 7*, 259-266.

Starkey Paint Company v. Springfield Life, 24 N.C. App. 507, 211 S.E.2d 498 (N.C. App. 1975).

State v. Montijo, 160 Ariz. 576, 774 P. 2d 1366 (Ariz App. 1989).

Test Rejects USS Iowa Sabotage. (1992, August 29). *Tampa Tribune*, p. 12.

Thompson v. Mayes, 707 S.W. 2d 951 (Ct. App. Texas 1986).

Turco, R.N. (1990). Psychological profiling. *International Journal of Offender Therapy and Comparative Criminology, 34*, 147-154.

U.S.S. IOWA Tragedy: An Investigative Failure (1990). Report of the Investigations Subcommittee and the Defense Policy Panel of the Committee on Armed Services, House of Representatives, 101st Congress, 2nd Session.

Norman Poythress, Randy K. Otto, Jack Darkes, and Laura Starr Department of Law and Mental Health, Florida Mental Health Institute, University of South Florida.

Mellisa G. Warren served as action editor for this article.

Correspondence concerning this article should be addressed to Norman Poythress, Department of Law and Mental Health, Florida Mental Health Institute, University of South Florida, 13301 Bruce B. Downs Boulevard, Tampa, FL 33612-3899.